Packaging Digital Information for Enhanced Learning and Analysis:

Data Visualization, Spatialization, and Multidimensionality

Shalin Hai-Jew
Kansas State University, U.S.A

A volume in the Advances in Educational Technologies and Instructional Design (AETID) Book Series

Managing Director: Lindsay Johnston
Editorial Director: Joel Gamon
Production Manager: Jennifer Yoder
Publishing Systems Analyst: Adrienne Freeland
Development Editor: Brett Snyder
Assistant Acquisitions Editor: Kayla Wolfe
Typesetter: Christina Barkanic
Cover Design: Jason Mull

Published in the United States of America by
Information Science Reference (an imprint of IGI Global)
701 E. Chocolate Avenue
Hershey PA 17033
Tel: 717-533-8845
Fax: 717-533-8661
E-mail: cust@igi-global.com
Web site: http://www.igi-global.com

Library of Congress Cataloging-in-Publication Data

Packaging digital information for enhanced learning and analysis : data visualization, spatialization, and multidimensionality / Shalin Hai-Jew, editor, Information Science Reference.
pages cm
Includes bibliographical references and index.
Summary: "This book brings together effective practices for the end-to-end capture and web based presentation of information for comprehension, analysis, and decision-making"-- Provided by publisher.
ISBN 978-1-4666-4462-5 (hardcover) -- ISBN 978-1-4666-4463-2 (ebook) -- ISBN 978-1-4666-4464-9 (print & perpetual access) 1. Information visualization. I. Hai-Jew, Shalin.
QA76.9.I52P33 2013
001.4'226--dc23
2013015457

This book is published in the IGI Global book series Advances in Educational Technologies and Instructional Design (AETID) Book Series (ISSN: 2326-8905; eISSN: 2326-8913)

British Cataloguing in Publication Data
A Cataloguing in Publication record for this book is available from the British Library.

All work contributed to this book is new, previously-unpublished material. The views expressed in this book are those of the authors, but not necessarily of the publisher.

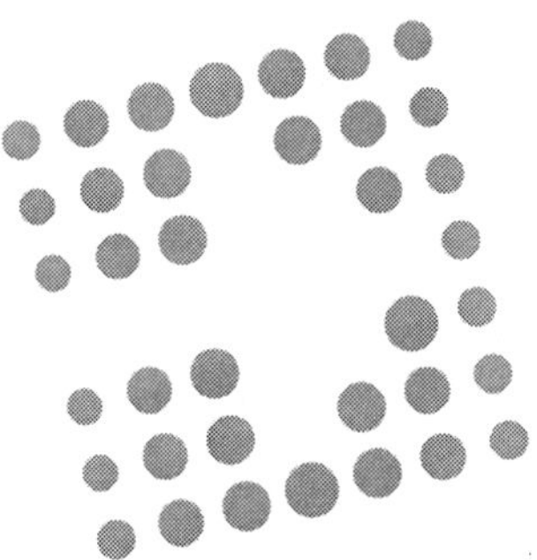

Advances in Educational Technologies and Instructional Design (AETID) Book Series

Lawrence A. Tomei
Robert Morris University, USA

ISSN: 2326-8905
EISSN: 2326-8913

Mission

Education has undergone, and continues to undergo, immense changes in the way it is enacted and distributed to both child and adult learners. From distance education, Massive-Open-Online-Courses (MOOCs), and electronic tablets in the classroom, technology is now an integral part of the educational experience and is also affecting the way educators communicate information to students.

The **Advances in Educational Technologies & Instructional Design (AETID) Book Series** is a resource where researchers, students, administrators, and educators alike can find the most updated research and theories regarding technology's integration within education and its effect on teaching as a practice.

Coverage

- Cognitive Theories
- Cultural Impacts
- Information and Communication Systems
- Knowledge Acquisition and Transfer Processes
- Knowledge Management Strategy
- Knowledge Sharing
- Organizational Learning
- Organizational Memory
- Small and Medium Enterprises
- Virtual Communities

IGI Global is currently accepting manuscripts for publication within this series. To submit a proposal for a volume in this series, please contact our Acquisition Editors at Acquisitions@igi-global.com or visit: http://www.igi-global.com/publish/.

The Advances in Educational Technologies and Instructional Design (ISSN 2326-8905) is published by IGI Global, 701 E. Chocolate Avenue, Hershey, PA 17033-1240, USA, www.igi-global.com. This series is composed of titles available for purchase individually; each title is edited to be contextually exclusive from any other title within the series. For pricing and ordering information please visit http://www.igi-global.com/book-series/advances-educational-technologies-instructional-design/73678. Postmaster: Send all address changes to above address.

Titles in this Series

For a list of additional titles in this series, please visit: www.igi-global.com

Packaging Digital Information for Enhanced Learning and Analysis Data Visualization, Spatialization, and Multidimensionality
Shalin Hai-Jew (Kansas State University, U.S.A)
Information Science Reference • copyright 2014 • 349pp • H/C (ISBN: 9781466644625) • US $175.00 (our price)

Cases on Communication Technology for Second Language Acquisition and Cultural Learning
Joan E. Aitken (Park University, USA)
Information Science Reference • copyright 2014 • 358pp • H/C (ISBN: 9781466644823) • US $175.00 (our price)

Exploring Technology for Writing and Writing Instruction
Kristine E. Pytash (Kent State University, USA) and Richard E. Ferdig (Research Center for Educational Technology - Kent State University, USA)
Information Science Reference • copyright 2014 • 368pp • H/C (ISBN: 9781466643413) • US $175.00 (our price)

Cases on Educational Technology Planning, Design, and Implementation A Project Management Perspective
Angela D. Benson (University of Alabama, USA) Joi L. Moore (University of Missouri, USA) and Shahron Williams van Rooij (George Mason University, USA)
Information Science Reference • copyright 2013 • 328pp • H/C (ISBN: 9781466642379) • US $175.00 (our price)

Common Core Mathematics Standards and Implementing Digital Technologies
Drew Polly (University of North Carolina at Charlotte, USA)
Information Science Reference • copyright 2013 • 364pp • H/C (ISBN: 9781466640863) • US $175.00 (our price)

Technologies for Inclusive Education Beyond Traditional Integration Approaches
David Griol Barres (Carlos III University of Madrid, Spain) Zoraida Callejas Carrión (University of Granada, Spain) and Ramón López-Cózar Delgado (University of Granada, Spain)
Information Science Reference • copyright 2013 • 393pp • H/C (ISBN: 9781466625303) • US $175.00 (our price)

Cases on Interdisciplinary Research Trends in Science, Technology, Engineering, and Mathematics Studies on Urban Classrooms
Reneta D. Lansiquot (New York City College of Technology of the City University of New York, USA)
Information Science Reference • copyright 2013 • 414pp • H/C (ISBN: 9781466622142) • US $175.00 (our price)

Cases on Inquiry through Instructional Technology in Math and Science
Lesia Lennex (Morehead State University, USA) and Kimberely Fletcher Nettleton (Morehead State University, USA)
Information Science Reference • copyright 2012 • 414pp • H/C (ISBN: 9781466600683) • US $175.00 (our price)

www.igi-global.com

701 E. Chocolate Ave., Hershey, PA 17033
Order online at www.igi-global.com or call 717-533-8845 x100
To place a standing order for titles released in this series, contact: cust@igi-global.com
Mon-Fri 8:00 am - 5:00 pm (est) or fax 24 hours a day 717-533-8661

This is for R. Max.

Editorial Advisory Board

Table of Contents

Preface xv

Acknowledgment xx

Section 1
Principled Strategies in Packaging Digital Contents

Chapter 1
Making Health Information Personal: How Anecdotes Bring Concepts to Life 1
Mitch Ricketts, Kansas State University, USA

Chapter 2
More than Just Data: The Importance of Motivation, Examples, and Feedback in Comprehending and Retaining Digital Information 37
Brent A. Anders, Kansas State University, USA

Chapter 3
Branching Logic in the Design of Online Learning: A Partial Typology 47
Shalin Hai-Jew, Kansas State University, USA

Section 2
Innovative Technologies and Techniques in Packaging Digital Contents

Chapter 4
Weaving Web 2.0 and Facial Expression Recognition into the 3D Virtual English Classroom 71
Ya-Chun Shih, National Dong Hwa University, Taiwan

Chapter 5
Utilizing Augmented Reality in Library Information Search 93
Robert Gibson, Emporia State University, USA

Chapter 6
E-LearningFacultyModules.org 103
Roger McHaney, Kansas State University, USA
Lynda Spire, Kansas State University, USA
Rosemary Boggs, Kansas State University, USA

Chapter 7
Multimodal Mapping of a University's Formal and Informal Online Brand: Using NodeXL to Extract Social Network Data in Tweets, Digital Contents, and Relational Ties 120
Shalin Hai-Jew, Kansas State University, USA

Section 3
Packaging Digital Contents for Perspective and Analysis

Chapter 8
Visualization of High-Level Associations from Twitter Data 164
Luca Cagliero, Politecnico di Torino, Italy
Naeem A. Mahoto, Politecnico di Torino, Italy

Chapter 9
Information Visualization Techniques for Big Data: Analytics using Heterogeneous Data in Spatiotemporal Domains.. 184
William H. Hsu, Kansas State University, USA

Chapter 10
Using Social Network Analysis to Examine Social Hierarchies and Team Dynamics on Instructional Design Projects 198
Shalin Hai-Jew, Kansas State University, USA

Chapter 11
Beyond Surface Relations: Using Maltego Radium® to Analyze Electronic Connectivity and Hidden Ties in the Internet Understructure 241
Shalin Hai-Jew, Kansas State University, USA

Section 4
Cases in Real-World Packaging of Digital Contents for Learning

Chapter 12
Immersion and Interaction via Avatars within Google Street View: Opening Possibilities beyond Traditional Cultural Learning 266
Ya-Chun Shih, National Dong Hwa University, Taiwan
Molly Leonard, National Dong Hwa University, Taiwan

Chapter 13
How Digital Media like TED Talks Are Revolutionizing Teaching and Student Learning 282
Gladys Palma de Schrynemakers, Long Island University – Brooklyn, USA

Chapter 14
Structuring an Emergent and Transdisciplinary Online Curriculum: A One Health Case.................. 299
Shalin Hai-Jew, Kansas State University, USA

Section 5
Digital Packaging for Young Learners

Chapter 15
Identification and Analysis of Primary School Children's Knowledge Acquisition: Using Knowledge Visualization Scenarios and Information Visualization Methodology 333
Søren Eskildsen, Aalborg University, Denmark
Kasper Rodil, Aalborg University, Denmark
Matthias Rehm, Aalborg University, Denmark

Chapter 16
Evaluating a Technique for Improving Letter Memory in At-Risk Kindergarten Students 355
Carol Stockdale, ARK Institute of Learning, USA

Compilation of References 373

About the Contributors 400

Index 406

Detailed Table of Contents

Preface xv

Acknowledgment xx

Section 1
Principled Strategies in Packaging Digital Contents

Chapter 1
Making Health Information Personal: How Anecdotes Bring Concepts to Life 1
Mitch Ricketts, Kansas State University, USA

Research suggests people often fail to understand the personal relevance of generalized health information. To make health information more meaningful, communicators can employ anecdotes that take the form of instructive stories about the illnesses or injuries of particular people. Appropriate anecdotes may help audiences internalize health information by triggering insights such as: "I see how that could happen to me…I'd better take action." Vivid anecdotes appear to activate many of the same neurological pathways that help us extract meaning from direct experience and observation. By eliciting vivid imagery, provoking deep thought, and forging lasting memories, anecdotes may shape beliefs and behaviors to nearly the same extent as a lived event. This chapter explores methods for integrating anecdotes into health messages to increase personal relevance and prompt important changes in health-related behavior.

Chapter 2
More than Just Data: The Importance of Motivation, Examples, and Feedback in Comprehending and Retaining Digital Information 37
Brent A. Anders, Kansas State University, USA

Increasing amounts of information are being generated and distributed to students and the public in general without regards for how this data will be processed, integrated, and recalled. This chapter seeks to present how, through the use of motivation, salient and multimodal examples, and properly created/regulated feedback, information presented can be much better learned and experienced so as to aid in overall comprehension and learning. The Attention, Relevance, Confidence, and Satisfaction (ARCS) model is highlighted when discussing how to motivate student and content viewers (Keller, 1987). Additional research findings with regards to the use of multimodalities, the use of examples, and proper implementation of feedback is also presented. Examples are provided as to how an educational facilitator might use this information in presentations and digital content distribution.

Chapter 3
Branching Logic in the Design of Online Learning: A Partial Typology 47
Shalin Hai-Jew, Kansas State University, USA

Online learning requires a clear structure to enhance learning, particularly for those with little background in the subject. Structurally, the design of online learning may involve branching and merging, forking and joining of multiple branches, and other combinations of branching, for a learner or learners. Instructional branching is a tool that enables the achievement of multiple objectives. These include the following: (1) An Adaptive Curriculum: Adapting a richer curriculum to reflect the complex realities of a field and the real world; (2) Learner Support: Accommodating learners, who often have diverse needs based on their capabilities, ambitions, areas of study, and needs; (3) Learner Collaboration Support: Promoting the building of learning teams for the acquisition of collaboration, co-learning, and co-design skills; (4) Respect for Learner Decision-Making: Respecting the decision-making of learners, particularly in scenarios of simulations, games, problem solving, case studies and analysis, microsite presentations, slideshows and lecture captures, design, and innovation; (5) Maximizing In-World Opportunities: Taking advantage of opportunities in the environment such as the availability of a guest speaker, the co-funding of a shared learning endeavor, a partnership with a business entity, fieldtrip options, and/or other created opportunities. This chapter addresses various known branching designs on two levels: (1) course curriculums and (2) Digital Learning Objects (DLOs). It offers a typology of branching at the course curriculum level. Further, it covers branching in the DLO level based on specific cases. It analyzes the various points at which a curriculum converges and when it diverges (branches). Finally, the chapter includes a section on the mindful design of branching: design of the branching, the transitions, and proper learning assessments.

Section 2
Innovative Technologies and Techniques in Packaging Digital Contents

Chapter 4
Weaving Web 2.0 and Facial Expression Recognition into the 3D Virtual English Classroom 71
Ya-Chun Shih, National Dong Hwa University, Taiwan

Of late, considerable attention has been given to the linking or "mashing up" of virtual worlds and Web 2.0 tools. The authors incorporated several Web 2.0 tools, including blogs, audioblogs, wikis, Facebook, Twitter, and Flickr, and a facial expression organizer together into the 3D Virtual English Classroom called VEC3D 5.0, thereby opening up new possibilities for collaborative language learning. In considering the needs of language learners, this study combines synchronous and asynchronous learning environments and methods to propose a blended language learning solution. VEC3D 5.0 offers the possibility of applying situated learning, multimodal communication, and facial expression recognition to language learning and teaching. VEC3D 5.0 has shown itself to possess tremendous potential as an optimal language learning environment. Integrating Web 2.0 applications in the form of open social networking and information sharing tools into VEC3D 5.0 supports collaborative and reflective language learning, and in particular, writing and cultural learning. The purpose of this study is to explore the application of a hybrid prototype solution, which combines the inherent strengths of both virtual environments and Web 2.0 applications, and to provide a framework for developing innovative pedagogies for experiential language learning in this context.

Chapter 5
Utilizing Augmented Reality in Library Information Search 93
Robert Gibson, Emporia State University, USA

A cross-disciplinary academic team at Emporia State University is currently in the process of developing and utilizing a mobile-based augmented reality application in the context of library information search. Specifically, the team is researching the use of mobile applications that can generate multi-sensory information retrieval relative to archives and special collections. Using this application, student and faculty researchers can physically point their mobile devices at an archival object that has been specifically marked with a photo-generated "tag" and, using specially designed software, access videos, photos, music, text, and other data that is germane to the object. This allows the archivist to preserve the object behind protective glass or other physical barriers, while allowing the information seeker to learn more about the object using embedded multimedia. This minimizes the potential for damage while providing extra dimensions of information. Of the many virtualizations currently under development are videos related to a rare novel and music compositions relative to rare sheet music – both currently housed within Special Collections at Emporia State University.

Chapter 6
E-LearningFacultyModules.org 103
Roger McHaney, Kansas State University, USA
Lynda Spire, Kansas State University, USA
Rosemary Boggs, Kansas State University, USA

A team at Kansas State University recently launched the E-Learning Faculty Modules wiki to enhance and support online faculty development. This project is customized for teaching in the Kansas State University distance-learning program but contains a broad set of information that might be useful to others. This site is constructed using wiki technology, which permits access, multimedia expressiveness, remote collaboration, tracking, and reversibility of postings. Other tools on the site are derived from MediaWiki and its open-source capabilities. The wiki includes an overall ontology, templates, categories, completed and seeded entries, input boxes, and menus that ensure users can easily use and join the community. Taken holistically, these attributes create an ideal venue for sharing ideas and encouraging synergistic improvement of teaching practices. This chapter describes the implementation process of E-LearningFacultyModules.org and gives insight into its purpose, features, and uses.

Chapter 7
Multimodal Mapping of a University's Formal and Informal Online Brand: Using NodeXL to Extract Social Network Data in Tweets, Digital Contents, and Relational Ties 120
Shalin Hai-Jew, Kansas State University, USA

With the popularization of the Social Web (or Read-Write Web) and millions of participants in these interactive spaces, institutions of higher education have found it necessary to create online presences to promote their university brands, presence, and reputation. An important aspect of that engagement involves being aware of how their brand is represented informally (and formally) on social media platforms. Universities have traditionally maintained thin channels of formalized communications through official media channels, but in this participatory new media age, the user-generated contents and communications are created independent of the formal public relations offices. The university brand is evolving independently of official controls. Ex-post interventions to protect university reputation and brand may be too little, too late, and much of the contents are beyond the purview of the formal university. Various offices and clubs have institutional accounts on Facebook as well as wide representation of their faculty, staff, administrators, and students online. There are various microblogging accounts on Twitter. Various photo and video contents related to the institution may be found on photo- and video-sharing sites, like Flickr, and there are video channels on YouTube. All this digital content is widely available and may serve as points-of-contact for the close-in to more distal stakeholders and publics related to the institution. A recently available open-source tool enhances the capability for crawling (extracting data) these various social media platforms (through their Application Programming Interfaces or "APIs") and enables the capture, analysis, and social network visualization of broadly available public information. Further, this tool enables the analysis of previously hidden information. This chapter introduces the application of Network Overview, Discovery and Exploration for Excel (NodeXL) to the empirical and multimodal analysis of a university's electronic presence on various social media platforms and offers some initial ideas for the analytical value of such an approach.

Section 3
Packaging Digital Contents for Perspective and Analysis

Chapter 8
Visualization of High-Level Associations from Twitter Data 164
Luca Cagliero, Politecnico di Torino, Italy
Naeem A. Mahoto, Politecnico di Torino, Italy

The Data Mining and Knowledge Discovery (KDD) process focuses on extracting useful information from large datasets. To support analysts in making decisions, a relevant research effort has been devoted to visualizing the extracted data mining models effectively. A particular attention has been paid to the discovery of strong association rules from textual data coming from social networks, which represent potentially relevant correlations among document terms. However, state-of-the-art rule visualization tools do not allow experts to visualize data correlations at different abstraction levels. Hence, the effectiveness of the proposed approaches is limited, especially when dealing with fairly sparse data. This chapter presents Twitter Generalized Rule Visualizer (TGRV), a novel text mining and visualization tool. It aims at supporting analysts in looking into the results of the generalized association rule mining process from textual data coming from Twitter supplied with WordNet taxonomies. Taxonomies are used for aggregating document terms into higher-level concepts. Generalized rules represent high-level associations among document terms. By exploiting taxonomy-based models, experts may look into the discovered data correlations from different perspectives and figure out interesting knowledge. Changing the perspective from which data correlations are visualized is shown to improve the readability and the usability of the generated rule-based model. The experimental results show the applicability and the usefulness of the proposed visualization tool on real textual data coming from Twitter. The visualized data correlations are shown to be valuable for advanced analysis, such as topic trend and user behavior analysis.

Chapter 9
Information Visualization Techniques for Big Data: Analytics using Heterogeneous Data in Spatiotemporal Domains.. 184
William H. Hsu, Kansas State University, USA

This chapter presents challenges and recommended practices for visualizing data about phenomena that are observed or simulated across space and time. Some data may be collected for the express purpose of answering questions through quantitative analysis and simulation, especially about future occurrences or continuations of the phenomena – that is, prediction. In this case, analytical computations may serve two purposes: to prepare the data for presentation and to answer questions by producing information, especially an informative model, that can also be visualized. These purposes may have significant overlap. Thus, the focus of the chapter is about analytical techniques for visual display of quantitative data and information that scale up to large data sets. It begins by surveying trends in educational and scientific use of visualization and reviewing taxonomies of data to be visualized. Next, it reviews aspects of spatiotemporal data that pose challenges, such as heterogeneity and scale, along with techniques for dealing specifically with geospatial data and text. An exploration of concrete applications then follows. Finally, tenets of information visualization design, put forward by Tufte and other experts on data representation and presentation, are considered in the context of analytical applications for heterogeneous data in spatiotemporal domains.

Chapter 10
Using Social Network Analysis to Examine Social Hierarchies and Team Dynamics on Instructional Design Projects 198
Shalin Hai-Jew, Kansas State University, USA

Social network diagrams have been an important part of understanding social dynamics from dyads all the way to human civilizations. In e-learning, social networks have been used to evaluate how online learners engage with each other and what the implications of that may be for the quality of learning. In this chapter, social networks are used to evaluate various social aspects of the development teams in their work. A number of contemporary Instructional Design (ID) projects, described briefly as comparative case studies in the chapter, are used as the contexts for these social networks and visualizations. While these depictions tend to be systemic-level ones, there are insights from considering the micro/ego-level views. The objectives of this chapter are to introduce one approach to the uses of social network visualizations in analyzing the internal and external social dynamics of instructional design across a number of institutions of higher education.

Chapter 11
Beyond Surface Relations: Using Maltego Radium® to Analyze Electronic Connectivity and Hidden Ties in the Internet Understructure 241
Shalin Hai-Jew, Kansas State University, USA

On the surface spaces of the WWW and Internet, organizations and individuals have long created a public face to emphasize their respective brands, showcase their credibility, and interact with others in often very public ways. These surface spaces include Websites, social media platforms, virtual worlds, interactive game spaces, content sharing sites, social networking sites, microblogging sites, wikis, blogs (Web logs), collaborative work sites, and email systems. Beneath the glittering surfaces are electronic understructures, which enable the mapping of networks (based on physical location or organization or URL), the tracking of inter-personal relationships between various accounts, the geolocation of various electronic data to the analog physical world, the de-anonymizing of aliases (to disallow pseudonymity), and the tracking of people to their contact information (digital and physical). Maltego Radium is a penetration testing tool that enables such crawls of publicly available information or Open-Source Intelligence (OSINT) to identify and describe electronic network structures for a range of applications. Further, this information is represented in a number of interactive node-link diagrams in both 2D and 3D for further insights. There is also an export capability for full reportage of the extracted information. This chapter introduces the tool and identifies some practical ways this has been used to "package" fresh understandings for enhanced awareness and decision-making in a higher education context.

Section 4
Cases in Real-World Packaging of Digital Contents for Learning

Chapter 12
Immersion and Interaction via Avatars within Google Street View: Opening Possibilities beyond Traditional Cultural Learning 266
Ya-Chun Shih, National Dong Hwa University, Taiwan
Molly Leonard, National Dong Hwa University, Taiwan

The optimal approach to learning a target culture is to experience it in its real-life context through interaction. The new 3D virtual world platform under consideration, Blue Mars Lite, enables users to be immersed in existing Google Maps Street View panorama, globally. Google Maps with Street View contains a massive collection of 360-degree street-level images of the most popular places worldwide. The authors explore the possibility of integrating these global panoramas, in which multiple users can explore, discuss, and role-play, into the classroom. The goal of this chapter is to shed new light on merging Google Street View with the 3D virtual world for cultural learning purposes. This approach shows itself to be a promising teaching method that can help EFL learners to develop positive attitudes toward the target culture and cultural learning in this new cultural setting.

Chapter 13
How Digital Media like TED Talks Are Revolutionizing Teaching and Student Learning 282
Gladys Palma de Schrynemakers, Long Island University – Brooklyn, USA

Launched in 1984, Technology, Entertainment, and Design (TED) Talks was successfully developed and implemented as a practical way to bring recognized experts together to discuss the latest developments and improve communication and collaboration across these fields. From its embryonic beginning, TED Talks has today expanded exponentially and is now a multi-media vehicle for delivering pioneering work to a global audience. For faculty wishing to bring user-friendly, cutting-edge research and ideas to the classroom, it can be an exciting teaching tool because students can draw from the real life experiences of outstanding professionals who are trailblazers in their fields. This chapter presents assignments that were created using TED Talks and provides a template that can be used to create unique assignments that are compatible with the needs and goals of the course. The template is designed to help faculty craft a learning experience that is embedded in an encouraging environment for innovative approaches and student involvement—where specific student learning objectives exist, along with approaches to assess student learning.

Chapter 14
Structuring an Emergent and Transdisciplinary Online Curriculum: A One Health Case.................. 299
Shalin Hai-Jew, Kansas State University, USA

Subject domains are in constant transition as new research and analysis reveal fresh insights, and occasionally, there may be paradigm shifts or new conceptual models. Transdisciplinary approaches may be understood as such a shift, with new approaches for conceptualization, analysis, and problem solving via recombinations of domain fields. Such transitory paradigm-shifting moments remove the usual touchpoints on which a curriculum is structured. There are often few or none of the accepted sequential developmental phases with identified concepts and learning outcomes in book chapters, thematic structures, and historical or chronological ordering. An emergent curriculum requires a different instructional design approach than those that have assumed curricular pre-structures. Based on a year-and-a-half One Health course build, this chapter offers some insights on the processes of defining and developing an emergent curriculum.

Section 5
Digital Packaging for Young Learners

Chapter 15
Identification and Analysis of Primary School Children's Knowledge Acquisition: Using Knowledge Visualization Scenarios and Information Visualization Methodology 333
Søren Eskildsen, Aalborg University, Denmark
Kasper Rodil, Aalborg University, Denmark
Matthias Rehm, Aalborg University, Denmark

Measuring a learning effect can be a difficult task and is not made any easier with all the parameters that can be taken into account. This chapter provides an insight into what to consider as interesting parameters when evaluating an interactive learning tool. The authors introduce a visual approach to enlighten children and teachers. This is done by visualizing logging data that has been collected during learning sessions with the Virtual Savannah software. They do not leave out traditional means like observation and usability testing, since they believe a holistic view is important, and a single method of data collection is not enough to base conclusions on. To understand the authors' approach, a short introduction on various perspectives on visualization is essential. The authors also discuss how multimedia can be used on a cognitive level to satisfy more pupils with different learning styles. Lastly, the authors present their approach and results from an in situ evaluation on primary school children.

Chapter 16
Evaluating a Technique for Improving Letter Memory in At-Risk Kindergarten Students 355
Carol Stockdale, ARK Institute of Learning, USA

This chapter focuses on a process for improving letter naming. Numerous studies have established the correlation between fluent letter naming and reading in young children (Badian, 2000; Catts, 2001; Faust, Dimitrovsky, & Shacht, 2003; Terepocki, Kruk, & Willows, 2002; Mann & Foy, 2003). Two schools using the same reading program were selected for the study. The 125 kindergarten children attending these schools were screened for letter naming fluency. The low scoring individuals in each school were randomly assigned either to a treatment or control group for the study. Pretesting addressed rapid letter recall, color naming, object naming, and receptive vocabulary. The children in the treatment groups received twelve twenty-minute instructional sessions teaching the children to attend to the distinctive features (unique parts) of each letter. The students in the treatment groups made significant gains in letter naming speed and accuracy compared to the control groups. Receptive language scores improved. Other measures had no significant correlation with letter naming proficiency in posttests.

Compilation of References 373

About the Contributors 400

Index 406

Preface

The idea for *Packaging Digital Information for Enhanced Learning and Analysis: Data Visualization, Spatialization, Predictiveness, and Multidimensionality* came to me as I was taking part in a regional conference in Hutchinson, Kansas. I had given a short talk on a software tool that enabled the mapping of data to geographical space. The small audience had been generous and asked me to give the "TMI" (Too Much Information) version of the talk, which included some musing on the challenges of collecting and analyzing valid data to draw more accurate conclusions. I had stayed over an extra night in the town in order to take in some of their local wonders—a space museum and a historical salt mine. This was in April 2012. By the time I had driven the few hours back to my town, I had decided to write a book prospectus based on the notes roughed out in the hotel room. Now, more than a year later, the text itself has coalesced with a broad range of creative and achieved researchers who are sharing their insights on how to package data and information for enhanced comprehension, and ultimately, decision-making.

AN INFORMATION-CENTRIC WORLD

In another sense, this idea of packaging digital information has been a long time in coming. In my past seven years of working as an instructional designer at Kansas State University, I have come across many different opportunities to consume and analyze data. I have learned that practitioners in different domain fields have inherent standards for research and the integration of new information in the field. They have differing ways to validate data. They also have deeply held assumptions about understanding information based on acculturation to their respective fields. These are ways of understanding that have evolved over time and long thinking and much academic combat. In their expert-based conceptual models, they have information ontologies or structures. To create coherence for learning, these Subject Matter Experts (SMEs) would require both explicit and implicit clarity. They would have to control for misunderstandings. They would have to help novice learners come to the correct conclusions. Those who have been in the classroom for years begin to understand where common misunderstandings may occur as learners strive to make sense of the new information. These challenges become more difficult in dynamic and changing systems, cross-domain learning, real-world decision-making, problem solving, and in innovating. Each new challenge results in additional layers of complexity. Further, very few active learning domains have all the foundational information mapped out. Rather, most fields are actively conducting research for deeper knowledge. In graduate-level education, SMEs need to further convey what is unknown and perhaps the known limits of knowability without closing off possibilities.

The SME ability to articulate the learning is only one part of the challenge. Another part involves actualizing their vision in digital form. SMEs can often describe an idealized presentation of their knowledge, but it may not be fully feasible, given the constraints of the technologies, the budget, the time constraints, and the scripting/coding constraints, among others. The numbers of file types (expressed in various file extensions) that may be used for delivery via the Web are finite, and there are de facto file types and accessibility standards.

Practically speaking, the design of a digital learning object requires a number of steps in order to achieve design coherence.

- The selectivity of data—inclusion or exclusion
- The order of the presentation (spatial, sequential, or other)
- The methods of the presentation (static or interactive; the selection of multimedia)
- The provided context and tone
- The cognitive scaffolding and other learning elements
- The evaluation methods

For any instructional design situation, there are a range of considerations. Depending on the project, some aspects come to the fore. The limitations (constraints) of software and technological sub-structures means that there is always a gap between the intentions of the subject matter expert and what is digitally rendered; further, there is also often a gap between the information delivered and what is perceived (in part because learners have not been trained in particular understandings).

By practice, there are conventions for digital packaging. For example, there is the "rule of threes" in the cropping of two-dimensional images. There are conventions in structuring non-fiction writing in rhetorical modes. Video scripts follow pre-set structures to capture viewer attention and contextualize the information. Trusted human or avatar hosts may serve as narrators to increase the veracity of a presentation. Slideshows follow dramatic storytelling trajectories. In various forms of modeling and simulations, the learning objects are designed to help learners perceive and understand relationships between variables and to see patterns, even at the cost of highly simplifying information.

To conceptualize the "packaging" of digital information, it helps to view information as a fluid and malleable substance. If treated in some ways, it takes on a form of its own. If treated in other ways, it may be transparent or opaque; it may take on a particular hue. Information may be elusive or very present and memorable. It may catalyze new ideas, or it may reaffirm existing understandings. It may inspire new thinking, or it may shut down learners. How people organize and present information affects how it is conceptualized and consumed.

While foundational design precepts are generally followed for various types of digital packaging, there is plenty of room for customizing for target learners or unique contexts; there is room for signature design. The examples suggested point to digital packaging around processed information. If there is an information pipeline, where raw data is captured and analyzed and processed into domain knowledge, the prior examples are usually used for data that has been highly processed into information. This digital design challenge is compounded with the presentation of new and raw data, which has not yet transmuted into some consensus understandings in a particular domain.

DIGITALLY PACKAGING RAW DATA

In this current age, a wide range of raw data is accessible. They stream in from sensor networks. They are collected on social media platforms, content sharing sites, microblogging sites, wikis, and email systems.

Learning management systems offer "big data" to analyze learner behaviors and profiles. Much of what is collected has defined usage for experts in a number of fields—for their awareness, research, analysis, and decision-making. Much of this data is delivered through user interface designs and componentized dashboards. Still other data, such as data extractions from social media platforms and the Internet, are portrayed as social network diagrams, which require some complex study in social network analysis to understand and exploit (These visuals are created by the extracted data through layout algorithms.). Data then is abstractions of the world; it is representational measures of particular aspects of the world. For this data to be relevant, users of those floods of data require clear understandings of what is being represented and what it might mean.

More and more, though, instructors and researchers are having to package digital contents from raw data and to make it make sense to colleagues and learners (This is especially so in cross-domain collaborations. Expertise in one domain field does not often transfer to expertise in others. However, there is a wide need to collaborate across fields. Designed data and information are then critical in helping others acclimate to a field.).

Ideally, area subject matter experts bring a seasoned expertise and an analytical aptitude to their reception (or rejection) of new data. They have the wherewithal to understand how the data was captured and then how it was rendered and delivered to the viewer. Depending on the data, there may be a range of possibly valid insights. The design challenge here involves how to present this data in a way that enables learners to make sense of it with accuracy. If a core competitive advantage in this modern age requires the ability to engage data practically, then surely, increasing data coherence for wide distribution is a critical goal. From the examples here and outside this work, it is clear that data coherence is achievable.

The content providers who provision raw data and processed information via the WWW and Internet have differentiated themselves from their competitors by their credibility, accuracy, speed, and methodologies. For most contents on any range of topics, there are only a handful or two of serious content providers. With such narrow streaming of data resources, it is all the more critical that such resources are digitally packaged with broadest usage and far-reaching clarity.

TARGET AUDIENCE

Those in higher education and K-12 are expected to use data analytics to enhance their decision-making for student learning and learning design. Therefore, it is critical for them to understand how to read complex data from Web interfaces.

Further, educators and instructional designers have to improve how they present complex data online so as to present their data with clarity and without miscommunication. Because data is used in many ways for many purposes, and most information today is delivered through Web and Internet, means for a broad audience, it is critical that there is a discussion on the optimal design approaches and practices.

The scholarly value of an edited collection is that those engaged in this work may share their learning and help propagate the best practices in this area to their colleagues. This work may also help those who are designing such systems to see educators' data analytics needs as a broad "use case" to improve the tools (both proprietary and open-source).

The potential audiences would be educators, trainers, instructional designers, Web designers, and graduate students. A strong design may stand the test of time (relatively speaking) with various fungible data and information contents.

AN OVERVIEW OF THE CONTENTS

Packaging Digital Information for Enhanced Learning and Analysis: Data Visualization, Spatialization, Predictiveness, and Multidimensionality was initially conceptualized to include a variety of approaches to the capturing of data and its representation to a broad audience. It was a stated goal to include work in K-20. In that sense, this would not capture data visualization for specialists who do not interface with the public. The initial call for chapter proposals included long sections on the disambiguation of data. It highlighted both static and dynamic information collection systems. It suggested spatialized information and digital mapping. It referred to the uses of data for trend-lining and predictive analytics. Finally, the element that would bring this together was the electronic visualization of the data—both on the Web and on desktop computing devices. This book achieved some of these initial objectives.

Every text is a work in motion. A collection is really a work by its respective authors, and *Packaging Digital Information for Enhanced Learning and Analysis...* captures a range of insights from the field. This provides a brief overview.

Section 1, "Principled Strategies in Packaging Digital Contents," includes works that articulate practical concepts and approaches to packaging digital materials. All of these insights are abstracted from actual practice. Dr. Mitch Ricketts's "Making Health Information Personal: How Anecdotes Bring Concepts to Life" (Ch. 1) shares an approach to creating visuals for teaching and learning about safety issues that brings in deep understandings of human perception, cognition, and learning. Brent A. Anders's "More than Just Data: The Importance of Motivation, Examples, and Feedback in Comprehending and Retaining Digital Information" (Ch. 2) elaborates on the human side of engaging with digital information for learning, based on the Attention, Relevance, Confidence, and Satisfaction (ARCS) model. Dr. Shalin Hai-Jew builds a partial typology of various types of branching logic applied in instructional design in "Branching Logic in the Design of Online Learning: A Partial Typology" (Ch. 3).

Section 2, "Innovative Technologies and Techniques in Packaging Digital Contents," focuses on creative applications of technologies for teaching and learning, information finding, training, and marketing outreach. Dr. Ya-Chun Shih describes an innovative mash-up of Web 2.0 and facial expression recognition in a 3D English classroom to bring authenticity to foreign language learning in "Weaving Web 2.0 and Facial Expression Recognition into the 3D Virtual English Classroom" (Ch. 4). Her chapter offers a variety of scenarios with creative applied curriculum. Dr. Rob Gibson describes the use of augmented reality to enhance library user experiences in "Utilizing Augmented Reality in Library Information Search" (Ch. 5). Dr. Roger McHaney, Lynda D. Spire, and Rosemary Boggs describe the multi-year collaborative project of creating a publicly available faculty module tool to enhance the quality of online teaching and learning at a university in "ELearningFacultyModules.org" (Ch. 6). This team describes the integration of an open-source wiki tool, MediaWiki, to actualize this vision of an interactive training resource. In "Multimodal Mapping of a University's Formal and Informal Online Brand: Using NodeXL to Extract Social Network Data in Tweets, Digital Contents, and Relational Ties " (Ch. 7), Dr. Hai-Jew describes the analysis of the formal and informal social presences of a university in its various manifestations on social media platforms through data extractions and graph data visualizations.

In Section 3, "Packaging Digital Contents for Perspective and Analysis," a group of authors engage with issues of capturing, visualizing, and analyzing complex data. Drs. Luca Cagliero and Naeem A. Mahoto's "Visualization of High-Level Associations from Twitter Data" (Ch. 8) introduces the Twitter Generalized Rule Visualizer (TGRV), which mines Twitter Tweets and expresses these as visual organizational structures. Dr. William H. Hsu provides an overview of a broad range of "Information

Visualization Techniques for Big Data: Analytics using Heterogeneous Data in Spatiotemporal Domains" in Chapter 9. Dr. Hai-Jew applies social network analysis to explore social hierarchies on instructional design projects in Chapter 10, titled "Using Social Network Analysis to Examine Social Hierarchies and Team Dynamics on Instructional Design Projects." Further, in "Beyond Surface Relations: Using Maltego Radium® to Analyze Electronic Connectivity and Hidden Ties in the Internet Understructure" (Ch. 11), Dr. Hai-Jew uses a penetration testing tool to surface information from academia for analytical purposes.

In Section 4, "Cases in Real-World Packaging of Digital Contents for Learning," researchers share their experiences using packaged digital contents in various learning contexts. If engineers are the ones who help bring new products into the world, the innovative faculty, administrators, and staff who connect the technological innovations with line-level practitioners in the field and learners are the other "bridging nodes" in complex innovation networks. Dr. Ya-Chun Shih and Molly Leonard, in "Immersion and Interaction via Avatars within Google Street View: Opening Possibilities beyond Traditional Cultural Learning" (Ch. 12), share a creative integration of real-world Google Street View scenes with avatar-based immersive foreign language (and culture) learning. Dr. Gladys Palma de Schrynemakers describes a project at her university that integrates uses of TED Talks resources for in-depth learning in "How Digital Media like TED Talks are Revolutionizing Teaching and Student Learning" (Ch. 13). Dr. Hai-Jew, in "Structuring an Emergent and Transdisciplinary Online Curriculum: A One Health Case" (Ch. 14) focuses on some strategies used to create an online curriculum about an emergent and evolving topic.

In Section 5, "Digital Packaging for Young Learners," researchers share their insights on creating both digital and analog objects for learning in augmented ways. Soren Eskildsen, Kasper Rodil, and Dr. Matthias Rehm describe a creative educational project "Identification and Analysis of Primary School Children's Knowledge Acquisition: Using Knowledge Visualization Scenarios and Information Visualization Methodology" (Ch. 15) deployed at a zoo. Finally, in Chapter 16, reading expert Dr. Carol Stockdale describes her research insights in using an analog technique for improving letter memory. Her chapter, "Evaluating a Technique for Improving Letter Memory in At-Risk Kindergarten Students," describes a tactual and visual analog technique which could be enhanced with digital methods for more effective learning.

Packaging Digital Information for Enhanced Learning and Analysis: Data Visualization, Spatialization, Predictiveness, and Multidimensionality captures a sense of the state-of-the-art in terms of data visualization, particularly as it is being practiced in the real world of teaching and learning and analysis.

Shalin Hai-Jew
Kansas State University, USA

Acknowledgment

Those dear readers who hail from academia will likely have a sense of the cooperative hard work of so many that has made this work possible. It helps to conceptualize *Packaging Digital Information for Enhanced Learning and Analysis...* not as a one-off but part of a long chain of efforts, all with learning and professional benefits along the way.

A singular chapter, which may be consumed with a fair amount of ease, requires a complex amount of dependencies to achieve. All the authors had to immerse in their respective domain fields. All had to conduct literature reviews. They had to mull the research and to design it. They had to actualize the research to standards (To do this, many had to use a range of technologies.). These authors have had to analyze their data. They had to package their chapters and visuals in a coherent way based on the conventions of the field. They had to revise their chapters after undergoing a double-blind peer review process. They had to meet some pretty stringent deadlines.

It may help for me to explain that whenever I put out a call for chapter proposals, I know that I am speaking not to a world of individuals who can speak to a particular issue with singular expertise and voices; I am speaking to an elite few with the rigorous higher education, the skill sets, the interest, and the good will to actually pursue the hard work and then ultimately to deliver solid chapters.

Anywhere along the way, writing teams have fallen apart. Projects have fallen to the wayside. Other priorities have intruded. Behind every work is a back story. These are the authors who persisted and turned out excellent chapters. I am grateful for their contributions.

Further, many at IGI Global have contributed to this text. Monica Speca served as editorial assistant to the project throughout most of its development cycle. Christine Smith came on during the production phase and saw the work through to its completion. I am grateful to them all for their kind support.

Shalin Hai-Jew
Kansas State University, USA

Section 1
Principled Strategies in Packaging Digital Contents

Chapter 1
Making Health Information Personal:
How Anecdotes Bring Concepts to Life

Mitch Ricketts
Kansas State University, USA

ABSTRACT

Research suggests people often fail to understand the personal relevance of generalized health information. To make health information more meaningful, communicators can employ anecdotes that take the form of instructive stories about the illnesses or injuries of particular people. Appropriate anecdotes may help audiences internalize health information by triggering insights such as: "I see how that could happen to me...I'd better take action." Vivid anecdotes appear to activate many of the same neurological pathways that help us extract meaning from direct experience and observation. By eliciting vivid imagery, provoking deep thought, and forging lasting memories, anecdotes may shape beliefs and behaviors to nearly the same extent as a lived event. This chapter explores methods for integrating anecdotes into health messages to increase personal relevance and prompt important changes in health-related behavior.

PREVENTING ILLNESSES AND INJURIES THROUGH THE MODIFICATION OF BEHAVIOR

Unhealthful behaviors represent an important public health problem in the United States and throughout the world. In fact, it is now widely recognized that unhealthful behaviors are among the leading causes of human death and disease (Ford, Zhao, Tsai, & Li, 2011; Mokdad, Marks, Stroup, & Gerberding, 2004; Woolf, & Aron, 2013; World Health Organization [WHO], 2011). Behaviors with the most deleterious impacts include tobacco use, poor eating habits, physical inactivity, alcohol consumption, unsafe actions that lead to injuries, unsafe sex, and the illicit use of drugs.

Over the years, public health professionals have developed a variety of interventions to influence relevant behaviors—often with positive impacts on human health (e.g., WHO, 2011). Examples of effective behavioral interventions include:

- Laws that require safe, responsible behavior (e.g., statutes prohibiting drunk driving).
- Policies that limit exposure to hazardous products and substances (e.g., the establishment of smoke-free public places).

DOI: 10.4018/978-1-4666-4462-5.ch001

- Built environments that support physical activity (e.g., the construction of safe and convenient walking routes).
- Public health messages that promote voluntary healthful behaviors (e.g., campaigns promoting breast self-examinations).

This chapter focuses on the last category of interventions—messages that promote healthful behaviors—and the realm of scholarship known as health communication.

A "RELEVANCE GAP" IN HEALTH INFORMATION: THE PROBLEM OF RELATING GENERAL INFORMATION TO PARTICULAR EVENTS

Health communication is an interdisciplinary profession committed to disseminating information that promotes safe and healthful decision making. Since health information is typically based on generalized epidemiological data, health communicators face the deceptively difficult task of helping learners comprehend the many ways in which *generalized* health concepts apply to *particular* events in everyday life. As an example, consider the current public health problem of distracted driving: Although drivers are routinely exposed to warnings about the number of deaths caused by inattention, many motorists continue to use cell phones, adjust radios, eat, and study maps while driving. The immense difficulty of applying health-related generalities to daily affairs is reflected in the finding that simply "learning the facts" often fails to trigger changes in peoples' behavior (e.g., Weare, 1992; Zeitlin, 1994).

One way health communicators can address the gap between generalized information and particular events is by *personalizing* health information through the use of anecdotes about singular health-related experiences in the lives of particular people. The goal of such personalization is to increase the likelihood that message recipients will internalize the health lessons, change their behavior, and enjoy better health.

A Mental Experiment

Before exploring methods for infusing generalized facts with personal relevance, we'll consider a brief "thought experiment" that illustrates the difficulty of applying broad generalizations to particular life events. To provide context for this "experiment," we'll examine two very different communication strategies for persuading adults to adopt behaviors that protect children from injuries caused by ride-on lawn mowers.

To prepare for our mental experiment, consider that childhood mower injuries comprise a serious public health issue in the United States, where thousands of children are injured by ride-on mowers every year (Hammig, Childers, & Jones, 2009; Smith & Committee on Injury and Poison Prevention, 2001; Vollman & Smith, 2006). Not only are these injuries common, but in some cases they have devastating consequences—particularly when a ride-on mower *runs over* a child. This can happen when a child is playing in an area where grass is being mowed. It can also happen if a child is riding on a mower and falls off—either while operating the machine or while riding as a passenger on an adult's lap.

Injuries such as these have led health communicators to develop messages aimed at persuading adults to keep children indoors while mowing and to never let children ride as passengers. Many of these messages are based on generalized information about the risks *to children in general*, as illustrated in the U.S. Consumer Product Safety Commission's (CPSC, n.d.b, p. 4) general warning shown in Figure 1.

Mental Experiment Task 1

As the first task in our mental experiment, take a moment to examine your subjective reaction to the message in Figure 1—a message based

Figure 1. Generalized information explaining that children should be kept out of the mowing area and never allowed to ride as passengers (CPSC, n.d.b, p. 4)

Riding Lawn Mowers and Children

Tragic accidents can occur if the operator of a mower is not alert to the presence of children. Children are often attracted to the machine and the mowing activity. **Never** assume that children will remain where you last saw them.

1. Keep small children out of the mowing area, and in the watchful care of a responsible adult other than the operator.
2. Be alert and turn the machine off if a child enters the area.
3. Before and while backing, look behind and down for small children.
4. Never carry children, even with the blade(s) shut off. They may fall off and be seriously injured or interfere with safe mower operation. Children who have been given rides in the past may suddenly appear in the mowing area for another ride and be run over or backed over by the machine.
5. Never allow children to operate the machine.
6. Use extreme care when approaching blind corners, shrubs, and trees, or other objects that may block your view of a child.

DO NOT CARRY PASSENGERS

entirely on generalized information. Here are some questions to guide your thoughts: How pertinent does the information in Figure 1 seem *with respect to the children you know and care about?* Does the information cause you to reflect on your own experiences (e.g., times when you or someone else was mowing at your home, in your neighborhood, or in a park)? Does the message persuade you to change *your* behavior in any way? For instance, how insistent will you now be about making sure no unsupervised children are present the next time you (or others) are mowing? How certain are you that from now on you will always say "no" if a child asks to ride on your lap or the lap of someone else who is mowing?

After reflecting on the generalized health information in Figure 1, read the health messages in Figures 2 and 3. These messages take an approach that is very different from that of Figure 1: Whereas Figure 1 emphasized the hazards of mowers to *children in general*, Figures 2 and 3 describe the true, representative cases of *individual children* who were tragically affected in ways discussed more generally by Figure 1.

Mental Experiment Task 2

The anecdotal health messages in Figures 2 and 3 are based on singular descriptions of events that happened to particular children. After considering these cases, reflect on the following questions to complete the thought exercise: How pertinent does the health message (keep children indoors during mowing and don't let them drive) seem now that you have read the anecdotes? Did anecdotes make it easier to imagine how a similar tragedy could

Figure 2. Anecdote used by the author in health interventions to explain why children should never be allowed to ride as passengers on mowers (© 2012 Mitch Ricketts, used with permission)

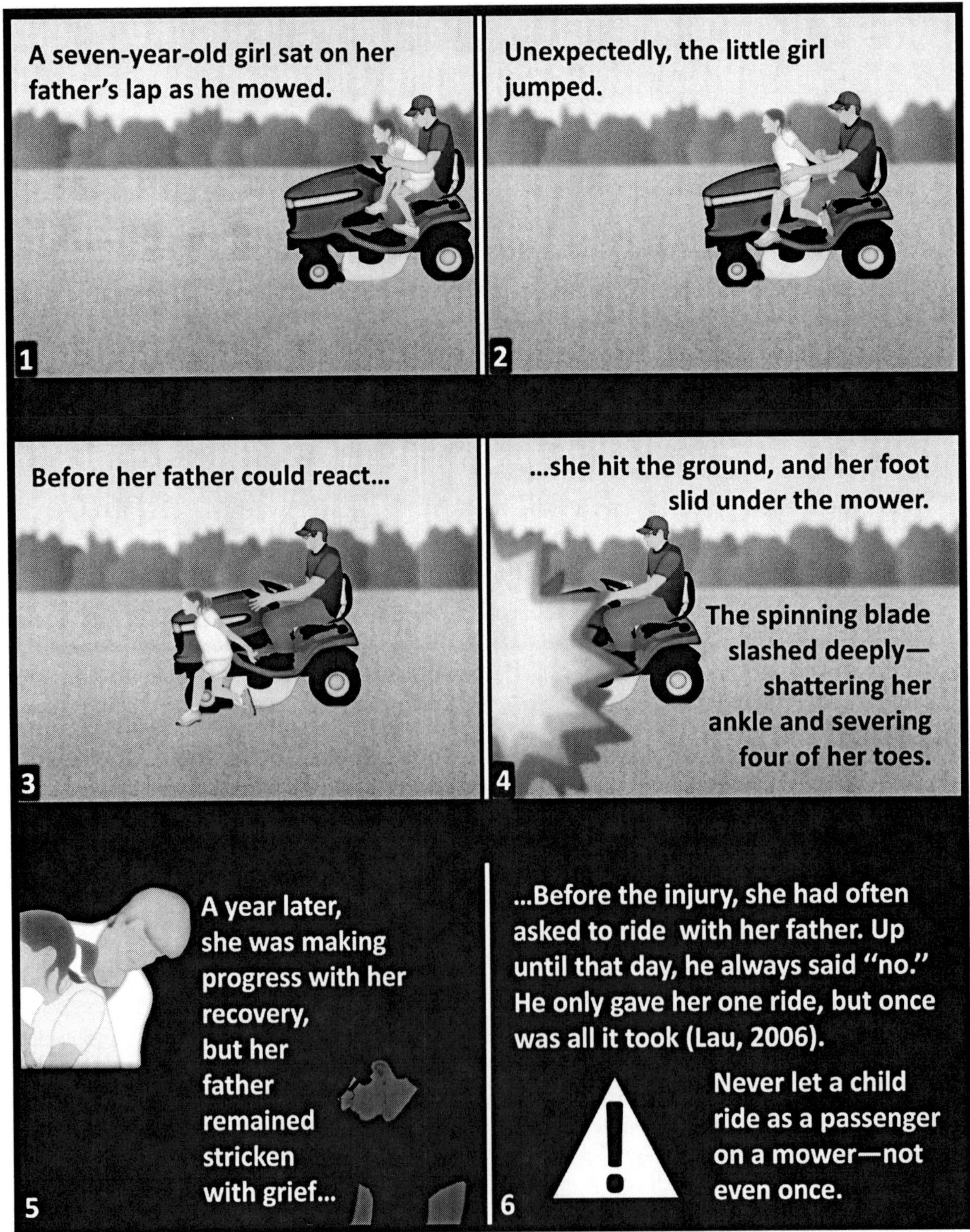

Figure 3. Anecdote used to explain why children should be kept out of the mowing area (© 2012 Mitch Ricketts, used with permission)

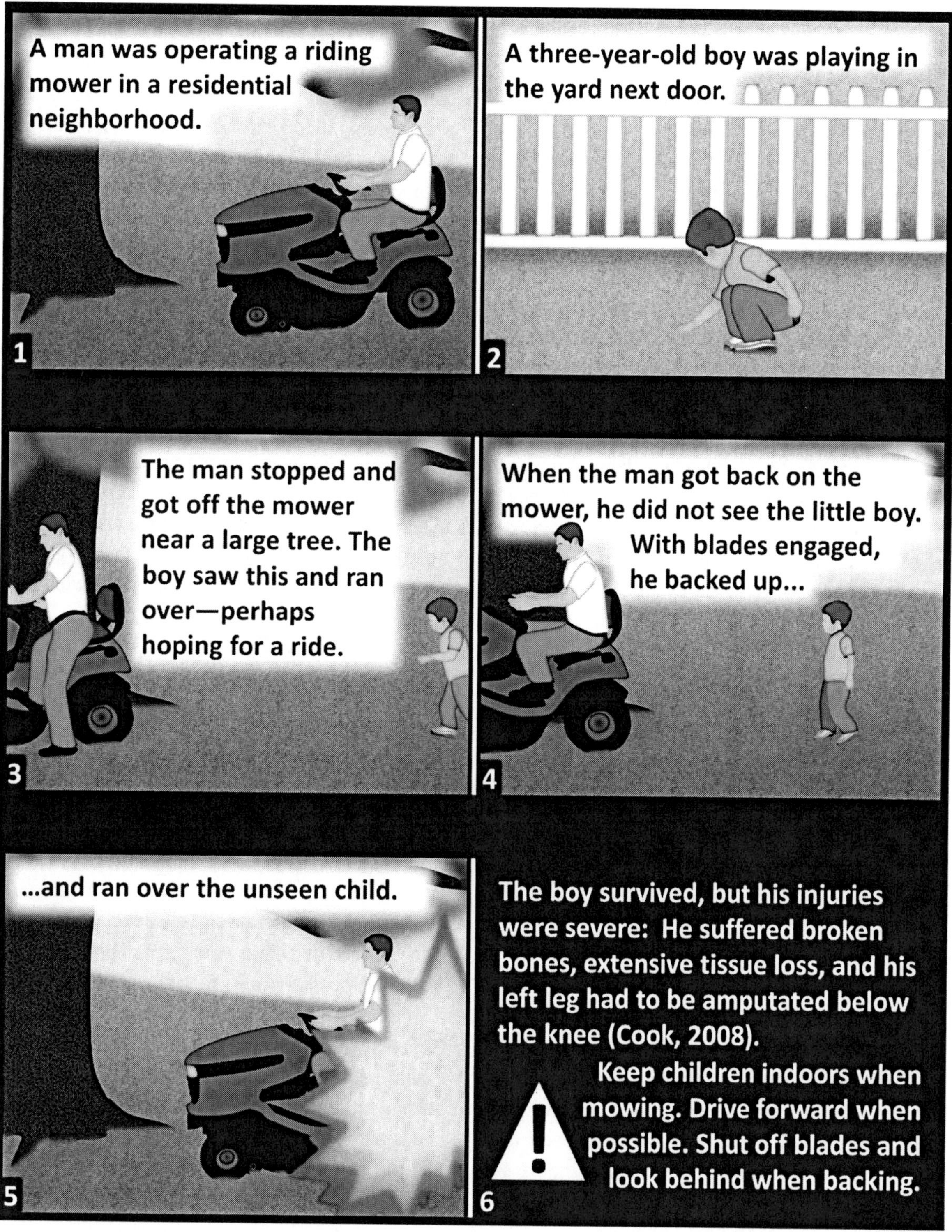

happen to *a child you know* and care about? Will you now give more thought to changing your own behavior when you or others are mowing in your yard, neighborhood, or park? If you found yourself reflecting and understanding more deeply when reading Figures 2 and 3 (compared with Figure 1), then you have just experienced the thought-provoking quality of anecdotes—also known as parables, narratives, and stories.

CHAPTER OVERVIEW

As demonstrated by the thought experiment, generalized information such as that shown in Figure 1 may be broadly applicable, yet it often seems unimportant and pedantic—perhaps because it fails to link general principles (e.g., keep children away) to an actual concrete experience (the injury of a particular child). In contrast, anecdotes trigger reflection and insight by relating abstract ideas to the tangible context of human events. The purpose of this chapter is to explore how anecdotes bring concepts to life by imparting personal meaning to generalized information. Chapter topics will include:

1. How learning from anecdotes relates to learning through personal experience and observation.
2. How anecdotes can trigger changes in behavior.
3. How to create effective health messages based on relevant anecdotes.

A Brief Word about Theory

The use of stories and anecdotes is not unique to any particular theory of health communication. In fact, anecdotal messages have been used in interventions based on a wide variety of theories and models, including the health belief model (Greene & Brinn, 2003), transtheoretical model (Jamner, Wolitski, & Corby, 1997), entertainment-education (Slater 2002); theory of planned behavior (Ashton, Houston, Williams, Larkin, Trobaugh, Crenshaw, & Wray, 2010), social cognitive theory (Houston, Cherrington, Coley, Robinson, Trobaugh, Williams, et al., 2011), and many others. Since anecdotal messages are not exclusively associated any theory or model of health behavior, the conceptual foundations of this chapter rest for the most part in the vast empirical literature of social learning and narrative communication.

THREE WAYS OF LEARNING FROM PARTICULAR EVENTS

To better understand the role of anecdotes in teaching and learning, it is helpful to consider some common ways people acquire knowledge in everyday life. First, we will explore learning that results from direct experience and observation. Then, we will discuss how learning from anecdotes relates to these forms of knowledge.

Learning from Personal Experience

As we will see, anecdotal learning shares many qualities with learning from direct experience. Therefore, we will briefly consider some ways in which personal experience affects behavior.

Much of what we know about the educational value of direct experience comes from research in the field of judgment and decision making. *In laboratory settings,* researchers often study experience-based decisions using a card game known as the Iowa Gambling Task, or IGT (Bechara, Damasio, Damasio, & Anderson, 1994). In the IGT, research participants win and lose money by drawing cards from various decks. Unknown to participants, some decks are designed to produce occasional large gains—but these gains are more than offset by persistent long-term losses. Other decks offer gains that are small but consistent, leading to long-term profit. Over a lengthy IGT session, a research participant draws about a hundred cards by choosing freely among the decks. Since participants are not told the decks differ, choosing profitably over time implies an ability to learn from experience. Researchers employing the IGT have confirmed that most adults do learn to choose from the better decks. In other words, experimental evidence suggests people do learn from experience—as long as they are not suffering from limitations such as neurological impairment, mental illness, or the influence of drugs (e.g., Buelow, & Suhr, 2009).

Outside the laboratory, learning from experience is often studied by asking people how their behavior has changed after major life events. Many of these studies have demonstrated that personal experience can trigger behavior change even when generalized information does not. In an investigation that mirrors the theme of our mental experiment, researchers in Ohio examined the causes and consequences of lawn mower injuries treated at Children's Hospital in Columbus (Vollman, Khosla, Shields, Beeghly, Bonsu, & Smith, 2005). Despite longstanding government warnings to keep children away from mowers, the hospital treated 85 youngsters for mower-related injuries during the investigation's four-and-a-half-year duration. Many of the injured children were quite young; in fact, the median age was 5 years, and some children were as young as 22 months. Injuries were often severe, with 40 percent of victims requiring inpatient treatment.

In line with the notion that people have trouble relating generalized information to particular events, Vollman and colleagues found clear evidence that prior to the children's injuries, their parents knew about, but were unaffected by, warnings similar to those shown in Figure 1. In fact, 100 percent of parents who responded to researchers' questions said they knew the risks prior to injury but allowed their children to participate in mowing activities anyway—even though many of these children were not yet old enough to attend school.

Most relevant for the purposes of our discussion is the finding by Vollman and colleagues that parents of the injured children *did* change their behavior after the injuries occurred—in other words, they learned from experience. Among parents who responded to researchers' inquiries, 86 percent said they adopted safety practices similar to those shown in Figure 1 after their children were injured. This included parents who stated they had begun keeping children inside while mowing and parents who no longer allowed children to ride as passengers on mowers.

Along with the findings noted above, research in a variety of settings supports three important conclusions:

1. People may not comprehend the personal relevance of information when concepts are presented in a general and abstract manner (e.g., Brickman,1978, Myers, Iscoe, Jennings, Lenox, Minsky, & Sacks, 1981).
2. Personal relevance is more easily learned when people experience consequences directly, and this learning often triggers changes in behavior (e.g., Ezingeard, & Bowen-Schrire, 2007; Grothmann & Reusswig, 2006; McBride, Emmons, & Lipkus, 2003; Perry & Lindell, 2008; Weinstein, 1989).
3. When faced with novel situations or difficult choices, people often make decisions based on lessons remembered from past events (e.g., Pillemer, 2001, 2003). Even when experiences are not fully remembered, they may trigger "gut feelings" that affect decisions in ways that remain outside our awareness (e.g., Damasio, Tranel, & Damasio, 1991).

Learning by Watching Others

Personal experience is a powerful teacher, but we can also learn by watching others. This is fortunate, because the consequences of some mistakes are so costly that we might not survive the learning process if we all had to discover everything on our own.

Among researchers in the field of social learning, terms such as *social influence, imitation,* and *observational learning* have rigorous—and sometimes disputed—definitions (Zentall, 2011, 2012). Rather than focusing on distinctions among these various types of learning, we will broadly consider any purposeful change in behavior that appears to be triggered, at least in part, by observing others. We will refer to this phenomenon informally as *learning-by-watching*.

More than a century ago, researchers sought evidence for learning-by-watching, often by examining the behavior of animals (e.g. Thorndike, 1898). Although researchers encountered many obstacles, Herbert and Harsh (1944) eventually reported convincing results in which house cats appeared to learn—or at least change their behavior—after watching others. Herbert and Harsh created a laboratory environment in which cats could gain access to food by manipulating levers, strings, turn tables, and foot pedals in particular ways. When naïve cats had to learn these tasks through personal trial and error, their skills developed slowly. In contrast, cats learned quickly when they watched other cats complete the tasks first, demonstrating a form of learning-by-watching that is now referred to as social influence.

Similar research in humans has demonstrated how *children* learn by watching adults and by observing each other. For instance, Bandura, Ross, and Ross (1961) demonstrated that children quickly copied the aggressive behaviors of a grownup, who famously pummeled and yelled at an inflatable clown doll named Bobo. With respect to learning-by-watching in *adults*, Santiesteban and Koran (1977) demonstrated that preservice teachers learned important instructional skills better if they first observed those skills being modeled by an experienced educator.

Studies such as these have established that when people learn new behaviors or refine existing skills, they often do so by watching others. A related issue involves the extent to which people learn to *avoid* certain behaviors if they witness others suffering adverse consequences as a result. Some early evidence on this issue came from an elaborate experiment reported by Heisler (1974). Briefly, Heisler found that college students were less likely to cheat on an exam if they saw another student being punished for dishonesty. The effect was greater when students *saw* a supposed classmate being punished, rather than merely being warned that there would be severe consequences for cheating. In other words, the experience of witnessing a single person's punishment led to greater internalization of consequences, compared with merely hearing how those consequences would apply to everyone. A recent meta-analysis including this and 20 similar studies confirmed that in a variety of contexts learning-by-watching does help people avoid behaviors that are likely to result in adverse outcomes—a phenomenon known as vicarious punishment (Malouff, Thorsteinsson, Schutte, & Rooke, 2009).

The Mirror Neuron System

For health educators, the concept of learning-by-watching implies that people's health-related habits are influenced by behaviors and consequences observed in others. The neurological mechanisms behind this process are far from clear; however, some scholars believe clues may be found in the growing body of literature on specialized brain cells known as "mirror neurons."

Mirror neurons were discovered by chance as researchers in Parma Italy monitored neurological activity in macaque monkeys (di Pellegrino, Fadiga, Fogassi, Gallese, & Rizzolatti, 1992). The original purpose of the Parma study was to identify neurons that became active in the brain's premotor cortex when monkeys engaged in goal-directed behavior such as grasping food or manipulating objects. Unexpectedly, researchers noticed that many of these same neurons also became active when monkeys *saw* a researcher perform a similar action. In other words, the neurons behaved in comparable ways regardless of whether a monkey performed the action itself or saw the action performed by someone else. The essence of the finding was that mirror neurons "reflect" others' actions within the brain.

The discovery of mirror neurons in monkeys triggered a cascade of research, and an analogous mirror neuron system was eventually confirmed in humans (Mukamel, Ekstrom, Kaplan, Iacoboni, & Fried, 2010). Many scholars now believe mirror neurons are at least partly responsible for our ability to understand the actions, intentions, and experiences of others—without which, observational learning would be impossible. A number of findings from this growing body of research are relevant to our discussion:

1. Mirror neurons fire in motor-related areas of the brain when we perform a particular goal-directed act *and* when we witness someone else engaging in a similar behavior. As a result, we understand others' behavior because their actions are mirrored in areas of our brains that represent our own body parts. By linking behaviors we see in others to internal representations of those same acts in ourselves, the mirror neuron system may help us understand others' actions "from the inside," giving us a "first-person grasp of the motor goals and intentions of other individuals" (Rizzolatti & Sinigaglia, 2010, p. 264).
2. Mirror neurons (or systems analogous to them) also fire in *pain*-related areas of the brain. These neurons fire not only when we experience pain (e.g., by a needle plunged into the hand), but also when we see someone else being injured in a similar way (Bastiaansen, Thioux, & Keysers, 2009; Keysers, Kaas, & Gazzola, 2010; Morrison, Lloyd, Pellegrino, & Roberts, 2004; Morrison, Tipper, Fenton-Adams, & Bach, 2012).
3. Additionally, mirror neurons (or analogous systems) fire in *emotion*-related areas of the brain when we experience emotions (e.g., disgust, joy, anger) and when we see someone else experiencing those emotions (Bastiaansen, et al. 2009; Chaminade, Zecca, Blakemore, Takanishi, Frith, et al. 2010; Jabbi, Bastiaansen, & Keysers, 2008; Keysers & Gazzola, 2009; Molenberghs, Cunnington, & Mattingley, 2012; Rizzolatti & Fabbri-Destro, 2009; Wicker, Keysers, Plailly, Royet, Gallese, & Rizzolatti, 2003).

This evidence has led many researchers to conclude that mirror neurons (or comparable systems) help us create empathetic mental representations of the experiences, actions, intentions, and emotions of others (e.g., Baird, Scheffer, & Wilson, 2011; Iacoboni, 2009; Keysers & Gazzola, 2009). Thus, the mirror neuron system may help explain observational learning by identifying neurological circuits through which we vicariously experience other people's successes and failures.

Learning From Anecdotes and Stories

Besides learning from direct experience and by watching others, we also benefit from hearing or reading about events we have not witnessed firsthand. For instance, researchers have found that women's decisions to schedule mammograms are often triggered by hearing about friends, family members, or others who have been diagnosed with breast cancer (Drossaert, Boer, & Seydel, 1996; Glanz, Resch, Lerman, Blake, Gorchov, & Rimer, 1992; King, Balshem, Ross, Rimer, & Seay, 1995; Vogel, Graves, Vernon, Lord, Winn, Peters, et al. 1990). As another example, Denscombe (2001) found that teenagers learn about alcohol, tobacco, and other drugs in part by listening to anecdotes told by friends and family members. Thus, some (but clearly not all) teenagers may be persuaded not to smoke by hearing about a friend's mother who suffers from smoking-related cancer.

Stronger evidence of learning-from-stories comes from formal experiments in which participants are systematically exposed to anecdote-based health messages. For instance, O'Donnell, O'Donnell, San Doval, Duran, and Labes (1998) conducted a study among patients attending a clinic for Sexually Transmitted Diseases (STDs). Some of the study's participants watched a video that conveyed health information through stories about people who used condoms to avoid exposure to STDs. Other participants did not see the video, but they did receive regular clinic services. Researchers found that participants were more likely to protect themselves from STDs if they had been shown the story-based health video. In fact, patients who saw the video contracted significantly fewer new STD infections during the study period, compared with patients who did not see the film.

Although patients in the STD study did appear to change their behavior, the study's design made it impossible to determine what components of the video-based treatment were responsible for that change. For instance, behavior could have changed because of exposure to health-related anecdotes in the film, or alternatively, because of factors unrelated to the anecdotes (including the extra generalized information and experimental attention received by participants who watched the video). To create a clearer test of anecdotal learning, Chang (2008) conducted a study in which all participants received similar amounts of information and attention. The only difference between treatments in Chang's study was that some participants received information through anecdote-based messages, while others received information without anecdotes. Health messages in this study were designed to inform participants about emotional depression. Some participants read messages that consisted entirely of generalized (non-anecdotal) content. Others read messages with identical content *and* a story about the struggles of a college student who suffered from depression. The major finding was that participants became more willing to seek professional help for depression if they read messages containing a personal anecdote.

Chang's study demonstrated that anecdotal health information prompted an internalization of the message and a willingness to seek professional help. However, it could be argued that *willingness* is not the same as actually *seeking* help (an overt behavior). To test the impact of stories on overt behavior, Ricketts, Shanteau, McSpadden, and Fernandez-Medina (2010) observed participants' actions after exposure to health messages. In separate experimental sessions, 54 teams of participants assembled a child's swing set according to instructions in a step-by-step manual. The manual contained safety messages and warnings related to common assembly mistakes that have caused serious injuries to children in the past. For instance, improperly installed bolts and S-hooks can snag clothing and cause children to be strangled. Other mistakes can result in structural weakness, causing the frames of swings to collapse on top of children (Tinsworth & McDonald, 2001; CPSC, 2010).

Participants were not aware that the true purpose of the study was to test the effectiveness of the safety messages and warnings. Instead, they knew only that their job was to assemble a swing set as though a child they cared about was going to use it. Participants were randomly assigned so that 18 teams used an assembly manual that contained traditional safety warnings written in a terse, authoritarian style (see Figure 4a). Another 18 teams used an assembly manual with the terse warnings *and* a generalized explanation of injuries that have happened to children (Figure 4b). The remaining 18 teams used an assembly manual with terse warnings *and* anecdotes about injuries that have happened to particular children (Figure 4c). To control for the effects of informational content, concreteness, and other factors, the generalized explanations (Figure 4b) and anecdotal messages (Figure 4c) were designed to be equivalent with respect to causal details, reading levels, the use

Figure 4. Examples of non-anecdotal and anecdotal safety messages: a) terse authoritarian warning; b) warning plus non-anecdotal message; c) warning plus anecdotal message. Ricketts et al. (2010) found that assemblers built safer swings when product manuals contained anecdotal messages similar to c.

a. WARNING: This product must be assembled according to the instructions in this manual. Failure to follow all instructions could result in collapse of the swing set during use.

b. WARNING: This product must be assembled according to the instructions in this manual. Failure to follow all instructions could result in collapse of the swing set during use.

Collapsing Swing Sets Can Injure Children. If a swing set collapses while a child is playing, the child may fall and the frame of the swing may even crash down on her. The child may suffer broken bones, internal injuries, and disfigurement. She may require extensive medical treatment. Death is even possible. Follow all instructions in the assembly manual. Swing sets may collapse if not assembled properly. Source: CPSC Recommendation #50711237.

c. WARNING: This product must be assembled according to the instructions in this manual. Failure to follow all instructions could result in collapse of the swing set during use.

Girl Seriously Injured in Swing Set Collapse. On July 4, 2005, a young girl was sitting on a swing in a park. Without warning, the entire swing set collapsed. The frame of the swing set crashed down, breaking her nose and several other bones in her face. Her injuries required extensive medical treatment. An investigation found that the swing set had not been assembled properly. Source: Consumer Product Safety Commission Case #50711237.

of personal pronouns, authoritative reference citations, etc.

After each team assembled the swing, researchers inspected it to identify preventable mistakes discussed in the safety messages. In support of the notion that anecdotes affect behavior, participants made about 20 percent fewer safety-related assembly errors when they used the assembly manual containing anecdote-based safety messages (compared with either of the other manuals). Interestingly, messages with generalized information (Figure 4b) were no more effective than terse warnings alone (Figure 4a)—a finding that once again suggests people may fail to comprehend the personal relevance of facts when they do not have the benefit of learning by experience, watching others, or exposure to anecdotes.

Many other researchers have found that health-related knowledge, attitudes, intentions, and behaviors can be influenced by relevant anecdotes (see Ricketts, 2007 for a review). Still, qualities that make anecdotes effective are far from clear.

One possibility is that we simply pay better attention to stories, perhaps because they are more interesting than generalized information. Support for this notion was found by Hastall and Knobloch-Westerwick (2012). These researchers created online magazines that included articles about health issues such as air quality, glaucoma, stress, and tainted food. Some articles included personal accounts of victims, while others were based entirely on generalized data. Research participants were free to browse the magazines at their own pace. Consistent with the notion that anecdotes are intrinsically interesting, participants in the study were more likely to read articles containing anecdotes, compared with those based entirely on generalized data. This is important, because health messages are unlikely to have an impact unless the audience pays attention.

Some researchers have suggested other reasons why stories may be effective; for instance, it has been demonstrated that stories have a tendency to trigger deep thought and to produce strong, coherent memories. Cox (2001) emphasized the thought-provoking quality of stories in connection with anecdotal medical cases used to train doctors: "Each local situation provides relevance, context and circumstantial detail…The listener pays close attention and is vicariously involved with working out what is wrong..." (p. 862). As learners work through challenging cases and anecdotes, strong memories may be forged, potentially affecting related decisions for years to come. In fact, researchers in many fields have argued that we often make decisions more or less automatically based on conscious and nonconscious memories of past cases (e.g., Norman & Brooks, 1997; Pliske & Klein, 2003; Schank & Abelson, 1977).

Stories can stimulate deep cognitive processing, trigger powerful mental images, affect perceptions of new situations, and influence behavior—qualities that have led some scholars to argue that a gripping story may have nearly as much personal impact as an actual event (De Young & Monroe, 1996; Mar & Oatley, 2008; Polichak & Gerrig, 2002; Stapel & Velthuijsen, 1996). In fact, researchers have found that when we read or hear about the experiences of others, we comprehend in part because our brains activate many of the same visual and motor circuits that would be engaged if we were experiencing events in the story first-hand (Speer, Reynolds, Swallow, & Zacks, 2009; Willems & Casasanto, 2011). Findings such as these seem to corroborate the claims of Green and Brock (2000, 2002, 2005), who argued that stories are powerful because they often seem as real as episodes from our own lives. In the words of Green and Brock, readers and listeners are subjectively *transported* into the story's setting. While immersed in the narrative, images may seem so vivid and emotions so strong that lines between story and personal experience become blurred. As a result, audiences may automatically incorporate the story's central message into their own beliefs and values.

Researchers have discovered many other qualities that make anecdotes effective for triggering behavior change. For instance, the natural structure of a story makes anecdotes easier to read, comprehend, and remember (e.g., Graesser, Hauft-Smith, Cohen, & Pyles, 1980; Zabrucky & Moore, 1999; Zabrucky & Ratner, 1992). Furthermore, vicarious engagement in a vivid story seems to break down resistance to persuasion, making audience members less likely to reject the central theme of a message and more confident in their own ability to overcome barriers and adopt healthful behaviors (e.g., Chang, 2008; Dillard, Fagerlin, Cin, Zikmund-Fisher, & Ubel, 2010; Kreuter, Holmes, Alcaraz, Kalesan, Rath, Richert, et al., 2010; McQueen, Kreuter, Kalesan, & Alcaraz, 2011).

In short, there appear to be many reasons why stories are effective. These include the intrinsically interesting nature of stories, the propensity of stories for triggering complex problem solving, the depth of memories forged by stories, the ability of stories to promote learning in ways that are reminiscent of direct experience and learning-by-watching, the ease with which we comprehend information in the context of a story, and the persuasive impact of hearing about a singular event that did (or could) happen.

USING ANECDOTES EFFECTIVELY IN SAFETY AND HEALTH MESSAGES

Although anecdotes can be compelling, effective communicators seldom rely on stories to the complete exclusion of other forms of information. A balanced mix of generalized facts, sprinkled with occasional anecdotes, is likely to be more effective than a purely one-dimensional approach. As noted by Sadoski (2001), "Knowledge includes particular examples and instances as well as the general definitions and principles that organize them. Learning concrete examples without abstract principles is piecemeal; learning abstract principles without concrete examples is empty..." (pp. 268-269). Generalized information *is* critical for understanding the facts surrounding complex issues. Rather than arguing against all use of abstract generalizations, this chapter recommends using anecdotes *in addition to* generalities so the broader implications of data will take on more personal meaning.

General Considerations for Message Development

Communicators must consider a variety of factors when developing health messages. In this section, we will consider how message effectiveness can be affected by audience characteristics and the presence of illustrations.

Audience Characteristics

Receptiveness to anecdotal messages may depend in part on an audience's prior level of awareness about a health issue. In this regard, anecdotes are well suited for raising consciousness among people who do not yet understand the personal relevance of a health topic. Generalized information, on the other hand, becomes more helpful once people have developed an interest in the issue (Braverman, 2008).

The impact of prior audience awareness was evident in a series of studies reported by Rook (1986, 1987). Participants in these studies were women, ranging in age from 34 to 79 years. Rook exposed the women to health messages about osteoporosis—a bone disorder that is most common in people over the age of 50. Some of the messages in Rook's studies were based on generalized information, while others were based on anecdotes about the experiences of particular women. Rook found that anecdotal osteoporosis messages were more persuasive among younger women, but not among those who were older. Rook explained this finding as follows: For *young* women, the risk of osteoporosis seems remote because it is unlikely to affect them until a time in the distant future. Among these women, anecdotes help personalize the risk, making an otherwise obscure topic seem relevant. For *older* women, the prospect of developing osteoporosis is more immediate and the risk already seems personal. As a result, these women are able to benefit from generalized health information without need for the personalizing effect of anecdotes.

Rook's studies demonstrated that anecdotal messages are especially useful when audiences do not yet understand the personal relevance of an issue. Other researchers have found anecdotal health messages to be particularly effective among certain cultural groups—especially if cultural relevance is woven into the central theme of the message. As an example, health communicators have successfully used culturally relevant stories to reach low-income Latinos with messages about early detection and prevention of colorectal cancer (Larkey & Gonzalez, 2007; Larkey, Lopez, Minnal, & Gonzalez, 2009). Culturally relevant anecdotal messages have also been used successfully to convey information about detection and prevention of breast cancer to low-income African American women (Erwin, Ivory, Stayton, Willis, Jandorf, Thompson, et al., 2003; Kreuter, et al., 2010).

To sum up, anecdotal messages can be effective in many situations, but they appear particularly well suited for triggering a sense of personal relevance and for creating culturally-appropriate interventions.

The Benefit of Illustrations

Messages that include both words *and* images belong to a general class of communications known as multimedia presentations. Extensive research has shown that audiences often understand complex information better when it is presented using a combination of words and images, rather than words or images alone (Mayer, 2009). In the context of multimedia learning, words may include spoken or written text, and images may include drawings, photographs, videos, animations, or other instructive artwork.

One example of beneficial illustrations was reported by Austin, Matlack, Dunn, Kesler, and Brown (1995). These researchers found that medical patients understood discharge instructions better when those instructions included both text and illustrations. Similarly, Delp and Jones (2008) found that patients released from an emergency department were more likely to read, understand, and follow wound care instructions when the text was illustrated with relevant cartoons. Finally, Houts, Doak, Doak, and Loscalzo (2006) reviewed a broad range of research and concluded that pictures can increase the effectiveness of health messages, particularly among low-literacy populations. Houts et al. further suggested that images should be free of unnecessary or distracting details, they should depict people who are similar to the intended audience, and they should relate to the main points of the message.

Features of Effective Anecdotes

In the previous section, we considered how audience characteristics and the presence of illustrations relate to message effectiveness. Here, we will examine particular features of narratives that make certain anecdotes more effective than others. These features include relevance, freedom from distracting content, a sense of chronology, clear cause-and-effect relationships, story characters with whom audiences can identify, an element of surprise, a sense that events in the story are subject to human control, and the possibility of alternative outcomes for the story's main characters.

Relevance

As discussed to this point, research demonstrates that relevant, representative anecdotes can increase the impact of health and safety messages. Here, we will consider evidence demonstrating an opposing effect; namely, that message impact may be undermined if anecdotes are irrelevant or distracting. A simple demonstration of this effect was reported by Harp and Mayer (1998), who asked research participants to read brief passages of text that described how lightning is created in thunderstorms. Some participants read passages in which all of the text and illustrations were directly related to the formation of lightning. Other participants read materials that contained additional anecdotes and illustrations that were *un*related to lightning formation. After reading the passages, participants were tested over their understanding of processes involved in the development of lightning. As might be expected, irrelevant anecdotes and illustrations detracted from learning and resulted in poor test performance.

The findings of Harp and Mayer represent an instance of a broader phenomenon known as the *seductive detail effect*. Seductive details consist of information that is interesting, but unrelated to the central purpose of a message (see Rey, 2012 for a recent review). Seductive details may divert attention or otherwise interfere with comprehension of the main lesson. To avoid the seductive detail effect, anecdotes must be carefully selected to reinforce or illustrate important points, and not detract from them.

As an example of distracting content that may inadvertently find its way into health messages, consider a series of experiments reported by Kyes, Brown, and Pollack (1991) and Wright and Kyes (1996). In this series of studies, research participants read health messages promoting the use of condoms as a method of safer sex. Overall, the researchers found that anecdotal messages could promote positive attitudes toward condom use—as long as the anecdotes did not distract audiences with sexual content that was unnecessarily erotic. For instance, attitudes toward condom use improved consistently when participants read non-erotic stories about a man and women *discussing* condoms. In contrast, improvement in attitudes was less consistent when participants read a story about an actual *sexual encounter* in which condoms were used. Apparently, the erotic content of the sexual-encounter story distracted some participants and prevented them from grasping the main point of the message.

In sum, anecdotes must be chosen and edited to focus attention on the main themes of a message. As illustrated in the condom study, pilot testing may be necessary to identify unanticipated distractions in anecdote-based messages.

Chronological Order and Cause-Effect Relationships

Although there are exceptions, people tend to comprehend stories better when events unfold in chronological order and when there are clear connections between causes and effects (e.g., Bower, Black, & Turner, 1979; De Young & Monroe, 1996; Pennington & Hastie, 1991). The importance of narrative order and causality has been examined frequently in the context of jury decisions. For instance, Voss, Wiley, and Sandak (1999) examined judgments by mock jurors, with the goal of identifying story components that must be present if evidence is to be perceived as convincing. Participants in this study read stories (summaries of evidence) that had been manipulated to (a) make the evidence less complete, (b) make cause-and-effect relationships less certain (e.g., by replacing the word *must* with *probably*), and (c) by scrambling the chronological order of events. An important finding was that mock jurors lost confidence in evidence when there were disruptions in chronological order or cause-and-effect relationships. (Interestingly, incompleteness—the absence of some information—did not impair the perceived quality of evidence.) The results of this and many other studies strongly suggest stories are most credible when they include a chain of causal events that unfolds in a natural order.

Applying this notion to health communication, it is important to consider that cause-and-effect relationships may be clearest when anecdotes involve *acute exposures* and *traumatic injuries*. For instance, Figures 2, 3, and 5 tell the stories of traumatic injuries caused by acute exposures (one-time events). These anecdotes leave little doubt as to causes, effects, and methods of prevention. In Figure 2, for example, the injury was clearly caused by the blade of the mower. Furthermore, the injury would certainly have been prevented if the child had been kept away and not allowed to ride on her father's lap. In Figure 3, the injury obviously would not have happened if the child had been kept out of the mowing area. In Figure 5, a properly-constructed railing would almost certainly have prevented the man's fall and his resulting death.

Cause-and-effect relationships may be somewhat less clear when cases involve *illnesses*—especially those caused by chronic exposures. Figures 6 and 7 describe illnesses for which there is strong (but not irrefutable) evidence of cause-and-effect. Figure 6 relates the story of an illness seemingly caused by an *acute* exposure (a single needle-stick), while Figure 7 describes an illness apparently caused by a *chronic* exposure (repeated low doses of a pesticide). Although there is reasonable evidence in both cases, it is possible to imagine alternative explanations for either illness. When audiences are not convinced that clear cause-and-effect relationships exist, messages will lack credibility and may be ineffective. To enhance credibility, it may be necessary to add some generalized data. For instance, Figure 6 states, "many healthcare workers have suffered diseases due to punctures from contaminated needles." Likewise, Figure 7 notes, "…research has shown that 2,4-D can damage the liver."

Some types of illnesses may have so many competing explanations that anecdotes should be minimized so attention can be focused almost exclusively on more convincing generalized data. Findings in line with this notion were obtained by Thrasher, Arillo-Santillán, Villalobos, Pérez-Hernández, Hammond, Carter, et al. (2012), who studied audience reactions to anti-smoking messages. Some messages in the study were non-anecdotal and discussed health effects as they apply to smokers in general. Other messages were anecdotal and discussed the experiences of particular smoking victims. An important finding of this study was that participants often rated the *non*-anecdotal messages as more credible, relevant, and powerful, compared with messages based on anecdotes. One possible interpretation of these findings is that anecdotes may have failed because there are simply too many competing explanations for any particular smoker's illness: Although there is clear statistical evidence that lung cancer, heart disease, and a variety of other maladies are more common among those who smoke, these same illnesses can also be caused by factors unrelated to smoking, including genetics, environmental exposures, and general physical condition. It is therefore practically impossible to state that any particular disease would definitely have been avoided if the person didn't smoke. For illnesses with many contributing factors, then, generalized (non-anecdotal) information may have greater veracity, simply because it is more compatible with the probabilistic nature of the evidence.

In short, anecdotal evidence is most credible when it includes a convincing sequence of cause-and-effect relationships. When cause-and-effect cannot be established, generalized information should be added to support the argument. In the most extreme examples, where illnesses have many potential causes, it may be necessary to minimize the use anecdotes and rely mainly on generalized information. Again, pilot testing with the target audience is important.

Attributes of Story Characters

It has been argued that stories are most persuasive when message recipients identify with, or experience a connection to, one or more characters within the story (e.g., Dal Cin, Zanna, & Fong, 2004; De Young & Monroe, 1996; Slater, 2002). Identification with story characters is a complex process that is not fully understood; nevertheless, research suggests audiences are more likely to identify with characters under the following circumstances:

1. Characters share demographic similarities with the audience; for instance, they are similar with respect to age, race, ethnicity, or gender (e.g., Jose & Brewer, 1984).
2. Characters are perceived as similar to the audience with respect to important values, beliefs, and life experiences (e.g., Oatley & Gholamain, 1997).
3. Characters are likeable, and the audience can imagine having a personal relationship with them (e.g., Slater, & Rouner, 2002).

Some research suggests audience members may be influenced even by seemingly minor similarities between themselves and story characters. For instance, Stapel, Reicher, and Spears (1994) reported the results of a study in which university

Figure 5. Traumatic injury with clear causation (© 2012 Mitch Ricketts, used with permission)

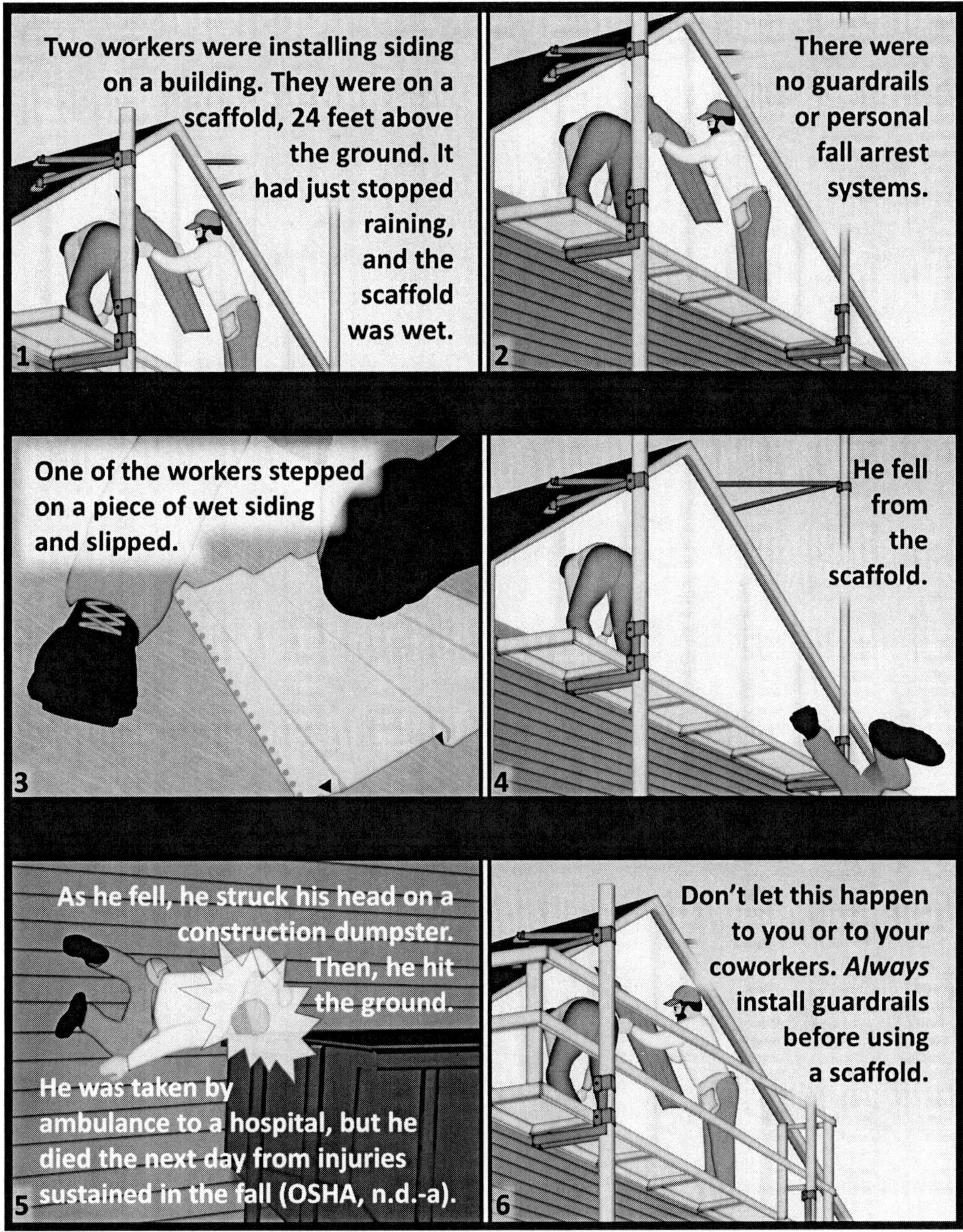

Figure 6. Illness with a probable causal link to an acute exposure (© 2012 Mitch Ricketts, used with permission)

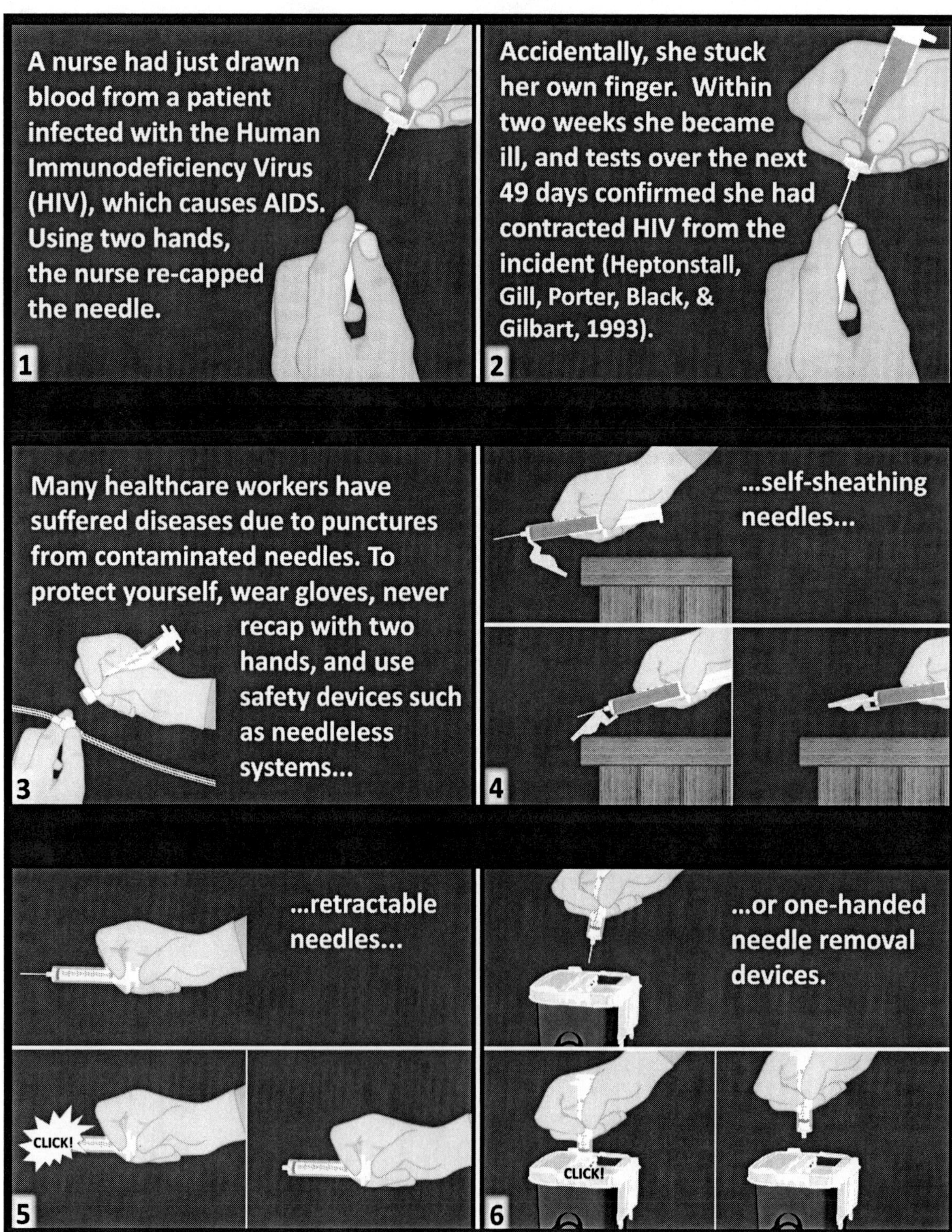

A nurse had just drawn blood from a patient infected with the Human Immunodeficiency Virus (HIV), which causes AIDS. Using two hands, the nurse re-capped the needle.
1
Accidentally, she stuck her own finger. Within two weeks she became ill, and tests over the next 49 days confirmed she had contracted HIV from the incident (Heptonstall, Gill, Porter, Black, & Gilbart, 1993).
2
Many healthcare workers have suffered diseases due to punctures from contaminated needles. To protect yourself, wear gloves, never recap with two hands, and use safety devices such as needleless systems...
3
...self-sheathing needles...
4
...retractable needles...
CLICK!
5
...or one-handed needle removal devices.
CLICK!
6

Figure 7. Illness with probable causal link to chronic exposure (© 2012 Mitch Ricketts, used with permission)

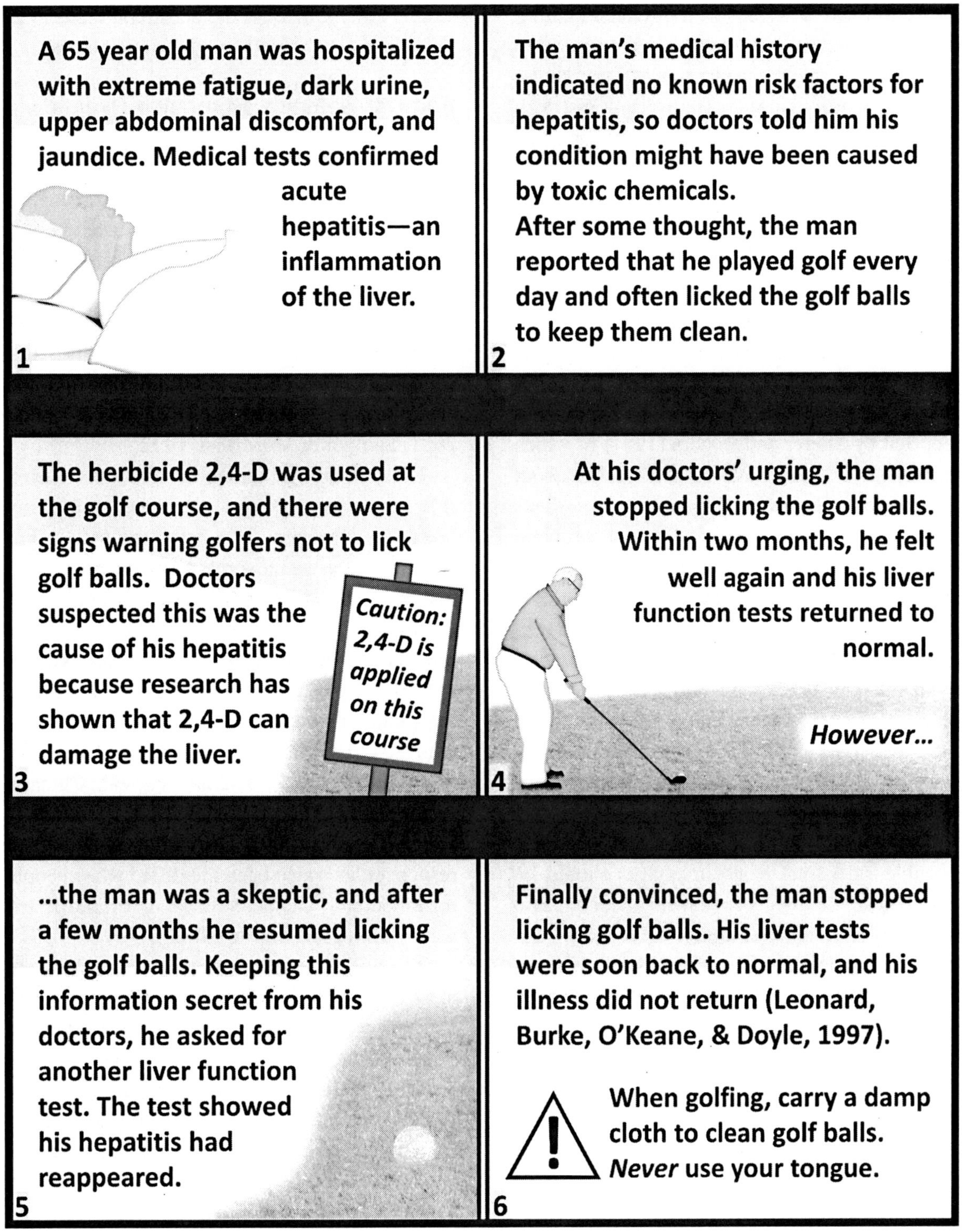

A 65 year old man was hospitalized with extreme fatigue, dark urine, upper abdominal discomfort, and jaundice. Medical tests confirmed acute hepatitis—an inflammation of the liver.

1

The man's medical history indicated no known risk factors for hepatitis, so doctors told him his condition might have been caused by toxic chemicals.
After some thought, the man reported that he played golf every day and often licked the golf balls to keep them clean.

2

The herbicide 2,4-D was used at the golf course, and there were signs warning golfers not to lick golf balls. Doctors suspected this was the cause of his hepatitis because research has shown that 2,4-D can damage the liver.

Caution: 2,4-D is applied on this course

3

At his doctors' urging, the man stopped licking the golf balls. Within two months, he felt well again and his liver function tests returned to normal.

However...

4

...the man was a skeptic, and after a few months he resumed licking the golf balls. Keeping this information secret from his doctors, he asked for another liver function test. The test showed his hepatitis had reappeared.

5

Finally convinced, the man stopped licking golf balls. His liver tests were soon back to normal, and his illness did not return (Leonard, Burke, O'Keane, & Doyle, 1997).

When golfing, carry a damp cloth to clean golf balls. *Never* use your tongue.

6

physics students read a story about a highway accident. Some participants read a story in which the victim was described as a physicist (similar to them). Others read a story that was identical in every respect, except the victim was described as either a construction worker or psychologist. Still others read a story with no clear description of the victim. Researchers found that participants judged the risk of highway accidents to be greater when they read stories in which the victim was described as more similar to themselves (i.e., a physicist). Comparable results were obtained in a separate study reported by Stapel and Velthuisen (1996).

As an example of the influence of more important attributes, such as story characters' identified values and experiences, consider an experiment reported by Sherer and Rogers (1984) in which university undergraduates read messages about alcohol abuse. Some participants read messages that focused on statistical facts about problem drinking and its effects. Other participants read messages that included anecdotes about two problem drinkers. Overall, participants who read anecdotal messages reported greater intentions to moderate their alcohol use—but only if the anecdotes' central characters (the problem drinkers) were described as similar to participants *and* as being very upset about the personal consequences of their drinking.

Reports such as these suggest that whenever possible, anecdotal health messages should be designed so the story's central character appears to have something in common with readers. On this basis, we might expect the message in Figure 5 to resonate most strongly with male construction workers, while the message in Figure 6 is likely to be taken most seriously by female nurses. In any case, audiences are *unlikely* to identify with characters who are portrayed as clearly different in ways audience members consider relevant. For instance, highly-skilled workers may fail to internalize a message if the central character is described as "young," "untrained," a "new worker," or otherwise less competent than the audience. Since these adjectives suggest the character is dissimilar (and perhaps defective), experienced workers might dismiss the anecdotal incident as something that could never happen to them.

Familiar Settings, Surprising Events

According to Schank and Abelson (1977), stories are most effective when they are familiar enough to be understood, but surprising enough to be interesting. *Familiar* contexts are important because they relate new information to prior knowledge—which often makes learning easier (e.g., Novak 2009). *Unexpected* events are powerful because they capture attention, elicit careful consideration, and create strong memories (e.g., Gendolla & Koller, 2001; Stangor & McMillan, 1992).

Brain-imaging studies confirm the notion that people take special note when something unexpected happens in a familiar context. For instance, when we see someone perform a familiar task (e.g., pouring wine), the occurrence of an unexpected event (spilling the wine) triggers an interaction between our mirror neuron system and other parts of the brain, signaling the action was unintentional, strange, or a mistake (Buccino, Baumgaertner, Colle, Buechel, Rizzolatti, & Binkofski, 2007; Malfait, Valyear, Culham, Anton, Brown, and Gribble, 2010; Rizzolatti & Fabbri-Destro, 2009). Distinctive neurological responses have also been identified when people read about story characters behaving in unexpected ways (Deen & McCarthy, 2010).

To sum up, research suggests anecdotes are most compelling when they portray events and contexts with enough familiarity that audience members can predict the intended outcome—thus ensuring their surprise at any unusual ending. Anecdotes with these characteristics apparently promote learning by challenging our prior beliefs and experiences. For instance, when reading Figure 3, parents and mower operators might be surprised to learn that small children are likely to run up behind mowers without being noticed. Likewise, golfers who read Figure 7 may be surprised to learn that golf balls can become contaminated with pesticide residues to the extent that they may cause serious illness if licked on a regular basis.

Personal Control and Responsibility for Events

There is considerable evidence that people are more inclined to change their health-related behaviors when outcomes are perceived as important and fully under their own control (e.g., Glanz, Rimer, & Viswanath, 2008). This means health messages should encourage preventive measures that can be implemented effectively *by message recipients;* otherwise, those recipients may not be able to identify clear courses of action.

To illustrate, the message in Figure 5 was developed for an audience consisting of construction *workers.* The message therefore encourages workers to take responsibility for their own safety and that of their coworkers by never working from a scaffold unless guardrails are in place. Had the message been developed for construction *supervisors*, on the other hand, it would advise them to take actions for which they are responsible, such as establishing and enforcing rules about guardrails on scaffolds. As another example, the message in Figure 7 was developed for *golfers*; thus, the final paragraph advises them to carry a damp cloth and refrain from using their tongues to clean golf balls—preventive measures that are fully under their own control. A parallel message for *golf course managers* would emphasize administrative responsibilities, such as reducing the use of pesticides, installing mechanical ball washing stations, and clearly communicating risks to golfers.

Personal responsibility can be highly motivating—especially when audience members believe they are accountable for the welfare of others. As an example, consider the sense of obligation for child safety that parents, property owners, and mower operators are likely to feel when they read the messages in Figures 2 and 3. The impact of personal responsibility for others was convincingly demonstrated in an experiment during which Solomon and DeJong (1988) showed a gonorrhea prevention video to male patients being treated for the disease at a clinic. The video included an anecdotal account of a man named Bob telling his girlfriend about his infection while also encouraging her to visit a doctor for testing and treatment. Later in the video, Bob related a separate incident he deeply regretted, in which he re-infected a woman because he didn't return to the clinic for a required test-of-cure after his symptoms disappeared. The video proved to be effective: Patients who watched it demonstrated greater knowledge about gonorrhea and were more likely to return to the clinic for a test-of-cure. The video's success was attributed in part to its emphasis on the harm that would come to women if men didn't follow the recommendations. This emphasis was included because pilot research with the audience indicated men who used the clinic felt a strong altruistic sense of responsibility to protect women.

Possibility of Alternative Outcomes

Researchers have found that health messages can be especially persuasive if they stimulate audiences to think about how people could have acted differently to avoid a tragedy (Gleicher, Boninger, Strathman, Armor, Hetts, & Ahn, 1995; Tal-Or, Boninger, Poran, & Gleicher, 2004). For instance, the message in Figure 2 is designed to elicit thoughts about how the injury would have been avoided if the father had refused to let his daughter ride along, as he had always done before: "He only gave her one ride, but once was all it took."

Contemplating alternative outcomes (i.e., "what might have been") is a phenomenon known as counterfactual thinking (Tal-Or et al. 2004). Counterfactual thinking may promote learning by triggering deep thought and mental rehearsal of actions that could prevent an adverse outcome.

Counterfactual thinking may also help us imagine the regret we would experience if a similar tragedy were to befall us. This is important because anticipated regret can have a powerful impact on current and future decisions (Connolly & Reb, 2005)

Sources of Health and Safety Anecdotes

Health communicators can obtain illness and injury stories from a variety of sources including news reports, medical journals, and health surveillance databases. The anecdotes in Figures 2 and 3 were adapted from news reports found with the help of ordinary Internet search engines. Reports such as these can also be located through commercial news clipping services. Since news reports may not be the most reliable sources for safety and health information, they should be used only when the facts of a case are obvious and undisputed.

Medical journals represent a more authoritative source of injury and illness anecdotes. As an example, the story in Figure 7 was summarized from a case that was reported in great detail in a medical journal. Similarly, the anecdote in Figure 6 is from a well-known case first reported in the early 1980s (Anonymous, 1984) and expanded upon in later reports. Since the byline "Anonymous" is unlikely to engender trust, a later citation was used in the health message (Heptonstall et al. 1993).

Searchable databases operated by government agencies often contain large numbers of injury and illness case reports. One of the largest publicly-accessible databases is the National Electronic Injury Surveillance System (NEISS), run by the CPSC (n.d.a). NEISS compiles hundreds of thousands of new case reports each year from hospital emergency rooms throughout the United States. The anecdote in Figure 4c is based on a report from this database.

Other publicly-accessible databases are operated by the Occupational Safety and Health Administration (OSHA, n.d.-b) and the National Institute for Occupational Safety and Health (NIOSH, n.d.). The OSHA database includes a large number and variety of reports involving workplace incidents. The anecdote in Figure 5 is based on an OSHA report. By comparison, the NIOSH database is smaller and less diverse, but NIOSH reports tend to include more detail. Finally, the American Association of Poison Control Centers (n.d.) publishes an annual report, with an appendix that includes anecdotal details for a number of representative poisoning cases.

Regardless of the source, illness and injury reports must usually be re-written to eliminate unnecessary details, minimize technical language, and to clarify cause-and-effect relationships. Furthermore, some reports may need to be purged of personal information to avoid disclosing the identities of victims, family members, and others who have suffered tragic consequences.

FUTURE DIRECTIONS

Anecdote-based interventions can be adapted to a variety of contexts, making these messages especially promising for future health communication efforts. As an example, illustrated anecdotes (such as those shown in this chapter) can be incorporated into presentational slides or printed handouts to stimulate discussion in face-to-face informational sessions. Illustrated anecdotes can also serve as the basis for animated instructional video sequences in Web-based interventions and distance education. As a final example, printed health messages based on illustrated anecdotes can be mailed to households or made available as "pickups" at community meeting places.

Interventions based on anecdotes are likely to become more commonplace as health communicators focus increasingly on the most vulnerable segments of society. For instance, American researchers have demonstrated that culturally-relevant story-based interventions can be particularly effective among vulnerable minority populations such as low-income African-Americans and Latinos (e.g., Erwin et al., 2003; Larkey & Gonzalez, 2007). Other vulnerable populations have been reached with a variety of story-based interventions worldwide. One example is the approach known as entertainment-education, which employs culturally-appropriate stories of fictional characters in popular television series, radio programs, and comic books. Entertainment-education has been used to promote important public health goals such as safer-sex behavior and cancer screening in developed and developing nations across the globe (Singhal, Cody, Rogers, & Sabido, 2004).

As anecdote-based health interventions proliferate, scholars will need to develop ever more effective methods of evaluating their impact. In that respect, past research findings have sometimes seemed contradictory, particularly with respect to anecdotes having markedly different characteristics. For instance, some scholars have noted that anecdotal messages may lead either to improved *or* impaired decision making, depending on how the messages are designed. Some of this apparent inconsistency can be resolved by considering the obviously different purposes of certain research laboratories. As a case in point, researchers in the *heuristics and biases* tradition often probe the limits of human reason by using anecdotes that are intentionally designed to confuse or promote bad choices. In these cases, impaired learning and poor decision making *should* be the expected outcome (e.g., Dennis & Babrow, 2005; Gibson, & Zillmann, 1994; Ubel, Jepson, & Baron, 2001). In contrast, when anecdotes are designed to clarify and focus attention on important health concepts, we should expect improvements in learning, motivation, decision quality, behavior. illness rates, or similar measures (e.g., de Wit, Das, & Vet, 2008; Hong, 2011; Larkey & Gonzalez, 2007; Larkey, et al. 2009; Ricketts et al. 2010).

Other seeming inconsistencies in research may be due in part to the wide range of narrative structures that are included under such broad headings as anecdotes, exemplars, stories, narratives, mental simulations, and entertainment-education. At one extreme, researchers may study the impacts of minimalist forms of anecdotes that consist only of single sentences or quotations with little or no contextual background. Researchers at the opposite extreme may study the more powerful impacts of classic novels, feature-length movies, and long-running soap operas.

Some apparent inconsistencies in research may also be due to methodological differences in the extent to which researchers engage participants in narrative events. The least engaging protocols merely require participants to passively read, watch, or listen to a story. The most engaging procedures require participants to create their own stories through mental simulation, story-writing, story-telling, stage-acting, or singing. Given the wide variety of narratives that have been studied, it seems unlikely that consistent findings will be obtained until results are grouped according to some well-defined taxonomy of story forms.

Still more seemingly inconsistent findings may relate to the variety of outcome variables that are typically evaluated. Educational researchers, for instance, are likely to examine recall of information, using objective tests that probe declarative knowledge. Public health researchers, in contrast, are likely to measure changes in behavior or changes in illness and injury rates. Persuasion and marketing scholars may examine still other outcomes, including changes in attitudes and purchasing intentions. When considering research results, it is important to distinguish among different categories of outcome variables because results with one type of outcome may not carry over to others. As a case in point, consider that anecdotal messages sometimes trigger important changes in behavior *without* being accompanied by corresponding gains in declarative knowledge (e.g., Ricketts et al, 2010; Solomon & DeJong, 1988; Solomon, DeJong, & Jodrie, 1988).

Worldwide, research has shed considerable light on methods for using anecdotes effectively in health messages. Nevertheless, results must always be interpreted in the context of research methodologies—particularly with respect to differences in narrative structures, audience engagement, and measured outcomes.

CONCLUSION

Anecdotes bring concepts to life by giving context and personal relevance to generalized information—apparently through many of the same neurological pathways that help us extract meaning from direct experience and observation. Although anecdote-based interventions can be effective in a variety of contexts, they have proven especially useful for reaching socially vulnerable populations throughout the world.

Research suggests anecdotal health messages may have the greatest impact when crafted according to the following principles:

1. Anecdotes and generalized information should be combined in a balanced manner to capitalize on the respective strengths of these two forms of communication. Initially, anecdotes can be used to capture attention and trigger deep reflection. Once an audience understands the personal relevance of the message, generalized information can be incorporated to provide a more thorough understanding of hazards, risk factors, and preventive measures.
2. Often, the most effective messages are multimedia communications—meaning they include a combination of words and images. Words in multimedia messages may include written or spoken language, and images may include drawings, photographs, videos, animations, and other instructive artwork.
3. It is important to select anecdotes carefully so they explain and highlight the most important points of a message, without creating distractions.
4. When composing anecdotal messages, it is usually best to describe story events in chronological order, with clear connections between causes and effects.
5. The best anecdotes have at least one important character with whom audience members can identify—either because of similarities with the audience or because the character is portrayed as someone with whom audience members can imagine having a personal relationship.
6. The best anecdotes describe events and settings that are familiar enough to be understood, and outcomes that are surprising enough to spark interest and trigger deep thought.
7. Anecdotes should emphasize preventive measures that fall within the control and responsibility of audience members.
8. To elicit deep reflection, anecdotes should imply alternative outcomes that would be possible if story characters had chosen different courses of action.

Although scholars have learned much about the use of anecdotes in health and safety messages, plenty of unanswered questions remain. In particular, more research is needed to better understand how diverse narrative structures and levels of audience engagement affect relevant outcomes including attitudes, intentions, knowledge, behavior, illnesses, and injuries.

REFERENCES

American Association of Poison Control Centers. (n.d.). *Annual reports*. Retrieved December 18, 2012, from http://www.aapcc.org/annual-reports/

Anonymous, . (1984). Needlestick transmission of HTLV-III from a patient infected in Africa. *Lancet*, *2*(8146), 1376–1377. PMID:6150372.

Ashton, C. M., Houston, T. K., Williams, J. H., Larkin, D., Trobaugh, J., Crenshaw, K., & Wray, N. P. (2010). A stories-based interactive DVD intended to help people with hypertension achieve blood pressure control through improved communication with their doctors. *Patient Education and Counseling*, *79*(2), 245–250. doi:10.1016/j.pec.2009.09.021 PMID:19833472.

Austin, P. E., Dunn, K. A., Kesler, C., & Brown, C. K. (1995). Discharge instructions: Do illustrations help our patients understand them? *Annals of Emergency Medicine*, *25*(3), 317–320. doi:10.1016/S0196-0644(95)70286-5 PMID:7532382.

Baird, A. D., Scheffer, I. E., & Wilson, S. J. (2011). Mirror neuron system involvement in empathy: A critical look at the evidence. *Social Neuroscience*, *6*(4), 327–335. doi:10.1080/17470919.2010.547085 PMID:21229470.

Bandura, A., Ross, D., & Ross, S. A. (1961). Transmission of aggression through imitation of aggressive models. *Journal of Abnormal and Social Psychology*, *63*(3), 575–582. doi:10.1037/h0045925 PMID:13864605.

Bastiaansen, J. A. C. J., Thioux, M., & Keysers, C. (2009). Evidence for mirror systems in emotions. *Philosophical Transactions of the Royal Society B. Biological Sciences*, *364*(1528), 2391–2404. doi:10.1098/rstb.2009.0058 PMID:19620110.

Bechara, A., Damasio, A. R., Damasio, H., & Anderson, S. W. (1994). Insensitivity to future consequences following damage to human prefrontal cortex. *Cognition*, *50*(1), 7–15. doi:10.1016/0010-0277(94)90018-3 PMID:8039375.

Bower, G. H., Black, J. B., & Turner, T. J. (1979). Scripts in memory for text. *Cognitive Psychology*, *11*(2), 177–220. doi:10.1016/0010-0285(79)90009-4.

Braverman, J. (2008). Testimonials versus informational persuasive messages: The moderating effect of delivery mode and personal involvement. *Communication Research*, *35*(5), 666–694. doi:10.1177/0093650208321785.

Brickman, P. (1978). Is it real? In Harvey, J. H., Ickes, W., & Kidd, R. F. (Eds.), *New directions in attributional research* (*Vol. 2*, pp. 5–34). Hillsdale, NJ: Lawrence Erlbaum Associates.

Buccino, G., Baumgaertner, A., Colle, L., Buechel, C., Rizzolatti, G., & Binkofski, F. (2007). The neural basis for understanding non-intended actions. *NeuroImage*, *36*, T119–T127. doi:10.1016/j.neuroimage.2007.03.036 PMID:17499159.

Buelow, M. T., & Suhr, J. A. (2009). Construct validity of the Iowa gambling task. *Neuropsychology Review*, *19*(1), 102–114. doi:10.1007/s11065-009-9083-4 PMID:19194801.

Chaminade, T., Zecca, M., Blakemore, S. J., Takanishi, A., Frith, C. D., & Micera, S. et al. (2010). Brain response to a humanoid robot in areas implicated in the perception of human emotional gestures. *PLoS ONE*, *5*(7), e11577. doi:10.1371/journal.pone.0011577 PMID:20657777.

Chang, C. (2008). Increasing mental health literacy via narrative advertising. *Journal of Health Communication*, *13*(1), 37–55. doi:10.1080/10810730701807027 PMID:18307135.

Connolly, T., & Reb, J. (2005). Regret in cancer-related decisions. *Health Psychology*, *24*(4S), S29–S34. doi:10.1037/0278-6133.24.4.S29 PMID:16045415.

Cook, T. (2008). Saskatchewan child nearly killed by riding mower. *The Canadian Press.* Retrieved November 28, 2012, from: http://www.thestar.com/News/Canada/article/427950

Cox, K. (2001). Stories as case knowledge: Case knowledge as stories. *Medical Education, 35*(9), 862–866. doi:10.1046/j.1365-2923.2001.01016.x PMID:11555224.

Dal Cin, S., Zanna, M. P., & Fong, G. T. (2004). Narrative persuasion and overcoming resistance. In Knowles, E. S., & Linn, J. A. (Eds.), *Resistance and persuasion* (pp. 175–191). Mahwah, NJ: Lawrence Erlbaum Associates.

Damasio, A. R., Tranel, D., & Damasio, H. (1991). Somatic markers and the guidance of behavior: Theory and preliminary testing. In Levine, H. S., Eisenberg, H. M., & Benton, A. L. (Eds.), *Frontal lobe function and dysfunction* (pp. 217–229). New York: University Press.

de Wit, J. B. F., Das, E., & Vet, R. (2008). What works best: Objective statistics or a personal testimonial? An assessment of the persuasive effects of different types of message evidence on risk perception. *Health Psychology, 27*(1), 110–115. doi:10.1037/0278-6133.27.1.110 PMID:18230021.

De Young, R., & Monroe, M. C. (1996). Some fundamentals of engaging stories. *Environmental Education Research, 2*(2), 171–187. doi:10.1080/1350462960020204.

Deen, B., & McCarthy, G. (2010). Reading about the actions of others: Biological motion imagery and action congruency influence brain activity. *Neuropsychologia, 48*(6), 1607–1615. doi:10.1016/j.neuropsychologia.2010.01.028 PMID:20138900.

Delp, C., & Jones, J. (2008). Communicating information to patients: The use of cartoon illustrations to improve comprehension of instructions. *Academic Emergency Medicine, 3*(3), 264–270. doi:10.1111/j.1553-2712.1996.tb03431.x PMID:8673784.

Dennis, M. R., & Babrow, A. S. (2005). Effects of narrative and paradigmatic judgmental orientations on the use of qualitative and quantitative evidence in health-related inference. *Journal of Applied Communication Research, 33*(4), 328–347. doi:10.1080/00909880500278137.

Denscombe, M. (2001). Critical incidents and the perception of health risks: The experiences of young people in relation to their use of alcohol and tobacco. *Health Risk & Society, 3*(3), 293–306. doi:10.1080/13698570120079895.

di Pellegrino, G., Fadiga, L., Fogassi, L., Gallese, V., & Rizzolatti, G. (1992). Understanding motor events: A neurophysiological study. *Experimental Brain Research, 91*(1), 176–180. doi:10.1007/BF00230027 PMID:1301372.

Dillard, A. J., Fagerlin, A., Cin, S. D., Zikmund-Fisher, B. J., & Ubel, P. A. (2010). Narratives that address affective forecasting errors reduce perceived barriers to colorectal cancer screening. *Social Science & Medicine, 71*(1), 45–52. doi:10.1016/j.socscimed.2010.02.038 PMID:20417005.

Drossaert, C., Boer, H., & Seydel, E. (1996). Perceived risk, anxiety, mammogram uptake, and breast self-examination of women with a family history of breast cancer: The role of knowing to be at increased risk. *Cancer Detection and Prevention, 20*(1), 76–85. PMID:8907207.

Erwin, D. O., Ivory, J., Stayton, C., Willis, M., Jandorf, I., & Thompson, H. et al. (2003). Replication and dissemination of a cancer education model for African American women. *Cancer Control, 10*(5), 13–21. PMID:14581900.

Ezingeard, J., & Bowen-Schrire, M. (2007). Triggers of change in information security management practices. *Journal of General Management, 32*(4), 53–72.

Ford, E. S., Zhao, G., Tsai, J., & Li, C. (2011). Low-risk lifestyle behaviors and all-cause mortality: Findings from the national health and nutrition examination survey III mortality study. *American Journal of Public Health*, *101*(10), 1922–1929. doi:10.2105/AJPH.2011.300167 PMID:21852630.

Gendolla, G. H. E., & Koller, M. (2001). Surprise and motivation of causal search: How are they affected by outcome valence and importance? *Motivation and Emotion*, *25*(4), 327–349. doi:10.1023/A:1014867700547.

Gibson, R., & Zillmann, D. (1994). Exaggerated versus representative exemplification in news reports. *Communication Research*, *21*(5), 603–624. doi:10.1177/009365094021005003.

Glanz, K., Resch, N., Lerman, C., Blake, A., Gorchov, P., & Rimer, B. (1992). Factors associated with adherence to breast-cancer screening among working women. *Journal of Occupational and Environmental Medicine*, *34*(11), 1071–1078. doi:10.1097/00043764-199211000-00008 PMID:1432296.

Glanz, K., Rimer, B. K., & Viswanath, K. (Eds.). (2008). *Health behavior and health education: Theory, research, and practice*. San Francisco, CA: Jossey-Bass.

Gleicher, F., Boninger, D. S., Strathman, A., Armor, D. A., Hetts, J. J., & Ahn, M. (1995). With an eye toward the future: The impact of counterfactual thinking on affect, attitudes and behavior. In Roese, N. J., & Olson, J. M. (Eds.), *What might have been: The social psychology of counterfactual thinking* (pp. 283–304). Mahwah, NJ: Lawrence Erlbaum Associates.

Graesser, A. C., Hauft-Smith, K., Cohen, A. D., & Pyles, L. D. (1980). Advanced outlines, familiarity, and text genre on retention of prose. *Journal of Experimental Education*, *48*(4), 281–290.

Green, M. C., & Brock, T. C. (2000). The role of transportation in the persuasiveness of public narratives. *Journal of Personality and Social Psychology*, *79*(5), 701–721. doi:10.1037/0022-3514.79.5.701 PMID:11079236.

Green, M. C., & Brock, T. C. (2002). In the mind's eye: Transportation-imagery model of narrative persuasion. In Green, M. C., Strange, J. J., & Brock, T. C. (Eds.), *Narrative impact: Social and cognitive foundations* (pp. 315–341). Mahwah, NJ: Lawrence Erlbaum Associates.

Green, M. C., & Brock, T. C. (2005). Persuasiveness of narratives. In Brock, T. C., & Green, M. C. (Eds.), *Persuasion: Psychological insights and perspectives* (2nd ed., pp. 117–142). Thousand Oaks, CA: Sage Publications.

Greene, K., & Brinn, L. (2003). Messages influencing college women's tanning bed use: Statistical versus narrative evidence format and a self-assessment to increase perceived susceptibility. *Journal of Health Communication*, *8*(5), 443–461. doi:10.1080/713852118 PMID:14530147.

Grothmann, T., & Reusswig, F. (2006). People at risk of flooding: Why some residents take precautionary action while others do not. *Natural Hazards*, *38*(1), 101–120. doi:10.1007/s11069-005-8604-6.

Hammig, B., Childers, E., & Jones, C. (2009). Injuries associated with the use of riding mowers in the United States, 2002-2007. *Journal of Safety Research*, *40*(5), 371–375. doi:10.1016/j.jsr.2009.07.005 PMID:19932318.

Harp, S. F., & Mayer, R. E. (1998). How seductive details do their damage: A theory of cognitive interest in science learning. *Journal of Educational Psychology*, *90*(3), 414–433. doi:10.1037/0022-0663.90.3.414.

Hastall, M. R., & Knobloch-Westerwick, S. (2012). Severity, efficacy, and evidence type as determinants of health message exposure. *Health Communication*. doi:doi:10.1080/10410236.2012.690175 PMID:22809248.

Heisler, G. (1974). Ways to deter law violators: Effects of levels of threat and vicarious punishment on cheating. *Journal of Consulting and Clinical Psychology*, *42*(4), 577–582. doi:10.1037/h0036709.

Heptonstall, J., Gill, O. N., Porter, K., Black, M. B., & Gilbart, V. L. (1993). Health care workers and HIV: Surveillance of occupationally acquired infection in the United Kingdom. *CDR Review*, *3*(11), R147–R158. PMID:7694732.

Herbert, M. J., & Harsh, C. M. (1944). Observational learning by cats. *Journal of Comparative Psychology*, *37*(2), 81–95. doi:10.1037/h0062414.

Hong, Y. (2011). *Narrative and frame in health communication: The influence of narrative transportation to promote detection behavior.* (Unpublished masters thesis). University of Alabama, Tuscaloosa, AL.

Houston, T. K., Cherrington, A., Coley, H. L., Robinson, K. M., Trobaugh, J. A., & Williams, J. H. et al. (2011). The art and science of patient storytelling—Harnessing narrative communication for behavioral interventions: The ACCE project. *Journal of Health Communication*, *16*(7), 686–697. doi:10.1080/10810730.2011.551997 PMID:21541875.

Houts, P. S., Doak, C. C., Doak, L. G., & Loscalzo, M. J. (2006). The role of pictures in improving health communication: A review of research on attention, comprehension, recall, and adherence. *Patient Education and Counseling*, *61*(2), 173–190. doi:10.1016/j.pec.2005.05.004 PMID:16122896.

Iacoboni, M. (2009). Imitation, empathy, and mirror neurons. *Annual Review of Psychology*, *60*, 653–670. doi:10.1146/annurev.psych.60.110707.163604 PMID:18793090.

Jabbi, M., Bastiaansen, J., & Keysers, C. (2008). A common anterior insula representation of disgust observation, experience and imagination shows divergent functional connectivity pathways. *PLoS ONE*, *3*(8), e2939. doi:10.1371/journal.pone.0002939 PMID:18698355.

Jamner, M. S., Wolitski, R. J., & Corby, N. H. (1997). Impact of a longitudinal community HIV intervention targeting injecting drug users' stage of change for condom and bleach use. *American Journal of Health Promotion*, *12*(1), 15–24. doi:10.4278/0890-1171-12.1.15 PMID:10170430.

Jose, P. E., & Brewer, W. F. (1984). Development of story liking: Character identification, suspense and outcome resolution. *Developmental Psychology*, *20*(5), 911–924. doi:10.1037/0012-1649.20.5.911.

Keysers, C., & Gazzola, V. (2009). Expanding the mirror: Vicarious activity for actions, emotions, and sensations. *Current Opinion in Neurobiology*, *19*(6), 666–671. doi:10.1016/j.conb.2009.10.006 PMID:19880311.

Keysers, C., Kaas, J. H., & Gazzola, V. (2010). Somatosensation in social perception. *Nature Reviews. Neuroscience*, *11*(6), 417–428. doi:10.1038/nrn2833 PMID:20445542.

King, E. S., Balshem, A., Ross, E., Rimer, B., & Seay, J. (1995). Mammography interventions for 65- to 74-year-old HMO women: Program effectiveness and predictors of use. *Journal of Aging and Health*, *7*(4), 529–551. doi:10.1177/089826439500700404 PMID:10165968.

Kreuter, M. W., Holmes, K., Alcaraz, K., Kalesan, B., Rath, S., & Richert, M. et al. (2010). Comparing narrative and informational videos to increase mammography in low-income African American women. *Patient Education and Counseling*, *81*(Suppl), S6–S14. doi:10.1016/j.pec.2010.09.008 PMID:21071167.

Kyes, K. B., Brown, I. S., & Pollack, R. H. (1991). The effect of exposure to a condom script on attitudes toward condoms. *Journal of Psychology & Human Sexuality*, *4*(1), 21–36. doi:10.1300/J056v04n01_04 PMID:12317687.

Larkey, L. K., & Gonzalez, J. (2007). Storytelling for promoting colorectal cancer prevention and early detection among Latinos. *Patient Education and Counseling*, *67*(3), 272–278. doi:10.1016/j.pec.2007.04.003 PMID:17524595.

Larkey, L. K., Lopez, A. M., Minnal, A., & Gonzalez, J. (2009). Storytelling for promoting colorectal cancer screening among underserved Latina women: A randomized pilot study. *Cancer. Culture and Literacy*, *16*(1), 79–87. PMID:19078934.

Lau, A. (2006). *Family warns of lawn mower dangers after girl loses foot.* Retrieved November 28, 2012, from http://www.newsnet5.com/dpp/news/Family-Warns-Of-Lawn-Mower-Dangers-After-Girl-Loses-Foot

Leonard, C., Burke, C. M., O'Keane, C., & Doyle, J. S. (1997). Golf ball liver: Agent orange hepatitis. *Gut*, *40*(5), 687–688. PMID:9203952.

Malfait, N., Valyear, K. F., Culham, J. C., Anton, J. L., Brown, L. E., & Gribble, P. L. (2010). fMRI activation during observation of others' reach errors. *Journal of Cognitive Neuroscience*, *22*(7), 1493–1503. doi:10.1162/jocn.2009.21281 PMID:19580392.

Malouff, J., Thorsteinsson, E., Schutte, N., & Rooke, S. E. (2009). Effects of vicarious punishment: A meta-analysis. *The Journal of General Psychology*, *136*(3), 271–286. doi:10.3200/GENP.136.3.271-286 PMID:19650522.

Mar, R. A., & Oatley, K. (2008). The function of fiction is the abstraction and simulation of social experience. *Perspectives on Psychological Science*, *3*(3), 173–192. doi:10.1111/j.1745-6924.2008.00073.x.

Mayer, R. E. (2009). *Multimedia learning* (2nd ed.). New York: Cambridge University Press. doi:10.1017/CBO9780511811678.

McBride, C. M., Emmons, K. M., & Lipkus, I. M. (2003). Understanding the potential of teachable moments: The case of smoking cessation. *Health Education Research*, *18*(2), 156–170. doi:10.1093/her/18.2.156 PMID:12729175.

McQueen, A., Kreuter, M. W., Kalesan, B., & Alcaraz, K. I. (2011). Understanding narrative effects: The impact of breast cancer survivor stories on message processing, attitudes, and beliefs among African American women. *Health Psychology*, *30*(6), 674–682. doi:10.1037/a0025395 PMID:21895370.

Mokdad, A. H., Marks, J. S., Stroup, D. F., & Gerberding, J. L. (2004). Actual causes of death in the United States, 2000. *Journal of the American Medical Association*, *291*(10), 1238–1245. doi:10.1001/jama.291.10.1238 PMID:15010446.

Molenberghs, P., Cunnington, R., & Mattingley, J. B. (2012). Brain regions with mirror properties: A meta-analysis of 125 human fMRI studies. *Neuroscience and Biobehavioral Reviews*, *36*(1), 341–349. doi:10.1016/j.neubiorev.2011.07.004 PMID:21782846.

Morrison, I., Lloyd, D., Di Pellegrino, G., & Roberts, N. (2004). Vicarious responses to pain in anterior cingulate cortex: Is empathy a multisensory issue? *Cognitive, Affective & Behavioral Neuroscience*, *4*(2), 270–278. doi:10.3758/CABN.4.2.270 PMID:15460933.

Morrison, I., Tipper, S. P., Fenton-Adams, W. L., & Bach, P. (2012). Feeling others' painful actions: The sensorimotor integration of pain and action information. *Human Brain Mapping*. doi:10.1002/hbm.22040 PMID:22451259.

Mukamel, R., Ekstrom, A. D., Kaplan, J., Iacoboni, M., & Fried, I. (2010). Single-neuron responses in humans during execution and observation of actions. *Current Biology*, *20*(8), 750–756. doi:10.1016/j.cub.2010.02.045 PMID:20381353.

Myers, M. L., Iscoe, C., Jennings, C., Lenox, W., Minsky, E., & Sacks, A. (1981). *Public version: Federal trade commission staff report on the cigarette advertising investigation.* Washington, DC: Federal Trade Commission. Retrieved October 12, 2012, from http://legacy.library.ucsf.edu/tid/jdr92d00/pdf

National Institute for Occupational Safety and Health. (n.d.). *Fatality assessment and control evaluation (FACE) program.* Retrieved December 12, 2012, from http://www.cdc.gov/niosh/face/default.html

Norman, G. R., & Brooks, L. R. (1997). The non-analytical basis of clinical reasoning. *Advances in Health Sciences Education : Theory and Practice*, *2*(2), 173–184. doi:10.1023/A:1009784330364 PMID:12386407.

Novak, J. D. (2009). *Learning, creating, and using knowledge: Concept maps as facilitative tools in schools and corporations.* Mahwah, NJ: Taylor and Francis.

O'Donnell, C. R., O'Donnell, L., San Doval, A., Duran, R., & Labes, K. (1998). Reductions in STD infections subsequent to an STD clinic visit: Using video-based patient education to supplement provider interactions. *Sexually Transmitted Diseases*, *25*(3), 161–168. doi:10.1097/00007435-199803000-00010 PMID:9524995.

Oatley, K., & Gholamain, M. (1997). Emotions and identification: Connections between readers and fiction. In Hjort, M., & Laver, S. (Eds.), *Emotion and the arts* (pp. 263–298). New York: Oxford University Press.

Occupational Safety and Health Administration. (n.d.a). *Accident inspection number 311958839.* Retrieved May 15, 2012, from http://www.osha.gov/pls/imis/establishment.inspection_detail?id=311958839

Occupational Safety and Health Administration. (n.d.b). *Fatality and catastrophe investigation summaries.* Retrieved December 12, 2012, from http://www.osha.gov/pls/imis/accidentsearch.html

Pennington, N., & Hastie, R. (1991). A cognitive theory of juror decision making: The story model. *Cardozo Law Review*, *13*, 519–557.

Perry, R. W., & Lindell, M. K. (2008). Volcanic risk perception and adjustment in a multi-hazard environment. *Journal of Volcanology and Geothermal Research*, *172*(3), 170–178. doi:10.1016/j.jvolgeores.2007.12.006.

Pillemer, D. (2003). Directive functions of autobiographical memory: The guiding power of the specific episode. *Memory (Hove, England)*, *11*(2), 193–202. doi:10.1080/741938208 PMID:12820831.

Pillemer, D. B. (2001). Momentous events and the life story. *Review of General Psychology*, *5*(2), 123–134. doi:10.1037/1089-2680.5.2.123.

Pliske, R., & Klein, G. (2003). The naturalistic decision-making perspective. In Schneider, S. L., & Shanteau, J. (Eds.), *Emerging perspectives on judgment and decision research* (pp. 559–585). New York: Cambridge University Press. doi:10.1017/CBO9780511609978.019.

Polichak, J. W., & Gerrig, R. J. (2002). Get up and win! Participatory responses to narrative. In Green, M. C., Strange, J. J., & Brock, T. C. (Eds.), *Narrative impact: Social and cognitive foundations* (pp. 71–95). Mahwah, NJ: Lawrence Erlbaum and Associates.

Rey, G. D. (2012). A review of research and a meta-analysis of the seductive detail effect. *Educational Research Review*, *7*, 216–237. doi:10.1016/j.edurev.2012.05.003.

Ricketts, M. (2007). *The use of narratives in safety and health communication.* (Unpublished doctoral dissertation). Kansas State University, Manhattan, KS.

Ricketts, M., Shanteau, J., McSpadden, B., & Fernandez-Medina, K. M. (2010). Using stories to battle unintentional injuries: Narratives in safety and health communication. *Social Science & Medicine*, *70*(9), 1441–1449. doi:10.1016/j.socscimed.2009.12.036 PMID:20176428.

Rizzolatti, G., & Fabbri-Destro, M. (2009). The mirror neuron system. In Bernston, G. G., & Cacioppo, J. T. (Eds.), *Handbook of neuroscience for the behavioral sciences* (*Vol. 1*, pp. 337–357). Hoboken, NJ: John Wiley and Sons, Inc. doi:10.1002/9780470478509.neubb001017.

Rizzolatti, G., & Sinigaglia, C. (2010). The functional role of the parieto-frontal mirror circuit: Interpretations and misinterpretations. *Nature Reviews. Neuroscience*, *11*(4), 264–274. doi:10.1038/nrn2805 PMID:20216547.

Rook, K. S. (1986). Encouraging preventive behavior for distant and proximal health threats: Effects of vivid versus abstract information. *Journal of Gerontology*, *41*(4), 526–534. doi:10.1093/geronj/41.4.526 PMID:3722739.

Rook, K. S. (1987). Effects of case history versus abstract information on health attitudes and behaviors. *Journal of Applied Social Psychology*, *17*(6), 533–553. doi:10.1111/j.1559-1816.1987.tb00329.x.

Sadoski, M. (2001). Resolving the effects of concreteness on interest, comprehension, and learning important ideas from text. *Educational Psychology Review*, *13*(3), 263–281. doi:10.1023/A:1016675822931.

Santiesteban, A. J., & Koran, J. J. (1977). Acquisition of science teaching skills through psychological modeling and concomitant student learning. *Journal of Research in Science Teaching*, *14*(3), 199–207. doi:10.1002/tea.3660140304.

Schank, R. C., & Abelson, R. P. (1977). *Scripts, plans, goals, and understanding*. Hillsdale, NJ: Lawrence Erlbaum Associates.

Sherer, M., & Rogers, R. W. (1984). The role of vivid information in fear appeals and attitude change. *Journal of Research in Personality*, *18*(3), 321–334. doi:10.1016/0092-6566(84)90016-3.

Singhal, A., Cody, M. J., Rogers, E. M., & Sabido, M. (Eds.). (2004). *Entertainment education and social change: History, research, and practice*. Mahwah, NJ: Lawrence Erlbaum.

Slater, M. D. (2002). Entertainment education and the persuasive impact of narratives. In Green, M. C., Strange, J. J., & Brock, T. C. (Eds.), *Narrative impact: Social and cognitive foundations* (pp. 157–181). Mahwah, NJ: Lawrence Erlbaum Associates.

Slater, M. D., & Rouner, D. (2002). Entertainment-education and elaboration likelihood: Understanding the processing of narrative persuasion. *Communication Theory*, *12*(2), 173–191.

Smith, G. A., & Committee on Injury and Poison Prevention. (2001). Technical report: Lawn mower-related injuries to children. *Pediatrics*, *107*(6), e106. doi:10.1542/peds.107.6.e106 PMID:11389304.

Solomon, M. Z., & DeJong, W. (1988). The impact of a clinic-based educational videotape on knowledge and treatment behavior of men with gonorrhea. *Sexually Transmitted Diseases*, *15*(3), 127–132. doi:10.1097/00007435-198807000-00001 PMID:2465581.

Solomon, M. Z., DeJong, W., & Jodrie, T. (1988). Improving drug-regimen adherence among patients with sexually transmitted disease. *The Journal of Compliance in Health Care*, *3*(1), 41–56.

Speer, N. K., Reynolds, J. R., Swallow, K. M., & Zacks, J. M. (2009). Reading stories activates neural representations of visual and motor experiences. *Psychological Science*, *20*(8), 989–999. doi:10.1111/j.1467-9280.2009.02397.x PMID:19572969.

Stangor, C., & McMillan, D. (1992). Memory for expectancy-congruent and expectancy-incongruent information: A review of the social and social developmental literatures. *Psychological Bulletin*, *111*(1), 42–61. doi:10.1037/0033-2909.111.1.42.

Stapel, D. A., Reicher, S. D., & Spears, R. (1994). Social identity, availability and the perception of risk. *Social Cognition*, *12*(1), 1–17. doi:10.1521/soco.1994.12.1.1.

Stapel, D. A., & Velthuijsen, A. S. (1996). Just as if it happened to me: The impact of vivid and self-relevant information on risk judgments. *Journal of Social and Clinical Psychology*, *15*(1), 102–111. doi:10.1521/jscp.1996.15.1.102.

Tal-Or, N., Boninger, D. S., Poran, A., & Gleicher, F. (2004). Counterfactual thinking as a mechanism in narrative persuasion. *Human Communication Research*, *30*(3), 301–328. doi:10.1111/j.1468-2958.2004.tb00734.x.

Thorndike, E. L. (1898). Animal intelligence: An experimental study of the associative processes in animals. *Psychological Monographs*, *2*(4), 1–109. doi:10.1037/h0092987.

Thrasher, J. F., Arillo-Santillán, E., Villalobos, V., Pérez-Hernández, R., Hammond, D., & Carter, J. et al. (2012). Can pictorial warning labels on cigarette packages address smoking-related health disparities? Field experiments in Mexico to assess pictorial warning label content. *Cancer Causes & Control*, *23*(S1), 69–80. doi:10.1007/s10552-012-9899-8 PMID:22350859.

Tinsworth, D. K., & McDonald, J. E. (2001). *Special study: Injuries and deaths associated with children's playground equipment*. Washington, DC: U.S. Consumer Product Safety Commission.

U. S. Consumer Product Safety Commission. (2010). *Public playground safety handbook (CPSC Publication No. 325)*. Washington, DC: Author.

U. S. Consumer Product Safety Commission. (n.d.a). *National electronic injury surveillance system (NEISS) on-line*. Retrieved November 15, 2012, from http://www.cpsc.gov/library/neiss.html

U. S. Consumer Product Safety Commission. (n.d.b). *Riding lawn mowers: Document no. 588*. Retrieved November 15, 2012, from http://www.cpsc.gov/cpscpub/pubs/588.pdf

Ubel, P. A., Jepson, & Baron, J. (2001). The inclusion of patient testimonials in decision aids: Effects of treatment choices. *Medical Decision Making*, *21*(1), 60–68. doi:10.1177/0272989X0102100108 PMID:11206948.

Vogel, V. G., Graves, D. S., Vernon, S. W., Lord, J. A., Winn, R. J., & Peters, G. N. et al. (1990). Mammographic screening of women with increased risk of breast cancer. *Cancer, 66*(7), 1613–1620. doi:10.1002/1097-0142(19901001)66:7<1613::AID-CNCR2820660728>3.0.CO;2-E PMID:2208012.

Vollman, D., Khosla, K., Shields, B. J., Beeghly, B. C., Bonsu, B., & Smith, G. A. (2005). Lawn mower-related injuries to children. *The Journal of Trauma, 59*(3), 724–728. PMID:16361919.

Vollman, D., & Smith, G. A. (2006). Epidemiology of lawn mower-related injuries to children in the Unted States, 1990-2004. *Pediatrics, 118*(2), 273–278. doi:10.1542/peds.2006-0056.

Voss, J. F., Wiley, J., & Sandak, R. (1999). On the use of narrative as argument. In Goldman, S. R., Graesser, A. C., & Vandenbroek, P. (Eds.), *Narrative comprehension, causality, and coherence: Essays in honor of Tom Trabasso* (pp. 235–252). Mahwah, NJ: Lawrence Erlbaum and Associates.

Weare, K. (1992). The contribution of education to health promotion. In Bunton, R., & Macdonald, G. (Eds.), *Health promotion: Disciplines, diversity and developments* (pp. 102–125). New York: Routledge.

Weinstein, N. D. (1989). Effects of personal experience on self-protective behavior. *Psychological Bulletin, 105*(1), 31–51. doi:10.1037/0033-2909.105.1.31 PMID:2648439.

Wicker, B., Keysers, C., Plailly, J., Royet, J. P., Gallese, V., & Rizzolatti, G. (2003). Both of us disgusted in my insula: The common neural basis of seeing and feeling disgust. *Neuron, 40*(3), 655–664. doi:10.1016/S0896-6273(03)00679-2 PMID:14642287.

Willems, R. M., & Casasanto, D. (2011). Flexibility in embodied language understanding. *Frontiers in Psychology, 2*(116), 1–11. PMID:21713130.

Woolf, S. H., & Aron, L. (Eds.). (2013). *U.S. health in international perspective: Shorter lives, poorer health*. Washington, DC: National Academies Press.

World Health Organization. (2011). *Global status report on noncommunicable diseases 2010*. Geneva, Switzerland: WHO.

Wright, S. S., & Kyes, K. B. (1996). The effects of safer-sex stories on college students' attitudes toward condoms. *Journal of Psychology & Human Sexuality, 8*(4), 1–18. doi:10.1300/J056v08n04_01 PMID:12347910.

Zabrucky, K., & Ratner, H. H. (1992). Effects of passage type on comprehension monitoring and recall in good and poor readers. *Journal of Literacy Research, 24*(3), 373–391. doi:10.1080/10862969209547782.

Zabrucky, K. M., & Moore, D. (1999). Influence of text genre on adults' monitoring of understanding and recall. *Educational Gerontology, 25*(8), 691–710. doi:10.1080/036012799267440.

Zeitlin, L. R. (1994). Failure to follow safety instructions: Faulty communications or risky decisions? *Human Factors, 36*(1), 172–181. PMID:8026839.

Zentall, T. R. (2011). Social learning mechanisms: Implications for a cognitive theory of imitation. *Interaction Studies: Social Behaviour and Communication in Biological and Artificial Systems, 12*(2), 233–261. doi:10.1075/is.12.2.03zen.

Zentall, T. R. (2012). Perspectives on observational learning in animals. *Journal of Comparative Psychology, 126*(2), 114–128. doi:10.1037/a0025381 PMID:21895354.

ADDITIONAL READING

Abbott, H. P. (2008). *The Cambridge introduction to narrative*. New York: Cambridge University Press.

Bandura, A. (2004). Health promotion by social cognitive means. *Health Education & Behavior*, *31*, 143–164. doi:10.1177/1090198104263660 PMID:15090118.

Brock, T. C., & Green, M. C. (Eds.). (2005). *Persuasion: Psychological insights and perspectives* (2nd ed.). Thousand Oaks, CA: Sage Publications.

Bruner, J. (1986). *Actual minds, possible worlds*. Cambridge, MA: Harvard University Press.

Bruner, J. (2002). *Making stories: Law, literature, life*. Cambridge, MA: Harvard University Press.

Cole, H. P. (1997). Stories to live by: A narrative approach to health behavior research and injury prevention. In Gochman, D. S. (Ed.), *Handbook of health behavior research IV: Relevance for professionals and issues for the future* (pp. 325–349). New York: Plenum Press. doi:10.1007/978-1-4899-0484-3_17.

Cole, H. P., Wiehagen, W. J., Vaught, C., & Mills, B. S. (2001). *Use of simulation exercises for safety training in the U.S. mining industry. DHHS (NIOSH) Publication No. 2001-141*. Cincinnati, OH: National Institute for Occupational Safety and Health.

Cullen, E. T., & Fein, A. H. (2005). *Tell me a story: Why stories are essential to effective safety training*. Cincinnati, OH: National Institute for Occupational Safety and Health.

De Young, R., & Monroe, M. C. (1996). Some fundamentals of engaging stories. *Environmental Education Research*, 2, 171–187. doi:10.1080/1350462960020204.

DiClemente, R. J., Salazar, L. F., & Crosby, R. A. (2013). *Health behavior theory for public health: Principles, foundations, and applications*. Burlington, MA: Jones and Bartlett Publishers.

Gerrig, R. J. (1993). *Experiencing narrative worlds*. New Haven, CT: Yale University Press.

Glanz, K., Rimer, B. K., & Viswanath, K. (Eds.). (2008). *Health behavior and health education: Theory, research, and practice*. San Francisco, CA: Jossey-Bass.

Goldman, S. R., Graesser, A. C., & Vandenbroek, P. (Eds.). (1999). *Narrative comprehension, causality, and coherence: Essays in honor of Tom Trabasso*. Mahwah, NJ: Lawrence Erlbaum Associates.

Green, M. C. (2006). Narratives and cancer communication. *The Journal of Communication*, *56*(Suppl. 1), S163–S183. doi:10.1111/j.1460-2466.2006.00288.x.

Green, M. C., Strange, J. J., & Brock, T. C. (Eds.). (2002). *Narrative impact: Social and cognitive foundations*. Mahwah, NJ: Lawrence Erlbaum Associates.

Hastie, R., & Pennington, N. (2000). Explanation-based decision making. In Connolly, T., Arkes, H. R., & Hammond, K. R. (Eds.), *Judgment and decision making: An interdisciplinary reader* (2nd ed., pp. 212–228). New York: Cambridge University Press.

Knowles, E. S., & Linn, J. A. (Eds.). (2004). *Resistance and persuasion*. Mahwah, NJ: Lawrence Erlbaum Associates.

Kogut, T., & Ritov, I. (2011). The identifiable victim effect: causes and boundary conditions. In Oppenheimer, D. M., & Olivola, C. Y. (Eds.), *The science of giving: Experimental approaches to the study of charity* (pp. 133–148). New York: Psychology Press.

Schank, R. C. (1990). *Tell me a story: Narrative and intelligence*. Evanston, IL: Northwestern University Press.

Schank, R. C. (1999). *Dynamic memory revisited*. New York: Cambridge University Press. doi:10.1017/CBO9780511527920.

Singhal, A., & Rogers, E. M. (1999). *Entertainment-education: A communication strategy for social change*. Mahwah, NJ: Lawrence Erlbaum Associates.

Spieholz, P., Clark, R., & Sjostrom, T. (2007). Fatality narratives: An effective way to convey hazard information. *Professional Safety*, *52*(4), 22–25.

(1995). InWyer, R. S. (Ed.). Advances in social cognition: *Vol. 8*. *Knowledge and memory: The real story*. Hillsdale, NJ: Lawrence Erlbaum Associates.

Zillmann, D., & Brosius, H. B. (2000). *Exemplification in communication: The influence of case reports on the perception of issues*. Mahwah, NJ: Lawrence Erlbaum Associates.

KEY TERMS AND DEFINITIONS

Anecdote: An account of at least one character involved in a sequence of events, with explicit or implied causal connections among those events. Characters can be people, animals, objects, or phenomena. In other words, an anecdote can involve human events *or* nonhuman occurrences (such as the decay of a radioactive atom, the development of a lightning bolt that strikes a tree, or the cannibalistic feeding of one star upon another, triggering a supernova explosion). Experimental findings can also be conveyed in the form of stories, with researchers and study participants as characters, and with causal relationships implied between events that are represented as independent and dependent variables. When described anecdotally, experiments can vividly illustrate particular instances of broader scientific concepts.

Counterfactual Thinking: The act of considering how a situation might have turned out differently. Anecdotal health messages may be more effective when they stimulate audience members to consider how story characters could have acted to prevent an adverse event.

Health Communication: The theory and practice of informing and influencing people about important health issues—ultimately leading to changes in behavior and improved health.

Health Education: See health communication.

Identification: The phenomenon of experiencing a personal connection with a character in a story. Some scholars believe audience members are more likely to internalize anecdotal information if they can easily identify with at least one of the story characters.

Mirror Neuron: A neuron (nerve cell) that fires when an animal (including humans) performs a particular goal-directed action *and* when the animal observes a similar action performed by another. Evidence suggests mirror neurons (or their analogues) may also exist in systems that are responsive to sensations and emotions. Mirror neurons apparently help us understand the intentions and experiences of others through an intuitive process that does not require conscious deliberation.

Multimedia Learning: The acquisition of knowledge from media that include a combination of words (printed or spoken) *and* images (still or moving). Evidence suggests people often learn better from a combination of words and images than from either words or images alone.

Narrative: See anecdote.

Parable: An anecdote with a clear lesson to be learned.

Story: See anecdote.

Transportation: The experience of being immersed or caught up in a story. Anecdotal messages are especially persuasive when audience members experience a narrative so vividly that it seems nearly as real as a lived event.

Vicarious Learning: The acquisition of knowledge, skills, or behaviors as a result of observing the consequences of another individual's actions. Vicarious learning is one mechanism by which anecdotes may trigger behavior change.

Chapter 2
More than Just Data:
The Importance of Motivation, Examples, and Feedback in Comprehending and Retaining Digital Information

Brent A. Anders
Kansas State University, USA

ABSTRACT

Increasing amounts of information are being generated and distributed to students and the public in general without regards for how this data will be processed, integrated, and recalled. This chapter seeks to present how, through the use of motivation, salient and multimodal examples, and properly created/regulated feedback, information presented can be much better learned and experienced so as to aid in overall comprehension and learning. The Attention, Relevance, Confidence, and Satisfaction (ARCS) model is highlighted when discussing how to motivate student and content viewers (Keller, 1987). Additional research findings with regards to the use of multimodalities, the use of examples, and proper implementation of feedback is also presented. Examples are provided as to how an educational facilitator might use this information in presentations and digital content distribution.

INTRODUCTION

Data are simply a conglomeration of content such as statistics, individual facts, and/or other types of information, but the real meaning and power lies in presentation of the data. There has always been a tendency for many in academia as well as many in complicated positions of government and the economy to gather and distribute lots of data/information to students, peers, and the public. Problems occur when little regard is given to how data will be understood or retained for integration and use with other information that a viewer may already have.

As a general public example, a piece of federal legislation came out that was 1,990 pages of data with zero diagrams, images, or video. It was only presented as a pure text document. I personally went around to my colleagues and asked about their thoughts on the issue of this particular legislation. All had opinions yet none had read it. "It's too long and boring," were the reasons most often given. In a very similar manner, many higher education and psychology research papers/information articles, as well as business reports and perspectives, and a fair amount of online training and courseware,

DOI: 10.4018/978-1-4666-4462-5.ch002

present information with nothing but pure textual data. This leaves students, peers and the public struggling to be motivated to go through the material as well being able to comprehend its contents.

By enhancing the way data is presented, comprehension as well as retention will be greatly improved. Modification and implementation of components such as motivational factors, example utilization, and feedback mechanisms can greatly improve the way informational data is understood and integrated within peoples' cognitive processes resulting in enhanced learning. These key elements are vital in packaging or putting together digital information to attain full comprehension and learning of the materials presented.

THE IMPORTANCE OF MOTIVATION

Motivation is a key component in virtually any human behavior, especially with regards to edification in that one can't learn/comprehend if one doesn't at first desire it or have a willingness to focus and pay attention to the information in the first place. In reviewing the literature dealing with learning/comprehension as applied to motivation, a plethora of theories and explanations are made available. One model that conglomerates multiple theories is that of the ARCS model which stands for Attention, Relevance, Confidence, and Satisfaction (Keller, 1987). Originally developed in 1979 and fully presented in 1987, Keller's ARCS model conglomerates and organizes Keller's macro theory of motivation and instructional design as well as expectancy-value theory and motivational ideas from education, psychology, and industry (see Figure 1).

Figure 1. Graphical example/representation of the ARCS model

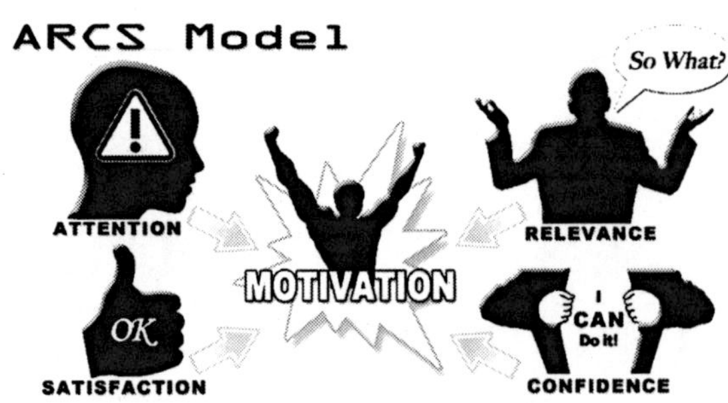

Motivational Component: Attention/ Interest

Attention, also described as interest, is a key aspect that needs to be addressed with regards to the packaging of digital information for enhanced learning. This attention-interest component is a vital element in motivation in that a student must at least look at or pay attention to the material in order to even begin the learning process (Keller, 1987; Suzuki, 2004). Interest, curiosity, fascination, are all positive things that can greatly increases people's desires and motivation (Kember, Ho, & Hong, 2008). The question then arises, how can interest or curiosity be enhanced? Interest can at least be initially peaked through the use of impactful images, hi-tech attention-grabbers (example: simulations, 3D elements, holograms, etc.), or emotionally charged content (storyline videos, case studies, etc.). It is important to remember though that using new technology or presenting information in an interesting and novel way will only be interesting until viewers or learners become familiar with this new technique or technology (Keller, & Suzuki, 2004). Getting a viewers attention is not the same as sustaining their attention, which is what would be needed to achieve learning and understanding (Keller, 1987). To sustain interest Keller recommends the use of inquiry and participation. Inquiry could be accomplished by presenting problem solving activities within the information being presented as a way to allow the viewer to "test" their own comprehension or capabilities in applying the data. Participation could be achieved through the use of specifically designed simulations and online games where information is used to achieve a desired outcome or progression.

Motivational Component: Relevance

There are many different aspects to consider with regards to data presentation and motivation. One key component is that of relevancy, meaning why is the data being presented important or valuable to the viewer. Literature review and research conducted by Kember, Ho, and Hong (2008), helped prove the importance of this aspect by interviewing 36 undergraduate students about what they perceived where the main aspects of teaching and learning that either motivated or demotivated them. *Relevance* proved to be one of the main things that aided in overall motivation with nearly 84% of those interviewed expressing negative feelings when relevancy was not used/expressed by the instructor. One interviewed student expressed "I think it is important to relate chemistry to daily life and that it has to be applicable to our daily life" (Kember, Ho, & Hong, 2008, p. 8). Additional research conducted by Ballanteyne, Bain, and Packer (1999) came to the same result while conducting research interviews with 44 college professors. As an example, one interviewed professor stated:

It gives me a buzz when I can relate the abstract to the practical or real world situations. I also find that students tend to be far more sympathetic to the learning process if they can match the abstract to the practical (Ballanteyne, Bain, & Packer, 1999, p. 10).

Relevancy is similar to valance as described in Vroom's Expectancy theory (1964). In Expectancy theory, the *valance* component is defined as the overall value/importance of accomplishing/completing a given task/goal/assignment/etc. In Vroom's explanation of motivation a mathematical formula is used where *valance* is used as a key component in determining overall motivation. By increasing the *valance* component (relevance/value) one would increase a persons' motivation to go through the digital content.

Although implicit reasons for relevancy may exist, explicit reasons need to be stated to maximize relevancy/value and therefore motivation. In other words people need to clearly see and understand the relevancy of the information being presented to be better motivated to go through it; that is read, listen, watch a video, go through a simulation, etc.

Motivational Component: Confidence

At first contemplation one may not think that confidence has anything to do with motivation, but in this case confidence is viewed as believing in one's own *effort* in learning/understanding, very similarly to Heider's Attribution Theory (1958) and Weiner's use of locus of causality (1974). Attribution deals specifically with how someone explains (attributes) successes or failures, meaning *what was the cause*. Locus of causality deals with understanding why a person behaves a certain way (Deci & Ryan, 1985). With these theories, the instructor creates an environment that helps foster the students' belief that it is through the students' own hard work and effort (all within their own control in that they are the cause) that they are able to learn and understand (see Figure 2).

The ARCS model provides multiple strategies to help exemplify this confidence within students. Through specific actions such as:

1. Providing clear learning requirements (and evaluation standards).

Figure 2. Graphical example/representation of the attribution theory

2. Presenting information/teaching in an increasingly more difficult manner (simple to hard so as to slowly learn more and more).
3. Providing a structured path with clear descriptions of effort needed.
4. Encouraging students to verbalize effort used or needed to accomplish task.
5. Providing opportunities to allow students to try and fail in a safe (low risk – loss of points, grade) environment both individually and with the whole class. (Keller, 1987).

Additional and more specific implementation ideas provided later in this chapter.

Motivational Component: Satisfaction

The final component within Keller's ARCS motivational model is satisfaction. This satisfaction deals with a sense of pleasure from the accomplishment of learning/understanding. This sense of pleasure can be viewed as a reward, which can be induced via both intrinsic and extrinsic means. Intrinsic is generally viewed as better in that pleasure is derived from a feeling of self-accomplishment, an internal feeling of success. Extrinsic rewards such as prizes, letter grades or other external things are generally viewed as less effective in that if these items were absent so too could the students' motivation. The ARCS model provides strategies to use both reward mechanisms for maximum effectiveness to induce satisfaction and enhance motivation. Allowing students to actually use a newly learned skill/technique in a realistic setting greatly reinforces what was learned and enhances students' satisfaction (intrinsic). Verbal reinforcements and making advanced students designated helpers for others are also very beneficial (extrinsic). Providing anticipated rewards for accomplishing boring type tasks can greatly help overcome monotony and boost satisfaction (extrinsic). Generally providing unexpected, non-contingent rewards for intrinsically interesting task performance can also provide increases to students' sense of satisfaction (intrinsic/extrinsic), (Keller, 1987).

Another big enhancer is the use of feedback. Providing feedback that is both informative and helpful as quickly as possible greatly enhances student satisfaction and aids in the learning process overall. As to the frequency of when intrinsic and extrinsic reinforcement should be provided, generally more frequently for students learning new tasks, less frequently for more advanced students (Keller, 1987).

Motivation: Digital Implementation

In implementing the ARCS model it is important to: 1. define any current or possible issues with motivation (is it interesting in itself, why would anyone want this information), 2. design the implementation (select from the many strategies available through the ARCS model or create new ones), 3. develop the elements needed (interesting graphics, realistic environments, other motivational elements and how they will be integrated in instructional content), and 4. evaluate (prior assessment, throughout and post, how can it be continually improved), (Keller, 1987).

Thanks to the Internet and the reduction in costs in creating content, impactful videos, stimulating simulations and higher-level games are widely available and could be used in not only grabbing student's attention and improving motivation, but to assist with instructing the material as well. Various paid and free resources are available including: YouTube (youtube.com), Vimeo (vimeo.com), TED Talks (www.ted.com/pages/initiatives_tedtalks), McGraw Hill Practice: multiplayer games and simulations (mhpractice.com), PBS Video (video.pbs.org), Archive.org (archive.org), BBC Video (www.bbc.co.uk/learningzone/clips), Zoom Video Communications (www.zoom.us), and Screenr: video cast/capture tool (www.screenr.com), just to name a few. As a side note, it is important to know and follow proper copyright guidelines when using any materials from any Website.

Using reflective online journals (example: blogger.com, squarespace.com, penmia.com, penzu.com), or creating Webquests (example: zunal.com) where the students are asked why the instructional material is relevant could be used to make the students actively engage in delineating course/class relevancy. As a twist and point of discussion, an instructor could pose the opposite question, "why is this course not important or relevant?" This could cause points of discussion and real thought for the students.

The use of online rubrics such as RubiStar (rubistar.4teachers.org) can provide clear learning requirements and evaluation standards so as to aid in students' confidence. Additionally, components of most learning management systems can assist in creating structured paths for students to follow as well as opportunities for additional knowledge acquisition or skills mastery through optional content and practice quizzes/exams, all of which will also help to improve student confidence levels. Daily messages of day done via text, audio, or video can also provide proper motivation to help build up students' attributional confidence and desire to learn.

Possible digital implementations of attaining the satisfaction component can be achieved through tools such as online badges for successful class/course achievement (examples: Digital Media and Learning Badges: dmlcompetition.net, Badge Stack: badgestack.com, Mozilla Open Badges: openbadges.org, For All Badges: forallbadges.com). Another technique to be used would be to simply designate high performing students as "helpers" in the class. Their names could be bolded or specially identified in some way within a learning management system's messaging board or chat-room system. Digital implementation of enhancing feedback is specifically discussed later in this chapter.

USE OF MULTIMODAL EXAMPLES

Highly motivated students are an important beneficial part of successful teaching and learning but clear instruction and explanations are also vital. Use of salient examples (representations) via stories, image, sound, or other media/techniques are crucial to turn abstract facts and content into meaningful items of understanding (Fisher & Ford, 2006). Although examples can be provided via the same medium/modality as the instructional content, additional benefits are achieved when multiple delivery mechanisms are used so as to engage as many senses as possible/appropriate (Doyle, 2011). In many instances simply using multimedia will excite/motivate viewers (Penuel, Means, & Simkins, 2000 & Marsh, 1992).

Below this paragraph, you will see content about the Great Pyramid of Giza in Egypt. It is presented in two different modalities: one as pure text and one mainly as an image. As you observe the information try to imagine being exposed to this content for the first time. In viewing the text on the left compared to the image on the right ask yourself: which medium makes more sense, which is easier to comprehend and incorporate with pre-existing information, which would make more of an impression, which is more interesting, which will be easier to remember and recognize or recall on an exam or during future utilization/application? (see Figure 3).

The Great Pyramid of Giza in Egypt is a large triangular structure used as the Pharaoh's tomb. It is 455 feet high, which is 150 feet taller than the Statue of Liberty that is 305 feet. The height of the pyramid is much higher than a person standing 6 feet tall.

Using one medium over the other is not necessary in that in most cases a combination of both is preferred so as to allow the brain exposure to multiple modalities to fully process the information. A key aspect to remember is that "information

Figure 3. The Great Pyramid of Giza in Egypt (Pharaoh's tomb)

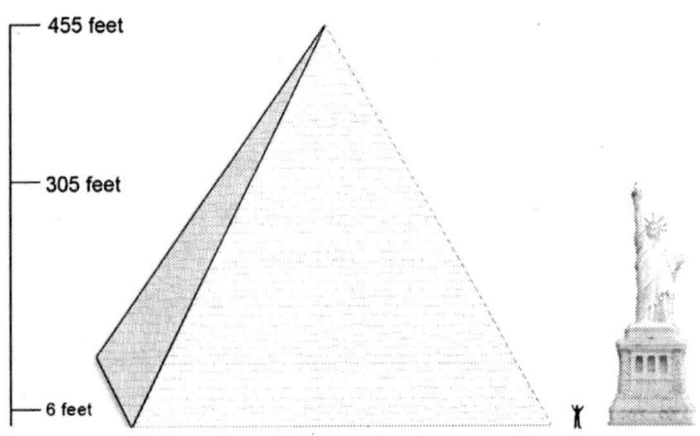

is not only represented in memory; it is processed" (Kozma, 1991, p. 181). Being exposed to content presented in multiple ways (such as text with image/video/audio) as well as with comparisons and examples, allows students to process the information more deeply and aids in later recall (Houts, et al., 2006 & Sadoski, 2001).

Another interesting example dealing with using multimedia examples to enhance learning comes from China. Many Chinese now happily use the TV show *Friends* to learn how to speak English as well as American culture (Lim, 2013) – read or listen to the article here: www.npr.org/2013/01/23/170074762/friends-will-be-there-for-you-at-beijings-central-perk. Similarly, Kaplan International Colleges conducted a study among their students and found that 82% said watching TV shows helped them learn English, with the number one show being *Friends* at 26% (Hofschroer, 2012) – read the article or view the great infographic linked towards the right and bottom of the article: www.marketwire.com/press-release/friends-helps-global-television-audience-learn-english-1732657.htm.

As a final example, think of the content already presented within this chapter. Do you remember the image representing the ARCS model? Do you recall an exclamation point on someone's head representing *Attention*, a guy shrugging his shoulders saying "so what" representing *Relevance*, a guy opening up his jacket superman-style to represent *Confidence*, and a thumbs up representing *Satisfaction*?

Was it easier to recall the information by seeing the image or was the text easier? Did the imagery make the information more salient and concrete? Multiple research conducted by Dr. Richard E. Mayer of the University of California, along with various colleges, have proven again and again the power of using multimedia to enhance learning (1989, 1990, 1991, 1992). Examples and imagery (especially via multimodal, multi-sensory means) greatly helps students' understanding which means that instructors and content creators should seek to implement it whenever applicable (Doyle, 2011).

Multimodal Examples: Digital Implementation

A listing of resources to find digital content (audio/video) has already been listed within the *Motivation: Digital Implementation* section. Some additional resources for images to use include: Flickr (http://www.flickr.com/creativecommons/), Free Digital Photos (http://www.freedigitalphotos.net/), Stock.XCHNG (http://sxc.hu), and Open Photo (http://openphoto.net/).

One can also create excellent graphics and animations through the use of a digital camera and advanced software or online tools such as Adobe Photoshop: high end, advanced photo editing software (adobe.com/products/photoshop.html), Pixlr: online photo editing (http://pixlr.com/editor), Blender: free animation and photo editing software (http://www.blender.org), Go Animate: simple but full featured online animated video maker (http://goanimate.com), another online animated video maker (http://www.xtranormal.com).

THE NEED FOR FEEDBACK

"Feedback is one of the most powerful influences on learning and achievement" (Hattie, & Timperly, 2007, p. 81). Although a very powerful statement, it is one that research has proven to be true (Doyle, 2011). At its core, feedback is two-way communication; in this case it is between the student and the instructor and back again.

To illustrate the power of two-way communication "feedback," a personal experience example is presented. As an instructor for the military I teach a course called Army Basic Instructor Course (ABIC). One of the classes I instruct deals specifically with proper communication techniques and the need for feedback via two-way communications. I get a volunteer from the student soldiers to stand in front of the class with his or her back turned to the rest of the class. The volunteer then attempts to give directions on drawing a series of simple geometric shapes (see Figure 4).

The reason this soldier's back is turned to the other students is that this is an example of pure one-way communication. No one is allowed to ask questions and the student instructing is not even allowed to receive or give feedback via facial expressions. After the instructions are given, I ask everyone to hold up their drawings. Huge variations are observed from one drawing to the next. I then use the Socratic method and pretend to be puzzled by this and state something like: "This is weird. The task was to draw a series of very simple geometric shapes, just a circle, a triangle, and some rectangles. Why is their so much variation?" The student responses are usually quite adamant that it wasn't a fair task in that they couldn't ask for clarification and that they couldn't get feedback as to whether or not they were doing the task correctly. I then tell them that I agree and that we will do it again. I state that this will be two-way communications. I ask the class if they should be allowed to ask questions throughout or if it would be better to wait until the end. The students always state that they want to be able to ask question immediately. "Oh," I state, "So you would find it better to have immediate feedback so as to gain usable information when it is needed?" They affirm the question and we start the task again. This time the student volunteer is allowed to look at the class and answer all questions. The students asked to draw a different series of geometric shapes, but this time there is a twist. The image they are directed to draw is displayed in Figure 5.

Figure 4. ABIC example 1

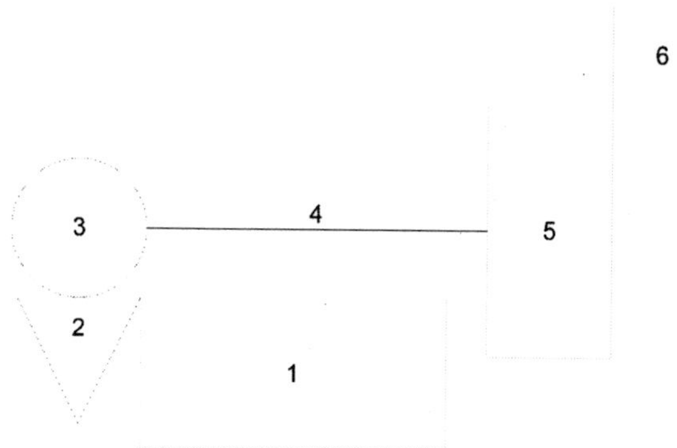

Figure 5. ABIC example 2

I tell the student giving the instructions to again to describe each shape in order and not to say that it looks like a snowman until one of the students realizes and states it. Half way through the task a student always says, "Oh, it looks like we are drawing a snowman." As soon as that happens the task becomes extremely easy and everyone is able to create an image that looks very similar when compared to the source image.

This task is done to allow the students the opportunity to experience first hand the frustrations of not having two-way communications with an instructor and not receiving timely feedback. It is done a second time with two-way communications so as to physically see how much better the task can be accomplished when questions are allowed throughout and usable feedback is provided. Additionally this task shows how in the process of feedback a comparative example was derived in that the geometric shapes looked like a snowman. This realization made it easier to process the instruction and successfully complete the task.

Another important aspect of feedback is the phraseology and approach used when actually giving the feedback to a student. A good approach is to be positive, focus on how to improve and if at all possible discuss strengths and weaknesses via a positive, negative, positive approach (Chur, Hansen, & McLean, 2006). Feedback "…is most powerful when it addresses faulty interpretations, not a total lack of understanding" (Hattie & Timperly, 2007, p. 82). Additionally, the value of peer feedback shouldn't be overlooked in that when done constructively it can enhance students' confidence as well as general student participation and engagement (Ertmer, et al., 2010; Smith & Higgins, 2006).

Feedback: Digital Implementation

Some ideas for digital implementations of feedback include:

Expressive Feedback Devices: Newer technologies provide the capability of not only showing feedback as to what a student got wrong, but why they got it wrong. Additional custom, personalized messages such as: "Overall you got 8 out 10 correct. This shows great effort. Note the reasons provided as to why you missed those two questions and try again," can enhance the effectiveness of the feedback process as well as tie in with motivational aspects of attribution.

Video: Use of online video, either synchronous or asynchronous can also allow for very expressive two-way interactions between student and instructor. Most learning management systems now have some sort of video component built in, but other video conferencing tools such as Zoom (http://zoom.us/) and Skype (http://www.skype.com) could also be used.

Peer Feedback: When done constructively can be effective as well. This can be accomplished either through direct expressions (such as commenting on a message board) or through rating schemes (such as those done via online message board rankings: four stars equals excellent).

Commenting Systems: Even the implementation of a simple commenting system provided at the bottom of a block of online instruction can provide very informative feedback in both directions so as improve understanding and learning. Care should be given so that all students/viewers understand proper netiquette as well as the purpose and power of the commenting system tool.

CONCLUSION

Instructors and content creators need to realize that it is *part* of their responsibility to help enhance motivation. They do this by: creating content and instruction that seeks to gain and maintain students' Attention, provide Relevancy, induce Confidence and a sense of self-attributed capabilities while fostering positive Satisfaction (via both intrinsic and extrinsic means). Additionally, instructors and content creators need to use multimodal examples to better describe and explain the content along with providing effective and timely feedback.

In describing the needed components of *Motivation, Examples,* and *Feedback* to transform mere data into actualized knowledge, the components start to blend together. In describing elements of *motivation,* aspects of *examples* were used (attention section) as well as aspects of feedback (satisfaction section). In describing the elements of *examples* it was also mentioned how having good multimedia can help explain content as well as *motivate* students to want to see more. In explaining *feedback*, aspects of motivation (attribution) and use of multimedia (examples) were also described. Therefore these components need to be considered, planned and implemented holistically so as to have maximum benefit and truly aid the viewers'/students' motivation and comprehension (see Figure 6).

Notice that this chapter tries to actually implement what it states by trying not to be boring and instead be motivating, by using many examples (using text as well as images with links to audio and video resources), and as for feedback, this chapter will be peer reviewed before it is publish. Going through and learning about this content isn't the end it is only the beginning. We, as educators and producers of content, need to act so as to integrate the stated components to enhance learning and understanding.

Figure 6. Motivation, examples, and feedback: integrated components to help induce successful learning

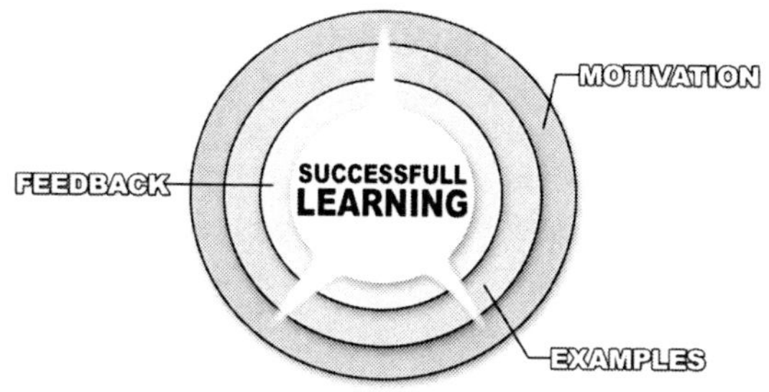

REFERENCES

Ballanteyne, R., Bain, J. D., & Packer, J. (1999). Researching university teaching in Australia: Themes and issues in academics' reflections. *Studies in Higher Education*, *24*(2), 237–257. Retrieved from http://search.ebscohost.com.er.lib.k-state.edu/login.aspx?direct=true&db=tfh&AN=1973925&site=ehost-live doi:10.1080/03075079912331379918.

Chur-Hansen, A., & McLean, S. (2006). On being a supervisor: the importance of feedback and how to give it. *Australasian Psychiatry*, *14*(1), 67–71. PMID:16630202.

Deci, E., & Ryan, R. (1985). *Intrinsic motivation and self-determination in human behavior*. New York: Plenum. doi:10.1007/978-1-4899-2271-7.

Doyle, T. (2011). *Learner-centered teaching: Putting the research on learning into practice*. Sterling, VA: Sylus Publishing.

Ertmer, P., Richardson, J., Lehman, J., Newby, T., Cheng, X., Mong, C., & Sadaf, A. (2010). Peer feedback in a large undergraduate blended course: perceptions of value and learning. *Educational Computing Research*, *43*(1), 67–88. doi:10.2190/EC.43.1.e.

Fisher, S. L., & Ford, J. K. (2006). Differential effects of learner effort and goal orientation on two learning outcomes. *Personnel Psychology*, *51*(2), 397–420. doi:10.1111/j.1744-6570.1998.tb00731.x.

Hattie, J., & Timperley, H. (2007). The power of feedback. *Review of Educational Research*, *77*(1), 81–112. doi:10.3102/003465430298487.

Heider, F. (1958). *The psychology of interpersonal relations*. New York, NY: John Wiley & Sons. doi:10.1037/10628-000.

Hofschroer, M. (2012). Friends helps global television audience learn English. *Marketwire*. Retrieved from http://www.marketwire.com/press-release/friends-helps-global-television-audience-learn-english-1732657.htm

Houts, P. S., Doak, C. C., Doak, L. G., & Loscalzo, M. J. (2006). The role of pictures in improving health communication: A review of research on attention, comprehension, recall, and adherence. *Patient Education and Counseling*, *61*(2), 173–190. doi:10.1016/j.pec.2005.05.004 PMID:16122896.

Keller, J., & Suzuki, K. (2004). Learner motivation and e-learning design: A multinationally validated process. *Journal of Educational Media*, *29*(3). doi:10.1080/1358165042000283084.

Keller, J. M. (1987). Development and use of the ARCS model of instructional design. *Journal of Instructional Development*, *10*(3), 2–10. Retrieved from http://www.jstor.org/stable/pdfplus/30221294.pdf doi:10.1007/BF02905780.

Kember, D., Ho, A., & Hong, C. (2008). The importance of establishing relevance in motivating student learning. *Active Learning in Higher Education*, *9*(3), 249–263. Retrieved from http://alh.sagepub.com.er.lib.k-state.edu/content/9/3/249.full.pdf doi:10.1177/1469787408095849.

Kozma, R. (1991). Learning with media. *Review of Educational Research*, *61*(2), 179–211. doi:10.3102/00346543061002179.

Lim, L. (2013). Friends will be there for you at Beijing's central perk. *National Public Radio*. Retrieved from http://www.npr.org/2013/01/23/170074762/friends-will-be-there-for-you-at-beijings-central-perk

Marsh, J. (1992). Menace or motivator? International Central Institute for Youth and Educational Television, 12(2).

Mayer, R. (1998). Systematic thinking fostered by illustration in scientific text. *Journal of Educational Psychology*, *81*, 240–246. doi:10.1037/0022-0663.81.2.240.

Mayer, R., & Anderson, R. (1991). Animations need narrations: An experimental test of dual-coding hypothesis. *Journal of Educational Psychology*, *83*, 484–490. doi:10.1037/0022-0663.83.4.484.

Mayer, R., & Anderson, R. (1992). The instructive animation: Helping students build connections between words and pictures in multimedia learning. *Journal of Educational Psychology*, *84*(4), 444–452. doi:10.1037/0022-0663.84.4.444.

Mayer, R., & Gallini, J. (1990). When is an illustration worth ten thousand words? *Journal of Educational Psychology*, *82*, 715–726. doi:10.1037/0022-0663.82.4.715.

Penuel, W. R., Means, B., & Simkins, M. (2000). The multimedia challenge. *Educational Leadership*, *58*(2), 34–38.

Sadoski, M. (2001). Resolving the effects of concreteness on interest, comprehension, and learning important ideas from text. *Educational Psychology Review*, *13*(3), 263–281. doi:10.1023/A:1016675822931.

Smith, H., & Higgins, S. (2006). Opening classroom interaction: the importance of feedback. *Cambridge Journal of Education*, *36*(4), 485–502. doi:10.1080/03057640601048357.

Vroom, V. (1964). *Work and motivation*. New York: Jon Wiley & Sons.

Weiner, B. (1974). *Achievement motivation and attribution theory*. Morristown, NJ: General Learning Press.

Chapter 3
Branching Logic in the Design of Online Learning:
A Partial Typology

Shalin Hai-Jew
Kansas State University, USA

ABSTRACT

Online learning requires a clear structure to enhance learning, particularly for those with little background in the subject. Structurally, the design of online learning may involve branching and merging, forking and joining of multiple branches, and other combinations of branching, for a learner or learners. Instructional branching is a tool that enables the achievement of multiple objectives. These include the following: (1) An Adaptive Curriculum: Adapting a richer curriculum to reflect the complex realities of a field and the real world; (2) Learner Support: Accommodating learners, who often have diverse needs based on their capabilities, ambitions, areas of study, and needs; (3) Learner Collaboration Support: Promoting the building of learning teams for the acquisition of collaboration, co-learning, and co-design skills; (4) Respect for Learner Decision-Making: Respecting the decision-making of learners, particularly in scenarios of simulations, games, problem solving, case studies and analysis, microsite presentations, slideshows and lecture captures, design, and innovation; (5) Maximizing In-World Opportunities: Taking advantage of opportunities in the environment such as the availability of a guest speaker, the co-funding of a shared learning endeavor, a partnership with a business entity, fieldtrip options, and/or other created opportunities. This chapter addresses various known branching designs on two levels: (1) course curriculums and (2) Digital Learning Objects (DLOs). It offers a typology of branching at the course curriculum level. Further, it covers branching in the DLO level based on specific cases. It analyzes the various points at which a curriculum converges and when it diverges (branches). Finally, the chapter includes a section on the mindful design of branching: design of the branching, the transitions, and proper learning assessments.

DOI: 10.4018/978-1-4666-4462-5.ch003

INTRODUCTION

For a curriculum to be relevant, it must help transfer both knowledge and skills that are relevant in the real world. It must reflect the world's complexity. If new learning changes old paradigms, clearly, the curriculum should reflect these findings. Further, it must support learners in their various learning and career objectives. A well designed curriculum must also enhance learners' skills in collaboration—intercommunications, co-learning, and co-design. A strong curriculum should respect learner decision-making and self-directedness in ways that increase learner self-motivations and self-efficacy. And finally, a strong curriculum should include the maximizing of learning opportunities in the environment. At the heart of these curriculum objectives is branching, or the capability of diversifying a curriculum through multiple paths.

This chapter addresses some of the strategies for designing branching divergence in online curriculums and DLOs. It looks at strategies for re-integrating learners after divergent learning experiences. To clarify, branching learning is not about skipping the prior planning of an online course. The sequence of a course should be fairly defined, even if there is plenty of branching learning. There is no excuse for disorganization. However, even within structured learning and a general trajectory, there is plenty of room for adaptivity and the accommodation of serendipitous learning opportunities. Branching learning may occur at any time in a learning sequence. It may involve single individuals, dyadic teams, and other sized teams. The branching should add value to the learning without eliminating or over-shadowing the fundamentals. Any branching should clearly contribute to the learning objectives of the course or digital learning object. This chapter will include the design of proper learning assessments for branched learning. One clarification: This chapter addresses how branching logic is used in instructor-led high-interactivity courses, not in automated learning setups.

BACKGROUND

"Branching logic" in instructional design refers to the reasoned design of different paths (relationships) through a learning experience. At various curricular junctures, once certain standards or conditions are met, to use logical connectives, learners may go forward along a particular branch, skip another branch ("not" or negation), take multiple branches ("and" or addition or conjunction; fork or join multiple paths simultaneously), magnify multiple learning paths (multiplication), "select" between branches ("or" or logical disjunction or inclusive disjunction or alternation), or branch or merge to a single path, based on their performance or preference or other learning-based factors.

In terms of instructional design practice, "branching logic" has not been developed to any high formalism. The academic research literature contains little in regards to branched learning. Often, there is the sense that branching is designed by faculty, Subject Matter Experts (SMEs), and instructional designers without too much external reference to learning theory or practice. Sometimes, branching is fleeting and unnoticed; at other times, it's a critical part of the course and the learning. A critical premise here is that e-learning path branching should be done with a clear pedagogical rationale.

The time assumption in the following depictions is that learners work towards progress at varying paces; other times, they may have to pause or stop temporally; for others, they may be stopping out permanently. Sometimes, the branching may begin early in a learning sequence and remain throughout the learning. Other times, the branching starts and stops during the learning sequence. For some, the branching occurs at the end of the learning sequence. The branching may be recursive; in other words, a learner may have to go backwards or review particular contents. The nature of time may be discrete, with hard deadline constraints for certain work to be achieved to have satisfactorily met the requirements of the branched learning. Or, the nature of time may be dense and continuous, with some flexibility in the application of deadlines. In this more flexible approach, as long as learners achieve some aspects of the required work according to certain normative rules, the deadlines may be more flexible and practical in the real world (Dignum & Kuiper, 1998 / 1999).

Two Levels of Branching Analyzed: Curricular (Macro) and Digital Learning Object (Micro)

Branching is done at the course curriculum level, with some classic types illustrated here. Branching is also instantiated in Digital Learning Objects (DLOs), including various simulations, games, problem-solutions, case studies, microsite presentations, slideshows and lecture captures, design and innovation, primary and secondary research, and procedural branching. Indeed, the capabilities of the authoring and design tools (particularly Website design, desktop lecture captures, and learning / course management systems) for various types of virtual learning enable a wide range of branching. Branching is usually expressed as an outline, storyboard, mock-up, or even a Website wireframe or working (draft) prototype. Finally, branching occurs in time and is often expressed in discrete time temporal semantics.

INSTRUCTIONAL DESIGN VARIATIONS ON BRANCHING LOGIC

This first section focuses on the branching typologies in course curriculums. This section offers a high-level view of longer-term learning sequences.

The various branching typologies in curriculums may be characterized as belonging to three different categories: The first is "High Convergence / Low Divergence; Low Branching." A range of conventional and traditional curriculums follow this model. The second group, and the largest, involves Medium Convergence / Medium Divergence; Medium Branching." These involve learning sequences with some divergence. Finally, the third group is High Divergence / Low Convergence; High Branching. These learning sequences are highly variant and often customized for learners. For transferability, these branching typologies were expressed abstractly, even though they were originally extracted from decades of curriculum work and analyses of course learning sequences.

High convergence (low divergence) means that learners are shepherded through a highly structured curriculum that leads to pre-defined and deterministic answers. High convergence has an inverse relationship with divergence, so a high convergence curriculum has low divergence or low branching. Likewise, low convergence (high divergence) is inversely related to divergence. A low convergence curriculum has high divergence, or a high level of branching and differentiation in learning paths. Curriculums and learning objects may be conceptualized as ranging on a continuum from high convergence (low divergence) on one end to low convergence (high divergence)(on the other.

What follows are visual depictions and textual descriptions of these patterned variations on branching logic, using Integrated Definition for Function (Process) Modeling (IDEFO). These are two-dimensional diagrams that use nodes and shapes to represent entities, lines to represent relationships, and descriptive text. These diagrams portray functions or processes within systems.

BRANCHING TYPOLOGIES IN CURRICULUMS

For all these types of branching, one can assume basic conditionalities: if-then, or if certain conditions are met, then a particular branching strategy is applied.

To set the baseline, it is helpful to consider the most common type of curriculum. A linear curriculum tends to typify high convergence / low divergence, with little to no branching. There is often a clearly defined start (opening) and end time (closure). This process structure is comparatively simple compared to branching logics, which may incorporate more information:

Formalization by a set of linear time models has the advantage of a very simple model structure. But the disadvantage is that the possible choices and the time points at which they should be made are not covered explicitly in the formalization itself. Branching time models represent these choices as points where the flow of time branches. However, a given branching time model may only describe a subset of the set of all possible behaviours (Engelfriet & Treuer, 2002, p. 390).

Within those limits, this chapter then offers some basic temporal branching structures in online learning. More complex and inclusive models may be made to describe a comprehensive curriculum, for example, but that is beyond the purview of this chapter. Further, this is not a formalist logical work but more of an abstract case.

Linear Curriculum

In a linear curriculum, there may be small accommodations for individual students based on their needs. Students who need some extra support should get it, and advanced learners with additional learning needs may be accommodated. There may be accessibility accommodations with multiple modes of accessing certain domain contents. In general, a linear curriculum adheres closely to the design: the syllabus is followed closely, with minute schedule adjustments possibly. This learning often addresses the foundational knowledge and skills (see Figure 1).

Figure 2 highlights a variety of variations on the theme of branching curriculums. These various models will be explored in more depth below.

Multiple Points of Entry

A Multiple Points of Entry branching scenario is typical for many college courses. Because of the high number of students without the sufficient skills to enter a college-level course, many are required to take pre-requisites prior to enrolling in the college courses. For others, if the disparity between entry expectations may be minimal, such differences may be addressed with a pre-module that may be deployed prior to the start of the official learning term (in Week Zero or the Pre-Week). Or there may even be additional supportive learning modules throughout the course to augment the learning. This cognitive scaffolding (mental structures and learning aids that enable a range of learning) enables a course to be accommodative of people at different learning levels. Oftentimes, the remedial or supportive aspects of an online course may be reviewed at the learner's convenience. The instructor may suggest that the learner access particular resources. The converse is also true: those already found to be advanced after a fairly thorough test of the pre-existing knowledge may be accommodated within the course by the addition of more complex versioning of assignments. For example, courses that serve both upper-level undergraduate and graduate students will often have different assignment requirements for each group (see Figure 3).

Figure 1. Linear curriculum (chronological)

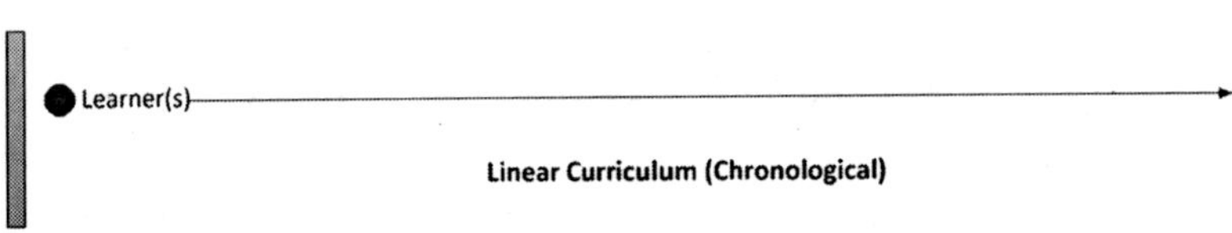

Figure 2. Medium convergence/medium divergence; medium branching

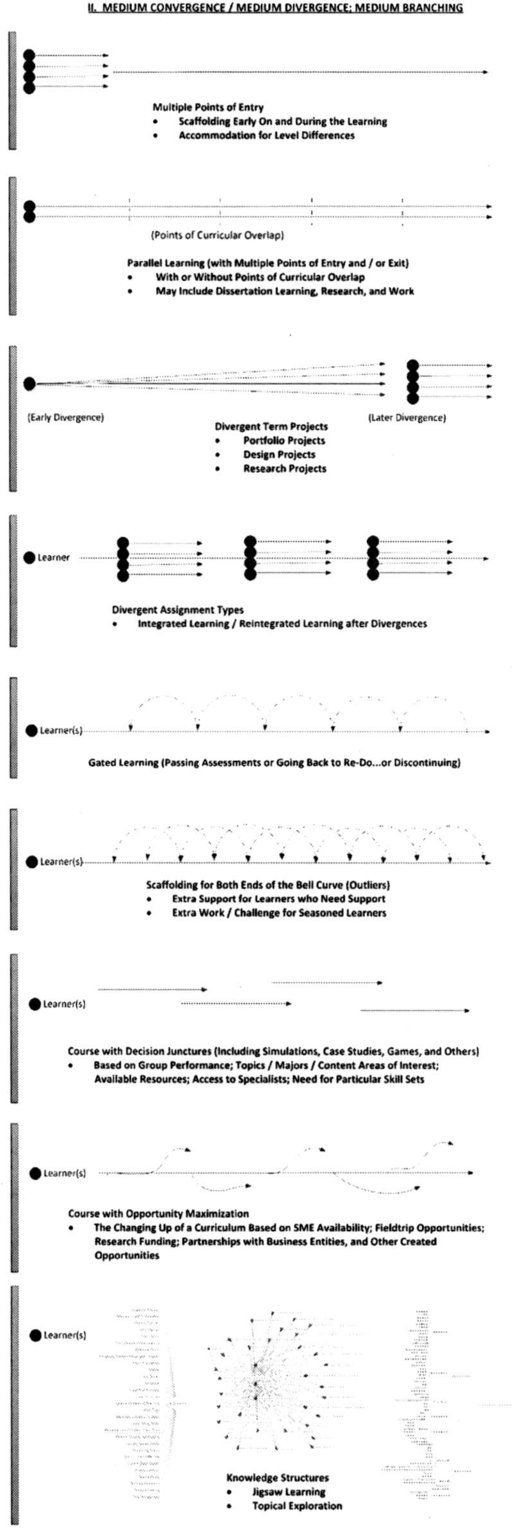

Parallel Learning

A Parallel Learning approach may be understood as a "multiple points of entry" approach. Here, learners enter a learning program at different levels, acquire the learning they need (simultaneously but sometimes without interacting with each other), and exit in an open way. Independent studies may fit into this model, and there may or may not be points of overlap between learners. While learners may take generally discrete and independent yet-synchronous paths, there may be some interdependencies in their learning. The time concurrency of the learning may or may not affect other learners. For example, in automated systems, learners may be tracked in and out, and the data analytics from their experiences may be used to redesign the system for more effective learning paths (for those with similar profiles) (see Figure 4).

The dissertation courses for learners in doctoral programs may be parallel learning. Here, learners take their own divergent research and paths after they have completed a shared curriculum. They may use different software tools. They may use varying research methods. They may obtain guidance and support from very different subject matter experts. The student's learning and professional ambitions inform the selected work. They have some shared curriculums, but in terms of their own research and dissertations, they may never overlap with many or most of their peers. Even the timelines of the doctoral students' work may vary greatly, with learners finishing in a variety of time frames. Parallel branching may also be understood as practicum learning with learners pursuing different specialization tracks and therefore taking on different learning experiences in professional workplaces, and under difference guidance.

Divergent Term Projects

The branching in terms of Divergent Term Projects is often used for courses with a high level

Figure 3. Multiple points of entry

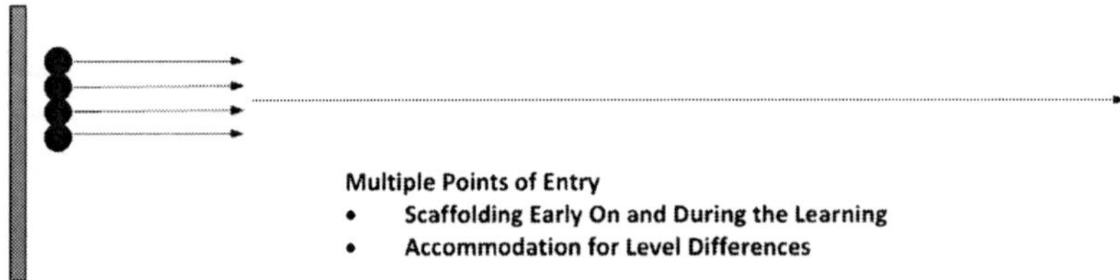

Figure 4. Parallel learning

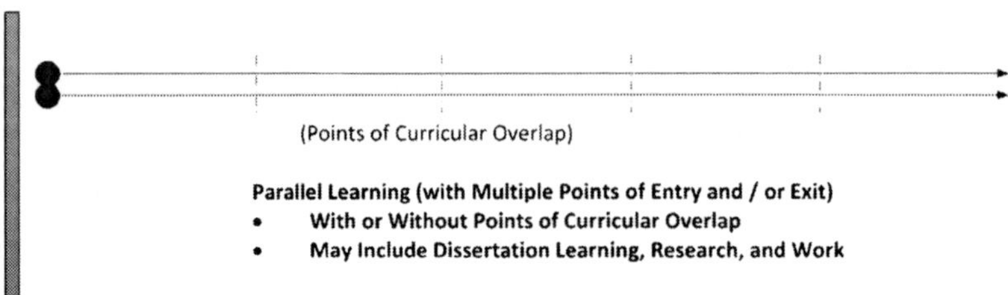

of divergent and innovative learning, such as portfolio-based design courses in architecture, engineering, art, music, interior design, and theatre. The idea is that is not one set answer, but there are a variety of ways to successfully design solutions (even though the work does have to meet certain criteria). While learners' projects diverge, there are similarities that will enable learning from each other's projects (see Figure 5).

In one research study, design students came up with more "holistic, flexible, and effective mental models" with a functional instructional approach (as contrasted to a more rigid structural teaching of the design process stages) (Mioduser & Dagan, 2007). The design course examined the impact of the two teaching approaches on learner mental models and then looked at how those models affected design thinking. The opening up of different design options expands "the space within which the design process proceeds" (Mioduser & Dagan, 2007, p. 142); instead of a linear solution, the learners use an optimal branching model as a description of the problem-solving process as "a solution space with branching nodes" (p. 141). Learners are better able to assimilate the complete functions of the design-functions-toolbox, including investigation, generating ideas, planning, drawing, selecting a solution, evaluation, and development.

Divergent Assignment Types

Another branching structure which is fairly common involves having divergent assignment types.

Figure 5. Divergent term projects

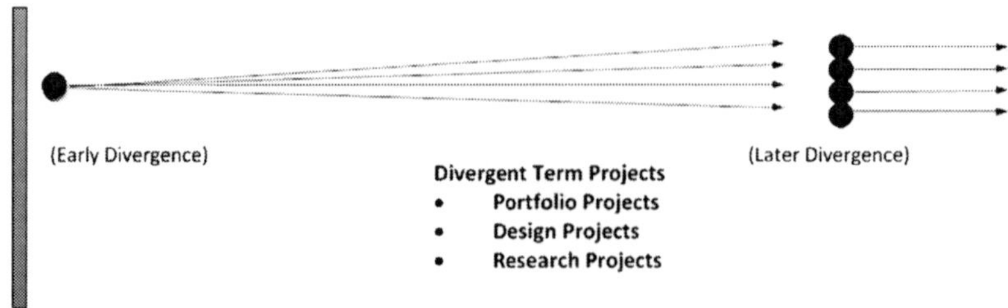

Various learners sign on for different assignments throughout the term and share the results of their work throughout the term. In this sense, learners diverge around the assignments but re-integrate or re-converge between those assignments to share their learning. Learners are seen to benefit from each other's assignments. One example of divergent assignment types would be a foundational writing course that allows learners to choose from among various rhetorical modes for their personal essay assignments; in this way, all learners can learn in depth about how different forms of writing may manifest with different contents and in the hands of different writers (see Figure 6).

Gated Learning

The Gated Learning branching construct involves a set of "hurdles" that learners must pass in order to pass the section of the course. This is a data-driven approach, with computer systems tracking learners and ensuring that they are on the right (automated) path. If they cannot get past the proverbial "gate," then they may have to review a module or a section of learning and take the assessment again. This is common for (usually annual) compliance trainings, which address a range of legal or regulatory changes that learners must know for their work. They have to show comprehension of the foundational contents (knowing the regulation or policy), decision-making savvy (interpreting particular situations), and certain types of competence (applying certain policies). Gated learning is also useful in highly sequentialized and high-dependency types of learning, which require meticulous foundational understandings of certain concepts before proceeding on to more complex ideas (see Figure 7).

The data collected on the back end may enable those who've designed the learning to further tailor the learning sequences for revision, particularly if learners are disproportionately confusing specific facts (which may indicate a challenging concept as well as potential problems in the curricular design about that particular issue) (Koller, 2012).

Figure 6. Divergent assignment types

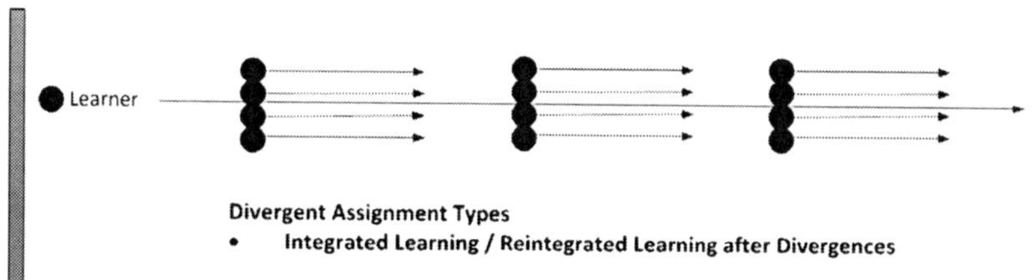

Figure 7. Gated learning

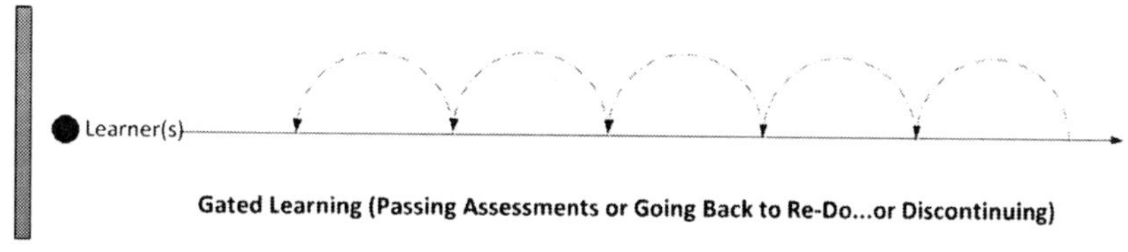

Scaffolding for Both Ends of the Bell Curve

Some simple branching occurs in Figure 8. Here, this refers to accommodations both for those at the left of the bell curve [the amateurs (those who only want to learn a targeted aspect of a field) and the novices (the new learners who are just starting to progress in a field)], and those at the right end (the high achievers). Here, learners branch off for developmental supports or value-added complex learning. Given the retention challenges for both groups, the accommodations for both should be a central part of all online learning.

Course with Decision Junctures

In a Figure 9, learners individually or separately go through a range of decisions. There are no pre-determined paths for their learning or necessarily even pre-laid tracks for people to follow. These decisions inform the steps to their learning in a semi-stochastic (non-deterministic) way. The types of learning in which such decisions affect the progress of the course include simulations, case studies, and games. Some faculty who co-build assessments with their learners (such as in doctoral programs, where learners inform the building of their high-value exams) design the critical design junctures into various learning sequences. For example, graduate students often have a voice in deciding part of their shared graduate curriculum. This is a kind of real-world "wayfinding" with their advisors' good will, expertise, and support.

Course with Opportunity Maximization

In Figure 10, the value-added branching occurs because of a faculty member and learners who focus on opportunities in the environment. For example, the faculty member has access to subject matter experts who may be brought in as guest speakers or portfolio judges or collaborators. The students may know of fieldtrip opportunities. This learning community may have access to research funding, partnerships with business entities, and other consciously created opportunities to enhance the learning by tapping social connections and resources in the larger environment.

Figure 8. Scaffolding for both ends of the bell curve (outliers)

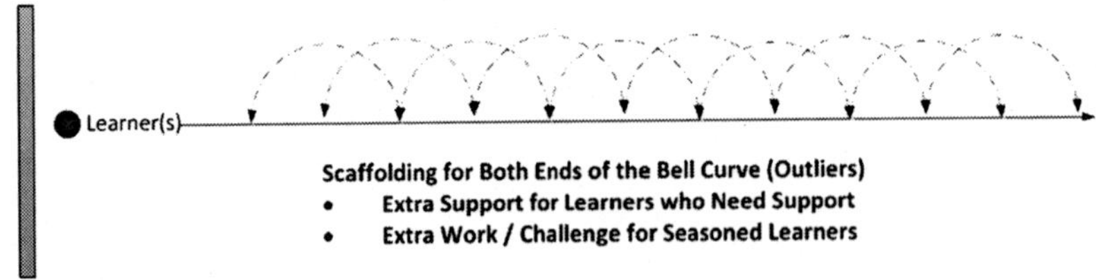

Figure 9. Course with decision junctures

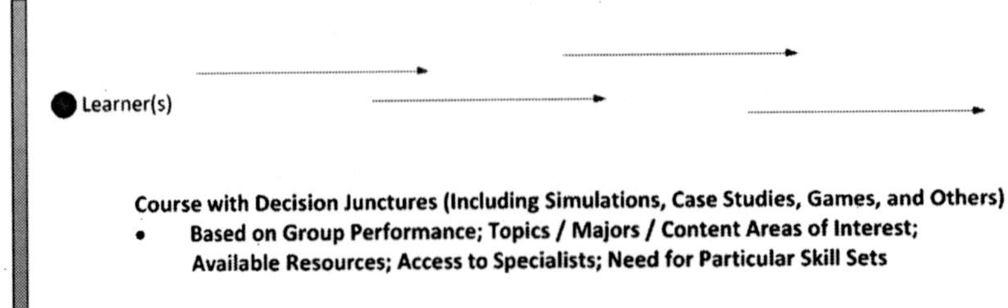

Figure 10. Course with opportunity maximization

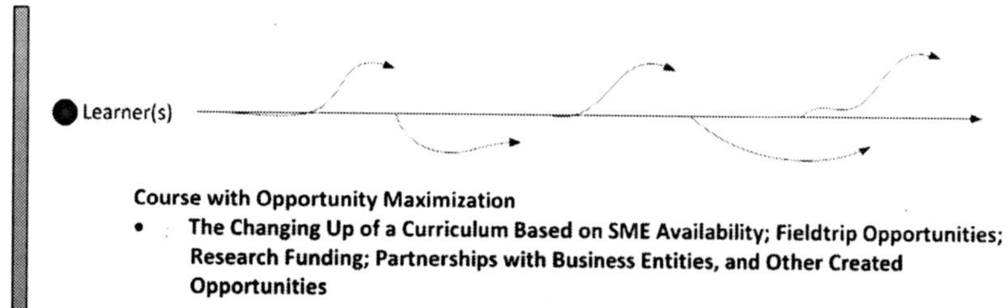

Knowledge Structures

Another type of branching structure involves knowledge structures (ontologies, taxonomies), with learners studying different branches and collecting information on those areas. Here, learners not only have to learn their areas well, but they need to understand the over-arching structures. They will share their knowledge areas with others to enhance the "jigsaw" learning (where each of the learners bring a piece of the "jigsaw puzzle" to help create a comprehensive picture or understanding). For example, in an entomology course, a 44-step dichotomous key involves a taxonomic morphological structure for insects (see Figure 11).

High Divergence with Little or No Overlap

Finally, in the third section, with high branching examples, High Divergence with Little or No Overlap describes one approach in which branching is the natural state. In self-discovery learning, for example, there is high divergence. Here learners do not necessarily impact each other's learning. Further, they may not even be aware of each other in a learning context. For the learners themselves, there may not be a clear through-path but only general ideas for way-finding. Their learning is a kind of unstructured mosaic or collage with mixes of relatedness and unrelatedness in their learning. One extreme example of this is the work of entrepreneurs in new domains, who must define

Figure 11. Knowledge structures

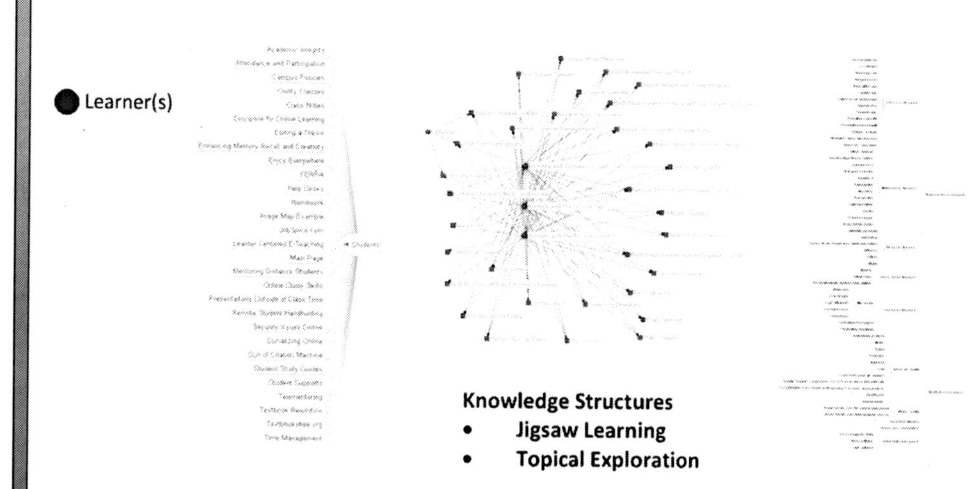

their own path. The potential for branching and sub-branching here is fairly infinite, out to the far edges of what is potentially relevant. This involves the cobbling of related components to create coherence in the learning (see Figure 12).

Dyads and Team Groupings

Finally, Dyads and Team Groupings reflect a dividing up of a course into separate groups early on (or during the term) for intensive training and learning in those groups. (Dyads are two-person pair teams.) The groups may have unique objectives and projects. The teams could be competitive teams (such as software design, robotics, Web design, or landscape architecture design teams); these groups may be co-competitors not only in the classroom but in various competitions, with actual prizes and amateur recognition. Their respective professional roles may be written into the assignment. They may be assigned to specific teams for certain learning objectives, skills attainment, or function, or they may be assigned by random chance. Often, the work is not close-ended, with a pre-determined conclusion. Instead, each of the team members will affect how the team functions. In such groupings, there are often convergences and reconvergences during the term to benefit the whole (see Figure 13).

DIGITAL LEARNING OBJECTS (DLOS)

The digital learning objects that will be considered in this branching context include (1) simulations, (2) games, (3) problem-solutions, (4) case studies, (5) microsite presentations, (6) slideshows

Figure 12. High divergence with little or no overlap

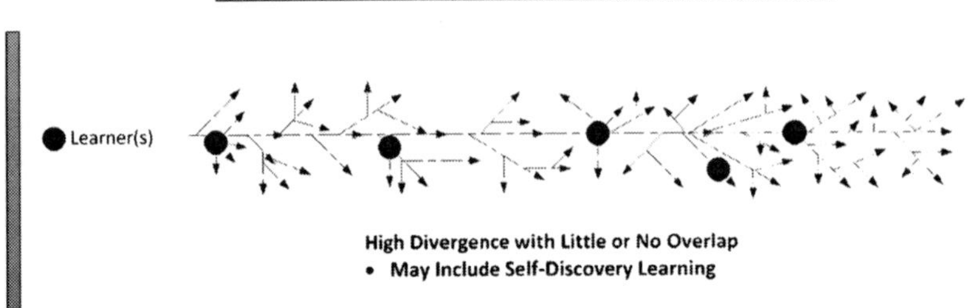

Figure 13. Dyads and team groupings

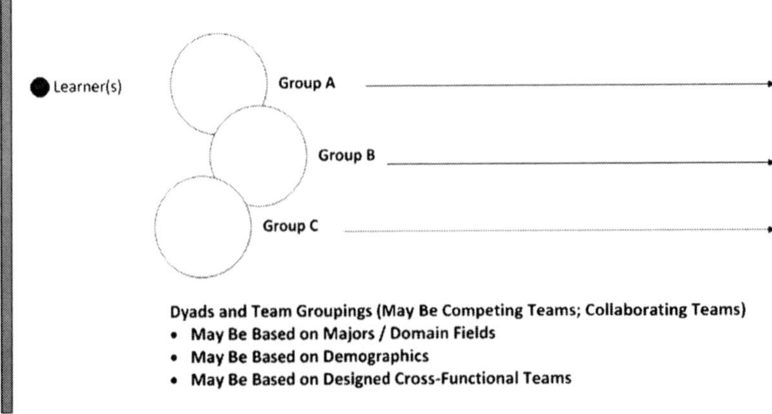

and lecture captures, (7) design and innovation work, (8) primary and secondary research, and (9) procedural branching. Some examples will be presented here as diagrams and flowcharts to show the various study branching divergences and convergences.

Simulations

Various types of online learning fit into the category of simulations. Some simulations are human-driven or participatory simulations, which are co-created by the learners who are sharing knowledge and interacting with each other. Participatory simulations include mock court sessions; historical event simulations; business simulations; virtual dramas (some acted out in virtual worlds through human-embodied avatars), and others. Further, participatory simulations may be in-world, in augmented reality spaces or consisting of spatially distributed individuals co-interacting through mediated and locative devices. Other simulations are fully online. These may include virtual laboratories that simulate real-world labs. (Remote labs involve Web-based access to physical laboratory equipment to conduct experiments.) Other virtual simulations involve the solving of mysteries that have been pre-branched, with critical decisions made at various junctures, which affect the later unfolding of the mystery. In discrete time, certain achievements must be met before learners proceed on past the juncture. Researchers differentiate between simple branching simulations that provide experiential learning "at a relatively low cost" and more high-end high-fidelity branching simulations that track learner states that drive the simulations (Ramachandran, Jensen, & Sincoff, 2010, p. 1).

The example of simulation branching here involves a partially-completed Digital Entomology Laboratory project. To conceptualize this, it will be helpful to think of a range of branching options based on learner needs and their learning objectives. This Lab was created to complement an undergraduate course in General Entomology by introducing insect morphology (form and function). The lab itself consists of a range of macro images of select insects. Figure 14 shows some of these through-paths.

Sequenced Learning describes an actual path through various insect paths. For example, one approach may help learners progress through an evolutionary path of a particular insect type. Or another sequence may take them through the critical pests for certain crops. Another sequence may involve insect structures as they progress from simple to complex. Another branch with this lab may involve responses to certain assignments. Learners may be assigned to examine particular morphological structures of insects in a particular region, for example. Or they may be assigned to examine the offensive and defensive structures of insects. They may be assigned to critique the sample images for proper insect pinning strategies. A problem-solution path involves using the information resources and photos to solve particular (often practical) problems. For example, a theoretical illustrated insect may be provided to students with various morphological structures, and students may need to describe how this imaginary insect might live in a real-world environment. An ad hoc branch use of this lab may involve a range of amateur or novice uses of the site to browse and learn. A field assignment branch could involve the capturing of insects and comparing them with the samples online to possibly "key" them by type. Another field assignment may involve observing insects in the natural environment to see how they engage with their surroundings. Or learners may visit a particular environmental niche to observe which insects they discover there. Perhaps learners may have a set of images of unkeyed insects that they have to figure out the type for based on known insect orders (kingdom, phylum, class, order, family, genus, and species); this keying could use a 44-step dichotomous key based on physical features of the insects. Learners may analyze various insect functions and forms for

Figure 14. User/learner tracks through a digital entomology lab

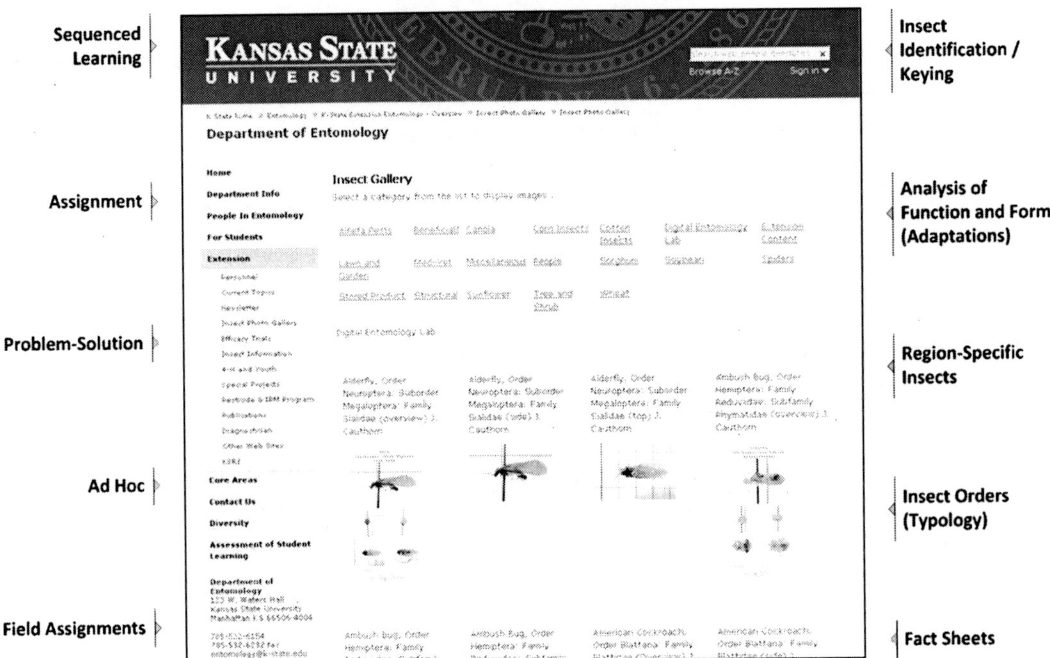

functionality and potential understandings of adaptation. Perhaps there are sets of region specific insects which may be studied for insights about the local environmental and climate conditions. Perhaps there are special collections of insect orders from different regions of the world. Perhaps there are fact sheets which may be reviewed and studied. There are a variety of ways to branch learning through a digital lab, with focuses on learning objectives, learner motivations, and available digital (and analog) tools.

Games

Immersive games have been used for various types of online teaching and learning. Many such games are pre-made off-the-shelf ones. For these, selected levels and experiences in a game are chosen. The learning is designed with a setup or preview, support during the game, and then a debriefing afterwards. There may be multiple runs of the game with different parameters. Additional learning materials may be created to change-up the game. Such games may be modded (modified) if portions of the game code or Application Programming Interface (API) are made available.

Or, games may be built over a virtual or physical structure. Many learning games have been built over virtual worlds. For example, in participatory games, human-embodied avatars may re-enact events, practice foreign languages, or play out particular roles. Simple participatory online games may be simply text-based with various individuals describing their own actions. Others, using mobile devices and locative software, build games over a physical space. Such augmented reality experiences may be built on a variety of high-powered social apps on iPads and iPhones, for example.

Still other games are custom-built using game design tools (or even simulation or general authoring tools). These may have automatic transitions along certain play paths based on decisions-made and actions taken. There may be manual segues as well between sections of a game. Because of the high cost-of-entry to game design and coding, this option is not as often used in higher education.

There are various types of branching in games. For many, they involve levels (rising, maintaining, or falling) to indicate knowledge and achievement and access to certain virtualized experiences with rising skills. Other educational games are about going through a range of experiences that increase the learning (knowledge and skills). Others are used to train individuals in inter-communications, strategizing, and cooperating.

Problem-Solutions

Various types of problem-solution assignments may manifest as brief works that cumulatively sum up into learning. Various types of math learning may fit into this category. Other types of problem-solutions are story problems that may have a few possible solutions. There may be open-ended and complex problems that have complex potential solutions or even no known solutions. Figure 15 provides some common branching options.

A "black box" branch involves a problem-solution with little structure in guiding the work. Unstructured problems are often used with high-level learners who have a broad understanding in their respective fields—such as senior undergraduates or graduate learners. Lock-step problem-solutions are used for convergent learning (learning that focuses on specific correct answers)—such as in some types of math, chemistry, and physics, where there may only be one correct answer for the particular problem. A "reverse engineering" sort of problem-solution begins with various products as solutions and then backtracks to try to understand the problem. An incremental learning sort of problem-solution offers scaffolding to help learners problem-solve. These aids may be material or directional or other forms of support offered along the way. Or the challenge may begin with a pre-made set of materials (as in some robotics challenges), which limit the scope of the competition. Finally, the co-design / cross-functional teams / competing teams approach involves the mix of people and their varying talents to help collectively solve a problem. These various branches may be mixed as well, for especially complex projects (such as those that may occur over learning terms or even the length of a full academic degree).

Case Studies

Case studies are used in a variety of fields to achieve various learning aims. Case studies in the health sciences are often factual works that highlight discoveries. These tend to be brief and written to a specialist audience. Case studies in the social sciences present real-world issues (either factually or theoretically) for learning and discussion, with "solutions" that may be non-obvious, complex, and /or elusive. Case studies may be stand-alone ones, or they may be part of a packaged sequence. They may be presented all-at-once with a debriefing to follow, or they may be incrementally revealed (with asymmetric information revealed), with multiple decision junctures (and differing end results based on the decisions). The conclusions of incrementally revealed case studies may be deterministic (with certain absolute occurrences if certain decisions are made), or they may be stochastic (somewhat randomly determined). A wide range of multimedia may be used to convey case studies, particularly in the social sciences. Case studies may be used for individual single-student study, or it may involve group work.

To examine some possible branching, the real-world case "Native Gaming in the U.S." is used. This case consists of three sections, each of which are stand-alone cases:

- **Case 1:** "All In? Economic Factors to Consider in Native Gaming."
- **Case 2:** "Smallpox or the New Buffalo: What's the Right Analogy for Indian Gaming?"
- **Case 3:** "Setting the Rules for Native Gaming."

Figure 15. Some branching types in problem-solution designs

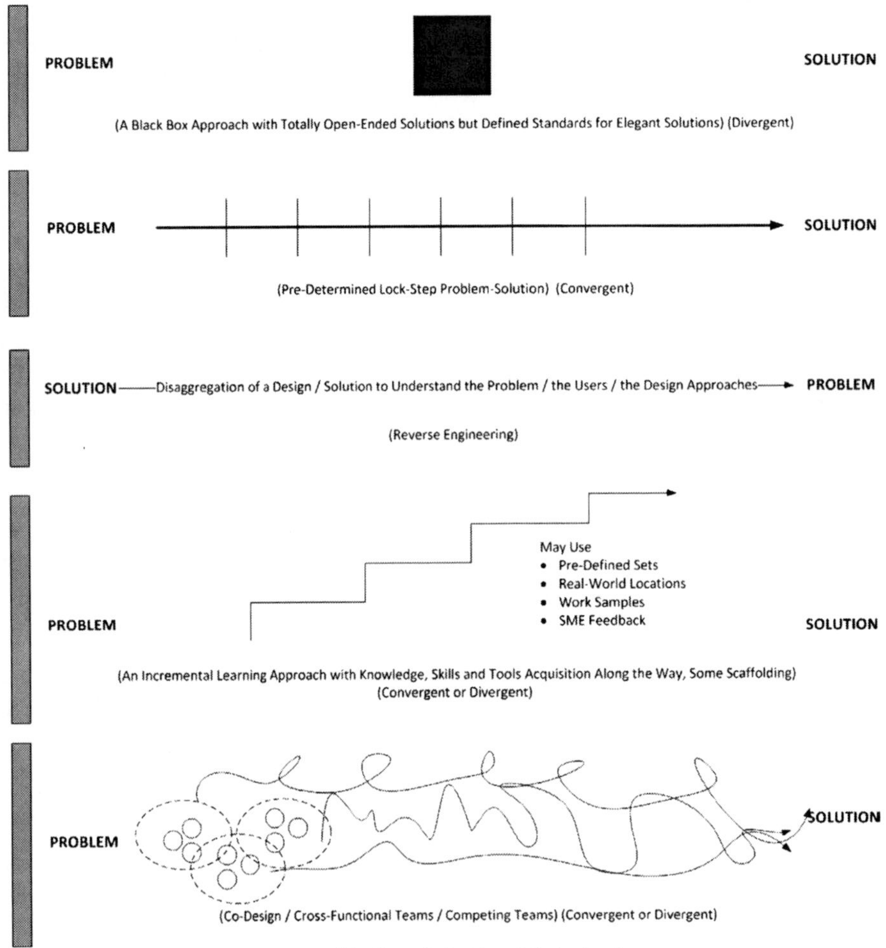

Figure 16 represents some of the ways learners may branch through this three-part case study. The image here is a screenshot of the Website where the parts of this case may be downloaded.

Learners may go through the cases in any order. The cases are not interdependent on each other, even though they are all related topically. Each of the cases has built-in study ideas, discussion questions, and in-community assignments. (These were built with the idea that learners would add value to each of the cases by updating them and collecting relevant information as a part of their studies. The cases all have outlinks to other resources. These cases have been used in face-to-face (F2F) trainings as well as virtual self-discovery studies. While the cases do come with some debriefing for faculty, there are no absolute right answers. The point is to have learners consider a range of factors.

Microsite Presentations

A microsite is a small Website that is used for a limited purpose. They may be used to augment an online article. They may contain a simulation. They may be used for a F2F presentation in order to offer visuals for the presenters but also to have a site for other conference-goers' reference.

Figure 16. Native gaming in the US: three interlinked and stand-alone cases

Native Gaming in the U.S.: Three Interlinked and Stand-alone Cases

(Some have used e-books on iPads as microsites for presentations.) For such microsites, there is branching that may occur within the site, such as the navigation between the site's pages, as well as outside the site. Figure 17 includes some screenshots from a real-world microsite created for a professional conference.

The outline at the "parent level" shows the overall trajectory of the presentation. These are organized in a developmental way, from simple to complex. Moving right across to the "child links" reveals more specific details, in-depth out-links, and activities. Each of these branches are topical ones.

Slideshows/Lecture Captures

A staple of Digital Learning Objects (DLOs) includes slideshows and lecture captures (often narrated slideshows with integrated videos, audio, and navigation of Websites). Branching structures may be built within these types of learning objects. Figure 18 uses a simple flowchart to describe the branching design. This particular project involved two main uses of the learning contents: 1) the distribution of the contents to professional trainers around the state to educate the public about how to support people with Traumatic Brain Injury (TBI) or Mild Traumatic Brain Injury (mTBI), and 2) the publishing of an automated learning Website to enable the general public to learn more about TBI and mTBI on their own, so as to better support their family members, friends, neighbors, and others.

Per the figure, learners first go through some introductory slides that introduce TBI and mTBI and then describe the various ways this may affect people's lives. At a decision juncture, the trainer, the learners, and / or the individual learners may choose to follow the stories of one of three real people with TBI or mTBI. The curriculum that follows is personalized to the interview subject, but the takeaway lessons are shared among the three. In a sense, the curriculum diverges to provide a (personality) framework for the shared curriculum that follows. Learners will then follow that same individual for the rest of the curriculum. There are unique aspects to each of the three (Subject A, B, and C) paths but also a shared core. This shows a deterministic trajectory, without chance moves to different learning (except for the F2F debriefing, possibly, because of the greater flexibility in the F2F setting with a trained trainer).

Figure 17. Branching in microsites used in presentations: an overall high-level trajectory, secondary development details, and interactivity

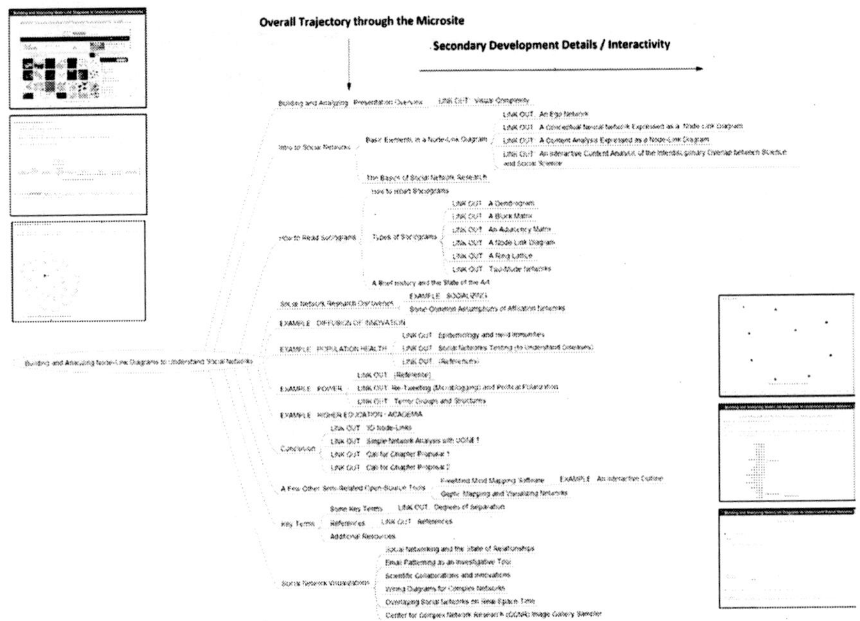

Branching in Microsites Used in Presentations: An Overall High-Level Trajectory, Secondary Development Details, and Interactivity

Figure 18. A branching structure for a traumatic brain injury project (flowchart)

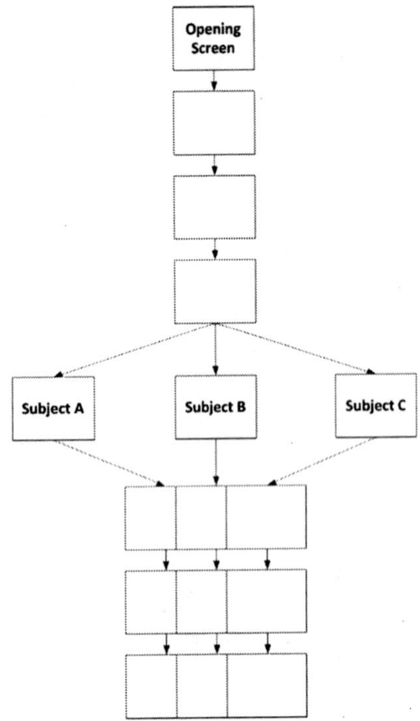

Design and Innovation

The packaging of a design and innovation assignment (often as part of a portfolio) enables plenty of room for both convergent and divergent learning (learning that focuses on a range of possible solutions or designs or answers). The convergent learning refers to the technical requirements of the project, which may be actualized by particular tools. The divergent aspect refers to how students actually solve the design challenge using a range of innovations of approaches, thinking, design, and development. The range of appropriate solutions may be infinite. Likewise, the branches that learners may use to arrive at their design decisions may also be myriad.

In fields that emphasize a "studio culture," the learning occurs based on creativity (built on a body of knowledge) balanced against critiques, for the creation of tangible objects and experiences. The student designers must be able to defend and justify their creations. Figure 19 defines some of these paths.

At the center rectangle is the design assignment. Many inputs go into this design. These include supporting lessons and work samples; incremental design assignments; practice analyzing designs, and feedback from faculty. These inputs are listed at the top right of the diagram. The learners themselves create a range of learning contents as part of their work. These include a research and design journal, a research paper, a design, and presentation materials about their design. Finally, the actual designs may be used in a variety of contexts in terms of the rectangles at the bottom of the diagram. These may include a campus display, portfolio, digital repository, publication, show, or even commercial use. This diagram shows the various branching ranges of possibilities with particular design assignments.

The various branches have unique requirements in terms of learner work and the support that may be needed to enable the work. This awareness of branching may benefit instructors in their design and support of learning, and it may benefit learners in their awareness of what is expected.

Primary and Secondary Research

The work of primary (creating original data and information through accepted and standardized methods) and secondary research (reviewing established research for relevant information) may be some of the most serendipitous. One lead, such as an author name or a reference to a model, in one source may lead to other sources. The following

Figure 19. Complex branching to and from a design assignment

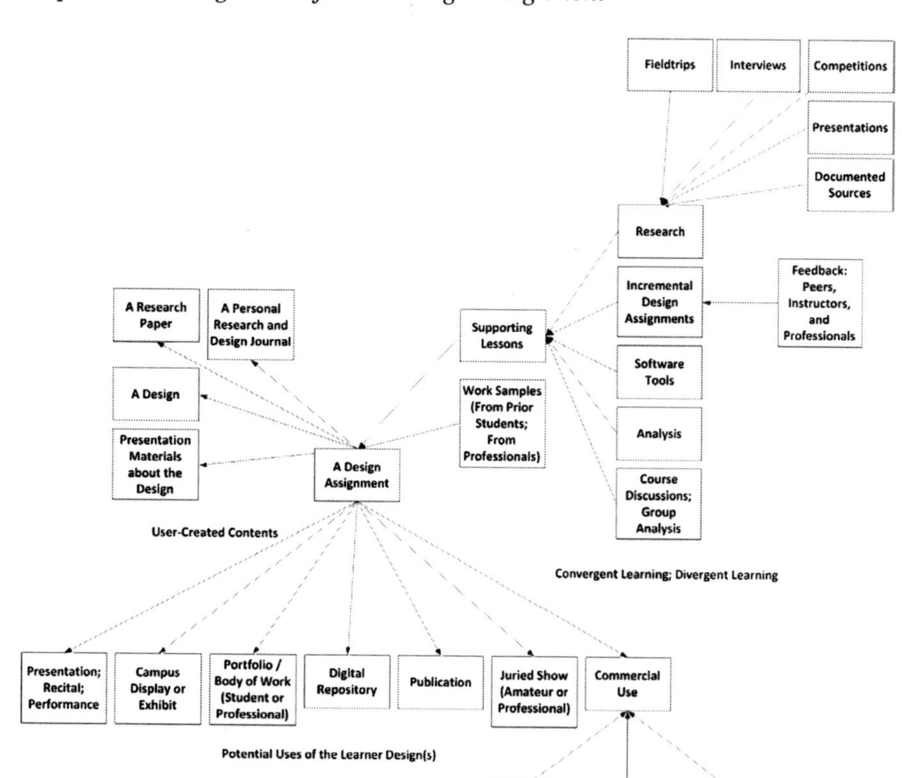

figure maps out the unfolding leads for an actual secondary research project about a global hacker collective and its spinoff organizations. To simplify, this will be represented in an abstract way in terms of the types of sources used to collect the data and information. Figure 20 shows an aggregated flow, with the original research conducted on the hacker collective and then the realization that the organization has multiple spinoffs, which were also researched, for the project.

For the entire project, the hacker collective and the two spinoff organizations studied. A wide range of sources were tapped. The email interviews were not fully exploited because of the need to keep the project fairly low-key and private (the hacker collective is known to hack individuals who do not portray them in the way they want). The project was launched while the author was taking a graduate course, so that was listed because the course informed some of the analysis (but not the direct research). Also, a serendipitous lecture informed the final project and resulted in a source citation, so that was included.

So which sources were the most rewarding for the particular project? A different sort of branching visualization may enhance understanding. Ninety-two sources were cited for the project. To be cited, a source has to have information that is original, with quotes or specific information from those sources.

Numerous other sources were used for insights or background information. However, of the sources vetted, there may have only been a use rate of 60%, which is fairly efficient (There have been research projects with use rates of only single-digit percentages.).

To conduct a node-link content analysis about which source types were the most effective, the author first created a data array / data matrix (spreadsheet or data table). In Table 1, the left column shows the various types of data contents used or cited. Across the top row are the various research sources. The numbers in the cells represent

Figure 20. Primary and secondary research branching (examining a global hacker collective)

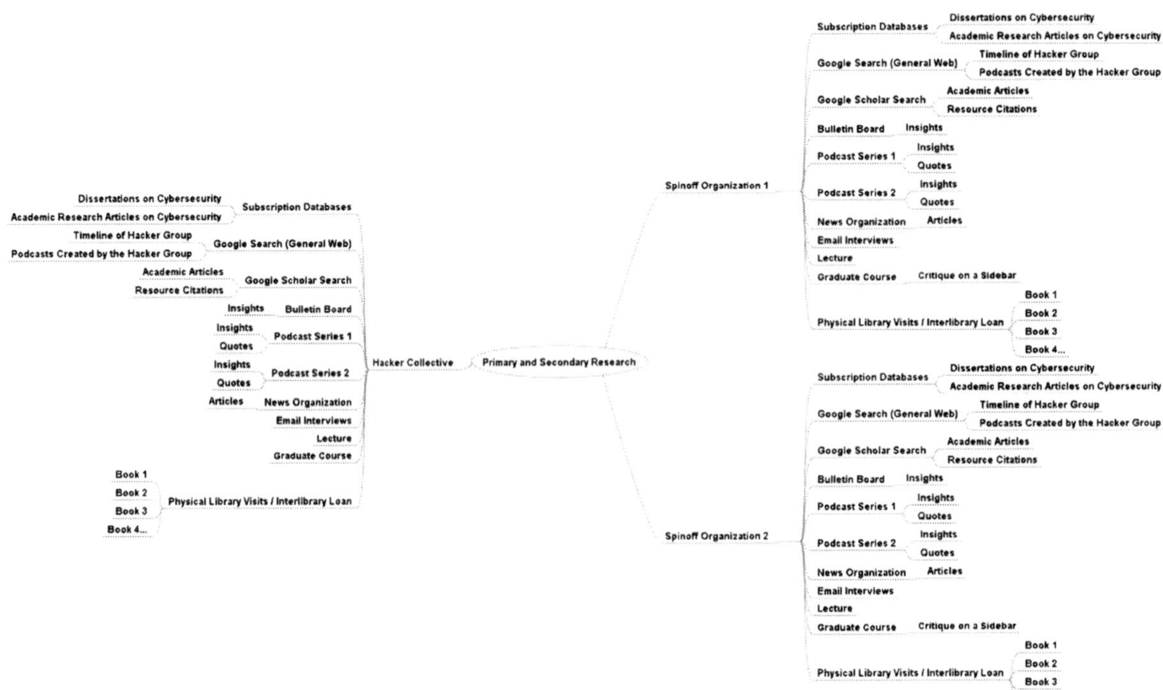

Table 1. Research sources analysis (data array)

Data Contents Used (below) General Research Sources (across)	Subscription Databases	Google Search (General Web)	Google Scholar Search	Bulletin Board	Podcast Series 1	Podcast Series 2
Articles and Papers	60	5	5	0	0	0
Dissertations	5	1	2	0	0	0
Timeline	0	1	0	0	0	0
Books	0	0	1	0	0	0
Informing Insights / No Citations	1	1	1	1	1	1
Data Contents Used (below) General Research Sources (across)	**News Organization**	**Email Interviews**	**Lecture**	**Graduate Course**	**Physical Library Visit / Interlibrary Loan**	
Articles and Papers	10	0	0	0	0	
Dissertations	0	0	0	0	0	
Timeline	0	0	0	0	0	
Books	0	0	0	0	8	
Informing Insights / No Citations	1	0	1	1	0	

the amounts of contents used from the particular source. So the intersection between Articles and Papers and Subscription Databases means that 60 articles and papers from various Subscription Databases were used in the final project (after extensive revision and editorial vetting).

The data array informed the node-link diagram: Figure 21.

There are apparently two centers of gravity in this diagram, one surrounding "Informing Insights / No Citations" (background information for the project, and then another segment for cited sources. The two main sources for cited contents are Articles and Papers and then Dissertations. The Timeline is a pendant node (a node which dangles from the network with only one link), which means it is peripherally connected to the network and is not a core information object type. Email Interviews are an isolate node (at the top left), which shows that it did not directly contribute to the core sources used. (An isolate node is totally disconnected from the rest of the network, which is indicated by the lack of a connector to any other node.) Physical libraries and interlibrary loan (bottom) were used to access books, which were identified through Google Scholar Searches and other methods.

While many types of sources informed the project by providing background material—a lecture, a graduate course, some podcast series, a bulletin board, a news organization, Google Searches, subscription databases, and Google Scholar searches, that knowledge was used on background only to inform the research, the organization of the project, and the contextualizing of the information. Background data and information are critical to inform how foreground data is analyzed and presented.

Procedural Branching

Another form of branching involves processes and procedures. While processes may be informational (descriptive, about how something generally progresses), others are directional processes or "how-to" types of procedures. For example,

Figure 21. Research sources analysis (the hacker collective project)

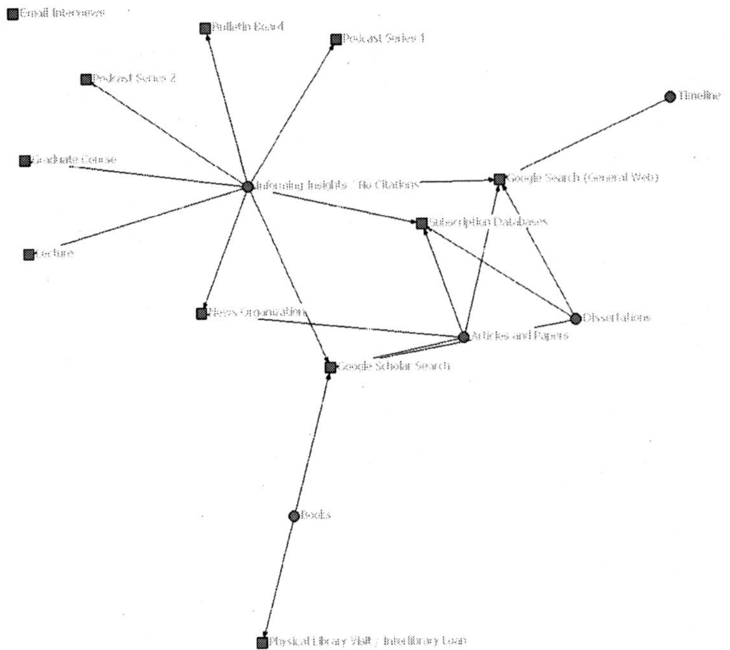

in a laboratory, there are precise steps that must be taken to achieve particular test results. Such procedures are critical for quality control. Further, there are many dependencies in processes to actualize certain objectives. To illustrate this type of branching in learning, an Event-driven Process Chain (EPC diagram) was created. In the logics literature, "events" are defined and represented in multiple ways in branching time but are generally indicative of causality and agency (Wölfl, 2005), which suggests both reasoned responses or behaviors and actors' volition. Figure 22 is expressed as an Event-Driven Process Chain (EPC) diagram.

This EPC diagram uses more of the formalisms in branching. The are "and" signs with the ^ sign, the "or" sign like a V, and the "xor" or ⊕ (exclusive or, or "exclusive disjunction," meaning one or the other, but not both).

This section provided some examples of branching logic in digital learning objects and some of the conventions of such branching. To back out a little further, branching may be applied to the sequencing of these various learning objects—with customized paths for different learners. Again, it is assumed that the segues between various learning objects are smooth and that the created learning achieves coherence.

Proper Learning Assessments

If branching is about strategic variations in learning in order to provide more diverse learning opportunities, then assessment of such learning has to be both about the assessment fit to the assignment and the fairness of the assessment. For example, rubrics are often used to assess portfolio work and projects. The rubrics are set at a sufficient level of abstraction in order to apply across a variety of projects and to accommodate a variety of strategies for problem-solving and design. Assessments should include clear feedback that will enrich both the mental modeling and the hands-on design work. Optimally, assessments should be built into the learning work from the beginning, so learners know what they will be assessed on. There generally is give-and-take between learners and their instructors in terms of assessments, so the assessment experience is supportive of the learner.

Figure 22. Topic selection for an academic publication (expressed as an event-driven process chain diagram)

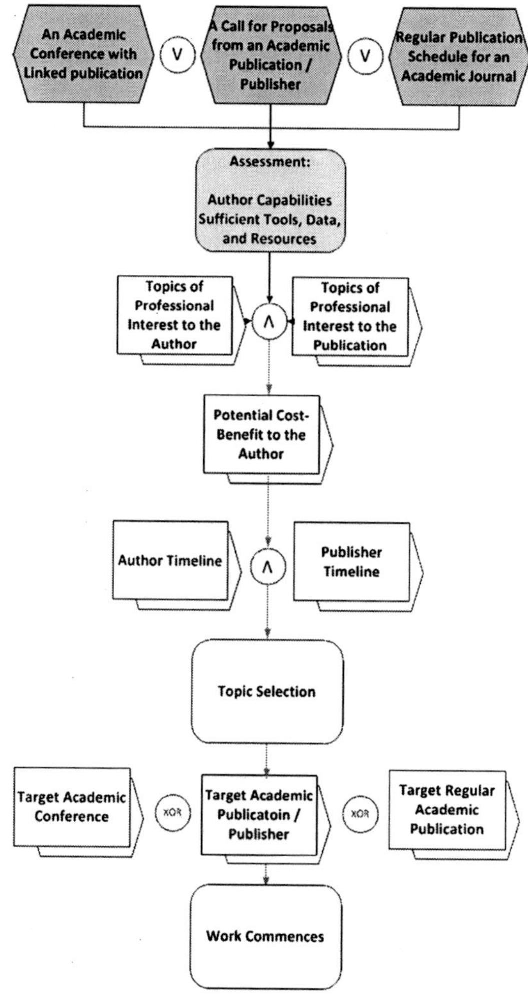

Factors to Take into Account when Branching

On one hand, branching does not seem unusual. It is used in an ad hoc way in many learning sequences. Because online learning often requires more conscious design, it is helpful to consider the role of branching as a kind of strategy in the packaging of online learning. Certainly, branching adds complexity and the potential for confusion. It helps to visualize learning as generally linear and chronological in time, with parts of the learning locked down and other parts free form and changeable. Branches may be designed into learning sequences in a componentized way.

To review, there are some basic reasons to branch. These involve the following aims:

1. **An Adaptive Curriculum:** Adapting a richer curriculum to reflect the complex realities of a field and the real world.
2. **Learner Support:** Accommodating learners, who often have diverse needs based on their capabilities, ambitions, areas of study, and needs.
3. **Learner Collaboration Support:** Promoting the building of learning teams for the acquisition of collaboration, co-learning, and co-design skills.
4. **Respect for Learner Decision-Making:** Respecting the decision-making of learners, particularly in scenarios of simulations, games, problem solving, case studies and analysis, microsite presentations, slideshows and lecture captures, design, and innovation.
5. **Maximizing In-World Opportunities:** Taking advantage of opportunities in the environment such as the availability of a guest speaker, the co-funding of a shared learning endeavor, a partnership with a business entity, fieldtrip options, and / or other created opportunities.

A review of some of the common types of branching in curriculums and then in learning objects has highlighted some important points.

- It is important to have a clear pedagogical rationale for branching. It is important to explain the rationales to learners (where necessary), so they understand the purpose(s) of the divergences.
- Curriculum designers should document the branching for clarity. Further, this documentation may benefit the hand-off to other designers or instructors.

- Every branch (every through-path) should be tested for any possible gaps in learning. Those gaps should be addressed.
- Every designed branch should be tested for efficacy for targeted learning. Every occasion that such learning is used, it is important for faculty to consider ways to hone the branches for more effective learning over time.
- Instructors should design assessments well to match the branches that various learners are taking, particularly if there is wide divergence. An example of such an assessment was a generalized rubric for assessing highly variant design or research projects.
- In faculty-led courses, such branching should not merely be mechanical. Thought and design should go into how divergent lessons may be integrated for all learners, so they may benefit from each other's learning (in a jigsaw learning design). Learning branches should be reintegrated or merged to the main curriculum for coherence.

FUTURE RESEARCH DIRECTIONS

Branching logic has been a built-in part of work for those who design interactive digital learning objects, simulations, serious educational games, and spatialized/locative interactive learning experiences (as in applications of mobile learning). This approach is used in mainline learning sequences as well but with much less recognition. This chapter offers an initial typology in instructional and curriculum design to support the application of thought-through design and sequentiality. Certainly, in future work, it is hoped that others would share their insights about branching strategies based on their respective work.

Future researchers could contribute insights about their methods to evaluate the efficacy of various branching techniques and their applications in various learning contexts. Other work could involve the creative uses of technologies to create effective branched learning.

The conventions of visual descriptions were based on a liberal interpretation of the Integrated Definition for Function (Process) Modeling (IDEFO) conventions. However, even a brief perusal of the literature has shown a number of conventions of visual / textual / symbolic expressions: tree-structures in game theoretic applications; algorithms in computer science; equations in philosophy; flow charts in the decision-sciences, and others. Because instructional design is a cross-disciplinary field, its practitioners should draw broadly from others in ways that are relevant to design.

CONCLUSION

This chapter offers an early look at curricular branching at both the course (macro) and the digital learning object (micro) levels. Curricular branching is used in various types of computer-based training (such as interactive videodiscs and Websites). This work is descriptive more than it is prescriptive although some takeaways have been drawn from the analysis of real-world curricular branching. Per the title, this chapter only offers a partial typology. There are likely still many other types of complex branching methods in designed instruction. The modeling of entire and complex curriculums are likely to show more complex branching structures.

Branching logic is a formalism from computer science, and there are conventions to modeling computation, but the concept is also helpful in expressing learning sequences in instructional and curricular design. While the concept and application are not as rigorous here as in computer science, in educational use, branching strategies and thinking can be highly helpful in structuring adaptive learning for a wide range of learners.

REFERENCES

Dignum, F., & Kuiper, R. (1999). Specifying deadlines with continuous time using deontic and temporal logic. *International Journal of Electronic Commerce, 3*(2), 67–85. Retrieved from http://www.jstor.org/stable/27750885.

Engelfriet, J., & Treur, J. (2002). Linear, branching time and joint closure semantics for temporal logic. *Journal of Logic Language and Information, 11*, 389–425. doi:10.1023/A:1019999621456.

Koller, D. (2012). What we're learning from online education. *TEDGlobal*. Retrieved from http://www.youtube.com/watch?v=U6FvJ6jMGHU

Mioduser, D., & Dagan, O. (2007). The effect of alternative approaches to design instruction (structural or functional) on students' mental models of technological design processes. *International Journal of Technology and Design Education, 17*, 135–148. doi:10.1007/s10798-006-0004-z.

Ramachandran, S., Jensen, R., & Sincoff, E. (2010). Simulation development and authoring: Why abstraction matters. In *Proceedings of the Interservice/Industry Training, Simulation, and Education Conference*. ITSEC.

Wölfl, S. (2005). Events in branching time. *Studia Logics: An International Journal for Symbolic Logic, 79*(2), 255–282.

KEY TERMS AND DEFINITIONS

Branching Logic: The reasoned design of different paths through a learning experience.

Conjunction: Addition.

Convergence: Coming together often to a fixed answer.

Decision Juncture: The point at which critical choices are made for a project or a learning sequence.

Divergence: Separate; develop in a different direction.

Exclusive Disjunction: Either-or, but not both.

Gated Assignment: A hurdle-based learning sequence that requires the proof of learning at various steps in the curriculum before being able to move on.

Logical Connectives: Formalized ways of showing relationships.

Logical Disjunction: Inclusive disjunction or alternation, the switching between different branches as equivalencies or pseudo-equivalencies.

Microsite: A small Website that is used for a limited purpose.

Negation: Not.

Profile (Learner): The description of a learner along with his/her learning achievements and projected needs.

Stochastic: Having a random probability distribution; unpredictable; not pre-determined and non-deterministic.

Wayfinding: Orientation to a learning space and navigating through it.

Xor: Exclusive or, exclusive disjunction.

Section 2
Innovative Technologies and Techniques in Packaging Digital Contents

Chapter 4
Weaving Web 2.0 and Facial Expression Recognition into the 3D Virtual English Classroom

Ya-Chun Shih
National Dong Hwa University, Taiwan

ABSTRACT

Of late, considerable attention has been given to the linking or "mashing up" of virtual worlds and Web 2.0 tools. The authors incorporated several Web 2.0 tools, including blogs, audioblogs, wikis, Facebook, Twitter, and Flickr, and a facial expression organizer together into the 3D Virtual English Classroom called VEC3D 5.0, thereby opening up new possibilities for collaborative language learning. In considering the needs of language learners, this study combines synchronous and asynchronous learning environments and methods to propose a blended language learning solution. VEC3D 5.0 offers the possibility of applying situated learning, multimodal communication, and facial expression recognition to language learning and teaching. VEC3D 5.0 has shown itself to possess tremendous potential as an optimal language learning environment. Integrating Web 2.0 applications in the form of open social networking and information sharing tools into VEC3D 5.0 supports collaborative and reflective language learning, and in particular, writing and cultural learning. The purpose of this study is to explore the application of a hybrid prototype solution, which combines the inherent strengths of both virtual environments and Web 2.0 applications, and to provide a framework for developing innovative pedagogies for experiential language learning in this context.

INTRODUCTION

In Taiwan, whether learners are situated inside or outside of the classroom setting, opportunities for in-depth exposure to target language and culture, naturalistic language acquisition and social interaction are usually limited. 3D Collaborative Virtual Environments (CVEs) serve as the context for situated language learning, as well as providing open social networking tools for collaborative language learning, in which learners form a community of practice. The purpose of this project is to make it easy for English as a Foreign Language (EFL) learners in Taiwan to connect with other learners, instructors and international English speakers, and through these interactions and the integration of Web 2.0 applications into a CVE, the 3D Virtual English Classroom (VEC3D 5.0), to foster students' language learning process and

DOI: 10.4018/978-1-4666-4462-5.ch004

autonomy. The idea of connecting these technologies originated from user needs.

Teaching language entirely in virtual worlds without using other available Web tools would limit the possibilities for gathering and sharing information, and generating new ideas, content, and discussion topics. The virtual world provides context for language learners. However, on its own, it is found to be somewhat lacking in terms of helping learners to acquire the target language. Moreover, it doesn't necessarily encourage prolonged engagement. To overcome these limitations, linking the virtual world with Web 2.0 stimulates further discussion, prolongs conversation, and provides more opportunities for collaboration and interaction. Combining Web 2.0 and VEC3D is seen as having potential for the development of new forms of language learning and acquisition. The combination also enables learners to broaden their social networks and co-construct knowledge through interaction and collaboration in online communities.

In order to support EFL learners' needs in terms of interaction, collaboration, social networking and information-sharing, we proposed a blended solution which combines VEC3D 5.0 and Web 2.0 applications. A group of Web 2.0 tools, including blogs, audioblogs, wikis, Facebook, Twitter, and Flickr, were integrated into the virtual environment to support collaborative and situated language learning, in particular, writing and cultural learning. We assume that writing development and cultural learning arise from interaction, "collaboration with more capable peers" (Vygotsky, 1978), and guidance from instructors. The development of both writing and cultural learning is the product of interaction and group dynamics in the learning process. Accordingly, we attempt to develop and integrate Web 2.0 dynamics into VEC3D 5.0, which is expected to facilitate the formation of a Web-based "community of practice" (Lave & Wenger, 1991) in a foreign language learning setting. Ultimately, the project's goal is to prepare students to be able to communicate in English naturally and effectively outside the classroom.

In addition to these elements, we also incorporated a facial expression analyzer, which facilitates our analysis of the English language learners' interactions, understanding and consciousness. Facial expressions provide nonverbal cues related to human emotions and behaviors, such as interaction, understanding and consciousness, all of which play important roles in language education. Facial expression analysis plays an important role in the language teaching process. Language instructors need to understand students' body language, as it can reveal a lot about the level of student interaction, the students' understanding, and the degree to which students are paying attention. Instructors can use this information to adjust their teaching to meet students' needs. The facial expression analyzer in VEC3D 5.0 lets English teachers know when it may be advantageous to adjust their speaking rate or teaching strategies to make input comprehensible to learners so as to meet learner needs. The VEC3D research team was able to take advantage of the facial expression analyzer's technical possibilities to expand on this idea and develop it within the framework of VEC3D 5.0.

BACKGROUND

Language learning and acquisition arise from interaction, which can take the form of guided interaction with instructors (Krashen, 1981), interpersonal interaction and interacting with the environment (Capocchi Ribeiro, 2002). The Interaction Hypothesis (Long, 1985, 1996) proposed that the acquisition of a second language lies in interpersonal and direct interaction, and emphasized the critical roles "comprehensible input" and "negotiated meaning" play in second language acquisition. Vygotsky (1978) stressed the importance of collaboration and social interaction in social learning, which leads to cognitive development.

Accordingly, language learning or acquisition is believed to be a product of social interaction and collaboration. Web 2.0 applications and virtual worlds foster high levels of user collaboration and social interaction, and, consequently, open up great possibilities for language learning. In this study, our curriculum and systematic design were informed by the social constructivist view of learning proposed by Vygotsky (1987). Human interaction and collaboration supported by Web 2.0 applications and virtual environments are assumed to be beneficial for language learning and/or acquisition.

WEB 2.0 AND LANGUAGE LEARNING

The term "Web 2.0" (O'Reilly, 2005) first came to use in 2004 and refers to all available second generation network services. Together, these can be conceptualized as a "participatory Web" (Decrem, 2006) or a "platform" (O'Reilly, 2005) for communication, information-sharing and collaboration on the World Wide Web. Web 2.0 applications, including video-sharing sites, social networking Websites (e.g., Twitter, Facebook), wikis, blogs, and so on, facilitate information-sharing, collaboration, interaction, and communication on a worldwide basis ("Web 2.0," n.d.). These applications provide Web-based platforms where people can meet, read, write, listen, speak, and share their experiences, talents and information.

Due to the communicative and collaborative nature of Web 2.0, the current popularity of its various applications has drawn considerable academic and practical interest in terms of how they relate to language learning. For example, emerging Web 2.0 applications have greatly expanded the research areas of Computer-Assisted Language Learning (CALL). Numerous researchers (e.g., Antenos-Conforti, 2009; Alm, 2006; Campbell, 2003, Godwin-Jones, 2003; Pinkman, 2005; Rosen & Kato, 2006; Stanley, 2006) have devoted their attention to the brand-new field of Web 2.0 assisted language learning, and have incorporated Web 2.0 tools into second or foreign language learning. According to Wang and Vasquez's comprehensive review study (2012), the most well-researched areas of Web 2.0 assisted second language (L2) learning, in descending order, are: L2 writing (e.g., Antenos-Conforti, 2009; Armstrong & Retterer, 2008; Kessler, 2009), attitudes and perceptions toward Web 2.0 tools (e.g., Chen, 2009; Dippold, 2009), and oral skills (Sun, 2009; Lord, 2008). The empirical results of studies in this field indicate that language learners benefit from the collaborative and communicative language learning Web (Dippold, 2009; Kessler, 2009), and Web 2.0 tools (i.e., blogs and/or wikis) have a positive influence on learners' writing skills (e.g., Franco, 2008; Lee, 2010).

Wang and Vasquez also indicate that the most-studied Web 2.0 tools in L2 learning field are blogs (e.g., Alm, 2009; Pinkman, 2005; Campbell, 2003), and wikis (e.g., Chen, 2009; Kessler, 2009), whereas the effect of social networking tools on language learning (e.g., Halvorsen, 2009; McCarty, 2009) has received less scholarly attention. The existing studies often attempt to shed light on how Web 2.0 tools might be combined to construct a dynamic language-learning environment. For example, class blogs, wikis, MySpace, and YouTube were used jointly (Alm, 2006); blogs and wikis were used in conjunction (Godwin-Jones, 2003); and Web 2.0 tools (i.e., blogs and podcasts) were combined with 3D virtual worlds (e.g., Second Life) (e.g., Vickers, 2007a, 2007b). According to the categorization proposed by Wang and Vasquez, a 3D virtual world is an existent type of Web 2.0 technology. In their comprehensive survey of research into the various applications of Web 2.0 technologies, these researchers highlighted the limitations of Web 2.0 assisted L2 learning:

...research on the application of Web 2.0 technologies to L2 learning is still quite limited. Specifically, blogs and wikis are "just the tip of

an integration" in the educational context (Oliver, 2010, p. 50). ...future research should investigate the less-studied Web 2.0 tools, such as Facebook, Twitter, and Second Life...in order to provide both researchers and practitioners with more information about various options for technology integration (Wang & Vasquez, 2012, p. 416).

To attempt to meet this challenge, our research team incorporated blogs, audioblogs, wikis, and social networking tools (Facebook, Twitter, and Flickr) into the 3D virtual world to facilitate language learning. Moreover, it is hoped that this study will allow other experts in this discipline to better understand how to integrate these Web 2.0 tools into a 3D virtual world in the context of language education, and encourage them to conduct follow-up studies.

One of the key elements of our platform is blogging. A blog is an online discussion Website where individuals (or, in some cases, groups) can author and publish various discrete or thematic entries, known as posts, on the World Wide Web. Audioblogging is an alternative form of blogging which employs uploading and embedding audiofiles. Other forms of blogging are moblogging (mobile blogging through the uploading and sharing of pictures taken using mobile devices, in addition to other content), and vlogging (video blogging, which includes the uploading and sharing of videos). Through blogging, users can reflect on their experiences and express their viewpoints and opinions publicly. Blog-Assisted Language Learning (BALL) has drawn much attention in the field of CALL recently. Researchers (Mynard, 2007; Yang, 2009; Metaferia, 2012) have indicated that blogs provide a reflective approach to language learning. Numerous studies have specifically explored the effect of using blogs on learners' language learning in terms of L2 reading and writing (e.g., Ducate & Lomicka, 2008), oral skills and learning strategies (i.e., Sun, 2009), learning communities (e.g., Yang, 2009), perceptions and attitudes (Soares, 2008), learning motivation and retention rates (Hsu & Wang, 2009), and so on.

The second element of our platform, wikis, allows users to create and edit collaboratively through a Web browser ("Wiki," n.d.). Wikis have been widely used and researched in language classroom settings, in particular, in the contexts of collaborative writing (skills) (e.g., Arnold, Ducate, & Kost, 2009; Elola & Oskoz, 2010; Hirvela, 1999; Kessler, 2009; Kessler & Bikowski, 2010; Lee, 2010; Mark & Coniam, 2008), language learners' identity (Choi, 2009) and factors affecting their collaboration (Zorko, 2009), and collective language development (Lund, 2008). The wiki-based Websites and collaborative activities have been found to facilitate learners' interaction and language use (Kessler & Bikowski, 2010), collaborative behaviors (Zorko, 2009), collaborative writing skills and revision behavior (Arnold, Ducate, & Kost, 2009), and language accuracy (Lee, 2010), amongst other things.

The third element, online social networking platforms (e.g., Facebook, Twitter), provide each user with an individual profile which is linked to others. These platforms facilitate social interaction among linked users, joining them together in an online community in which they can share real-life experiences, common interests, and opinions. Several studies have examined Web-based social networking in the context of language learning. For instance, researchers and pacticitioners used Twitter to facilitate the development of community, classroom dynamics, cultural interest, positive experiences (Antenos-Conforti, 2009), and communicative and cultural competence (Borau, Ullrich, Feng, & Shen, 2009). Researchers have investigated the development of a sense of community and socio-pragmatic competence (Blattner & Friori, 2009), the development of learners' identity, autonomy, and critical literacy (Halvorsen, 2009; Harrison & Thomas, 2009), and the integrative motivation EFL learners have toward learning English language (McCarty, 2009) within the context of social networking sites. Flickr is another popular social networking Website which is widely regarded as serving the same type of function. This Web-based photo management and sharing application allows users to create their own content (i.e., images), and share them with other members in an online community. Moreover, it allows users to collaborate on projects through creating, sharing, and searching for photos. Campbell (2007) investigated the pedagogical potential of Flickr, and introduced various language class activities using Flickr to motivate language learners. However, as mentioned previously, the impact of these social networking tools on language learners is still relatively uncharted territory, especially in comparison to the attention that has been given to blogs and wikis.

VIRTUAL ENVIRONMENTS AND LANGUAGE LEARNING

A virtual environment or world is a computer-based simulated environment which allows people to interact and communicate with others synchronously in an immersive and collaborative virtual space. Users, embodied by different forms of avatars, are able to explore, socialize, and interact with other avatars, with the environment itself, and with the myriad virtual objects within the environment. Since the functionality of an online 3D virtual world, such as Second Life, corresponds closely to the definition of Web 2.0 as a social platform for generating content, collaboration, and sharing information, online 3D virtual worlds are looked upon as constituting either a type of Web 2.0 tool (e.g., Wang and Vasquez, 2012), or a "prototype of [a] Web 3.0 tool" (Stanley, 2006). Some researchers (e.g., Cashmore, 2006) suggest that the distinction between Web 2.0 and online virtual worlds, such as Second Life is blurred. However, many researchers exclude virtual worlds from the categorization of Web 2.0, and treat these two terms as being distinct from each other. In order to present the concept of the integration of Web 2.0 and a 3D virtual world, we treat the two elements, Web 2.0 and the 3D virtual world, as distinct, both conceptually and practically.

Virtual Environments provide interactive environments and numerous occasions, both planned and spontaneous, for social interaction, collaboration, and authentic communication, all of which are critical components of effective language learning and acquisition. Practitioners and researchers have investigated the role played by 3D virtual worlds in language education. Previous studies of virtual environment assisted language have focused on different aspects of language learning, such as reading and writing skills (e.g., Warren, Stein, Dondlinger, & Barab, 2009; Warren, Barab, & Dondlinger, 2008), communicative competence and intercultural awareness (e.g., University of Utrecht, 2009), oral proficiency/skills (e.g., Deutschmann, Panichi, Molka-Danielsen, 2009; Koenraad, 2007, 2008), negotiation of meaning (e.g., Toyota, 2002; Peterson, 2006), cultural learning (e.g., Henderson, 2008), Spanish pragmatics (i.e., Sykes, 2009), and language learner attitudes (Kuriscak & Luke, 2009). Conspicuous by its absence from the foregoing list, however, is empirical research into the integration of Web 2.0 with virtual environments along with their pedagogical implementation in the context of language learning, a field which is only in its infancy.

INTEGRATION OF WEB 2.0 AND VIRTUAL ENVIRONMENTS FOR LANGUAGE LEARNING

Combining various Web 2.0 tools and 3D immersive virtual environments to facilitate dynamic language learning is a promising research trend. The SurReal Quests project (Vickers, 2007a, 2007b), for instance, combines Second Life (which provides social interaction and communication opportunities), traditional Websites, and Web 2.0 tools (e.g., blogs and podcasts), which allow for the sharing of information and user-created content, to facilitate both classroom learning and distance learning. A typical SurReal Quests task called "Travel Podcast" is mentioned in Avatar Language Blog (Vickers, 2007a). Both Second Life and real-life locations (e.g., Krakow) were selected for the topic-specific "virtual quests", and Web 1.0 and 2.0 applications were used to complete assigned "Web quests". Within this context, the learning process generally involves four stages: 1) planning, 2) researching about the locations via traditional Websites, blogs, podcasts, forums, and interviewing local people and exploring the destination via Second Life, 3) drafting and editing content for the follow-up podcast recordings, and 4) recording and uploading podcasts to accomplish both virtual quests and Web quests (Vickers, 2007a, "Combination of Advantages," para. 1). The above-mentioned blog post indicates that the benefits which this combination brings to learners are "rich information" (especially via researching through the Web), and "active and social communication" as facilitated by Second Life ("Combination of Advantages," para. 1). Inspired by the possibilities of this combination, we incorporate Web 2.0 tools into the 3D virtual environment in an EFL learning context in an effort to gain insight how these technologies may be used to advance users' language learning.

As shown by Figure 1, within the framework of a collaborative learning space, VEC3D 5.0, a blended learning environment, occupies a space midway between Web 2.0 tools and the virtual world, integrating the best features of both technologies to facilitate two kinds of learning: reflective language learning, as enabled by Web 2.0 tools through sharing user created content, and immersive language learning, as a product of experiences in the virtual world. In terms of communication, Web 2.0 tools allow users to interact asynchronously, while the virtual space mirrors this with the possibility of synchronous interaction.

Figure 1. Concept map

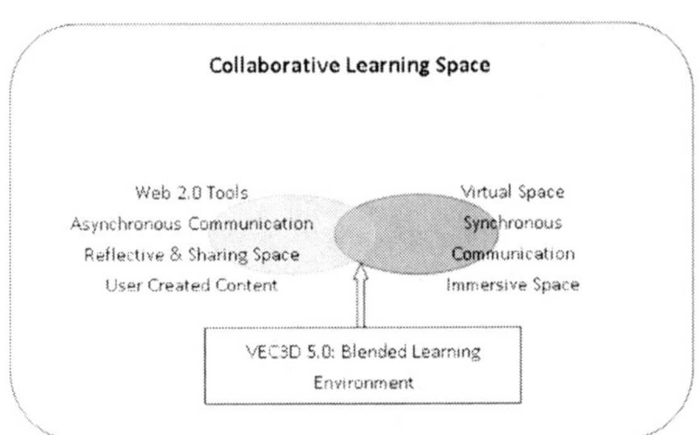

THE ROLE OF CONSCIOUS AWARENESS IN LANGUAGE LEARNING

Conscious awareness plays a role in language learning, in the sense that language learners need to possess at least a minimal level of conscious awareness during language learning or acquisition. Schmidt (1990) identifies three levels of awareness, with corresponding roles in input processing: 1) the level of "noticing"; 2) "paying attention"; and 3) "unconscious process of abstraction," all of which lead to "subliminal learning," "incidental learning," and "implicit learning" (as cited in Jung, 2009; Schmidt, 1990), respectively. Follow-up empirical studies are needed to determine the possible existence of a relationship between conscious awareness and language learning, as suggested by Schmidt:

...noticing is the necessary and sufficient condition for converting input to intake. Incidental learning, on the other hand, is clearly both possible and effective when the demands of a task focus attention on what is to be learned. Even so, paying attention is probably facilitative, and may be necessary if adult learners are to acquire redundant grammatical features (Schmidt, 1990, Abstract section).

Schmidt (1993) posits that conscious awareness plays a necessity role in a learner noticing or being aware of the forms and functional meanings within the social contexts in the broader process of acquiring pragmatic competence. Researchers (e.g., Borg, 1994) have tried to uncover the best language awareness methodology with which to develop learners' further understanding of language, language use and culture. The research that expands on earlier studies related to conscious awareness in language learning distinguishes between awareness of form and meaning, and cross-cultural awareness.

In the present study, it is assumed that conscious (language) awareness is necessary in writing training and in the development of cross-cultural awareness, the two main pedagogical goals of the proposed project. Language learners were guided by a native English-speaking instructor in an effort to develop their conscious knowledge, and to understand the features of their language use and skills, as well as the associated linguistic meanings and concepts, through exploiting group dynamics and exploring the virtual environment. With the help of the facial expression analyzer provided by VEC3D 5.0, instructors are able to monitor learners' conscious awareness. This is a key feature of the platform, considering the critical role conscious awareness is presumed to play in foreign language learning and acquisition.

SYSTEMATIC DESIGN AND IMPLEMENTATION

3D Virtual Environment

The Virtual English Classroom (VEC3D) (Figure 2) is an immersive and interactive 3D virtual world designed for English language learning. Users, represented by different 3D avatars, can move through the virtual world, interacting with other user-controlled avatars using text-based and voice chat. The most recent version of VEC3D integrates 3D graphics, text- and voice-based communication, and video conferencing within the framework of 3D virtual environment architecture. It immerses language learners in various 3D virtual scenes, such as classrooms, meeting rooms, and virtual reconstructions of real-world scenes, such as the university's campus lake view, to provide opportunities for situated language

Figure 2. VEC3D interface

learning. VEC3D offers benefits for language learners by allowing them autonomy in their use of multimodal communications, and by allowing them to interact and communicate with each other through avatars or video-conferencing to achieve a variety of shared learning goals. What distinguishes VEC3D from other virtual worlds is the seamless integration of different technologies, which offers users more autonomy. In other words, multiple communication modes can be selected by users, depending on their needs in specific situations. For researchers and practitioners, VEC3D represents an experimental prototype for the expansion of the communicative functions of a 3D virtual world and integrating different technologies into it.

INCORPORATION OF WEB 2.0 TOOLS INTO VEC3D 5.0

We implemented a blended language learning environment that combined Web 2.0-based tools with a 3D virtual world, VEC3D 5.0 (see Figure 3). The idea to integrate these technologies was inspired by Second Life Blogs, in which the Second Life online community creates information regarding new experiences and events, and shares their experiences using Second Life. A typical virtual world is primarily designed for synchronous communication, however, we anticipate that users also need to be able to reflect on their experiences of using the virtual world, share related information with the community, and prolong their engagement with the virtual community. Thus, our platform allows users to access several different Websites where they can do exactly that. By incorporating Web 2.0 tools in this manner, we satisfy user needs for information-sharing, reflection, and the sharing of user-created content.

This project presents collaborative writing and cultural experiential learning as an instructional model within a blended learning environment; namely, the integration of a 3D virtual world and the aforementioned Web 2.0 applications. Language learning results from interaction within the socio-cultural context. In particular, writing and culture learning are inherently collaborative and experiential. The team has investigated the possibility of integrating Web 2.0 tools into VEC3D 5.0 to foster the development of learners' writing and cultural understanding. In this project, we hypothesized that collaborative language learning activities could be designed and implemented to enhance learners' writing performance and facilitate their cultural learning through engaging them in various activities held in the blended learning environment, VEC3D 5.0.

The implementation of the user interface of VEC3D 5.0 was based on DXUT (DirectX Utility Library). Compared with Windows and Direct3D API (Application Programming Interface), DXUT simplifies the complicated process of interface construction. Seven buttons were created for the VEC3D 5.0 interface. The learners identified one Web 2.0 tool with each of the buttons, which were then used for accessing the Web 2.0 tools and Skype. The implementation process consisted of four steps:

1. Assigning an ID to the button.
2. Adding the button to the VEC3D window.
3. Specifying the position and size of the button.
4. Linking a Web 2.0 address to the button.

The interface of VEC3D 5.0 is shown in Figure 3. Seven transparent buttons are located on the left side of the VEC3D window. Clicking on these buttons allows users to connect to and to access blogs, Facebook, Twitter, audioblog, Flickr, wikis, and Skype. Two buttons located on the bottom right-hand corner of the VEC3D 5.0 window enable users to start and stop the Webcam. Live facial images are only evaluated, transferred, and displayed if the Webcam is enabled.

Figure 3. VEC3D 5.0 interface

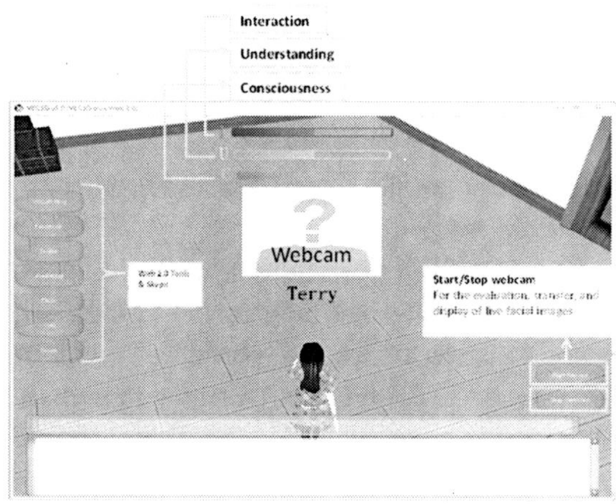

INCORPORATION OF FACIAL EXPRESSION RECOGNITION INTO VEC3D 5.0

By integrating the research team's own proprietary facial expression recognition technology (Yang, Cheng, & Shih, 2010) into VEC3D 5.0, we allow instructors to monitor the levels of students' *understanding* (U), *interaction* (I), and *consciousness* (C). Being able to read and analyze students' facial expressions can help instructors to monitor their students' moods and level of motivation at any given time, and can give the instructor insight into the level at which students are learning the target material. This can be especially valuable in the case of students who are lagging behind their peers, as it allows the instructor to decide on what pedagogical action needs to be taken, thereby bridging the gap between learning and instruction. With the addition of facial expression recognition capability to the virtual space, the instructor is better able to guide and facilitate the learning process.

The proposed system represents an upgrade to VEC3D with the addition of facial expression recognition and analysis capabilities. Three colored bars are located above the live facial image which is captured by a Webcam and displayed in the VEC3D 5.0 interface (see Figure 3). The facial images, along with the analyzed learning statuses, are transmitted and shown in the virtual classroom. Figure 3 shows the interface as it appears to both students and the teacher. The system allows every user to enable the facial expression recognition system (that is, to transfer, display and evaluate live facial images), and see the recognition information by clicking the "Start Record" button. Users can likewise disable the recognition system by clicking the "StopWebcam" button. These three bars above the facial image indicate the levels of *Interaction, Understanding, and Consciousness*, respectively, for each student. Facial feature extraction in conjunction with spatial relation filtering can accurately locate facial features and the resulting system has the ability to reliably recognize and categorize facial expressions.

"Negative" facial expressions, such as yawns, point to low motivation, sleepiness, frustration and other negative feelings or moods, including disinterest, boredom, anxiety and so on. It is important for teachers to recognize when students are exhibiting such signals and adjust their teaching to meet student needs and lower what Krashen (1982) referred to as their "affective filter". Krashen indicated that ideal language input occurs when this "affective filter" is low. High levels of motivation and self-confidence and low levels of frustration and anxiety act to lower the affective filter, and when a student has a low affective filter, this allows for more language input. The proposed system helps teachers to detect likely indicators of students' negative mental states during the foreign language teaching process.

As previously mentioned, the proposed system allows teachers to detect student's *interaction(I)*, *understanding(U)*, and *consciousness(C)*. In addition, VEC3D 5.0 makes it possible to monitor, record, and understand every student's learning status, and to estimate the duration of his or her attention span. Specifically, the estimated probabilities of the occurrence of six facial expressions (Blink, Wrinkled Brow, Shake, Nod, Yawn, and

Talk) jointly determine the students' scores in terms of *interaction(I)*, *understanding(U)*, and *consciousness(C)*. For instance, a score indicating a high degree of *interaction(I)* suggests a learner's active participation in the virtual community, whereas a low *understanding(U)* score suggests that the topic and content may be perceived as difficult by students, meaning the instructor might need to re-identify the learner's entry skills. Low *consciousness(C)* scores are assigned by the system when a student adopts an expression like "eyes half-closed," suggesting his or her boredom or tiredness and a low level of awareness or taking notice. With the help of the estimated scores provided by the system, language teachers are able to adjust their teaching pace and methods, help lagging students to catch up, and close the gap between learning and instruction. Additionally, the system makes it possible for instructors to observe and record student performance longitudinally. For more detailed technical specifications and discussion of the validity of the facial expression recognition system, please refer to the recent work entitled "Facial Expression Recognition for Learning Status Analysis" (Yang, Cheng, & Shih, 2010).

CURRICULUM DESIGN

Task-based events were designed and implemented to link Web 2.0 applications (including wikis, blogs, Facebook, Twitter, and Flickr) with VEC3D 5.0, to create a blended environment where students can practice reflective thinking, writing, and real-time social communication. We adopt an experiential learning approach (Kolb, 1984) in terms of task design, and incorporate a variety of synchronous and asynchronous communication tasks to allow learners to gain experience in communication and use this as a vehicle for language learning and development. To arouse students' interest and motivation to learn a foreign language, we created various virtual environments. For instance, learners were asked to conduct ethnographic interviews with the native-English speaking instructor (embodied as an avatar), to participate in synchronous learning events, and to reflect on the experiences they had during their immersion and interactions with others in the virtual environment.

Based on the Experiential Learning Theory, Kolb's experiential learning model (1984) (see Figure 4) involves two intersecting continuums (i.e., process and perception) forming four quadrants, and a learning cycle with four learning stages, one of which is situated at each end of the two continuums: (a) Active Experimentation (doing); (b) Concrete Experience (feeling); (c) Reflective Observation (watching), and (d) Abstract Conceptualization (thinking). The process continuum involves how learners approach tasks, for example, by acting or by observing. The perception continuum involves how learners feel or think about tasks. Learners can enter the learning cycle at any of the four starting points (i.e. on either continuum, at any of the four learning stages).

Kolb's learning cycle can be used as a framework for considering the different synchronous and asynchronous learning stages which learners

Figure 4. A learning cycle proposed by Kolb (adapted from Kolb, 1984)

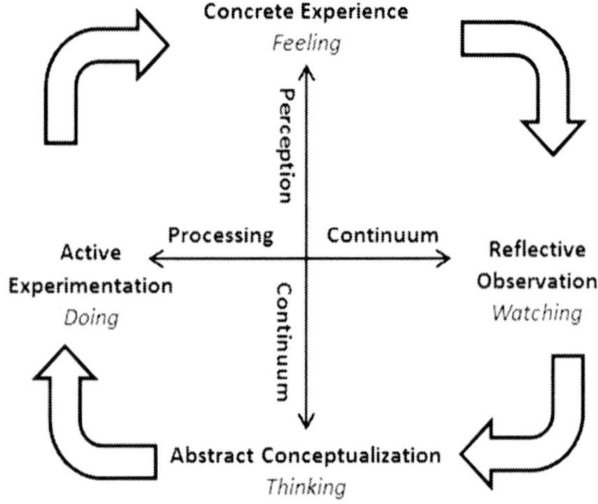

pass through. Based on Kolb's cycle, we have created a number of different scenarios designed to satisfy students' different learning styles and goals. Learners are expected to gain experience through participation in different experiential settings, while taking advantage of both the synchronous and asynchronous components of VEC3D 5.0. The tasks are designed to engage learners in the virtual environment, in the hope that the experience they gain from real-time interaction in the virtual environment will provide a strong foundation for their continued reflective learning, along with increased opportunities for asynchronous collaboration.

Example elements of the curriculum are provided below:

Scenario 1: Traveling

Active experimentation (synchronous): Students are embodied as avatars, and explore the virtual environment.

Concrete experience (synchronous): Students have the experience of travel through conversing with knowledgeable persons (e.g., a native English-speaking instructor) who serve as tour guides as they explore the various settings.

Reflective observation (synchronous and asynchronous): Students observe how people communicate with native English speakers, and record their thoughts and reflections via blogs.

Abstract conceptualization (asynchronous): Students download audio files from Websites (e.g., podcasts), visit audioblogs, and hear audio tour guides introduce locations.

Scenario 2: Ethnographic Interviews

Abstract conceptualization (asynchronous): Students explore the cultural heritage of an ethnic group (e.g., Taiwan's indigenous tribes) through Wikipedia.

Active experimentation (synchronous): Students are immersed in the virtual environment, embodied as avatars, and conduct one-on-one interviews with the local people (who can be role-played by native English speakers).

Concrete experience (asynchronous): Students build up cultural experience through contact with the instructor, who serves as an expert and communicates with the students via Twitter or Facebook (usually in the form of Q & A).

Reflective observation (synchronous and asynchronous): Students engage in immersive observation to understand behaviors and social rituals of the target culture in a real-life or virtual setting, take snapshots (for later sharing through Flickr), and record their thoughts and reflections via blogs. Students describe people they met, places they visited, (virtual) objects or scenes they saw, events they joined in, and what they heard in their blogs.

Scenario 3: Contextual Inquiry – Music Recording Studio

Abstract conceptualization (asynchronous): Students gain an understanding of the process of recording through researching via wikis.

Reflective observation (synchronous): Students watch musicians perform a task, such as recording an album, in a real-life or virtual studio.

Concrete experience (synchronous and asynchronous): Students ask the musicians questions about what they do on-site and how they do it, and/or raise questions through Facebook or Twitter.

Active experimentation (asynchronous): Students visit a real-world studio, try their hand at recording, and share the experience through blogging and posting their recordings (via audioblogging).

Scenario 4: Paddling a Boat on the Lake

Concrete experience (synchronous and asynchronous): A coach guides students as they paddle a virtual or real-life boat on a lake, and/or the students visit the coach's blog, audioblog, Facebook page or Twitter Website, where the coach teaches paddling skills and the skills necessary to control virtual vehicles in the virtual world.

Active experimentation (synchronous): Students paddle a (virtual) boat on the lake.

Reflective observation (synchronous and asynchronous): Students observe how other people paddle their boats on the lake, and reflect on their own experiences through blogging.

Abstract conceptualization (asynchronous): Students read wikis to gather information about paddling technique.

Task design and implementation were conducted with a view to helping students improve their writing ability and broaden their cross-cultural understanding through exploration, discussion, interaction and comparison of their own culture and the target culture. In addition, interacting with a native English-speaking instructor, as well as with other non-native speakers in VEC3D 5.0, provided EFL learners with ample opportunity to develop their communication skills and (cross-) cultural understanding and awareness. Task-based events were designed and implemented to link Web 2.0 applications including blogs, wikis, Facebook, Twitter, and Flickr with VEC3D 5.0 to improve writing performance and enhance cultural learning. Examples of collaborative language learning and task-based activities are categorized by task title, summarized, and presented in Table 1.

The tasks allowed EFL learners to immerse themselves in a virtual environment such as the *Campus Lake* in VEC3D 5.0 (see Figure 2), and to describe people they met, places they visited, virtual objects or scenes they saw, events they joined in, and what they heard. Whatever they experienced or perceived in the virtual space served as the focus of their follow-up reflection and discussion via Web 2.0 tools. Two screenshots of students and their instructor interacting through Twitter (see Figure 5) and VEC3D Blogs (see Figure 6) are presented following the conclusion of this paragraph. The tasks entitled *A Trip to a Lake,* and *Boat vs. Dragon Boat* are described in Table 2 and Table 3, respectively. Throughout both tasks, students are working towards the expected learning outcomes and task goals: developing writing and communication skills and cross-cultural understanding and awareness by using the 3D virtual space synchronously, and the Web 2.0 tools asynchronously.

THE POSSIBILITY OF BLENDED SOLUTIONS

Recent discussion and research into Web 2.0 applications and 3D virtual environments served as the impetus for us to turn our attention to explor-

Table 1. Task list: examples

Tasks	Summary
1. My First Experience	Learners describe their impressions of VEC3D 5.0.
2. A Trip to a Lake	Participants share their experiences of virtual travelling to the Campus Lake and paddling a virtual boat on the lake.
3. Canadian Food	Students describe Canadian food and cooking.
4. Christmas Celebration	Learners join a celebration of Christmas and winter fun in VEC3D 5.0.
5. Chess vs. Chinese Chess	Participants learn to play chess in order to understand the target culture, compare this culture to their own, and share personal experiences via VEC3D 5.0.
6. Turkey vs. Peking Duck	Students participate in cross-cultural activities involving cooking and food preparation via VEC3D 5.0.
7. Boat vs. Dragon Boat	Learners take a virtual trip by boat via VEC3D 5.0, and share the experience of celebrating the Dragon Boat Festival.

Figure 5. Student interaction through Twitter

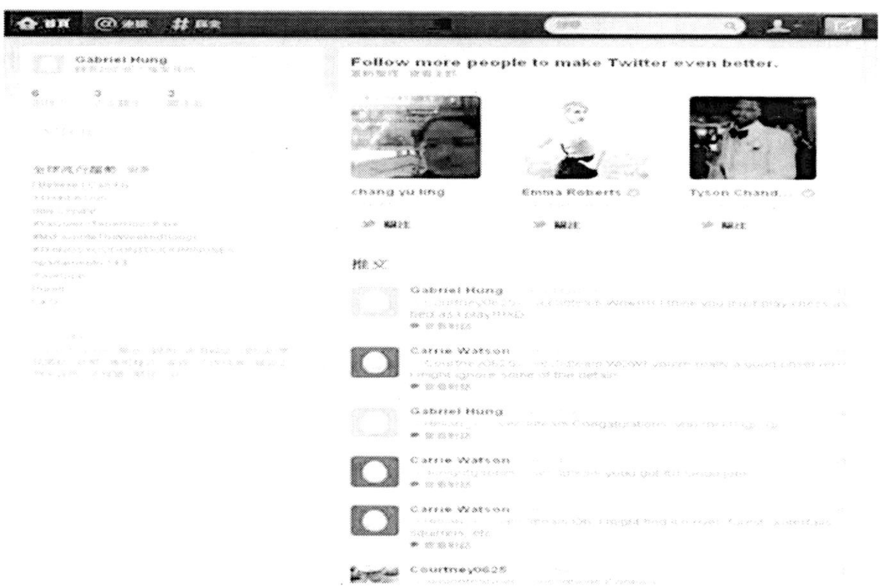

Figure 6. Student interaction through VEC3D blog

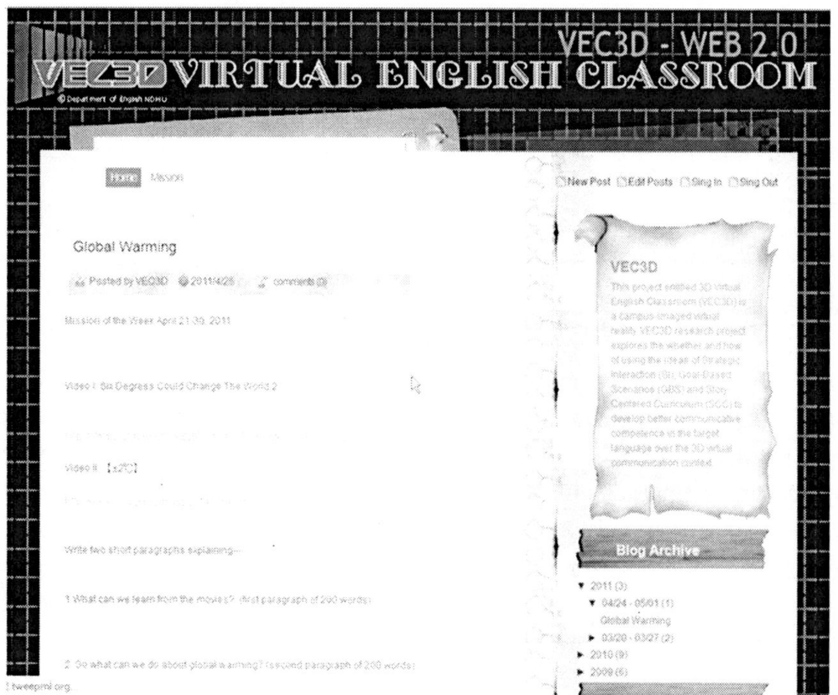

Table 2. An example of a task

Scenario	**Traveling**
Task	A Trip to a Lake
Main Goals	To practice and improve writing skills and performance To be able to communicate more effectively in everyday life
	1. Active experimentation (synchronous): Students view YouTube videos embedded on the VEC3D 5.0 Website. Students, embodied as avatars, explore scenery in VEC3D 5.0 (scene: Campus Lake), and take a snapshot to be named "Lake Fun," and join the discussion via VEC3D 5.0. 2. Concrete experience (synchronous): Students have the experience of travel through conversing with a native English-speaking instructor who serves as a tour guide as they explore the virtual scene, the Campus Lake. 3. Reflective observation (synchronous and asynchronous): Students observe how other classmates communicate with the instructor, and record their thoughts and reflections via their blogs. 4. Abstract conceptualization (asynchronous): Students download audio or video files from Websites (e.g., podcasts), and hear audio tour guides introduce the related locations.

Table 3. An example of a task

Scenario	Paddling a Boat on the Lake
Task	Boat vs. Dragon Boat
Main Goals	To be able to interact effectively with people of different cultures and backgrounds To develop students' cultural competence as well as (cross-) cultural understanding and awareness To practice and improve students' writing and communication skills
	1. Concrete experience (synchronous and asynchronous): A native English speaking instructor guides students as they paddle a virtual (or real-life boat) on *Campus Lake* (see Figure 2), and the students visit blogs and Twitter Websites, where they share their experiences of boating on the lake. 2. Active experimentation (synchronous): Learners take a virtual trip by boat via VEC3D 5.0. Students paddle a virtual or real-life boat on the lake. 3. Reflective observation (synchronous and asynchronous): Students observe how other people paddle their virtual or real-life boats on the lake, and reflect on their own experiences through blogging. They share the experience of celebrating Dragon Boat Festival, and take snapshot(s) which they then post on their blogs, share through Flickr, and/or tweet about on Twitter. This is accomplished by students clicking on the "VEC3D Blog," "Flickr," and "Twitter" buttons, respectively. 4. Abstract conceptualization (asynchronous): Students read wikis to gather information about paddling technique and Dragon Boat Festival, and compare the differences between Dragon Boats and other kinds of boats, in addition to considering cultural differences.

ing the possibility of using these technologies to facilitate language learning, in terms of, inter alia, collaborative writing performance, cultural learning, user identity, formation of virtual community, group or classroom dynamics, and motivation.

We therefore incorporated Web 2.0 tools and a facial expression recognition system into VEC3D 5.0, a blended learning environment, which gives rise to the possibility of both situated language learning and collaborative language learning. Currently, we are conducting an ongoing case study to discover more about EFL graduate students' interaction, writing, and cultural learning process. Using data collection strategies including interviews, observations, and collection of written texts (blog entries and tweets) as well as Qualitative Data Analysis (QDA) allows us to discover the interaction process in collaborative learning groups and to investigate the possible development of a virtual community (of practice) and cultural understanding in this innovative setting.

This paper presents preliminary results from the ongoing case study. The blended learning environment, VEC3D 5.0, has the potential to become a useful tool for language learning and the gaining of cultural understanding. Participants were impressed with the level of integration of synchronous and asynchronous communication modes, as well as the platform's ability to provide multiple communication channels and valuable language and culture learning opportunities. Additionally, VEC3D 5.0 provided ample opportunities for the negotiation of meaning and helped shaped students' identities as English language users as they participated in virtual events within the virtual community of practice which was developed during the interaction process. A strong sense of community enhanced the quality of their interactions, as well as fostering their commitment to learning, their mutual support, and their willingness to share thoughts, ideas and feelings with other members.

Linking VEC3D with Web 2.0 tools helped the learners to elaborate, reflect upon, and extend their ideas as a result of their experiences in the virtual world and the group relationships which were formed and continued beyond the timeframe of the events held in the virtual world. The use of blogs and Twitter, for instance, created an ideal situation for learner autonomy as well as for collaborative writing and culture learning through doing, participating and interacting. Due to the limit on the length of a message (i.e. a tweet is limited to 180 characters) Twitter is of limited use as a vehicle for written expression. However, the use of Twitter in conjunction with the other communication tools of VEC3D 5.0 allowed learners to fully express themselves and exercise their autonomy, while simultaneously facilitating group dynamics. The learners' enhanced interest in the target culture, motivation toward culture learning and cultural understanding also point to the potential benefits of using VEC3D 5.0, especially when the native English speaking instructor serves as a virtual tourist or culture guide and provides culture-related information and/or assistance on planning a trip. Following such experiences, the learners were able to reflect on and share them through blogging and tweeting. Taken together, all of these characteristics hint at the possibilities embodied by a blended environment.

FUTURE RESEARCH DIRECTIONS

The integration of the virtual environment and Web 2.0 technologies in language learning has great potential for building EFL learners' confidence and writing ability, supporting the development of virtual community, strengthening learners' identities as English users and boosting their motivation toward language learning, increasing cross-cultural awareness, and facilitating the acquisition of cultural information.

Recent research regarding the integration of Web 2.0 tools and virtual environments is still in its infancy, but it has become a hot topic in CALL circles around the world. The primary aim of this project is to provide researchers and practitioners with a hybrid prototype platform and a knowledge base for future studies. The VEC3D research team intends to make valuable contributions to the existing body of knowledge based on our previous and current work. To investigate this issue in greater depth, further fieldwork and studies have already been initiated by the project leaders and the research team, and other research is planned for the future.

CONCLUSION

The educational virtual world is expanding rapidly, and the integration of facial expression technology and Web 2.0 tools into 3D virtual environments is a relatively nascent area of exploration. We look forward to integrating VEC3D 5.0 into future English classrooms and making online English language learning an enjoyable and fruitful experience for learners. As it stands, VEC3D 5.0 has been created to promote English language learning, especially through writing practice and the development of cultural understanding. The VEC3D research team is conducting ongoing research to investigate the efficacy of VEC3D 5.0 on EFL learners in this regard.

ACKNOWLEDGMENT

The research has been heavily supported by a grant from the Taiwan National Science Council.

REFERENCES

Alm, A. (2009). Blogging for self-determination with L2 learner journals. In Thomas, M. (Ed.), *Handbook of research on web 2.0 and second language learning* (pp. 202–221). Hershey, PA: IGI Global. doi:10.4018/978-1-60566-190-2.ch011.

Antenos-Conforti, E. (2009). Microblogging on Twitter: Social networking in intermediate Italian classes. In Lomicka, L., & Lord, G. (Eds.), *The next generation: Social networking and online collaboration in foreign language learning* (pp. 59–90). San Marcos, TX: CALICO.

Armstrong, K., & Retterer, O. (2008). Blogging as L2 writing: A case study. *AACE Journal, 16*(3), 233–251.

Arnold, N., Ducate, L., & Kost, C. (2009). Collaborative writing in wikis: Insights from culture projects in intermediate German classes. In Lomicka, L., & Lord, G. (Eds.), *The next generation: Social networking and online collaboration in foreign language learning* (pp. 115–144). San Marcos, TX: CALICO.

Avatar Languages Blog. (n.d.). *SurReal language quests*. Retrieved January 31, 2013, from http://www.avatarlanguages.com/blog/surreal-language-quests/

Blattner, G., & Friori, M. (2009). Facebook in the language classroom: Promises and possibilities. *International Journal of Instructional Technology & Distance Learning, 6*(1). Retrieved January 31, 2013, from http://www.itdl.org/journal/jan_09/article02.htm

Borau, K., Ullrich, C., Feng, J., & Shen, R. M. (2009). Microblogging for language learning: Using Twitter to train communicative and cultural competence. In M. Spaniol et al. (Eds.), *8th International Conference on Web Based Learning - ICWL 2009* (pp. 78–87). Berlin: Spinger-Verlag. Retrieved January 31, 2013, from http://www.carstenullrich.net/pubs/Borau09Microblogging.pdf

Borg, S. (1994). Language awareness as a methodology: Implications for teachers and teacher training. *Language Awareness, 3*(2), 61–71. doi:10.1080/09658416.1994.9959844.

Campbell, A. (2003). Weblogs for use with ESL classes. *The Internet TESL Journal, 9*(2).

Campbell, A. (2007). Motivating language learners with Flickr. *The Internet TESL Journal, 11*(2).

Capocchi Ribeiro, M. A. (2002). *An interactionist perspective to second/foreign language learning and teaching*. (ERIC Document Reproduction Service No. ED 469392. Cashmore, P. (2006). *Second life +web 2.0= virtual world mashups!* Retrieved January 31, 2013, from http://mashable.com/2006/05/30/second-life-Web-20-virtual-world-mashups/

Chen, Y. C. (2009). *The effect of applying wikis in an English as a foreign language (EFL) class in Taiwan*. (Doctoral Dissertation). University of Central Florida, Orlando, FL. Retrieved January 31, 2013, from http://etd.fcla.edu/CF/CFE0002227/Chen_Yu-ching_200808_PhD.pdf

Choi, J. (2009). Asian English language learners' identity construction in an after school literacy site. *Journal of Asian Pacific Communication, 19*(1), 130–161. doi:10.1075/japc.19.1.07cho.

Decrem, B. (2006). Introducing flock beta 1. *Flock official blog*.

Deutschmann, M., Panichi, L., & Molka-Danielsen, J. (2009). Designing oral participation in Second Life: A comparative study of two language proficiency courses. *ReCALL*, *21*(2), 206–226. doi:10.1017/S0958344009000196.

Dippold, D. (2009). Peer feedback through blogs: Student and teacher perceptions in an advanced German class. *ReCALL*, *21*(1), 18–36. doi:10.1017/S095834400900010X.

Ducate, C. L., & Lomicka, L. L. (2005). Exploring the blogosphere: Use of web logs in the foreign language classroom. *Foreign Language Annals*, *38*(3), 410–421. doi:10.1111/j.1944-9720.2005.tb02227.x.

Ducate, C. L., & Lomicka, L. L. (2008). Adventures in the blogosphere: From blog readers to blog writers. *Computer Assisted Language Learning*, *21*(1), 9–28. doi:10.1080/09588220701865474.

Elola, I., & Oskoz, A. (2010). Collaborative writing: Fostering foreign language and writing conventions development. *Language Learning & Technology*, *14*(3), 51–71. Retrieved January 31, 2013, from http://llt.msu.edu/issues/october2010/elolaoskoz.pdf

Franco, C. (2008). Using wiki-based peer-correction to develop writing skills of Brazilian EFL learners. *Novitas-ROYAL*, *2*(1), 49–59.

Godwin-Jones, R. (2003). Blogs and wikis: Environments for on-line collaboration. *Language Learning & Technology*, *7*(2), 12–16.

Godwin-Jones, R. (2008). Web-writing 2.0: Enabling, documenting, and assessing writing online. *Language Learning & Technology*, *12*(2), 7–13.

Halvorsen, A. (2009). Social networking sites and critical language learning. In Thomas, M. (Ed.), *Handbook of research on web 2.0 and second language learning* (pp. 237–255). Hershey, PA: IGI Global. doi:10.4018/978-1-60566-190-2.ch013.

Harrison, R., & Thomas, M. (2009). Identity in online communities: Social networking sites and language learning. *International Journal of Emerging Technologies & Society*, *7*(2), 109–124.

Henderson, J., Fishwick, P., Fresh, E., Futterknecht, F., & Hamilton, B. D. (2008). *An immersive learning simulation environment for Chinese culture*. Paper presented at the Interservice/Industry Training, Simulation, and Education Conference (I/ITSEC). New York, NY.

Hirvela, A. (1999). Collaborative writing: Instruction and communities of readers and writers. *TESOL Journal*, *8*(2), 7–12.

Hsu, H. Y., & Wang, S. K. (2009). The effect of using blogs on college students' reading performance and motivation. In T. Bastiaens et al. (Eds.), *Proceedings of World Conference on E-Learning in Corporate, Government, Healthcare, and Higher Education 2009* (pp. 1308–1313). Chesapeake, VA: AACE.

Jung, J. Y. (2009). Attention, awareness, and noticing: The role of consciousness and the selective fossilization hypothesis. *Teachers College, Columbia University Working Papers in TESOL &. Applied Linguistics*, *9*(2), 58–59.

Kessler, G. (2009). Student-initiated attention to form in wiki-based collaborative writing. *Language Learning & Technology*, *13*(1), 79–95. Retrieved January 31, 2013, from http://llt.msu.edu/vol13num1/kessler.pdf

Kessler, G., & Bikowski, D. (2010). Developing collaborative autonomous language learning abilities in computer mediated language learning: Attention to meaning among students in wiki space. *Computer Assisted Language Learning*, *23*(1), 41–58. doi:10.1080/09588220903467335.

Koenraad, A. L. M. (2007). *3D and language education*. Retrieved January 31, 2013, from http://www.koenraad.info/vrall-2/3d-and-language-education-1/view

Koenraad, A. L. M. (2008). How can 3D virtual worlds contribute to language education? Focus on the language village format. In *Proceedings of the 3rd International WorldCALL Conference (WorldCALL 2008)*. Retrieved January 31, 2013, from http://www.koenraad.info/vrall-2/how-can-3d-virtual-worlds-contribute-to-language-education/view

Kolb, D. A. (1984). *Experiential learning: Experience as the source of learning and development*. Upper Saddle River, NJ: Prentice-Hall.

Krashen, S. (1981). *Second language acquisition and second language learning*. Oxford, UK: Pergamon Press.

Krashen, S. (1982). *Principles and practice in second language acquisition*. Oxford, UK: Pergamon.

Kuriscak, L. M., & Luke, C. L. (2009). Language learner attitudes toward virtual worlds: An investigation of Second Life. In Lomicka, L., & Lord, G. (Eds.), *The next generation: Social networking and online collaboration in foreign language learning* (pp. 115–144). San Marcos, TX: CALICO.

Lave, J., & Wenger, E. (1991). *Situated learning: Legitimate peripheral participation*. Cambridge, UK: Cambridge University Press. doi:10.1017/CBO9780511815355.

Lee, L. (2008). Focus-on-form through collaborative scaffolding in expert-to-novice online interaction. *Language Learning & Technology, 12*(3), 53–72. Retrieved January 31, 2013, from http://llt.msu.edu/vol12num3/lee.pdf

Lee, L. (2010). Exploring wiki-mediated collaborative writing: A case study in an elementary Spanish course. *CALICO Journal, 27*(2), 260–276.

Long, M. (1985). Input and second language acquisition theory. In Gass, S., & Madden, C. (Eds.), *Input in second language acquisition* (pp. 177–393). Rowley, MA: Newbury House Publishers, Inc..

Long, M. (1996). The role of the linguistic environment in second language acquisition. In Ritchie, W., & Bhatia, T. (Eds.), *Handbook of second language acquisition* (pp. 413–468). San Diego, CA: Academic. doi:10.1016/B978-012589042-7/50015-3.

Lord, G. (2008). Podcasting communities and second language pronunciation. *Foreign Language Annals, 41*(2), 364–379. doi:10.1111/j.1944-9720.2008.tb03297.x.

Lund, A. (2008). Wikis: A collective approach to language production. *ReCALL, 20*(1), 35–54. doi:10.1017/S0958344008000414.

Mark, B., & Coniam, D. (2008). Using wikis to enhance and develop writing skills among secondary school students in Hong Kong. *System, 36*, 437–455. doi:10.1016/j.system.2008.02.004.

McCarty, S. (2009). Social networking behind student lines in Japan. In Thomas, M. (Ed.), *Handbook of research on web 2.0 and second language learning* (pp. 181–201). Hershey, PA: IGI Global. doi:10.4018/978-1-60566-190-2.ch010.

Metaferia, T. F. (2012). Using blogs to promote reflective language learning. *Journal of Language and Culture, 3*(3), 52–55.

Mynard, J. (2007). A blog as a tool for reflection for English language learners. *ASIAN EFL Journal, 24*, 1–6.

O'Malley, J. M., & Chamot, A. J. (1990). *Learning strategies in second language acquisition*. Cambridge, UK: Cambridge University Press. doi:10.1017/CBO9781139524490.

O'Reilly, T. (2005). What is web 2.0. *O'Reilly Network*. Retrieved January 31, 2013, from http://www.oreillynet.com/pub/a/oreilly/tim/news/2005/09/30/what-is-Web-20.html

Oliver, K. (2010). Integrating web 2.0 across the curriculum. *TechTrends, 54*(2), 50–60. doi:10.1007/s11528-010-0382-7.

Peterson, M. (2006). Learner interaction management in an avatar and chat-based virtual world. *Computer Assisted Language Learning*, *19*(1), 79–103. doi:10.1080/09588220600804087.

Pinkman, K. (2005). Using blogs in the foreign language classroom: Encouraging learner independence. *The JALT CALL Journal*, *1*(1), 12–24.

Raith, T. (2009). The use of weblogs in language education. In Thomas, M. (Ed.), *Handbook of research on web 2.0 and second language learning* (pp. 274–291). Hershey, PA: IGI Global. doi:10.4018/978-1-60566-190-2.ch015.

Rosen, L., & Kato, K. (2006). *Building community, improving oral proficiency: A wiki case study.* Retrieved January 31, 2013, from http://www.actfl.org/files/ACTFL06handouts/Session371.pdf

Scharle, A., & Szabo, A. (2000). *Autonomy in language learning: A guide to developing learner responsibility*. Cambridge, UK: Cambridge University Press.

Schmidt, R. W. (1990). The role of consciousness in second language learning. *Applied Linguistics*, *11*(2), 129–158. doi:10.1093/applin/11.2.129.

Schmidt, R. W. (1993). Consciousness, learning and interlanguage pragmatics. In Kasper, G., & Blum-Kulka, S. (Eds.), *Interlanguage pragmatics* (pp. 21–42). Oxford, UK: Oxford University Press.

Schon, D. (1983). *The reflective practitioner: How professionals think in action*. London: Temple Smith.

Soares, D. A. (2008). Understanding class blogs as a tool for language development. *Language Teaching Research*, *12*(4), 517–533. doi:10.1177/1362168808097165.

Stanley, G. (2006). Podcasting: Audio on the internet comes of age. *Teaching English as a Second or Foreign Language, 9*(4). Retrieved January 31, 2013, from http://www-writing.berkeley.edu/TESL-EJ/ej36/int.html

Sun, Y. (2009). Voice blog: An exploratory study of language learning. *Language Learning & Technology*, *13*(2), 88–103.

Sykes, J. M. (2009). Learner requests in Spanish: Examining the potential of multiuser virtual environments for L2 pragmatic acquisition. In Lomicka, L., & Lord, G. (Eds.), *The next generation: Social networking and online collaboration in foreign language learning* (pp. 115–144). San Marcos, TX: CALICO.

Toyoda, E., & Harrison, R. (2002). Categorization of text chat communication between learners and native speakers of Japanese. *Language Learning and Technology, 6*(1), 82-99. Retrieved January 31, 2013, from http://llt.msu.edu/vol6num1/pdf/toyoda.pdf

University of Utrecht. (2009). *NIFLAR project home page*. Retrieved January 31, 2013, from http://cms.let.uu.nl/niflar

Vickers, H. (2007a). *SurReal language quests*. Retrieved January 31, 2013, from http://avatar-languages.com/blog/?p=14

Vickers, H. (2007b). SurReal quests: Enriched, purposeful language learning in second life. *The Knowledge Tree*. Retrieved January 31, 2013, from http://kt.flexiblelearning.net.au/tkt2007/Ed.-15/surreal-quests-enriched-purposeful-language-learning-in-second-life

Vygotsky, L. S. (1978). *Mind and society: The development of higher psychological processes*. Cambridge, MA: Harvard University Press.

Vygotsky, L. S. (1987). Thinking and speech. In R. W. Rieber & A. S. Carton (Eds.), The collected works of L. S. Vygotsky: Vol. 1: Problems of general psychology (pp. 39-285). New York: Plenum.

Wang, S., & Vasquez, C. (2012). Web 2.0 and second language learning: What does the research tell us? *CALICO Journal*, *29*(3), 412–430.

Warren, S. J., Barab, S. A., & Dondlinger, M. J. (2008). A MUVE towards PBL writing: Effects of a digital learning environment designed to improve elementary student writing. *Journal of Research on Technology in Education*, *41*(1), 121–147.

Warren, S. J., Stein, R. A., Dondlinger, M. J., & Barab, S. A. (2009). A look inside a muve design process: Blending instructional design and game principles to target writing skills. *Journal of Educational Computing Research*, *40*(3), 295–321. doi:10.2190/EC.40.3.c.

Web 2.0. (n.d.). *Wikipedia*. Retrieved January 31, 2013, from http://en.wikipedia.org/wiki/Web_2.0

Wiki. (n.d.). *Wikipedia*. Retrieved January 31, 2013, from http://en.wikipedia.org/wiki/wiki

Yang, M. T., Cheng, Y. R., & Shih, Y. C. (2011). Facial expression recognition for learning status analysis. In *Proceedings of the International Conference on Human-Computer Interaction (HCI 2011)* (LNCS), (vol. 6764, pp. 131-138). Orlando, FL: Springer.

Yang, S. H. (2009). Using blogs to enhance critical reflection and community of practice. *Journal of Educational Technology & Society*, *12*(2), 11–21.

Zorko, V. (2009). Factors affecting the way students collaborate in a wiki for English language learning. *Australasian Journal of Educational Technology*, *25*(5), 645–665.

ADDITIONAL READING

Aguilar, F. R. (2007). Top of the pods: In search of a podcasting pedagogy for language learning. *Computer Assisted Language Learning*, *20*(5), 471–492. doi:10.1080/09588220701746047.

Alm, A. (2006). CALL for autonomy, competence and relatedness: Motivating language learning environments in Web 2.0. *The JALT CALL Journal*, *2*(3), 29–38.

Barab, S. A., Thomas, M., Dodge, T., Carteaux, R., & Tuzun, H. (2005). Making learning fun: Quest Atlantis, a game without guns. *Educational Technology Research and Development*, *53*(1), 86–107. doi:10.1007/BF02504859.

Black, J. (1993). *The effects of auditory and visual stimuli on tenth graders' descriptive writing*. Retrieved January 31, 2013, from http://www.eric.ed.gov/PDFS/ED364887.pdf

Dede, C., Ketelhut, D., & Ruess, K. (2006). *Designing for motivation and usability in a museum-based multi-user virtual environment*. Retrieved January 31, 2013, from http://www.gse.harvard.edu/~dedech/muvees/documents/AELppr.pdf

Elola, I., & Oskoz, A. (2008). Blogging: Fostering intercultural competence development in foreign language and study abroad contexts. *Foreign Language Annals*, *41*(3), 454–477. doi:10.1111/j.1944-9720.2008.tb03307.x.

Elola, I., & Oskoz, A. (2013). A social constructivist approach to foreign language writing in online environments. In Levine, G., & Phipps, A. (Eds.), *Critical and intercultural theory and language pedagogy* (pp. 185–201). Boston: Cengage Heinle.

Kern, R., & Warschauer, M. (2000). Introduction: Theory and practice of network-based language teaching. In Warschauer, M., & Kern, R. (Eds.), *Network-based language teaching: Concepts and practice* (pp. 1–19). Cambridge, UK: Cambridge University Press. doi:10.1017/CBO9781139524735.003.

Kim, D. (2010). Incorporating podcasting and blogging into a core task for ESOL teacher candidates. *Computers & Education*, *56*(3), 632–641. doi:10.1016/j.compedu.2010.10.005.

Lim, K. Y. T. (2009). The six learnings of second life: A framework for designing curricular interventions in-world. *Journal of Virtual Worlds Research*, *2*(1), 3–11.

Linden Research Inc. (n.d.). *Second life*. Retrieved January 31, 2013, from http://secondlife.com/

Lord, G. (2008). Podcasting communities and second language pronunciation. *Foreign Language Annals*, *41*(2), 364–380. doi:10.1111/j.1944-9720.2008.tb03297.x.

Lund, A., & Rasmussen, I. (2008). The right tool for the wrong task? *Computer-Supported Collaborative Learning*, *3*, 387–412. doi:10.1007/s11412-008-9050-8.

Maranto, G., & Barton, M. (2010). Paradox and promise: MySpace, Facebook, and the sociopolitics of social networking in the writing classroom. *Computers and Composition*, *27*, 36–47. doi:10.1016/j.compcom.2009.11.003.

McCarty, S. (2005). Spoken Internet to go: Popularization through podcasting. *JALT CALL Journal*, *1*(2), 67–74.

O'Bryan, A., & Hegelheimer, V. (2007). Integrating CALL into the classroom: The role of podcasting in an ESL listening strategies course. *ReCALL*, *19*(2), 162–180. doi:10.1017/S0958344007000523.

Peterson, M. (2010). Learner participation patterns and strategy use in second life: An exploratory case study. *ReCALL*, *22*(3), 273–292. doi:10.1017/S0958344010000169.

Sykes, J., Oskoz, A., & Thorne, S. (2008). Web 2.0, synthetic immersive environments, and mobile resources for language education. *CALICO Journal*, *25*(3), 528–546.

Sze, P. (2006). Developing students' listening and speaking skills through ELT podcasts. *Education Journal*, *34*(2), 115–134.

Thomas, M. (Ed.). (2009). *Handbook of research on web 2.0 and second language learning*. Hershey, PA: IGI Global. doi:10.4018/978-1-60566-190-2.

Warren, S. (2006). Researching a MUVE for teaching writing: The anytown experience. In C. Crawford et al. (Eds.), *Proceedings of Society for Information Technology and Teacher Education International Conference 2006* (pp. 759–764). Chesapeake, VA: AACE.

Warren, S. J., Dondlinger, M. J., & Barab, S. A. (2008). A MUVE towards PBL writing: Effects of a digital learning environment designed to improve elementary student writing. *Journal of Research on Technology in Education*, *41*(1), 113–140.

KEY TERMS AND DEFINITIONS

Blog Assisted Language Learning (BALL): Blog is an abbreviated form of Weblog ("Web" for Internet; and "log" for journal), and is a new application that is a current trend in language learning. Blogs facilitate collaborative language learning over the Internet and can inspire language teachers, especially writing teachers. A blog is a public Web site set up by individual users to be edited, and updated with entries allowing for expression in the forms of text, graphics, audio, and video.

Collaborative Virtual Environment (CVE): CVE is the acronym for Collaborative Virtual Environment. CVEs, usually built in Virtual Reality Modeling Language (VRML), are created to support multi-user collaboration and interaction regardless of the distance, and have currently been used in educational settings. Participants are embodied in avatars and use chat boxes and/or voice chat to communicate with others in CVEs.

Computer Assisted Language Learning (CALL): CALL is the acronym for Computer Assisted Language Learning and is defined as (the study of) the use of computers in language learning and teaching. Computer technology in the language-learning domain is a promising field in Information and Learning Technology, as well as in Language Instruction.

English as a Foreign Language (EFL): English is taught to people who learn the language for different reasons in non-English-speaking countries.

Facial Expression Recognition: Facial expression recognition involves a systematic process performed by computers, which mainly consists of face detection, facial feature extraction, and facial expression interpretation.

Second Life (SL): Second Life © is a registered trademark of Linden Research, Inc. Second Life (SL) is a computer-generated three-dimensional multi-user virtual environment (MUVE). Users are called residents and are embodied as avatars who interact with one another through text chat, voice chat, avatar gestures, instant messaging, and notecards in SL. Second Life allows residents to discover a vast virtual world, socialize with others, trade virtual properties, and join events and activities held by various communities.

Web 2.0: The term "Web 2.0" originates from "a brainstorming session between O'Reilly and MediaLive International" (O'Reilly, 2005). Web 2.0, including Web applications, such as blogs, wikis, video-sharing Web sites, is used to foster collaboration, interaction, communication and information sharing on the World Wide Web.

Chapter 5
Utilizing Augmented Reality in Library Information Search

Robert Gibson
Emporia State University, USA

ABSTRACT

A cross-disciplinary academic team at Emporia State University is currently in the process of developing and utilizing a mobile-based augmented reality application in the context of library information search. Specifically, the team is researching the use of mobile applications that can generate multi-sensory information retrieval relative to archives and special collections. Using this application, student and faculty researchers can physically point their mobile devices at an archival object that has been specifically marked with a photo-generated "tag" and, using specially designed software, access videos, photos, music, text, and other data that is germane to the object. This allows the archivist to preserve the object behind protective glass or other physical barriers, while allowing the information seeker to learn more about the object using embedded multimedia. This minimizes the potential for damage while providing extra dimensions of information. Of the many virtualizations currently under development are videos related to a rare novel and music compositions relative to rare sheet music – both currently housed within Special Collections at Emporia State University.

INTRODUCTION

Information search has an interesting history – especially as it relates to libraries and user interactions when engaging with information and data retrieval systems. Aside from advances in the mechanics of information search and retrieval, several scholars have researched the evolving psychology of how users engage in information seeking strategies within libraries and media centers. Notable researchers in this field include Carol Kuhlthau who crafted the *Information Search Process* (ISP) model (2001); Brenda Dervin whose *Sense Making Strategies* are still widely used in information retrieval (1976); Marcia Bates who introduced *Browsing and Berry Picking Techniques* related to information search behaviors among library patrons (2005); *The Big Six Information Literacy Process* designed for school library media specialists by Michael Eisenberg and Bob Berkowitz; and Nick Belkin whose *Anomalous States of Knowledge,* also known as the ASK model, provided the construct for many contemporary search engines, including "ASK Jeeves" (1980). Emerging systems such as faceted search, voice-assisted information retrieval, QR Codes, and semantic-based search engines, including Wolfram Alpha, Hakia, Swoogle, Powerset and

DOI: 10.4018/978-1-4666-4462-5.ch005

other similar systems promise enormous potential for retrieving information from the corpus (Radhakrishnon, 2009).

The two primary taxonomies related to information seeking strategies are known as *Information Science* and *Information Retrieval*. Information Science is a field of study that is primarily concerned with the analysis, collection, classification, manipulation, storage, retrieval, movement, and dissemination of information. In short, this is the field of study most closely approximating traditional library science. Information Retrieval, on the other hand, is involved with obtaining information resources relevant to an information need and related to a collection or body of resources. This field of study most closely approximates *Human-Computer Information Retrieval* (HCIR) and human-factors psychology. For many years, these fields of study were considered completely independent of one another. Librarians were exposed to principals of Information Science in their graduate programs, whereas computer scientists were focused on the Information Retrieval systems and how information seekers extracted data through various interfaces and human-computer interaction systems.

However, these two fields of research and inquiry are beginning to converge. Increasingly, the field of *Information Science* is intersecting with the field of *Information Retrieval*. For example, the dissemination of information is often managed through an information retrieval system – usually a computer or mobile application of some sort. We see these systems each time we enter a library and ask personnel at the Reference Desk for search assistance. However, the majority of these systems (OCLC, WorldCat, LexisNexis, Academic Search Complete, etc.) remain primarily text-based. Queries must still be manually keyed using the correct syntax in order to retrieve a data set that is relative to the query.

What are beginning to emerge in libraries are new modes of information retrieval that do not necessarily require keyboard entry. For example, voice-assisted search, QR-coded information retrieval, and other forms of inquiry are beginning to take root. These systems allow the library staff to embed additional data stores into the various library artifacts and corpus. While still far from providing patrons unlimited search opportunities within the library, they do provide a glimpse into how librarians will likely codify, classify, and store information in the very near future. The promise of these types of systems is that a variety of information modalities can be retrieved and presented to the information seeker relative to the search query – well beyond text. For example, images, videos, music, or any other type of information can be embedded into the corpus and retrieved along with the query. Groundbreaking work in this area by Gary Marchionini at the University of North Carolina has generated research related to human-information systems, interface design, digital libraries, and interaction design (OCLC, 2012). In 1998, Marchionini and researchers from the Interaction Design Laboratory and the School of Information and Library Science at North Carolina developed a ground-breaking retrieval system entitled the *Open Video Project* based on metadata that allows information seekers to locate video-based archives. According the project Web site, "the purpose of the Open Video Project is to collect and make available a repository of digitized video content for the digital video, multimedia retrieval, digital library, and other research communities." (p. 1) However, the system may have been developed a bit too early to leverage contemporary mobile-based information retrieval technology. Clearly, the direction libraries are moving is toward systems that allow patrons to transport and utilize information search systems anywhere within the library ecosystem. The ability for patrons to retrieve this contextualized information using these types of powerful, portable devices offers libraries new opportunities to embed additional information into any number of artifacts.

This chapter will introduce new perspectives regarding these mobile search systems. Specifically, the author will provide examples of how mobile-based augmented reality applications are being developed and used within the context of archival and special collections in an academic library setting. The goal of the project is threefold:

1. Develop experiential search applications related to specific and rare collections within the library.
2. Promote the use of mobile search systems – specifically, systems that provide data to information seekers in a variety of media formats.
3. Promote patronage at Archives and Special Collections.

BACKGROUND

According to the *2011 Horizon Report*—a longitudinal, annual investigation of emerging technology that is jointly sponsored by the EDUCAUSE Learning Initiative (ELI) and the New Media Center (NMC), Augmented Reality is poised to make a pronounced emergence in the educational spectrum—notwithstanding public libraries, museums, school library media centers, and various archive and special collections departments. Augmented Reality (AR) refers to the "addition of a computer-assisted contextual layer of information over the real world" (Horizon Report, 2011, p. 16). Augmented reality is not necessarily limited to mobile or handheld devices. The recent introduction of Google Glass(es) and other forms of wearable augmented reality devices provides a similar experience as mobile products (Sterling, 2013). These wearable devices even allow the user to control certain appliances through the augmentation.

Augmented reality for mobile devices is commonly referred to as *Location Aware Mobile Technology* (Farkas, 2010). Interpreted, these devices can identify the user's location through the use of built-in Global Position System (GPS) technology, thus allowing the user to interact with the environment in whatever context and wherever they may be located at that moment. In the retail sector, this technology allows the user to locate restaurants and shops, hotels, street locations, review property values for real estate, etc. Conceptual videos illustrating the potential of the technology in the retail and transportation sectors have already been developed.

Early prototypes of augmented reality applications began to appear in the latter half of the last decade. For example, when Nissan launched the Cube—a square-looking compact vehicle—they simultaneously launched an augmented reality application entitled the *Nissan Cube Interactive Brochure* (Retrieved from http://nissan.t-immersion.com/). Still a bit ahead of Smartphone capabilities at the time of its launch, the application required that users install a DVD that invoked the user's on-board computer camera. Using specially-designed placard cards with images of the vehicle interior, exterior, cargo bay, etc. the camera would identify embedded 'markers' (small icons placed somewhere within the image) that triggered a 3-D view of the vehicle that appeared to hover above the card – while still within the virtual space. Users were able to rotate the card relative to the camera position and angle, thus changing the view of the 3-D vehicle representation. One placard even opened the back hatch of the vehicle and invoked a music track. Another placard illustrated the vehicle interior, which triggered a 3-D view of the dashboard and seats. Another placard allowed the user to press a key on the keyboard which changed the colors of the vehicle. However, these vehicle placards are arguably more novelty than legitimate information relative to the vehicle. Aside from the engaging 3-D representations and animations, there was really no additional layers of contextualized information regarding the vehicle.

Another popular augmented reality application that utilized specially designed markers was developed by General Electric. Entitled the *Smart Grid Augmented Reality* (http://ge.ecomagination.com/smartgrid/#/augmented_reality), this application allowed users to engage in one of two sustainability environments – solar and wind. Users printed a special line art image—a graphical representation of a solar panel—which served as a visual marker that triggered the augmented environment. When held in front of a computer camera while the *Smart Grid Augmented Reality* application Web site is running, the marker triggers additional interactive components that appear to emerge from the printed paper itself – again, hovering in a virtual space just above the paper. This representation was not visible in the physical environment. The representation of the 3-D image is only visible from within the computer screen. If a microphone is attached to the computer, users can literally blow into the device and see the wind turbines increase their rotation speed. The augmentation also includes audio elements (birds, crickets, and other sounds) that can be heard as well. Like the Nissan Cube application, the augmented environment is rendered using 3-D modeling and animation software, rather than video of an actual environment.

Large retail outlets, such as IKEA, are now embedding augmented reality markers in their hard-bound product catalogs which allow users to envision how the furniture product looks with content inside (Wired, 2012). Other companies embarking on the augmented reality craze include Zugara's Webcam Social Shopper (at-home interactive purchasing experience), Lego (virtual product pre-assembly prior to point-of-sale), Zagat (store location finder), Foodtracer (food ingredients), and much more (Kuang, n.d.).

While these applications are intriguing, they are really intended for general novelty, product information, and marketing. Still, they illustrate a glimpse of the potential for augmented environments. The exciting prospect for these applications is their availability and promise in the mobile spectrum. Having access to augmented reality applications on a Smartphone, for example, offers unlimited information retrieval opportunities in unlimited environments.

AR IN LIBRARY INFORMATION SEARCH

The use of augmented reality applications in the context of library and information search processes is not necessarily new. Rather, it is evolving. Ceynowa (2011), a Bavarian library researcher noted in the conference proceedings *Vision 2020: innovative policies, services and tools* that his library has embarked on utilizing a custom application known as *Ludwig II* that provides multi-sensory information relative to the image that is captured on the device's screen.

Much of this interest is driven from the increasingly sophisticated applications that are emerging in this spectrum. Indeed, multiple AR applications loosely related to information search are beginning to emerge. For example, Yovcheva, Buhalis, and Gatzidis (2012) indicate that augmented reality applications are beginning to emerge in such industries as tourism. (Retrieved from http://www.ifitt.org/admin/public/uploads/eRTR_SI_V10i2_Yovcheva_Buhalis_Gatzidis_63-66.pdf).

Greg Sterling who writes for *Search Engine Land* has declared augmented reality to be a form of information search (2009). According to Sterling, multiple applications are beginning to arrive on Smartphones, including *Layar*, *TwitARound*, *Acrossair* and others. Some of the earliest iterations were mobile applications that allowed for scanning of bar codes. Referred to as QR Codes, these specialized images contained links to Web sites, text, or Short Message Service (SMS)-based information.

Another use of augmented reality in the context of library and information search was developed by a team at the University of Oulu in Finland called *SmartLibrary* (http://virtuaalikampus.oulu.fi/English/smartlibrary.html) – a *wayfind-*

ing mobile application that helps users locate the shelf holding the resource they desire within the library. Wayfinding refers to techniques used by people to orient themselves in a physical space and navigate from place-to-place. Used in the context of libraries, wayfinding applications leverage the phone's built-in GPS technology to help orient the user to various resources.

Bo Brinkman from Miami University has developed an application he's entitled Shelvr (http://www.shelvar.com/) which purportedly improves shelf-reading and library asset management. When the mobile device is pointed at the book stack, Shelvr provides augmented overlays that allow the user to reposition the books in the correct call number sequence. Each book is encoded with a marker that interacts with the software, allowing the user to see contextualized information regarding its correct shelf location. Shelvar then illustrates to the user which direction to move the asset relative to its call number.

Another interesting augmented reality application utilized by librarians is entitled Tagwhat (http://www.tagwhat.com/) which allows users to add contextual location data to digital objects in a library collection, and make that data discoverable through a combined map and camera component within the application (Hadro, 2012). Tagwhat purports to be the most comprehensive feed of hyper-local content in the world, allowing the user to instantly find and deliver actionable content regarding places in the user's locale.

However enticing these applications are to utilize, the research team at Emporia State was particularly interested in developing an augmented reality application that allows users to point the Smartphone or mobile device at a library artifact and retrieve contextual information relative to that artifact in real time. In essence, providing the library patron an opportunity to engage with that artifact without the necessity of handling or potentially damaging the object. This is a particular a concern in Special Collections, Archives, and Rare Books section of the library. While the library staff desire patronage in Special Collections, they also must be sensitive to the potential for irreparable damage due to accidents, changes in temperature and environmental conditions, oils and salts emitted from human skin, etc. Currently, artifacts can only be observed in controlled environments, and must employ safeguards that ensure they are appropriately handled. It is often difficult for patrons to engage with the object in these controlled environments.

To manage these concerns while still being sensitive to the needs of the information seeker, archivists are exploring the use of augmented reality applications. Several of these applications are beginning to emerge – especially those that leverage advances in mobile technologies and the processing power embedded within mobile devices. Using mobile-based technologies, the archivist can generate an unlimited amount of supplemental information that is accessed in the virtual space. This not only provides the information seeker contextualized information, but it allows the library staff to maintain environmental control over the object.

One such technology is a mobile-based augmented reality product that allows the information seeker to point the device at the objects and generate a variety of contextual information. This technology utilizes a specially designed mobile application entitled *Aurasma*. Launched in 2011 in the United Kingdom, Aurasma is a relatively new augmented reality application that allows the user to generate visual markers within live objects and scenes. These markers then trigger video, animations, and other enhanced media elements. Called "auras," a recent video presentation on TED (Technology, Education, Design) illustrates how easy it is to generate a virtual reality asset using Aurasma (Retrieved from http://www.ted.com/talks/matt_mills_image_recognition_that_triggers_augmented_reality.html).

The team at Emporia State University, comprised of instructional systems designers, videographers, archivists, and reference librarians, elected to utilize Aurasma to develop a series of augmented environments specific to Archives and Special Collections. Specifically, the team was interested in developing auras related to some unique and interesting objects within the collection, including:

- Very rare novels, including a first-edition novel written by Mark Twain.
- University artifacts, including the foundation stone from the first administration building and a Phi Sigma Epsilon fraternity paddle.
- Diaries, including the Penelope "Nellie" Covert Papers and the Cecil Carle Collection. One of the first Black women in Emporia – dating back to 1850.
- Sheet music, including the Eugene Grissom Papers. Grisson served as a member of the Constitutional Convention of 1865.
- Original drawings by Robert McCloskey who was an American writer and illustrator of children's books in the latter half of the last century.
- Unidentified textile object from the Caroline Broomand Papers.
- Wooden university mascot carvings from the Norman O. Walrafen's Walnor Crafts Wood Crafts.
- A *Dance Card* from Nadine Patterson and Bill Obley Papers. Dance Cards were used in the late 19th century by a woman to record the names of the gentlemen with whom she intends to dance each successive dance at a formal dance.

Several years earlier a research team at the library had entertained a similar approach for archives and special collections using a series of photographs that are stitched together to make a continuous 360 degree image. When viewed through special software on a computer, the user was able to manipulate the object in a virtual space. While very useful for certain 3-D objects, such as pottery, textiles, and prints, the technology was limited to viewing the object only through rotation and zoom. No additional contextual information regarding the object could be embedded into the photos – aside from text. Using the aforementioned technology, users were only able to view the objects when they had access to a computer. Often, this was outside the Archival and Special Collections area. Furthermore, it did not necessarily promote patronage as users were able to view the objects outside the library and without support or information from the archival librarians. While certainly satisfying the goal of preserving the artifacts using an augmentation of the actual object, it did not provide contextualized information; information in a variety of formats; nor promote patronage to the physical library.

SOLUTIONS AND RECOMMENDATIONS

Using auras, the research team envisions a completely new approach to developing contextualized information search for library artifacts and data. This is particularly useful as it relates to the portable processing power now available in Smartphones and other types of mobile devices. The goal is to drive patronage to the Archives and Special Collections areas of the library, while providing those researchers and information seekers rich, contextualized information regarding rare artifacts.

Using the software application *Aurasma*, the team is developing a series of augmented reality environments for a variety of library artifacts and rare collections. For example, an aura is currently being developed for a rare Mark Twain novel. Other rare books are currently in consideration. Developers will embed visual markers into the environment that triggers the augmentation. These 'markers' must be unique – similar to a Quick Reference (QR) code. No two QR codes are identical or the user may retrieve the incorrect data when the code is scanned using a mobile device. Aurasma works using the same principal. The visual markers – which are essentially photos of the object or environment, serve as the placeholder to invoke the augmentation. When the software sees the visual marker, the augmentation is activated. These augmentations can include video, audio, still images, animations, music, etc.

In order to initiate the augmentation, the user first installs the free Aurasma application, which is available for a variety of devices and operating systems. After initializing the product, the user points his/her Smartphone at the archival object. The developers embed specific videos, music tracks, and other data into these markers that appear on the user's mobile device and provide additional contextual information.

Figure 1 illustrates how the application works in the context of a special collection. In this example, the user points his/her Smartphone at an illustration from renowned children's book illustrator Robert McCloskey. The development team has generated an Aurasma marker – a still photographic image of the object. When the phone is pointed at the object, the Aurasma application will spawn additional, contextual information regarding the object. In this example, the aura is a short video clip of the author—highlighting many of his famous works and providing a short biographical sketch regarding his life, career, and information regarding one of his books entitled *Make Way for Ducklings*—a Caldecott Book Award winner. This type of data would not be available by simply visiting the archive or rare books collection and observing the book in a glass case or through physical examination.

Figure 2 illustrates how the aura works when pointed at a rare book from the corpus written by Mark Twain. In this example, the aura spawns contextualized information regarding Twain, his stage in life when he was writing the novel, the context of the novel, and a short segment regarding how the library came to possess the book. A short video biography regarding Twain is spawned and played for the information seeker.

Figure 3 illustrates how the aura works when pointed at sheet music from the *Eugene Grissom Papers.* In this example, the aura spawns a musical performance conducted by members of the Emporia State Musical Department – playing select arrangements from the archival pieces. This provides the information seeker a sense of how the arrangements sound – even if they are unable to read sheet music.

The auras are relatively easy to develop and construct. The mechanical process simply involves

Figure 1. Robert McCloskey children's book illustrator

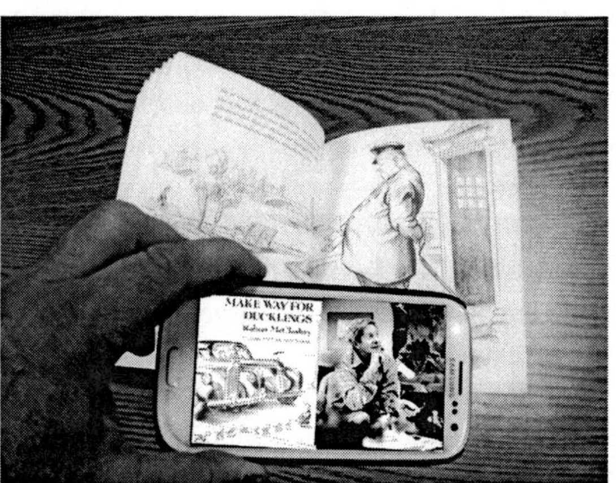

Figure 2. Rare Twain novel

Figure 3. Eugene Grissom papers

capturing a marker of the object and associating that marker with the contextual information – video, music, etc. That additional layer of information is associated using hyperlinks or other pointers. The challenge lies with the archivist to select the components that best illustrate the artifact, and assemble those components into a useable format. That process normally requires the expertise of the videographer, photographer, animator, or musicians to regenerate the contextual information layer. Assuming a biographical sketch is developed, the segment may require a script, storyboarding, narration, video, photography, and other components. Unless the information seeker is interested in detailed information regarding the artifact—as opposed to general information—the contextual layer must present salient information regarding the object in a compressed time frame. Too long, and the information seeker may lose interest. Too short, and the information seeker may not feel as though enough information regarding the object or subject was presented.

There are other downsides to this technology as well. For one thing, the technology is still very device dependent. Certain mobile technologies will not yet support augmentation, potentially disqualifying patrons from accessing the contextual data layers. This type of technology is limited to powerful mobile devices that are Web capable and have the ability to install applications. In addition, the very nature of the technology is predicated on access using single, stand alone devices. This discounts the ability for group or collaborative research – particularly if the members of the group are located in disparate locations. And since the technology is dependent on the ability to point the mobile device at the asset, the information seeker must normally be physically located in the same area as the asset. However, representations of the asset presented online may suffice in certain instances.

Finally, the technology still does not yet satisfy true information search. Normally, an information seeker looks for a variety of information and data regarding the subject or topic. This can lead the seeker into various, indiscriminate information seeking paths. The augmentation, while powerful and multi-sensory, does not yet support this indiscriminate, ramdom information seeking process.

FUTURE RESEARCH DIRECTIONS

Future research should be directed toward how advances in augmented reality technology can be included in other types of library applications. For example, if all books and articles in the library—digital or physical—are coded with visual markers when they are acquired in the collection, it is conceivable that patrons will have the ability to scan any book or artifact on any shelf in the library and retrieve metadata associated with that asset. This marks a convergence between Web 3.0—the Semantic Web—and information technology search using mobile-based technology. The Semantic Web—or the Web of data as it is commonly referred—encodes information with rich metadata. That metadata can then be accessed using any number of search processes, including voice, text, or advanced search systems.

As the augmented reality evolves, archivists and special collections librarians should research how they can leverage the technology to include additional layers of information. The current limitation of the technology is that the user is limited to whatever contextual information the developer has elected to include in the marker. So, the information seeker is still really not in control of the information seeking process. That is, the query is dictated to the user in the form of the contextualized elements that are selected, developed, and presented. While useful, it does not provide much flexibility, autonomy, or 'serendipitous' information search; that is, the exploration and location of information based on other information.

Future augmented environments will likely include the ability for the user to choose from multiple types of information sources. For example, if the user points her mobile device at a rare book, the archivist will be able to embed multiple types of simultaneous data layers, including video, photography, text, music, animation, etc. This enables the user to choose the type of data to retrieve, or to construct their own search parameters and retrieve information that combines multiple data sets. This is a powerful and exciting opportunity for librarians.

Augmented Reality is particularly useful in the context of archives and special collections given the sensitivity of the collection. This technology provides librarians a unique ability to develop rich data associated with any type of library artifact. By adding this layer of data, librarians can then explore and study how information seekers acquire information. A wealth of research opportunities presents itself when examining these processes. For example, empirical data can be collected and analyzed regarding the processes users invoke when engaging contextualized information when conducting research. Students, faculty, and other academicians can be examined in control and treatment groups to study the effectiveness of the technology in retrieving information. Human-computer experts can be engaged to determine how the user utilized the technology; the time it required to retrieve the information; and the overall user experience.

CONCLUSION

Augmented reality applications are still very much in their infancy. The applications that are currently being marketed and used provide an amazing layer of contextualized data; however, we have only really begun to explore the possibility of how this technology can be leveraged in education and research. Based on prototypical augmented environments that are still in development for business and industry applications, it is very possible that these products will evolve in their sophistication and capabilities to include a rich layer of contextual data relative to a variety of physical environments.

Libraries and librarians are poised to leverage this technology. By their very nature, they have a wealth of information and data that can be harnessed to leverage powerful mobile applications – including, but not limited to augmented reality. Advanced information search processes that capitalize on the Semantic Web will most certainly converge with mobile technologies. When this convergence occurs, users will engage in information seeking strategies using entirely new tools and processes. More information seekers will engage with libraries and their corpus independent of reference librarians – the traditional help desk in libraries. The need to seek assistance with information search will change markedly. Users will likely engage with the collection using their own devices and using their own information seeking strategies.

Augmented reality may provide these users with additional tools and technologies to assist in that search process. This means that the role of the librarian will likely change to being a person who acquires, curates, and constructs the information sources for the patrons, as opposed to the person that has traditionally directed users to the information sources. It's conceivable that the role of archivist librarians will change in profound ways as this technology matures.

Augmented reality was not necessarily conceived with libraries in mind. However, this environment would be an excellent location to begin experimentation and research regarding how these technologies can be used in information seeking strategies. Clearly, how users engage with information is evolving. The more librarians can understand how to harness that technology, the better they will be able to develop rich search strategies and dynamic data archives.

REFERENCES

Bates, M. J. (2005). Berrypicking. In Fisher, K. E., Erdelez, S., & McKechnie, L. (Eds.), *Theories of Information Behavior*. Medford, NJ: Information Today.

Belkin, N. J. (1980). Anomalous states of knowledge as a basis for information retrieval. *The Canadian Journal of Information Science*, *5*, 133–143.

Ceynowa, K. (2011). *Mobile applications, augmented reality, gesture-based computing and more – Innovative information services for the internet of the future: The case of the Bavarian state library.* Retrieved from http://conference.ifla.org/past/ifla77/122-ceynowa-en.pdf

Dervin, B. (1976). *Information for sense-making*. Paper presented to the Symposium of the Committee on Public Information in the Prevention of Occupational Cancer, National Research Council, National Academy of Sciences. Washington, DC.

Farkas, M. (2010). *Your reality, augmented.* Retrieved from http://americanlibrariesmagazine.org/columns/practice/your-reality-augmented March, 2013.

Horizon Report. (2011). Retrieved from http://wp.nmc.org/horizon2011/sections/augmented-reality/#0

Kuang, C. (n.d.). Five to-die-for augmented reality shopping apps. *FastCompany*. Retrieved from http://www.fastcodesign.com/1313133/five-to-die-for-augmented-reality-shopping-apps

Kuhlthau, C. C. (2001). The use of theory in information science research. *Journal of the American Society for Information Science and Technology*, *52*, 62–73. doi:10.1002/1532-2890(2000)52:1<62::AID-ASI1061>3.0.CO;2-J.

OCLC. (2012). *Libraries as read/write services.* Retrieved from http://www.oclc.org/research/events/dss/marchionini.html

Overview of Smartphone Augmented Reality Applications for Tourism. (n.d.). Retrieved from http://www.ifitt.org/admin/public/uploads/eRTR_SI_V10i2_Yovcheva_Buhalis_Gatzidis_63-66.pdf

Radhakrishnan, A. (2009). *9 semantic search engines that will change the world of search.* Retrieved from http://www.searchenginejournal.com/semantic-search-engines/9832/

Sterling, B. (2013). *Augmented reality: New patent allows for Google Glass to control appliances.* Retrieved from http://www.wired.com/beyond_the_beyond/2013/03/augmented-reality-new-patent-allows-google-glass-to-control-appliances/

Sterling G. (2009). Retrieved from http://searchengineland.com/augmented-reality-is-also-a-form-of-search-23859

Chapter 6
E-LearningFacultyModules.org

Roger McHaney
Kansas State University, USA

Lynda Spire
Kansas State University, USA

Rosemary Boggs
Kansas State University, USA

ABSTRACT

A team at Kansas State University recently launched the E-Learning Faculty Modules wiki to enhance and support online faculty development. This project is customized for teaching in the Kansas State University distance-learning program but contains a broad set of information that might be useful to others. This site is constructed using wiki technology, which permits access, multimedia expressiveness, remote collaboration, tracking, and reversibility of postings. Other tools on the site are derived from MediaWiki and its open-source capabilities. The wiki includes an overall ontology, templates, categories, completed and seeded entries, input boxes, and menus that ensure users can easily use and join the community. Taken holistically, these attributes create an ideal venue for sharing ideas and encouraging synergistic improvement of teaching practices. This chapter describes the implementation process of E-LearningFacultyModules.org and gives insight into its purpose, features, and uses.

1. OVERVIEW

Higher education has undergone incredible changes in the past fifteen years with the advent of distance education. Traditional universities have risen to the challenge of providing access to degrees and certificates to students in locations away from campuses. The fairly finite group of students served by universities in the past exploded with students from across the country and world knocking at their virtual doors. Fierce competition from higher educational institutions of all varieties has come along with the opportunity to serve expanded student populations. Students now shop for desired programs, affordable education and courses to fit into degrees from other universities. On this international stage, universities have to ensure that all courses are of the highest quality using benchmarks established within the online education world. Of course, this may require faculty members to gain new skills so they can provide effective online instruction which will help enable students to achieve course objectives and this can be an institutional challenge (Bower, 2001). The idea of the E-Learning Faculty Modules wiki was conceived by a committee to help K-State faculty,

DOI: 10.4018/978-1-4666-4462-5.ch006

staff, and administrators gain the needed skills to be successful in an online environment.

At Kansas State University, a strategy aimed at providing tools for faculty already teaching online and those ready for the challenge of online instruction has taken the form of a wiki designed to serve faculty at all levels of expertise in online teaching. This wiki format was approached through an anytime, anyplace mindset with the goal of faculty access to information from offices, home or other remote locations. It was designed to allow faculty to boost their knowledge, build new skills, gain confidence and understand the complexity of moving from traditional classroom teaching to online teaching. This opportunity to learn by sharing experiences and expertise with peers was viewed as essential (Clay, 1999). Principles of good practice and the latest developments in wiki technology were used to ensure a stable and user-friendly platform.

The project was designed and completed by a team of faculty members, instructional designers and continuing education professionals. The project, called E-Learning Faculty Modules, started rather simply with three main modules—one for beginning online instructors (0-2 years of online teaching experience), one for intermediate level instructors (3-5 years of experience), and the third for expert faculty who had taught for a number of years but wanted to employ new technologies and methods of teaching. These three main sections were called *Beginners Studio*, *E-Learning Central,* and *Advanced Workshop*. As the project progressed, other sections were added. A *Getting Started* module that features online instructors who share experiences and knowledge was developed for beginning online instructors. A welcome and introduction from the university provost was added, as was a section named *Rules of the Road* that noted regulations related to distance education from different accrediting agencies. *Stand Alones* on pertinent topics such as accessibility, honesty and integrity, assessment, and fair use and copyright were created as well as sections called *E-Quality*, *Faculty Share*, *Best Practices*, *Take Five*, and *General Reference Resources*.

The development team made decisions that shaped the wiki. During the first year the team met on a monthly basis but later these meetings were replaced with small project teams focused on specific tasks. The project design and implementation process continues to remain fluid as new ideas are explored and developed. A marketing plan for the wiki was developed so instructors and others on campus could become aware of this resource.

On October 19, 2010, Kansas State University publically released E-Learning Faculty Modules (see Figure 1) with the overall goals of boosting faculty knowledge, building new skills for online instructors, enhancing confidence, developing standards for instructional approach, and providing a better understanding of the complexity required to move from traditional classroom teaching to online teaching.

The Website, located at elearningfacultymodules.org (http://www.elearningfacultymodules.org) provides the virtual space for faculty and staff to interact with a set of resources that can enhance their online teaching experiences. While the wiki is not universally used by K-State online instructors, feedback has been encouraging. Many faculty members and administrators now refer to "the faculty modules" in conversations. It even has been used by instructors as a teaching tool for education courses.

2. WIKIS REVISITED

Wikis belong to a class of online software sometimes called Web 2.0. They are symbolic of the Web's collaborative power and were among the first applications to benefit from the efforts of like-minded people developing Websites filled with co-created, informative content. To do this, a wiki provides an interactive environment where users build and edit Web pages with a browser

Figure 1. E-learning Faculty Modules main page

from an Internet-connected location (Cummings, 2008; Richardson, 2009). Most wikis provide a variety of features that facilitate the creation and editing of new material, provide a means to group material into topic or subject areas, link pages, and cross reference material. In addition to text-based material, Wikis often support graphics, images, audio files, video clips, hyperlinks, embedded documents, and other Web page features. Wikis can be open to the public or carefully controlled to give editing privileges to specific users.

The word *wiki* is based on the Hawaiian language term for *fast.* The first wiki was developed by Ward Cunningham who used collaborative Web technology to create a shared repository of software design knowledge for his team of software developers. He wanted the stored material to be accessible to those using it and he wanted developers with a vested interest in its accuracy to be able to make changes. His wiki was called the *Portland Pattern Repository* and it captured tacit knowledge so software developers could learn from each other and avoid reinventing solutions to problems. Cunningham's approach became recognized in software development circles as an example of Web 2.0 in practice (Leuf and Cunningham, 2001; McHaney, 2011). The idea caught the public's imagination and soon found use in many organizations and groups (Bishop, 2004; Deursen and Visser, 2002).

Soon after Cunningham's initial development, *Wikipedia* was founded. This Web-based, free-content, collaborative encyclopedia was founded by Jimmy Wales and Larry Sanger in 2001. They wanted to "*create and distribute a multilingual free encyclopedia of the highest quality to every single person on the planet in his or her own language*" (Wikipedia, 2012). Wikipedia became the fifth most popular Website (in 2012) and proves group-created knowledge repositories are a viable method of codifying, maintaining, improving, and collecting information. In 2012, it had more than 3.7 million articles in English, 15 million users, and 260 languages. Further, Wikipedia demonstrates that allowing a group of users to create and edit a Web page encourages democratization of the Web (McHaney, 2012a).

A number of different software systems are used to develop wiki applications. The most popular is MediaWiki, a free Web-based software application developed by Wikimedia Foundation and a large community of users. MediaWiki is used by Wikipedia and thousands of other Websites (McHaney, 2012a). It was developed in the PHP programming language and relies heavily on a backend database system (most commonly MySQL). MediaWiki was first released in 2002 and coincided with the publication of Wikipedia. Since that time more than 700 configuration settings, 600 automated tools, and 1,800 extensions have been added. MediaWiki supports a large number of languages, Website configurations, edit tracking, and talk pages (MediaWiki, 2012). It is licensed under the GNU General Public License (GPL).

In addition to Wikipedia, a large number of private and public wikis exist in a variety of application areas. For instance, in businesses, wikis are being used for internal collaborative document development. These documents provide a knowledge repository that remains even if employees leave. American Express used wiki technology to develop an executive travel wiki which enabled employees to share hints about corporate travel and the procedures required to receive reimbursement for expenses. Other organizations use wikis as internal documentation for in-house systems and software applications. Still others promote the use of wikis by customers to help produce documentation of products or software (McHaney, 2012b). According to researchers Majchrzak, Wagner and Yates (2006), business wiki users are either synthesizers or adders. Synthesizers provide information needed by others in an organization and adders enter information needed to accomplish their jobs.

In the academic world, wikis have been used for collaborative grant writing, academic unit documentation, committee reports and work, strategic planning documentation, and as knowledge repositories. Wikis also are popular in the classroom and have been used by instructors to develop collaborative writing projects for students (McHaney, 2012b). Wikis are often at the center of learning communities and provide a means to codify knowledge (Gilbert, Chen and Sabol, 2008).

Wikis serve as an example of social constructivism (Notari, 2005; Seitzinger, 2006) and are structured to facilitate knowledge construction through communal activities, online discussion, and reflection. The net result can be a synergistic increase in group learning rather than an individual quest for knowledge (Parker & Chao, 2007). This makes a wiki ideal for the development of an online learning community.

A primary criticism of wiki use involves the ease with which inaccurate information can be added to the site. For instance, Wikipedia often has been the subject of criticism for its potential to include faulty information and for furthering commercial or political causes. In these instances, it becomes the responsibility of the wiki master to take both corrective and preventative action.

3. CONCEPT DEVELOPMENT

Online courses are a relatively new tool in higher education's portfolio of teaching practices (Keegan, 1996). Instructional design in this area has re-imagined the possibilities which include collaborative communication tools, wikis, blogs, online video, shared documents, and numerous apps. The wide spectrum of tools, techniques, and practices has made it important for an institution to find new ways to ensure quality and share techniques among instructors, administrators and staff (Simpson, 2013).

Universities have utilized a variety of approaches to ensure high quality in online teaching (Chapman & Henderson, 2010). In addition, national organizations have taken on the cause of supporting universities as they embrace distance education. Several universities and organizations that have demonstrated strong approaches to faculty support are shown in Table 1.

Table 1. Influential universities and organizations in distance education

West Virginia University OIT: Provides the general Pros/Cons for online learning; suggested methodologies for faculty; tips from other faculty who also teach online. http://oit.wvu.edu/itrc/faculty/tips/
Oklahoma State University: Institute for Teaching and Learning Excellence: Provides a full course for educators to go through to find the best practices for learning about how to manage and implement online courses. http://itle.okstate.edu/index.php/online-instruction
The University of California-Irvine: Provides instructor orientation and training to new online instructors. http://sites.uci.edu/instructors/applying/training-orientation-for-all-instructors/overview/
Maryland Online: Developed and recommends faculty take an online training course, Certificate for Online Adjunct Teaching (COAT); also available to other institutions. www.marylandonline.org/coat
Regis University: Offers an optional online resource site, Passport to Course Development. http://www.youtube.com/watch?v=wKO-oMgy6FM
University of Wisconsin-Madison: Expands knowledge and skills in distance teaching and learning with an annual conference, professional certificates, individual courses and custom courses for groups of 10 or more. http://depd.wisc.edu/info
The Sloan-C Certificate: Uses the Sloan-C pillars of quality in online education (learning effectiveness, scale, faculty and student satisfaction and access). http://sloanconsortium.org/certificate
Illinois Online Network: offers a master Online Teacher Certificate for faculty development based on the MVCR (Making the Virtual Classroom a Reality) series of online faculty development courses. This program is not required for instructors who teach online at the University of Illinois. http://www.ion.uillinois.edu/courses/students/mot.asp
ASTD (American Society for Training Development): Provides an e-learning instructional design certificate in a two-day workshop. http://www.astd.org/Education/Certificate-Programs/E-Learning-Instructional-Design-Certificate

It was against this backdrop that E-Learning Faculty Modules wiki conceptually originated. Recognizing the need for online teaching resources at Kansas State, leaders from the Kansas State University Division of Continuing Education assembled a group of professionals that included faculty and instructional designers as well as continuing education staff members involved in distance education. That group was charged with development of a tool that could be used successfully by distance instructors teaching online. Participating faculty had successful histories of teaching online and were invited because they had reputations of being innovative, enthusiastic and dedicated to the distance-learning concept. The centralized organizational model of the university meant the instructional designers were located in a single unit and they formed an extremely vital piece of the team. They provided background in a variety of learning techniques and approaches. The continuing education professionals brought a strong knowledge of student and faculty needs. The varied makeup of the team proved central to the success of the project as each brought different skills, outlooks, and talents to the team.

All team members volunteered their time to the project. It was not any team member's primary responsibility. In addition, content for the wiki came from K-State staff, faculty, and administrators who agreed to create certain pieces of the project. Using campus experts who agreed to work on the project presented challenges but it also added to the richness of the content. The team liked to say that the wiki was *created by K-Staters for K-Staters*.

The group determined the wiki format and designed a project plan which was presented and accepted by campus administrators in May, 2010. The plan for three initial levels of information—beginner, intermediate, and advanced—provided the backdrop for the team's effort as the work was planned, content was created and the wiki launched.

Initial discussions covered the audience scope and whether to open the wiki to the world or to keep it private for use by Kansas State faculty. After much debate, the team determined the wiki would be designed with the K-State faculty in mind as the team wanted to use terminology, resources, and policies specific to K-State. An additional concern addressed by the team involved content related to issues such as copyright, accessibility and other university-specific policies. This information needed to remain accurate and had to be locked to ensure no edits could be made without specific review and permission.

The decision was made to develop an area entitled Faculty Share that would be available for content addition by those outside the development team and university. This permitted others to contribute to the wiki but not to edit or change entries that had been created by the team members. A system that required new users to request an account was implemented to help limit spam entries which had become an early problem for the wiki master. This allowed the team to minimize monitoring of the wiki content additions.

4. IMPLEMENTATION OF E-LEARNINGFACULTYMODULES.ORG

The K-State implementation team developed a strategy for building a high quality, engaging wiki-based Web site to enhance learning. In general, the team wanted to ensure that users would have the opportunity to enhance the site with their experiences while benefiting from the experiences of others. This approach was meant to facilitate the sharing of intellectual resources and encourage users to contribute new material knowing added content would remain available with a Creative Commons™ license (http://creativecommons.org/). In general, the implementation strategy followed the process used in building ELATEwiki.org (Hai-Jew and McHaney, 2010) and included the following aspects: paradigm development; content ontology; risk assessment; technological considerations; and sustainability.

4.1. Paradigm for ELearningFacultyModules.org

The implementation team engaged in paradigm development for the Website which included brainstorming desired contents and developing an identity for the Website. The primary idea was to create an engaging site filled with resources for online instructors at K-State. The team focused on potential content areas ranging from beginners with no experience to advanced instructors with high levels of online experience. It was determined the site would be best served if the experiences and knowledge of more seasoned instructors could be collected and made available to those just starting out in the online environment. Additionally, advanced material created by instructional designers and other experts would provide a rich set of resources.

The implementation team discussed various identities for the site options and after numerous suggestions determined ELearningFacultyModules.org would convey the site's meaning and provide a memorable domain name (that was also available for purchase). The domain was secured by K-State and registered for use. A K-State graphic artist created prototypes for a logo and the implementation team selected two for use on the site (See Figures 2 and 3).

Figure 2. Website logo

Figure 3. Banner logo

4.2. Wiki Software Selection and Installation

The implementation team researched and discussed various wiki software and hardware configurations before an implementation decision was reached. The team was familiar with the implementation of ELATEwiki.org (McHaney, 2009) and determined that using the same platform for wiki software would reduce complexity and simplify hosting. The consensus was that MediaWiki (http://www.mediawiki.org/wiki/MediaWiki), the open-source wiki technology that underlies Wikipedia™, would be used. The software was installed by K-State's Office of Mediated Education (OME) (http://ome.ksu.edu/) on a K-State server with a clustered environment having two nodes (to ensure a higher level of uptime). The server was prepared by pre-loading PHP 5.2.17 and MySQL database software version 5.5.13. Version 1.15.3 of Wikimedia software was loaded and configured.

4.3. Content Ontology

"Ontologies are unambiguous representations of concepts, relationships between concepts (such as a hierarchy), ontologically significant individuals, and axioms" (Hepp, Siorpaes, & Bachlechner, 2007, p. 55). The implementation team determined an initial ontology needed to consider a variety of users with varying degrees of sophistication related to online teaching. The site needed to provide new users with a sense of becoming comfortable with online teaching. Moderately experienced users would use the site for inspiration, new ideas, and for quality-enhancements to their teaching practice. Expert users would be able to obtain new ideas from peers and instructional designers and contribute ideas to share with others. These goals were accomplished using a structure that started with three Main Modules called *Beginner's Studio*, *E-Learning Central,* and *Advanced Workshop*. Figure 4 provides a view of this ontology and its main categories. Table 2 offers example topics from each main category.

Other components were also created as a result of the initial ontology. These included *Stand Alone Modules*, *Take Five*, *Rules of the Road*, *Introduction* by the Provost and later an area for the Kansas State Quality Checklist.

4.4. Wiki Ontology Implementation

The site was developed to utilize Wikimedia features and implement the desired ontology. The wiki was implemented in two dimensions. First, a macro structure was developed to provide an overall categorization of areas. This macro view grouped content into Beginners' Studio, E-Learning Central, Advanced Workshop, Faculty Share, Best Practices, Take Five, General Refer-

Figure 4. Main sections in ontology for E-Learning Faculty Modules

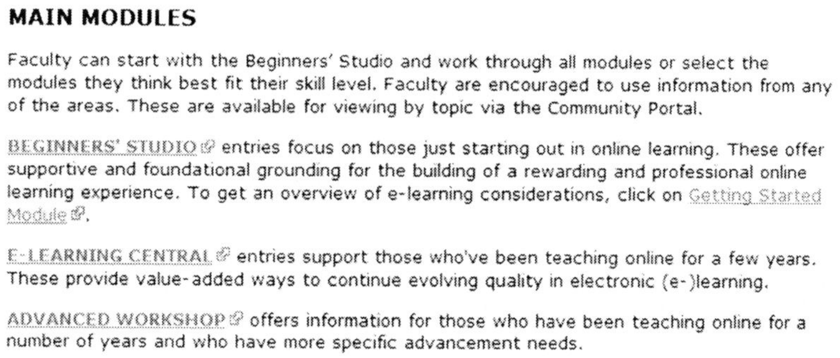

MAIN MODULES

Faculty can start with the Beginners' Studio and work through all modules or select the modules they think best fit their skill level. Faculty are encouraged to use information from any of the areas. These are available for viewing by topic via the Community Portal.

BEGINNERS' STUDIO entries focus on those just starting out in online learning. These offer supportive and foundational grounding for the building of a rewarding and professional online learning experience. To get an overview of e-learning considerations, click on Getting Started Module.

E-LEARNING CENTRAL entries support those who've been teaching online for a few years. These provide value-added ways to continue evolving quality in electronic (e-)learning.

ADVANCED WORKSHOP offers information for those who have been teaching online for a number of years and who have more specific advancement needs.

Table 2. Selected examples from each main module

BEGINNERS' STUDIO	E-LEARNING CENTRAL	ADVANCED WORKSHOP
Collaboration	Active Learning	Academic Writing and Publishing
Communication and Feedback Policies	Learning Management System	Advanced Online Assessment Techniques
Contingency Plans	Micro-Blogging Assignments	Building Digital Learning Objects
Course Evaluation	Rubrics	Educational Games
Creating a Course Syllabus	Social Networking Tool	Educational Simulations
Icebreakers	Storyboarding	Mobile Learning
Learner Interaction	Student Retention	Self-Discovery Learning

ence Resources, and Rules of the Road. These topics were instantiated with category tags, which also makes it possible for a particular content page to be a member of multiple categories. Figure 5 provides an example of a category tag viewed in the wiki's edit mode for a page called *Icebreakers*.

In order to easily develop an entry for one of the major categories, hyperlinks were provided on the wiki's main page navigation bar. Figure 6 illustrates.

Each hyperlink opens a new page creation area. Each area provides choices from a set of pre-tagged templates suited to potential topics being developed in each category. Figure 7 provides an example of the category choices provided for the Beginner's Studio area. Each choice provides a different default tag set as a starting point but can still be fully customized by the wiki contributor.

The pre-inserted tags differentiate the various pages so users can conduct searches more easily. Creating a new page results in the instantiation of the underlying template and opens a new page in the edit mode. The templates are Wikimedia wikitext page structures with features designed to make content easier to enter and to increase user productivity while eliminating frustration with technical details. Figure 8 illustrates a template for the 'Instructor Administration Strategies and Support' within the Beginner's Studio category. Similar templates exist for the other categories. While a general structure is provided, the wiki development team believed it was important to leave the content largely unstructured so authors

Figure 5. Editing an entry categorized as "beginner"

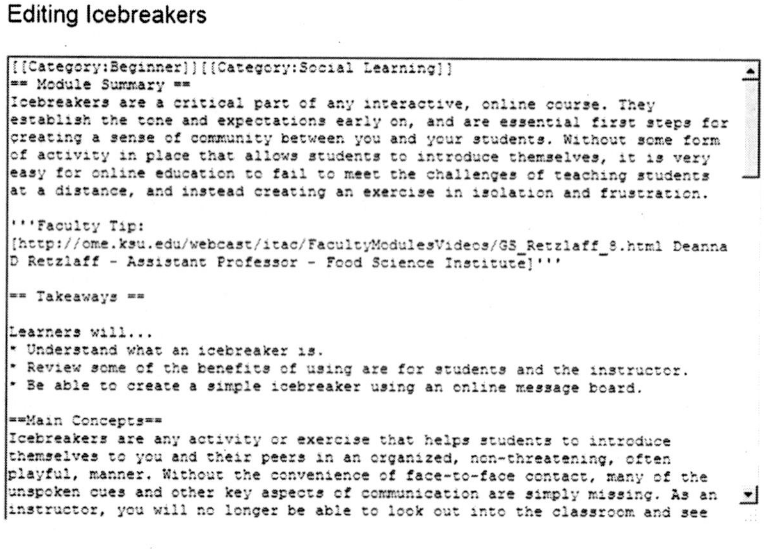

Editing Icebreakers

```
[[Category:Beginner]][[Category:Social Learning]]
== Module Summary ==
Icebreakers are a critical part of any interactive, online course. They
establish the tone and expectations early on, and are essential first steps for
creating a sense of community between you and your students. Without some form
of activity in place that allows students to introduce themselves, it is very
easy for online education to fail to meet the challenges of teaching students
at a distance, and instead creating an exercise in isolation and frustration.

'''Faculty Tip:
[http://ome.ksu.edu/webcast/itac/FacultyModulesVideos/GS_Retzlaff_8.html Deanna
D Retzlaff - Assistant Professor - Food Science Institute]'''

== Takeaways ==

Learners will...
* Understand what an icebreaker is.
* Review some of the benefits of using are for students and the instructor.
* Be able to create a simple icebreaker using an online message board.

==Main Concepts==
Icebreakers are any activity or exercise that helps students to introduce
themselves to you and their peers in an organized, non-threatening, often
playful, manner. Without the convenience of face-to-face contact, many of the
unspoken cues and other key aspects of communication are simply missing. As an
instructor, you will no longer be able to look out into the classroom and see
```

Figure 6. Navigation bar links for page creation

Create Pages

- Beginners' Studio
- E-Learning Central
- Advanced Workshop
- E-Quality
- Faculty Share
- Best Practices
- Take Five
- General Reference Resources
- Rules of the Road

Figure 7. Example category choices for page creation

CreateBeginners

The Beginners' Studio offers an entry point for faculty who are new to e-learning.

Contributing to Beginners' Studio

This page provides a template to facilitate the development of new pages for the Beginners' Studio pages. If you would like to create a page that does not exist on this Wiki, use the appropriate category template below to start adding information! Simply enter the name of the page you wish to create and Click **Create**. You will be taken to the new page where you can make your edits then save the page to the wiki.

Create Instructor Administration Strategies and Support Page

Create

Create Pedagogy Page

Create

Create Digital Contents Page

Create

Create Social Learning Page

Create

Create Technologies Page

Create

Create Policies and Practices Page

Create

would have the freedom to develop material in a way that made sense. The only titles entered on the templates are for required elements such as 'Module Summary', 'Takeaways', and so forth. Additionally, pages can be added to the wiki without the use of the templates using standard Wikimedia commands.

Figure 8. Template for "instructor administration strategies and support" page in the beginner's studio

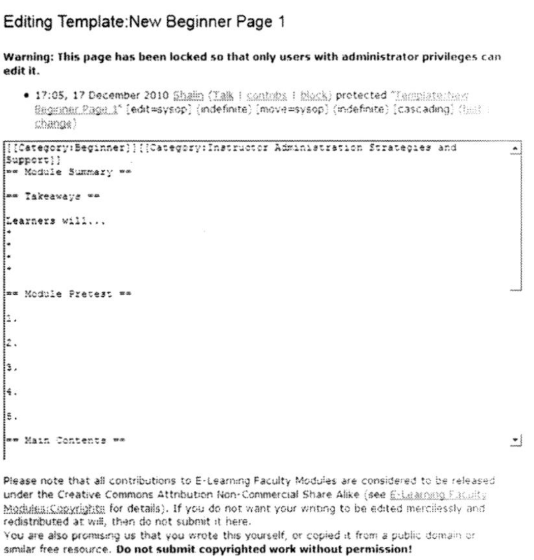

Editing Template:New Beginner Page 1

Warning: This page has been locked so that only users with administrator privileges can edit it.

- 17:05, 17 December 2010 Shalin (Talk | contribs | block) protected "Template:New Beginner Page 1" [edit=sysop] (indefinite) [move=sysop] (indefinite) [cascading] (hist | change)

```
[[Category:Beginner]][[Category:Instructor Administration Strategies and Support]]
== Module Summary ==

== Takeaways ==

Learners will...
*
*
*
*

== Module Pretest ==

1.

2.

3.

4.

5.

== Main Contents ==
```

Please note that all contributions to E-Learning Faculty Modules are considered to be released under the Creative Commons Attribution Non-Commercial Share Alike (see E-Learning Faculty Modules:Copyrights for details). If you do not want your writing to be edited mercilessly and redistributed at will, then do not submit it here.
You are also promising us that you wrote this yourself, or copied it from a public domain or similar free resource. **Do not submit copyrighted work without permission!**

Figure 9 provides a list of categories currently in the ontology. New categories can be added and the overall graphic ontology map expanded as needed. Over time, the implementation team believes users will attach more content-specific tags. Wikimedia will automatically provide hyperlinks to groups of related articles this way.

Figure 9. Current categories in ontology

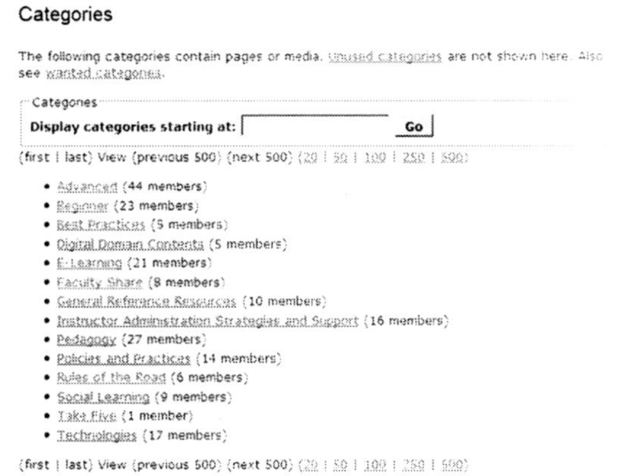

Categories

The following categories contain pages or media. Unused categories are not shown here. Also see wanted categories.

Categories
Display categories starting at: Go

(first | last) View (previous 500) (next 500) (20 | 50 | 100 | 250 | 500)

- Advanced (44 members)
- Beginner (23 members)
- Best Practices (5 members)
- Digital Domain Contents (5 members)
- E-Learning (21 members)
- Faculty Share (8 members)
- General Reference Resources (10 members)
- Instructor Administration Strategies and Support (16 members)
- Pedagogy (27 members)
- Policies and Practices (14 members)
- Rules of the Road (6 members)
- Social Learning (9 members)
- Take Five (1 member)
- Technologies (17 members)

(first | last) View (previous 500) (next 500) (20 | 50 | 100 | 250 | 500)

The ontology was supplemented with additional sections including: Introduction by Provost, Stand Alone Modules, E-Quality, Faculty Share, Best Practices, Take Five, General Reference Resources, and Rules of the Road. These are described in more detail in the following sections.

4.4.1. Introduction by the Provost

The provost recorded a message for the E-Learning Faculty Modules wiki that both introduces the wiki and reveals the administration's interest in high quality online courses offered at a distance. This introduction has given the site credibility with the campus and integrated it with other ongoing teaching and learning efforts on campus.

4.4.2. Stand-Alone Modules

Because of the crucial nature of certain topics related to online teaching, the team decided that more comprehensive information on certain topics was needed to give faculty members a sturdy platform as they developed courses. It was agreed to start with the development of the *Stand Alone* modules related to accessibility for all learners, assessment of student learning, honesty and integrity, and fair use and copyright. These Stand Alone modules were designed to offer faculty members an experience of 60 minutes or less as they accessed content developed by campus experts. The content is partially presented in video format and usually includes additional hyperlinks to Web resources and Web activities. Opportunity for reflection after viewing the Stand Alone modules is provided. Completion of the Stand Alone modules and the Getting Started module eventually became a requirement for faculty receiving course development funding through the Division of Continuing Education grant process. Additional Stand Alone modules are in development. The Library Services module was made available in February 2013. Figure 10 offers a view of the Stand Alone modules wiki page.

4.4.3. E-Quality

As the importance, visibility, and continuing growth of online instruction continues to emerge, Kansas State University, like other universities, has attempted to define quality in online courses. The *E-Quality* area will provide faculty members with benchmarks established within the online education world. With the knowledge gained through attendance at many professional development sessions, a group of staff and faculty worked together to develop an E-Quality Checklist to be used by faculty and instructional designers when creating or revising online courses (Appendix 1).

Figure 10. Stand-Alone Modules wiki page

STAND ALONE E-LEARNING MODULES FOR FACULTY

We encourage K-State faculty receiving grant funds for the development of online courses to review the following critical modules. These Stand Alone modules offer faculty members an experience of 60 minutes or less that address topics pertinent to online distance education. Content comes from campus experts and is partially presented in video format. Each stand alone module may include additional hyperlinks to web resources and web activities. These may serve as pre- or post-activities to the content presented in the video segments. Opportunity for reflection after viewing the stand alone modules will be provided. Assessment opportunities will also exist within each module.

Because of the crucial nature of the topics, completion of several Stand Alone modules will be required for those who are receiving DCE grant development money. The required modules are listed below and are also in a KSOL class site. Faculty who receive DCE grant money will be added to the KSOL class to review the modules and then complete short quizzes related to each topic. For more information on the DCE RFP process or to be added to the KSOL class, contact Rosemary Boggs, rboggs@k-state.edu, 785-532-5724.

GETTING STARTED: This Getting Started Module may be accessed at the following location Getting Started Module. This multimedia slideshow with videos highlights some basics of quality e-learning.

ACCESSIBILITY FOR ONLINE LEARNERS: Accessibility is a critical legal requirement for online courses. This module provides a brief overview of some accessibility concerns. A video entitled Accessibility by Jason Maseburg-Tomlinson provides specific information about K-State's Disability Support Services. Additional information about accessibility requirements for online courses is also provided.

FAIR USE AND COPYRIGHT: Intellectual Property addresses IP issues related to both the build of an online course and the uses of copyrighted contents by the learners and instructor; this page sets a basic context. An overview of Copyright Basics is available as well as information on Fair Use, Alternatives to Copyrighted Materials, Your Responsibilities, and Copyright & Using Media in the Online Classroom. Information about K-State Copyright Consultation Services is also provided.

ASSESSMENT OF ONLINE STUDENT LEARNING: This is a link to a video on Assessment and Student Learning in an Online Environment. This module includes a video on What Works. Information on assessment methods such as wikis, message boards, writing activities, and e-portfolios make up the rest of this module.

HONESTY AND INTEGRITY IN ONLINE LEARNING: Academic Integrity vs. Dishonesty focuses on the requirements of the Honor and Integrity expectations of the campus and some strategies for achieving this in online learning. Additional information about Honesty and Integrity in Online Learning is also provided.

- What is the K-State Honor and Integrity System
- Honor Pledge Violations in Online Learning
- Proactive Measures Against Violations in Your Class
- Confronting and Reporting a Violation
- Resources for Working with Students with a Violation

LIBRARY RESOURCES AND SERVICES: The library provides a wide variety of resources and support services for online instructors and learners. Faculty are encouraged to make some resources available to their students in online courses. Cool Tools highlights a variety of tools available to students, in a colorful digital flyer. Faculty and Graduate Services highlights the services available to both faculty and graduate students. Finally, this student flyer lets learners know what services the library will provide for them. Faculty may review Distance Education Faculty's Top 10 Points about Library Services highlights a countdown of library services.

For more about the K-State Libraries, please see the page created by K-State Librarians.

For further information on any of these topics please contact Rosemary Boggs rboggs@ksu.edu to request access to the K-State Online class entitled "Faculty Modules for Distance Teaching".

This checklist was developed at K-State and is offered to faculty members who use it to ensure that elements of their online courses contain key quality indicators. Resources used with the checklist are housed in this particular area of the wiki and are specific to Kansas State University. Plans are to expand this section of the wiki with good examples of the items mentioned in the checklist. For example, a welcome message that a faculty member uses in her online class will be posted. Video or interactive html will be used to show best practices and quality online delivery.

4.4.4. Faculty Share Area

The E-Learning Faculty Modules site specifically was built for K-State faculty and staff as a training tool for teaching distance classes. Therefore, much of the information posted by campus experts must be monitored and can only be changed with special permission. Even with that stipulation, the goal is for K-State faculty to share information, teaching experiences and digital resources with other faculty. The *Faculty Share* area facilitates this interaction as faculty members are encouraged to post on a particular topic with others then adding their expertise. The Faculty Share area offers an informal way for faculty to connect with others on campus. Those who request an account and are given rights to the wiki can post to this area. Figure 11 provides a view of the Faculty Share area of the wiki.

4.4.5. Best Practices

The *Best Practices* section is a collection of best strategies from online courses, short courses, and trainings. This section is currently under construction. Figure 12 provides a view of the Best Practices area of the wiki.

Figure 11. Faculty Share

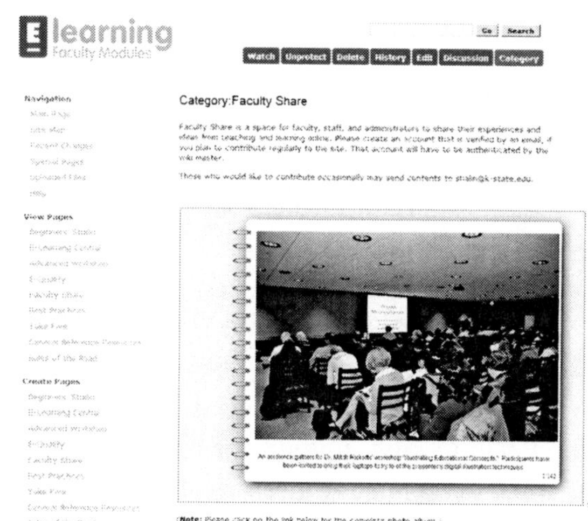

4.4.6. Take Five

Technology rapidly changes and new instructional tools often become available. The *Take* Five section of the E-Learning Faculty Modules is devoted to highlighting, in five minute clips, teaching

Figure 12. Best Practices

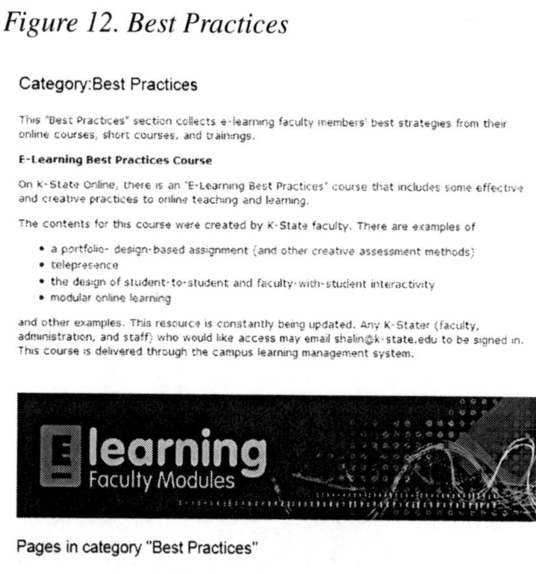

Category:Best Practices

This "Best Practices" section collects e-learning faculty members' best strategies from their online courses, short courses, and trainings.

E-Learning Best Practices Course

On K-State Online, there is an "E-Learning Best Practices" course that includes some effective and creative practices to online teaching and learning.

The contents for this course were created by K-State faculty. There are examples of

- a portfolio- design-based assignment (and other creative assessment methods)
- telepresence
- the design of student-to-student and faculty-with-student interactivity
- modular online learning

and other examples. This resource is constantly being updated. Any K-Stater (faculty, administration, and staff) who would like access may email shalin@k-state.edu to be signed in. This course is delivered through the campus learning management system.

learning
Faculty Modules

Pages in category "Best Practices"

The following 5 pages are in this category, out of 5 total.

B

- Building Effective Study Guides for Online Learning and Assessment
- Building and Analyzing Node-Link Diagrams to Understand Social Networks

P

- Planning before Executing in Multimedia

techniques specific to particular technologies. K-State IT staff, instructional designers and faculty members share their expertise and knowledge and are available for further discussion if online instructors require more information. Figure 13 provides a view of the Take Five Section and Table 3 contains information about the segments in this section.

Table 3. Take Five topics and presenters

Wikis	Dr. Roger McHaney
Immersive Simulation	Dr. Roger McHaney
Video Creation	Brent Anders
Blogs	Dr. Linda Yarrow
K-State Online Analytics	Scott Finkeldei
Open Educational Resources	Dr. Brian Lindshield
Under construction	
Twitter	Dr. Noel Schulz
E-Portfolios	Dr. Royce Ann Collins
Electronic Participation Rubrics	Dr. Doris Wright Carroll
Producing Mobile Friendly Materials for iPad or Smart Phones	Dr. Andy Bennett
Accessibility Tools	Jason Maseberg-Tomlinson

4.4.7. General Reference Resources

A *General Reference* section was added to provide additional resources useful for online teaching. This section contains a glossary of terms and updated e-learning information. Figure 14 provides a view of this section of the wiki. In addition, at the end of each Stand Alone module, contact information is given for K-State experts who developed the material and can provide further detail.

4.4.8. Rules of the Road

Excellent instruction involves certain key themes whether delivered in a face- to- face, blended or online format. In many instances different delivery methods are more effective with different tools, techniques and, in some cases, policies. To ensure faculty are aware of these nuances, current policies from the university, state, and federal agencies directly related to distance instruction are posted in the *Rules of the Road* section. This section helps provide faculty members with an awareness of Rules of the Road and an understanding of the implications of each. Figure 15 provides a view from this part of the wiki.

Figure 13. Take Five

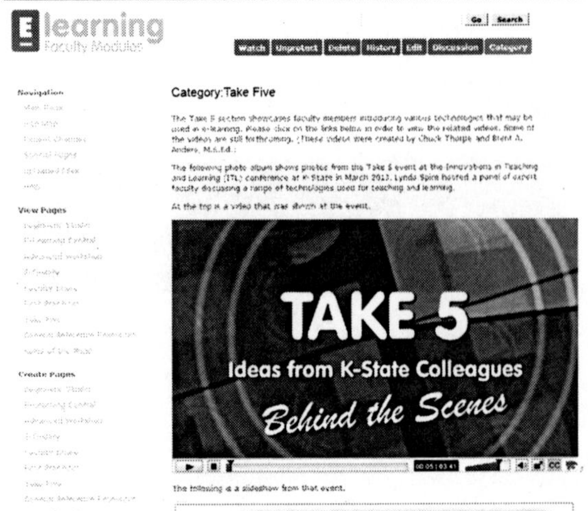

Figure 14. General Reference Resources

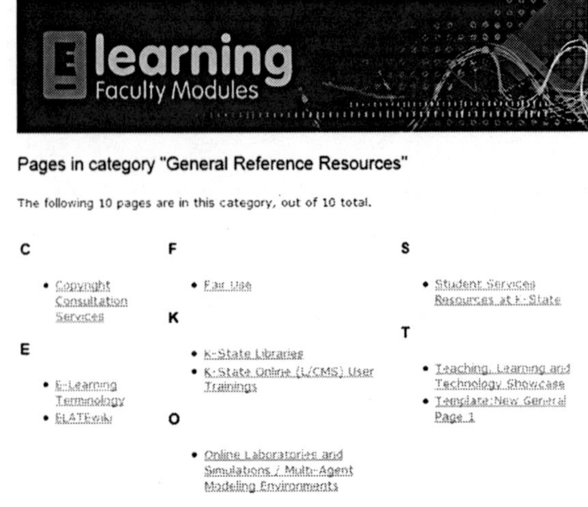

Figure 15. Rules of the Road

Category:Rules of the Road

This area of the wiki consists of a compilation of policies related to online instruction. The content of this section is divided into five sections: Division of Continuing Education, Kansas State University, Kansas Board of Regents, Higher Learning Commission and the United States Department of Education. In many cases, there is a brief explanation of the policy with a link to the actual policy. Online education has recently received a lot of attention from many agencies and many new policies exist. As a result, it is extremely important that all K-State faculty members teaching online be familiar with the information in this part of the wiki.

Lynda Spire (lspire@k-state.edu) is the individual in charge of this area. Any ideas for content in this area should be sent to her.

Pages in category "Rules of the Road"

The following 6 pages are in this category, out of 6 total.

D

- Division of Continuing Education

H

- Higher Learning Commission

K

- Kansas Board of Regents
- Kansas State University

T

- Template:Rules of the Road

U

- United States Department of Education

4.5. Wiki Oversight and Quality

Collaboration is at the heart of wiki development. With collaboration comes a variety of challenges, particularly regarding oversight and quality. Theoretically, a wiki is intended to attract users and develop a sense of community that will enforce accuracy and ensure quality (McHaney, 2009). However, a wiki provides a fertile ground for free content posting and spammers seek out wikis for a variety of reasons. In general, the spam falls into several categories. One area is *malicious damage*. This is done for fun by hackers or it may be done systematically to determine how quickly the changes are undone. This allows perpetrators to gage if more serious posting efforts are likely to remain or be quickly removed. The second category of spam relates to *posting advertising pages*. To the individuals involved, a wiki represents free server space where they can post material for themselves or their clients. This is probably the most common type of damage done to a wiki and may be perpetrated by individuals or through the use of automated programs. The third type of damage is *embedded links*. The hacker will add links to reference lists, into article bodies, and in other locations to link back to their sites or their clients' sites. The motivation here is to raise their search engine ranks by having more links back to their site from established locations (McHaney, 2012a). To combat spam and to vet new content, the implementation team believed direct oversight was needed and that the area where content could be added by those not on the team be limited to the Faculty Share Area. The team designated several administrators to handle administrative, non-academic related aspects of wiki management and to review new content.

5. LAUNCH STRATEGY

A multiphase launch strategy was used to introduce the E-Learning Faculty Modules wiki. While a team was formed to plan a formal announcement of the project, each person on the wiki development team also put forth efforts to share the project with constituents. Presentations at university conferences, introduction of the wiki to administrators, and articles for campus publications were used to make the campus aware. The instructional designers on the team used the wiki as they worked with faculty members and the Division of Continuing Education coordinators assigned to each university college also ensured that their faculty was informed. As newer additions were made to the wiki, they were also introduced. Although the wiki has been in existence for two years, efforts are still made to share this tool with faculty who may be new to the university or just moving to online teaching. See Figures 16 and 17 for a postcard used for publicity.

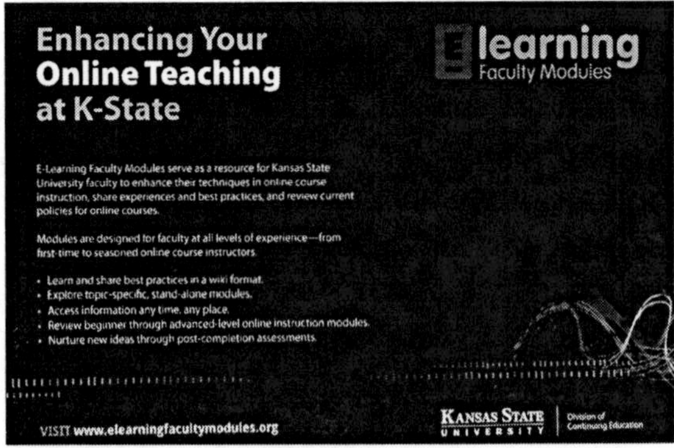

Figure 16. Postcard used for publicity (front)

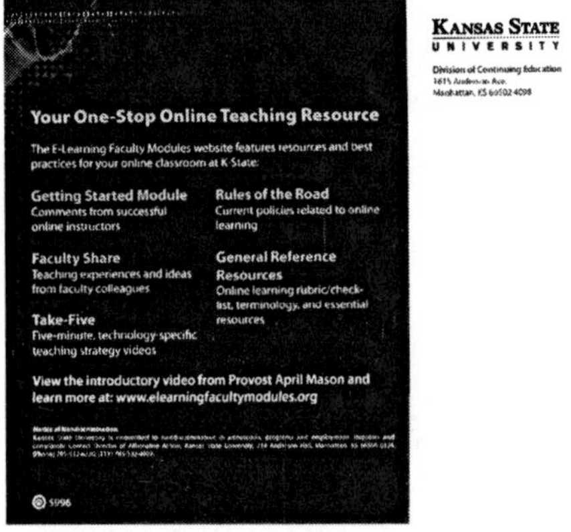

Figure 17. Postcard used for publicity (back)

6. CLOSING COMMENTS

The E-LearningFacultyModules Website was launched on October 19, 2010. It was in its fledgling stage and has since matured into today's more comprehensive site. Since it was publically released, it has been visited over 50,000 times. While use of the wiki is available to any faculty member, The Division of Continuing Education at Kansas State University now requires distance learning faculty to review and complete five of the most important *Stand Alone* modules prior to receiving new course development grants. The wiki has been used as a teaching tool by some instructors teaching classes on online instruction, and articles and presentations about the project continue to be made. The wiki project never will be completed, as new content and sections are constantly being added by the team. Wikis were conceptualized as a tool for sharing and it is hoped and expected that more faculty members will become accustomed to sharing their experiences in the *Faculty Share* area with colleagues from across campus.

The development team worked hard to conceptualize and produce the wiki. All of the team members offered their time to the project and though none of the team members had this project as their major assignment, all worked with volunteers from campus who donated their time to produce wiki content. Implementation is continuing with the development of videos and other material for posting on the site. It is believed this wiki will have a great impact on the quality of teaching at Kansas State University and is a positive step in the direction of higher quality and consistency of delivery in online courses. All involved take pride in the project which was developed by K-Staters for K-Staters.

The E-Learning Faculty Modules wiki is an example of a training tool that other universities dealing with the issue of providing high quality distance courses could develop. Any institution could use this model and develop components pertinent to their school. One of the key reasons the project developers chose this model was so they could design the content to meet Kansas State University needs and incorporate pre-existing components into the wiki.

ACKNOWLEDGMENT

E-Learning Faculty Modules exists because of the support of Dr. Sue Maes of the Division of Continuing Education (DCE) at K-State. The development team that created the wiki included: Lynda Spire, Phyllis Epps, Rosemary Boggs, Shalin Hai-Jew, Ronald Jackson, Trina McCarty, Roger McHaney, Bettie Minshall, Swasati Mukherjee,

Barb Newhouse, Charles Thorpe, Ben Ward, and Sue Williams. Faculty Resource committees included: Laura Bonella, Frederick Burrack, Martin Courtois, Vicki Clegg, Jason Coleman, Gayle Doll, Scott Finkeldei, Dorinda Lambert, Jason Maseburg-Tomlinson, Jenny Oleen, Joelle Pitts, Heather Reed, Camilla Roberts, Beth Turtle, and Karen Westman.

REFERENCES

Bishop, T. (2004). *Microsoft notebook: Wiki pioneer planted the seed and watched it grow.* Retrieved from http://www.seattlepi.com/business/158020_msftnotebook26.html

Bower, B. L. (2001). Distance education: Facing the faculty challenge. *Online Journal of Distance Learning Administration*, *4*(2).

Chapman, B. F., & Henderson, R. G. (2010). E-learning quality assurance: A perspective of business teacher educators and distance learning coordinators. *Delta Pi Epsilon Journal*, *52*(1), 16–31.

Clay, M. (1999). Development of training and support programs for distance education instructors. *Online Journal of Distance Learning Administration*, *2*(3).

Cummings, R. E. (2008). What was a wiki and why do i care? A short and usable history of wikis. In Cummings, R. E., & Barton, M. (Eds.), *Wiki Writing: Collaborative Learning in the College Classroom*. Ann Arbor, MI: University of Michigan Press. doi:10.3998/dcbooks.5871848.0001.001.

Deursen, A. V., & Visser, E. (2002). The reengineering wiki. In *Proceedings 6th European Conference on Software Maintenance and Reengineering* (CSMR), (pp. 217-220). IEEE Computer Society.

ELATEwiki. (n.d.). Retrieved from http://www.ELATEwiki.org

ElearningFacultyModules.org. (n.d.). Retrieved from http://elearningfacultymodules.org

Gilbert, D., Chen, H. L., & Sabol, J. (2008). Building learning communities with wikis. In Cummings, R. E., & Barton, M. (Eds.), *Wiki Writing: Collaborative Learning in the College Classroom*. Ann Arbor, MI: University of Michigan Press.

Hai-Jew, S., & McHaney, R. W. (2010). ELATEwiki: Evolving an e-learning faculty wiki. In Luppicini, R., & Haghi, A. K. (Eds.), *Cases on Digital Technologies in Higher Education: Issues and Challenges*. Hershey, PA: IGI Global. doi:10.4018/978-1-61520-869-2.ch001.

Hepp, M., Siorpaes, K., & Bachlechner, D. (2007, September). Harvesting wiki consensus: Using wikipedia entries for knowledge management. *IEEE Internet Computing*, 54–65. doi:10.1109/MIC.2007.110.

Keegan, D. (1996). *Foundations of distance education*. New York: Routledge.

Leuf, B., & Cunningham, W. (2001). *The wiki way: Quick collaboration on the web*. Boston: Addison-Wesley.

Majchrzak, A., Wagner, C., & Yates, D. (2006). *Corporate wiki users: Results of a survey*. Paper presented at the Symposium on Wikis. New York, NY.

McHaney, R. W. (2009). Implementation of ELATEwiki. *EDUCAUSE Quarterly*, *32*(4). Retrieved from http://www.educause.edu/EDUCAUSE+Quarterly/EDUCAUSEQuarterlyMagazineVolum/ImplementationofELATEwiki/192968.

McHaney, R. W. (2011). *The new digital shoreline: How web 2.0 and millennials are revolutionizing higher education*. Stylus Publishing.

McHaney, R. W. (2012a). The web 2.0 mandate for a transition from webmaster to wiki master. In *Open-Source Technologies for Maximizing the Creation, Deployment, and Use of Digital Resources and Information* (pp. 193–218). Hershey, PA: IGI Global. doi:10.4018/978-1-4666-2205-0.ch012.

McHaney, R. W. (2012b). *Web 2.0 and social media for business*. Ventus.

Mediawiki. (2012). Category: MediaWiki configuration settings. *MediaWiki*. Retrieved from http://www.mediawiki.org/wiki/Category:MediaWiki_configuration_settings

MediaWiki.org. (2012). Retrieved from http://www.mediawiki.org/wiki/MediaWiki

Notari, M. (2006). How to use a wiki in education: Wiki-based effective constructive learning. In *Proceedings of the 2006 International Symposium on Wikis* (pp. 131-132). New York: Association for Computing Machinery.

Parker, K. R., & Chao, J. T. (2007). Wiki as a teaching tool. *Interdisciplinary Journal of Knowledge and Learning Objects,* (3), 57-72.

Richardson, W. (2009). *Blogs, wikis, podcasts, and other powerful web tools for classrooms* (2nd ed.). Thousand Oaks, CA: Corwin Press.

Seitzinger, J. (2006). *Be constructive: Blogs, podcasts, and wikis as constructivist learning tools*. Learning Solutions e-Magazine.

Simpson, O. (2013). *Supporting students in online, open & distance learning*. New York: Routledge.

Wikipedia. (2012, November 30). *Wikipedia.* Retrieved from http://en.wikipedia.org

APPENDIX

K-State Quality E-Learning Checklist

http://elearningfacultymodules.org/uploaded/QualityELearningChecklist.pdf

Chapter 7
Multimodal Mapping of a University's Formal and Informal Online Brand:
Using NodeXL to Extract Social Network Data in Tweets, Digital Contents, and Relational Ties

Shalin Hai-Jew
Kansas State University, USA

ABSTRACT

With the popularization of the Social Web (or Read-Write Web) and millions of participants in these interactive spaces, institutions of higher education have found it necessary to create online presences to promote their university brands, presence, and reputation. An important aspect of that engagement involves being aware of how their brand is represented informally (and formally) on social media platforms. Universities have traditionally maintained thin channels of formalized communications through official media channels, but in this participatory new media age, the user-generated contents and communications are created independent of the formal public relations offices. The university brand is evolving independently of official controls. Ex-post interventions to protect university reputation and brand may be too little, too late, and much of the contents are beyond the purview of the formal university. Various offices and clubs have institutional accounts on Facebook as well as wide representation of their faculty, staff, administrators, and students online. There are various microblogging accounts on Twitter. Various photo and video contents related to the institution may be found on photo- and video-sharing sites, like Flickr, and there are video channels on YouTube. All this digital content is widely available and may serve as points-of-contact for the close-in to more distal stakeholders and publics related to the institution. A recently available open-source tool enhances the capability for crawling (extracting data) these various social media platforms (through their Application Programming Interfaces or "APIs") and enables the capture, analysis, and social network visualization of broadly available public information. Further, this tool enables the analysis of previously hidden information. This chapter introduces the application of Network Overview, Discovery and Exploration for Excel (NodeXL) to the empirical and multimodal analysis of a university's electronic presence on various social media platforms and offers some initial ideas for the analytical value of such an approach.

DOI: 10.4018/978-1-4666-4462-5.ch007

INTRODUCTION

Web 2.0, the so-called Read-Write Web, has been lauded as a major vector for human connectivity. This social Web has enabled mediated connections between people regardless of distance, nationality, social backgrounds, or languages. Social media platforms are online spaces designed for human social interactions, and many of them attract different user bases. These include social networks, multimedia (photo -, video-, slideshow- and other) sharing sites, blogging sites, microblogging sites, wikis, discussion forums, virtual worlds, and mash-ups of various functionalities of the above. The sites all have different functionalities, vetting of human identities, interface designs, and terms of agreement (end user license agreement or EULAs). Currently, sites like Facebook and Twitter are some of the most trafficked Websites in the world, accessible on a range of mobile and other computing devices.

Ideally, socio-technical systems, which are designed for human interactions and engagement, should be designed to enhance human actualization and social support for others (Lanier, 2010). For all the efforts at proper management of such sites, there are examples of anti-social behavior: content pollution, self-promotion, malicious content, copyright infringements, pornography, and spam. There are attempts to game the system or compromise information. Further, not all accounts are humans; rather, there are accounts set up for robots ('bots), cyborgs (people and robots posting contents together), and humans.

The social connections that arise through social media platforms have been described in various ways. For many, these are "loose ties," with light connections between people who are essentially strangers. There are instances of "weak cooperation" between individuals who express themselves through videos and photos, often without direct awareness of each other until certain digital artifacts are published and shared. Others are sparked by social media to participate in mass events like flash mobs. Strangers play augmented reality games on their mobile devices and interact with each other within the rules of the game. The movement of peoples en masse to social media platforms has been a distinct phenomenon among youth, many of whom are university students. This means that universities that want to engage their students in electronic spaces would benefit from being aware of where their students are engaging and knowing how to teach them.

Data extractions (or crawls) from social media sites may shed light on these various online communities, their structures, and their functions. This knowledge may support university outreach and (formal and informal) branding endeavors.

A REVIEW OF THE LITERATURE

To offer a brief overview: research into social networks started in the early 20th century within sociology. Researchers started to create quantitative measures of network relationships in the 1930s with sociometry. Psychologists contributed to this work in the 1940s by formally defining cliques (or subnetworks). In the 1950s and 1960s, anthropologists started applying social network analysis to their work. Some researchers integrated elements of game theory and economics into their social network analyses—for a highly multi-disciplinary approach. Various researchers have since contributed rich research and theorizing about social networks. In the 2000s, the computing sciences offered ways to analyze and visualize social networks.

To contextualize, there are some basic governing logics and underlying assumptions. One central concept is that much of human endeavor occurs in social groupings and fairly stable human relationships (defined by social roles, bureaucratic structures, social practices, and others). Human groups tend to be fairly hierarchical, and those with power accrue much more than others in terms of decision-making, power, information, and resources. They are theorized to have a clearer sense of a social network than others who are relatively less privileged in terms of positions. Human connections matter. People do not connect randomly, but they tend to build relationships in homophilous ways, with similarity being attracted to similarity (or "preferential attachment"). On some work teams, heterophily (the like of differences) is preferred to ensure a diverse skill set and variant perspectives. Social network analysis involves the analysis of the structural aspects of such connections. The proximity of an individual's nodes suggests a direct influence; network analysis shows that an influential node may have distal influence as well (influence at a distance). The structure of a network may shed light on its capabilities.

Other canonical concepts examine how resources, practices, and ideas "diffuse" or flow through a network along certain human channels. A flow may be stopped at a particular node based on particular threshold effects (a signal not reaching a particular threshold for that node to respond). That said, information may also flow around a non-responsive node through lines of acquaintance, trust, and familiarity.

People are said to be separated from each other by "degrees of separation" or certain hops from node-to-node to connect with another. "Power laws" are at play in many scale-free social networks in which a small percentage of nodes are the most powerful, popular, influential, and rewarded, with a "long tail" of others who are not. "Small world" networks are described as having small clusters of people who are close to each other (with dense ties or edges), and then a few degrees of separation among even stranger nodes.

Figure 1 provides a sense of a simple node-link depiction. At the near-center is the focal node, or the ego around which there is an ego neighborhood. This neighborhood of direct ties consists of so-called "alters". A one-degree trawl of the network includes a listing of all those with direct ties to the focal node. A 1.5 degree crawl involves

Figure 1. Degrees or levels in social networks

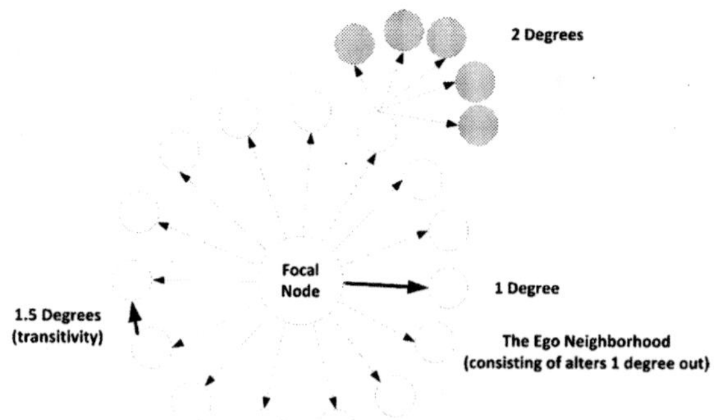

transitivity or the connections between the alters themselves. (If a -> b, and b-> c, then a-> c.) A two-degree capture of the focal node's network involves not only the ego neighborhood but all the ego neighborhoods of the alters for that focal node.

Social network analysis is supported by the so-called Two-Step Flow of Information model (also known as the Multistep Flow Model), which suggests that most people rely on "opinion leaders" whom they know and trust to vet their intake of news—in order to have a sense-making frame for that information. The forwarding of links and news headlines is one way that this intermediation occurs.

In terms of graph visualizations, social networks are depicted as node-link diagrams. On a two-dimensional graph, nodes represent entities or egos; links represent relationships (of varying types, intensities, and frequencies). Here, a core-periphery dynamic is in play. Layout algorithms place the most powerful nodes ("fat nodes") at the center of the two-dimensional space, and the least connected or engaged nodes ("thin nodes") are in the periphery. A node may be influential in one community but peripheral in another. Peripheral nodes should not be seen as "marginal" simply because they are not central in one grouping; many such nodes serve as critical bridging (boundary-spanning) nodes between communities and provide powerful value that way. Social networks that are densely connected are theoretically considered positive for democratization, with a more egalitarian flow of information and resources. These networks are considered to have interaction effects, and differing degrees of mutual influence. However, many densely tied networks tend to be quite homogeneous. Weak-tie networks are thought to be more outward looking, welcoming, and diverse.

Also, nodes change positions in a network over time, so there is a temporal element. Depending on the salience of an event, a particular peripheral node may gain centrality...but lose it over time, when it is no longer the focus of a particular event or activity. (Sometimes, node influence is depicted by the physical size of the node in the graph). A graph visualization is only one tool among many to understand social networks. These are inevitably used in connection with graph metrics, contextual information, and other research-based data.

In social network analysis, there are varying levels of analysis. Traditionally, these may be understood as the individual node (or entity); dyads (pairs of two nodes), triads (groups of three nodes), and motifs (various sub-structures in various combinations of nodes); the clique (or sub-network), and the entire social network. While this may sound straightforward, there are challenges to defining the boundaries of social networks. Table 1 provides an overview of these levels of analysis and some measures that are applied.

To elaborate, cognitive social networks focus on perceptions of the network at the ego node, motif, clique, and network levels. Here, the point-of-view matters and will affect what is able to be seen of the network from the particular location of a node, entity, or group in the structure. The more active and powerful nodes have the most accurate perspectives of the network and often show themselves to be the most effective informants. Kaplan (2012) writes of geography and human culture: "A good place to understand the present, and to ask questions about the future, is on the ground, traveling as slowly as possible" (p. xiii). In a sense, understanding a human geographical network may involve working at very local levels with particular informants or groups of informants.

Researchers have begun to analyze the "sociology of online knowledge" by using electronic research (Meyer & Schroeder, 2009). Such research may be done with artificial as well as real-world data. Real-world data extractions from microblogging sites, for example, are tied to "naturalistic interactions" and are similar to information seeking in more traditional environments (Efron & Winget, 2010, n.p.). In the past few years, social network analysts have started studying social media platforms and extrapolating social network structures (network topologies) from "crawled" data extractions. This is seen as providing empirical bases for particular observations of public communities, their communications, their shared multimedia objects, and other elements. Electronic communications may enhance the efficiencies in the movements of information, and they may even alter the structures of networks. Online Social Networks (OSNs) are seen to display small world and scale-free properties, with power law applications (highly privileged few nodes).

SOCIAL MEDIA PLATFORMS

To understand online social network analysis, it is important to consider the various types of social media platforms that are in wide use today. These various types have been presented on a continuum from most static (least-often updated by users) to the most dynamic (most-often updated by users). At the most static are digital content sharing platforms; then Web logs and video logs (and the more old-school forums); wikis; open-source collaborative work sites; email networks; social networking sites, and microblogging / Short Message Service (SMS) sites. These are conceptualized as general communications vehicles and not particular dedicated ones. This is a generalit

Table 1. Four general levels of structural analysis in social network analysis and analytical factors

Local Node-Level Measure				
	Individual Node (Agent, Ego, or Entity)	**Dyads, Triads, and other Motifs**	**Clique (including Sub-Cliques, Sub- Networks, or Islands)**	**Social Network**
Degree centrality	In-degree / out-degree	Frequency counts	In-degree / out-degree	In-degree / out-degree
Bias	Tendencies or propensities of the node particularly in relation to decision-making (and thresholds before actions may be sparked); nodes are depicted as "multiplex" or multi-faceted		Cultural or behavioral tendencies of the respective cliques and sub-cliques	Cultural or behavioral tendencies of the respective social network
Type of node	Types of nodes		Multimodal analysis	Multimodal analysis
Global Network Structure Measures				
	Individual Node (Agent, Ego, or Entity)	**Dyads, Triads, and other Motifs**	**Clique (including Sub-Cliques, Sub- networks, or Islands)**	**Social Network**
Betweenness centrality				The total number of shortest paths for each pair of dyadic nodes (with the understanding that information and resources move between the shortest paths in a social network); the importance of a node as a recipient of information
Closeness centrality				The geodesic path distance between a node and every other node
Eigenvector centrality (diversity)				The distance between a node and every other node, with those connected to higher-value or popular nodes equated with a greater value; the importance of a node in a network
Clustering coefficient				The aggregating for multiple nodes based around definitions of similarity or proximity or other closeness factor among an ego neighborhood's proximate nodes; transitivity
Geodesic distance of the network (diameter)				The farthest distance between the furthermost nodes in a social network
Motif (censuses)		Various types of identified structures of relationships among different numbers of vertices (nodes)	Internal structures and patterns	Internal structures and patterns

so there will certainly be exceptions in different platforms and their levels of activity.

Figure 2 provides a generalized view of social media, writ large. Semi-static networks may be crawled occasionally for a particular slice-in-time view. The more often digital contents and messages are updated, the more critical it is to conduct more frequent data crawls of the site to update the information. For critical events, data crawls are continuous with real-time captures of information.

An abstraction of the process of data extraction from social media platforms and the ensuing analysis is depicted in Figure 3. The visual is to be read left-to-right. At the far left is the contextual analysis to set the baseline for the university's presence on social media sites and the outreach, branding, and marketing needs. Here, it is important to identify university-related accounts and search terms as leads for various data crawls. (In some written accounts, this is called the "crawl frontier" for social media sites.) Separate strategies are applied for each of the social media platforms because of how the platforms collect data, how the Application Programming Interfaces (APIs) work, how the data extraction software functions, and what the layout algorithms mean in terms of the encapsulated calculations. The actual data extractions are then actualized. These take from under an hour to many days depending on the size of the network being acquired. The data is processed, and social network visualizations are created. The data is analyzed in conjunction with other related information. The analysts then apply their specialty to the data in order to design outreaches. Those plans are actualized, their results are measured, and the process may repeat.

There are wide ranges of variations in how this research may be conducted. There may be pre-processing of data before visualizaitons are run; there may be post-processing as well. Further, there may be a wide range of research questions that may be asked.

NODEXL OPEN-SOURCE SOFTWARE TOOL

A popular open-source tool that enables the crawling of some current social media platforms is Network Overview, Discovery and Exploration for Excel (NodeXL) (formerly .NetMap), created under the auspices of the Social Media Research Foundation (http://www.smrfoundation.

Figure 2. Semi-static to dynamic continuum of social media platforms

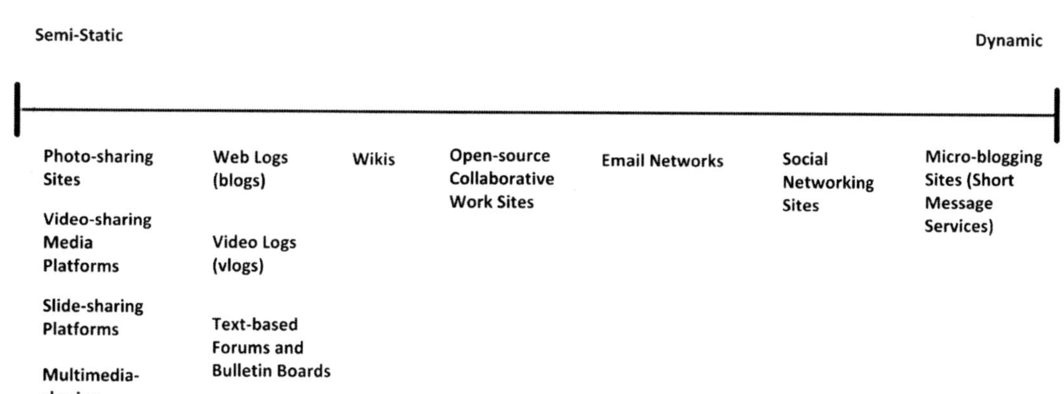

org/), with a tagline of "Open Tools, Open Data, Open Scholarship for Social Media," and released through the CodePlex site (http://nodexl.codeplex.com/). The makers of this tool have worked with developers to access the APIs of major social media platforms, who make such public data more widely accessible because it helps drive traffic to the social media platform (Jung & Lee, 2010). The tools that may currently be accessed are Facebook (limited), Twitter, Flickr, and YouTube. Additional Web crawls may be possible with the addition of a plugin from Uberlink's The Virtual Observatory for the Study of Online Networks (VOSON) (http://www.uberlink.com/), which makes its servers available for Web crawling and the social network depictions of http networks (only if the seed URLs are approved by their team). Wikis, blogs, and email accounts may be crawled as well but entail further complexities (Hansen, Smith, & Schneiderman, 2011). This software tool provides a range of options for social network analysis and visualizations. (Other "helper applications" may add value to social media by enabling other types of data extractions.)

The type of data capture here is known as Representational State Transfers (REST). These are slice-in-time captures, not streaming or dynamic captures.

To maintain the privacy protections promised by various social media platforms, crawlers that download information from social media sites are privacy-compliant (Catanese, DeMeo, Ferrara, Fiumara, & Provetti, 2011). This is so for NodeXL as well. Research into privacy on social media platforms shows that users tend to be ambivalent about privacy. Even so, privacy concerns have not been found to restrain people from participating in social networking platforms, in part, because there are misconceptions about people's privacy rights and powers in online sites. Many have an outsized sense of their amount of control over their private information. Researchers found "evidence of members' misconceptions about the online community's actual size and composition, and about

Figure 3. Extracting data from social media platforms for formal and informal branding analysis

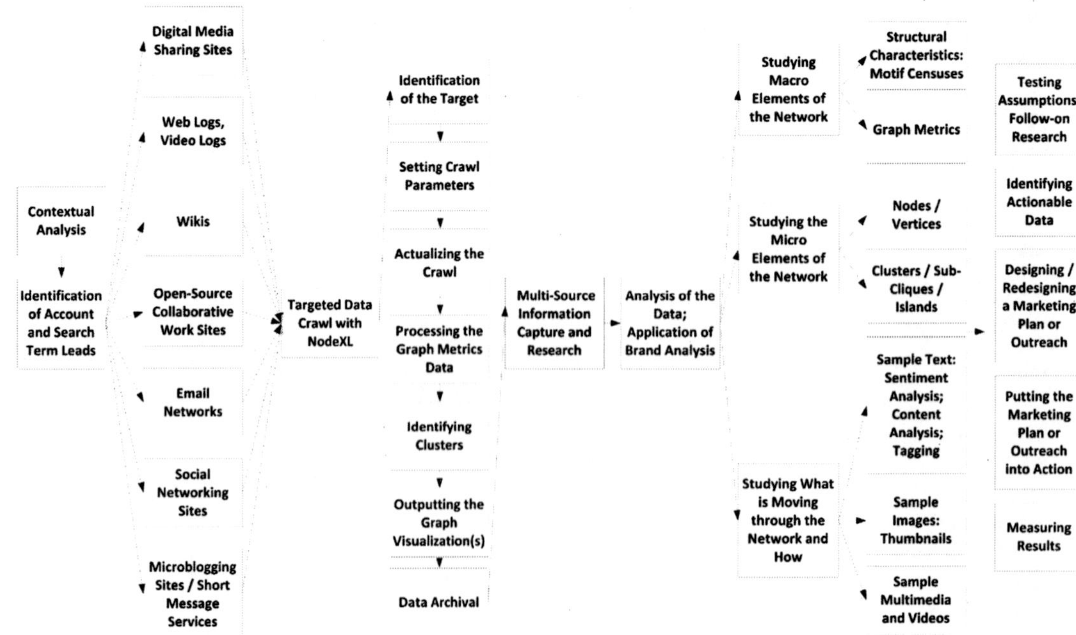

the visibility of members' profiles" (Acquisti & Gross, 2006, p. 1).

Figure 4 shows NodeXL on pause per the requirements of the social media platform's download limitations during a data crawl. This NodeXL template is built over the Excel tool, and all Excel functionalities may be applied to any dataset created from the NodeXL add-in (plug-in).

Effectively conducting a data crawl involves a depth of knowledge and various dependencies on multiple computer systems. New researchers would do well to put the tool through its paces by conducting many dozens of data crawls on the respective social media platforms before striving to make initial exploratory observations. Further, it helps to have a real-world expectation for how long a crawl may take. Those that are too large will result in no usable information capture. Those that are too small will be too limited to draw any semi-valid conclusion. It may help to have a dedicated machine to conduct the crawls, so the crawl is not interrupted. To get a sense of the complexity of this, a quote from one of the NodeXL's programmer's back-of-the-envelope rough calculations was quoted from the NodeXL community site. Wangela wrote in May 10, 2012:

Can you estimate how long it will take to "import from Twitter user's network" if I choose the following options:

- User has 15,000 followers, is following 7,000.
- Add a vertex for both followers and following.
- Add an edge for each followed/following relationship.
- 1.5 levels.
- I have a Twitter account and have authorized it.

(Note: I tried this with much more rigorous options (2 levels, replies and mentions relationships, include latest tweet column) and it kept having to retry each hour, but only got a partial network after about 15 hours and is taking a long time to show the graph for a sheet with 196K edges, so I

Figure 4. A screenshot of the NodeXL® add-in to Microsoft Excel®

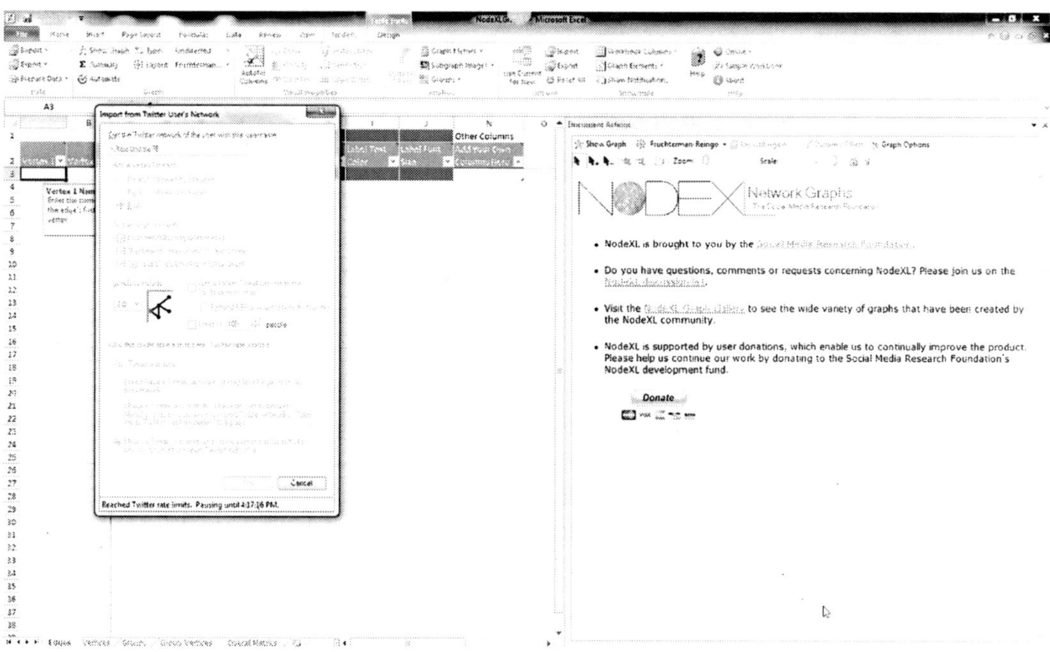

gave up. The file so far is 82 MB. I want to try this again with the proposed lesser options but don't want to start the task if I'm not going to be able to finish it tomorrow.) ("Size Limits on Twitter Import," 2012)

tcap479, identified as a Coordinator, writes on May 10, 2012:

- For 1.0 starting point, the IDs of the user's followers and followings are obtained 5,000 at a time, so 22,000 followers and followings for user take 5 requests.
- Follower and friend names are obtained 100 at a time, so 22,000 follower and following names take 220 additional requests.
- For the 1.5 connections, must get follower and following IDs for each of the 22,000 followers and followings. Assuming each of the followers and followings has no more than 5,000 followers and followings, this requires 22,000 additional requests.
- Total requests: At least 22,225.
- Maximum requests allows before a one-hour pause: 350.
- Minimum number of one-hour pauses: 64.

Answer: It will take at least 3 days. And that assumes that Twitter won't arbitrarily kick you out in the middle of getting the network, which it has been known to do at times of high traffic. ("Size Limits on Twitter Import," 2012)

Some of the social media platforms offer faster data crawls if individuals have an account on their system. Some not only require an account but also application for "whitelisting," so the machines may prioritize which crawls should go faster (in trade for the user's identity through email-verified accounts or other types of authentication.).

The NodeXL tool, as of this publication, does not have an initial indicator of the size of a network crawl. A dataset may be re-run to collect new information using the old or new parameters (Smith, Schneiderman, Milic-Frayling, Rodrigues, Barash, Dunne, Capone, Perer, & Gleave, 2009). All crawls are necessarily somewhat constrained because of various limitations of the software tools, social media platforms, and commonplace computers.

Academic Scholarship and Social Media

In some ways, the social media platforms have been a support for academic culture. The media platforms are used for widespread research in terms of e-governance and public policymaking (Kolcz, 2012). Social media platforms enable collaborations between political elites and users of social media (Auer, 2011, p. 709). Various communities of learning coalesce around persistent social media, through which their collaborations are shared and archived.

Microblogging sites are used for Massively Open Online Courses (MOOCs), stand-alone courses, and as augmentation to online and blended courses. Scholars use Twitter to cite scholarly works, particularly in fast-moving discourses (Priem & Costello, 2010). Academics use microblogging sites like Twitter to promote their careers:

Findings indicate that scholars participating on Twitter (1) shared information, resources, and media relating to their professional practice; (2) shared information about their classroom and their students; (3) requested assistance from and offered suggestions to others; (4) engaged in social commentary; (5) engaged in digital identity and impression management; (6) sought to network and make connections with others; and (7) highlighted their participation in online networks other than Twitter. These findings assist the field in understanding the emerging practice of scholarly participation in online networks (Veletsianos, 2012, p. 336).

The researcher identified a number of themes in scholars' Twitter practices: "information, resource, and media sharing; expanding learning opportunities beyond the confines of the classroom; requesting assistance and offering suggestions; living social public lives; digital identity and impression management; connecting and networking; presence across multiple online social networks" (Veletsianos, 2012, p. 342). Social networking sites are used to create learning communities with individuals with shared interests. Student work, both individual and group, is showcases on wikis, blogs, and content-sharing sites (both video- and photo-sharing). Plenty of academic contents are shared on multimedia-sharing sites. Academic conferences encourage the uses of microblogging sites as a public and unofficial back-channel for communications, with a resulting electronic "event graph" from the interactions. Microblogged messages are collated using particular hashtags (indicated by a # and a keyword) often linked to the event or sponsoring organization. Some researchers are studying some of the different structural patterns from such events (Hansen, Smith, & Schneiuderman, 2011). Other researchers have suggested that the electronic residuals from conferences have limited usefulness post-event, particularly for those who were not part of the direct event (Ebner, Mühlburger, Schaffert, Schiefner, Reinhardt, & Wheeler, 2010).

For learners, social media platforms may mitigate "friendsickness," which may occur with the "loss of connection to old friends when a young person moves away to college" (Paul & Brier, 2001, as cited in Ellison, Steinfield, & Lampe, 2007, p. 1148). Using social media, college students may maintain their friend ties from high school. They may find emotional resilience and support online. Another researcher found Facebook at the center of the "identity politics" of being a student, which plays a critical role in the addressing of role conflicts that students experience "in their relationships with university work, teaching staff, academic conventions" (Selwyn, 2009, p. 157). In a survey of undergraduate students, social networking sites were found to support student formation and maintenance of social capital, friendship bonding, and bridging social circles; Facebook use was linked to "measures of psychological well-being" (Ellison, Steinfield, & Lampe, 2007, p. 1143). Social networking sites have been particularly helpful for those college students with lower self-esteem bridge social capital through heterogeneous social networks created online (Steinfield, Ellison, & Lampe, 2008).

Individual satisfaction with the level of social support that they attain in social networks varies. It is not necessarily density or sparseness of ties that lead to satisfaction (both have been shown to be related to satisfaction, depending on the type of network and the membership and the members' respective needs). Stokes (1983) identified the importance of having a trusted confidant in the network.

KANSAS STATE UNIVERSITY IN SOCIAL MEDIA

To apply social network analysis in an academic setting, to understand a university's social presence on multiple platforms, data extractions will be conducted on a range of accounts and multimedia contents from social media platforms.

Kansas State University (K-State) was founded in 1863. It has 1,275 academic staff. This year, 19,385 undergraduates and 3,885 post-graduates are attending this land grant institution. A slightly different number is offered by the Registrar's Office, which suggests that K-State has 24,378 students enrolled in the most recent term. It has a $374 million endowment. Its official color is royal purpose, and its members are known as Wildcats. Its mascot is Willie the Wildcat. Kansas State University's mission statement reads:

The mission of Kansas State University is to foster excellent teaching, research, and service that develop a highly skilled and educated citizenry necessary to advancing the well-being of Kansas, the nation, and the international community. The university embraces diversity, encourages engagement and is committed to the discovery of knowledge, the education of undergraduate and graduate students, and improvement in the quality of life and standard of living of those we serve.

To map some of the formal and informal social media presences linked to Kansas State University, the researcher identified various accounts directly and indirectly related to K-State. The research does not claim to capture all accounts in all venues. As a matter of fact, this was only a convenience sample or selection of the available social media contents related to this university.

Microblogging Relationships and Messaging

Twitter, which was founded in 2006, is the most popular microblogging service on Earth, with emulator sites in other countries. Its approach is simple. It offers a 140-character short message service (SMS) to distribute Tweets to all those who follow particular Tweetstreams. On Twitter, there is the full spectrum of communications: personal and private messages, so-called "mass personal" messages (mediated personal messages), and highly public messages to curate networks of people around shared interests.

The lifespan of most contents is ephemeral and transient. The most long-lived re-tweeted URLs last for 200 days (Wu, Hofman, Mason, & Watts, 2011). The authors point out that ".05% of the population accounts for half of all posted URLs in Twitter (another sign of the power law); elite users of Twitter tend to be homophilous and to follow each other. That said, the Library of Congress is also archiving all the 170 billion Tweets created so far for posterity, for research, and for analysis—into perpetuity.

K-State Search Network on Twitter

First, a search for "K-State" was made on Twitter in early 2013. This would capture any mention of K-State. What resulted was a social network with 1,115 vertices, with 5,018 edges (high connectivity) of following / followed, re-tweets, and mentions (see Table 2).

The data from the crawl is depicted using the Fruchterman-Reingold force-based algorithm. In Figure 5 there is a clear center-periphery dynamic with the most deeply connected nodes in the center. This network is predominantly single-centered but has 383 clusters or groups, for a highly diversified group of clusters in the network.

Table 2. K-State search on Twitter (graph metrics)

Graph Metric	Value
Graph Type	Directed
Vertices	1115
Unique Edges	5018
Edges With Duplicates	760
Total Edges	5778
Self-Loops	1290
Reciprocated Vertex Pair Ratio	0.240310078
Reciprocated Edge Ratio	0.3875
Connected Components	366
Single-Vertex Connected Components	319
Maximum Vertices in a Connected Component	689
Maximum Edges in a Connected Component	5178
Maximum Geodesic Distance (Diameter)	11
Average Geodesic Distance	3.335514
Graph Density	0.003477953
Modularity	Not Applicable
NodeXL Version	1.0.1.229

Figure 5. K-State search on Twitter (graph)

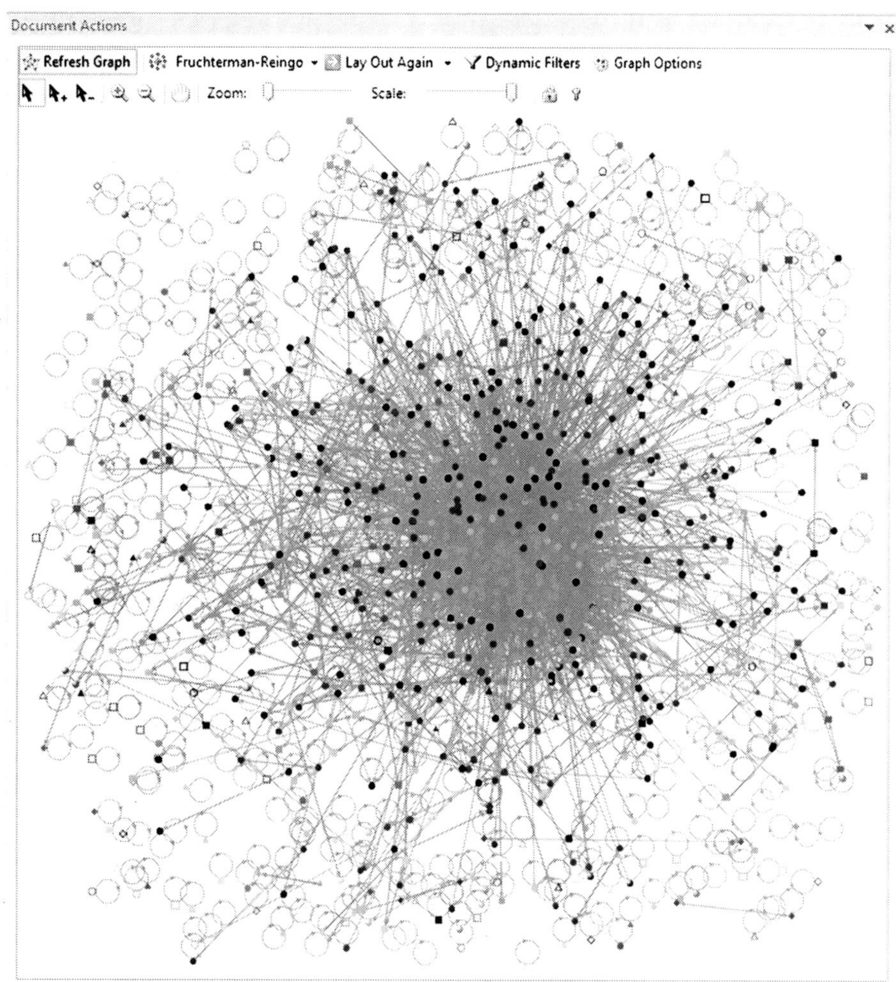

The same data is also portrayed using a Harel-Koren Multi-Scale layout algorithm in Figure 6. This also shows high density in the center but offers clearer senses of which nodes are clustered based on the spatial placement of the various nodes, along with their colors and shapes.

Hashtag #KState Search Network on Twitter

An unlimited #KState (hashtag KState) search was conducted on Twitter in early 2013 to see what sort of microblogging chatter might be occurring on Twitter. (The researcher was aware that "kstate" could also be used to indicate Kennesaw State University, but there was not a simple way—even using Boolean operators—to disambiguate the term further.) An informal perusal of some of the messages did seem to show a majority of the microblogging messages were in relation to Kansas State University though. The messages dealt with a friendly collegiate sports rivalry (see Table 3).

The hashtag #KState search network on Twitter crawl found 62 clusters of communicators using the #kstate to label the message. Indeed, the transience of the messages and moods flowing

Figure 6. K-State search on Twitter (graph 2)

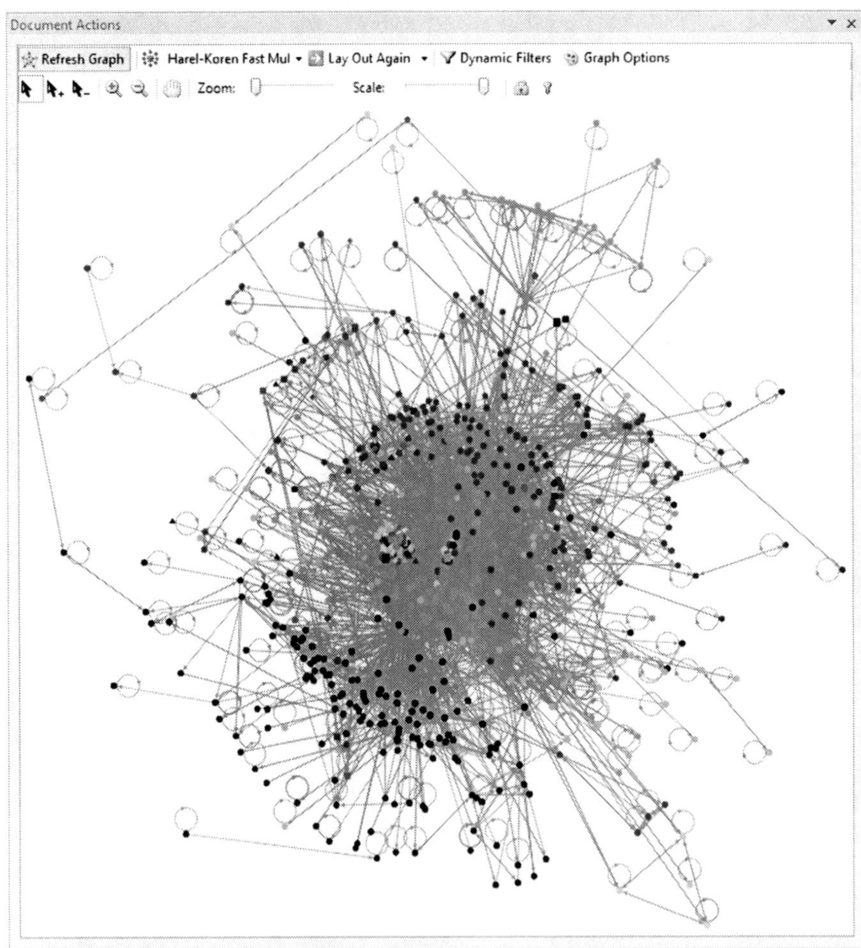

around a particular hashtagged term is common and often influenced by real-world events spilling into electronic spaces. Figure 7 shows a Harel-Koren Fast Multiscale algorithm depiction in graph form.

K-State President (kstate_pres) User Network on Twitter

Another strategy in mapping a university's social media presence involves identifying key people and mapping their networks. For example, a university president not only has a critical leadership role but also symbolic importance. Kansas State University's president models a progressive use of social network connectivity (see Table 4).

During a relatively quiet period, 12,228 vertices with 13,502 edges were captured. (An earlier crawl had found 80,000 vertices—but that was at the height of enthusiasm about a college sports event. The researcher decided to go with one that is a more typical data extraction.) Figure 8 is a visualization from the Fruchterman-Reingold force-based visualization algorithm. Ten clusters were extracted, suggesting a fairly homogeneous network.

The same data was used for a different visualization, expressed in Figure 9 as a vertical sine wave. There are varying levels of effectiveness for using particular visualizations for particular data sets and crawls on various social media platforms.

Table 3. Hashtag #KState search network on Twitter (graph metrics)

Graph Metric	Value
Graph Type	Directed
Vertices	1037
Unique Edges	9368
Edges With Duplicates	855
Total Edges	10223
Self-Loops	1140
Reciprocated Vertex Pair Ratio	0.306401766
Reciprocated Edge Ratio	0.469077391
Connected Components	52
Single-Vertex Connected Components	47
Maximum Vertices in a Connected Component	981
Maximum Edges in a Connected Component	10153
Maximum Geodesic Distance (Diameter)	9
Average Geodesic Distance	2.663492
Graph Density	0.008262809
Modularity	Not Applicable
NodeXL Version	1.0.1.229

K-State News (k_state_news) User Network on Twitter

A two-degree unlimited-person crawl of the KStateNews user network on Twitter (https://twitter.com/KStateNews) showed 10,551 vertices with 12,992 edges. The official account has 1,838 Tweets, 53 following, and 7,271 followers (see Table 5).

This K-State News user network data resulted in Figure 10 visualization using the Fruchterman-Reingold force-based layout algorithm. This visualization is especially revealing because there are such disparate clusters (8 in total), some connected in a thin way with critical bridging connectors. There does not seem to be much in the way of overlaps in this network. This could suggest some structural risks in the loss of particular nodes.

The NodeXL Graph Gallery enables a public version of the graph that is interactive. When a cursor is placed on a particular node, the name of that communicator on Twitter is highlighted. In the actual data set, hovering over a node brings up not only the name of the Tweeter but the contents of their most recent message (recorded in the .xlsx file in a separate column).

In Figure 11 scrolling into the graph above will reveal the proximity of the relationships between the various vertices. There is a zoom feature which enables a close-in view of the various nodes and their interconnectivity. See Figure 12 for a close-in view.

K-State on Facebook

The author would be remiss in not mentioning Facebook, which is a major force in social media today. Currently, the Social Network Importer for NodeXL does not enable crawling Facebook networks except for the user's own account's ego network. According to the official NodeXL site, though, just such a tool is forthcoming for the crawling of fan pages.

K-State Sports (kstatesports) User Network on Twitter

Kansas State Athletics is a source of pride (and funding) for Kansas State University. Its formal account (https://twitter.com/kstatesports) has 9,011 Tweets, 234 following, and 28,728 followers. It is a highly active account with Tweets going out

Figure 7. #KState search network on Twitter (graph)

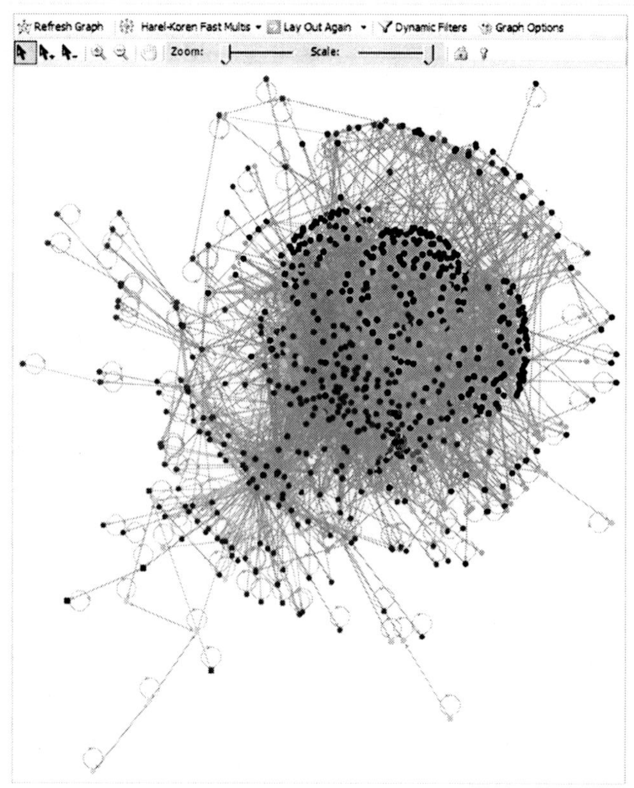

multiple times a day during intense moments of the respective sports seasons. A two-degree data crawl was captured, with no limits on the numbers of persons in the capture, but the software only captured a partial directional graph. The social network for kstatesports involved 37,581 vertices, with 40,944 unique edges (see Table 6).

There were 7 clusters or groups identified by the software. This social network is expressed as a horizontal sine wave in Figure 13.

KSREsupport User Network on Twitter

The K-State Research & Extension Support (https://twitter.com/ksresupport) site is an apparently semi-public work group that rides on an open-source microblogging platform. At the time of the data crawl, the account only had 213 Tweets, 67 followers, and 18 following (followed by the account). The most recent message had been Tweeted that day. The graph metrics are summarized in the NodeXL table (Table 7). This crawl found 19,894 nodes or vertices in a 2.0 degree data extraction.

When related groups were extracted, 14 clusters were found. These are depicted on a grid below. Some of the clusters are more insular (fewer overlapping dots of different colors) while others are more integrated with diverse members of other clusters, according to the grid visualization in Figure 14.

Grids are a type of graph that resembles treemaps to a degree, where the amount of space covered reflects the size of a particular cluster.

Table 4. K-State president user network on Twitter (graph metrics)

Graph Type	Directed
Vertices	12620
Unique Edges	13502
Edges With Duplicates	16
Total Edges	13518
Self-Loops	0
Reciprocated Vertex Pair Ratio	0.022091088
Reciprocated Edge Ratio	0.043227239
Connected Components	1
Single-Vertex Connected Components	0
Maximum Vertices in a Connected Compo-nent	12620
Maximum Edges in a Connected Component	13518
Maximum Geodesic Distance (Diameter)	4
Average Geodesic Distance	2.30551
Graph Density	8.48342E-05
Modularity	Not Appli-cable
NodeXL Version	1.0.1.229

K-State Collegian (kstatecollegian) User Network on Twitter

The Kansas State Collegian is the university's student newspaper. As such, it is a critical learning tool for journalism students. Further, it is a critical voice for students' points-of-view. This two-degree unlimited-persons crawl of the network highlighted 12,732 vertices, with 13,733 unique edges. The official account (https://twitter.com/kstatecollegian) shows that it has 2,734 Tweets, 216 following, and 2,826 followers. The most recent posting was the day before the crawl, which shows quite a bit of activity. The topics of this Twitter feed generally consisted of retweets of shortened URLs to published stories, requests for social media responses for forthcoming stories, student-related campus events, and comments about impending weather, at the time of this crawl. Only five clusters were found, suggesting a fairly heterogeneous network (see Table 8).

Figure 15 is a visual depiction of this social network using the Harel-Koren Fast Multiscale algorithm in NodeXL.

Figure 15 shows a network with some possible fragility, such as bridging nodes that are choke-points for possible information or connectivity to larger communities in this social network. A higher rate of connectivity instead of single linkages or edges to various nodes would possibly enhance the social integration of those engaging the K-State Collegian.

K-State Football Feedr (KstateFBFeedr) on Twitter

Other Twitter accounts seem to be automated robots that collect data and distribute it to subscribers. One such account is the K-State Football Feeder account (https://twitter.com/KstateFBfeedr). Such accounts capitalize on public information. The URL for this site (http://fanfeedr.com/ncaa-football/kansas-st-wildcats) was a "dead link." A data crawl may be achieved on a 'bot account as it is with those that are led by people or even cyborgs (people and 'bots together) (Chu, Gianvecchio, Wang, & Jajodia, 2010). Such accounts are not uncommon to collect news and information in an automated way to keep people in the loop (see Table 9).

A crawl of this account in early February, 2013, shows 10,742 vertices, with 13,470 edges. The social network is expressed as a graph using the Fruchterman-Reingold force-based layout algorithm, which shows 10 clusters or groups.

Figure 8. K-State president user network on Twitter (graph)

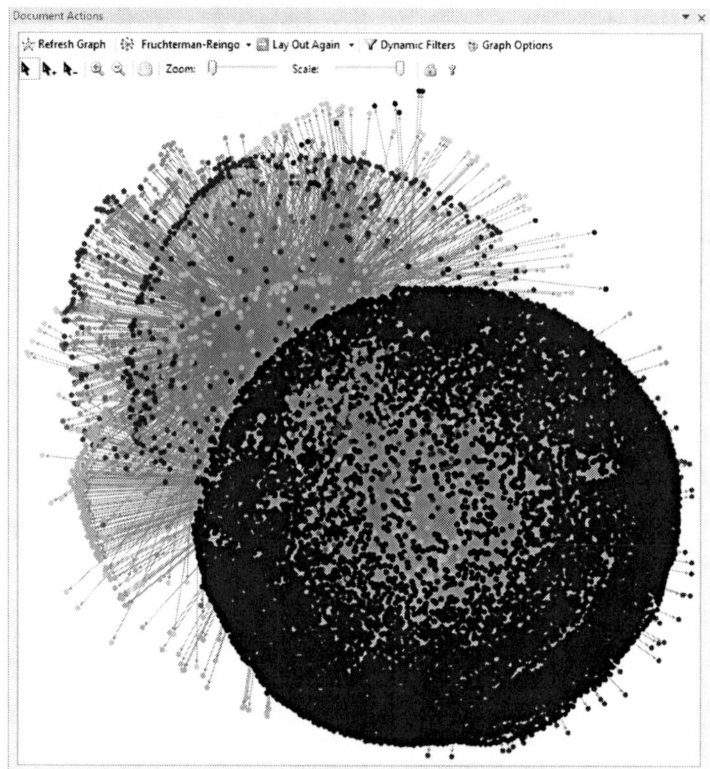

Figure 9. K-State president user network on Twitter (a vertical sine wave)

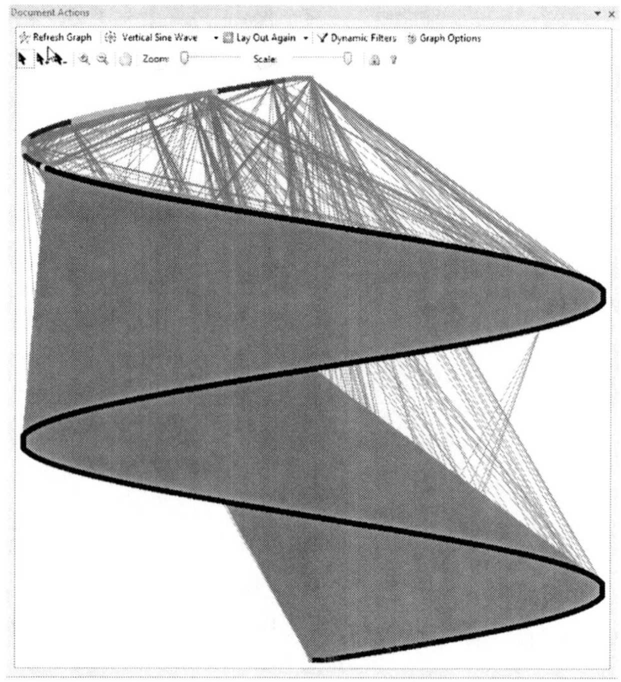

Table 5. K-State news user network on Twitter (graph metrics)

Graph Metric	Value
Graph Type	Directed
Vertices	10551
Unique Edges	12992
Edges With Duplicates	40
Total Edges	13032
Self-Loops	0
Reciprocated Vertex Pair Ratio	0.009386394
Reciprocated Edge Ratio	0.018598217
Connected Components	1
Single-Vertex Connected Components	0
Maximum Vertices in a Connected Component	10551
Maximum Edges in a Connected Component	13032
Maximum Geodesic Distance (Diameter)	4
Average Geodesic Distance	2.559059
Graph Density	0.000116896
Modularity	Not Applicable
NodeXL Version	1.0.1.229

With only 10 unique groups, this is not a highly diversified network. (However, there is more diversity in this group than for the K-State basketball statistics social network.) Figure 16 shows this social network depicted using a Fruchterman-Reingold force-based layout algorithm.

Real people may still maintain conversations and interactivity around a robot-driven account, in this case, because of a shared appreciation of college football.

Figure 10. K-State news user network on Twitter (graph)

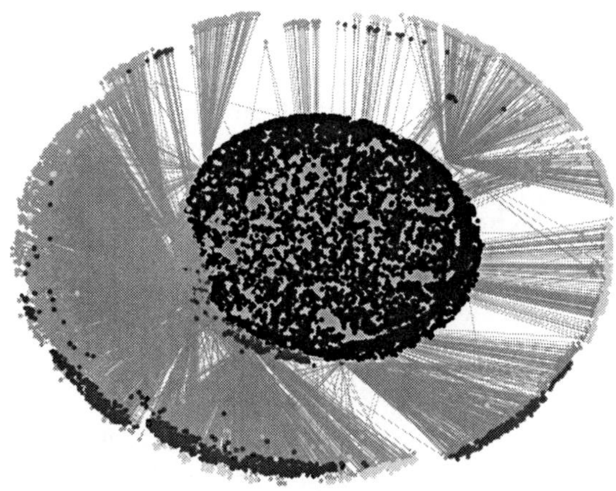

Figure 11. K-State news user network on Twitter (interactive graph)

K-State Wildcats Basketball (@KStateUpdateBB) User Network on Twitter

The KStateUpdateBB (https://twitter.com/KStateUpdateBB) account also seems to be a commercial account consisting of statistics collected by a 'bot and distributed to those who follow the account. The logo consists of a robot wearing a shirt with a Wildcat logo. This microblogging account consists of 2,861 Tweets, with 13 following, and

Figure 12. A close-up of the K-State news user network on Twitter

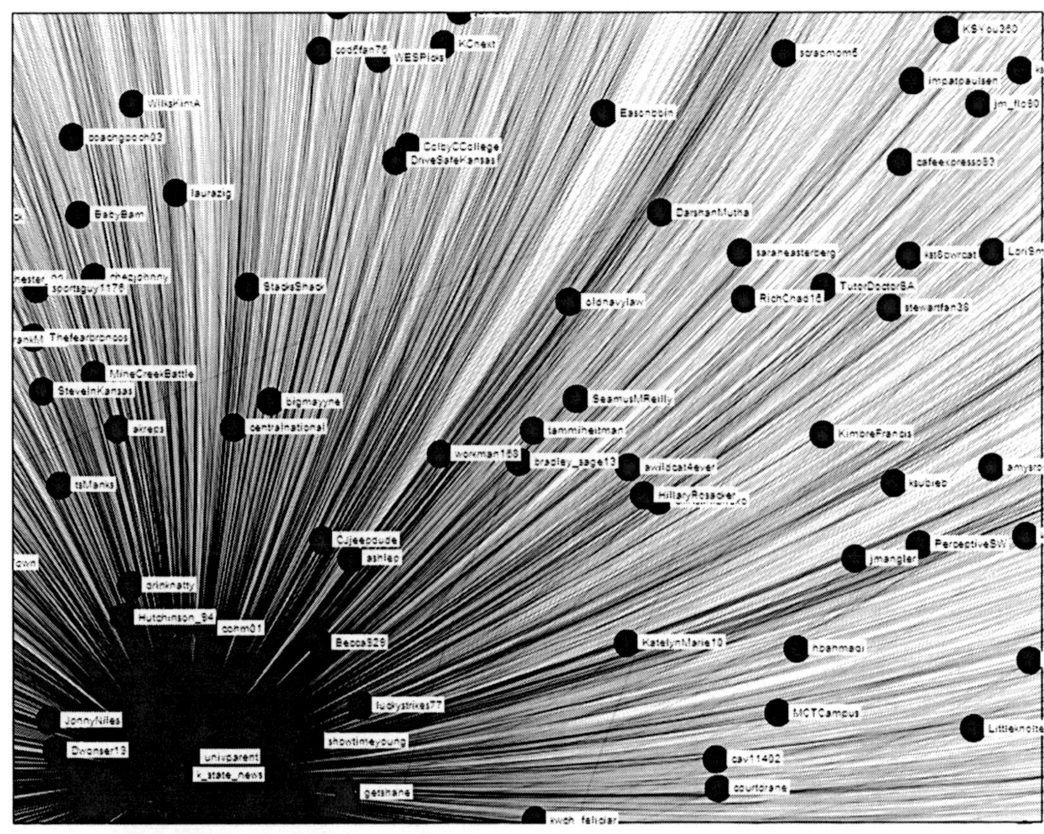

693 followers. An unlimited-persons crawl was conducted with a two-degree capture and resulted in the following graph metrics: 884 nodes and 984 unique edges (see Table 10).

There were ten clusters identified in the analysis, which does not indicate a very heterogeneous network. Of these, there seem to be two major groupings only. This K-State Wildcats Basketball user network is depicted using a Harel-Koren Fast Multiscale network graph (see Figure 17).

K-State Proud (K-State-Proud) User Network on Twitter

K-State Proud is described as a student organization of students helping each other. This organization funds a range of scholarships ("student opportunity awards") for learners. This organization's Twitter site (https://twitter.com/KStateProud) has 221 Tweets, 97 following, and 1,686 followers. The formal site for this student-led organization is http://www.found.ksu.edu/k-stateproud/. An unlimited-persons two-degree crawl of the user network for this organization found 13,258 nodes or vertices, connected by 13,746 links or edges (see Table 11).

Women of K-State (WomenofKState) User Network on Twitter

Started in January 2012, the Women-of-K-State (https://twitter.com/WomenofKState) user network is an endeavor of the university's First Lady (and member of the engineering faculty), Dr. Noel Schulz. This endeavor not only offers mentoring for female administrators, faculty, and staff, but

Table 6. K-State athletics (kstatesports) user account on Twitter (graph metrics)

Graph Metric	Value
Graph Type	Directed
Vertices	37581
Unique Edges	40944
Edges With Duplicates	16
Total Edges	40960
Self-Loops	0
Reciprocated Vertex Pair Ratio	0.002227062
Reciprocated Edge Ratio	0.004444227
Connected Components	1
Single-Vertex Connected Components	0
Maximum Vertices in a Connected Component	37581
Maximum Edges in a Connected Component	40960
Maximum Geodesic Distance (Diameter)	4
Average Geodesic Distance	2.393323
Graph Density	2.89968E-05
Modularity	Not Applicable
NodeXL Version	1.0.1.229

there are recreational activities and fun events. This user account has 82 Tweets, 48 following, and 89 followers. The account has approximately 2- 5 messages a month. An unlimited-person two-degree crawl of this network found the following, in a partial extraction: a network of 35,141 vertices, with 48,385 unique edges (see Table 12).

The network is fairly intimate, with the two nodes at the farthest points of path-distance from each other at four hops. Both the university's first

Figure 13. K-State athletics (kstatesports) user account on Twitter in a horizontal sine wave

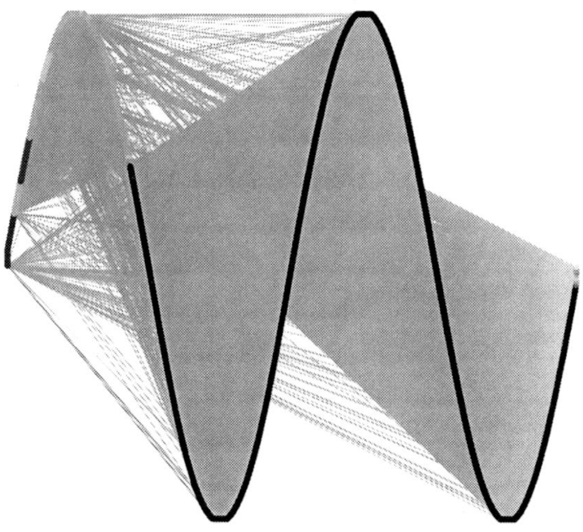

lady (@kstate_1stlady) and president (@kstate_pres) are active on this network (that would be Drs. Noel Schulz and Kirk H. Schulz). This social network is depicted using a Fruchterman-Reingold force-based layout algorithm in Figure 19.

Figure 19 shows a visualization of the 21 related clusters in this social network. The differing clusters may be understood as representational of various interest groups.

K-State Student Union Program Council (kstateUPC) User Network on Twitter

The K-State Student Union Program Council (UPC) schedules a range of entertaining, educational, and cultural activities and events for students and the larger Manhattan, Kansas, community. The events are substance-free ones, so they are inclusive of those of college age who do not drink. The formal Website for the K-State Union Program Council is http://www.k-state.edu/upc.

The official Twitter page for the kstateUPC user account is https://twitter.com/kstateUPC. At the time of the data crawl in early February 2013, the account had 840 Tweets. There were 1,071

Table 7. KSREsupport user network on Twitter (graph metrics)

Graph Metric	Value
Graph Type	Directed
Vertices	19894
Unique Edges	30647
Edges With Duplicates	1286
Total Edges	31933
Self-Loops	0
Reciprocated Vertex Pair Ratio	0.222719598
Reciprocated Edge Ratio	0.364302001
Connected Components	1
Single-Vertex Connected Components	0
Maximum Vertices in a Connected Component	19894
Maximum Edges in a Connected Component	31933
Maximum Geodesic Distance (Diameter)	4
Average Geodesic Distance	3.753718
Graph Density	7.86832E-05
Modularity	Not Applicable
NodeXL Version	1.0.1.229

following and 854 followers. The social network had 18 clusters or groups. The crawl resulted in 9,169 vertices or related accounts, and these were connected by 13,608 links (edges). The diameter of the network was 4, which suggested short paths connected the two farthest-most nodes in the network (see Table 13).

The kstateUPC user network extraction showed that there were 18 clusters in this network. This is dramatically illustrated in the Harel-Koren Fast Multiscale layout algorithm in Figure 20.

Figure 14. KSREsupport user network on Twitter in a grid

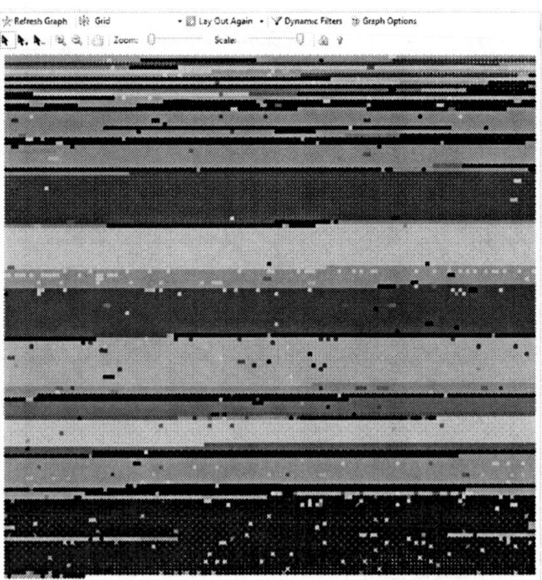

Kansas State University Salina (kstatesalina) User Network on Twitter

The K-State Salina branch campus (http://salina.k-state.edu/) focuses on arts, sciences, and business; aviation; engineering technology; family studies and human services; social work; a professional masters of technology, and continuing education. Its official Twitter account "kstatesalina" (https://twitter.com/kstatesalina) features 365 Tweets, 131 following, and 707 followers. The most recent posting was within a week and a half of the data crawl. A two-degree 400-persons (limited) data extraction found 62,216 vertices and 89,942 unique edges (The limitation was put into place after multiple unlimited crawls resulted in crashed computer systems and lost data.) (see Table 14).

This social network had 66 clusters, which indicates relatively high diversity in the social network. The K-State Salina user network on Twitter

Table 8. K-State collegian user network on Twitter (graph metrics)

Graph Type	Directed
Vertices	12732
Unique Edges	13733
Edges With Duplicates	12
Total Edges	13745
Self-Loops	0
Reciprocated Vertex Pair Ratio	0.007553535
Reciprocated Edge Ratio	0.014993813
Connected Components	1
Single-Vertex Connected Components	0
Maximum Vertices in a Connected Component	12732
Maximum Edges in a Connected Component	13745
Maximum Geodesic Distance (Diameter)	4
Average Geodesic Distance	**3.000885**
Graph Density	**8.4761E-05**
Modularity	Not Applicable
NodeXL Version	1.0.1.229

is depicted in Figure 21, using the Fruchterman-Reingold layout algorithm.

K-State Olathe (KStateOlathe) User Network on Twitter (Crawl 1)

The Olathe Innovation Campus opened in Olathe, Kansas, in April 2011. It features a curriculum with a focus on a range of distance master's programs; it also features special learning on animal health and food safety. Its official Twitter account

Figure 15. K-State collegian user network on Twitter (graph)

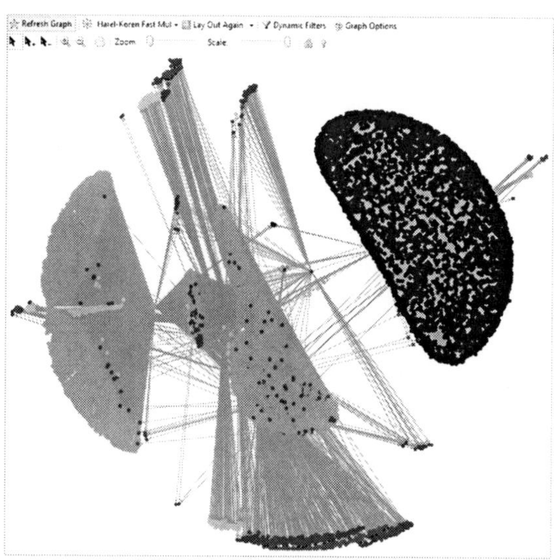

(located at https://twitter.com/KStateOlathe) only has 10 Tweets, with 30 following, and 49 followers. A partial crawl of its network was achieved in mid-February and was limited to 1,000 persons because of the failure of several attempts at an unlimited two-degree (level) crawl. The partial crawl resulted in the identification of 36,366 node, with 59,269 edges. The diameter of this social network is 4. With so few followers and yet so many vertices and ties, this suggests that some of the alters in the social network are highly connected individuals (or entities) with many connections (links) (see Table 15).

A visualization of this social network found 17 clusters. These are depicted below as a horizontal sine wave in Figure 22. Each of the different color and shape groupings indicate a different cluster. The gray vertices show the ties between the various clusters.

K-State Olathe (KStateOlathe) User Network on Twitter (Crawl 2)

A second simultaneous run on the KStateOlathe user network on Twitter was run at 2.0 degrees and

Table 9. KstateFBFeedr user network on Twitter (graph metrics)

Graph Metric	Value
Graph Type	Directed
Vertices	10742
Unique Edges	13470
Edges With Duplicates	0
Total Edges	13470
Self-Loops	0
Reciprocated Vertex Pair Ratio	0.014765707
Reciprocated Edge Ratio	0.029101707
Connected Components	1
Single-Vertex Connected Components	0
Maximum Vertices in a Connected Component	10742
Maximum Edges in a Connected Component	13470
Maximum Geodesic Distance (Diameter)	4
Average Geodesic Distance	3.184187
Graph Density	0.000116745
Modularity	Not Applicable
NodeXL Version	1.0.1.229

with no limits—to see what differences there may be with the 1,000-persons limited crawl. Again, the account at the time (a day later from the first crawl) still had 10 Tweets, 30 following, and 49 followers—which are deceptively low numbers. The degree of the crawl (2.0) adds much complexity because these pull in all the networks of the ego node's neighborhood or "alters." A no-limit crawl means that there is no artificial stop on the

Figure 16. KstateFBFeedr user network on Twitter (graph)

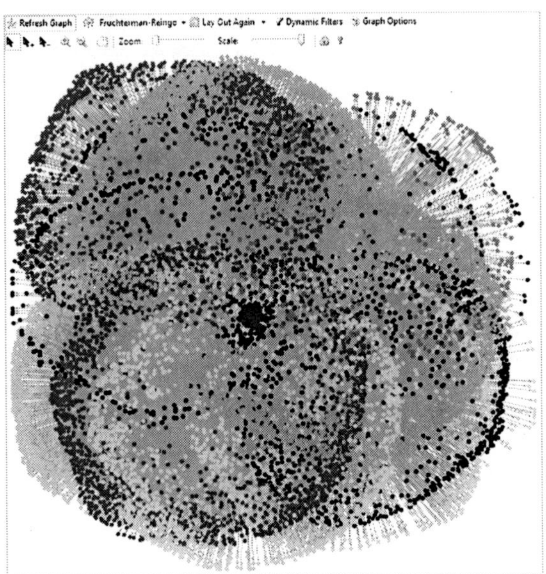

number of persons (nodes) represented in the crawl (see Table 16).

Eight clusters were identified as contrasted to the 17 found of the social network with a more limited crawl. It may be that with a larger data set, what appeared to be variances were less pronounced, and there were some consolidations of prior groupings. In Figure 23, this data was represented as a horizontal sine wave to echo the original social network visualization with the limited crawl.

K-State Cancer Research (KStateCancerRes) on Twitter

The K-State Cancer Research (KStateCancerRes) user account on Twitter has 410 Tweets, 67 following, and 144 followers at the time of the data crawl in February 2013. This account was crawled three different times in February 2013. It was crawled in an unlimited-persons way for 1 degree, 1.5 degree, and 2.0 degree, and the differences in the findings are presented in Figure 24. The URL

Table 10. K-State Wildcats basketball (KStateUpdateBB) user network on Twitter (graph metrics)

Graph Metric	Value
Graph Type	Directed
Vertices	884
Unique Edges	984
Edges With Duplicates	0
Total Edges	984
Self-Loops	0
Reciprocated Vertex Pair Ratio	0.041269841
Reciprocated Edge Ratio	0.079268293
Connected Components	1
Single-Vertex Connected Components	0
Maximum Vertices in a Connected Component	884
Maximum Edges in a Connected Component	984
Maximum Geodesic Distance (Diameter)	3
Average Geodesic Distance	2.330358
Graph Density	0.001260614
Modularity	Not Applicable
NodeXL Version	1.0.1.229

for the official Twitter site is https://twitter.com/KStateCancerRes.

In ring lattices, or circles, the vertices are placed in a circle. The edges are the lines connecting elements of the circle. Visually, these provide a quick snapshot of the density of both the vertices and the ties (edges or arcs). A data extraction was done to analyze the KStateCancerRes (K-State Cancer Research) user network on Twitter, based on the three levels of degrees enabled by NodeXL. A one-degree crawl only identifies all the ties directly connected to the account. A 1.5 degree crawl includes both the alters in an ego neighborhood as well as the ties between the alters (for a measure of transitivity). A 2.0 degree crawl includes the ego neighborhood of the focal node, the ties between alters in the neighborhood, and the direct ties of the alters, which adds exponential complexity.

Figure 17. K-State Wildcats basketball (KStateUpdateBB) user network on Twitter (graph)

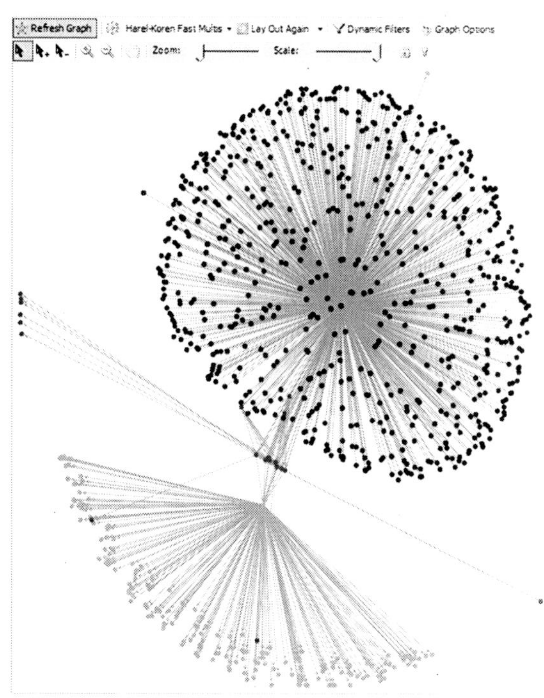

At the far left, the 1-degree unlimited-persons data crawl shows 180 vertices, with 218 unique edges. A 1-degree or 1-level crawl only captures the focal ego node (KStateCancerRes) and its alters (directly connected ego neighborhood). The maximum geodesic distance (diameter) of this network is only 2, with a graph density of 0.006828057. The 1-degree crawl had 4 clusters; the 1.5-degree crawl had 3 clusters; the 2-degree crawl had 3 clusters.

Table 11. K-State proud user network on Twitter (graph metrics)

Graph Metric	Value
Graph Type	Directed
Vertices	13258
Unique Edges	13746
Edges With Duplicates	0
Total Edges	13746
Self-Loops	0
Reciprocated Vertex Pair Ratio	0.005486065
Reciprocated Edge Ratio	0.010912265
Connected Components	1
Single-Vertex Connected Components	0
Maximum Vertices in a Connected Component	13258
Maximum Edges in a Connected Component	13746
Maximum Geodesic Distance (Diameter)	4
Average Geodesic Distance	2.406957
Graph Density	7.82083E-05
Modularity	Not Applicable
NodeXL Version	1.0.1.229

At the center ring lattice is a 1.5 degree unlimited-persons data crawl of the same network in the same time frame. This is a multi-directional network which shows transitivity or the connectivity between the alters in the ego neighborhood (how well connected the ego neighborhood alters are to each other). The graph metrics are very similar on some variables: 180 vertices and 117 unique edges. However, the edges with duplicates have jumped from 4 to 5,906, and the total edges from 222 to 6,023.

Figure 18. K-State proud user network on Twitter (graph)

Finally, at the far right ring lattice is a 2.0 degree crawl, with involves the ego node's direct neighborhood, the connections between the alters, and then the ego neighborhoods of the alters, two levels out from the center. This capture increases the numbers of the vertices or nodes exponentially, from 180 (1 degree) to 180 (1.5 degrees) to 28,514. There are 28,899 unique edges, with no edges with duplicates, for a total of 28,899 edges or links. The diameter or maximum geodesic distance has gone to 4, with 2.17 as the average geodesic distance. The graph has a density of 3.56. There are three main clusters, so there is not a wide diversity of types within this cultivated network. Even visually, the changes in the capture parameters result in a wide range of variation in the captured data, with fast-expanding complexities.

K-State Soccer Club (k_stateSoccer) User Network on Twitter

The K-State Soccer (k_stateSoccer) user network on Twitter represents both female and male teams at K-State, according to their official site on Twitter

Table 12. "Women of K-State" user network on Twitter (graph metrics)

Graph Metric	Value
Graph Type	Directed
Vertices	35141
Unique Edges	48385
Edges With Duplicates	116
Total Edges	48501
Self-Loops	0
Reciprocated Vertex Pair Ratio	0.01273153
Reciprocated Edge Ratio	0.025142952
Connected Components	1
Single-Vertex Connected Components	0
Maximum Vertices in a Connected Component	35141
Maximum Edges in a Connected Component	48501
Maximum Geodesic Distance (Diameter)	4
Average Geodesic Distance	3.362832
Graph Density	3.92297E-05
Modularity	Not Applicable
NodeXL Version	1.0.1.229

(https://twitter.com/k_stateSoccer). This account has 110 Tweets, with 369 following, and 93 followers. (This was the only account analyzed that had more following than followers.) At the formal page, the account represents K-State Club soccer teams and came with the hash tags: #KState #soccer #EMAW ("Every Man a Wildcat"). A perusal of the messages show announcements of events, kudos, and well wishing. The K-State Soccer Club has an official presence on Facebook as well, at https://www.facebook.com/#!/KStateClubSoccer.

Figure 19. "Women of K-State" user network on Twitter (graph)

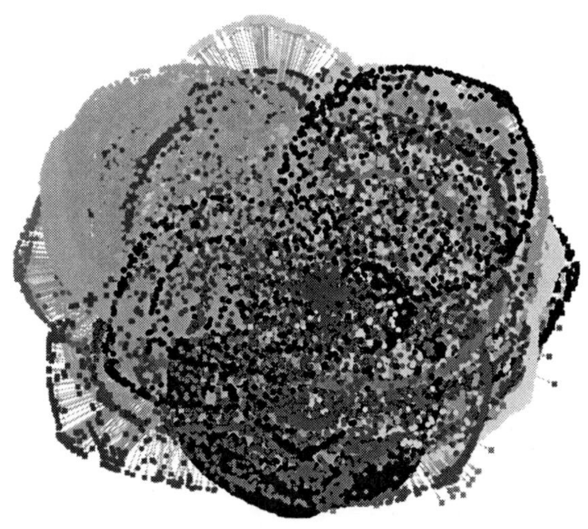

The data crawl was achieved in mid-February and set at a 1,000-persons crawl and a two-degree (levels) of capture. (Multiple initial unlimited-persons crawls were attempted with multiple system crashes, so a limited crawl was created.) This crawl found 9,895 vertices, with 13,076 unique edges (links) (see Table 17).

A visualization of this network using the Fruchterman-Reingold force-based layout algorithm is available in Figure 25. Twenty-one clusters were found in this K_stateSoccer user network, which is quite diverse for a student club's Twitter network.

SOCIAL SHARING CONTENT ANALYSIS

The phenomenon of "social sharing" of user-generated contents has emerged as another facet of Web 2.0. In these social media platforms, images, videos, and other digital contents are uploaded and tagged with metadata based on "bottom-up user-proposed tagging convention" (Chang, 2010). The contributors are often independent-minded

Table 13. K-State union program council (kstate-UPC) network on Twitter (graph metrics)

Graph Metric	Value
Graph Type	Directed
Vertices	9169
Unique Edges	13608
Edges With Duplicates	0
Total Edges	13608
Self-Loops	0
Reciprocated Vertex Pair Ratio	0.030284676
Reciprocated Edge Ratio	0.058788948
Connected Components	2
Single-Vertex Connected Components	0
Maximum Vertices in a Connected Component	9167
Maximum Edges in a Connected Component	13607
Maximum Geodesic Distance (Diameter)	4
Average Geodesic Distance	3.395783
Graph Density	0.000161882
Modularity	Not Applicable
NodeXL Version	1.0.1.229

and individually motivated and working individually to share information, in what has been termed "weak cooperation" in collective production. In other cases, whole groups collaborate around shared projects and publish their contents for others. There are acts of co-creation of digital works. The social aspects of this content sharing involve a co-experience (such as viewing videos

Figure 20. K-State union program council (kstateUPC) network on Twitter (graph)

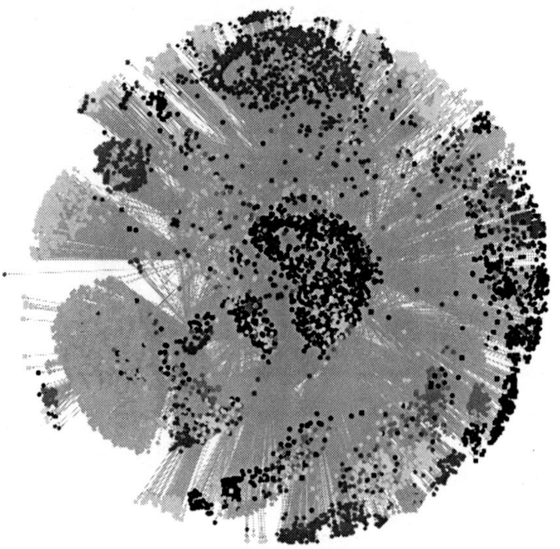

together in virtual film festivals). There are shared communications around digital contents. There are response photos or videos to others' works in a kind of public mass media discourse. Social media interactions involve a range of relationships: object-to-object, objects-to-people, people-to-objects, and people-to-people. Data crawls may be obtained in each of these directions. Based on digital contents, people organize actions, socialize, and create understandings.

The corpus of information may be depicted as content networks. User accounts may be mapped along with those with whom they are connected in terms of co-commenting or video linking. In photo- or video-sharing sites, contents may be analyzed based on metadata tags and how related they are to others (in semantic clusters) to identify content clusters (see Table 18).

K-State Videos on YouTube (Google)

In Figure 26 this content network is depicted using the Harel-Koren Fast Multiscale layout algorithm.

Table 14. K-State salina (kstatesalina) user network on Twitter (graph metrics)

Graph Type	Directed
Vertices	62216
Unique Edges	89942
Edges With Duplicates	392
Total Edges	90334
Self-Loops	0
Reciprocated Vertex Pair Ratio	0.006285236
Reciprocated Edge Ratio	0.012491957
Connected Components	1
Single-Vertex Connected Components	0
Maximum Vertices in a Connected Component	62216
Maximum Edges in a Connected Component	90334
Maximum Geodesic Distance (Diameter)	4
Average Geodesic Distance	3.858298
Graph Density	2.32868E-05
Modularity	Not Applicable
NodeXL Version	1.0.1.229

Figure 21. K-State salina (kstatesalina) user network on Twitter (graph)

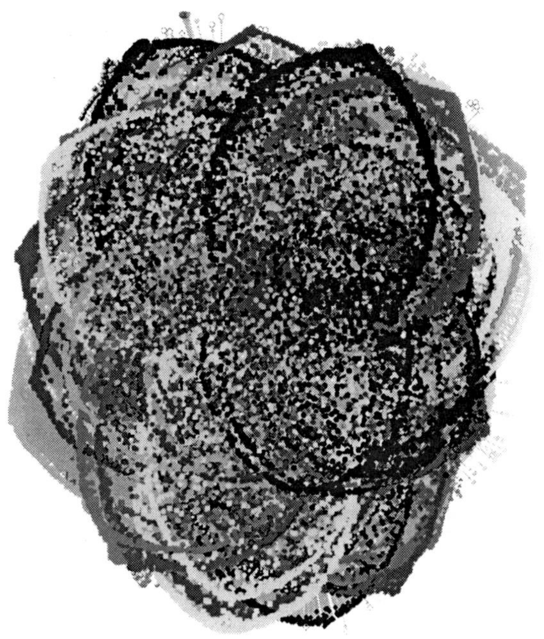

K-State Libraries' Photostream on Flickr

Multi-media content sharing sites enable the creation of collections of digital contents. The K-State Libraries photostream (user account) on Flickr (http://www.flickr.com/photos/kstatelibraries/) was mapped to examine the social network (see Table 19).

The unlimited data crawl at two-degrees found that the K-State Libraries photostream on Flickr had a social network consisting of 5,766 nodes or vertices, and 7,848 unique edges. A perusal of the main page showed various collections of information, some focused around the financial contributors to the library and others around particular data collections. In Figure 27 this social network is depicted in a grid format.

This crawl resulted in the identification of 7 clusters based on the semantic relatedness of the metadata tags. This same information is shown as a Harel-Koren Fast Multiscale graph in Figure 28.

K-State Search Network on Flickr

A search for "K-State" on the Flickr multimedia content site shows a fairly stable network of 561 nodes, with 1,507 edges. Two unlimited runs were done, and both resulted in similar data crawls and similar numbers, even though two months had passed between the data crawls (see Table 20).

The contents were mostly photos as Flickr had only recently introduced the video feature. The

Table 15. K-State olathe user network on Twitter (lim. 1000) (graph metrics)

Graph Metric	Value
Graph Type	Directed
Vertices	36366
Unique Edges	59269
Edges With Duplicates	3873
Total Edges	63142
Self-Loops	0
Reciprocated Vertex Pair Ratio	0.091432698
Reciprocated Edge Ratio	0.167546196
Connected Components	1
Single-Vertex Connected Components	0
Maximum Vertices in a Connected Component	36366
Maximum Edges in a Connected Component	63142
Maximum Geodesic Distance (Diameter)	4
Average Geodesic Distance	3.619615
Graph Density	4.57099E-05
Modularity	Not Applicable
NodeXL Version	1.0.1.229

information clustering shows semantic clusters around reading, nature, weather, sports, Kansas State University, and activities. There is also some clear semantic drift in terms of moving to distal ideas such as sports in S. America. (This Harel-Koren Fast Multiscale algorithm used to lay out the data in Figure 29 shows a range of associations with "K-State" as understood by mostly amateur photographers and metadata taggers.

Figure 22. K-State olathe user network on Twitter (lim. 1000) (graph)

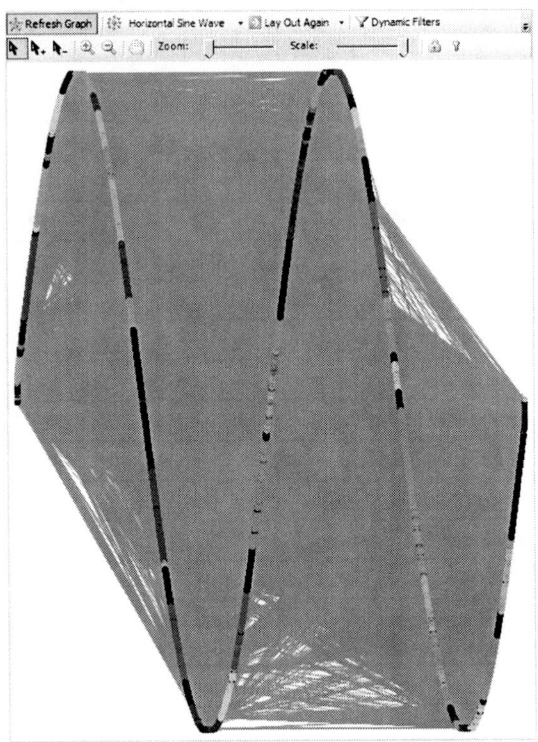

Established relational paths are critical for the delivery of new contents. One research study about Flickr looked at its growth data. The researchers found the following:

Over 50% of the observed new links in Flickr are between users that have, a priori, some network path between them (the remainder of the observed new links are between users which are, a priori, disconnected). For these new links among already connected users, Figure 5 shows the cumulative distribution of shortest-path hop distances between source and destination users. It reveals a striking trend: over 80% of such new links connect users that were only two hops apart, meaning that the destination user was a friend-of-a-friend of the source user before the new link was created (Mislove, Koppula, Gummadi, Druschel, & Bhattacharjee, 2008, p. 5).

Table 16. K-State olathe user network on Twitter (no limits crawl) (graph metrics)

Graph Metric	Value
Graph Type	Directed
Vertices	45569
Unique Edges	53291
Edges With Duplicates	84
Total Edges	53375
Self-Loops	0
Reciprocated Vertex Pair Ratio	0.01295322
Reciprocated Edge Ratio	0.02557516
Connected Components	1
Single-Vertex Connected Components	0
Maximum Vertices in a Connected Component	45569
Maximum Edges in a Connected Component	53375
Maximum Geodesic Distance (Diameter)	4
Average Geodesic Distance	2.934201
Graph Density	2.56842E-05
Modularity	Not Applicable
NodeXL Version	1.0.1.229

Figure 23. K-State olathe user network on Twitter (no limits crawl) (graph)

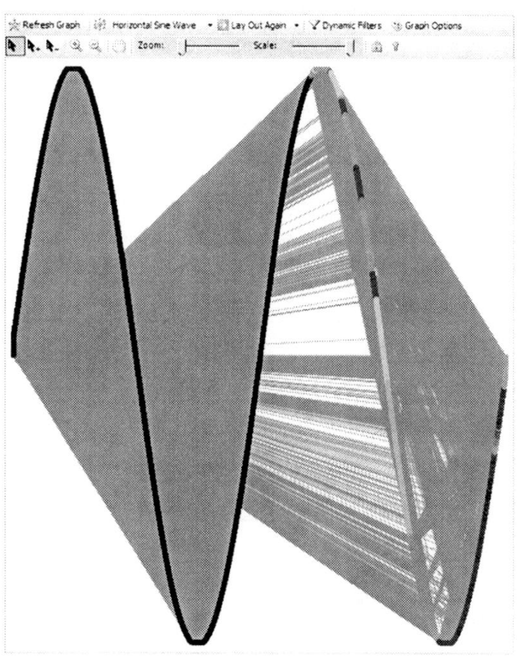

Figure 24. Three ring lattices of the KState-CancerRes user network on Twitter (in varying degrees)

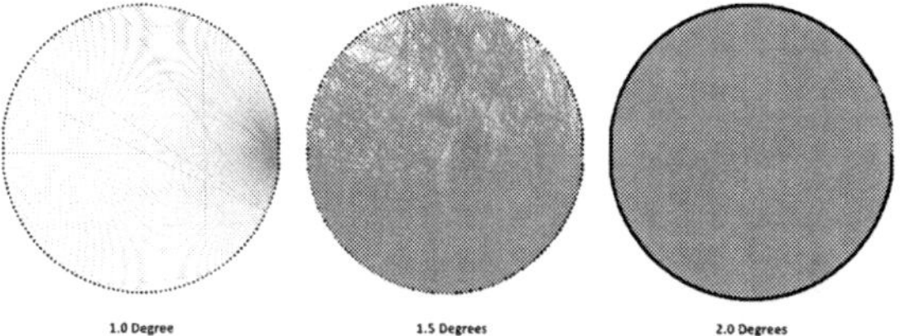

Prior links matter. Social proximity matters. Like roads, relational social network paths may involve some long-standing connectivity.

Delimitations

The essential work of data extractions from social media platforms is the mapping of the human terrain, with humans acting as unwitting sensors in the network. Certainly, there are limitations to crawling social media platforms to understand a formal brand presence as well as an informal one. Comprehending these limitations will enhance the understandings that may be drawn from this empirical network analysis approach.

The nature of social media: One limitation stems from the nature of social media and human presences. Not all people choose to go online. Those who opt-in tend to be less cynical (mistrustful of others' motives) and more optimistic dispositionally and tend to be more pro-social and

Table 17. K-State soccer user network on Twitter (graph metrics)

Graph Metric	Value
Graph Type	Directed
Vertices	9895
Unique Edges	13076
Edges With Duplicates	0
Total Edges	13076
Self-Loops	0
Reciprocated Vertex Pair Ratio	0.008250443
Reciprocated Edge Ratio	0.016365861
Connected Components	1
Single-Vertex Connected Components	0
Maximum Vertices in a Connected Component	9895
Maximum Edges in a Connected Component	13076
Maximum Geodesic Distance (Diameter)	4
Average Geodesic Distance	3.694039
Graph Density	0.000133563
Modularity	Not Applicable
NodeXL Version	1.0.1.229

supportive of others; they tend to be more generous with social and emotional support (Kaplan, Bradley, & Ruscher, 2004). Those who engage in social sharing in mediated environments may be a powerful resource in times of social stress. People self-select into sharing online. Of that group, a subset makes their presences semi-public or public (with a segment who engage totally privately). The data crawls are unable to access private networks; only public information is available. Of the public

Figure 25. K-State soccer user network on Twitter (graph)

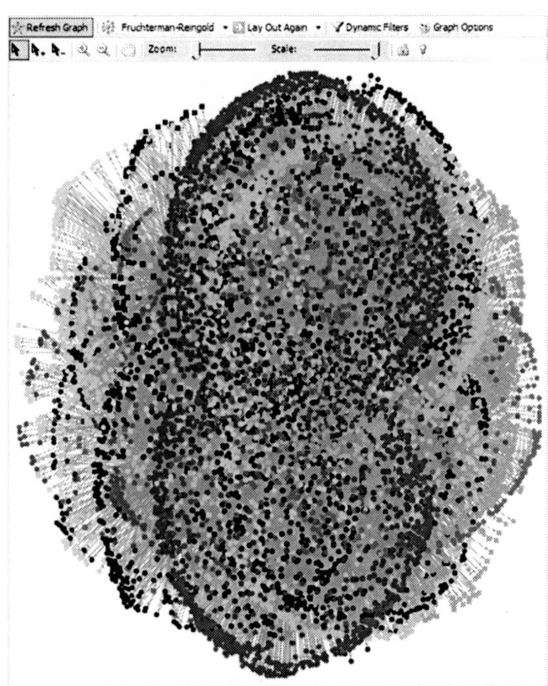

group, only a small percentage is participatory. Many follow others' accounts as lurkers without ever interacting in a mediated way. This means that the few who actually share in microblogging or digital content sharing have an outsized effect in social networks. This means that those who are private or silent will not register on a social media data crawl. What is intangible or invisible must be quantifiable to some degree as uncertainty. The views of those who are offline or who are inactive online will have to be elicited in other ways. Also, there have been signs of social media fatigue. Sufficiently popular social network platforms that attract a high number of users will likely vary over time, if history is any indication.

How well does the electronic world map to the larger external one? Do social media platforms really strengthen the role of identity and self-concept and self-exploration? In some cases, fairly closely; in others, not so much. A study was done to test how accurate online profiles were in the nonymous

Table 18. K-State video search on YouTube (graph metrics)

Graph Metric	Value
Graph Type	Undirected
Vertices	733
Unique Edges	61656
Edges With Duplicates	2731
Total Edges	64387
Self-Loops	0
Reciprocated Vertex Pair Ratio	Not Applicable
Reciprocated Edge Ratio	Not Applicable
Connected Components	4
Single-Vertex Connected Components	0
Maximum Vertices in a Connected Component	694
Maximum Edges in a Connected Component	63930
Maximum Geodesic Distance (Diameter)	7
Average Geodesic Distance	2.573515
Graph Density	0.23417127
Modularity	Not Applicable
NodeXL Version	1.0.1.229

Facebook space to the individual in terms of expressions of personality. The authors were testing the "idealized virtual-identity hypothesis." Were online presences mirrors to the real world with personal information "found in personal environments, private thoughts, facial images, and social behavior, all of which are known to contain valid information about personality"? The researchers found that online Facebook presences, with reputational data and information from individuals' acquaintances, mapped fairly closely to peoples identities in Facebook profiles on the dimensions of extraversion, agreeableness, conscientiousness, neuroticism, and openness. The authors came to their conclusion after comparing observer ratings of Facebook profiles and correlations of their observations with the actual personality and the idealized self. This group affirmed the extended real-life hypothesis by identifying the electronic space as an extension of the real world, with people's depictions of themselves on Facebook reflecting "no evidence of self-idealization." The profile owner's ideal self-ratings "did not predict observer impressions above and beyond actual personality." The authors write:

Figure 26. K-State video search on YouTube (graph)

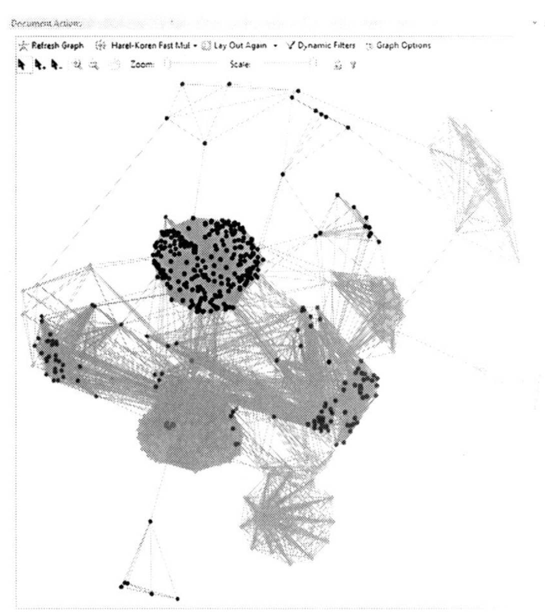

In contrast, even when controlling for ideal-self ratings, the effect of actual personality on OSN (online social network) impressions remained significant for nearly all analyses. Accuracy was strongest for extraversion (paralleling results from

Table 19. K-State libraries photostream on Flickr (graph metrics)

Graph Metric	Value
Graph Type	Directed
Vertices	5766
Unique Edges	7848
Edges With Duplicates	36
Total Edges	7884
Self-Loops	11
Reciprocated Vertex Pair Ratio	0.007307692
Reciprocated Edge Ratio	0.014509355
Connected Components	1
Single-Vertex Connected Components	0
Maximum Vertices in a Connected Component	5766
Maximum Edges in a Connected Component	7884
Maximum Geodesic Distance (Diameter)	4
Average Geodesic Distance	2.861327
Graph Density	0.000236365
Modularity	Not Applicable
NodeXL Version	1.0.1.229

face-to-face encounters) and openness (similar to research on personal environments).

Accuracy was lowest for neuroticism, which is consistent with previous research showing that neuroticism is difficult to detect in all zero-acquaintance contexts (Funder, 1999; Kenny, 1994). These results suggest that people are not using their OSN profiles to promote an idealized virtual identity. Instead, OSNs might be an

Figure 27. K-State libraries photostream on Flickr (grid visualization)

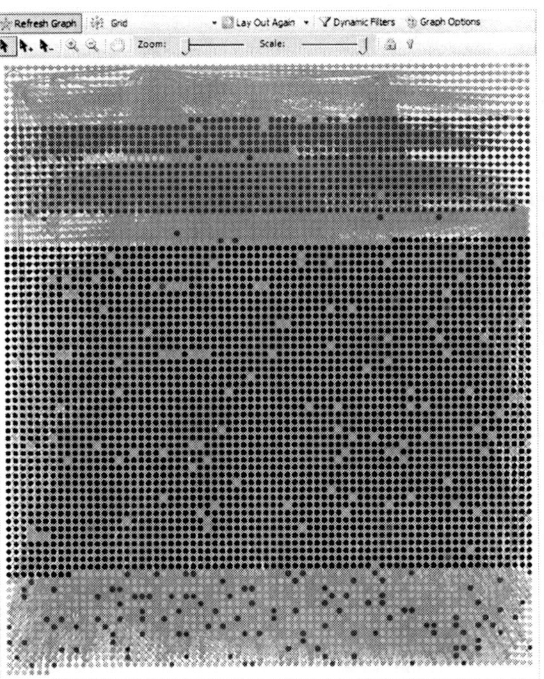

Figure 28. K-State libraries photostream on Flickr (graph)

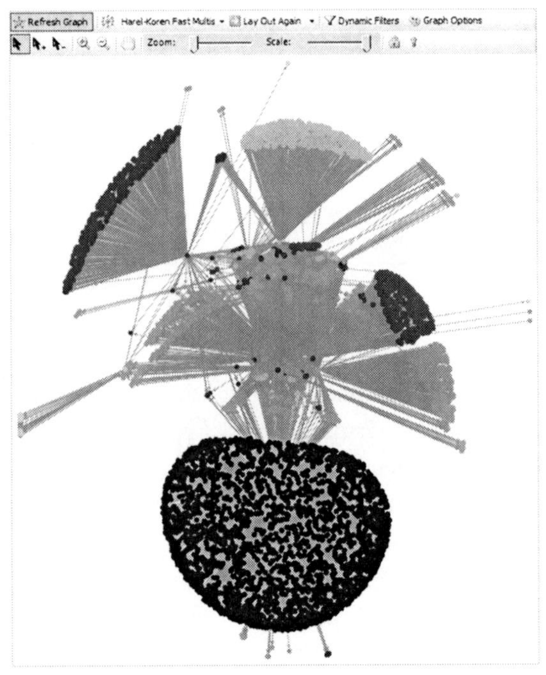

Table 20. K-State search network on Flickr (graph metrics)

Graph Metric	Value
Graph Type	Directed
Vertices	561
Unique Edges	1507
Edges With Duplicates	0
Total Edges	1507
Self-Loops	0
Reciprocated Vertex Pair Ratio	0.02726653
Reciprocated Edge Ratio	0.053085601
Connected Components	1
Single-Vertex Connected Components	0
Maximum Vertices in a Connected Component	561
Maximum Edges in a Connected Component	1507
Maximum Geodesic Distance (Diameter)	4
Average Geodesic Distance	3.072054
Graph Density	0.004796919
Modularity	Not Applicable
NodeXL Version	1.0.1.229

efficient medium for expressing and communicating real personality, which may help explain their popularity. (Back, Stopfer, Vazire, Gaddis, Schmukle, Egloff, & Gosling, 2009, n.p.)

Other researchers show that consumers of social media information may apply a healthy skepticism about others networks when there is an overabundance of connections, which may be seen as raising doubts about the focal individual's actual "popularity and desirability" (Tong, Van Der Heide, Langwell, & Walther, 2008). That said, people are interpreted by the company they keep. While social media spaces are places for identity performances, these performances contain some checks and double-checks for the validation of identity.

What occurs electronically may reveal something of what is happening in the real world, but there is not a one-to-one correlation between what is seen electronically and what is happening in the real and the actual. Researchers show how there is even a wide discrepancy between professed or declared friends and acquaintances in electronic social networks vs. the actual interconnections (intercommunications and reciprocated ties) between individuals (Huberman, Romero, & Wu, 2008). The authors point to what they call "the networks that matter" as those who act as friends than those who merely claim to be. Links between people alone do not mean actual interactions.

Technological limitations: Another limitation comes from the available technologies. Whether open-source or proprietary, publicly-available software programs for such data crawls all have their limits. One limit involves the size of the crawl. Capturing a social network at two-degrees means that the capture inly involves the direct ego neighborhood of a focal node, and then the ego neighborhoods of the alters. Anything beyond that circle is outside the bounds of the data capture (Those who have more high-powered machines may capture and analyze more and to a higher level of rigor.).

Their performance depends on the computer's Random Access Memory (RAM) and Central Processing Unit (CPU). Further, there are limits in Excel, depending on the version, which also adds constraints. One of the NodeXL coordinators wrote on the NodeXL Discussion Forum: "For very large data sets we recommend that users consider the more powerful tools like Python/NetworkX or RSNA or iGraph. If you need a much more powerful machine for a short period of time I suggest exploring the Amazon EC2 service

Figure 29. K-State related tag search network on Flickr (graph)

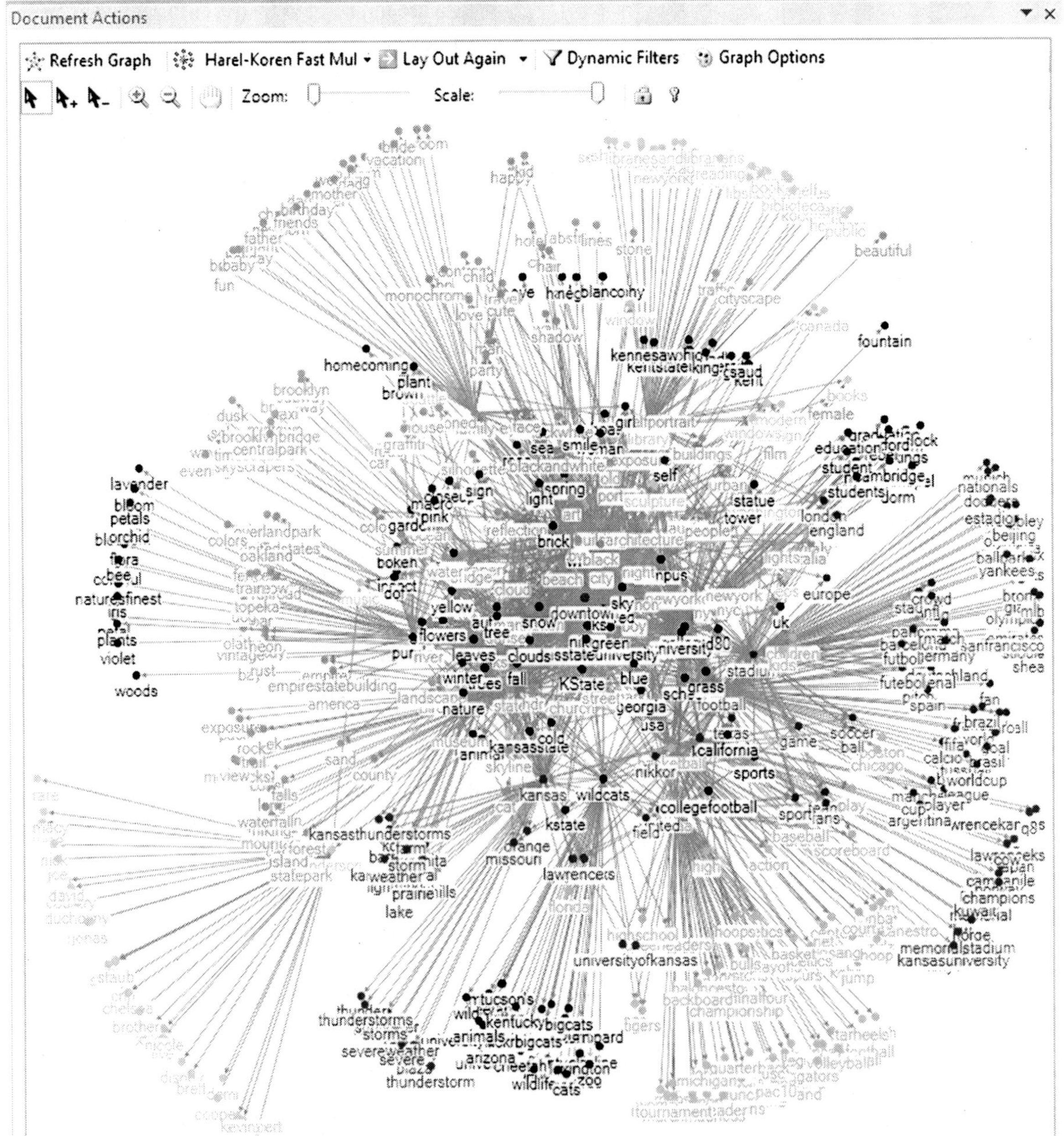

(aws.amazon.com)" (Smith, Jan. 1, 2013). Such software requires high computational processing, which is often beyond the limits of even the most high-end desktop and laptop computers. (In most universities, high performance computing is set aside for better-paid science research.) The "big data" extractions and analyses require much in the way of computational resources and time; there are challenges of scale. There are other dependencies for full data extractions. The software acquires and downloads information through APIs which enable access to social media platforms, which have to limit access to their resources in order to meet needs.

Partial data extractions: Because of the computational expense of social media crawls, most samples of networks are only partial. A partial crawl could be generalizable if social networks were expressible as patterned fractals, but currently, they are not. Each network is a unique case because so little is known of the various types of networks and their patterns (expressed as motif censuses or machine counts of these structures). This means that pattern mining can only inform researchers of so much. In terms of Large-Scale Network Analysis (LSNA), it is important then to crawl the whole network and collect as much information as possible for generalizability about the network topology (structure of entities and relationships). In this early stage, there are a handful of theories about pattern mining social networks, and many of these theories are as-yet untested. Suffice it to say that the concept here is that a social network topology is to human interactions as geography has been to human civilizations; the topology provides a context and constraints, and it is an influencing factor for human interactions but does not wholly determine human outcomes. The storing of large online social network datasets also incurs computational load or cost.

These strategies for data crawls of social media platforms may be applied to email repositories (albeit only with the permission of the email account holder), public wikis, public blogs, threaded discussions (from learning management systems and other types of forums) and http networks. This information may have value for a variety of internal and external uses, even if not all of that data may be publishable.

High learning curves: Social Network Analysis (SNA) entails some 80 – 100 years of research to understand thoroughly. The theories in use are complex, and there are no fully consensus-accepted theories. For example, the methods for the identification of an influential node in a network—a fundamental or canonical assumption—are not widely accepted; these standards vary depending on the type of social network. There has been research that has shown that even with saturation coverage of a product, with millions of Tweets, it may not necessarily result in any direct sales (Schaefer, 2012). Another example involves the analysis of "cold spots" or tie absences in networks. Researchers need to distinguish between a lack of data and data confirming the absence of a tie. The quantification of influence is still in debate. Engaging in social network analysis is cognitively demanding of researchers.

Various social network analysis and visualization tools are complex to use. They are computationally intensive. That said, they do enable the capturing of various "motif censuses." They enable the pruning of node sets and the analysis of smaller branches of the social network. Dynamic filters may be employed to highlight particular aspects of a social network in relation to the network itself or to other branches of the network. Nodes may be removed from a network to see what would happen as the network re-configures around the absence. Social analysis software tools enable closer analysis of particular focal nodes and ego-node neighborhoods. Various algorithms for drawing graphs from a dataset differ greatly, and differing interpretations may be made based on the visualizations.

What this all means is that researchers need to hone their skills for the most effective data crawls. Just extracting a social network structure may be insufficient, for example; capturing the actual microblogging messages and thumbnails would be helpful in gleaning more information for qualitative, quantitative, and mixed methods research. Researchers have to apply creative and validated methodologies to elicit information (from multiple information streams, including trace data, survey data, and others) and then to analyze the data. In a so-called "data hungry" approach, they need to be able to triangulate data for insights. They need to be able to define the social context and cultural elements to understand social networks. They need to be able to test and validate or invalidate understandings.

Another next step is to develop more sophisticated analysis of what is knowable. What assertions may be made about particular nodes in the network and their relative influences? What may be asserted about the interrelationships between nodes? What may be asserted about a social network's capabilities based on its structure and the resources moving through it (and the paths that the resources are taking)? How may a professional social network be strengthened?

Validation and invalidation of theories: The work of validating or invaliding social network analysis insights vary. There does not seem to be any accepted percentage of a network captured that would be considered a valid sampling.

The research so far has begun with grounded theory (what is observable) and moved to abstractions (moving from specific to general). It has also worked the other way, with theorists proposing hypotheses, conducting research, and drawing conclusions. Others use the triangulation of data method, by collecting copious amounts of information and testing theories against various data sets. There have also been theorists who have offered theories that have not yet been tested. This may well be expected in a fairly nascent field (particularly in the analysis of online social networks).

Some practitioners in this field have asserted that a social network analysis is not truly validated until an intervention is conducted on the in-world population to see how the network behaves post-vention. For example, the sending out of a "lever" (a friendly agent) to influence an unfriendly one directly or indirectly, proxemically or distally, may be one such test—assuming measureable and observable reactions may be seen. Another example of this is in the attempts by law enforcement to disrupt or fragment terror networks. Some believe that removal of an influential node may fragment or break apart a network; others suggest that the network will generally only readjust around the absence of an influential leader and may even become stronger. Such ideas are applied to the creation of societal resilience in the face of natural or human-made disasters. How may a social network or community be made more resilient? There is research on the structuring of innovation teams (less connected is better) to create new approaches, and then there is research on structuring company compliance trainings (highly connected is better).

Actionable information: Network effects occur when people move en masse to particular behaviors and spaces, and in that act, add value. The network effects of people going to social media platforms to interact means that universities have to move there, too, to engage and to understand the effects of their outreach endeavors. They need to track the effects of their faculty's research, their funding campaigns, their launching of new academic programs, and other endeavors. Too often, there are outreach endeavors made without any "closing the loop" to understand effects on their stakeholders.

Then, too, the new awareness from SNA may lead to ideas for other engagements or actionable information. This is where branding and marketing understandings need to be delved into with more depth. How may universities start positive trends or spark social cascades? Which influential nodes should universities reach out to to promote research or public good will or access to resources? How may university fund-raisers be made more effective by tapping into social networks? How may universities support their students and other stakeholders better using social media? Where should universities put resources in terms of digital content development for content sharing sites? What should universities do with the awareness of what is out on social media even if they do not have direct control? ["Freedom of the Internet" is a core value for "online expression, assembly and association" (Fontaine & Rogers, 2011, p. 5). Further, the archival properties of the Internet ensure that "long-tail content" may be accessible on dedicated sites into perpetuity.]

Information updates: Even though this approach is highly data-intensive, this work involves information that is transient and often fast-moving. This would suggest that information would need to be constantly updated for it to be valid. A slice-in-time view is only applicable for a particular period before the power of current relationships fades (through tie entropy and dissolution).

A sequence of data captures for a particular account may result in some insights from "auto-correlation" methods, where cross-correlations are made of a signal with itself. At various time intervals, what are the differences between various measures of an account?

Finally, there are endeavors towards actualizing real-time monitoring of electronic social networks and the information flowing through them. This would theoretically enable not only an understanding of social network structures but the dynamism within in terms of both structure and content flows. Such analysis includes temporal patterning of communications around various news, weather, and human-made events, from a head period to a trend peak to the ending of an event (Naaman, Becker, & Gravano, 2011).

There have been studies on the analysis of how trends heat up, popularize through word-of-mouth and forwarded messages, and then dissipate or transmute into something else. There are moves to enhance geosocial analysis, which links social networks to both dynamic space and dynamic time, for deeper understandings. There are endeavors towards predictive analysis—such as focusing on a particular node as a possible future leader or understanding social network trajectories (rarely simply linear progressions) or predicting the probabilistic future for particular social networks (such as political groups). There are also analyses of tie antecedents or precursors to network position or the creation of certain edges (relationships).

FUTURE RESEARCH DIRECTIONS

With the exponential popularization of a range of social media platforms and the capturing of so much electronic data (public as well as trace), there is plenty of latent information from social media to exploit in ways that are beneficial to the conduct of a university in reaching out to its many constituencies.

This chapter focuses on extractive social (and content) network analysis to enhance branding efforts by a university. This is by no means representative of the limits of what is knowable. Rather, this offers a brief look at what is easily accessible currently. A simple value-added research approach could involve downloading the communicated texts and running them through a text analysis tool. The data sets could be run through other social network graphing tools for different kinds of statistical analysis.

One example of the integration of locative information is cartoblography, which combines microblogging information overlaid over a map (with words depicted as larger in size based on text frequency found in the data crawl) (Field & O'Brien, 2010). Tweet maps are combinations of textual data (ranked by frequency) with geolocation data. The introduction of spatial elements in network analysis suggests the ability to analyze for proximity or adjacency influences. Locative events may be analyzed.

There are tools that enable multi-nodal Dynamic Network Analysis (DNA) through live data feeds (with people as sensors) to detect and capture emergent or real-time events (for situational awareness through "social awareness streams" as termed by Naaman, Becker, & Gravano, 2011); independent cascades or word-of-mouth riffs; activity peaks and declines. With sufficient vigilance, entire events may be detected from originating spark to the final quiet. Some researchers are mapping conversations around particular topics and analyzing who is engaging with those topics—whether individuals who are parts of formal networks, clustered nodes, or those from unrelated nodes—to label structural, coordinated, or uncoordinated trends. Researchers are looking to create publicly available tools for real-time analysis of data moving through evolving networks. Much progress has been made in the machine analysis of sentiment as expressed in "opinion lexicon" text and symbols (and other psycholinguistic phenomena). Other software programs strive to read human intent based on their textual language contents and frequency of posts. There have been remote reads of individuals' learning styles preferences, personality dispositions (based on the Five Factor Model, including neuroticism, extraversion, openness to experience, agreeableness, and conscientiousness) emotional states, and organizational roles and responsibilities based on their positions in social media networks. Various computer programs have been created to read information moving through social networks to identify "confirmed truths" vs. "false rumors" (Mendoza, Poblete, & Castillo, 2010, p. 77).

Not only have there been innovations in computing research, but as more researchers are read into the capabilities of this approach, it's possible that currently unforeseen questions may arise that may further push innovations. Online social network analysis will certainly evolve as new insights are achieved and new theories proposed and technologies evolve. It may be possible to provide electronic doppelgangers of whole digital communities from origination to sunset.

CONCLUSION

The application of social network analysis to data extracted from social media sites is a promising approach to understanding a university's formal and informal branding in electronic spaces. This chapter brings together some of the latest knowledge in the field in terms of computational social network analysis and social media research. However, it is critical to knowledge that this approach entails a high learning curve. As such, this is not an easy-to-integrate approach. Any decision-makers who would be read into this approach would have to be introduced to some pretty complex theory and statistical analysis.

The potential benefits of this approach outweigh the known costs, however, given the richness of the data and the impossibility of acquiring this information in other ways. This approach of mapping online social networks enables a more comprehensive branding approach; it enables the generating and developing of leads.

ACKNOWLEDGMENT

I am grateful to my university's social networks that make this a very joyful place to work. Thanks to the NodeXL team for a fantastic tool that simplifies the work of researchers. Thanks to the various social media platforms for their generous and open approach to the world in making Application Programming Interfaces (API) available. Let no one say that social network analysis is easy or simple. It took me more than a year of reading in-depth and experimenting with a range of social network analysis software tools before being able to apply this approach to a very simple application.

REFERENCES

Acquisti, A., & Gross, R. (2006). *Imagined communities: Awareness, information sharing, and privacy on the Facebook*. Retrieved from http://link.springer.com/chapter/10.1007%2F11957454_3?LI=true

Auer, M. R. (2011). The policy sciences of social media. *Policy Studies Journal: the Journal of the Policy Studies Organization*, *39*(4), 709–736. doi:10.1111/j.1541-0072.2011.00428.x.

Back, M. D., Stopfer, J. M., Vazire, S., Gaddis, S., Schmukle, S. C., Egloff, B., & Gosling, S. D. (2010). *Facebook profiles reflect actual personality, not self-idealization*. Psychological Science Online First. doi:10.1177/0956797609360756.

Catanese, S. A., De Meo, P., Ferrara, E., Fiumara, G., & Provetti, A. (2011). Crawling Facebook for social network analysis purposes. In *Proceedings of WIMS '11*. Sogndal, Norway: WIMS.

Chang, H.-C. (2010). A new perspective on Twitter hashtag use: Diffusion of innovation theory. In *Proceedings of ASIST 2010*. Pittsburgh, PA: ASIST.

Chu, Z., Gianvecchio, S., Wang, H., & Jajodia, S. (2010). Who is tweeting on Twitter: Human, bot, or cyborg. In *Proceedings of ACSAC '10*. Austin, TX: ACSAC.

Ebner, M., Mühlburger, H., Schaffert, S., Schiefner, M., Reinhardt, W., & Wheeler, S. (2010). Getting granular on Twitter: Tweets from a conference and their limited usefulness for non-participants. In Reynolds, N., & Turcsányi-Szabó, M. (Eds.), *KCKS 2010, IFIP AICT 324* (pp. 102–113). IFIP International Federation for Information Processing. doi:10.1007/978-3-642-15378-5_10.

Efron, M., & Winget, M. (2010). Questions are content: A taxonomy of questions in a microblogging environment. In *Proceedings of ASIST 2010*. Pittsburgh, PA: ASIST.

Ellison, N. B., Steinfield, C., & Lampe, C. (2007). The benefits of Facebook 'friends': Social capital and college students' use of online social network sites. *Journal of Computer-Mediated Communication*, *12*, 1143–1168. doi:10.1111/j.1083-6101.2007.00367.x.

Field, K., & O'Brien, J. (2010). Cartoblography: Experiments in using and organizing the spatial context of micro-blogging. *Transactions in GIS*, *14*(s1), 5–23. doi:10.1111/j.1467-9671.2010.01210.x.

Fontaine, R., & Rogers, W. (2011). Internet freedom: A foreign policy imperative in the digital age. Washington, DC: Center for a New American Security.

Hansen, D., Smith, M. A., & Schneiderman, B. (2011). EventGraphs: Charting collections of conference connections. In *Proceedings of the 44th Hawaii International Conference on System Sciences*. IEEE.

Hansen, D. L., Schneiderman, B., & Smith, M. A. (2011). *Analyzing social media networks with NodeXL: Insights from a connected world*. Amsterdam: Elsevier.

Huberman, B. A., Romero, D. M., & Wu, F. (2008). Social networks that matter: Twitter under the microscope. *Social Computing Laboratory, HP Labs*. Retrieved on Feb. 9, 2013, from http://www.hpl.hp.com/research/scl/papers/twitter/

Jung, G., & Lee, B. (2010). Analysis on social network adoption according to the change of network topology: The impact of 'Open API' to adoption of Facebook. In *Proceedings of the 12th International Conference on Electronic Commerce (ICEC), Roadmap for the Future of Electronic Business* (pp. 23 – 32). ICEC.

Kaplan, R. D. (2012). *The revenge of geography: What the map tells us about coming conflicts and the battle against fate*. New York: Random House.

Kaplan, S. A., Bradley, J. C., & Ruscher, J. B. (2004). The inhibitory role of cynical disposition in the provision and receipt of social support: The case of the September 11th terrorist attacks. *Personality and Individual Differences*, *37*, 1221–1232. doi:10.1016/j.paid.2003.12.006.

Kolcz, A. (2012). Large scale learning at Twitter. In Simperl, E. et al. (Eds.), *ECWC 2012 (LNCS)* (*Vol. 7295*). Berlin: Springer.

Lanier, J. (2010). *You are not a gadget*. New York: First Vintage Books.

Mendoza, M., Poblete, B., & Castillo, C. (2010). Twitter under crisis: Can we trust what we RT? In *Proceedings of the Workshop on Social Media Analytics (SOMA '10)*, (pp. 71-79). Washington, DC: SOMA.

Meyer, E. T., & Schroeder, R. (2009). Untangling the web of e-research: Towards a sociology of online knowledge. *Journal of Informetrics*, *3*, 246–260. doi:10.1016/j.joi.2009.03.006.

Mislove, A., Koppula, H. S., Gummadi, K. P., Druschel, P., & Bhattacharjee, B. (2008). Growth of the Flickr social network. In *Proceedings of WOSN '08*. Seattle, WA: ACM.

Naaman, M., Becker, H., & Gravano, L. (2011). Hip and trendy: Characterizing emerging trends on Twitter. *Journal of the American Society for Information Science and Technology*, *62*(5), 902–918. doi:10.1002/asi.21489.

Priem, J., & Costello, K. L. (2010). How and why scholars cite on Twitter. In *Proceedings of ASIST 2010*. Pittsburgh, PA: ASIST.

Schaefer, M. (2012). *Return on influence: The revolutionary power of Klout, social scoring, and influence marketing*. New York: McGraw Hill.

Selwyn, N. (2009). Faceworking: Exploring students' education-related use of Facebook. *Learning, Media and Technology*, *34*(2), 157–174. doi:10.1080/17439880902923622.

Size Limits on Twitter Import. (2012). Retrieved from http://nodexl.codeplex.com/discussions/348565

Smith, M. (2013). *A cloud large-data processing function? NodeXL discussion board*. Retrieved Feb. 12, 2013, from http://nodexl.codeplex.com/discussions/428064

Smith, M. A., Schneiderman, B., Milic-Frayling, N., Rodrigues, E. M., Barash, V., & Dunne, C. ... Gleave, E. (2009). Analyzing (social media) networks with NodeXL. In *Proceedings of C&T '09*, (pp. 255-263). University Park, PA: C&T.

Steinfield, C., Ellison, N. B., & Lampe, C. (2008). Social capital, self-esteem, and use of online social network sites: A longitudinal analysis. *Journal of Applied Developmental Psychology*, *29*, 434–445. doi:10.1016/j.appdev.2008.07.002.

Stokes, J. P. (1983). Predicting satisfaction with social support from social network structure. *American Journal of Community Psychology*, *11*(2), 141–182. doi:10.1007/BF00894363.

Tong, S. T., Van Der Heide, B., Langwell, L., & Walther, J. B. (2008). Too much of a good thing? The relationship between number of friends and interpersonal impressions on Facebook. *Journal of Computer-Mediated Communication*, *13*, 531–549. doi:10.1111/j.1083-6101.2008.00409.x.

Veletsianos, G. (2012). Higher education scholars' participation and practices on Twitter. *Journal of Computer Assisted Learning*, *28*, 336–349. doi:10.1111/j.1365-2729.2011.00449.x.

Wu, S., Hofman, J. M., Mason, W. A., & Watts, D. J. (2011). Who says what to whom on Twitter. In *Proceedings of the World Wide Web 2011*. Hyderabad, India: IEEE.

ADDITIONAL READING

Hansen, D. L., Schneiderman, B., & Smith, M. A. (2011). *Analyzing social media networks with NodeXL: Insights from a connected world*. Amsterdam: Elsevier.

NodeXL Graph Gallery. (n.d.). Retrieved from http://nodexlgraphgallery.org/Pages/Default.aspx

NodeXL: Network Overview, Discovery, and Exploration for Excel. (n.d.). Retrieved from http://nodexl.codeplex.com/

KEY TERMS AND DEFINITIONS

Add-In: A set of software components that may be added to a software application to add functionality; plug-in.

Application Programming Interface (API): A protocol used as an interface by software to communicate with each other (for interactions, such as the exchange of services or information).

Arc: An undirected link between two vertices or nodes.

Cluster: A unique grouping of nodes or entities based on shared interests or similarities.

Data Crawl: Automated (but usually human directed) data extraction, such as from a social media site.

Data Extraction: The downloading of data from a social media platform; a data crawl.

Data Harvesting: The culling and exploitation of data from a socio-technical system for assessment.

Directed: Links with arrowed ends to show the directionality of a relationship between two nodes.

Diameter: The farthest path distance between extreme-most nodes in a network.

Edge: A link that may be directed (with arrows on the ends) or undirected (without arrows on the end).

Edge (Betweenness) Centrality: The number of shortest paths through an edge in a graph or network (as an indicator of how traveled that edge is in terms of resources or information moving through the network); a value indicating edge betweenness centrality.

Eigenvector Centrality: Various measures which analyze the value of a node's ties to other nodes, with popular node connections seen as more valuable.

Equivalence: Similarity in structure (such as in-degree and out-degree); similarity in some other dimension.

Geodesic Distance: The shortest paths (in terms of numbers of edges or links) between two vertices or nodes.

Graph: A two-dimensional space on which entities and relationships are depicted, usually in node-link diagrams.

Hashtag: A tag consisting of the hash sign # and alphanumeric characters included in a microblogging message to help organize the contents.

Heterophily: The preference or "like" of differences in others; the phenomenon of finding others likeable who are different from oneself.

Homophily: The preference or "like" of similarity in others; the phenomenon of finding others likeable who are similar to oneself.

Lever: A friendly agent who might influence unfriendly ones directly or indirectly.

Link: A tie, edge, or arc that represents a relationship.

Mass-Personal: A public and mediated personal form of interconnectivity.

Multimodal: Involving multiple types of vertices or nodes.

Node: A vertice, representing an individual, group, or entity.

Node-Link Diagram: A 2D diagram that consists of nodes (entities, egos, or agents) and links (lines, edges, or arcs), which represent entities and relationships.

Nonymous: Having an acknowledged name, named (the opposite of anonymous).

Path: A "walk" through a social network or between vertices (or nodes).

Predictive Analytics: Various techniques used to make predictions of the future.

Random walk: A chance-based movement through a social network along paths with all paths having an equal chance of being used; an unpatterned movement of information through a network.

Social Network: A human grouping expressed as an abstracted network.

Social Network Analysis (SNA): The science of studying social structures and human interrelationships to achieve various aims.

Topology (of Networks): The structure of a network; the arrangement of nodes and links representing the structure of a network.

Undirected: Links (without arrowed ends) between nodes which indicate symmetric binary relations.

Walk: The movement of resources or information through a social network along particular paths (whether random or determined or other).

Section 3
Packaging Digital Contents for Perspective and Analysis

Chapter 8
Visualization of High-Level Associations from Twitter Data

Luca Cagliero
Politecnico di Torino, Italy

Naeem A. Mahoto
Politecnico di Torino, Italy

ABSTRACT

The Data Mining and Knowledge Discovery (KDD) process focuses on extracting useful information from large datasets. To support analysts in making decisions, a relevant research effort has been devoted to visualizing the extracted data mining models effectively. A particular attention has been paid to the discovery of strong association rules from textual data coming from social networks, which represent potentially relevant correlations among document terms. However, state-of-the-art rule visualization tools do not allow experts to visualize data correlations at different abstraction levels. Hence, the effectiveness of the proposed approaches is limited, especially when dealing with fairly sparse data. This chapter presents Twitter Generalized Rule Visualizer (TGRV), a novel text mining and visualization tool. It aims at supporting analysts in looking into the results of the generalized association rule mining process from textual data coming from Twitter supplied with WordNet taxonomies. Taxonomies are used for aggregating document terms into higher-level concepts. Generalized rules represent high-level associations among document terms. By exploiting taxonomy-based models, experts may look into the discovered data correlations from different perspectives and figure out interesting knowledge. Changing the perspective from which data correlations are visualized is shown to improve the readability and the usability of the generated rule-based model. The experimental results show the applicability and the usefulness of the proposed visualization tool on real textual data coming from Twitter. The visualized data correlations are shown to be valuable for advanced analysis, such as topic trend and user behavior analysis.

INTRODUCTION

Data Mining and Knowledge Discovery (KDD) focuses on extracting useful information from large datasets (Tan & al., 2005). Descriptive data mining techniques (e.g., clustering, association rule mining) entail discovering interesting and hidden patterns from the analyzed data. In the last several years a significant research effort has been devoted to applying data mining techniques to textual data published on social networks. In particular, the analysis of the textual User-Generated Content (UGC) published on Twitter (http://twitter.com) has achieved promising results

DOI: 10.4018/978-1-4666-4462-5.ch008

in the context of user behavior profiling (Li et al., 2008; Mathioudakis & Koudas., 2010) and topic trend discovery (Cheong & Lee., 2009; Cagliero & Fiori, In press).

Association rule mining (Agrawal & al., 1993) is a widely exploratory data mining technique that allows discovering valuable correlations among data. An association rule is an implication A → B, where A and B are sets of items occurring in the source data. In the context of textual data analysis, a rule represents an implication between a couple of term sets occurring in the analyzed document. To make the rule mining process computationally tractable, a minimum support threshold is commonly enforced to select only the associations among terms that occur frequently in the analyzed data. As a drawback, traditional rule mining algorithms (e.g., Apriori (Agrawal & Srikant, 1994), FP-Growth (Han et al., 2000)) are sometimes ineffective in mining valuable knowledge, because of the excessive level of detail of the mined information. For instance, when coping with real-world textual data, most of the associations among terms occur rarely in the analyzed data and, thus, may be discarded by enforcing a minimum support threshold. To overcome this issue, Agrawal & Srikant (1995) proposed to discover generalized association rules. Generalized rules are rules that may also contain high level (generalized) terms. By exploiting a taxonomy (i.e., a set of is-a hierarchies) built over the analyzed textual documents terms are aggregated into higher level concepts, which are more likely to be frequent in the analyzed data. Hence, generalized rules represent underlying term correlations at different abstraction levels. Generalized rule mining from textual data has already been addressed in different application contexts, among which social data analysis (Cagliero & Fiori, In Press) and biomedical literature analysis (Berardi et al., 2005).

To support analysts in the knowledge discovery process a parallel relevant research effort has been devoted to proposing visual tools adapted to several well-known KDD tasks. In the context of association rule mining, the proposed systems are commonly focused on either visualizing the mining results effectively to ease the expert validation task (Leung et al. 2008; Wong et al., 1999; Meng, 2010) or allowing experts to drive the data mining process (Fayyad et al., 2001; Li et al. 2011). However, to the best of our knowledge, the problem of visualizing generalized rules mined from textual data coming from social networks has never been investigated so far.

This Chapter presents a novel visualization tool, called *Twitter Generalized Rule Visualizer* (TGRV), which allows experts to explore the result of the generalized rule mining process from textual data coming from Twitter effectively. Twitter textual messages published by Web users and ranging over the same topic are retrieved through the Twitter Application Programming Interfaces (APIs) and integrated in common repositories. Next, frequent generalized association rules are discovered from the generated datasets by exploiting a WordNet taxonomy built on the analyzed data. Finally, a graph-based rule visualization model, namely the *Generalized Rule Graph*, is generated to allow experts to explore the mined rules from different perspectives. Generalized Rule Graph nodes represent term sets of arbitrary size, while the oriented edges represent strong associations between node couples. Analyzing the Generalized Rule Graph from different perspectives allows analysts to avoid exploring the whole set of frequent rules. For instance, changing the abstraction level at which rules are analyzed allows experts to overcome the limitations of traditional rule visualizers, which often provide unsatisfactory results when coping with fairly sparse data (Meng, 2010).

The applicability of the proposed system has been evaluated on real textual data coming from the Twitter microblogging system. TGRV is shown to effectively support experts in performing targeted social network analysis. In particular, the suitability of the proposed approach in supporting user behavior and topic trend analysis has been evaluated with the help of a domain expert.

This Chapter is organized as follows. Section "Related works" compares our work with the most recent related approaches. Section "The Twitter Generalized Rule Visualizer" presents the architecture of the TGRV system and describes its main blocks. Section "Experimental validation" assesses the capability of the proposed system in supporting knowledge discovery from the Twitter user-generated content. Section "Future research directions" presents future development of this work, while Section "Conclusions" draws conclusions.

RELATED WORKS

This section overviews the main state-of-the-art approaches relative to the following research topics: (1) visualization, (2) generalized association rule mining, and (3) data mining from user-generated content.

Visualization

Visualization was conceived to propose visual tools adapted to several well-known KDD tasks (Simoff et al., 2008; Fry, 2007). These tools actively contribute to the knowledge discovery process as they give understandable data and pattern representations and, thus, facilitate interaction with experts. In recent years, visual tools became major data mining system components, because of the increasing role of experts within the KDD process.

In Keim (2002) the authors present a classification of the information visualization and visual data mining techniques. *Information visualization* focuses on exploring large data volumes, while *visual data mining* helps experts to deal with the flood of information. A significant research effort has been devoted to addressing the task of smart data visualization (e.g., Keim, 2000; Havre et al. 2002; Grinstein et al., 1989; Chernoff, 1973; Ropinski et al., 2011). To visualize complex data, modern scientific visualization tools commonly utilize advanced mathematical models. For instance, EXVIS (Grinstein et al., 1989) and Chernoff Faces (Chernoff, 1973) are examples of traditional glyph-based methods. Glyphs are graphical entities whose visual features, such as shape, orientation, color and size, are used for encoding the analyzed data features. Hence, glyphs are often used for interactive data exploration (Ropinski et al., 2011). Similarly, in Keim (2000) a pixel-oriented 2D data model is proposed. Despite these models have been designed to visually represent large data collections, they often do not scale well with data dimensionality (Oliver et al., 2007). The goal of this Chapter significantly differs from the one of all of the above-mentioned works as it concerns generalized association rule visualization rather than data visualization.

A parallel research issue is visual data mining (Fayyad et al., 2001). It has the two-fold aim at visualizing the information provided by the mining results and allowing experts to select the most notable information. Several attempts to support the exploration of the extracted frequent patterns by means of visualization tools has been made (Liu et al. 2005; Liu et al., 1999; Liu, 2005; Blanchard et al., 2003; Leung et al. 2008; Wong et al., 1999). They present visualization systems based on either textual, 2D, or 3D pattern visualization models, which provide different data viewpoints. For instance, MineSet (MineSet, 2012) is an example of commercial visualization tool. Depending on the adopted rule representation strategy, rule visualization approaches may be classified as follows: 2D grid view (Wong et al., 1999), 3D information landscape view (Blanchard, 2003), or the node link view (Liu et al., 2005). In the grid view, the screen is framed into smaller cells, each one corresponding to a distinct rule. Instead, in the information landscape view, a 3D grid, in which item sets are mapped, is represented (Wong et al., 1999). Finally, the node link view represents association rules as links among nodes in a graph-based model. Link color and width are exploited to represent the values of the most commonly used rule quality indexes (Liu et al., 2005). Furthermore, in Chakravarthy and Zhang (2003) the authors focus on integrating tabular 2D and 3D graphical visualizations into a unified model.

Recently, advanced rule visualization systems tailored to specific applications have also been proposed. For instance, Meng (2010) addresses the problem of fuzzy association rule visualization, while in Leung et al. (2008) the authors address the issue of visualizing frequent itemsets as polylines to improve the readability of the mined patterns compared to the raw textual form. In Li et al. (2011) pattern mining and trajectory analysis are jointly exploited to visualize animal movements. The discovered patterns are plotted on 2D plane or embedded into other visualization tools (e.g., Google Maps, Google Earth). Along with the visualized results, some statistics, if available, are presented to provide to users more insights into the achieved results. However, the effectiveness of the previously mentioned approaches strongly depends on the analyzed data distribution. For instance, when coping with fairly sparse textual data, the effectiveness of the proposed systems is biased by the highly detailed granularity level at which rules have been extracted. Hence, the generated models become either hardly readable or not informative enough. Marcos et al. (2011) made a preliminary attempt to overcome the above issue by representing generalized association rules extracted from data supplied with taxonomies. However, rules having common antecedent or consequent are grouped together and visualized as a single subset. Hence, the information at the lowest granularity levels is not easily accessible. This Chapter also addresses generalized rule visualization from textual data. Unlike Marcos et al. (2011), rules are visualized in a graph-based model and their granularity level could be selected by the analyst by exploring both the input taxonomy and the rule-based model.

Generalized Association Rule Mining

Generalized association rule mining is the task of discovering association rules (Agrawal & Srikant, 1995) that represent high-level correlations among data. By exploiting a taxonomy (i.e., a set of is-a hierarchies) that aggregates data items into upper level generalizations, generalized association rules are generated by combining items belonging to different abstraction levels. Generalized rules may allow supporting experts in making decision better than traditional rules, because they provide a high level view of the analyzed data and also represent the knowledge covered by their low level infrequent descendants.

The first generalized association rule mining algorithm, namely Cumulate, was presented in Agrawal and Srikant (1995). It is an Apriori-based algorithm (Agrawal et al., 1993; Hilage & Kulkarni, 2012) that generates high level patterns by considering, for each item, all of its parents in the hierarchy. One step further towards a more efficient extraction process for generalized association rule mining was based on new optimization strategies (Han & Fu., 1999; Hipp et al., 1998). In Hipp et al. (1998) a faster support counting is provided by exploiting the TID intersection computation, which is common in rule mining algorithms designed for the vertical data format. In Han and Fu (1999) an optimization based on top-down hierarchy traversal and multiple-support thresholds is proposed. It aims at identifying in advance generalized itemsets that cannot be frequent by means of an Apriori-like approach. To further increase the efficiency of generalized rule mining algorithms, in Pramudiono et al. (2004) an FP-tree based algorithm is proposed, while in Sriphaew and Theeramunkong (2002) both subset-superset and parent-child relationships in the lattice of generalized itemsets are exploited to avoid generating meaningless patterns. More recently, in Baralis et al. (2010) the authors propose an algorithm that performs support-driven itemset generalization, i.e., a frequent generalized itemset is extracted only if it has at least an infrequent (rare) descendant. Similar to Baralis et al. (2010), Cagliero (2011) adopts a support-driven itemset aggregation strategy to discover significant pattern changes in a dynamic context. To constrain the extraction of generalized rules, a confidence-based constraint has also been proposed (Baralis et al., 2012). It aims at preventing the generation of misleading high-confidence rules and, thus, improving the quality and the compactness of the mining result.

This work focuses on visualizing frequent generalized itemsets mined from Twitter textual data. The proposed visualization approach is taxonomy-driven, i.e., the taxonomy exploited to drive the generalized rule mining process is also used by the domain experts for selecting the most suitable data granularity level at which rules should be analyzed.

Data Mining from User-Generated Content

A significant research effort has been devoted to analyzing the content and the structure of online communities and social networks in order to discover fruitful knowledge about community user behaviors and topic trends. For instance, in Benevenuto et al. (2011) click-stream data is analyzed to identify most common Web user activities, such as universal searches, message sending, and community creation, while in Guo et al. (2009) the evolution of the online communities and the lifetime of their User-Generated Content (UGC) are investigated. In recent years, the application of data mining techniques to discover relevant social knowledge from the UGC has become an appealing research topic. For instance, significant research efforts have been devoted to (1) developing new recommendation systems to enhance the quality of product promotions (Xue et al., 2009), (2) improving the understanding of online resources (Li et al., 2008; Yin et al., 2009), and (3) building query engines that take advantage of the emerging semantics in social networks (Heymann et al., 2008).

The problem of discovering hidden associations among Twitter User-Generated Content (UGC) has already been investigated (Cagliero & Fiori, In press; Cheong & Lee, 2009). For instance, in Cheong and Lee (2009) trend patterns extracted from Twitter are exploited to identify users who contribute towards the discussions on specific trends. Similarly, TwitterMonitor (Mathioudakis & Koudas, 2010) focuses on the detecting topic trends from Twitter streams. This system first identifies and clusters the "bursty" keywords (i.e., the keywords that appear in tweets at unusually high rates), and then performs contextual knowledge extraction to compose an accurate description of the identified trends. Instead, the system proposed in Cagliero and Fiori (2013) addresses topic trend analysis from Twitter data by exploiting generalized association rules. Unlike (Cagliero & Fiori, 2013; Cheong & Lee, 2009; Mathioudakis & Koudas, 2010), the Chapter proposes a generalized rule mining and visualization system targeted to Twitter UGC analysis.

THE TWITTER GENERALIZED RULE VISUALIZER

TwiGenRule Viewer is a data mining system that focuses on supporting the discovery and exploration of frequent generalized rules mined from textual data coming from Twitter. Generalized rules, which represent high level correlations among textual terms, are visualized by exploiting a graph-based model and explored by domain experts. Rules exploration at different abstraction levels is driven by the input taxonomy, which aggregates low level document terms into higher level concepts. In Figure 1 the system architecture is depicted, while the main system blocks are described briefly in the following.

Twitter data retrieval and processing: This block aims at retrieving and preprocessing the

Figure 1. The TGRV system architecture

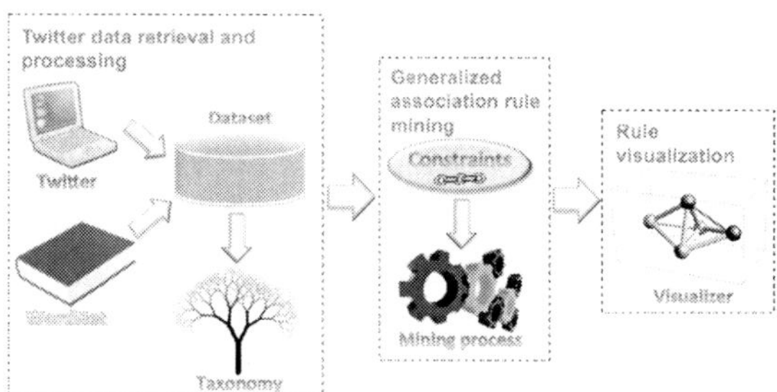

textual content coming from Twitter. Collections of Twitter messages (i.e., tweets) ranging over the same topic are crawled by exploiting the Twitter Application Programming Interfaces (APIs). Then, tweets are preprocessed in order to make them suitable for the subsequent mining phase. Furthermore, a WordNet taxonomy, which aggregates terms into higher level concepts, is built on the preprocessed data.

Generalized association rule mining: This block focuses on discovering frequent generalized rules from the previously generated textual dataset. Generalized rules represent potentially relevant term correlations holding at different abstraction levels. To guarantee the quality of the mined rule set, rule extraction is driven by established rule quality constraints (e.g., minimum support and confidence thresholds).

Rule visualization: The last block focuses on visualizing the extracted rules by exploiting a graph-based model to ease the rule-based model exploration. Graph nodes represent term sets of arbitrary size, while oriented edges represent strong associations between node couples. Expert visualization may be driven by the input taxonomy. In particular, rules belonging to different abstraction levels may be visualized separately to allow rule exploration from different viewpoints. Furthermore, visualization constraints relative to the presence/absence of specific item combinations may be also enforced.

In the following sections a more detailed description of the main TGRV blocks is given.

Twitter Data Retrieval and Preprocessing

This block addresses the retrieval and preprocessing of the tweets posted on Twitter (http://twitter.com). Tweets are user-generated textual messages publicly visible by default. Twitter APIs are general-purpose tools that allow the efficient retrieval of tweets from the Web. However, tweets are provided in a data format which is commonly unsuitable for further analysis. Furthermore, clustering tweets published in close time periods (e.g., during the last 12 hours) or ranging over the same topic is a challenging task. TGRV exploits a tweet crawler that automatically retrieves and collects tweets ranging over a specific topic by setting a number of filtering parameters. The filtering parameters may include every selection criterion provided by the Twitter APIs. The searching parameters regard either the tweet content (e.g., the contained keywords) or their context of publication (e.g., the GPS position of the user). The crawler continuously monitors the stream and retrieves tweets according to the required parameters.

Since textual data retrieved by the Twitter Stream APIs (Application Programming Interfaces) is not suitable for being directly analyzed by a rule miner, an ad-hoc preprocessing phase is needed. In particular, to suit the raw tweet textual content to the following generalized rule mining process, some preliminary data cleaning and processing steps have been applied. More specifically, stopwords, numbers, links, non-ascii characters, mentions, and replies are eliminated from the textual content. Then a traditional stemming algorithm based on WordNet (WordNet, 2012) is applied to reduce words to their root form (i.e., the stem). Each preprocessed tweet is mapped to a set of terms, each one corresponding to a distinct stem.

Definition 1 (Transactional Twitter Dataset): Let TW be a tweet set. The transactional Twitter dataset T associated with TW is a set of transactions T_i, one for each tweet tw_i T. Each transaction

$T_i=\{t_1, t_2, \ldots, t_n\}$ is a set of terms (i.e., stemmed words) relative to tw_i.

For instance, the tweet "This is the simplest message from New York City!" is mapped to the corresponding transaction {this, simple, message, New York City} composed of 4 distinct terms.

To enable the generalized rule mining process a taxonomy is built over a transactional dataset T. A taxonomy is a set of generalization hierarchies. Each generalization hierarchy is a tree-based structure whose leaf nodes are terms in T, while its upper level nodes, named *generalized terms*, aggregate items in T into higher level concepts. The level of a generalized term *tr* with respect to is defined as the height of the 's subtree rooted in *tr*.

For instance, recalling the previous example, in Figure 2 two generalization hierarchies that aggregate terms relative to specific cities and time stamps are generalized as the corresponding region and state and 3-hour and 12-hour time slots, respectively. Similarly, other generalization hierarchies may be defined on terms having different semantics. For instance, animals may be generalized as the corresponding specie and class. TRGV exploits a semi-automatic, analyst-driven approach to generating taxonomies over the transactional Twitter datasets. To build generalization hierarchies over the tweet content terms, the WordNet lexical database (WordNet, 2012) is queried to retrieve the most relevant semantic relationships holding between term couples. More specifically, TGRV considers hypernyms (is–part-of relationships) or hyponyms (i.e., is-a-subtype-of relationships) to generate meaningful generalization relationships. For instance, since the semantic relationship <New York City> is-part-of <New York State> is retrievable from the WordNet database, then term New York City may be generalized as New York State. Furthermore, the database querying process is deepened to find all the possible upper level aggregations (e.g., < New York City> is-a-subtype-of <U.S.A.>), which allow generalizing New York City as USA. In general, a taxonomy may include items that are generalized by several generalization hierarchies. However, for the sake of simplicity in the following we exclusively consider taxonomies in which items belong to at most one generalization hierarchy.

The data mining process applied on the transactional Twitter dataset supplied with a taxonomy is described in the following.

Generalized Association Rule Mining

This block aims at discovering high-level data recurrences, in the form of frequent generalized rules, from the preprocessed Twitter transactional dataset.

Generalized association rule mining is commonly accomplished by means of a two-step process (Agrawal & Srikant, 1995): (1) Frequent generalized itemset mining, driven by a minimum support threshold, and (2) generalized association rule generation, starting from the previously extracted frequent generalized itemsets.

Frequent Generalized Itemset Mining

When coping with textual data, a *k-itemset* (i.e., an itemset of length k) is defined as a set of *k* distinct terms occurring in a Twitter transactional dataset. For instance, {*message, New York City*} is an example of 2-itemset. When dealing with textual data enriched with taxonomies, a *generalized k-itemset* is defined as a set of *k* distinct terms *or* generalized terms. For instance, according to the taxonomy reported in Figure 2, {message, U.S.A.} is an example of generalized 2-itemset. Notice that itemsets are a special case of generalized itemsets which exclusively include not generalized terms.

Itemset mining is typically driven by the well-known support quality index (Agrawal et al., 1993). To define the generalized itemset support, we first introduce the concept of generalized itemset matching.

Definition 2 (Generalized itemset matching): Let *T* be a Twitter transactional dataset and Γ taxonomy defined on terms in *T*. A generalized

Figure 2. Examples of generalization hierarchies

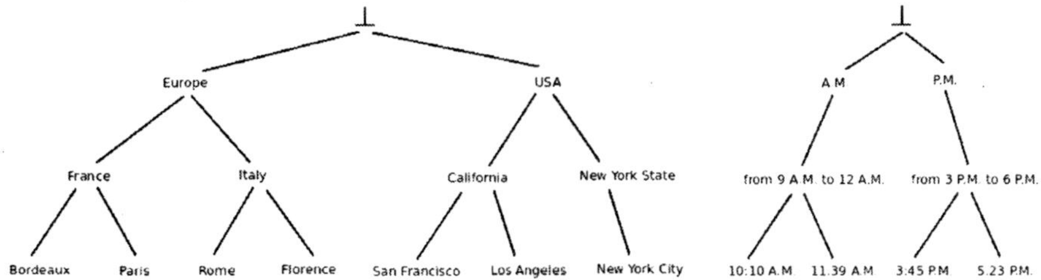

itemset X *matches* an arbitrary transaction *t* in *T* if and only if for each (possibly generalized) term *tr* in X:

- *tr* is a leaf node in Γ and it is contained in *t* or
- *tr* is a not leaf node in *T* and there exists a descendant *dtr* of *tr* with respect to Γ such that *dtr* is contained in *t*.

Definition 3 (Generalized itemset support): Let *T* be a Twitter transactional dataset and Γ taxonomy defined on *T*. The support of a generalized itemset X in T is equal to the ratio between the number of transactions *t* matched by *X* and the total number of transactions in *T*.

Hence, the support of a not generalized itemset represents its observed frequency in the analyzed dataset. Given a minimum support threshold *minsup*, a generalized itemset whose support is equal to or above a given threshold is said to be *frequent*.

Given a Twitter transactional dataset *T*, a taxonomy Γ, and a minimum support threshold *minsup*, frequent generalized itemset mining entails discovering all frequent generalized itemsets from *T*.

Generalized Association Rule Extraction

Generalized association rules are implications among term set couples, possibly including generalized terms. A more formal definition follows.

Definition 4 (Generalized association rule): Let *A* and *B* be two generalized itemsets such that $A \cap B = \varnothing$. A generalized association rule is represented in the form $A \rightarrow B$, where A and B are the body and the head of the rule, respectively.

A and *B* are also denoted as antecedent and consequent of the generalized rule $A \rightarrow B$. For example, *{New York State}* $\rightarrow$ {Message} represents a co-occurrence between a couple of generalized items.

Generalized association rule discovery is commonly driven by minimum rule support and confidence thresholds (Agrawal & Srikant, 1995), whose formal definitions follow.

Definition 5 (Generalized association rule support): Let *T* be a Twitter transactional dataset and $A \rightarrow B$ a generalized association rule. The support of $A \rightarrow B$ in T is defined as the support $A \cup B$ in *T*.

The support index represents the prior probability of $A \cup B$ (i.e., its observed frequency in the analyzed textual data).

Definition 6 (Generalized association rule confidence): Let *T* be a Twitter transactional dataset and $A \to B$ a generalized association rule. Let $s(A \cup B)$ be the support of $A \to B$ in *T*. Its confidence is given by

$$\frac{s(A \cup B)}{s(A)}$$

The confidence of a rule $A \to B$ is the conditional probability of the generalized itemset B given A. For example, the generalized rule *{New York State}* $\to$ {Message} (sup=10%, conf=50%) has a support equal to 10% because terms *New York State* and *Message* co-occur in 10% of the analyzed data (possibly at different abstraction levels). The rule confidence is 50% because *Message* occurs half of the times in which *New York State* occurs. Hence, the confidence index estimates the implication strength.

Given a Twitter transactional dataset *T*, a taxonomy Γ, a minimum support threshold *minsup*, and a minimum support threshold *minconf*, the frequent generalized association rule mining problem entails discovering all generalized association rules that satisfy both *minsup* and *minconf* in *T*.

A brief description of the algorithm integrated in TGRV for extracting the frequent generalized rules is given in the following.

The Algorithms

The mining algorithm takes in input the Twitter transactional dataset, a taxonomy, and, eventually, some mining constraints (e.g., minimum support and confidence thresholds). It discovers the generalized association rule set satisfying the enforced constraints. To prevent the discarding of relevant but infrequent knowledge, the itemset generalization process is driven by a taxonomy.

The mining task follows the usual two-step approach (Agrawal & Srikant, 1995): (1) *Extraction of the frequent generalized itemsets*, and (2) *generation of the corresponding generalized rules*. Since the first step is considered the most computationally intensive knowledge extraction task (Agrawal & Srikant, 1994), several algorithms, e.g., *Cumulate* (Agrawal & Srikant, 1995), *GenIO* (Baralis et al., 2010), *ML_T2LA-C* (Han & Fu, 1999), have been proposed to accomplish this task effectively. Next, generalized association rules are generated by applying a traditional rule mining algorithm (e.g., Agrawal & Srikant, 1994) on the extracted itemsets. The TGRV framework may potentially integrate every itemset mining algorithm. Currently, TGRV exploits a traditional generalized itemset mining algorithm, namely *Cumulate* (Agrawal & Srikant, 1995), which discovers all frequent generalized rules. To perform rule generation, TGRV exploits our implementation of the Apriori rule-mining algorithm (Agrawal & Srikant, 1994), named as *RuleGen* in the following. The main algorithm features are outlined below.

Cumulate: Cumulate is a traditional generalized itemset mining algorithm first presented in Agrawal & Srikant (1995). The Cumulate itemset mining step is based on Apriori algorithm (Agrawal & Srikant, 1994). Unlike Apriori, it performs an exhaustive taxonomy evaluation (i.e., it extracts itemsets for every level of the taxonomy) to generate generalized itemsets as well as traditional (low level) ones. Cumulate is a level-wise algorithm. At each iteration, it generates only the frequent, possibly generalized, itemsets of a given length. At arbitrary iteration k, three steps are performed: (1) Candidate generation, in which all the candidate k-itemsets are generated from the set of (k-1)-itemsets, (2) Taxonomy evaluation, which aggregates itemsets into their higher level versions, and (3) Candidate Generalized itemset support counting, performed by means of a dataset scan. Once a candidate itemset is generated, its generalized candidate versions are generated by evaluating the taxonomy. Finally, only those generalized itemsets whose support exceeds the minimum support threshold are kept.

A pseudo code of the generalization process is reported in Algorithm 1. The algorithm takes in input two parameters: a generalized itemset *X* and a taxonomy . The generalization of an itemset *X* is performed by generalizing each item *i* in *X* (lines 2-4). An item is generalized by climbing up the taxonomy stepwise (function Generalize_item(*i*,) in line 3). Since every ancestor node of *i* in the taxonomy is an item generalization, the taxonomy evaluation procedure stops when the top of the taxonomy is reached. All itemsets obtained by replacing one or more items in *X* with their generalized versions are ancestors (i.e., generalized itemsets at higher abstraction level) of *X*. Hence, the generalization of an itemset *X* may produce a set of generalized itemsets (line 5). The complete set of mined generalized itemsets is returned.

Taxonomy Evaluation

Algorithm 1: Taxonomy evaluation procedure:
Input: A generalized itemset *X*, a taxonomy Γ.
Output: All generalizations *Comb*.

1. ***Gen_items*** **=** $\varnothing$
2. **for each** item *i* in *X* **do**
3. *Gen_items* = *Gen_items* U Generalize_item(*i*, Γ)
4. end for
5. *Comb* = generate_comb(*Gen_items*)
6. **return** *Comb*

For instance, according to the taxonomy reported in Figure 2, *{message, New York City}* is generalized as *{message, New York State}* and *{message, USA}*. Generalized itemset versions are usually characterized by a higher support with respect to each of their descendants as they represent high level knowledge.

RuleGen: Given the complete set of frequent generalized itemsets, RuleGen generates frequent and high-confidence generalized rules based on the Apriori algorithm (Agrawal & Srikant, 1994). The Apriori rule generation algorithm (Cf. Algorithm 3) exploits a level-wise approach to generating association rules, where each level corresponds to the number of items that belong to the rule consequent. Initially, all the high-confidence rules having only one item in the rule consequent are extracted. These rules are used for generating new candidate rules. Since the confidence index of the rules generated from the same itemset has the anti-monotone property, candidate rules of length *k* are generated by merging two (*k-1*)-length rules that share the same prefix in the rule consequent (Agrawal & Srikant, 1994).

Although RuleGen exclusively enforces support and confidence thresholds to drive the generalized rule mining process, different and more complex mining constraints (e.g., lift, interest (Tan et al., 2005)) may be easily integrated as well.

Rule Visualization

To make strategic decisions, domain experts are used to explore the generated rule-based models. However, since rules are usually extracted from textual datasets characterized by a high dimensionality and size, a textual representation of the mined patterns is usually neither easily manageable nor interpretable by not expert readers. Furthermore, in the context of generalized rule mining, analysts may be not only interested in a simple representation of each single rule, but even in the descent relationships between rules extracted at different abstraction levels.

We propose a novel graph-based visualization model, which allows analysts to easily explore the generalized rule mining result from different viewpoints. The representation consists of a graph, namely the *Generalized Rule Graph*, in which nodes represent frequent generalized itemsets, while edges represent associations between node couples. A more formal definition follows.

Definition 7 (Generalized Rule Graph): Let *T* be a Twitter transactional dataset and $\grave{e}$ a taxonomy built on *T*. Let *minsup* and *minconf* be a minimum support and confidence thresholds. Let *R* be the set of generalized rules satisfying both *minsup* and *minconf*. A generalized rule graph *G* is a graph whose nodes are frequent generalized itemsets which are antecedents or consequents of at least one rule in *R*. For each generalized rule $A \rightarrow B$ contained in R there exists an oriented edge in *G* from *A* to *B*.

Since when coping with large and high dimensional textual data the corresponding set of frequent generalized rules may be potentially large, TGRV allows generating three complementary views of the Generalized Rule Graph.

Item-constrained viewpoint: The first viewpoint allows the analyst to focus her/his attention on the subsets of rules containing a specific item combination. For instance, consider a visualization constraint like the following one: *{New York State}* → {*}. It states that all rules containing New York State as antecedent and every other item combination as consequent should be visualized. Hence, only rules like *{New York State}* → {Message} are visualized.

Level-constrained viewpoint: The second viewpoint allows analysts exploring all the rules having items with a specific generalization level. Consider, as an example, the taxonomy reported in Figure 2. Visualizing only the rules that contain *at least* one item of level 3 may allow selecting rules like *{USA}* → {Message}. Instead, by considering rules having *only* item of level 2 a rule like *{New York State}* → {from 9 a.m. to 12 a.m.} may be visualized. In the latter case, more specific rules (e.g., *{USA}* → {9.30 a.m.}) or more general ones (e.g., *{USA}* → {a.m.}) are disregarded.

Item- and level-constrained viewpoint: The last viewpoint allows the expert to explore rules satisfying a conjunction of the previously mentioned visualization constraints. For instance, considering again *{New York State}* → {*}, the expert may would like to explore rules containing a specific generalized term or any of its descendants. Hence, rules like *{New York City}* → {Message} are visualized as well.

Note that the selectivity of the selected rule visualization perspective depends on the characteristics of the analyzed data distribution. The visualization model allows the expert to move from one viewpoint to another to have a better insight into the mining result.

EXPERIMENTAL VALIDATION

In the previous sections, we introduced and thoroughly described the Twitter Generalized Rule Visualizer (TGRV) system. To experimentally evaluate its applicability we performed experiments on two real datasets coming from Twitter.

This section is organized as follows. Section "Evaluated datasets and taxonomy" describes the main characteristics of the analyzed datasets and the corresponding taxonomies. Section "Real-life use-cases" presents two real-life use-cases for the proposed system, while Section "Characteristics of the mined patterns" analyzes the characteristics of the discovered rules.

All the experiments were performed on a 3.2 GHz Pentium IV system with 8 GB RAM, running Ubuntu 12.04.

Evaluated Datasets and Taxonomy

To retrieve the real Twitter data we monitored the public stream endpoint offered by the Twitter API over the time period [2012-09-07, 2012-09-23] and we tracked a selection of keywords ranging over different topics (e.g., education, social events). The crawler establishes and maintains a continuous connection with the stream endpoint to collect and store the Twitter data. In our crawling session, we generated two different Twitter transactional datasets, namely *Social* and *Politics*, ranging over social and political themes, respectively. Table 1 summarizes their main characteristics. To build a 5-level taxonomy over the tweet textual content, we exploited the WordNet lexical database (WordNet, 2012).

Real-Life Use-Cases

In this section, we analyze the applicability of the TGRV system in a real-life context with the help of a domain expert. In the following, we present two representative use-cases for the proposed system: the first one concerns the problem of topic trend discovery and analysis from Twitter data; the second one addresses the issue of highlighting significant Twitter user behaviors.

Topic trend analysis: The first scenario of usage for the proposed system concerns the discovery and the analysis of the topics that are currently matter of contention on Twitter.

Consider, as an example, a domain expert who is in charge of discovering from the Social dataset the subjects of topical interest for Twitter users. Mining rules like the ones depicted in Figure 3 may suggest to the expert that the education is currently matter of contention on the Web. Hence, Twitter users are likely to be currently interested in news, articles, or blogs relative to school or teaching. Note that both the not generalized rule *{Student}* → {School} and the high level (generalized) ones *{Person}* → {Educational institution} are discovered by enforcing a minimum support threshold equal to 3% and a minimum confidence threshold equal to 70%. Instead, when lowering the support threshold (e.g., minsup = 1%), the more specific rule becomes infrequent and, thus, it is discarded. However, the corresponding generalized version is kept. Hence, the information associated with the more general topic is still maintained and could be exploited by the domain expert for performing targeted analysis.

Figure 3. Social dataset. Portion of the generalized rule graph: minsup = 3%. Minconf = 70%.

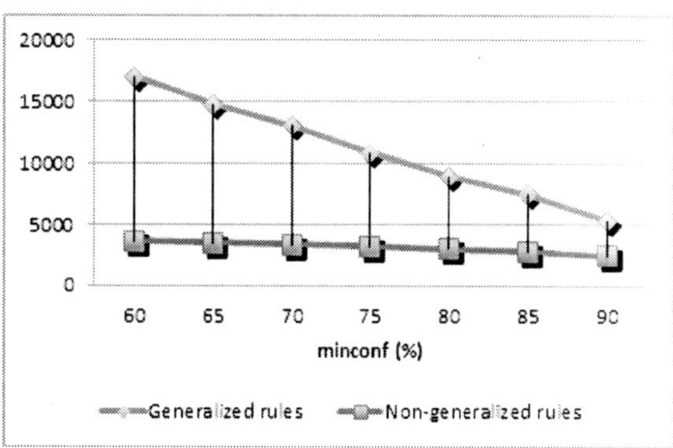

TGRV provides an insight into the underlying data correlations, which cannot be easily achieved by using traditional rule visualization approaches. In fact, since the traditional rule visualization approaches are unable to show both low level and high level rules at the same time, the capability of the domain experts to explore the discovered knowledge from different perspectives remains limited. For instance, the expert may wonder analyzing high level (more general) data correlations first. Then, she/he may perform a selective

Table 1. Dataset characteristics

Dataset Name	No. of Transactions	Total distinct words	Min. words per transaction	Avg. words per transaction	Max. words per transaction
Social	6340	3263	1	15	109
Politics	1400	577	1	14	79

drill-down on a subset of more specific rules. This reduces the complexity and improves the quality of the decision making process. For instance, since Education appear to be a subject of topical interest for Twitter users, experts may further investigate the user interest in some more specific related subjects (e.g., school, university, teaching). On the other hand, if the analysis is targeted to planning an advertising campaign, the analyst may promote the products/services that are somehow related to the currently most appealing topics. Similarly, news agencies may also the Twitter user interest to plan the daily news offer.

Consider now the *Politics* dataset. Visualizing rules relative to specific upcoming political events (e.g., American President elections, European Union meetings) may allow experts to better understand the interest of the Web users in some specific topics. For instance, since many rules contain keywords "President" and "Vote" it turns out that the attention of the Web community is mainly focused on the upcoming American elections. Although the analyzed collection is rather sparse, the visualization tool allows experts to explore many high level term correlations which are deemed valuable for targeted actions. For instance, even if the correlation between *President* and *New York City* is infrequent in the analyzed dataset by enforcing a minimum support threshold equal to 1% the corresponding high level correlation between *President* and *U.S.A. East Coast* is anyhow extracted. Hence, visualizing generalized rules beyond traditional ones positively contributes to the knowledge discovery process.

User behavior analysis: The generalized rules mined from the Politics dataset allow the experts to highlight hidden and potentially interesting user behaviors.

Rule *U.S.A. Elections* → *Europe* indicates that European users are particularly interested in the American elections. Hence, European news agencies should focus their attention on foreign politics because such events are becoming of topical interest. Note that, although the former rule provides a high level and quite general information, the expert may perform a drill-down and figure out more detailed information. For instance, rule *American Elections* → *North West Spain* provides a more specific insight into the provenance of the users who are mainly interested in the same topic. To exploit such knowledge, news agencies may adapt the news service provisioning based on the user provenance. For instance, they may set up context-aware services whereby news ranging over different topics is sent to users coming from different regions and countries. The quality of the extracted rule may be exploited to drive the selection of the most significant topics. For instance, topics occurring in high-support and high-confidence rules are more likely to represent potentially interesting news subjects.

Mobile companies may also exploit the information extracted from the Twitter datasets for different purposes. For instance, they may tailor mobile service provisioning to the actual user interest and activities. Through the analysis of the Twitter user-generated content, companies may figure out the most recurrent user behaviors. For instance, if Twitter users are used to post their messages during the evening mobile service shaping may adapt the dedicated service bandwidth to the actual service usage. In parallel, the experts may plan personalized service offers, which take into account the actual user interests. For instance, if a user is currently posting messages about politics, online magazines ranging over the same topic can be promoted. Analyzing high level data correlations allows experts to promote service/product categories, e.g., all magazines ranging over a specific topics (Economics, Politics), rather than offering a specific service or product.

Characteristics of the Mined Rules

TGRV visualizes frequent generalized rules extracted from the analyzed Twitter transactional datasets. Since the enforcement of the minimum support and confidence thresholds may affect the characteristics of the mining result significantly, we analyzed the cardinality of the mined set by varying the values of both constraints.

Figure 4 reports the number of rules mined from the real-life dataset Politics, taken as representative, by setting the minimum confidence threshold to 70% and by varying the minimum support threshold in the range [1%, 10%]. Similarly, Figure 5 reports the number of rules mined from the same representative dataset by setting the minimum confidence threshold to 3% and by varying the minimum confidence threshold in the range [60%, 90%]. As expected, the number of mined rules increases more than linearly when lowering the support threshold due to the combinatorial increase of the number of generated combinations (Baralis et al., 2010). Oppositely, increasing the confidence threshold value on average reduce the cardinality of the mined set. In Figures 4 and 5 we also partitioned the extracted rules in generalized and not, i.e., rules containing at least one generalized term and not. At relatively high support thresholds (e.g., 8%), the cardinality of the set of generalized rules is comparable with the one of the not generalized rule set. Instead, when lowering the support thresholds, many not generalized rules become infrequent with respect to the support threshold, while the generalized rules are still mined because they represent more general information. Hence, the cardinality of mined generalized rules becomes significantly larger than the number of the not generalized ones (e.g., around 80% against 20% at *minsup*=1%).

Figure 4. Politics dataset. Impact of the support threshold on the number of mined rules.

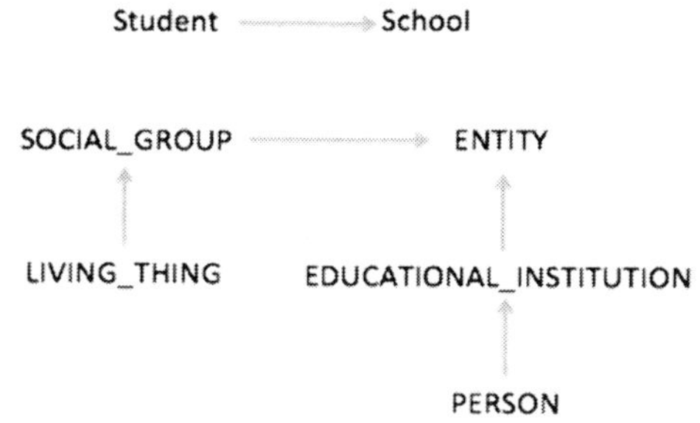

Figure 5. Politics dataset. Impact of the confidence threshold on the number of mined rules.

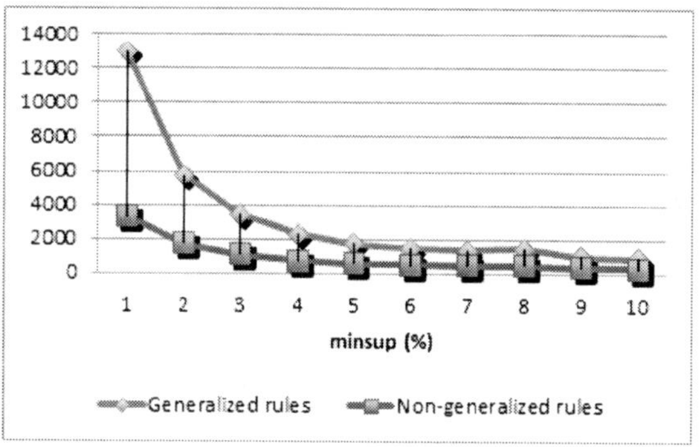

FUTURE RESEARCH DIRECTIONS

The approach presented in this chapter has been experimentally evaluated on real-life Twitter textual data. However, we plan to investigate the applicability of the proposed tool in different application contexts as future work. For instance, in the context of medical data analysis, doctors and scientists are commonly interested in analyzing the results of the data mining process from different perspectives. For instance, medical exams are usually categorized in different classes and high level correlations between exams may be discovered and exploited to evaluate the adherence of medical treatments to standard guidelines. On the other hand, census data relative to patients with common diseases may be analyzed in order to discover unexpected data correlations at different abstraction levels.

In the context of network traffic analysis the proposed visualization system could also find interesting applications. For instance, to discover and analyze unexpected network traffic flows analysts may aggregate IP addresses into their corresponding subnets in order to discover data correlations at higher granularity levels. Once an unexpected flow has been detected, they may perform a drill-down to analyze the low level data correlations relative to the corresponding individual IP addresses.

CONCLUSION

This chapter presents TGRV, a data mining system that addresses generalized rule mining and visualization from Twitter textual content. Twitter messages are retrieved from the Web and analyzed to discover high correlations among terms. A graph-based visualization model is proposed to show the underlying term correlations at different abstraction levels. TGRV performance has been evaluated on real-life Twitter datasets with the help of a domain expert. The usefulness of the proposed approach has been evaluated in two real-life use-cases relative to topic trend discovery and user behavior analysis.

REFERENCES

Agrawal, R., Imieliski, T., & Swami, R. (1993). Mining association rules between sets of items in large databases. *SIGMOD Record*, *22*(2), 207–216. doi:10.1145/170036.170072.

Agrawal, R., & Srikant, R. (1994). Fast algorithms for mining association rules in large databases. In J. B. Bocca, M. Jarke, & C. Zaniolo (Eds.), *Proceedings of the International Conference on Very Large Data Bases* (pp. 487-499). San Francisco, CA: Morgan Kaufmann.

Agrawal, R., & Srikant, R. (1995). Mining generalized association rules. In *Proceedings of the International Conference on Very Large Data Bases* (pp. 407-419). San Francisco, CA: Morgan Kaufmann.

Baldi, M., Baralis, E., & Risso, F. (2005). Data mining techniques for effective and scalable traffic analysis. In *Proceedings of the International Symposium on Integrated Network Management* (pp. 105-118). IEEE Press.

Baralis, E., Cagliero, L., Cerquitelli, T., D'Elia, V., & Garza, P. (2010). Support driven opportunistic aggregation for generalized itemset extraction. In *Proceedings of the 2010 IEEE Conference on Intelligent Systems* (pp. 102-107). IEEE Press.

Baralis, E., Cagliero, L., Cerquitelli, T., & Garza, P. (2012). Generalized association rule mining with constraints. *Information Sciences*, *194*, 68–84. doi:10.1016/j.ins.2011.05.016.

Baralis, E., Cagliero, L., Cerquitelli, T., Garza, P., & Marchetti, M. (2009). Context-aware user and service profiling by means of generalized association rules. In *Proceedings of the Conference on Knowledge and Engineering Systems* (pp. 50-57). Springer.

Benevenuto, F., Rodrigues, T., Cha, M., & Almeida, V. (2011). Characterizing user navigation and interactions in online social networks. *Information Sciences*.

Berardi, M., Lapi, M., Leo, P., & Loglisci, C. (2005). Mining generalized association rules on biomedical literature. In *Proceedings of the 18th International Conference on Innovations in Applied Artificial Intelligence* (IEA/AIE'2005). London: Springer-Verlag.

Blanchard, J., Guillet, F., & Briand, H. (2003). Exploratory visualization for association rule rummaging. In *Proceedings of the 4th International Workshop on Multimedia Data Mining MDM/KDD2003*, (pp. 107-114). Washington, DC: MDM/KDD.

Cagliero, L. (2011). Discovering temporal change patterns in the presence of taxonomies. *IEEE Transactions on Knowledge and Data Engineering*, 99.

Cagliero, L., & Fiori, A. (2013). Generalized association rule mining from Twitter. In *Intelligent Data Analysis*. Amsterdam: IOS Press.

Chakravarthy, S., & Zhang, H. (2003). Visualization of association rules over relational DBMSs. In *Proceedings of the 2003 ACM symposium on Applied Computing* (pp. 922–926). ACM.

Cheong, M., & Lee, V. (2009). Integrating web-based intelligence retrieval and decision-making from the twitter trends knowledge base. In *Proceedings of the Second ACM Workshop on Social Web Search and Mining* (pp. 1-8). ACM Press.

Chernoff, H. (1973). The use of faces to represent points in k-dimensional space graphically. *Journal of the American Statistical Association*, *68*(342), 361–367. doi:10.1080/01621459.1973.10482434.

Couturier, O., Mephu Nguifo, E., & Noiret, B. (2005). A formal approach to occlusion and optimization in association rules visualization. In *Proceedings of VDM of IEEE 9th International Conference on Information Visualization*. IEEE Press.

Fayyad, U., Grinstein, G. G., & Wierse, A. (2001). *Information visualization in data mining and knowledge discovery*. San Francisco, CA: Morgan Kaufmann Publishers Inc..

Fry, B. (2007). *Visualizing data*. Sebastopol, CA: O'Reilly Media.

Grinstein, G., Pickett, R. M., & Williams, M. G. (1989). EXVIS: An exploratory visualization environment. In *Proceedings of Graphics Interface '89*. London: IEEE.

Guo, L., Tan, E., Chen, S., Zhang, X., & Zhao, Y. E. (2009). Analyzing patterns of user content generation in online social networks. In *Proceedings of the 15th ACM SIGKDD International Conference on Knowledge Discovery and Data Mining*, (pp. 369-378). ACM.

Hamasaki, M., Matsuo, Y., Nishimura, T., & Takeda, H. (2009). Ontology extraction by collaborative tagging. In *Proceedings of World Wide Web* (pp. 427–437). IEEE.

Han, J., & Fu, Y. (1999). Mining multiple-level association rules in large databases. *IEEE Transactions on Knowledge and Data Engineering*, *11*(5), 798–805. doi:10.1109/69.806937.

Han, J., Pei, J., & Yin, Y. (2000). Mining frequent patterns without candidate generation. In *Proceedings ACM-SIGMOD International Conference Management of Data* (pp. 1-12). ACM Press.

Havre, S., Hetzler, E., Whitney, P., & Nowell, L. (2002). Themeriver: Visualizing thematic changes in large document collections. *IEEE Transactions on Visualization and Computer Graphics*, *8*, 9–20. doi:10.1109/2945.981848.

Heymann, P., Ramage, D., & Garcia-Molina, H. (2008). Social tag prediction. In *Proceedings of the 31st Annual International ACM SIGIR Conference on Research and Development in Information Retrieval* (pp. 531-538). ACM Press.

Hilage, T. A., & Kulkarni, V. (2012). Review of literature on data mining. *International Journal in Research and Reviews in Applied Sciences*, *10*(1), 1–14.

Hipp, J., Myka, A., Wirth, R., & Guntzer, U. (1998). A new algorithm for faster mining of generalized rules. In *Proceedings of the 2nd European Symposium on Principles of Data Mining and Knowledge Discovery* (pp. 72–82). IEEE.

Keim, D. A. (2000). Designing pixel-oriented visualization techniques: Theory and applications. *IEEE Transactions on Visualization and Computer Graphics*, *6*, 59–78. doi:10.1109/2945.841121.

Keim, D. A. (2002). Information visualization and visual data mining. *IEEE Transactions on Visualization and Computer Graphics*, *8*, 1–8. doi:10.1109/2945.981847.

Lau, R. Y. K., Song, D., Li, Y., Cheung, T. C. H., & Hao, J. (2009). Toward a fuzzy domain ontology extraction method for adaptive e-learning. *IEEE Transactions on Knowledge and Data Engineering*, *21*(6), 800–813. doi:10.1109/TKDE.2008.137.

Leung, C.-S., Irani, P., & Carmicheal, C. (2008). Wifisviz: Effective visualization of frequent itemsets. In *Proceedings of the VIII IEEE International Conference on Data Mining (ICDM '08)*, (pp. 875–880). IEEE Press.

Li, X., Guo, L., & Zhao, Y. (2008). Tag-based social interest discovery. In *Proceedings of the 17th International Conference on World Wide Web* (pp. 675-684). ACM Press.

Li, Z., Han, J., Ji, M., Tang, L.-A., Yu, Y., Ding, B., … Kays, R. (2011). Movemine: Mining moving object data for discovery of animal movement patterns. *ACM Transactions on Intelligent Systems Technologies, 2*, 37:1–37:32.

Liu, B., Hsu, W., Wang, K., & Chen, S. (1999). Visually aided exploration of interesting association rules. In *Proceedings of the 3rd Pacific-Asia Conference on Knowledge Discovery and Data Mining* (pp. 380-389). IEEE.

Liu, B., Ma, Y., & Lee, R. (2001). Analyzing the interestingness of association rules from the temporal dimension. In *Proceeding of the International Conference on Data Mining*, (pp. 377-384). IEEE Press.

Liu, Y., & Salvendy, G. (2005). Visualization to facilitate association rules modeling: A review. *Ergonomia IJE&HF*, *27*(1), 11–23.

Mathioudakis, M., & Koudas, N. (2010). TwitterMonitor: Trend detection over the twitter stream. In *Proceedings of the 2010 International Conference on Management of Data* (pp. 1155-1158). ACM Press.

Meng, H. S., & Fong, S. (2010). Visualizing e-government portal and its performance in WEBVS. In *Proceedings of the Fifth International Conference on Digital Information Management (ICDIM)* (pp. 315-320). IEEE Press.

MineSet. (2012). Retrieved from www.sgi.com/software/mineset

Pramudiono, I., & Kitsuregawa, M. (2004). FP-tax: Tree structure based generalized association rule mining. In *Proceedings ACM SIGMOD Workshop on Research Issues in Data Mining and Knowledge Discovery* (pp. 60-63). ACM Press.

Ropinski, T., Oeltze, S., & Preim, B. (2011). Visual computing in biology and medicine: Survey of glyph-based visualization techniques for spatial multivariate medical data. *Computer Graphics*, *35*(2), 392–401. doi:10.1016/j.cag.2011.01.011.

Simoff, S. J., Behlen, M. H., & Mazeika, A. (2008). Visual data mining: An introduction and overview. In Simoff, S. J., Behlen, M. H., & Mazeika, A. (Eds.), *Visual Data Mining (LNCS)*. Springer-Verlag. doi:10.1007/978-3-540-71080-6_1.

Sriphaew, K., & Theeramunkong, T. (2002). A new method for finding generalized frequent itemsets in association rule mining. In *Proceedings of the VII International Symposium on Computers and Communications* (pp. 20-26). ACM Press.

Tan, P., Kumar, V., & Srivastava, J. (2002). Selecting the right interestingness measure for association patterns. In *Proceedings ACM SIGMOD International Conference on Knowledge Discovery and Data Mining* (pp. 32-41). ACM Press.

Tan, P.-N., Steinbach, M., & Kumar, V. (2005). *Introduction to data mining*. Reading, MA: Addison-Wesley.

Wong, P. C., Whitney, P., & Thomas, J. (1999). Visualizing association rules for text mining. In *Proceedings of the 1999 IEEE Symposium on Information Visualization* (INFOVIS '99), (pp. 120-128). Washington, DC: IEEE Computer Society.

WordNet Lexical Database. (2012). Retrieved from http://wordnet.princeton.edu

Xue, Y., Zhang, C., Zhou, C., Lin, X., & Lin, Q. (2009). An effective news recommendation in social media based on users' preference. In *Proceedings of the International Workshop on Education Technology and Training* (pp. 627-631). IEEE Computer Society.

Yahia, B., Mephu, S., & Nguifo, E. (2004). Emulating a cooperative behavior in a generic association rule visualization tool. In *Proceedings of the16th IEEE International Conference on Tools with Artificial Intelligence (ICTAI'04)*. Boca Raton, FL: IEEE Press.

Yin, Z., Li, R., Mei, Q., & Han, J. (2009). Exploring social tagging graph for web object classification. In *Proceedings of the 15th ACM SIGKDD International Conference on Knowledge Discovery and Data Mining* (pp. 957-966). ACM Press.

ADDITIONAL READING

Agrawal, R., & Psaila, G. (1995). Active data mining. In *Proceedings of the First International Conference on Knowledge Discovery and Data Mining* (pp. 3-8). ACM Press.

Cagliero, L., & Fiori, A. (2011). Knowledge discovery from online communities. In *Social Networking and Community Behavior Modeling: Qualitative and Quantitative Measures*. Academic Press. doi:10.4018/978-1-61350-444-4.ch007.

Cerquitelli, T., Fiori, A., & Grand, A. (2011). *Community-contributed media collections: Knowledge at our fingertips*, 21.

Cunha, E., Magno, G., Comarela, G., Almeida, V., Gonçalves, M. A., & Benevenuto, F. (2011). *Analyzing the dynamic evolution of hashtags on twitter: A language-based approach*. ACL HLT.

Eisenstein, J., O'Connor, B., Smith, N. A., & Xing, E. P. (2010). A latent variable model for geographic lexical variation. In *Proceedings of the 2010 Conference on Empirical Methods in Natural Language Processing*, (pp. 1277-1287). IEEE.

Han, J. (2009). Data mining. In Liu, L., & Tamer, M. (Eds.), *Encyclopedia of Database Systems* (pp. 595–598). New York: Springer.

Ienco, D., & Meo, M. (2008). Towards the automatic construction of conceptual taxonomies. In *Proceedings of the 10th International Conference on Data Warehousing and Knowledge Discovery* (pp. 327-336). Berlin: Springer-Verlag.

Java, A., Song, X., Finin, T., & Tseng, B. (2007). Why we twitter: Understanding microblogging usage and communities. In *Proceedings of the 9th WebKDD and 1st SNA-KDD 2007 Workshop on Web Mining and Social Network Analysis*, (pp. 56-65). SNA-KDD.

Kasneci, G., Ramanath, M., Suchanek, F., & Weikum, G. (2009). The YAGO-NAGA approach to knowledge discovery. *SIGMOD Record*, *37*(4), 41–47. doi:10.1145/1519103.1519110.

Kimball, R., Ross, M., & Merz, R. (2002). *The data warehouse toolkit: The complete guide to dimensional modeling*. New York: Wiley.

Kwak, H., Lee, C., Park, H., & Moon, S. (2010). What is Twitter, a social network or a news media? In *Proceedings of the 19th International Conference on World Wide Web*, (pp. 591-600). IEEE.

Lam, H. Y., & Yeung, D. Y. (2007). A learning approach to spam detection based on social networks. In *Proceedings of the Fourth Conference on Email and Anti-Spam* (pp. 81-94). AIDAA.

Lee, C., Kwak, H., Park, H., & Moon, S. (2010). Finding influentials based on the temporal order of information adoption in twitter. In *Proceedings of the 19th International Conference on World Wide Web*, (pp. 1137-1138). IEEE.

Mislove, A., Marcon, M., Gummadi, K. P., Druschel, P., & Bhattacharjee, B. (2007). Measurement and analysis of online social networks. In *Proceedings of the 7th ACM SIGCOMM Conference on Internet Measurement*, (pp. 29-42). ACM.

Neshati, M., & Hassanabadi, L. S. (2007). Taxonomy construction using compound similarity measures. In *Proceedings of the 2007 OTM Confederated International Conference on the Move to Meaningful Internet Systems* (pp. 915-932). Berlin: Springer-Verlag.

Olivier, C., Tarek, H., Sadok, B. Y., & Engelbert, M. N. (2007). A scalable association rule visualization towards displaying large amounts of knowledge. In *Proceedings of the 11th International Conference Information Visualization (IV '07)*. IEEE Computer Society.

Phelan, O., McCarthy, K., Bennett, M., & Smyth, B. (2011). Terms of a feather: Content-based news recommendation and discovery using twitter. In *Proceedings of Advances in Information Retrieval* (pp. 448–459). IEEE. doi:10.1007/978-3-642-20161-5_44.

Qamra, A., Tseng, B., & Chang, E. Y. (2006). Mining blog stories using community-based and temporal clustering. In *Proceedings of the 15th ACM International Conference on Information and Knowledge Management*, (pp. 58-67). ACM Press.

Rodrigues Barbosa, G. A., Silva, I. S., Zaki, M., Meira, W., Jr., Prates, R. O., & Veloso, A. (2012). Characterizing the effectiveness of Twitter hashtags to detect and track online population sentiment. In *Proceedings of the 2012 ACM Annual Conference Extended Abstracts on Human Factors in Computing Systems Extended Abstracts*, (pp. 2621-2626). ACM.

Sakaki, T., Okazaki, M., & Matsuo, Y. (2010). Earthquake shakes Twitter users: Real-time event detection by social sensors. In *Proceedings of the 19th International Conference on World Wide Web*, (pp. 851-860). IEEE.

Tanbeer, S., Ahmed, C., & Jeong, B.S. (2010). Mining regular patterns in data streams. *Database Systems for Advanced Applications*, 399-413.

Wang, J., Li, Q., Chen, Y. P., & Lin, Z. (2010). User comments for news recommendation in forum-based social media. In *Information Sciences* (pp. 4929–4939). London: Elsevier.

Woon, W., & Madnick, S. (2009). Asymmetric information distances for automated taxonomy construction. *Knowledge and Information Systems*, *21*(2), 91–111. doi:10.1007/s10115-009-0203-5.

KEY TERMS AND DEFINITIONS

Association Rule Mining: Association rule mining is a widely used exploratory technique to discover relevant correlations hidden in the analyzed data.

Data Mining and Knowledge Discovery: The Data mining and Knowledge Discovery (KDD) is the process of extracting patterns from data and exploiting them to support analyst decision making.

Data Visualization: The task of proposing visual tools suitable for supporting KDD tasks.

Frequent Itemset: Set of data items occurring frequently in the analyzed dataset.

Information Visualization: Visualization and exploration of large volumes of data.

Itemset Generalization Process: The itemset generalization process is the task of aggregating items into higher level concepts by exploiting a taxonomy built on the analyzed data.

Social Network Analysis: Analysis of the structure of social networks and online communities and mining from social network user-generated content to support the knowledge discovery process.

Taxonomy: A taxonomy is a representation of a set of is-a relationships between concepts in a knowledge domain.

User-Generated Content: Textual and multimedia content (e.g., photos, videos, posts, tags) published by Web users on social networks and online communities.

Visual Data Mining: The process of exploiting advanced visualization tools to support experts in dealing with the flood of information generated by a data mining session.

Chapter 9
Information Visualization Techniques for Big Data:
Analytics using Heterogeneous Data in Spatiotemporal Domains

William H. Hsu
Kansas State University, USA

ABSTRACT

This chapter presents challenges and recommended practices for visualizing data about phenomena that are observed or simulated across space and time. Some data may be collected for the express purpose of answering questions through quantitative analysis and simulation, especially about future occurrences or continuations of the phenomena – that is, prediction. In this case, analytical computations may serve two purposes: to prepare the data for presentation and to answer questions by producing information, especially an informative model, that can also be visualized. These purposes may have significant overlap. Thus, the focus of the chapter is about analytical techniques for visual display of quantitative data and information that scale up to large data sets. It begins by surveying trends in educational and scientific use of visualization and reviewing taxonomies of data to be visualized. Next, it reviews aspects of spatiotemporal data that pose challenges, such as heterogeneity and scale, along with techniques for dealing specifically with geospatial data and text. An exploration of concrete applications then follows. Finally, tenets of information visualization design, put forward by Tufte and other experts on data representation and presentation, are considered in the context of analytical applications for heterogeneous data in spatiotemporal domains.

1. TRENDS IN DATA VISUALIZATION

1.1. Learning and Analytics Tasks

This section provides a brief history of information visualization for educational and scientific applications, followed by a survey of challenges and tools encountered in visualizing data.

DOI: 10.4018/978-1-4666-4462-5.ch009

1.1.1. Brief History of Prediction

Information visualization is the study of (interactive) visual representations of abstract data to reinforce human cognition. ("Information visualization", Wikipedia, 2013) Abstract data include both numerical data such as geospatial locations or other physical measurements, and non-numerical data such as text. However, information visualization differs from scientific visualization:

Munzner (2008) advises using the term "infovis (for information visualization) when the spatial representation is chosen", and "scivis (scientific visualization) when the spatial representation is given". According to Friendly (2009), scientific visualization is primarily concerned with the "visualization of three-dimensional phenomena (architectural, meteorological, medical, biological, etc.), where the emphasis is on realistic renderings of volumes, surfaces, illumination sources, and so forth, perhaps with a dynamic (time) component".

Input data for visualization includes observational data, collected for the express purpose of answering questions through quantitative analysis, and simulated data, which is generated using a mathematical model. One particular type of simulated data consists of future occurrences or continuations of the phenomena – that is, prediction. Modeling of phenomena for the purpose of forecasting predates computational realization of the methods used, including econometrics (Frisch, 1929) and statistical hypothesis testing (Neyman & Pearson, 1933; Fisher, 1935). Some of the earliest methods for nonlinear time series prediction were extrapolation, interpolation, and smoothing methods derived by: Wiener (1949); Brown (1956), Holt (1957), and Winters (1960); and Box and Jenkins (1970). These contributions comprise fundamental representation and estimation methods that underlie spectral analysis approaches to signal identification, including autoregressive moving average (ARMA) process models.

Although specifically geared towards time series and geospatial data, the visualization approaches covered in this chapter are generally applicable to a variety of data sets and to the behavior and output of many type of machine learning algorithms. Hall et al. (2009) give a much more detailed catalogue of the models and algorithms implemented in the Waikato Environment for Knowledge Analysis (WEKA), to which we refer the interested reader. Predictive visualization, the aspect of information visualization that especially focuses on the continuation of time series beyond historical observations, often poses questions of evaluation using previous unseen data. Watson and Wixom (2009) describe architectures for this type of analytical modeling, among others, in the domain of business intelligence (BI). Business intelligence comprises theories, methodologies, and technologies that serve to transform raw data into information for business decision making. Similar uses of prediction and visualization can be found in most fields where sequences and time series are observed as signals. This includes neuroscience, where such measurements are fundamental, giving rise to the work of scientists such as Elger and Lehnertz (1998).

1.1.2. Challenges of Heterogeneity in Big Data

The term heterogeneous data refers to variables that are fundamentally diverse in character, particularly their source and means of acquisition. One of the key challenges to working with heterogeneous data is that multiple dimensions and a very high volume of data may result from differences in data provenance (origin and preprocessing history). This issue gives rise to the problem of designing visual representations that can consistently support the display of such data. Heer, Kong, and Agrawala (2009) present adjustable parameters such as layering and chart sizing, and discuss the perceptual effects of introducing such degrees of freedom. Monmonier (1990) discusses methods from statistics for coping with the additional technical challenge of working with spatial data over time.

A further challenge is that of big data, a generic term used to refer to data of high complexity (especially intrinsic complexity), the value that can be derived from the data using various analytical methods, and longitudinal information. Mike 2.0 (2013) notes furthermore that big data does not necessarily mean extremely large in size, if the other aspects of analytical task complexity are high. Kumar et al. (2005) present some specific approaches to scaling up visualizations to large data sets, such as introducing trend lines, quartile boxes, etc. The provenance of big data, like that of visualization data, plays an important role.

Cox and Ellsworth (1997) discuss facets of complexity, distinguishing between big data collections, which "typically arise in fields with acquired data, as from remote sensors and satellite imaging", and big data objects, which "typically are the result of large-scale simulations in such areas as Computational Fluid Dynamics (CFD), Structural Analysis, Weather Modeling, and Astrophysics". With respect to collections, they note that data within them often:

- Tend to be "distributed among multiple sites".
- Are stored within "collections of heterogeneous databases (each the repository for data acquired or processed at that site)".
- Have "generally incompatible data interfaces and representations" and are "generally not self-describing".
- Admit "no platform-independent definition of the data types in the underlying data, and the relationship between them" (e.g., no well-defined relational data model).
- Do not have "meta-data that facilitate discovery and use" stored with them (e.g., describing where and when they were collected, what calibration was applied, what their units, are etc.). Such metadata "may (and probably should) also include compressed and/or condensed representations of the underlying data" to "enable browsing of a large collection".
- Are difficult to retrieve or locate: "Visualization can serve an important role in data location, in particular by compressing summary information in a format that can be visually understood quickly".
- Admit large storage requirements, "requiring partitioning between disk and tape" (or between secondary and tertiary storage in general).
- Admit "poor locality in the queries for the data (since, for example, requests may be to diverse variables measured at arbitrary times). Any particular request is more likely to require data from tap than from disk", meaning that responses may need to be freshly computed or observed rather than retrieved from archives.
- Require "raw bandwidths required to satisfy requests [that] may be quite large for any actively used collection. These include bandwidths from tape to disk, from disk to memory, from memory to network, and across the network."

An independent set of characteristics for data objects is that they present challenges to:

- **Data modeling:** Multi-dimensionality, lack of a standardized representation and interfaces for structured data (as above). "As a result, visualization codes typically must handle multiple file formats and data representations."
- **Data model evolution:** Dynamicity of representations including relational schemas and formats, *e.g.*, alternative grid structures in Computational Fluid Dynamics.

Specific additional challenges for big data objects are:

- **Data management:** "There is generally not a clean division between the data models (where they exist) and data management". This requires "special handling of data sets that do not fit in main memory". In more current terminology, there is a resultant lack of good data description languages as used in semistructured data (especially XML, which includes a standard for document type definitions).

- **"Data too big to be memory-resident":** "Often a single data object does not fit in main memory." CFD applications earlier than the late 1990s produced time-varying data objects on the order of 10 gigabytes (Gb) and those of 1997 were 100-200Gb. As of 2013, this typical figure has grown by three decimal orders of magnitude to 300+ terabytes (Tb).
- **"Data too big for local disk (perhaps even for remote disk)":** This meant hundreds of gigabytes (more than 650, approximately 7×10^{11} bytes) in 1997 and hundreds of terabytes to petabytes (10^{14}-10^{15} bytes) at the time of this writing.
- **"Bandwidth and latency":** The need, resulting in part from the preceding challenges, to find alternatives to secondary storage-based virtual memory with a high bandwidth, low latency data pathway between the data store and main memory.

Steele and Illinsky (2010) survey and catalog the above challenges in several modern domains, viewing these requirements in the context of functional and aesthetic criteria. Cuzzocrea, Song, and Davis (2011) further discuss the challenges inherent in dealing with large-scale multidimensional data analytics, especially moving towards NoSQL query languages and Map-Reduce platforms such as Hadoop. A 2011 panel at the DOLAP conference on online analytical processing that discussed visualization issues, among other aspects of analytics, advocated an emphasis on decision support context and the ability to explore multidimensional spaces.

1.1.3. Current and Emerging Technologies for Visualizing Data

Goldstein and Roth (1994) introduced a hierarchical framework for data browsing, comprising an interface mechanism they called the Aggregate Manipulator (AM). Combined with the Dynamic Query (DQ) mechanism of Ahlberg, Williamson, and Shneiderman (1992), this system has served as a widely adopted paradigm, much like the model-view-controller framework of Reenskaug (1979) among Graphical User Interface (GUI) developers.

The term visual analytics was coined to describe "an outgrowth of the fields of information visualization and scientific visualization that focuses on analytical reasoning facilitated by interactive visual interfaces" (Kovalerchuk & Schwing, 2004; "visual analytics", Wikipedia, 2013). Active clientele of this technology include developers of business decision support technology. In particular, the use of visualization in e-commerce has recently risen, exemplified by Customer Relationship Management (CRM) and business intelligence tools that incorporate data mining-based analytics and visualization. (Cadez et al., 2000) Cannataro and Talia (2003) present an architecture they call the knowledge grid that implements a scalable infrastructure for widespread access to online services as visualization or analytics.

Meanwhile, Keim et al. (2006) note in a survey article that visual analytics "combines strengths from information analytics, geospatial analytics, scientific analytics, statistical analytics, knowledge discovery, data management and knowledge representation, presentation, production and dissemination, cognition, perception, and interaction". They also discuss the following specific open problems of visualization in detail:

1. Synthesis of heterogeneous types of data.
2. Human interpretability requirements.
3. Data transformations and integration constraints.
4. "Problem solving, decision science, and human information discourse".
5. Semantics for future analytical tasks and decision-centered visualization (a key feature of user modeling, adaptation, and personalization).

6. Promotion of user acceptability by "addressing the challenges of new systems to be pervasive, embedded, nomadic, adaptable, powerful, intentional and eternal" *cf.* MIT Project Oxygen (2004).
7. Integration into intelligent user interfaces.
8. Derivation of objective evaluation criteria.

Summarizing common design tenets that for the above requirements, Keim *et al.* derive the following "visual analytics mantra".

1.2. Taxonomies: Scientific, Data, and Information Visualization

As Munzner (2008) notes, the term scientific visualization is distinct from information visualization, in that scientific visualization aims at rendering phenomena, to a given spatial representation. That is, scientific observations entail a set of requirements and a specification – sometimes constrained by the instrumentation or use cases, such as Geographic Information Systems (GIS) software. Information visualization typically leaves more degrees of representational freedom to the designer, having performance criteria related to usability and graphical excellence, rather than using predetermined constraints. Finally, data visualization gives some of the design freedom of information visualization but involves abstraction of raw observation data to some schematic form, and generally involves less preprocessing, analysis, and annotation of the source data.

2. ASPECTS OF SPATIOTEMPORAL DATA

We now discuss some aspects of data that include a spatial ("length-scale") or temporal ("time-scale") measure. Theses spatiotemporal data are most frequently presented in map and timeline form, but can be captured and represented in other ways.

2.1. Space and Time

A spatiotemporal sequence is a data set whose points are ordered by location and time. Spatiotemporal sequences arise in analytical applications such as time series prediction and monitoring, sensor integration, and multimodal human-computer intelligent interaction. Learning to classify time series is an important capability of intelligent systems for such applications. Many problems and types of knowledge in intelligent reasoning with time series, such as diagnostic monitoring, prediction (or forecasting), and control automation can be represented as classification. The machine learning task that yields the capability of forecasting is described using the term modeling, while higher-level descriptive characterization of the time series is referred to as understanding. Spatiotemporal physical data can include scientific and engineering measurements at microscopic or sub-microscopic orders of spatial magnitude, and similarly small orders of temporal magnitude. Some domains such as genome biology and particle physics admit both information visualization and scientific visualization. Infovis may be feasible using descriptive statistics or summary attributes of an entire entity such as the genome of an entire organism, whereas scivis may use a standard visual metaphor such as a ladder depiction of the DNA double helix or the colored-ball molecular renderings produced by RasMol (2013).

2.1.1. Capturing and Creating Spatial Data: Georeferencing

Extracting spatially-referenced events, even using structured data sources, entails a straightforward but data-intensive georeferencing task: looking up the coordinates (latitude and longitude) of locations where events are reported to have occurred. These may be identified as buildings or landmarks. The resulting coordinates are placed into a spatial database management system (SDBMS) for visualization using software libraries and services, as shown in Figure 1. Such a system uses two access layers with a unified representation and Geographic Information System (GIS) data model: one based on a geospatial markup language such as Google's Keyhole Markup Language (KML) and a file-based Application Programmer Interface (API), while the second layer is based on a server-side interface to a relational database implementing the schema.

2.1.2. Capturing Temporal Data

Figure 1 also depicts the data integration between the map and timeline visualization subsystems. The seizure event in April, 2010 is represented on the map by a pop-up note, on the monthly scale timeline (upper right) by a circled dot, and on the yearly scale timeline (lower right) by a circled point.

2.1.3. Predictive Analytics: Forecasting, Modeling, and Understanding

A *spatiotemporal* sequence is a data set whose points are ordered by location and time. Spatiotemporal sequences arise in analytical applications such as time series prediction and monitoring, sensor integration, and multimodal human-computer intelligent interaction. Learning to classify time series is an important capability of intelligent systems for such applications. Many problems and types of knowledge in intelligent reasoning with time series, such as diagnostic monitoring, prediction (or *forecasting*), and control automation can be represented as classification. The machine learning task that yields the capability of forecasting is described using the term *modeling*, while higher-level descriptive characterization of the time series is referred to as *understanding*.

Figure 1. Map and timeline visualization of meth lab seizure events (2004-2011) using Google Maps and MIT SIMILE. Seizures from the first half of 2010 are depicted, with one event selected.

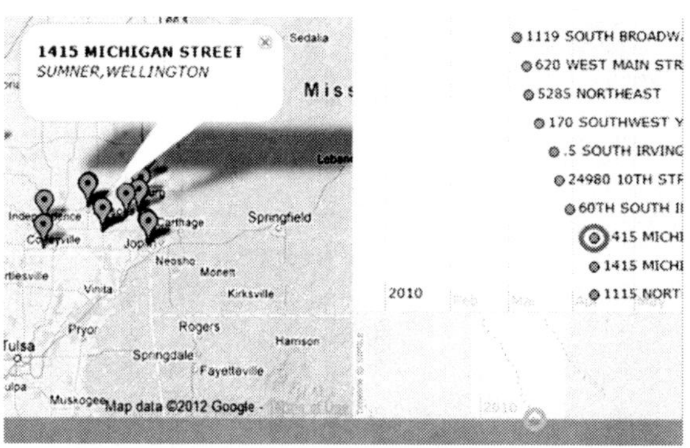

2.2. Big Data: Multidimensionality and the Need for Scalability

Visualization can help make both multi-dimensional data and the results of an analytical or optimization algorithm more accessible. Oftentimes, it is used to project data and objects into a lower dimension space to make the data set more manageable. It can also help the user grasp the broad characteristics of the data. The complexity challenges of big data applications underscore a need to limit the growth of the complexity of visualization. Like analytics algorithms for text and numerical data, visualization algorithms must generally have worst-case asymptotic running time linear in the problem size.

2.3. Heterogeneity

Software tools for visualization also play a key role in coping with heterogeneity, as they allow disparate aspects to be hidden. This is comparable to projecting only the shared attributes of two tables in a relational database, corresponding to the intersection of their schemas. The key challenge in visualization is accounting for relevant and interesting differences in disparate parts of a data set in order to reveal variation in the data to the user. Some text domains exhibit *semantic heterogeneity*, a disparity in the sense or meaning of terms used. Coping with this is an open research problem in general, but presents a specific set of issues for visualization, in that showing the differences (and similarities) does not necessarily confer an ability to disambiguate a model manually – *i.e.*, based on inspection.

3. TECHNIQUES FOR ANALYZING AND LEARNING FROM BIG DATA

3.1. Thematic Maps

The object of thematic mapping is to depict phenomena and trends in a geospatial context. Toward this end, most frameworks allow data to be superimposed or blended with a color or grayscale map that depicts region boundaries, baseline, *etc.* This includes choropleth maps with dynamically computable color palettes.

Figure 2 is a choropleth map depicting the rate of death attributed to heart disease by county in the USA from 2000 through 2006. This map, which was published by the Centers for Disease Control, takes inter-county population distribution (but not intra-county population distribution) into account by normalizing to a death rate per 100,000 individuals. For information retrieval applications, it does not provide any drill-down interface *cf. HealthMap* or similar event visualization services. One of the reasons for the development of the geospatial visualization components of an event monitoring system is to facilitate information retrieval and multimodal information access using well-established visualization techniques such as thematic mapping and small multiples.

3.2. Text Analytics: Visualizing Natural Language

3.2.1. Text Annotation and Markup

Named Entity Recognition (NER) seeks to locate and classify atomic elements in text into pre-

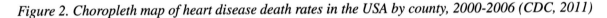

Figure 2. Choropleth map of heart disease death rates in the USA by county, 2000-2006 (CDC, 2011)

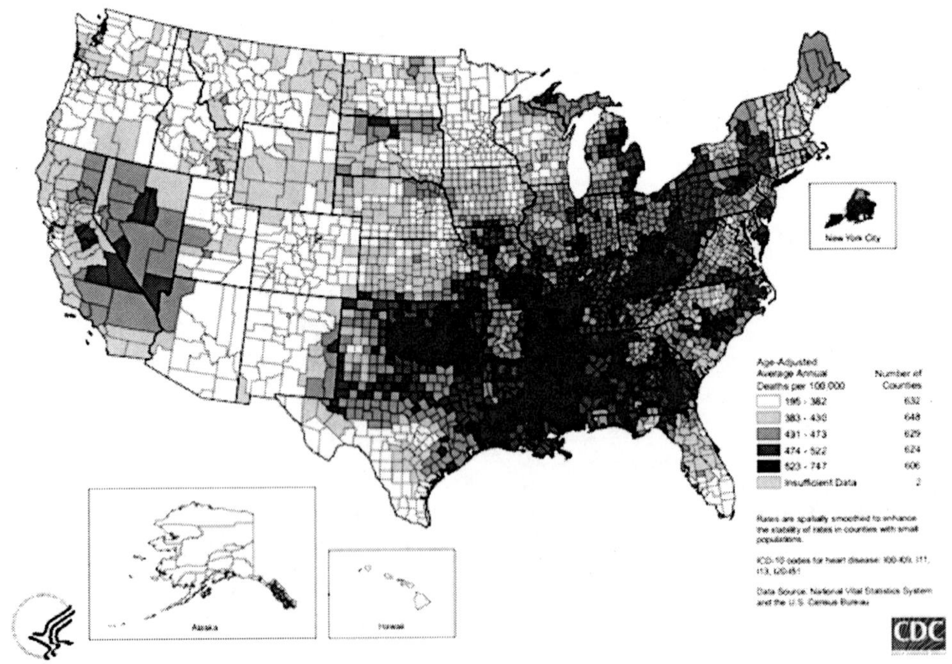

defined categories such as the names of persons, organizations, locations, etc. The list of categories can be extended to include disease names in the biomedical paradigm. Most NER research consists of taking an unannotated, unstructured block of text such as:

Chancellor Ridcully hired three new faculty to work at Unseen University in Ankh-Morpork.

And producing an annotated output such as:

{Chancellor Ridcully}\PERSON hired {three new faculty}\QUANTITY to work at {Unseen University}\ORGANIZATION in {Ankh-Morpork}\LOCATION.

In addition to people, organizations, and locations, quantities and dates are often included in NER systems. Quantities are particularly relevant to textual IE in the domain of epidemiology because of the many units of measurement (length, area, volume, mass and weight, monetary units, time, etc.) that are required and the variety of agents (infectious agents and host organisms) that may be named.

Research indicates that NER systems developed for one domain do not typically perform well on other domains. Early work in NER systems in the 1990s was aimed primarily at extraction from journalistic articles. Attention then turned to processing of military dispatches and reports. Since about 1998, there has been a great deal of interest in entity identification in the molecular biology, bioinformatics, and medical natural language processing communities. The most common entity of interest in that domain has been names of genes and gene products. The Stanford Named Entity Recognizer (Stanford NER) labels sequences of words in a text which are the names of things, such as person and company names, or gene and protein names. The software provides a general (arbitrary order) implementation of linear chain Conditional Random Field (CRF) sequence models, coupled with well-engineered feature extractors for Named Entity Recognition. Included are a good 3-class (PERSON, ORGANIZATION, LOCATION) named entity recognizer for English (in versions with and without additional distributional similarity features) and another pair of models trained on the CoNLL 2003 English training data.

3.2.2. Processing Tasks: Information Extraction and Topic Modeling

Coreference resolution (abbreiviated *coref*) is the problem of deciding which of multiple expressions in a sentence or document refer to the same object, quantity, or entity. For example, in the sentence "NIH policy was that if a submitted proposal was not funded, a review report would be generated for it by the study section assigned to it," the anaphoric reference "it" refers to the submitted proposal.

Coreference resolution is a significant, though not essential task in spatiotemporal event extraction; an example can be found in the statement, "informed estimates suggest that up to 17,000,000 children suffer from hunger throughout the USA, many of them living in poverty". The QA task of determining how many animals this sentence says were killed, and the textual entailment task of determining whether the children live in the United States, are relatively straightfoward, whereas the coreference resolution task of identifying what subset of entities were said to be impoverished is more difficult. Thus, a high-level event wherein "17 million children suffer from hunger in the USA" can be detected even without coreference resolution, whereas the more challenging problem of tagging "locales where children in poverty suffer from hunger" requires it.

3.2.3. From Tag Clouds to Opinion Mapping

Tag clouds are simple visualizations of documents that depict words used in a single document or a collection of documents, scaled in descending order by frequency of occurrence. Often, differences in word orientation, size, *etc.* are emphasized. Figure 3 shows a tag cloud published as part of a *Voice of America* report on cyber-bullying, generated from students' own survey responses.

Figure 3. Tag cloud of teen's descriptions of bad behaviors they have seen online (Voice of America, 2011)

A major limitation of tag clouds is that it does not show distributions comparatively, between two or more documents (or collections), and does not admit simple comparison between clouds. In order to produce a more informative visualization of word distributions, some form of topic modeling is needed, which as discussed above can also support geographic mapping of sentiments.

3.3. Heterogeneous Information Networks

Heterogeneous Information Networks (HIN) are a type of graph-based model of communication and trust that include a large proportion of all social networks. Research on heterogeneous information networks as led to a convergence of methodologies for network modeling, incorporating classification, learning and reasoning with graphical models, frequent subgraph mining, relational representation, and link annotation, among other techniques. Many intelligent systems applications to information extraction, Web search, and recommendation call for inferences to be made regarding the existence, type, or attributes of links. Some tasks, such as question answering using information networks, may require that inferences be based upon partial link information and made under uncertainty about participating entities and relationships.

3.3.1. Visualization of Large and Interesting Graphs

Application areas that often exhibit a need for heterogeneous information network analysis include:

- **Information diffusion and sharing systems:** Sensor networks, social media (opinions and sentiments, meme propagation, viral content, political commentary, *etc.*)
- **Behavioral modeling:** Community recruitment and mass activity, large-scale patterns, traffic, spatiotemporal effects.
- **Content-management systems:** Version control, wikification.
- **Social recommender systems:** Communities, experts, friends, products, reviewers, providers.
- **Application areas:** Cybersecurity (information flow, trust networks, attack graphs, mechanism design), bioinformatics and biomedicine (genomics, proteomics, metabolomics), epidemiology.

3.3.2. Descriptive Analytics of Graphs

As shown in Figure 4 and Figure 5, visualization can also help differentiate key features of different specified topologies, particularly when the connectivity is generated by a random or semirandom process. These include the maximum and minimum degrees, number of connected components, and centrality of the graph.

3.3.3. Emerging Techniques

Active research areas that are relevant to heterogeneous information networks include:

- Community detection and formation modeling.
- Ranking-based clustering methods: learning to rank in information networks.

Figure 4. Different graph topologies, visualized (part 1 of 2) – Havel-Koren fast multiscale graph, horizontal sine wave, spiral graph, uniform random graph

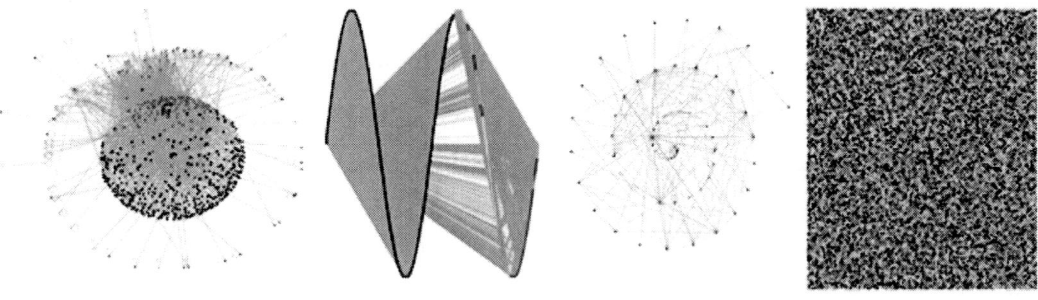

Figure 5. Different graph topologies, visualized (part 2 of 2) – sparse (2-D) vs. dense (3-D) Havel-Koren fast multiscale graph

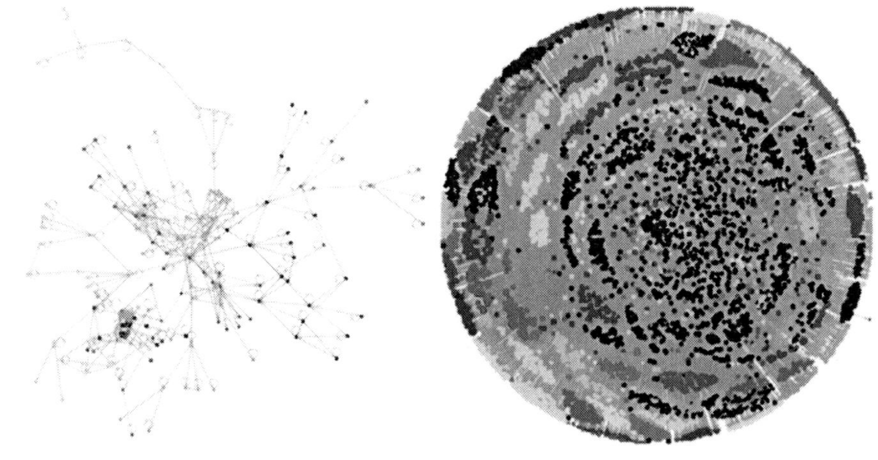

- Path-based similarity measures and relationship extraction.
- Modeling of link types and relationship strength.
- Applications to modeling of Weblogs, social media, social networks, and the semantic Web.
- Frequent pattern mining in graph and sequence data.
- Statistical relational learning.
- Trust networks and information sharing.

4. CASE STUDIES OF THEMATIC MAPS

4.1. Epidemiology: Historical and Predictive

Predictive epidemiology refers to the analytical study of disease dynamics to predict future outbreaks in space and time so that effective mitigation strategies can be implemented to curb the recurrence of epidemics. Since epizootic diseases such as the Foot and Mouth Disease (FMD), which periodically or sporadically break out within livestock populations, raise several political, administrative, economic and welfare issues, it is imperative to analyze the disease dynamics to facilitate adequate preventive measures, especially in countries that report recurring epidemic outbreaks instances. Figure 6 depicts a simulation described in (Roy Chowdhury, Scoglio, & Hsu, 2011) that was used to generate all of the states other than the upper-left hand corner.

4.2. Text Information Retrieval and Extraction: Sentiment Analysis

The specific aims of the techniques surveyed in this section are as follows:

Aim 1: Extend known algorithms for named entity recognition and relationship extraction, to produce basic summaries of entities and relationships mentioned in texts. The technical objective is to tag where basic entities and opinions are mentioned in freely available text (including both user posts and profiles), then map these tagged elements in space, time, and by topic, to acceptable levels of precision and recall.

Aim 2: Adapt basic known techniques to a particular domain of interest – specifically, extracting data from text discussions that are archived from the dark Web (including blogs and forums) using Web crawlers. This entails developing a means of handling entities and quantitative data that have not previously been extracted from text. Another functional requirement is some mechanism for entity reference resolution, *e.g.*, abbreviations and synonyms, for known terms. Finally, a domain-specific ontology of relevant aspects or attributes of the domain of discourse is proposed. This includes topics frequently discussed in blogs and forums, to better facilitate information retrieval applications such as question answering about the domain and gathering recommendations from subject matter experts.

Aim 3: Develop methods for sentiment analysis and improve existing ones, to summarize opinions and discover patterns. The technical objective is to relate demographic data extracted from text and

Figure 6. Simulation-based visualization of spread models for foot-and-mouth disease (Chowdhury, Scoglio, & Hsu, 2011)

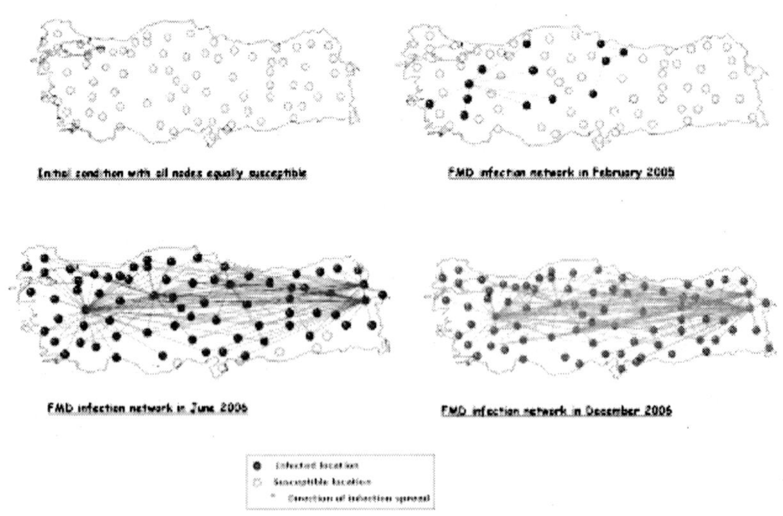

profiles to qualitative data – namely, the polarity of text at the document, sentence, or aspect level, aggregated across demographic categories such as geographic region of residence. Objects of interest for sentiment analysis include recommended solutions, but can extend to aspects of the domain.

4.3. Event Tracking: Clandestine Labs

The problem of event visualization based on structured data, in the form of time-referenced and georeferenced relational tuples, and on unstructured data, in the form of free text. Information extraction systems based on Named Entity Recognition (NER) and relationship extraction have enabled detection of events mentioned in free text and extraction of structured tuples describing the location, time, along with other attributes of an event. Identifying hotspots and trends, however, remains an open problem. One limitation is the absence of ground truth for high event activity. In some cases this is due to a lack of well-defined criteria for activity and relevance, while in some it is due to limitations in existing annotation interfaces.

We first present a basic approach to event visualization. Our general framework makes use of mapping tools such as *Google Maps*, the Google Web toolkit, and timeline visualization tools such as *MIT SIMILE*. It also builds upon previous work on gazetteer-based event recognition and syntactic patterns for semantic relationship detection. Next, we show how a system developed originally for visualization of animal disease outbreaks reported in online news documents can be adapted to display reports of methamphetamine lab seizures compiled by regional law enforcement. We briefly outline the development of a domain-specific data description language for increased portability and ease of information integration. We then discuss the role of topic modeling and information retrieval approaches in filtering and ranking events.

A key technical contribution of this work is the application of topic modeling algorithms in order to compute the posterior probability of a particular spatial location, time unit, or combination given the type of event, which is treated as a topic. This allows the data to be interrogated systematically in order to display geographic regions that are more prone to events of interest. A potential application of this is to construct a time composite map of administrative divisions within a state or province, or a spatial composite time series by month or year, showing active regions. These can be visualized using a *choropleth map*: a map in which regions (geographic regions in this case) are coded by colors or grayscale intensity levels. These represent a variable of interest – in this case, event frequency. Finally, the ability to estimate marginal likelihoods over locations and times given the event type parameters can also be used to filter events, to display only those that fall within a specified frequency range. For example, the system can be configured to search for seizures of methaphetamine production labs in counties or districts where they are common or rare.

5. EFFECTIVE PRACTICES FOR INTEGRATIVE INFORMATION VISUALIZATION

The basis tenets of information graphic design as related, critically analyzed, and demonstrated by Tufte (1990, 1997, 2001, 2003, 2006), are as follows:

1. Show the data.
2. Induce the reader to think about the *substance* rather than about:
   a. Methodology.
   b. Graphic design.
   c. Technology of graphic production.
   d. Something else.
3. Avoid distorting what the data have to say.
4. Present many numbers in a small space.

5. Make large data sets coherent.
6. Encourage the eye to compare different pieces of data.
7. Reveal the data at different levels of detail, broad to fine.
8. Serve a clear purpose: description, evaluation, tabulation, decoration.
9. Be closely integrated with statistical and verbal descriptions of data.

In this section, we review some realizations of this high-level vision in the specific domains of information graphics for big data analytics and spatiotemporal applications.

5.1. Information Graphic Design: Enhancing Learning and Analysis

Matlow (2000), a practitioner, instructor, and educational administrator in graphic design, describes the challenges of introducing computation into a graphic design curriculum at Harrow College, which merged in 1990 with the Polytechnic of Central London. These include the paradigm shift "from `page' to `screen'" and the evolution of curricula. The article gives a critical analysis of contextual studies, a comparative ethnographic and cultural approach that was applied to digital media with poor initial results. It discusses how a critical theory module was successfully added to this curriculum, focusing on enabling technologies for social action and cognitive aspects of computer-mediated communication. This module went beyond incorporating technical aspects of digital arts to explore the role of language in structuring and creating meaning in cultural adaptation to technology. In particular, key topics regarding human-computer interaction and human factors, technical claims and open questions concerning computational intelligence and philosophy of mind, including the possibility of strong AI, were raised. Matlow concludes by pointing out that this kind of integrative curriculum holds positive potential for enhancing the education of digital arts practitioners, but also offers a timely warning for present-day designers of Massively Online Open Course (MOOC) material about the disparity between ease of delivery and the difficulty of ensuring the quality of content.

5.2. Tufte's Principles Applied to Spatiotemporal Big Data

Tufte's principles have been extensively applied to the visual display of quantitative information (Tufte, 2001), object visualization and thematic maps (Tufte, 1990), visualization of processes and storylines (Tufte, 1997), the improvement of presentation graphics (Tufte, 2003), and the critical exploration of evidence, especially for decision-making (Tufte, 2006). Of the four primary books on information graphics by Tufte (1990, 1997, 2001, 2006), *Envisioning Information* (Tufte, 1990) in particular emphasizes spatiotemporal aspects, though the other three also cover specific aspects of map visualizations and geospatial data to a degree.

Gahegan *et al.* (2001) describe the establishment of a Commission on Visualization by the International Cartographic Association, reporting on "the use of visualization within exploratory analysis, data mining and geocomputation, with the overall focus directed to the task of knowledge construction". This paper depicts a waterfall model of knowledge discovery (here referred to as the "knowledge construction process") proceeding from more data-driven and pattern-driven to more model-based and process-driven. In an extensive survey of exploratory visual analysis and exploratory data analysis, the Commission's report also characterizes stages of reasoning, from more abductive in emphasis to more inductive and finally more deductive (analytical) and theory-guided. Aside from being very similar to the waterfall model of development in software engineering and knowledge engineering, this cascade process follows some computational models of cognitive processes, particularly machine learning and inference.

REFERENCES

Cadez, I., Heckerman, D., Meek, C., Smyth, P., & White, S. (2000). Visualization of navigation patterns on a web site using model-based clustering. In R. Ramakrishnan, S. J. Stolfo, R. J. Bayardo, & I. Parsa (Ed.), *Proceedings of the 6th ACM SIGKDD International Conference on Knowledge Discovery and Data Mining (KDD 2000)* (pp. 280-284). Boston, MA: ACM Press.

Cuzzocrea, A., Song, I.-Y., & Davis, K. C. (2011). Analytics over large-scale multidimensional data: The big data revolution! In A. Cuzzocrea, I.-Y. Song, & K. C. Davis (Eds.), *Proceedings of the ACM 14th International Workshop on Data Warehousing and On-Line Analytical Processing (DOLAP 2011)* (pp. 101-104). Glasgow, UK: ACM Press.

Elger, C. E., & Lehnertz, K. (1998). Seizure prediction by non-linear time series analysis of brain electrical activity. *The European Journal of Neuroscience*, *10*(2), 786–789. doi:10.1046/j.1460-9568.1998.00090.x PMID:9749744.

Goldstein, J., & Roth, S. F. (1994). Using aggregation and dynamic queries for exploring large data sets. In E. Dykstra-Erickson & M. Tscheligi (Eds.), *Proceedings of the SIGCHI Conference on Human Factors in Computing Systems (CHI 2004)* (pp. 23-29). Boston, MA: ACM Press.

Hall, M., Frank, E., Holmes, G., & Pfahringer, B. (2009). The WEKA data mining software: An update. *ACM SIGKDD Explorations Newsletter*, *11*(1), 10–18. doi:10.1145/1656274.1656278.

Heer, J., Kong, N., & Agrawala, M. (2009). Sizing the horizon: the effects of chart size and layering on the graphical perception of time series visualizations. In *Proceedings of the 27th International Conference on Human Factors in Computing Systems (CHI 2009)* (pp. 1303-1312). Boston, MA: ACM Press.

Keim, D. A. (2006). Challenges in visual data analysis. In E. Banissi, K. Börner, C. Chen, G. Clapworthy, C. Maple, A. Lobben, J. Zhang (Eds.), *10th International Conference on Information Visualisation (IV 2006)* (pp. 9-16). London, UK: IEEE Press.

Kumar, N., Keogh, E., Lonardi, S., & Ratanamahatana, C. A. (2005). Time-series bitmaps: A practical visualization tool for working with large time series databases. In *Proceedings of the 5th SIAM International Conference on Data Mining (SDM 2005)* (pp. 531-535). Newport Beach, CA: SIAM.

Mario, C., & Talia, D. (2003). The knowledge grid. *Communications of the ACM*, *46*(1), 89–93. doi:10.1145/602421.602425.

Monmonier, M. (1990). Strategies for the visualization of geographic time-series data. *Cartographica: The International Journal for Geographic Information and Geovisualization*, *27*(1), 30–45. doi:10.3138/U558-H737-6577-8U31.

Steele, J., & Iliinsky, N. (Eds.). (2010). *Beautiful visualization: Looking at data through the eyes of experts*. Cambridge, MA: O'Reilly Media.

Watson, H. J., & Wixom, B. H. (2007). The current state of business intelligence. *IEEE Computer*, *40*(9), 96–99. doi:10.1109/MC.2007.331.

Chapter 10
Using Social Network Analysis to Examine Social Hierarchies and Team Dynamics on Instructional Design Projects

Shalin Hai-Jew
Kansas State University, USA

ABSTRACT

Social network diagrams have been an important part of understanding social dynamics from dyads all the way to human civilizations. In e-learning, social networks have been used to evaluate how online learners engage with each other and what the implications of that may be for the quality of learning. In this chapter, social networks are used to evaluate various social aspects of the development teams in their work. A number of contemporary Instructional Design (ID) projects, described briefly as comparative case studies in the chapter, are used as the contexts for these social networks and visualizations. While these depictions tend to be systemic-level ones, there are insights from considering the micro/ego-level views. The objectives of this chapter are to introduce one approach to the uses of social network visualizations in analyzing the internal and external social dynamics of instructional design across a number of institutions of higher education.

INTRODUCTION

Social network science is a field which has evolved over the past seven decades. Early thinkers who contributed to social network concepts include sociologists David Émile Durkheim (social pathologies), Ferdinand Tönnies ("*gemeninschaft* and *gesellschaft*" / community and society), and Georg Simmel (social geometry, the metropolis). The study of social networks started in the 1930s with the work of Jacob Moreno, who originated the "sociogram"—a connection diagram which shows people's connections with each other. John Barnes (a British anthropologist) originated the term "social network" in the 1950s. Over the years, the field has evolved with broad influences from sociology, political science, organizational studies, discrete mathematics, and recently, computer science's network analysis and graph theory (from math).

Today, social network research is highly interdisciplinary. It is used to theorize; to research; to analyze phenomena, and to make decisions. In higher education, social networks have been ana-

DOI: 10.4018/978-1-4666-4462-5.ch010

lyzed in terms of organizational change. They have also been studied in the context of online learning to look at the various social networks that form around academic discourses; for example, learners who are central in a network tend to achieve higher grades, but those on the periphery are more willing to explore new network linkages (bringing with that the possibility of new, advantageous, and boundary-spanning ties through weak links) (Cho, Gay, Davidson, & Ingraffea, 2007). Henttonen (2010) conducted a deep literature review in the study of social networks on groups as a unit of analysis and highlighted some emerging themes in terms of group structures and team performance. In this chapter, social network analysis will be applied to how instructional design teams coalesce and function on a number of real-world projects, which occurred within the last seven years.

While social networks may be depicted visually in a variety of ways, they will be displayed here as node-link diagrams (a type of line graph), which consist of nodes (also known as "egos" or "actors" or "vertexes") and links (lines, edges, or arcs). Nodes (expressed as dots) represent entities, and links (expressed as lines) represent the relationships between them. These elements are expressed on a two-dimensional (2D) plane on the x and y axes. They may be read from top to bottom, left to right, from the center outwards, from the periphery inwards, and in a range of other spatialized ways. The spatial layout of these entities and relationships contain meaning depending on the type of node-link diagram. In one conceptualization, the nodes closest to the core are the most critical in a network. Those in the semi-periphery and the periphery are less critical to the mission of that particular organization. (Sometimes, nodes are moved slightly to improve legibility and visual coherence.) The centrality of a node is seen as indicative of various features, including the "(potential for) autonomy, control, risk, exposure, influence, belongingness, brokerage, independence, power and so on" (Borgatti & Everett, 2006, p. 467). The measure of centrality differs based on different models, but in this chapter refers to betweenness or the connectivity of a node with others in the network, which suggests a high amount of resources flowing to that node (high in-degree or amount of in-flow of information and resources from other nodes). Because this work did not analyze traffic flow per se but only linkages, this is only using betweenness as a centrality measure, which is in line with social network science conventions.

Some assumptions of social network science are that human relationships matter, from the micro ego-node (egocentric point-of-view) level to the macro systemic large-scale structure. Some social groupings coalesce in an ad hoc way. Other groups are organized. People generally are attracted by shared likenesses or "homophily" (McPherson, Smith-Lovin, & Cook, 2001). This underlying concept informs the idea that a person may be identified by "the company he / she keeps". However, various social groupings, particularly work-related ones, may be heterophilous because of the need for cross-functional team collaborations. (Some researchers have argued that people have a tendency towards novelty and complexity, and these may mean acquaintances who are fundamentally different or variant from themselves.) There are many small world networks with short average path lengths over the entire graph and a strong degree of clustering or local ego neighborhoods (Watts, 2003); this means that people are connected by a few short paths to anyone else in what is known as the well known "six degrees of separation." (Theoretically, strong clustering often means distant path lengths between individuals. There is usually an inverse correlation between clustering and path lengths.) The thickest ties are those in which the resources and information move two-ways between nodes (in which the relationships are reciprocated) in an active way. In organizational research, the "walk" of communications through a network tend to map fairly closely to the organizational structure, which suggests both hierarchy and role-based ratiionales for communications (Adamic & Adar, 2005).

The units of analysis may be any part of the sociogram from egos to dyads (two related nodes) to subclusters to clusters (cliques), all the way to the entire network. Ego (node) attributes are important because they may capture how that node functions—how it intakes resources and information, and what it actually does with those resources. (In this way, a node-link diagram is a kind of neural network of human decision-makers and actors.) Real-world personalities will function based on past patterns of behaviors.

Information and resources are conceptualized to flow through these networks. The abstraction of real-world relationships into social network diagrams is done to reveal hidden structures and patterns. In social networks, people influence each other in seen and unseen ways with especially powerful influences with proxemic nodes (Christakis & Fowler, 2009). This assumes that individuals function in a social context, which they influence and by which they are influenced. Social relationships are created strategically and tactically, and they involve some investments by both sides. Ties may be non-directional in some depictions, or they ("directed networks," "directional graphs," or "digraphs") may be directional, which shows the direction(s) in which resources and information flow through the nodes. The nature of a social network may be described by its constituent nodes, the density of path ties, the clustering of various nodes, and what flows through the network. Within these networks may be partitioned into islands (sub-cliques) or ego neighborhoods with denser connectivity among its members than with those outside the island.

In this sociocentric worldview, people's interrelationships and exchanges matter. They affect the capabilities of a social network. For example, in a variety of industries, teams improve performance when they share knowledge creation and network socially in a strategic way (Janhonen & Johanson, 2011). In engineering product development teams, information sharing leads to creativity, but too much social network efficiency has a negative effect on team creativity; rather, direct contacts are more efficacious for high-skilled innovation work (Kratzer, Leenders, & Van Engelen, 2010). Reputations matter, which inform trust, which enables people to collaborate. Power (measured by the proxies of resources and information) moves through systems and coalesce in certain nodes, which may be gatekeepers to enable certain types of work. There may be some interchangeability between nodes with "automorphic equivalence" or "structural equivalence" (or similar node-link social structures) which might suggest that they may be substitutable or interchangeable. Some social networks may be sufficiently malleable to be rewired for new capabilities (Hanneman & Riddle, 2005).

Analysis of social networks may point to certain structural "holes" in the network which may be exploited based on introduction of other nodes or the disposition of certain existing nodes. [In work places, structural holes in work groups are found to harm the teams' work performance (Cummings & Cross, 2003).] Brokerage roles include titles such as coordinator, consultant ('itinerant broker'), gatekeeper, or representative; these roles are defined by the memberships of the egos in certain groups and how they interact both within-group and with out-groups. For example, a *tertius gaudens* (the "third who rejoices") exploitation may occur when an actor (or player) acts as a broker between two other nodes and benefits from the "disunion" of the other two, in an observation by George Simmel (1923). The disunion between two nodes is a structural hole in which a third may step in to exploit the relationship as mediator or broker. (Practically, an escrow service, an auction house, divorce attorneys, and such, may be conceptualized as a third node in a *tertius gaudens* strategy.) In this concept, all relationships are transactional and with-cost; there are no frictionless connections. A *tertius iungens* strategy (or "the third who joins") may be read as either beneficial in creating a dense network of nodes engaged in innovation (Obstfeld, 2005).

The more diverse and heterogeneous groups are, the more capable they are regarding a range of adaptive capabilities because they have a greater variety of skill sets to draw from. Strong ties indicate close interactivity; weak ties show light and even distant interactivity. Those who are members of disparate groups may serve as "weak tie" bridges between different entities, leading to potentially potent connections and collaborations. An isolate node is not connected with any other node in a network but is still conceptualized as part of the network. (There are logical arguments for the power of delinking from a network at certain times.) A pendant is a node that hangs on the edge of a network by one connection. A thin node may have few connections. A fat node has many incoming connections (in-degree, in-ties) but fewer outgoing connections (out-degree, out-ties), which indicates power, popularity, renown, and also limited subordinate reportage to others. An influential node often has multi-connectivity or plural pathways through which to connect and interact with others. It has an "accumulative advantage" in terms of social ties and power resources, in this social structure. An island is a sub-network or sub-cluster of nodes that are densely connected with each other but less densely connected with the larger networks. The closer a network is, the more resilient it is if it's communications and resources moving through the network. (Resilience, in systems theory, includes system attributes "as diversity, ability to self-organize, system memory, hierarchical structure, feedbacks and non-linear processes" (Cumming, Barnes, Perz, Schmink, Sieving, Southworth, Binford, Holt, Stickler, & Van Holt, 2005, p. 975). These authors note that "resilience" may be understood as the amount of change that the system may undergo while maintaining its structural and functional integrity. Further, the system's ability to learn and adapt is another aspect of system resilience. However, the denser a network is (the more ties between nodes), the weaker it is if it's contagious and life-threatening diseases moving through the network.

Networks may be highly formal or informal; short-term, medium-term, or long-term; hierarchical and rigid or distributed and loosely connected. There may be high or low transitivity in networks, which indicates the likelihood of connectivity between nodes of A connecting with C when A -> B and B -> C. In other words, how much transference of relational ties are there in the social networks? Various software programs enable the application of statistical techniques to analyze social networks and examine the various types of relationships in a social network (through network censuses) to describe the networks. Few real-world social networks conform perfectly to the theories. Further, most networks are not purely static; they are evolving and dynamic. The ways that sociograms capture complexity is that complex information may be captured in a dynamic visualization linked to a timeline (and trendline data), or sequential still visualizations. Some social network visualizations offer explanatory power about relationships in the world; some may even offer some predictive power (such as demographic visualizations indicating probable trends).

Finally, a social network may not be understood in isolation. A sociogram is informed by context and analysis. The narrative that explains a social network is critical to the explanatory power of the data visualization. This introduction sets up the basic intuitions behind social networks. Finally, these static social network structure mining approaches show a flattened work team reality. To "re-hydrate" the actual and dynamic full team reality, it would be important to bring in more information streams for explanatory power.

BACKGROUND

The information that informs the development of a social network node-link visualization may come from a variety of sources. The data array may be informed by any number of research fields. Some software programs enable the easy ingestion of trace electronic information (such as text) from various types of Websites to surface hidden patterns in human behaviors and communications.

In a review of the literature, there are some basic steps to social network research. The first step involves conceptualizing a relevant research question in a particular area or multi-disciplinary domain. Next, it is important to formulate a hypothesis from the available information and theory. Third, a researcher has to create a research design. Often, this may involve identifying a particular social group to study. Fourth, the researcher needs to collect relevant information (from surveys, historical research). This information will inform the "drawing" of the social network diagram. Or, in this phase, an analyst may conceptualize a sociogram as a hypothesis (based on educated and informed logical inference), such as from game theory; this visualization could serve as a hypothesized description of a social network. Fifth, the researcher sets up an electronic data array (an example follows shortly). Sixth, the researcher inputs the information into a social network software tool and may apply various types of analyses (both statistical and non-parametric). Next, the researcher outputs a social network diagram—and may experiment with multiple visualizations. Eighth, the researcher analyzes the data array, the social network, and other data—and may add contextual details to fully flesh out the descriptiveness of the social network. Finally, the researcher finalizes the social network depiction and presents the work to professional peers. (Other steps may involve a testing of the model, but this will suffice at least for a one-cycle approach to the creation of a social network diagram.) Figure 1 highlights these research steps.

In a workplace, proximity matters. People collaborate with those who are physically closer because such interactions may mitigate a range of work-based challenges; their proximity encourages more frequent intercommunications (Kraut, Egido, & Galegher, 1988). Beyond that, people tend not to collaborate. There are "regional advantages" which enable people with disparate interests to meet and share ideas and collaborate (Saxenian, 1994/1996).

Analysis of Instructional Design Projects

This chapter uses social network visualizations from over a dozen real-world instructional design projects that the author was engaged in over the past seven years. The social network data are derived from work files and project notes. The social network visualizations were designed to extract critical features of the various project teams and their internal and external interactions. The selected instructional design projects were all achieved for institutions of higher education in multiple states and for various federal and local grant funders.

1. Native American Case Studies
2. Technical Writing Course Team

Figure 1. An overview of the process for social network research

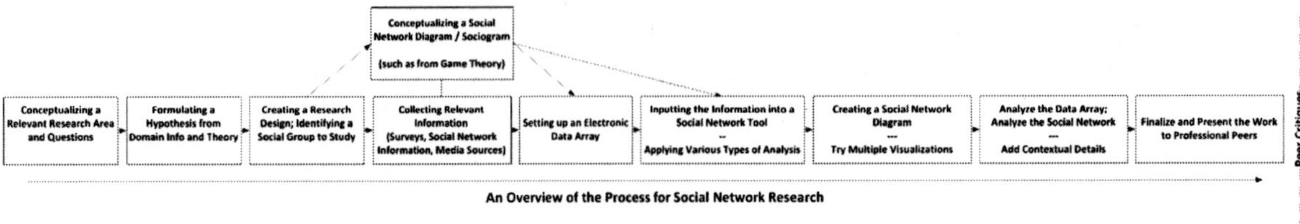

3. An Automated Biosecurity Training
4. Axio™ Demo Course
5. University Life Café
6. Appendix G (Grievance Policy) Training
7. Academic Dishonesty Co-Authored Article
8. Introduction to Public Health
9. Global Health
10. E-Learning Best Practices
11. E-Learning and Teaching Exchange (ELATEwiki)
12. Digital Entomology Lab
13. Introduction to One Health
14. Traumatic Brain Injury
15. E-Learning Faculty Modules

No focal ego node is considered central; no ego neighborhood "alters" are pre-defined. Rather, the actual network visualizations came from quantified data about relationships within and without the project team.

There are manual ways to create the data arrays for the network diagrams. In Table 1 shows how the left column identifies the main members of the internal development team for a One Health course, and the entities across the time are the various external stakeholders to this project. (The labels have been abstracted to anonymize the information. Some researchers have expressed concerns about the research done on social networks since the nodes represent individuals, who are often identified or identifiable, particularly if one has access to other databases of information, with personally identifiable information (PII). There are debates about how much privacy protections need to be in place (Kadushin, 2005). De-identified data about individuals often may be used for individual re-identification with only a few data points. In this situation, individuals are identified by roles without individual identifiers. Only general information is used to describe the projects. The software used for the visualizations was UCINET (Borgatti, Everett, & Freeman, 2002).

The following section contains a brief overview of the particular instructional design case, then a social network visualization (a reconstruction of team dynamics in compressed summary time), and an analysis of that visualization along with some implications (All the other data arrays / matrices will be offered in the Appendix, in the sequential order of the presented cases.).

Table 1. A data array from the "intro to one health" visualization

	External Funding Agency	External Funder 2	Internal Funder 1	Evaluation Office	College Deans	On-Campus Subject Matter Experts (SMEs)	Off-Campus SMEs	One Health Leaders (Nationally)	Third-Party Content Creators
Principal Investigator (PI) / Administrator	1	1	1	1	1	1	1	1	1
PI / Clinician / Professor	0	0	0	0	1	1	0	0	0
One Health Administrator / Veterinarian	0	0	0	1	1	1	1	0	0
Instructional Designer	0	0	0	0	0	1	0	0	1
Videographer 1	0	0	0	0	0	0	0	0	0
Videographer 2	0	0	0	0	0	0	0	0	0

A few more observations should be made about these particular social networks. These are all work-based, which means that they are highly defined (both egocentrically and from the network level), sparse (vs. dense), and artificially bounded based on the workplace context, resource limitations, and functional needs of the respective projects. (Some work relationships may represent "strong ties" in the sense that the relationships are long-term, fairly close, stable, and often legally binding; however, work relationships may represent "weak ties" in the sense that the relationships are short-term, transitory, perfunctory, and impersonal.) These node-links were defined *ex post*, so these social networks may be understood in a fixed-in-time format; they are not currently evolving. All of these may be understood as "islands" within larger social networks to which the development teams were beholden: funding agencies, learning constituencies, academic networks, and others. To incorporate the various teams, a necessary level of simplicity was applied, involving the functional teams and other basic information.

1. **Native American Case Studies:** A group of faculty from multiple institutions and multiple states were brought together to create Native American case studies for Native American students in the Puget Sound tribes in Washington State. The idea was to create learning materials from the world in a way that would pass muster with the tribal elders (in terms of aligning with their worldviews, in order to strengthen the retention of Native American learners in higher education). The case studies would be created by small teams, vetted by the larger group, revised, and then used in a publicly available Website as points of discussion for the students. The case studies were to introduce a contemporary issue (along with its historical roots) and enable relevant and valid questions for student consideration (and possible research). Figure 2 features the core members involved in the creation of a case and the external stakeholders and constituents—along with the related ties.

Figure 2. Native American case study team and various stakeholders and constituents

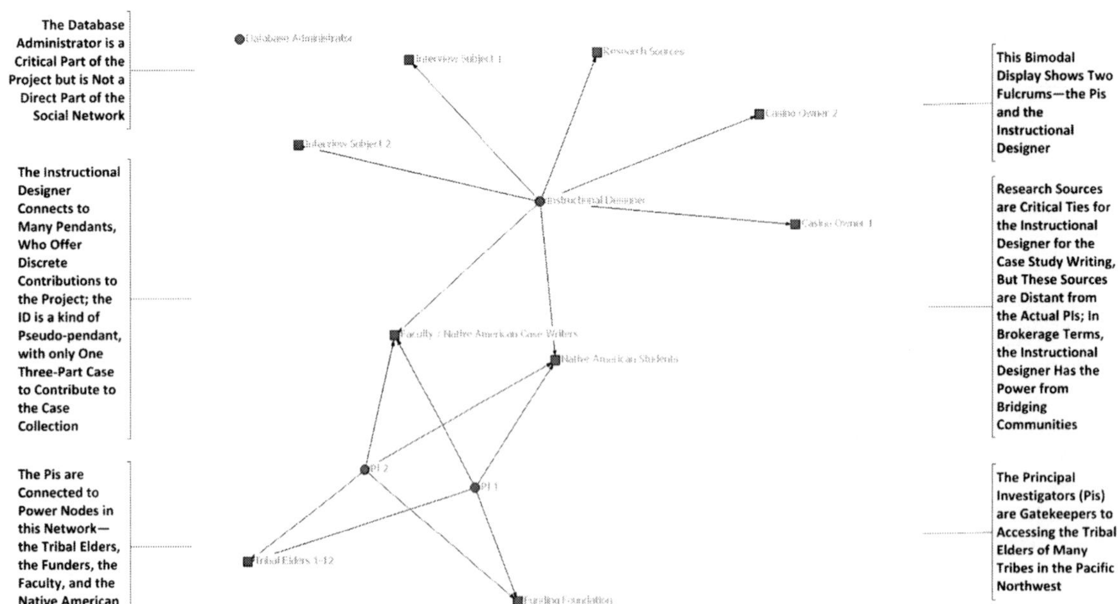

The social network depiction here shows a bimodal display with the instructional designer separate from the two grant Principal Investigators (PIs). This bimodalism reveals the geographically separation between the teams (with the Instructional Designer [ID] flying in multiple times to train and immerse in Native American culture, research, and then present the case). It further reveals the disparate groups that are thinly connected through brokers such as the PIs, who work as gatekeepers to the tribal elders and the funding foundations.

Figure 3 shows the Native American students as the core concern of the tribal elders, project PIs, the program faculty, and Native case authors. From the instructional design view though, the case authors are on the periphery and are a functional out-group. Those in-between are gatekeepers of sorts. This image reflects the case writers' lack of continuing work with the learners except for the case authors who also served as faculty to the Native learners or the project administrators who had continuing research relationships with the students and others. This is not to suggest that this is necessarily negative, as long as there is sufficient critique of the cases and feedback from learners about the efficacy of the cases (In this project, the instructors and administrators provided superb feedback to the case writers about how the cases were used, the discourse that was engendered, and the feedback that students had.).

Figure 3. Native American case studies core-periphery diagram

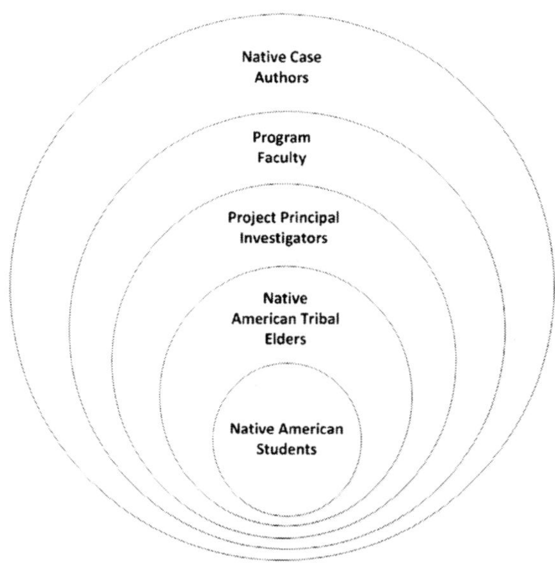

2. **Technical Writing Course Team:** Three faculty members, Subject Matter Experts (SMEs) on the selected topic, were culled from a statewide consortium of online instructors to build an online course on technical writing. The team used the criteria for a range of colleges (members of the consortium) to build the online course: its contents, assessments, interactivity, and other elements. As a distributed team which never met face-to-face, the team experienced a network sociality. Wittel (2001) writes:

In network sociality the social bond at work is not bureaucratic but informational; it is created on a project-by-project basis, by the movement of ideas, the establishment of only ever temporary standards and protocols, and the creation and protection of proprietary information. Network sociality is not characterized by a separation but by a combination of both work and play. (p. 51)

The work was indeed ephemeral, and once the project was completed, the team members no longer had a reason to inter-communicate. Figure 4 demonstrates a network with sparse ties, partly due to the geographically distributed nature of the work.

In this line social network's power dynamic, the course creator who was also the lead faculty member for the course has a much stronger central role because of his/her connections to the learners. This lead instructor (in a changing role) also has more responsibilities in terms of connecting with the bookstore and student beta testers (who help

Figure 4. Online technical writing course SME team

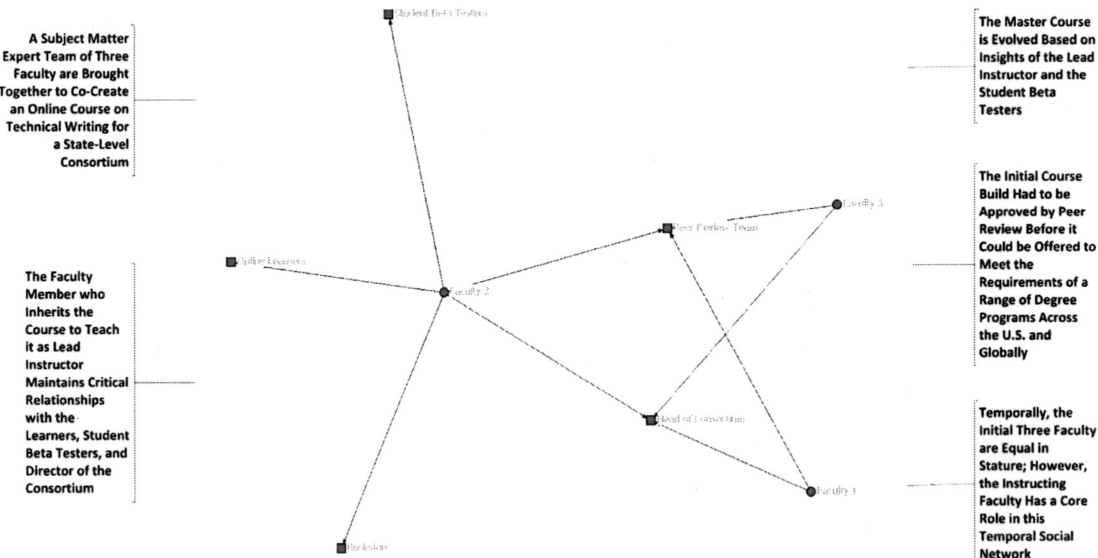

evolve the online course over time). While the peripheral faculty members are important in getting the course to launch and past the peer review team and the director of the online learning consortium, their roles are only for a time, and that is reflected in their peripheral status in this network.

A Subject Matter Expert Team of Three Faculty are Brought Together to Co-Create an Online Course on Technical Writing for a State-Level Consortium
The Faculty Member who Inherits the Course to Teach it as Lead Instructor Maintains Critical Relationships with the Learners, Student Beta Testers, and Director of the Consortium
The Master Course is Evolved Based on Insights of the Lead Instructor and the Student Beta Testers
The Initial Course Build Had to be Approved by Peer Review Before it Could be Offered to Meet the Requirements of a Range of Degree Programs Across the U.S. and Globally
Temporally, the Initial Three Faculty are Equal in Stature; However, the Instructing Faculty Has a Core Role in this Temporal Social Network

3. **An Automated Biosecurity Training:** A federally funded biosecurity project focused on training 12,000 learners working in U.S. agriculture to identify signs of Select Agents in the nation's dispersed agricultural land. This automated training was to be created by three universities working in concert. The instructional designer was brought in past the three-year mark after the curriculum was supposed to have been delivered. Little progress had been made in those three years, even though there were weekly phone meetings. The project was complex and required the use of a Cisco Systems Reusable Learning Object (RLO) structure and metadata collection. There was also a new customized software system that would be used. The project was finally delivered and made functional, even though the PI at one university was removed by the other PIs because of non-delivery of work. Figure 5 is a freeze-frame of the social dynamics of the project, condensed in time.

This static cross-sectional depiction does not capture the dramatic shifts in the team membership due to the project having to go into an extension and then a crisis of leadership. One instructional designer worked from one of the main campuses, and the other telecommuted from an hour and a half away. The structure of this network shows the peripheral status of the commuting instructional designer in terms of his / her impact on the project.

4. **Axio™ Demo Course:** A university had created a Learning / Course Management System (L/CMS) and was marketing it to other colleges and groups around the state. To showcase the various functionalities, the office asked

Figure 5. The biosecurity development team's social network in a time of crisis

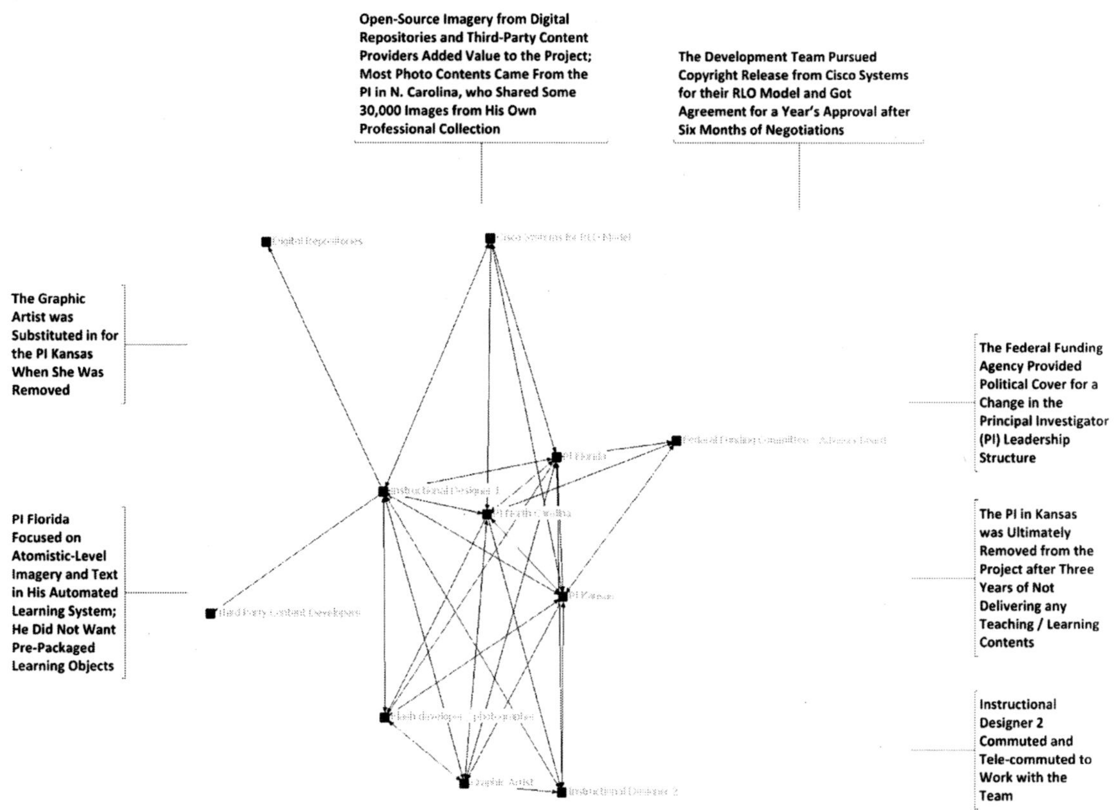

its three instructional designers to create an automated course that would demonstrate the system's capabilities in a kind of "tour" within the space. The instructional designers turned to their faculty clients and requested usage of their modules. They were interested in demonstrating the various authoring tools that could be used to create digital contents. The data array was created with binary graphing, identifying a node as a "yes" (1) or a "no" (0) about whether or not it is tied to a certain phase. Figure 6 serves as a social-functional analysis of a development team.

This two-mode network (one which has entities and events) shows not only the development team members but also the five phases of the project (albeit in a flattened singular slice-in-time approach):

Phase 1: Brainstorming
Phase 2: Content Development
Phase 3: Alpha Testing
Phase 4: Beta Testing
Phase 5: Rollout and Publicity

In this social network depiction, individuals are critical at various phases. However, when that phase passed, their criticality may have subsided. While the IT Associate Director had a critical role in starting the project, he is outside of the core development team—or those who actually did the work. The three instructional designers played central roles in the work phases. They were the bridges to various content providers, represented by the faculty. On the periphery were code developers and a software help documentation writer who provided critical work at various phases.

Figure 6. Axio™ demo course: a development team and their participation in five phases

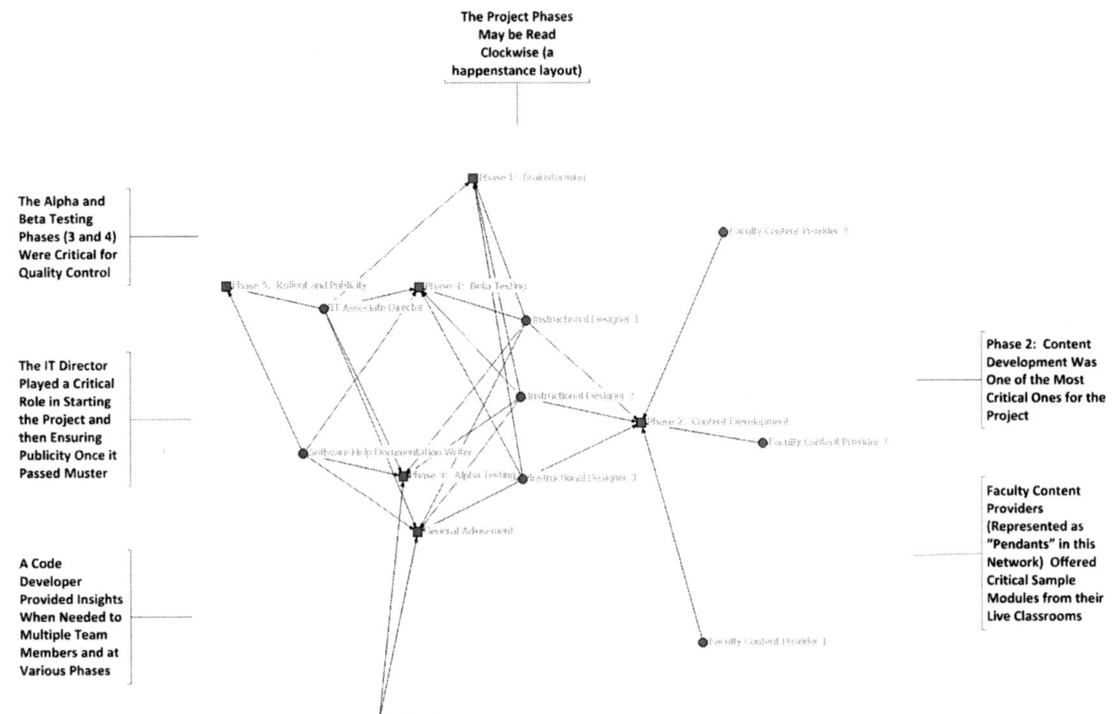

5. **University Life Café:** The University Life Café started out as a two-campus endeavor, but when one PI was unable to deliver work that met the requirements of the grant, the other PI petitioned the federal funding agency for a shift of the work to one campus (The original grant writer was removed from the project and relegated to the periphery and then removed from the network.). This was a complex project that involved the participation of a range of stakeholder-informants on various advisory committees that included individuals on campus concerned about the mental, emotional, and physical well-being of students. Students also served on this team. There was a lot of coordination required in terms of connecting with legal counsel, Information Technology (IT) personnel, videographers and actors, an instructional designer, and others, who would put together a suicide prevention / emotional resiliency Website for the university. The importance of privacy protections made the design and building work even more complicated. The use of the site by potentially fragile individuals meant that the university had to tie its quick response team in to the site's functions. It had to enable a publicly facing use of anonymous handles while being able to track users from the back end (in case of a need for a fast response). Figure 7 is a complex social network with a complex array of both supporters to a project and its stakeholders.

Work-based social networks show a confluence of coordination needs with a project. Initially, the instructional designer played a key role in researching and executing on the site—including connecting with media specialists, IT specialists, and

Figure 7. The university life café development team and its internal and external publics

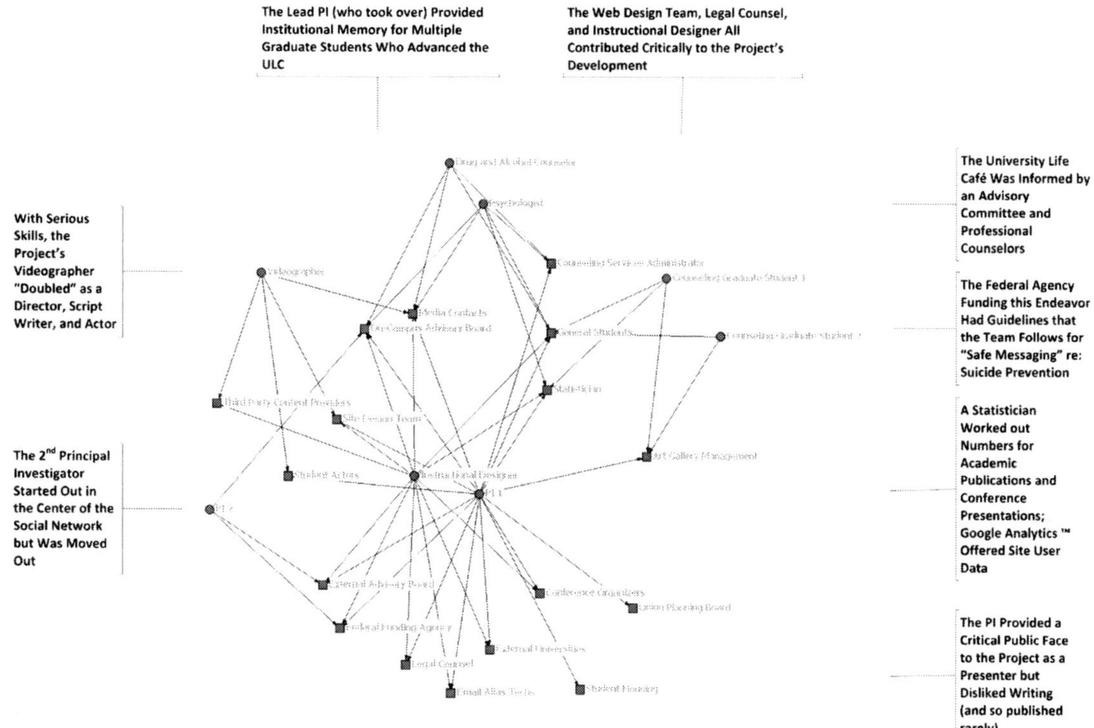

legal counsel. The PI focused on working with the campus constituencies. Finally, as the instructional designer moved off project and the continuing work was taken on by graduate students in counseling, the main PI maintained the institutional memory of the project and trained future graduate students working on the site. In the years since the site's launch, little new content has been added. A Google Analytics™ analysis has shown some large spikes and drops in usage.

6. **Appendix G (Grievance Policy) Training:** In order to abide by university policies, legal counsel needed to set up an automated training for faculty and staff who would be serving on a university-level committee hearing staff grievances and ultimately providing a recommendation to the university president for resolution of the matter. The lawyer wanted to build a verbatim training by introducing the policy in parts and then explaining the main takeaway points. She wrote the entire training and asked an instructional designer to add imagery and script the contents into a stand-alone module. She also wrote the assessment. The instructional designer was asked to create a simple way for people to verify that they'd been trained.

The phases of the work included the following steps:

1. Project Conceptualization
2. Content Writing
3. Scripting
4. Critique
5. Revision
6. Launch and Outreach
7. Updating

Figure 8 highlights the social network as it engaged with these work phases.

Figure 8 shows a simple social network with the legal counsel at the core. The instructional designer is a pendant here because of a very strictly limited role. Some projects are fairly direct. The work is part of the in-house services of the instructional designer. The PI here takes on a centralized role in virtually all phases of the work. A second phase was added to a project when the policy changed, and the digital learning object needed updating. However, the core power dynamic remained the same.

7. **Academic Dishonesty Co-Authored Article:** An instructional designer had worked on an Honor and Integrity course for learners who had been found to engage in academic dishonesty (as established by a student-led panel that considered the evidence). The instructional designer saw a call for articles that focused on academic dishonesty and thought that the university's Honor Pledge and the course would make an engaging article. By then, the original faculty member of the course had left the institution, and the leadership in the Honor and Integrity Office had changed. To promote this article, the instructional designer contacted both the original instructor to request use of her model (with full byline citation) and contacted the head of the Honor and Integrity office to see if she would be willing to be primary author (The primary authorship goes to the one who has more standing to address an issue vs. the one who has done more of the work sometimes) (see Figure 9).

This sparse line social network diagram shows the importance of the corresponding author role even though the corresponding author may well not be the primary author. Various individuals

Figure 8. Appendix G dyadic team and work phasing

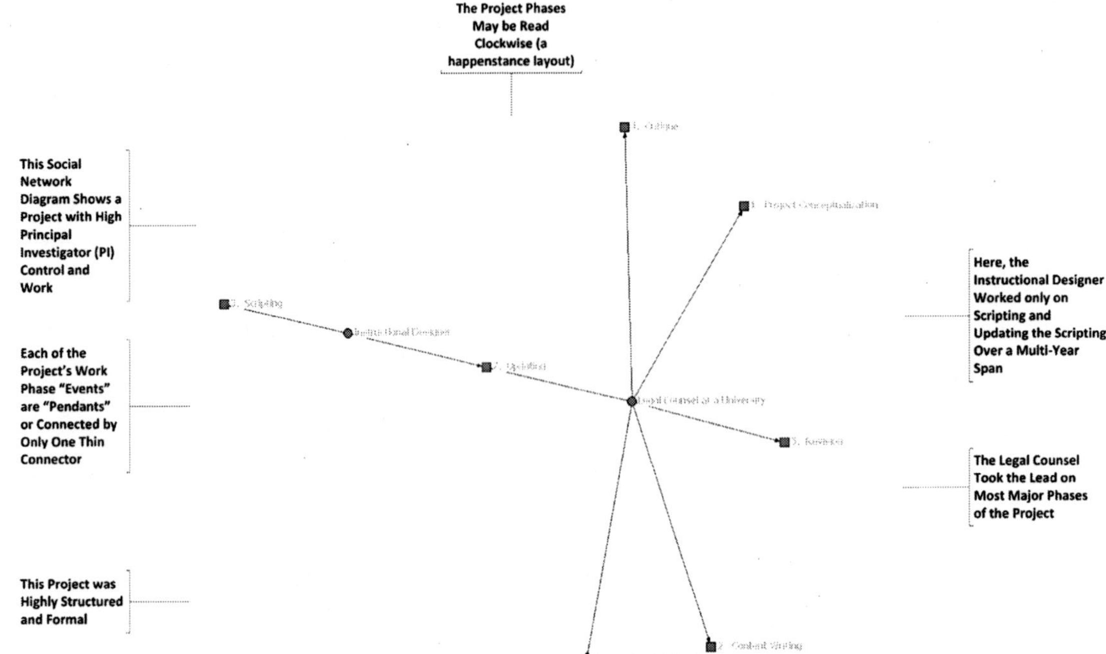

Figure 9. Academic dishonesty article co-authorship

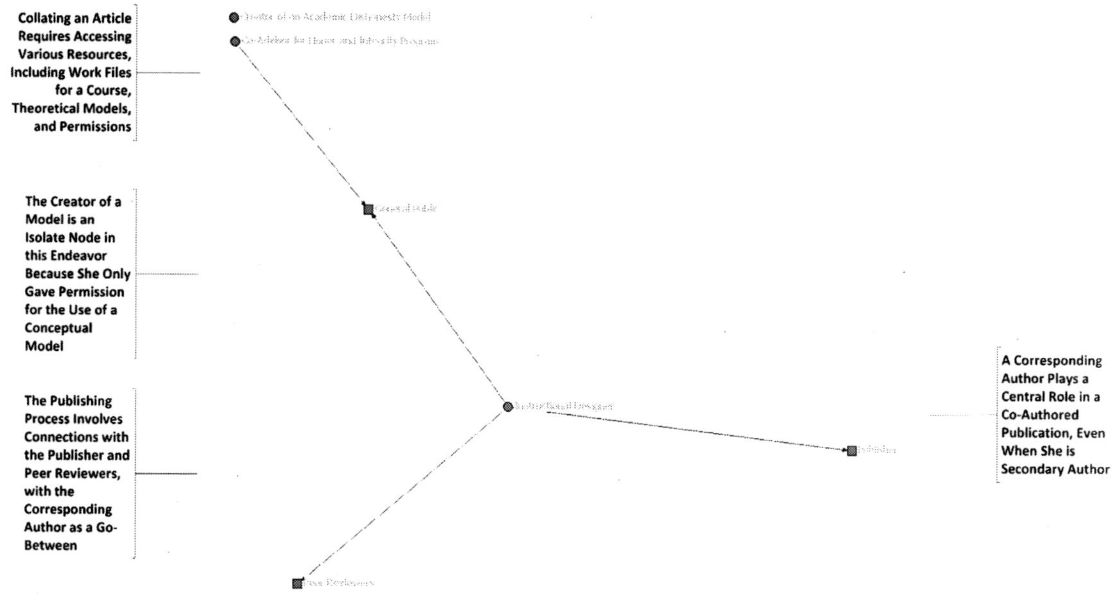

have to be consulted to bring the pieces of an article together.

8. **Introduction to Public Health:** The "Introduction to Public Health" project was a multi-institutional collaboration with expertise from a university and four colleges. This collaborative approach not only promoted the connections between those with related expertise but would strengthen 2 x 2 ("two by two") graduate pipeline / transfer ties between the colleges and the destination university (which was also the lead on the project). The team worked to respect the various areas of expertise. They met early on in the project to define the project stylebook and to assign modules for which the teams would write slideshows. The cross-functional team met again to critique the work by the various smaller teams that co-authored the pieces. The two PIs both were hands-on in the work. They dealt with a range of management and bureaucracy-based issues in terms of having the course offered on multiple campuses with differing tuition rates and different faculty members. Figure 10 shows a breakdown of the modules in the course and the various contributions of the dispersed multi-organizational teams to the work.

This two-mode social network is expressed as a ring lattice (a social network expressed with the nodes placed in a circle, based on "trellis graphics" which display information on a certain data structure). The two main PIs have thick ties to a range of individuals. They had a strong hand in every module of the curriculum as leaders and critiquers. The dyadic and triadic teams that co-authored particular modules were more often than not co-located on the same campus.

Some floating isolate nodes came from one of the colleges, who listed a range of staff—maybe to justify the college's contribution or maybe because of ambiguity about the project's needs early on or even possibly for political coverage for individuals.

Figure 10. Introduction to public health internal team participation ring lattice

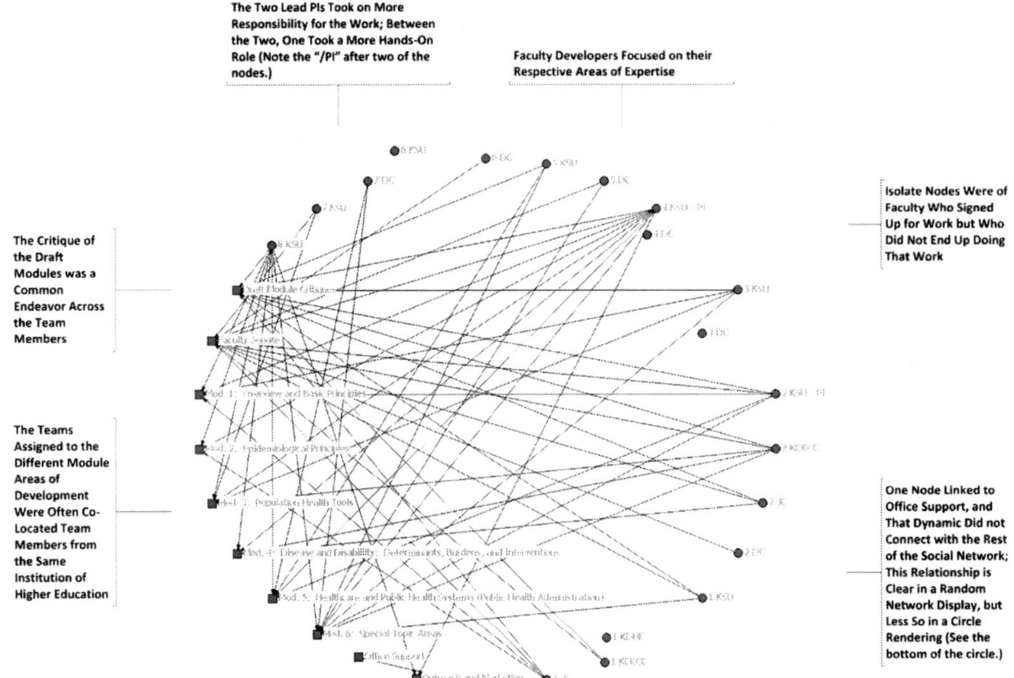

9. **Global Health:** The global health course was spearheaded by a leader who had decades of expertise in veterinary medicine and global public health. She had ties to a range of critical stakeholders: global health organizations, grant funders, and the graduate students. She was physically separate from the actual development team, which worked stateside while she lived abroad. During her multiple-times-a-year visits stateside, she would meet with the team and participate in interviews or chroma-key / green-screen video taping for the project, which involved both curriculum development and the creation of a global health game. Figure 11 showcases the complex power dynamics.

This team has two general power centers, one stateside and one abroad. The global health expert's ties to various stakeholders is represented by the pendant links to her at the right. The development team working stateside is represented in the "island" to the left. The instructional designer was the gatekeeper to the global health expert. Network science has implications for population health. It is used in part for epidemiology (the work of disease detectives who conduct contact tracing and traceback to find the origin of an outbreak) and has implications for herd immunities (such as inoculating a percentage of a population in order to protect those who do not immunize) (Fine, Eames, & Heymann, 2011). Network science has shown that distant health dangers are actually much closer than people may conceptualize.

10. **E-Learning Best Practices Course:** The e-learning best practices course was conceptualized by an IT director to offer yet another route for faculty members to acquire some of the best practices in online teaching and learning by offering a showcase of online professors' inventive approaches. She brought

Figure 11. The global health development team and its stakeholders social network

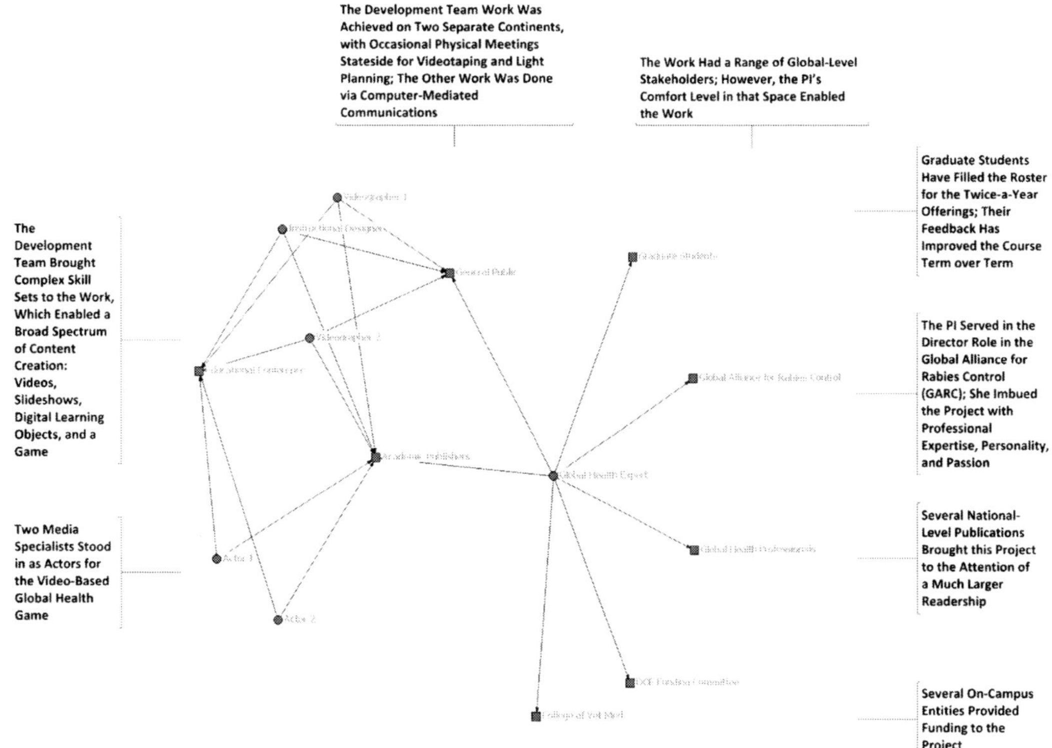

on board the three instructional designers in her office. The showcase course would be based on the quality e-learning matrix developed at the university. It would sample widely from across campus in order to be as inclusive of learning domains as possible.

The parts of the course included the following:

1. Course Info Policies and Requirements
2. Course Content and Technology Usage
3. Learner Interactions
4. Learner Support
5. Assessment and Evaluation

Figure 12 focuses on the role of the various members of the development team in contributing to the various parts of this online, automated course.

This social network analysis examines the contributions of each to the various modules of the course: This shows the importance of bringing in various disparate skill sets (as indicated by the pendant node contributors). Further, there may be an observation here about Jim Collins' idea of getting the right people on the bus—those who have an interest in the topic and are willing to invest their talents and social connections to actualizing the course.

11. **E-Learning and Teaching Exchange Wiki (ELATEwiki):** The E-Learning and Teaching Exchange wiki (ELATEwiki) was originated to offer a participatory space for online faculty to share expertise. Dr. Roger McHaney brainstormed a simple ontology: Instructors, Course Issues, Students, and Tools. He went on to serve as wiki master.

Figure 12. E-learning best practices course: two-mode network about the dev team and project contribution

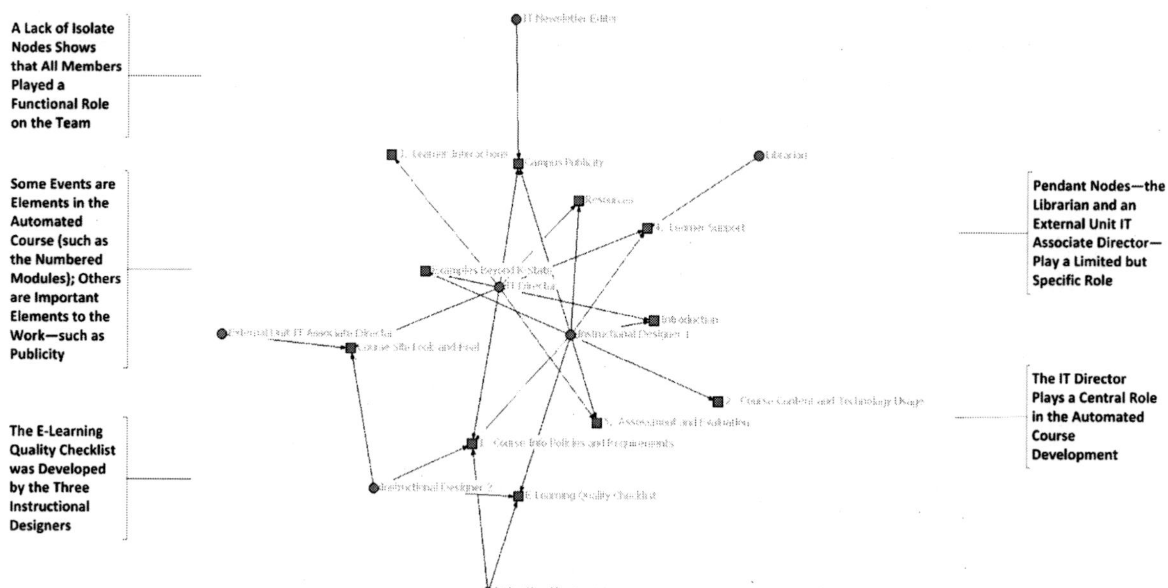

The knowledge structure has since evolved with students and staff contributing most of the contents. While the site itself has garnered plenty of visits, few have been full contributions by practicing faculty members. Figure 13 shows how a team engages with external constituencies as the public-facing aspects of their work.

This social network shows in part the way leaders on a project have to harness disparate skills from across campus to actualize a project. There is a need for the political cover of the Division of Continuing Education (DCE) director. Further, there has to be good will from all quarters to push forward an unfunded project. Figure 14 further refines the visualization.

Here, this focuses on the team ties to the public. The publicly facing side of this team highlights those with the hands-on collaboration work. This includes both members of the university community and those off-campus in the general public.

12. **Digital Entomology Lab:** An entomology professor was putting an undergraduate course online. This course had a lab component to study insect form and function (morphology) in the face-to-face setting. When the online course itself was completed, the instructional designer and professor decided to write a grant to pursue further funds to put the lab component online. The team hired a student photographer for the macro photography. The work proceeded with an initial site created. However, the development team did not have the Web developer support that was expected, and the endeavor ended up with only a partially completed digital lab. Figure 15 highlights a reality on many projects—or the shortage of funds and resources to actualize the work.

That a project in academia is poorly funded is not a surprise for most. Again, those in the core of a social network are those with staying power. Initially, the photographer and instructional de-

Figure 13. ELATEwiki dev team and external ties

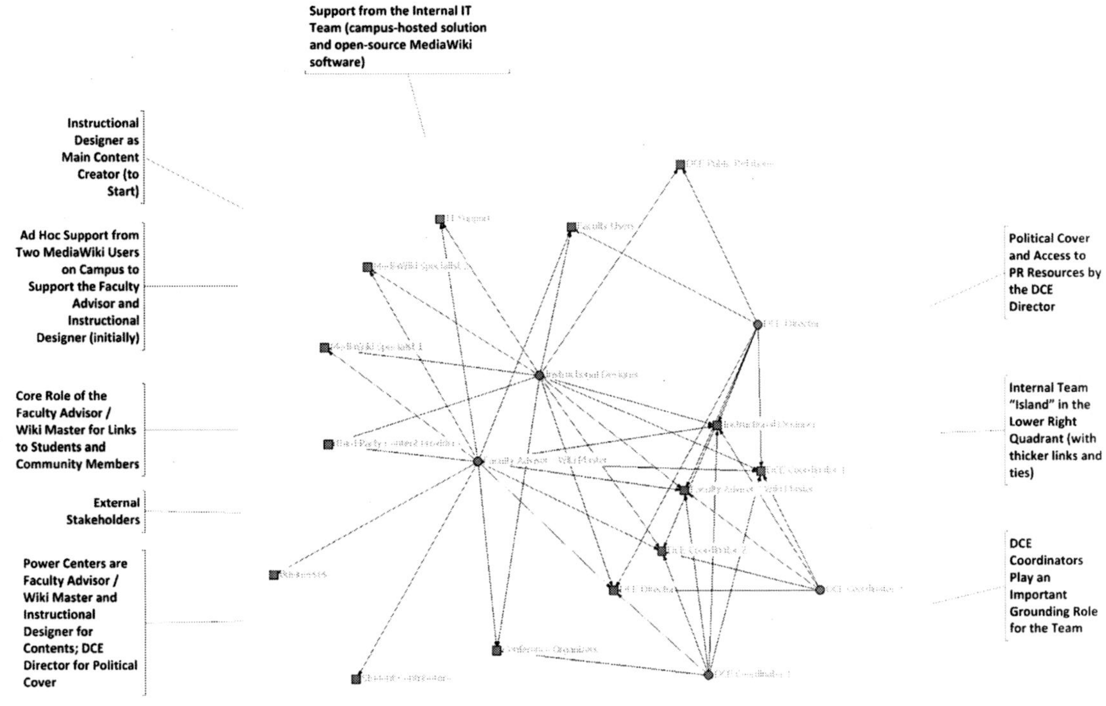

Figure 14. ELATEwiki dev team and external ties only

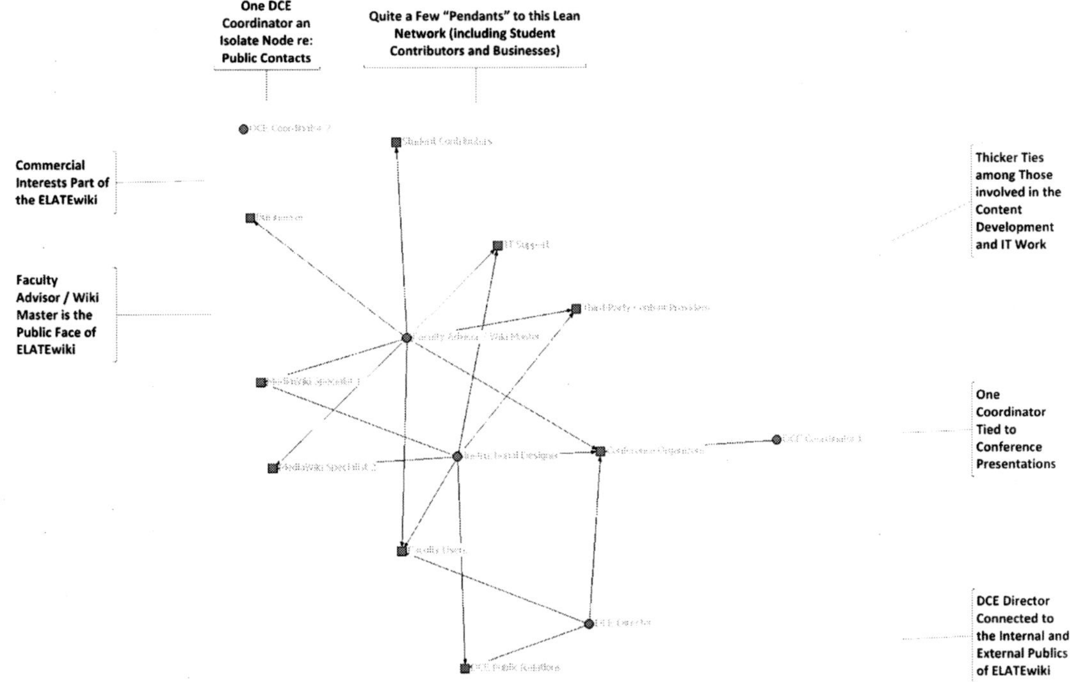

signer had important roles, but both disappeared off the project upon its completion, and now, if the visual were to be created, it would only be the PI / Entomologist who has a vested interest in the project. He is currently pursuing further funding for the effort.

13. **Introduction to One Health:** The "Introduction to One Health" course development involved working with an emergent curriculum that shows the connections between human, animal, and environmental health. The fielded team involved a lead PI / administrator (a former genetic scientist), a clinical scientist, a veterinarian (who would later become the instructor for the course), and an instructional designer. This was an unusual course build in the sense that the development cycle was a year and a half. Most the digital learning contents (slideshows, videos, and links to articles) had to be created from reams of contemporary research. This transdisciplinary approach melded the expertise of a diverse range of subject matter experts in the so-called hard sciences. As such, it required a high level of PI intellectual pedigree and powerful political connections across campus. Figure 16 highlights a special case in instructional design—of a well-funded and ambitious project, which tested the team members skills.

This online course development was possible really only because of the lead PI / administrator brought a breadth of expertise, administrative sophistication, and SME connections to the work. Her role is indicated in terms of her degree cen-

Figure 15. The digital entomology lab team and their resources seeking

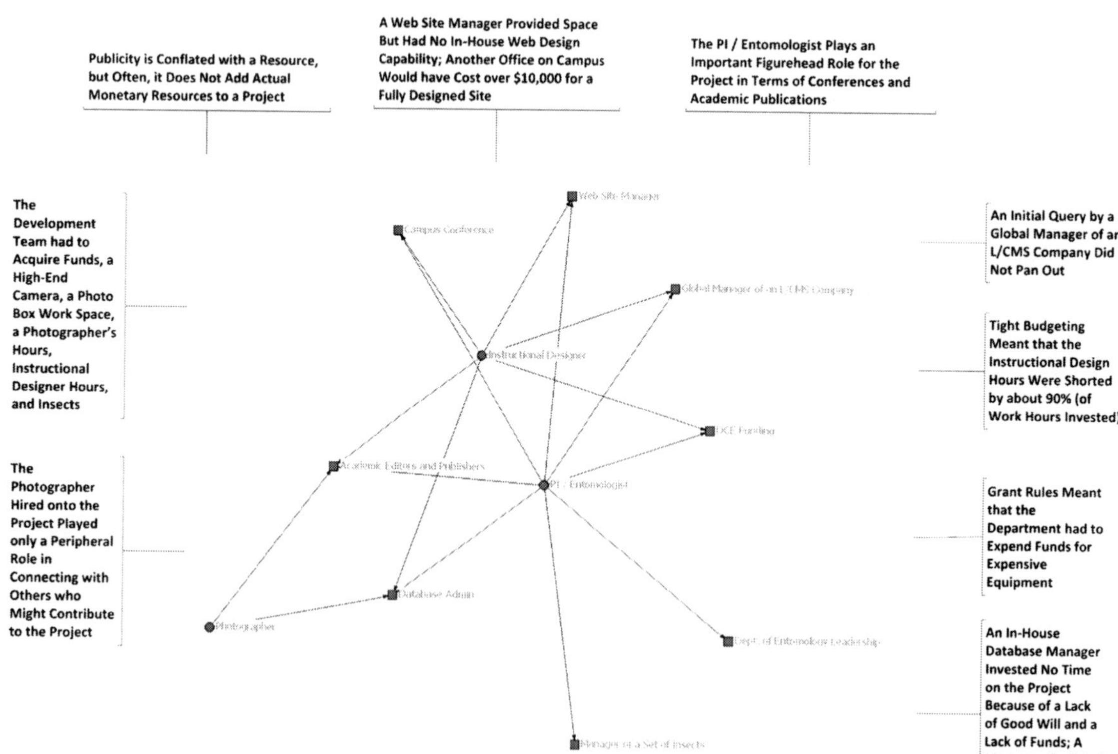

trality in the network, which indicates her structural prestige and advantageous position. Her embeddedness or integration in multiple networks helped move the project forward. Further, those who are out in the social network hinterlands may be just a short path away from someone else in the network if they work through the PI node (for example, if an instructional designer would like to ask a question of a faculty member or external SME). Her cross-domain knowledge served the team well especially when it came to vetting the slideshows, which drew heavily from the research literature. This social network involved a heavy network load of data that were processed into digital learning objects.

This network served as a prime example of the "diffusion of innovation" in the sense that the team functioned as a learning organization. While all came at science with some level of expertise, the learning curve was steep for at least a few members of the team. Each team member learned during the development with since the work drew from human medicine, animal medicine, and environmental health. The team adopted many One Health concepts in their work. The curriculum itself assumes a kind of adoption rate by professionals in a number of fields who may collaborate with others outside their domains as others adopt trans-domain practices.

14. **Traumatic Brain Injury:** The Traumatic Brain Injury project was led by two PIs with a vision for integrating interviews of people with TBI into the curriculum. The focus of the curriculum would be to educate the larger community about how to be more

Figure 16. The "introduction to one health" development team and the criticality of connections to subject matter experts

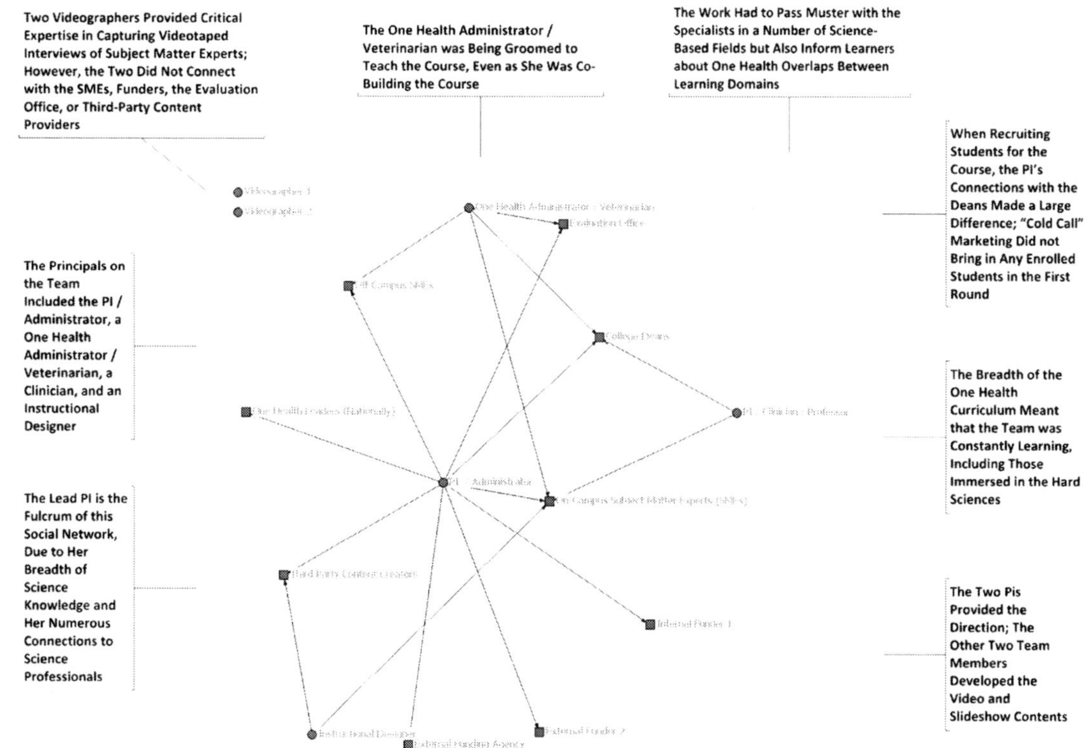

accommodating and supportive for people with TBI. As the project evolved, the main focus of the work shifted to the video captures all around the state. The work of the instructional designer was relegated to transcription and capturing images and supporting delivery of the contents from a Website and also a DVD. Those who were central to the project were the two PIs, who designed their own curriculum, and a videographer who traveled all over the state to capture videos for the project (and was planning on creating a documentary with some of the used and unused footage). Figure 17 highlights a strategy used in some instructional design projects to keep those with various skill sets apart but simultaneously working towards the aims of the project.

This social network depicts the core team members and their contributions to the various stages of the work. The stages are described as follows:

1. Grant Writing
2. Curricular Design
3. Interviews of Individuals with TBI
4. Video Production
5. Video Transcription
6. Video Post Production
7. Site Design and DVD Packaging
8. Branding
9. Publicity, Presentations, and Publications

What this visualization shows is that the PIs determine the social hierarchy because it is their project. They choose who to put on the team and what the members will do. Further, on this particular project, the PIs were very interested in protecting their work. On the development team, they compartmentalized the work, with very little overlap between members of the team after the first meeting.

The PIs cut the video snippets into short pieces to make them more difficult for others to download and misuse. They used branching logic in the learning not only for the learning but to preserve some of the originality of the learning experience off of their Website (in a way that would not be as easy to recreate). They created an interactive Flash video for part of the training—which was designed for both live trainers in the field engaged in Face-to-Face (F2F) learning as well as automated use by site visitors.

15. **E-Learning Faculty Modules:** A mid-level administrator was inspired by a conference she attended to create a self-learning resource for online teaching faculty as part of the organization's training. She brought together a group of advisory faculty, Division of Continuing Education coordinators, an IT administrator, and instructional designers to build the E-Learning Faculty Modules. She hosted regular meanings to unify the group, which may be seen in Figure 18. Those central to this endeavor were the instructional designers who created a majority of the contents, and a faculty advisor and the inspired dean.

A further visualization was created to explore the relationship between the internal development team and internal and external publics for the resource. Faculty members have a strong power base in this social network in the sense that many nodes feed resources towards the faculty. While the site was created for internal use at a university, because the contents were hosted on a locked-down but publicly available Website. Figure 19 shows the importance of shepherding a project through political territory—such as the fraught area of faculty training.

In Figure 19, this social network shows an internal team "island" of developers with denser ties among themselves and then another hub of

Figure 17. The traumatic brain injury project and compartmentalization

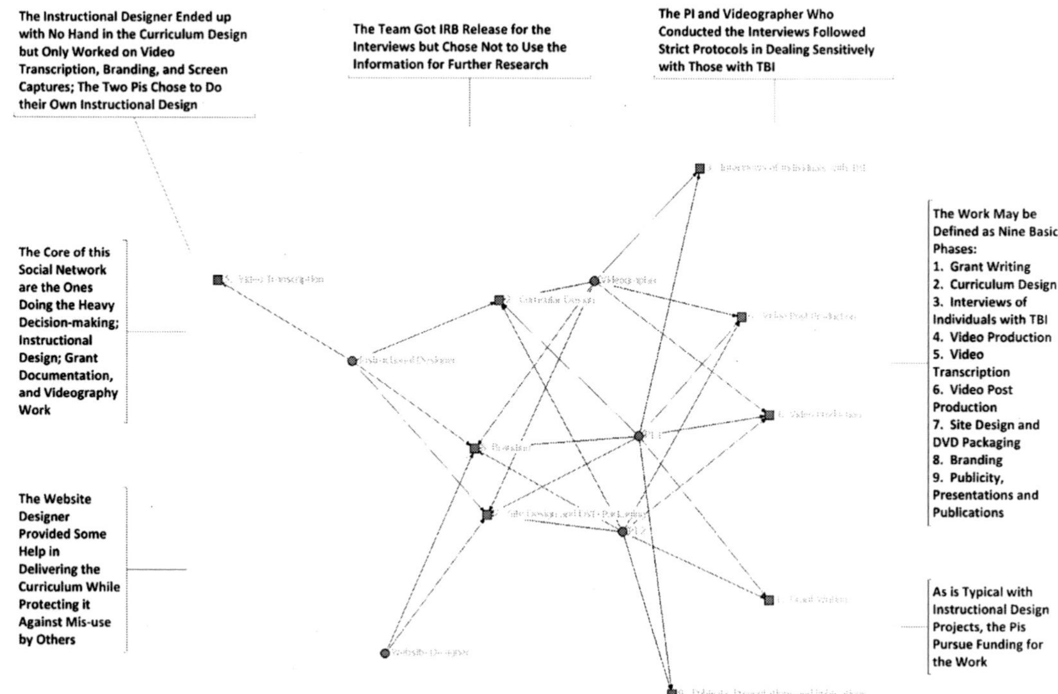

Figure 18. E-learning faculty modules internal development team

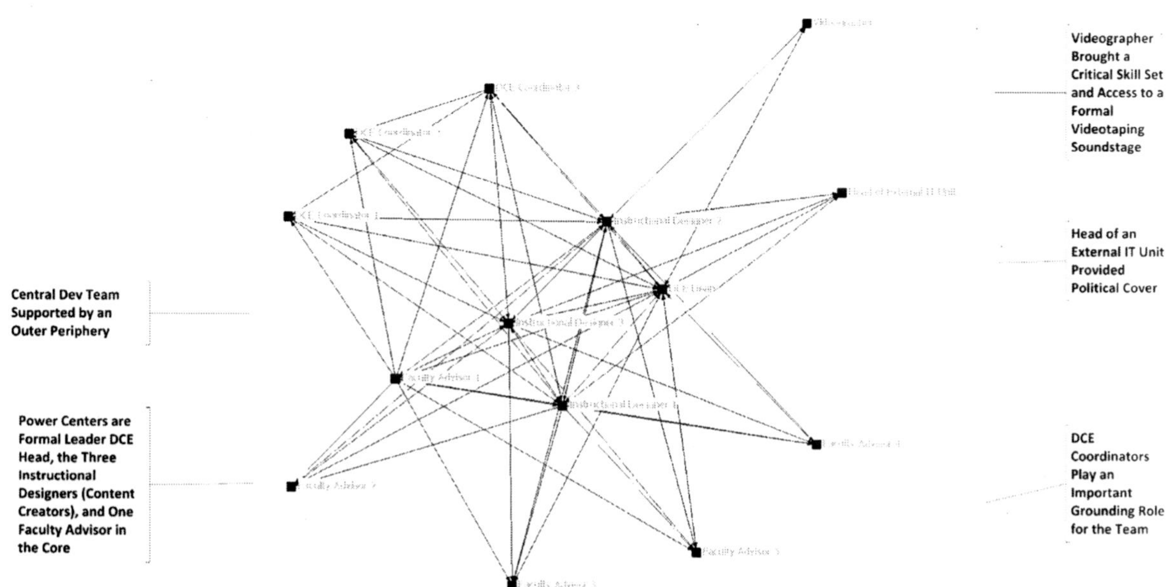

faculty members, which resembles a simple star network at the lower left.

Finally, Figure 20 shows how the team members engaged with the functional development work. The various entity nodes cluster around particular similar functions. Those who work with digital media are clustered with the instructional designers, and at the bottom right are those engaged with critique, public presentations, and political work. This project has lasted for two years and is continuing sporadically into the third year.

SOME LIMITS TO THE STUDY

In one sense, these visualizations use a kind of circular logic. The information that is put into the software is merely re-configured and re-output from a data matrix to a 2D spatial visualization on a graph. No "new" information has been created per se. Rather, the reiteration of the information in a visual format enables researchers to change their own awareness of what the data are actually conveying. In other words, their sensemaking has been enhanced with this software tool. Researchers then are using inductive logic by collating large amounts of information and making inferences from that.

Each of these depictions may be conceptualized as hypotheses of how the team structures may look in terms of how resources and information and power moved through them. These depictions show expected centrality of certain nodes based on their interrelationships with other notes and their level of connectivity. The narrative descriptions of each provided some background to each project.

In a workplace (as a social context), there are generally shared interests in pursuing certain objectives. The complex multiplex (mulfi-faceted) aspects of the ties between nodes were not explored here. There are often closer and richer relationships between some individuals than others, but

Figure 19. E-learning faculty modules development team relationships with external stakeholders

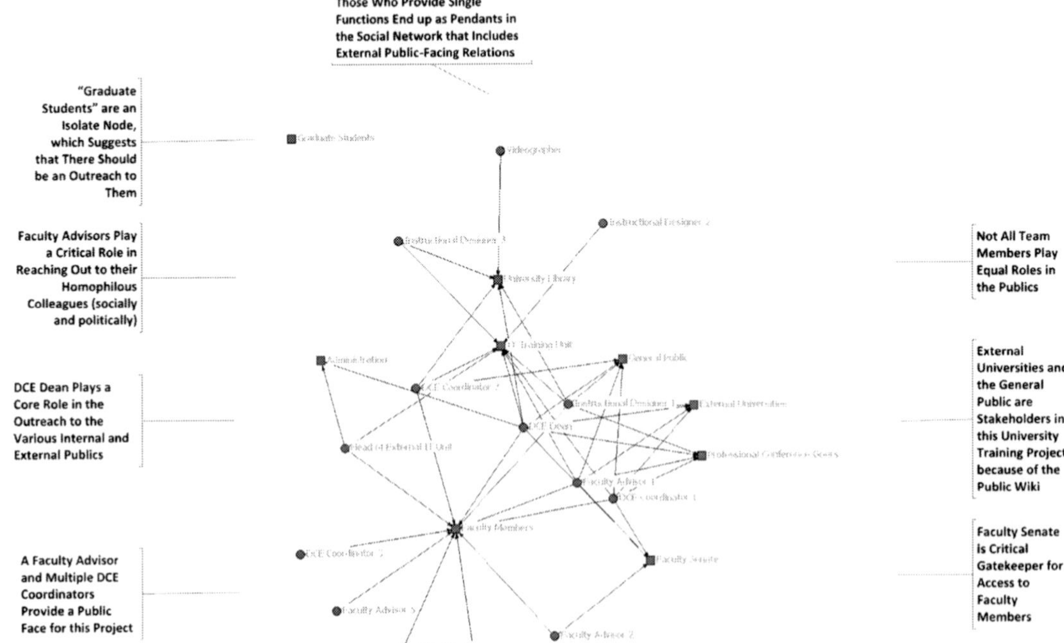

Figure 20. E-learning faculty modules two-mode network: team entities and functional events

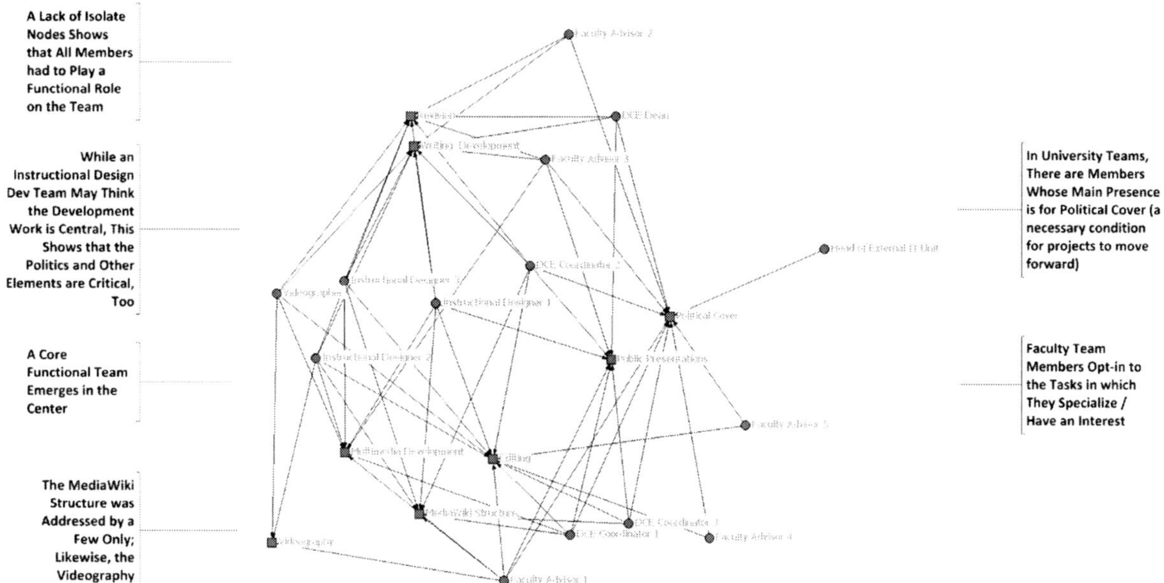

because weighted linkages were not used, and other types of node attributes were not included beyond roles, other aspects of these social networks were not probed. Further, the compositions of the various social networks are defined by respective workplace / project-based positions. In that sense, the compositions of each of the teams were determined by the PI and the limits of the workplace context (in terms of access to human resources). The stochastic or random dynamism in such a context may be minimalized by the designed context. While there will be endogenous and exogenous effects on the social networks, the workplace affords an overarching structure that provides some regulation of the group. For examples, members of a network who leave by attrition may be substituted for by another. Node attributes—such as years of professional experience, education, personality, demographics, and other descriptive elements—were not discussed.

These depicted social networks are fairly sparse. They are described from the perspective of one insider who served on all the projects and who referred to documentary work files. Some research suggests that people's recalls of schemas and larger patterns of group interactivity are more accurate than their memories for individual performances (Krackhardt, 1987). However, the research literature also points to non-trivial forgetting of "a significant proportion of their close contacts" (Brewer, 2000, p. 29), which is a critical point to consider in evaluating this research but also in future work. (This is where reliance on proposals of work, email records, and other forms of documentation may enhance the quality of the collected data). The projects themselves lasted only some months in a few cases to several years in others.

Social network depictions are only as good as the data used to create the model. Having multiple perspectives informing a social network may enhance the visualization. For example, multiple team members may contribute to the visualization. A number of work files may be triangulated (or cross-referenced) for stronger validity and analytical robustness.

Further, to verify these social network depictions, it would be important to collect information to find actual data to test against the expected data. How did resources move through the networks? How did the respective nodes behave? What were the perspectives of others on the respective teams? After all, node attributes (the characteristics of each team member) will affect how the nodes function in the network. Node attributes affect "flow characteristics" in a social network. The nature of what is moving through social networks also affects the "centrality" of various nodes (Borgatti, 2005), but those nuances were not considered here. (By "what," these include things like funding, resources, ideas, social relationships, information, messages, reputation and social prestige, political power, access, and work-place opportunities.)

Finally, this chapter offers single and local cases, not larger data sets. The generalizability of the findings may be limited because of the low "n" and brief case-based features. There was not analysis of cutpoints (points of weakness in a social network) or strategies to exploit structural holes in the networks in part due to the simplicity of the networks and in part due to the completed nature of the work projects and finally because there was not a rationale for exploiting such work-based networks.

The UCINET software enables easy scalability to larger social networks with a wide range of tools to surface features of those work-based communities. Tools for the topology of large-scale social networks were not exploited here but could be applied to larger-scale analyses of work places or work domains. These tools may identify islands or sub-cliques; network density; various paths for information and resource flows, and other aspects.

SOLUTIONS AND RECOMMENDATIONS

The exercise of creating social network diagrams of various curricular design and development teams as well as co-authorship projects have highlighted some realities of instructional design work. The projects vary in terms of how centralized decision-making can be. PIs determine how much sharing they want to engage in in terms of work as well as how much is shared in terms of communication. How PIs structure the work will determine how much clique-ishness is manifested in the work. If those in leadership and in the work team make a point to intercommunicate (and maybe even over-communicate), many potential structural rifts may be addressed and mitigated. Further, conscious introductions of "alters" in an ego neighborhood may enhance the work of people from cross-disciplinary fields. Having a social networking view of a live project may help instructional designers try to shape their work environments—to have more input into the decision-making process, to encourage the assignment of work that skills (vs. de-skills), and to add value to the project.

FUTURE RESEARCH DIRECTIONS

The key insight of this chapter is that social network analysis may be applied to temporary work teams to understand the power dynamics in that circumstance and to use that knowledge to facilitate the effective work. This is an unusual "unit of analysis," with many work-place social networks focused on ego networks of individual employees or the bounded networks of whole organizations. Larger and distributed projects may be analyzed using automatic data extraction tools that track emails, social networks, electronic contents, and other digital expressions of group work; whole conferences may be mapped electronically through EventGraphs. Combined advances in sociology and computer science work in statistically and geometrically describing social networks have advanced analytical possibilities (Hansen, Schneiderman, & Smith, 2011).

The application of network analysis to instructional design work presents potential directions for how to disperse power among the group members over time. Network analysis may present opportunities for mitigating weak links in a work team structure by increasing structured communications. Nodes that may be non-functioning or problematically placed within a hierarchy may be moved to more constructive parts of a network, or cross-training between nodes may occur to increase work team resilience. Automated network functionality—extrapolated from intercommunications and other variables—may be built into online work sites to inform the team of their apparent inter-relationships and interactions. Systems may be defined with sufficient research to formalize the observations into appropriate and refined models. Such meta-perspectives may enhance the group's work. Such tools may enhance the self-awareness of groups in their electronically mediated work.

Having an exogenous (vs. egocentric) perspective of a team and its required functionalities may be helpful on a project in the pre-, during, and post- phases. In the pre-phase, per Figure 21, the team leader and other participants may more consciously design the team's structure. They may use the visualizations as a tactic for team building and role awareness, with a focus on interactivity. Industries have applied network thinking in reaching out to disparate social networks, groups, and individuals to create specialist "innovation networks" (Cotton, 2009).

Figure 21. Using social network diagrams in various work project phases

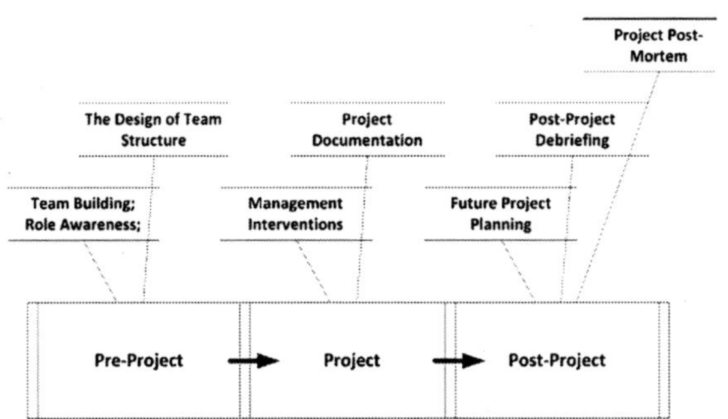

During the project, social network visualizations may be used in the project documentation; management may use the visualizations for team interventions. Finally, post-project, sociograms may be used for a project post-mortem or debriefing, and / or the information may be used for future project planning. Outside evaluators (of the project) may use such depictions to elicit feedback from the team members and to provide insights on improving future teamwork.

The team should be "read into" the uses of social network diagrams, though, to enhance the related analytical and decision-making work. While much of social network diagramming is intuitive, there are some nuances in how to understand the depictions, which may involve some complexity. There is research work in this direction. For example, Durugbo (2012) presents a model for user participation in organizations as social networks that may also provide a work forward to analyzing the workflow processes for certain workplaces or projects.

CONCLUSION

Applied social network modeling, with its visual and textual components, offers much potential for work team awareness, understanding, analysis, and decision-making. This analysis of various transitory instructional design project teams offers a systems view of the social relations among the team members; the social hierarchy; the team functionality and resource and workflows. These structures shed light on workplace dynamics and may suggest ways to re-arrange such structures for improved work efficiencies. Social network diagrams may be used as an analytical tool for heuristic (experience-based) research in work places.

A NOTE ABOUT THE CHAPTER'S ANNOTATED SOCIAL NETWORK DIAGRAMS

The social network diagrams were created by first creating a data array in an Excel spreadsheet. Then, that was placed into UCINET™ and saved as a data file. The file was then visualized using UCINET's NetDraw™. That image was captured using Gadwin Print Screen's screen capture technology, and the image was placed into Microsoft Visio, which was used to place annotations on the diagram. The diagram was saved out as a .jpg image. Then, Adobe Photoshop® was used to transcode the image into the proper image type for publication.

ACKNOWLEDGMENT

Thanks to Jerome Sibayan for introducing UCINET to me and then encouraging my learning acquisition of the actual tool, which required many months of study and experimentation. A lot of work is required to understand the software, its functionalities, and then the sociological research behind the structures. I am still learning. I am grateful to Colleague 2 Colleague (C2C) for hosting my presentation "Building and Analyzing Node-Link Diagrams to Understand Social Networks" in early August 2012 in Overland Park, Kansas. Thanks to all the principal investigators (PIs) that I've worked with on the various projects, especially those that encouraged professional growth and learning.

REFERENCES

Adamic, L., & Adar, E. (2005). How to search a social network. *Social Networks*, *27*, 187–203. doi:10.1016/j.socnet.2005.01.007.

Borgatti, S. P. (2005). Centrality and network flow. *Social Networks*, *27*, 55–71. doi:10.1016/j.socnet.2004.11.008.

Borgatti, S. P. (2006). A graph-theoretic perspective on centrality. *Social Networks*, *38*, 466–484. doi:10.1016/j.socnet.2005.11.005.

Borgatti, S. P., Everett, M. G., & Freeman, L. C. (2002). *UCInet for windows: Software for social network analysis*. Boston, MA: Harvard.

Brewer, D. D. (2000). Forgetting in the recall-based elicitation of personal and social networks. *Social Networks*, *22*, 29–43. doi:10.1016/S0378-8733(99)00017-9.

Cho, H., Gay, G., Davidson, B., & Ingraffea, A. (2007). Social networks, communication styles, and learning performance in a CSCL community. *Computers & Education*, *49*, 309–329. doi:10.1016/j.compedu.2005.07.003.

Christakis, N. A., & Fowler, J. H. (2009). *Connected: The surprising power of our social networks and how they shape our lives*. New York: Little, Brown and Company.

Cotton, B. (2009). Innovation networks: A report on creating a specialist professional social network, offline and online, to foster innovation in the new media sector. [LNCS]. *Proceedings of Online Communities*, *5621*, 312–321. doi:10.1007/978-3-642-02774-1_34.

Cumming, G. S., Barnes, G., Perz, S., Schmink, M., Sieving, K. E., & Southworth, J. ... Van Holt, T. (2005). An exploratory framework for the empirical measurement of resilience. Ecosystems, 8, 975- 987. DOI: doi:10.1007/s10021-005-0129-z.

Cummings, J. N., & Cross, R. (2003). Structural properties of work groups and their consequences for performance. *Social Networks*, *25*, 197–210. doi:10.1016/S0378-8733(02)00049-7.

De Nooy, W., Mrvar, A., & Batagelj, V. (2011). *Exploratory social network analysis with Pajek: Structural analysis in the social sciences*. Cambridge, UK: Cambridge University Press. doi:10.1017/CBO9780511996368.

Durugbo, C. (2012). Modeling user participation in organisations as networks. *Expert Systems withApplications*, *39*, 9230–9245. doi:10.1016/j.eswa.2012.02.082.

Fine, P., Eames, K., & Heymann, D. L. (2011). Herd immunity: A rough guide. *Clinical Infectious Diseases*, *52*(7), 911–916. doi:10.1093/cid/cir007 PMID:21427399.

Hanneman, R. A., & Riddle, M. (2005). *Introduction to social network methods*. Riverside, CA: University of California.

Hansen, D. L., Schneiderman, B., & Smith, M. A. (2011). *Analyzing social media networks with NodeXL: Insights form a connected world*. Amsterdam: Elsevier.

Henttonen, K. (2010). Exploring social networks on the team level—A review of the empirical literature. *Journal of Engineering and Technology Management*, *27*, 74–109. doi:10.1016/j.jengtecman.2010.03.005.

Janhonen, M., & Johanson, J.-E. (2011). Role of knowledge conversion and social networks in team performance. *International Journal of Information Management*, *31*, 217–225. doi:10.1016/j.ijinfomgt.2010.06.007.

Krackhardt, D. (1987). Cognitive social structures. *Social Networks*, *9*, 109–134. doi:10.1016/0378-8733(87)90009-8.

Kratzer, J., Leenders, R. T. A. J., & Van Engelen, J. M. L. (2010). The social network among engineering design teams and their creativity: A case study among teams in two product development programs. *International Journal of Project Management*, *29*, 428–436. doi:10.1016/j.ijproman.2009.09.007.

Kraut, R., Egido, C., & Galegher, J. (1988). *Patterns of contact and communication in scientific research collaboration*. ACM Press. doi:10.1145/62266.62267.

McPherson, M., Smith-Lovin, L., & Cook, J. M. (2001). Birds of a feather: Homophily in social networks. *Annual Review of Sociology*, *27*, 415–444. Retrieved from http://www.jstor.org/stable/2678628?origin=JSTOR-pdf doi:10.1146/annurev.soc.27.1.415.

Obstfeld, D. (2005). Social networks, the Tertius iungens orientation, and involvement in innovation. *Administrative Science Quarterly*. Retrieved from http://asq.sagepub.com/content/50/1/100.abstract. doi: 10.2189/asqu.2005.50.1.100

Saxenian, A. (1994). *Regional advantage: Culture and competition in silicon valley and route 128*. Boston: Harvard University.

Watts, D. J. (2003). *Six degrees: The science of a connected age*. New York: W.W. Norton & Company.

Wittel, A. (2001). Toward a network sociality. *Theory, Culture & Society*, *18*(6), 51–76. doi: doi:10.1177/026327601018006003.

KEY TERMS AND DEFINITIONS

Actor: An individual with agency who acts within a social network (and is represented as a node or point).

Acyclic Network: A network which does not contain any cycles (such as networks of article citations which only refer in one direction—in the past—to refer to published works).

Adjacency: The phenomena of being close neighbors/nodes in a social network.

Adjacency Matrix: A matrix in which individuals who are next to each other in a social space are listed together side-by-side (and thus the adjacency label); this matrix looks at the effects of proximity.

Adoption Curves: A distribution which shows the rate of acceptance or adoption of a new idea, technology, practice, or other aspect.

Affiliation: The nature of interactions between vertices (nodes).

Affiliation Network: A two-mode social network that consists of actors and events (as mutually exclusive categories, with no crossover in information type).

Affinity: A liking or sympathy for others; a sense of closeness.

Alter (Connections): Directly connected nodes to a focal or "ego" node; also known as neighbors in an ego network.

Amplifier: A factor that magnifies or enlarges another force or message or energy.

Arcs: Directed lines (with arrows on one or both ends) in a directed graph or directed sociogram, with a clear sender and a clear receiver.

Asymmetry: An imbalance in a social relationship (or directed ties); potentially an unreciprocated relationship in which one side perceives a bonded tie and the other side does not.

Attribute: A descriptor (descriptive variable) of a node; may lead to preferences or biases.

Automorphic (Structural) Equivalence: The parallel structures existing between nodes and links; the concept of substitutability between nodes with similar structures (and presumed capabilities); a sense of similarity of roles within a social network.

Backtesting: Testing the verifiability of a model by comparing what the model would suggest would happen given certain historical inputs as contrasted with what actually happened in those historical situations.

Balanced/Imbalanced Networks: A theory of networks that suggests certain types of relationships within the network, with the idea that most networks work towards balance.

Betweenness Centrality: A measure of a node's or ego's centrality in a network (the number of shortest paths from all vertices to all others that pass through that node).

Bias: A preference of a vector or node in a social network.

Binary Graph: A graph which represents nodes as either a "yes" or "no"/present or non-present (binary) about a particular variable or phenomena.

Block (Bi-Component): Elements (or divisions) of connected nodes in a graph that may be separated into components with the deletion of cutpoints.

Blocking the Matrix: Partitioning parts of a social network represented in a matrix to create blocks; sectioning off the matrix into partitions.

Bonded Ties: A reciprocal (co-present or co-occurring) relationships between two vertices or nodes (with the relationship represented as a double-headed arrow).

Broadcast Search: Projecting a generalized message with a search request to the entire network.

Broker: An individual who negotiates between two other parties; a go-between who manages informational or other resources/assets.

Circle Graphs: A diagram that places the vertices or nodes in a circle in order to highlight the actual connectors (lines, edges) between the various vertices or nodes; this form shows the highest concentrations of connections.

Citation Network: A social network of research citations showing which works are the most popular (or the most often cited).

Clique: A substructure in a social network in which every element of the set is connected to every other member of that set at a distance greater than one; a maximal fully-connected subgraph which is a part of a larger graph or social network (with other variable definitions based on various analyses).

Closed Trail: A walk between two actors that begins and ends with the same actor.

Closed Walk: A sequence of connections between two actors with clearly defined start and end points.

Cluster: Groups of people represented as individual vertices who share dense close ties in local neighborhoods because of shared mutual interests; cohesive subgroups with various types of affiliations.

Cohesion: The structural cohesion of a social network is determined by the degrees of vertices (the numbers of connectors leading to and from the vertices, which may be averaged out to describe the network's structural cohesion); a highly cohesive network can move information / messages much more efficiently.

Complete Network: A network with maximum density (theoretically where all possible vertices are connected? A network with high cohesive ties?).

Connected Phase: A point at which a network changes from a disconnected phase to one where a critical point (or a "tipping point") has been reached where a sufficient number of nodes have converted to accepting a new practice, and there are sufficient numbers to maintain momentum on its own or to accelerate momentum of conversions.

Constellation: A node-link diagram that depicts data that is associative or hierarchical.

Constraint: A limitation or restriction; something that constrains.

Contamination: The process of diffusion of something (an idea, a technology, a practice, a meme, or other element) through a social network.

Co-Present or Co-Occurring: Ties between vertices which require the participation of the involved nodes in a particular event; bonded ties.

Critical Mass: A sufficient amount of nodes (adopters) that may enable a network to achieve a "tipping point" or sufficient momentum to be self-sustaining in the acceptance of a new innovation (in a diffusion of innovation model).

Cutpoints: Places in a network where the removal of a node would divide the structure into unconnected parts; weak links / brokers / bridges between otherwise disconnected groups in a graph.

Cycle: A restricted walk of three or more actors (nodes), all of whom are distinct except for the origin/destination actor.

Cyclic Network: A network with clusters that are generally within one rank with equality among the vertices.

Data Array: The setup of a data set in a spreadsheet (or multiple spreadsheets) with variables listed across the top row and each of the following rows below as individual records, with unique identifiers running down the left column (a classic rectangular data array).

De-Duplication: Removing any repeated data from a data set to ensure clean data.

Degrees of Separation: The concept that people may be connected by close ties in a "small world" through low degrees of separation in the "human Web" (an initial idea by Dr. Stanley Milgram); the famous "six degrees of separation" suggests that people are only six steps away from anyone else in the world by the six steps (in a concept expressed by Frigyes Karinthy and popularized in a play by John Guare).

Density: The number of lines (connectors) in a simple network, described as a proportion of the maximum possible number of lines or ties (a percentage of extant lines or arcs divided by all possible lines or arcs).

Diameter (of a Social Network): The length of the longest path between connected actors; the span of the network (as an indicator of size).

Diffusion: The spreading of an innovation, disease, practice, information, or some other element through a social network (often enhanced by the density of the social network).

Directed Graph (Digraph): A node-link diagram that has directional lines (the presence or absence of arrow-heads at the line ends) or arcs indicating directional aspects of relationships (including whether the connections are reciprocated or not).

Directed Search: Reaching out to a targeted few in a social network to locate particular information or resources.

Direction: The course or impetus of a relationship.

Dyad: A pair of vertices (nodes) and the lines linking them.

Eccentricity: A measure of how far one node is from the furthest other in a social network (the mean and standard deviation of their geodesic distances to describe their closeness to other actors).

Edges (Ties, Lines, or Links): Line indicators in a social network that indicate relationships between individuals, cliques, and groups in that social network; undirected ties (lines without arrows showing directionality on the ends).

Ego: A focal node, a vertex that represents a specific individual or agent (from whose perspective the other aspects of the network may be viewed) and the various alters connected to that node (others in the "neighborhood"); an ego may also refer to groups, organizations, or even whole countries or societies.

Ego Network: A social network of various individuals with a special focus on the local (neighborhood) connections of individual actors; a vertex (node) and its neighbors, including all the lines among the selected vertices (nodes).

Embeddedness: The closeness of a particular node in an ego-network with other members, characterized by dense local sub-structure connections; the extent to which actors are in social structures with "dense, reciprocal, transitive, strong ties" (Hanneman & Riddle, 2005, Ch. 9, "Ego networks," p. 1).

Equivalence: A state of similarity between vertices with "zero dissimilarity" (or similarity of a lesser degree).

Eulerian Circuit or Cycle: A Eulerian trail (a path in a graph which visits every line exactly once which starts and ends on the same node or vertex.

Fat Node: A vertex or node which has high in-degrees of lines or arcs or edges as well as high out-degrees of lines, showing high connectivity and assumed popularity and influence.

Geodesic: The shortest path between two vertices or nodes (one of the ways that resources and materials move through a network).

Graph: A systematic and condensed representation of information; a set of vertices or nodes and a set of lines between pairs of vertices (including some non-lines between vertices).

Hierarchical Clustering: A form of cluster analysis that builds a hierarchy of cluster based on criteria such as affinity or relatedness (used in genomic data), often expressed in a dendrogram.

Immediacy Index: A measure of a publication's power in terms of the citations to the contents within the year of its publication (a rate based on the immediacy of response within the publication year).

Impact Factor: A measure of a journal's power in terms of how many other articles cite that work.

In-Group: A social group to which an ego node belongs.

In-Degree: The amount of lines leading in to a particular node; volume of ties pointing to a node from other nodes.

Innovation: A high-innovation individual is a person with a low threshold for adoption of a new technique or technology; the tendency to be susceptible to new ideas moving through a social network.

Intellectual Pedigree: The association of an individual with other thinkers or practitioners in a field (in an affinity).

Interdependence: A mutually reciprocal relation between entities.

Island: A maximal subnetwork of vertices (ego neighborhoods) connected by lines with values greater than the lines to vertices outside the subnetwork; a large cluster of highly interactive nodes with fewer connections to the outside.

Isolate: A node which is not connected to other nodes in a network; a node which is on the periphery of a social network without anything in the way of a connection or relationship tie.

Isomorphic Equivalence: The visual equivalency of structure between ego nodes.

Legible: Able to be read; clear.

Length (of a Walk): The number of relations contained within a walk.

Linegraph: A nodelink diagram that indicates relationships by lines in between connected nodes.

Lines: Edges (without arrows, in an undirected social network diagram) and arcs (with arrows, as "directed lines" in a digraph).

Loop: Reflexive connections from one node back to itself.

Matrix: A visualization of multivariate data consisting of rows and columns, with cells at the intersection of a row and a column; here each row and each column represent one vertex; a filled cell means the presence of a phenomenon while a blank cell means the absence of a phenomenon (in a binary); these can be reconfigured to be sorted by various descriptors of the groups to identify patterns.

Multiplier Effect: An entity or resource whose use will magnify or amplify the impact.

Multiplex Data: A stack of actor-by-actor matrices with similar defined factors, enabling comparability.

Multiplex Relations: Multiple relationships among multiple vertices to show more complex relationships (as contrasted to "simplex" relations).

Neighborhood: The area around an "ego" including the "alters" that are linked to the focal ego node; this includes a connection up to some maximum path length (with a minimum of at least one step of connection); includes all the ties among all of the actors to whom the ego has a direct connection; these may be indicated by color or a circle or some other indicator (or sometimes no indicator at all).

Neighbors: The "alters" or direct nodes connected to an ego node in a neighborhood.

Network Analysis: Learning about social networks based on analyses of various aspects of the relational ties between the individuals in the network.

Network Load: The amount of traffic or information or other network resources that move through a network.

Network Size: The number of original nodes or egos (or individuals, groups, organizations, or societies) in the network.

Node: A point or vertex in a social network which represents an individual (or actor) within that network.

Node Load: The measure of load placed on a given node to show its importance to the network; load is based in part on how connected that node is to other nodes (and the directions of the relationships between nodes.

Nonbiological Affinity: The ties between individuals who were influenced by the same predecessors and so are considered to belong to the same family or tradition in a field.

N-Step Neighborhood: The size of an ego's neighborhood including all nodes at a path length of N, inclusive of all the connections among those actors (most neighborhood path lengths are 1, which include the egos and their adjacent nodes).

Null Dyads: A pair of vertices (nodes) without any lines between them (no connectors).

Ordinal Data: Rank-ordered data.

Outdegree: The number of lines or edges leading from a particular node.

Out-Group: A social group to which an ego does not belong.

(Pure) Out-Tree: A sociogram in which all actors are embedded into a single component as one structure, with no reciprocated ties and each node with an in-degree of one (or each actor has one boss, in a unified command, except the ultimate boss).

Partition: A part; a section.

Path: A walk in which each actor and relation in the graph may be used at most one time (except for a closed path in which the first actor is also the ending actor); a Eulerian path defines a once-through of a network that touches every path/line once except for the starting node or vertex.

Pendant: A case or node which is connected to the graph by only one tie; this has earned its name because such cases will "dangle" off more central cases that are heavily connected.

Percolation Theory: The concept that sudden changes seem to occur after a certain amount of percolation of changes, at which a tipping point is reached in connected clusters in a random graph.

Perfect Hierarchy: A social network in which all arcs (directional lines) point up, and none point down; an acyclic social network (a network without cycles or without arcs pointing down returning to a starting point); a perfect hierarchy suggests that all such networks have a concentration of power at the top with resources and information moving up and a potential enervating of the peripheries.

Periphery: The outer edge of a social network, usually represented by nodes that are not connected to others in the network or are connected thinly to others.

Permutation: The reordering or sorting or renumbering of vertices of a network to highlight particular descriptions of the network (with other patterning).

Popularity: The state of being recognized, appreciated, and liked by many.

Power Curve: An exponential curve that shows a high incidence of the phenomena early on but with a steep drop-off and then a long tail (said to represent various phenomenon in the world such as the popularity of particular Websites in a particular domain, with a few dominating).

Power Law: A mathematical relation between two quantities, when the frequency of an event varies as a power of an attribute; a power law distribute starts at its maximum value and decreases to infinity; this features a long tail leading towards infinity with a slower decay than the decay rate for a normal distribution, which suggests a greater likelihood of extreme events or variability.

Predictive Analytics: The uses of data to anticipate future behaviors, events, and trends, among other things (This is a kind of "forward testing.).

Property (Bias): Tendencies as defined by node descriptors; tendencies extrapolated from node descriptors.

Proximity: Closeness or nearness based on various dimensions: physical, spatial, relational, structural; temporal; emotional, or otherwise; vicinity.

Random Network: The nature of a network if the null hypothesis for the contents cannot be rejected; what a random network would look like (with each of the nodes having an equal opportunity of being chosen in this randomized network).

Rank: Stratification within social groups (whether discreetly or indiscreetly expressed) that may be inferred by the way information moves in a social network.

Reachability: Any set of connections which trace from a source to the target actor.

Salience: Importance, criticality, most noticeable.

Scale-Free Networks: Networks that display power laws.

Semi-Path: "A semi-walk in which no vertex in between the first and last vertex of the semi-walk occurs more than once" (de Nooy, Mrvar, & Batagelj, 2005, p. 78).

Semi-Walk: A sequence of lines from vertex u to vertex v such that "the end vertex of one line is the starting vertex of the next line and the sequence starts at vertex us and ends at vertex v" (de Nooy, Mrvar, & Batagelj, 2005, p. 77).

Sensitivity: The ability to respond to slight environmental or other changes.

Simple Graph: An undirected graph (nodes without lines).

Sink Vertex (or "Sink"): In an acyclic network (usually used for networks in time), a vertex with in-degree links (as the receiver of ties) but zero out-degree (which suggests an ending vertex on the periphery of a network or at least at the end of a main path analysis).

Small World Phenomena: The existence of a social network in which there are clusters of nodes which enable the connection between one node and another through a few number of steps; a social network in which strangers may be connected through a mutual acquaintance; technically defined to be "a network where the typical distance L between two randomly chosen nodes (the number of steps required) grows proportionally to the logarithm of the number of nodes N in the network" ("Small-world network," Wikipedia) where.

Social Prestige: Social recognition or respect.

Social Roles: A set of connected behaviors and obligations for individuals in a social situation (may be formal or informal).

Sociogram: A social network represented as a graph (bar charts, pie charts, trend charts, line charts, and others), node-link diagram, or other informational graphic display.

Sociometry: The study of relationships among people, usually quantitative tools.

Source Vertex: In an acyclic network (usually used for networks in time), a vertex with zero indegree (no lines going into it, suggesting that these are originating vertexes).

Strong Component: A maximally connected (cyclic) sub-network in which each vertex can reach any other vertex (with pairs of lines going in both directions to all vertices).

Strong Link: An interpersonal tie that is close, long-standing, and over-which many resources may be exchanged.

Structural Hole: A triad of three nodes with one connected to the two nodes, who are not directed connected to each other.

Structural Prestige: The "social respect" indicated by the importance and power of a node in a social network.

Subnetwork: A social cluster within a network.

Symmetry: The sense of a balanced relationship (directed ties) in which two individuals (nodes) share the same sort of tie (bonded or non-bonded).

Thin Node: A vertex with a low degree of connectivity with other vertices; low connectivity; low popularity.

Threshold: A minimum limit which must be attained to create a certain effect.

Trail: A walk between two actors (nodes in a social network) that includes a given relation no more than once (one of the trajectories of traffic in a social network).

Transitivity: A state of: when A = B and B = C, then A = C (from algebra).

Transposition: Switching the locations of two different objects with each other; reversing the order of objects.

Tree: A structure within social networks which do not contain any semicycles or cycles; a structure often used to show genealogies in time.

Trellis Graphic: A data visualization that represents information on an underlying physical structure (like a lattice).

Triad: Three vertices (nodes) which may be combined in a range of ways by the lines between them.

Triad Census: A listing of the triads in a social network (based on the types found as compared to the numbers expected); four possible types of triadic relationships are possible—with no ties, one tie, two ties, or three ties (in a nondirected network).

Triadic Closure: The idea that if Node A knows B and B knows C, then Node C is more likely to know A than just anyone picked at random.

Undirected Lines (Edges): Unordered or undirected pair of vertices or nodes.

Universal Classes: Groupings of networks which share broad assumptions and about which descriptive generalizations may be made.

Universality: The idea of shared descriptions between various social networks.

Valued Graph: A graph that represents how the various individuals surveyed think or feel about a particular issue in terms of a ranked measurement.

Vector: An entire social network matrix or part of a larger matrix; a singular column of data (that is part of a matrix).

Vertex (Vertices, Plural): The common end point of two or more rays or line segments; a corner or a point where lines meet (a point where three or more edges meet, in solid geometry); the highest or lowest points in a parabola (as in a quadratic equation).

Walk: The most general connection between two actors, usually a sequence of actors (nodes) and relations that begins and ends with actors; a sequence of nodes.

Weak Link: A weak tie between nodes; a link that is weakly traveled or weakly used.

APPENDIX

Native American case study team and various stakeholders and constituents (shown in Table 1.)

Table 1. Native American Case Studies

	Funding Foundation	Tribal Elders 1-12	Native American Students	Faculty / Native American Case Writers	Casino Owner 1
PI 1	1	1	1	1	0
PI 2	1	1	1	1	0
Instructional Designer	0	0	1	1	1
Database Administrator	0	0	0	0	0

Online technical writing course SME team (shown in Table 2.)

Table 2. Technical Writing Course Team

	Head of Consortium	Peer Review Team	Online Learners	Bookstore	Student Beta Testers
Faculty 1	1	1	0	0	0
Faculty 2	1	1	1	1	1
Faculty 3	1	1	0	0	0

The biosecurity development team's social network in a time of crisis is shown in Table 3.

Table 3. An Automated Biosecurity Training

	PI Kansas	PI Florida	PI North Carolina	Instructional Designer 1	Instructional Designer 2	Graphic Artist	Flash developer / photographer	Federal Funding Committee / Advisory Board	Third Party Content Developers	Digital Repositories	Cisco Systems for RLO Model
PI Kansas	--	1	1	1	1	1	1	1	0	0	1
PI Florida	1	--	1	1	1	1	1	1	0	0	1
PI North Carolina	1	1	--	1	1	1	1	1	0	0	1
Instructional Designer 1	1	1	1	--	1	1	1	0	1	1	1
Instructional Designer 2	1	0	0	1	--	0	0	0	0	0	0
Graphic Artist	0	1	1	1	1	--	1	0	0	0	0
Flash developer / photographer	1	0	0	1	0	1	--	0	0	0	0
Federal Funding Committee / Advisory Board	1	1	1	0	0	0	0	--	0	0	0
Third Party Content Developers	0	0	0	0	0	0	0	0	--	0	0
Digital Repositories	0	0	0	0	0	0	0	0	0	--	0
Cisco Systems for RLO Model	1	1	1	1	0	0	0	0	0	0	--

Axio™ demo course: a development team and their participation in five phases shown in Table 4.

Table 4. Axio™ Demo Course

	Phase 1: Brainstorming	Phase 2: Content Development	Phase 3: Alpha Testing	Phase 4: Beta Testing	Phase 5: Rollout and Publicity	General Advisement
IT Associate Director	1	0	1	1	1	1
Instructional Designer 1	1	1	1	1	0	1
Instructional Designer 2	1	1	1	1	0	1
Instructional Designer 3	1	1	1	1	0	1
Code Developer	0	0	1	0	0	1
Software Help Documentation Writer	0	0	1	1	1	1
Faculty Content Provider 1	0	1	0	0	0	0
Faculty Content Provider 2	0	1	0	0	0	0
Faculty Content Provider 3	0	1	0	0	0	0

The university life café development team and its internal and external publics (Table 5.)

Table 5. University Life Café

	On-Campus Advisory Board	External Advisory Board	Federal Funding Agency	Counseling Services Administrator	Student Housing	Union Planning Board	Art Gallery Management	Student Actors	Site Design Team	Email Alias Techs	Legal Counsel	Third Party Content Providers	Statistician	External Universities	Conference Organizers	Media Contacts	General Students
PI 1	1	1	1	1	1	1	1	1	1	1	1	0	1	1	1	1	1
PI 2	1	1	1	0	0	0	0	0	0	0	0	0	0	0	0	0	0
Instructional Designer	1	1	1	0	0	0	0	0	1	1	1	1	1	1	1	1	1
Psychologist	1	0	0	1	0	0	0	0	0	0	0	0	1	0	0	1	1
Drug and Alcohol Counselor	1	0	0	1	0	0	0	0	0	0	0	0	0	0	0	1	1
Counseling Graduate Student 1	0	0	0	0	0	0	1	0	0	0	0	0	1	0	0	0	1
Counseling Graduate Student 2	0	0	0	0	0	0	1	0	0	0	0	0	0	0	0	0	1
Videographer	0	0	0	0	0	0	0	1	1	0	0	1	0	0	0	1	0

Appendix G dyadic team and work phasing (Table 6.)

Table 6. Appendix G (Grievance Policy) Training

	1. Project Conceptualization	2. Content Writing	3. Scripting	4. Critique	5. Revision	6. Launch and Outreach	7. Updating
Legal Counsel at a University	1	1	0	1	1	1	1
Instructional Designer	0	0	1	0	0	0	1

Academic dishonesty article co-authorship shown in Table 7.

Table 7. Academic Dishonesty Co-Authored Article

	Publisher	Peer Reviewers	General Public
Co-Advisor for Honor and Integrity Program	0	0	1
Instructional Designer	1	1	1
Creator of an Academic Dishonesty Model	0	0	0

Introduction to public health internal team participation ring lattice shown in Table 8(anonymized data)

Table 8. Introduction to Public Health

	Office Support	Mod. 1: Overview and Basic Principles	Mod. 2: Epidemiological Principles	Mod. 3: Population Health Tools	Mod. 4: Disease and Disabillity: Determinants, Burdens, and Interventions	Mod. 5: Healthcare and Public Health Systems (Public Health Administration)	Mod. 6: Special Topic Areas	Draft Module Critiques	Faculty Senate	Outreach and Marketing
1 DC	1	0	0	0	0	0	0	0	0	0
2 DC	0	0	0	0	0	0	0	0	1	0
3 DC	0	0	0	0	0	0	0	0	0	0
4 DC	0	0	0	0	0	0	0	0	0	0
5 DC	0	0	0	0	0	0	1	0	1	0
6 DC	0	0	0	0	0	0	0	0	1	0
7 DC	0	0	0	0	0	1	1	0	0	0
1 JC	0	1	1	0	0	0	0	1	1	0
2 JC	0	0	0	0	1	0	0	1	1	0
1 KDHE	0	0	0	0	0	0	0	0	0	0
1 KCKCC	0	0	0	0	0	0	0	1	1	0
2 KCKCC	0	0	0	1	1	0	1	1	1	0
1 KSU	0	0	0	0	0	0	1	1	1	0
2 KSU / PI	0	1	0	0	0	1	1	1	1	0
3 KSU	0	1	0	1	0	0	1	1	0	0
4 KSU / PI	0	1	1	1	1	1	1	1	1	1
5 KSU	0	0	0	0	0	1	1	1	0	0
6 KSU	0	0	0	0	0	0	0	0	0	0
7 KSU	0	0	0	1	0	0	0	0	1	0
8 KSU	0	1	1	1	1	1	1	1	0	1

The global health development team and its stakeholders social network (Table 9.)

Table 9. Global Health

	College of Vet Med	DCE Funding Committee	Global Health Professionals	Graduate Students	Global Alliance for Rabies Control	General Public	Academic Publishers	Educational Conference
Global Health Expert	1	1	1	1	1	1	1	0
Instructional Designer	0	0	0	0	0	1	1	1
Videographer 1	0	0	0	0	0	1	1	1
Videographer 2	0	0	0	0	0	1	1	1
Actor 1	0	0	0	0	0	0	1	1
Actor 2	0	0	0	0	0	0	1	1

E-learning best practices course: two-mode network about the dev team and project contribution in Table 10.

Table 10. E-Learning Best Practices

	Introduction	1. Course Info Policies and Requirements	2. Course Content and Technology Usage	3. Learner Interactions	4. Learner Support	5. Assessment and Evaluation	Resources	Examples Beyond K-State	E-Learning Quality Checklist	Course Site Look-and-Feel	Campus Publicity
IT Director	1	1	0	1	1	1	1	1	0	1	1
Instructional Designer 1	1	1	3	0	3	3	1	1	1	0	1
Instructional Designer 2	0	1	0	0	0	0	0	0	1	1	0
Instructional Designer 3	0	1	0	0	0	0	0	0	1	0	0
External Unit IT Associate Director	0	0	0	0	0	0	0	0	0	1	0
Librarian	0	0	0	0	1	0	0	0	0	0	0
IT Newsletter Editor	0	0	0	0	0	0	0	0	0	0	1

ELATEwiki dev team and external ties shown in Table 11.

Table 11. E-Learning and Teaching Exchange (ELATEwiki)

	Instructional Designer	Faculty Advisor / Wiki Master	DCE Coordinator 1	DCE Coordinator 2	DCE Director	Student Contributors	Third-Party Content Providers	Businesses	IT Support	DCE Public Relations	MediaWiki Specialst 1	MediaWiki Specialist 2	Conference Organizers	Faculty Users
Instructional Designer		8	3	3	3	0	1	0	1	1	1	1	1	1
Faculty Advisor / Wiki Master	8	--	3	3	3	1	1	1	1	0	1	1	1	1
DCE Coordinator 1	3	3	--	3	3	0	0	0	0	0	0	0	1	0
DCE Coordinator 2	3	3	3	--	3	0	0	0	0	0	0	0	0	0
DCE Director	3	3	3	3	--	0	0	0	0	1	0	0	0	1

ELATEwiki dev team and external ties only (shown in Table 12.)

Table 12. Digital Entomology Lab

	Student Contributors	Third-Party Content Providers	Businesses	IT Support	DCE Public Relations	MediaWiki Specialist 1	MediaWiki Specialist 2	Conference Organizers	Faculty Users
Instructional Designer	0	1	0	1	1	1	1	1	1
Faculty Advisor / Wiki Master	1	1	1	1	0	1	1	1	1
DCE Coordinator 1	0	0	0	0	0	0	0	1	0
DCE Coordinator 2	0	0	0	0	0	0	0	0	0
DCE Director	0	0	0	0	1	0	0	1	1

Table 13 shows the digital entomology lab team and their resources seeking.

Table 13. Introduction to One Health

	Dept. of Entomology Leadership	DCE Funding	Web Site Manager	Database Admin	Manager of a Set of Insects	Global Manager of an L/ CMS Company	Campus Conference	Academic Editors and Publishers
PI / Entomologist	1	1	1	1	1	1	1	1
Instructional Designer	0	1	1	1	0	1	1	1
Photographer	0	0	0	1	0	0	0	1

The "introduction to one health" development team and the criticality of connections to subject matter experts (shown in Table 14.)

Table 14. Traumatic Brain Injury

	External Funding Agency	External Funder 2	Internal Funder 1	Evaluation Office	College Deans	On-Campus Subject Matter Experts (SMEs)	Off-Campus SMEs	One Health Leaders (Nationally)	Third-Party Content Creators
PI / Administrator	1	1	1	1	1	1	1	1	1
PI / Clinician / Professor	0	0	0	0	1	1	0	0	0
One Health Administrator / Veterinarian	0	0	0	1	1	1	1	0	0
Instructional Designer	0	0	0	0	0	1	0	0	1
Videographer 1	0	0	0	0	0	0	0	0	0
Videographer 2	0	0	0	0	0	0	0	0	0

The traumatic brain injury project and compartmentalization shown in Table 15.

Table 15. E-Learning Faculty Modules

	1. Grant Writing	2. Curricular Design	3. Interviews of Individuals with TBI	4. Video Production	5. Video Transcription	6. Video Post Production	7. Site Design and DVD Packaging	8. Branding	9. Publicity, Presentations and Publications
PI 1	1	1	1	1	0	1	1	1	1
PI 2	1	1	0	1	0	1	1	1	1
Videographer	0	1	1	1	0	1	1	1	0
Instructional Designer	0	1	0	0	1	0	1	1	0
Website Designer	0	0	0	0	0	0	1	1	0

E-learning faculty modules internal development team (shown in Table 16.)

Table 16.

	DCE Dean	Instructional Designer 1	Instructional Designer 2	Instructional Designer 3	Videographer	Faculty Advisor 1	Faculty Advisor 2	Faculty Advisor 3	Faculty Advisor 4	Faculty Advisor 5	DCE Coordinator 1	DCE Coordinator 2	DCE Coordinator 3	Head of External IT Unit
DCE Dean	--	1	1	1	1	1	1	1	1	1	1	1	1	1
Instructional Designer 1	1	--	1	1	0	1	1	1	1	1	1	1	1	1
Instructional Designer 2	0	1	--	1	1	1	1	1	1	1	1	1	1	1
Instructional Designer 3	0	1	1	--	0	1	1	1	1	1	1	1	1	1
Videographer	1	0	1	0	--	0	0	0	0	0	0	0	0	0
Faculty Advisor 1	1	1	1	1	0	--	1	1	1	1	1	1	1	0
Faculty Advisor 2	1	0	0	0	0	0	--	0	0	0	0	0	0	0
Faculty Advisor 3	1	0	0	0	0	0	0	--	0	0	0	0	0	0
Faculty Advisor 4	1	0	0	0	0	0	0	0	--	0	0	0	0	0
Faculty Advisor 5	1	0	0	0	0	0	0	0	0	--	0	0	0	0
DCE Coordinator 1	1	1	1	1	0	0	0	0	0	0	--	0	0	0
DCE Coordinator 2	1	1	1	1	0	0	0	0	0	0	0	--	0	0
DCE Coordinator 3	1	1	1	1	0	0	0	0	0	0	1	1	--	0
Head of External IT Unit	1	1	1	1	0	0	0	0	0	0	0	0	0	--

E-learning faculty modules development team relationships with external stakeholders (shown in Table 17.)

Table 17.

	Faculty Senate	Faculty Members	Administration	IT Training Unit	University Library	Graduate Students	General Public	External Universities	Professional Conference-Goers
DCE Dean	1	1	1	1	1	0	1	1	1
Instructional Designer 1	0	1	0	1	1	0	1	1	1
Instructional Designer 2	0	0	0	1	0	0	0	0	0
Instructional Designer 3	0	0	0	1	1	0	0	0	0
Videographer	0	0	0	0	1	0	0	0	0
Faculty Advisor 1	1	1	0	1	0	0	1	1	1
Faculty Advisor 2	1	1	0	0	0	0	0	0	0
Faculty Advisor 3	0	1	0	0	0	0	0	0	0
Faculty Advisor 4	0	1	0	0	0	0	0	0	0
Faculty Advisor 5	0	1	0	0	0	0	0	0	0
DCE Coordinator 1	1	1	0	1	0	0	1	1	1
DCE Coordinator 2	0	1	0	1	1	0	1	0	0
DCE Coordinator 3	0	1	0	0	0	0	0	0	0
Head of External IT Unit	0	1	1	1	0	0	0	0	0

E-learning faculty modules two-mode network: team entities and functional events (shown in Table 18.)

Table 18.

	Writing Development	Editing	Revision	Multimedia Development	Public Presentations	MediaWiki Structure	Videography	Political Cover
DCE Dean	1	0	1	0	1	0	0	1
Instructional Designer 1	1	1	1	1	1	1	0	0
Instructional Designer 2	1	1	1	1	0	1	1	0
Instructional Designer 3	1	1	1	1	0	1	0	0
Videographer	1	1	1	1	0	0	1	0
Faculty Advisor 1	0	1	0	1	1	1	1	1
Faculty Advisor 2	1	0	1	0	0	0	0	1
Faculty Advisor 3	1	0	1	1	1	0	0	1
Faculty Advisor 4	0	1	0	0	0	0	0	1
Faculty Advisor 5	0	1	0	0	0	0	0	1
DCE Coordinator 1	0	1	0	1	1	1	0	1
DCE Coordinator 2	1	1	1	0	1	1	0	1
DCE Coordinator 3	0	1	0	0	1	1	0	1
Head of External IT Unit	0	0	0	0	0	0	0	1

Chapter 11
Beyond Surface Relations:
Using Maltego Radium® to Analyze Electronic Connectivity and Hidden Ties in the Internet Understructure

Shalin Hai-Jew
Kansas State University, USA

ABSTRACT

On the surface spaces of the WWW and Internet, organizations and individuals have long created a public face to emphasize their respective brands, showcase their credibility, and interact with others in often very public ways. These surface spaces include Websites, social media platforms, virtual worlds, interactive game spaces, content sharing sites, social networking sites, microblogging sites, wikis, blogs (Web logs), collaborative work sites, and email systems. Beneath the glittering surfaces are electronic understructures, which enable the mapping of networks (based on physical location or organization or URL), the tracking of inter-personal relationships between various accounts, the geolocation of various electronic data to the analog physical world, the de-anonymizing of aliases (to disallow pseudonymity), and the tracking of people to their contact information (digital and physical). Maltego Radium is a penetration testing tool that enables such crawls of publicly available information or Open-Source Intelligence (OSINT) to identify and describe electronic network structures for a range of applications. Further, this information is represented in a number of interactive node-link diagrams in both 2D and 3D for further insights. There is also an export capability for full reportage of the extracted information. This chapter introduces the tool and identifies some practical ways this has been used to "package" fresh understandings for enhanced awareness and decision-making in a higher education context.

INTRODUCTION

Like the stitching on the back of a piece of embroidery, the understructure of electronic spaces, interrelationships between accounts, and other types of electronic information show something about the embroiderer, his or her interests, his or her skill sets, and his or her influences—in a way that complements surface information. The understructure presents insights on the patterning of interrelationships; it may suggest other threads to follow in learning more about the entities online. The understructure then offers yet another layer of publicly available information, all sent "in the clear," to help people understand, analyze, and make decisions. In game theory, in

DOI: 10.4018/978-1-4666-4462-5.ch011

asymmetric information situations, not knowing is a "dominated strategy." There are no benefits to maintaining blind spots, particularly if the information is fairly easily available.

For example, an emergent network may be analyzed by conducting a hashtag search of a particular trending topic on a microblogging site to find out who (which accounts) is busy Tweeting about this issue. To understand an individual on Facebook, it may help to extract the data of his or her social network to better understand the depth of inter-relationships. To probe an organization with a strong online presence, it may help to map its network to find out where it is situated, who some of its main staff are (and their contact information), and its basic network structure.

The art of studying this electronic understructure involves the analysis of trace and other data in order to extrapolate details and draw some initial conclusions about interrelationships and network structures. Electronic spaces offer empirical *in vivo* (in-field or "in the body") relational information (based on actual links, actual connections, and actual relationships based on electronic documentation) that is behavior- and action-based and not hypothetical or professed details only. These are often considered self-organizing networks that just emerged from interested parties; others are formal creations that are curated and maintained by leaders. In a sense, this information is about "light leakage" or "behavior leakage," the unintended release of information that is a byproduct of common (and even unthinking) interactions. The concept here is that any communication reveals something about the communicator especially for astute observers. Finally, another assumption of this approach is the "cyber-physical confluence," the space where the cyber and the real intersect (Arnaboldi, Guazzini, & Passarella, 2013, p. 1). This concept suggests that there is some connectivity between cyberspace and the physical world.

Some research has borne out that more than half of profiles in social networking sites align with real-world features of individuals, and digital information on the Social Web is often credible (Rowe, 2010). Other researchers have probed microbloggers' and bloggers' psychological profiles and personalities based on the contents of their messages. What individuals do and do not disclose about themselves may also be revelatory—by inference. Chen (2013) found that extroversion was a key personality trait in those who self-revealed on social networking sites.

Further, online engagements with others have had salutary psychological and social benefits: "Intensity of Facebook use in year one strongly predicted bridging social capital outcomes in year two, even after controlling for measures of self-esteem and satisfaction with life," observe Steinfield, Ellison, and Lampe (2008, p. 434). These researchers observe that students with lower self-esteem may be empowered to form and interact in the "large, heterogeneous networks that are sources of bridging social capital" (2008, p. 434). Other researchers found positive effects of social networking on college students learning:

Online social networking not only directly influences university students' learning outcomes, but also helps the students attain social acceptance from others and adapt to university culture, both of which play prominent roles in improving their learning outcomes (Yu, Tian, Vogel, & Kwok, 2010, p. 1494).

Other researchers have found that learners who are more central to a network tend to be more likely to ask for help and to be targeted by peers in their help-seeking; further, more central students in a social network tend to "have better learning achievement" (Lin & Lai, 2013, p. 40). Researchers have been focusing on the post-adoption usage of the social networking sites (SNSes) by learners for continuing benefits and potential future connections with professional colleagues.

People's sense of self is reliant in part on their social identities. In-group and out-group dynamics may have an impact on how various individuals in social networks interact and how they share information.

So while there is some cyber-physical confluence, the extent of that "relationship" or potential dynamic may differ on the issues being researched. Still, even though there is a lack of assumed one-for-one confluence between the cyber and the actual, there are clear competitive advantages to avoiding seduction by the polished messages of the overstructure and engaging an additional information stream that includes insights about less obvious electronic connections. Electronic understructure research data may be used to make some cautious extrapolations (or informal intuitions or "whispers") about real-world offline phenomenon, governments, organizations, personalities, and emergent events.

REVIEW OF THE LITERATURE

Network analysis is an approach that has been applied to a number of fields: biology, environmental sciences, sociology, engineering, management, information technology, and other fields. At its most basic, this involves a systems analysis of entities and their relationships (linkages) over time (or in a slice-in-time). How networks are structured may indicate something of their capabilities and their limits. Network analysis is usually not used in isolation but is bolstered by complementary streams of data.

Social networks: A catchphrase of the current age involves networks. Networks are groups of people in various forms of community and interaction, much of it mediated by electronic communications and brought in closer through lower and lower degrees of separation (the path or paths through which two nodes have to traverse in order to contact each other). People are understood to be members of multiple communities and groups, and they play various social roles in each. In some, they may play a major or central role; in others, they may serve on the periphery. People are also understood to be highly hierarchical in their social relationships. The more powerful an individual in a network, the more informed he or she is, and the more he or she is thought to be accurately informed about that network. (By definition, a powerful node is highly centralized, with high in-degree of contacts providing information for him or her and lower out-degree or outgoing information to others—usually higher up in a social hierarchy. An influential node is considered to receive and wield the application of resources to various endeavors. Central decision-making resides with a powerful node.) People compete with each other (particularly those close by) to build social capital and to establish social standing. Power is also thought to come with influence, the ability to affect those both proxemically and socially near but also those who are far away (particularly those who "follow" the individual or who choose to be influenced, through this form of social transmission).

In terms of preference, non-kin social networks seem to cluster around homophily or human bonding around similar others (like being attracted to like). This phenomenon of preferential selection is also known as assortative mixing. Friendship associations often tend to be homophilous. (The assumption of "the company you keep" (your associates) as a social interpretation of an individual relies on this assumption of homophily. The assertion: If a social network is analyzed in depth, there may be some generalizations that may be made about a mystery individual in that group who is an unknown.) There are human groups which are highly heterophilous, with preferential selection by difference (disassortative mixing); this may be found, for example, in mixed teams that achieve particular complex innovations or other work goals. Another feature of networks is whether they are high-density or low-density in terms of the connectivity between their members. Dense networks are thought to be more effective for the propagation of ideas, but low-density or sparse networks are thought to be better for innovations.

Networks are expressed in a number of textual, numerical, and visual ways. They are described narratively; they are described through graph metrics; finally, they are expressed as 2D or 3D graphs that may be static or interactive.

A narrative description often sets the context for the description of the graph, explains the relevance of the graph metrics for the network, and contributes further insights. These may include insights about the culture of the network and its social control mechanisms, for example. Or there may be discussions of network externalities and external effects on the network itself. Graph metrics of a network involve any range of quantized data that describe the network. (For social networks, for example, there are basic graph metrics that provide an overview of the network like numbers of vertices, numbers of edges, geodesic distance, graph density, and so on. Further, there may be motif censuses that consist of counts of certain structures found in the network—such as types of triadic interrelationships. There are ways to identify "strategic holes" in a network which may be exploited. Using a machine for pattern recognition of types of structures in a network is often much more effective than just eye-balling a graph given the complexity of graph analysis.

The graphs are node-link (entity-relationship) diagrams that are not read on an x or y axes (or x, y, and z axes) but more in terms of the relationships between the various nodes in relation to each other. Node-link diagrams may also be described as vertices-and-edges diagrams. (Those network diagrams that relate to social networks are called "sociograms.") The same information about a network may be depicted in over a dozen different types of visuals based on differing layout algorithms. The same information may look highly variant visually. The visual layout of networks is important because various relationships and dynamics may be more easily understood through the image. In some graphs, the center-periphery dynamic shows the centrality and degree betweenness of the respective nodes. The closeness or distance between selected nodes may be seen. There would be defined direct ties vs. indirect ties. Particular branches of the graph may be identified for closer analysis. Graphs may be depicted in visual layers, with various aspects of the network highlighted in different overlapping layers. The sizes of the nodes may vary based on their importance; the depth or intensity of relationships may be described in the visual as well. "Pendant" nodes are those that are peripheral to a network and connected by only one link or edge. "Isolate" nodes are those that are not actually connected through a link but are still part of a network by membership.

Some early research has helped to demythify some basic assumptions. Former researchers used to conflate popularity of a node with high-influence, but there have been more recent findings which suggest that popularity and even high positive word-of-mouth may not mean individuals will respond with the desired purchasing behaviors (Schaefer, 2012). Other researchers have shown that a thin node may be highly influential as a "bridging node" between different disparate populations, so they have a high value even if their connections are sparse.

Social networks may also be understood from various points-of-view. An internal node-level point-of-view from within a network is a kind of *sousveillance* (inverse surveillance or watchful vigilance from inside or below; participant surveillance). A more objectivist external view of a network may be surveillance. Node-to-node surveillance may be conceptualized as a kind of interpersonal electronic surveillance. Self-surveillance is self-awareness for marketing and branding and may be used as part of self-awareness of electronic telepresence, social grooming, and the cultivation of electronic ties. Vertical surveillance may be done from top-down or bottom-up; horizontal surveillance is achieved on the same level organizationally. In terms of levels of analysis, networks may be viewed in totality, in part, in particular branches, or more deeply clustered subnetworks or islands, or at the node level. To analyze at various levels of analysis, other tools and information streams will have to be brought into play—for deeper high-resolution insights.

Depending on the context of the network, the various standards for the definitions of various terms of network membership, linkage or connection, and node (entity) centrality would clearly vary. This is particularly so in data extractions from various electronic networks based on the parameters of the crawl and the coding of the data extraction software.

Finally, social networks are mapped not only to understand the structured interrelationships but to understand how resources and information (and exchanges) move through these hierarchies along particular social paths. Affiliations initially were thought to be costless, but later researchers realized that for the models to map to the world, they would have to calculate the social and other costs of maintaining relationships. In that sense, relationships may be conceived of as transactional, with a consideration of costs-and-benefits, to a degree.

Cyberspace affords new forms of social life and bonds through different types of technologies. Still, fundamentally, people tend to have limited (even scarce) attentional resources, even if these are augmented by technologies that enable them to "follow" others automatically. Human attentional resources may extend to their social networks, with an actual Dunbar's number, based on bounded human capacities to socialize. Some researchers suggest that limits to the sizes of social networks may be due to expected tensions once communities reach a certain size and diversity (Binder, Howes, & Sutcliffe, 2009). The authors note that tensions may arise when individuals are messaging a limited intended audience, but the wide public access to many public accounts on social networking sites often mean unintended communications to others, who may take offense at certain types of messaging. (In some work-based social networks, there are optimal and limited sizes based on the need for interactive efficiency and group functionalities.)

A "network effect" is understood to occur when a particular critical mass has accumulated around particular shared interests and may result in incremented benefits to the various members of that network. Researchers have been exploring the power of network effects that may amass through Web 2.0 applications that may convey extraordinary competitive advantage (Aggarwal & Yu, 2012).

Researchers have made progress in understanding how innovations diffuse through human networks; they have observed how ideas propagate socially through formal and informal channels. Further, different nodes have different tendencies to carry an innovation forward, depending on various thresholds of responsiveness. The nature of various nodes make some more suggestible than others. One example is the possibility of ideas or behaviors going "viral"; much advertising and outreach consists of efforts for positive Word-of-Mouth (pWOM). Social Network Analysis (SNA) data are used with other information to set a full context. It is important to understand what messages are moving through social network topologies. For example, sentimental analysis may be conducted on microblogged, blogged, or wiki-posted and other messages to capture a sense of people's motivating emotions. Word frequency counts may be used to extrapolate the popularity of a message. Popular memes may be analyzed because of their cultural reproductive potential.

Electronic network analysis: In the age of Web 2.0, it is said that two-thirds of the global online population is active in social networks and blogs. It is estimated that people spend at least 10 percent of their waking time on the Internet. The analysis of electronic networks on the Internet may range in scope from the macro to the micro. At the macro level may be the technology understructure related to a particular government or large region. So-called "http networks" may be macro-level networks. Global trends and phenomenon are macro-level. At the micro level may be analyses of organizations, ego neighborhoods (or "personal networks") of particular individuals or groups on social network platforms (microblogging sites, social networking sites, online collaborative sites, virtual worlds, interactive game spaces, email systems, wikis, blogs, and other socio-technical spaces where humans interact with others).

One line of inquiry for electronic network analysis involves the identification of what is "hidden." Are there "sleeper" sub-networks of interest that may not be aware of each other which could be encouraged to connect and collaborate for mutual benefit? Are there hidden potentials in relationships between members of a network? Is there a node which is forming as emergent leadership? Emergent events may start out as micro ones but evolve into macro ones. Electronic networks may be highly dynamic, with some potential for unpredictable and high-impact Black Swan events (Taleb, 2007, 2010).

THE SOFTWARE TOOL: MALTEGO RADIUM

Electronic network analysis would not be possible if it weren't for the development work that has gone into various tools that enable the mapping of networks across various sites and the Internet itself. One of these tools is Maltego Radium, which released its first version in 2008.

The slick branding and mediated packaging of a software tool may advocate for particular uses of the tool, but often, there are unintended uses by adopters of a tool. This is the case with Maltego Radium (v. 3.3.3), a penetration testing tool that maps digital footprints on the Internet. This tool captures Open-Source (publicly available) Intelligence (OSINT) about organizations, Websites, and individual identities through its slick "machines" and "transforms" to increase "knowability". The machines are sequences of transforms, which extract data from the public Web and "transform" them from one type to others...which enables the extraction of geolocation data from EXIF data in imagery which may have been posted as Twitpics on Twitter, a microblogging site; organization or company networks with their various servers mapped; aliases linked to personally identifiable information (PII), and other relatively interchangeable electronic elements. As data extractions are achieved, this data is depicted in an evolving multi-modal (multiple types of information) node-link visualization (2D or 3D); users may visualize these networks as any of a half-dozen node-link graphs and automapped tree hierarchies (with root entities, leaf entities, and branching connections), all of them interactive. (The graph types are described as the following: Block, Hierarchical, Circular, Organic, and Interactive organic.)

The commercial version of this tool accesses Paterva company servers for the crawls and offers back results often with blistering speeds. Maltego Radium, with a v.1 release in 2008, then enables electronic network analysis of organizations, people, technology systems, and informational content. Maltego Radium uses Java and runs on Windows, Mac, and Linux.

This software tool has its origins in penetration ("pen") testing and has had new rollouts debut at various international security conferences. The "penetration" of a network or socio-technical system refers to the unauthorized access or break-in of a protected network, often involving attacks on hardware (device or machine exploits), software (malware, password cracking), and wetware (people, through social engineering, phishing, spear phishing, and others).

For the "white hat" defenders of networks, they use tools like Maltego Radium to understand their risk environment by scanning and mapping their publicly viewable perimeter. They analyze their technology systems to see what is publicly seeable and what the potential "attack vectors" of the so-called perimeter systems (and what inferred attack strategies) might be. This and other tools enable them to design various countermeasures, which may be both offensive and defensive. These efforts may involve a range of measures: working with law enforcement, policy-setting, electronic surveillance, the deployment of honey pots, staff training, professional partnerships, efficient intercommunications and reportage of exploits and system compromises, and other endeavors.

Maltego Radium enables the data extraction of multimodal data. These data are considered "unstructured" or "loosely structured" because of the wide mix of electronic content types. This capability of capturing and cross-referencing various types of data for relationships enables a range of other types of work than penetration testing and network security.

To review, this tool enables the scanning of network ties (social, technological, content, and others). It enables the tie-in of spatiality and geolocation to various entities' identities and network information. It enables the identification of aliases and pseudonyms to personally identifiable information (PII) and potentially, an identifiable individual, ultimately making the Internet and Web more nonymous spaces. It enables the identification of devices used on a network. It maps various aspects of Internet infrastructure, like domains, DNS (Domain Name System) names, netblocks, and IP addresses. It enables core transformations of various types of electronic data into other types for a broad collection of related information based on interactivity and affiliations. It also captures relationships between documents and files.

Maltego Radium features a range of "machines," which are sequences of "transforms" which are targeted acquisitions of information from online. A "company stalker" captures the email addresses of a domain. Domains may be footprinted at three different levels: L1 as a fast footprint; L2 as a "mild" footprint, and an L3 as an "intense" footprint. A software user may identify a person's email address with only a name, although this feature will pull even closed accounts and accounts unrelated to the individual (an issue of noisy data). The "Prune Leaf Entities" machine prunes all leaves, those entities without outgoing links and just one incoming link—to enable the viewing of interactivity in the initial network. A "Twitter Digger" enables the use of a phrase as a Twitter alias and strives to link that to identifying information. The "Twitter GeoLocation" machine helps identify a person's location based on multiple information streams. A "Twitter Monitor" machine monitors the microblogging site through its rate-limited API for particular hashtags (#) and named entities mentioned (@). A "URL to Network and Domain Information" is a mapping of an Internet domain.

This software also enables "transforms." These involve the capture of various types of related electronic information and transforming data types of one kind to another. These may be run on various nodes for more in-depth information. Further, a range of transforms (including "all" for the node type) may be run. "Devices" such as phones or mobile devices connected to accounts on a network may be identified. An "Infrastructure" transform includes autonomous systems, DNS names, domain information, IPv4 addresses, MX records (DNS mail exchange), NS records (a DNS name server record), netblocks, URLs (uniform resource locators), and Websites. The "Location" transform may be used to choose a location on "Mother Earth" to find domains. "Affiliation" networks may be extracted from public accounts on Facebook and Twitter, currently. Finally, "Personal" transforms enable the capture of information linked to aliases, (online) documents, email addresses, images (through EXIF or "Exchange Image File" data extractions), persons, phone numbers, or phrases. Individuals who can code using the Maltego Scripting Language (MSL) may conduct customized transforms; they may create macros (various sequences of data crawls) via the Palette Manager. (To clarify, the software itself does not require any command line coding. However, additional extra-software functionalities may require such work.)

The data resulting from an extraction may be saved as .mtz files or .mtgx files (proprietary or native Maltego Radium files). As a security researcher touch, the software enables the encryption of the crawl as an AES-128 (Advanced Encryption Standard 128) file type.

The tool has a Detail View and a Property View that adds more information about the various parts of a network when users put their cursor over a particular node of the network. This is one way to see close-in node-level multiplex data. Another way to access this information is to export a full report about the crawl, in which case the data is then depicted in a .pdf report.

This software may accept both Maltego Radium files and tabular files (including .csv, .xlsx, and .xls files). Various file types may be saved using Maltego Radium: data sets, reports, and graphs. Two-dimensional graph imagery may be exported as .gif, .png, .bmp, and .jpg file types.

It is important to note that a Radium user often gives up his or her identity (Internet Protocol address at minimum) when conducting a data crawl of others' networks. The surveiller faces counter-surveillance. Organizations and networks (their network administrators) have it in their interests to know who is scanning their networks and possibly prospecting for a potential later attack. It's telling that the software itself requires disclaimers of liability for certain crawls.

Maltego Radium brings together various functionalities that may be done separately with separate customized programs, like Google Search, Network Solutions' WHOIS, NodeXL's social media platform data extractions, and then data visualization tools… but not as quickly, efficiently, or as elegantly.

Conducting a data mining crawl: What are the steps to conducting a data mining crawl, to capture the electronic network data? In a general sense, the researcher begins with a research question. He or she runs various "machines" and "transforms" using Maltego Radium. The data extraction may include more pre-processing work—the setting of new parameters, the addition of new data crawls—next. Then, he or she outputs a data visualization, which is then analyzed. If further data are necessary, then those are extracted. Then, data post-processing occurs with different visualizations extracted. Various analyses may be applied to the extracted data. Finally, the research is output and/or decisions related to the crawl are made. These steps are reflected in the flowchart in Figure 1.

This process may be seen as a recursive one depending on the needs of the research.

ELECTRONIC NETWORK ANALYSIS IN ACADEMIA

In many academic institutions of higher education, there are three main areas of focus for faculty: (1) teaching and learning, (2) research, and (3) social contribution. These three broad areas will be used to examine some ways that electronic network analysis may be applied to an academic setting. Finally, there will be a fourth catch-all category, (4) management, which will include other university organizational applications of electronic network analysis.

Teaching and learning: In terms of teaching and learning, network analysis has a variety of applications. One of the foremost ones is in the analysis of ego networks and topic-based networks. Data extrapolations from online sites may be used to find learning communities for students. They may be used to examine the dynamics in online (or offline) study- or work-based collaboration networks. To enhance learner retention, many institutions of higher education encourage their faculty and staff to engage their various constituencies using social networking tools. Such online communities may be analyzed using electronic social network analysis tools.

Research: Regarding academic research, network analysis and datamining may enhance the work of faculty and researchers. First, these tools and methods may be used to enhance the research

Figure 1. Steps to a data mining crawl

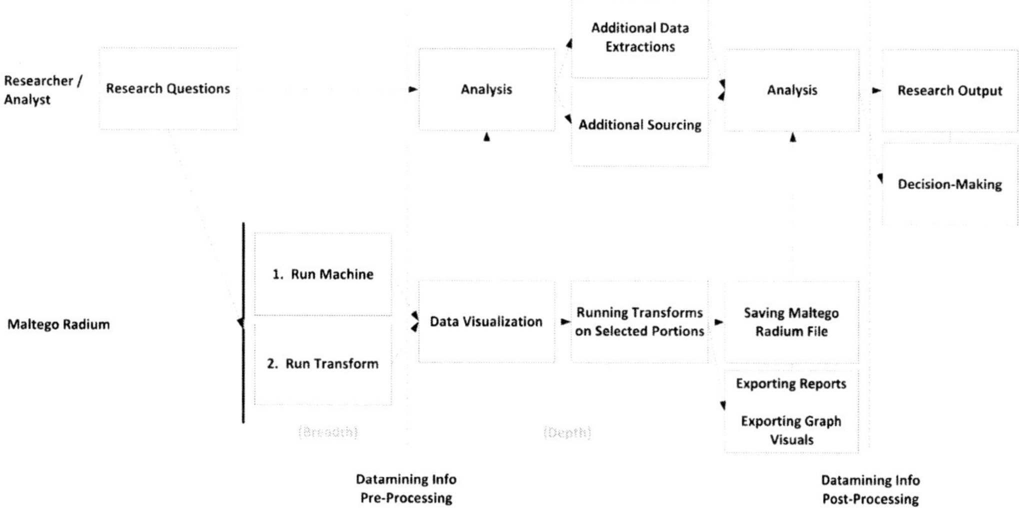

through computational research and analysis. This assumes that if social networks are mapped that private information may be de-identified (such as in crawls of email networks). There is a need to protect user privacy while conducting research in the virtually connected world (Hoser & Nitschke, 2010). Professional ties for faculty and researchers may be enhanced with the identification of fellow experts in various countries or contexts; the mapping of professional organizations; and the identification of online communities or networks of practice. Authorship networks may be mapped to identify the state of a research domain or of cross-domain research. Competency mapping may be achieved to understand the capabilities of a particular university or domain or industry in other countries. Data extractions of content networks may be completed to understand information dissemination or the diffusion of innovation in particular networks. Open-source project collaborations may be mapped to identify major contributors in those networks.

Social contribution: For the third area of focus, social contribution, electronic network analysis may be done to understand the thinking of public groups on various issues. This approach has a strong history in e-governance. Trending ideas may be extracted from microblogging and other online communal sites.

Electronic network mapping may also enhance work in academic organizations by creating an electronic mirror of the university itself in terms of its telepresence in various social and technological spaces. What messages are being conveyed by the university, both formally *and informally*? (Around every university, there are a number of student organizations and clubs, informal networks, sports and other fan clubs, work groups, and other informal sites.) Who are the most active members of the various online communities (microblogs, Websites, social networking sites, wikis, blogs, repositories / referatories, virtual worlds, and other spaces)? Organizationally, understanding what its position is in the social network milieu may be part of the 360-degree view of the organization and may protect against blind spots.

Not only may be the public be better understood, but the information for electronic network analysis will enable the creation of outreach and marketing strategies to external organizations—with clearer understandings of their human structures and their contact information.

The geographical analysis features may enable a university or academic organization to map the domains at various physical locations.

Management: Electronic network analysis may enhance efforts at fund-raising by providing staff with clearer understandings of organizations and their members. An online datamining tool enables ways to disambiguate people; in a real-world situation, individuals were creating fraudulent accounts to register in college courses in order to access federal tuition funding; a datamining analysis enabled the identification of patterning that could possibly indicate fraudulent accounts for further investigation.

To explore some of the possibilities of applying Maltego Radium to an academic setting, some data extractions were conducted. These are not in-depth analyses that show specific inferences that may be made; rather, these are done to highlight some of the capabilities of the tool in terms of data crawls and data visualization outputs. Actual real-world analyses will involve a more in-depth crawl of various entities from each of the network in order to be able to draw some tentative conclusions and to find leads to follow.

MACHINES

A "Company Stalker" machine captures a range of information about the electronic footprint of a particular company or organization. In this case, an academic publishing company specializing in science and engineering fields was selected, IGI Global, with its main Website (http://www.igi-global.com/). The data extraction identifies the network domain, related URLs, core personnel and their related email address and phone numbers. Figure 2 highlights some of these findings. This is depicted as a comprehensive graph view. The legend at the bottom right indicates the various types of information captured: person, email address, phone, document, domain, URL, and Website. In a zoomed-in view, the various entities may be analyzed...and further crawled with relevant transforms.

Company Stalker

A force-based visualization of the same information from the company stalker crawl in Figure 3.

Finally, a more structured view of the company stalker data follows in Figure 3. This visu-

Figure 2. A "company stalker" crawl of IGI Global with core periphery dynamics

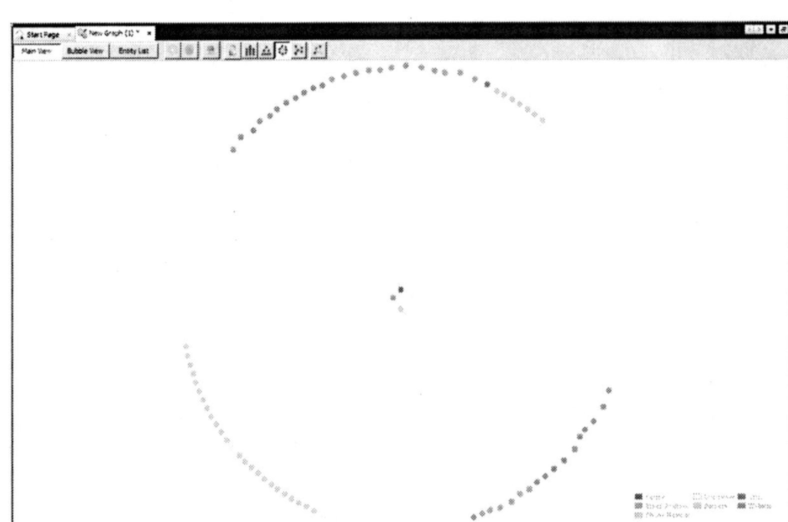

Figure 3. A "company stalker" crawl of IGI Global with force-based relational layout (version 2)

alization includes readable icons at this particular level of resolution (see Figure 4).

Figure 5 shows the entities in a close-up way. Many of these entities may be explored further with additional transforms. In the figure, the telephone numbers have been blurred out.

A footprinting of an entity involves identifying the network understructure. The L1 (of three possible) level is the lightest level of a data extraction. For the next few footprinting endeavors, the www.k-state.edu site was footprinted. Figure 6 shows a hierarchical view of this data extraction.

Footprint L1

A fast crawl of the .edu domain with a parameter set to 12 results ends up with the following graph. This is a macro-level online footprint, which may be interpreted for size and structure. Figure 7 is in the circular layout mode.

An L1 level crawl of the .edu domain with a limit of 255 entities shows a much more unwieldy view. In the "organic" visualization, this shows more granular information about this domain. Figure 8 shows a more in-depth capture of the domain.

Figure 4. A "company stalker" crawl of IGI Global with readable icons (version 3)

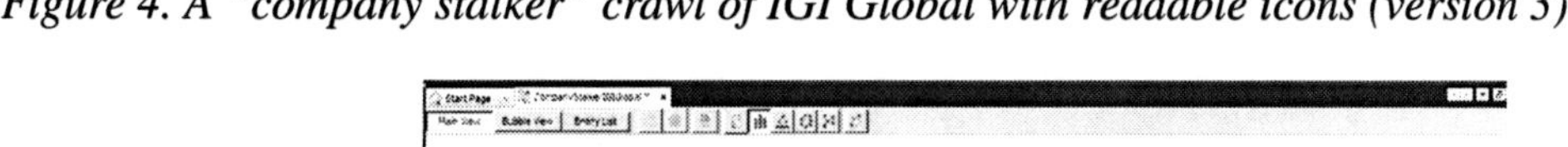

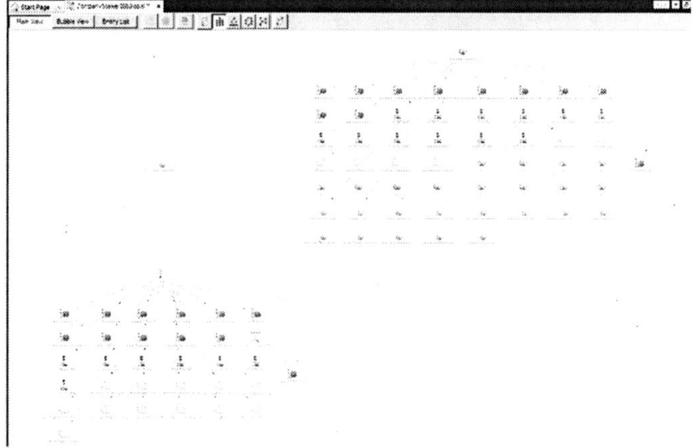

Figure 5. A "company stalker" crawl of IGI Global with readable icons in a zoomed-in view (version 4)

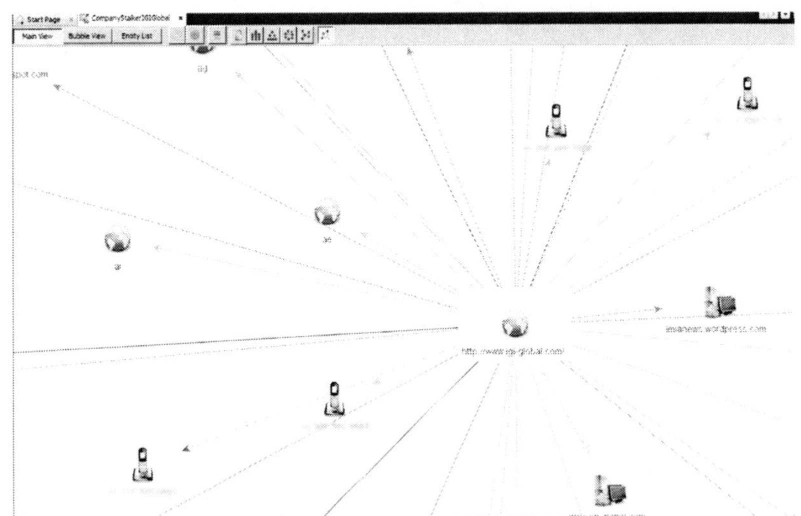

Figure 6. An L1 level assessment of Kansas State University's online footprint

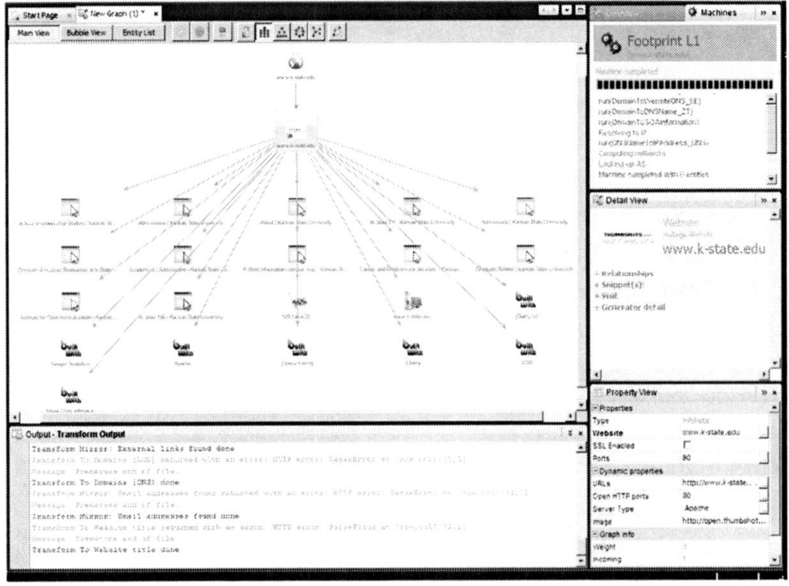

An L2 level assessment of K-State's online footprint results in Figure 9. Figure 9 shows a zoomed-in view.

Footprint L2

Figure 10 shows a more structured view of the same data as in Figure 9. These details include information on a range of the following: autonomous systems on the Internet, Domain Name Server (DNS) server names, IPv4 addresses, name server records, netblocks, domains, MX records (DNS mail exchange records), email addresses, and Websites. This one, by contrast, is a zoomed-out view.

Figure 7. An L1 level assessment of .edu macro online footprint

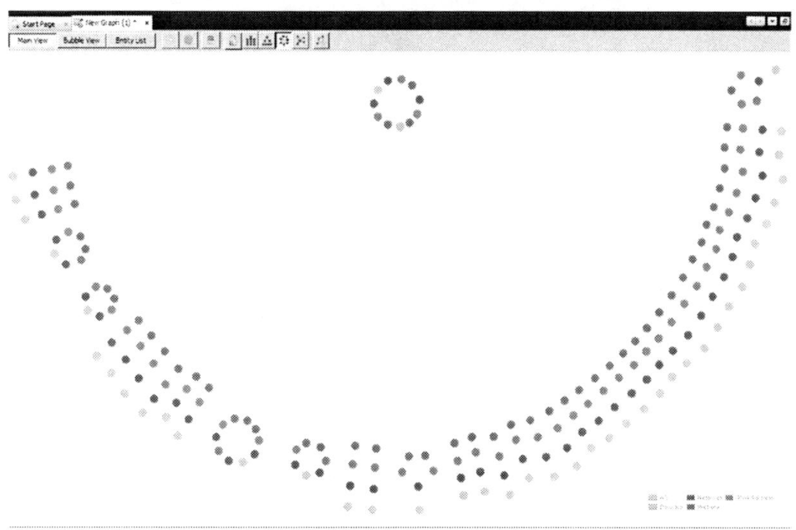

Figure 8. An L1 level assessment of .edu macro online footprint (with 255 entities)

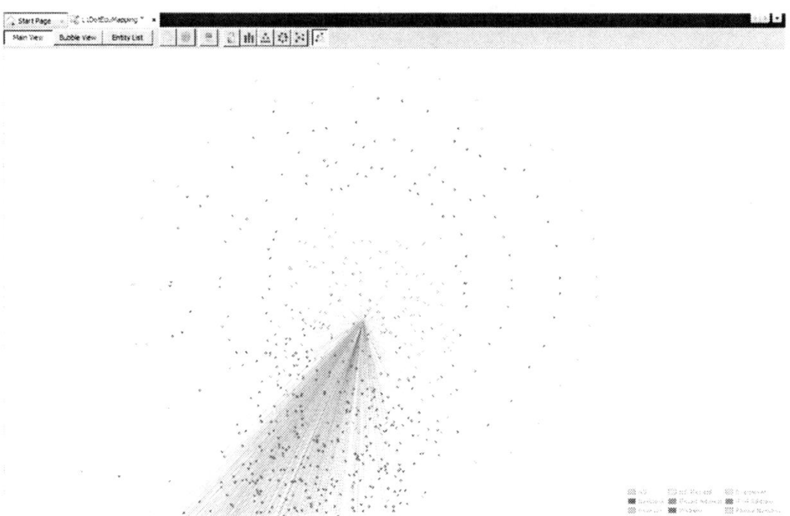

An L3 level extraction of the university's online footprint captures many of the base technologies used to create parts of this network Figure 11 spotlights some of the technologies used to build this university's Internet footprint.

Footprint L3

Figure 12 shows a zoomed out view of the university's online footprint augmented with additional data extractions.

Person – Email Address

A "Person-Email Address" search connects an individual with a range of possible connected email accounts across a range of email providers. (This machine requires further inquiries to explore different accounts.) Figure 13 shows the results of a recent data extraction, with quite a few accounts which clearly do not belong to this individual. It is important to filter results in order to get closer to the valid data.

Figure 9. An L2 level assessment of Kansas State University's online footprint

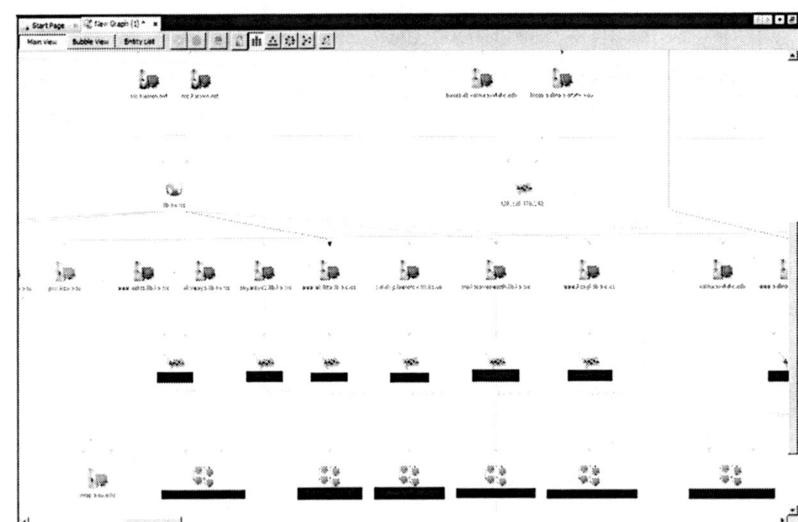

Figure 10. An L2 level assessment of Kansas State University's online footprint structured view

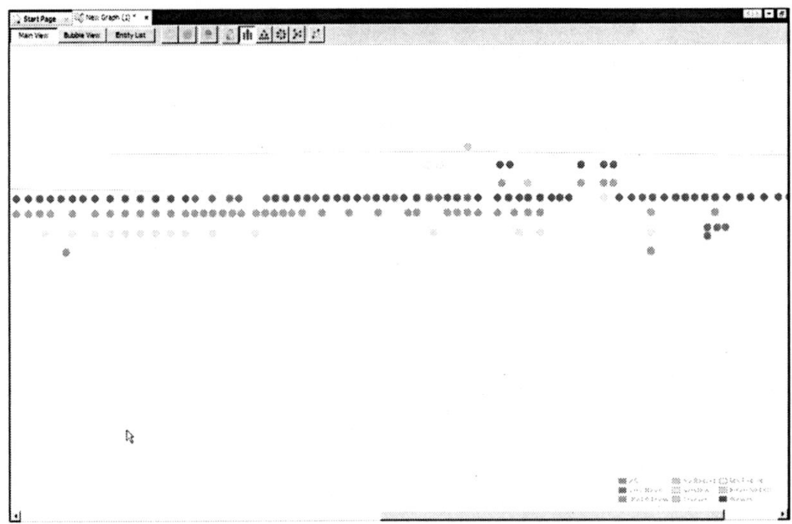

In the spirit of testing a tool against known data, the author did a crawl of her email accounts and found a range of leads, even those to a defunct email account. One additional benefit of this machine was that the name did not need more disambiguating. Figure 14 shows a tree diagram with additional searches conducted on some of the extended entities. The original search term was input at the top node.

Prune Leaf Entities

The "Prune Leaf Entities" feature removes entities (nodes or vertices) that are connected to the network by single links and which do not connect to other elements in the graph, to enable some further analysis. In some ways, this pruning of leaf entities de-noises the data in order to find more interactive elements.

Figure 11. An L3 level assessment of Kansas State University's online footprint

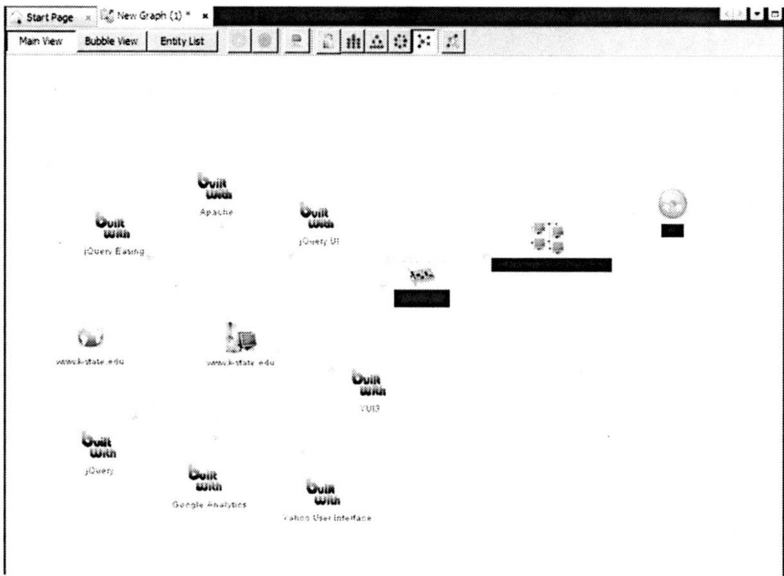

Figure 12. An L3 level assessment of Kansas State University's online footprint with additional transforms

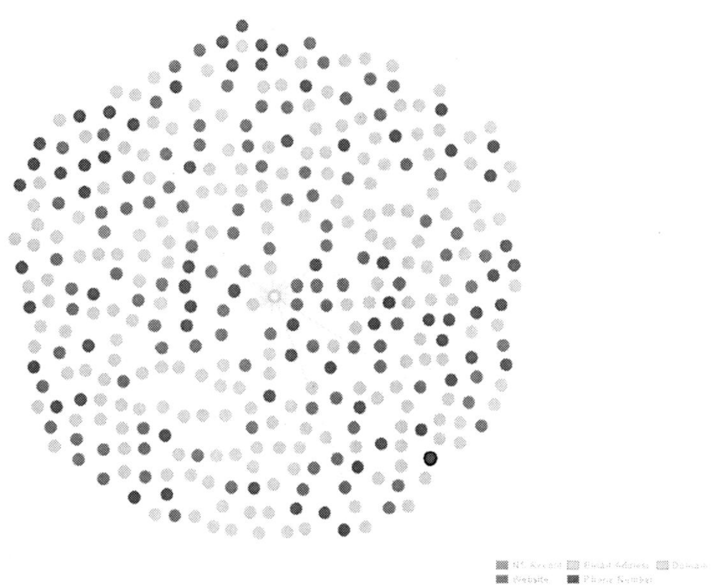

Twitter Digger

The Twitter Digger works on a phrase that may be explored on the microblogging site, Twitter. In this case, "kstate" was used as the phrase, and it was expected to surface geographically diverse comments. Indeed, recent comments came from two continents, according to this data extraction. Figure 15 has surfaced a range of types of information: Twit (Tweet text), devices used, phrases,

Figure 13. Discovering the email contacts for Phyllis Epps

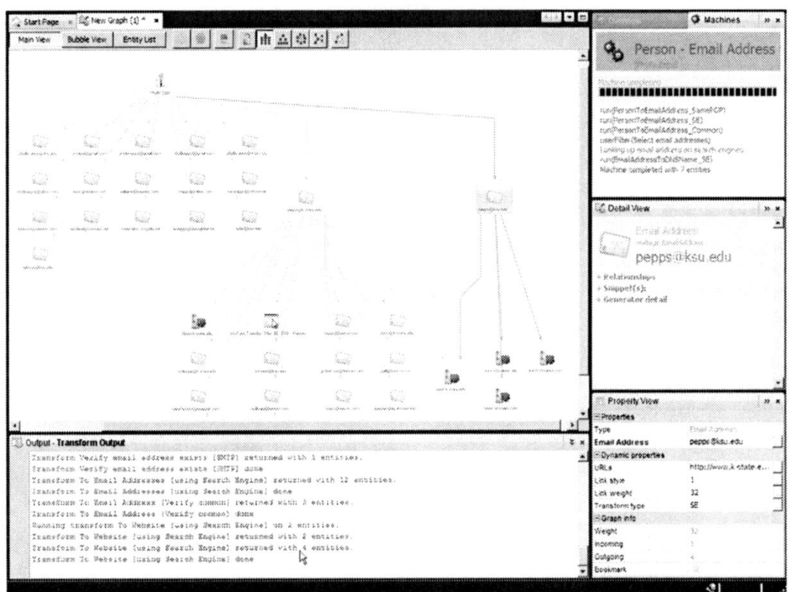

Figure 14. A search of the author's email accounts

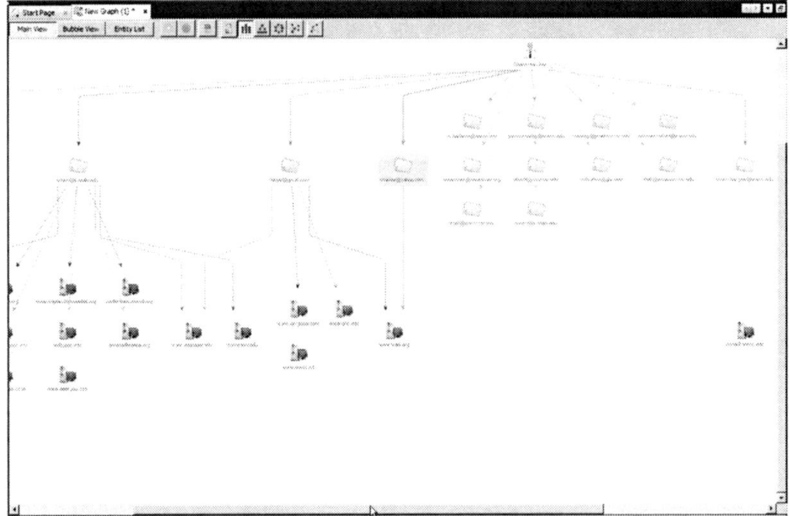

identities, persons, locations, URLs, hashtags, images (Twitpics), and affiliations.

To track a Twitter microblogging account to a physical location, Maltego Radium offers a machine to capture that data. Figure 16 captures a range of information and suggests a probable physical location. In this case, there were a number of locations linked to this network (with phone numbers with area codes linked to physical locations), but there were too many leads at the time of the crawl to result in one defined location.

Twitter Geo Location

A "MOOC" ("massive open online course") is a course type that is gaining popularity currently. To find out how this topic was trending on Twitter, a hashtag search of "#MOOC" was conducted. This brought up a list of Tweets, active accounts that had communicated using this and related hashtags, and Twitpics related to the topic. Also, URLs that were Tweeted were captured. Figure 17 provided a sense of this issue over a limited time period. The Twitter Monitor machine enables a capture of what is trending and possibly the individuals who may be leaders in the discussion for a time (Some of this may be findable using both Twitter tools and other apps.).

Figure 15. A Twitter digger search of the phrase "kstate"

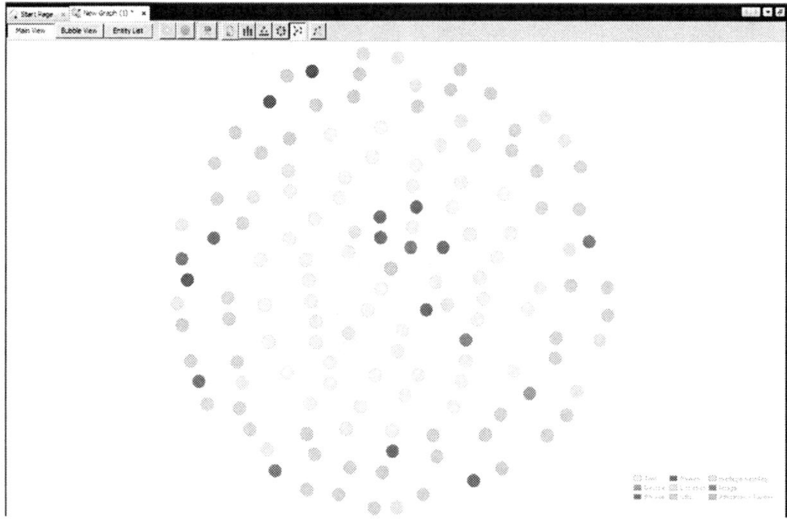

Figure 16. Twitter geo location for "educause"

Twitter Monitor

The same "#MOOC" data is output as a force-based diagram in Figure 18. Force-based layouts create a sense of repulsion between vertices or nodes, which enables there to be more clarity between them particularly in dense networks.

To get a sense of Maltego Radium's network and domain crawls, a datamining crawl of http://www.educause.edu was conducted. Figure 19 surfaced information about the technologies used to build the network and domain.

URL to Network and Domain Information

Further, to test the ability of the tool to map the electronic networks underlying a geographical location, the domain of the location "Manhattan, Kansas" was run. Figure 20 shows the results of that run.

To get a sense of the K-State social networking profile, the official K-State fan page on Facebook was mapped. The official page (located at https://www.facebook.com/KState) had 94,763 likes at the time of the data extraction. The cover page shows a broad diversity of interests and complexity. Institutions of higher education likely show very different presences on various social media platforms. Figure 21 shows some of the main participants and their contact information, among other details.

Finally, on Twitter, the kstate_pres account was crawled to identify the owner of the account. Further, this captured other technical details of the account (see Figure 22).

Solutions and Recommendations

As it stands, Maltego Radium may be used as a tool for discovery, for asking questions, and for looking at relationships. It will be critical to regard the results as the start of an inquiry process, not an end point. The treatment of these data mines has also been fairly superficial. It is beyond the purview of the chapter to add more analytical depth. It would seem helpful to test the tool's insights and capabilities against real-world realities.

SOME LIMITATIONS

What these data extractions and visualizations show are various relational structures that are

Figure 17. Twitter monitor for "MOOC"

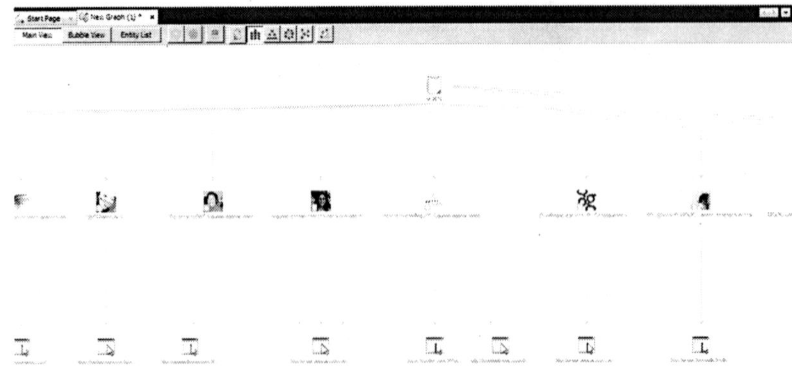

Figure 18. Twitter monitor of "MOOC" as a force-based graph

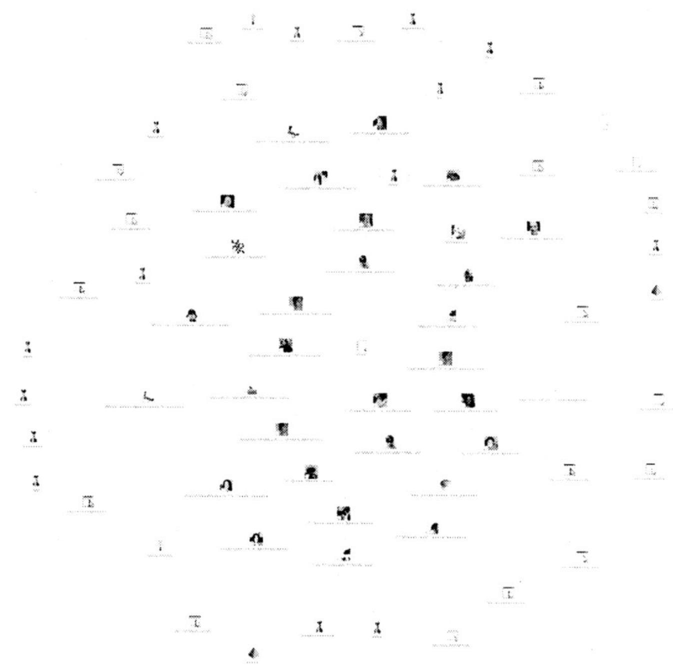

Figure 19. URL to network and domain search for educause.edu

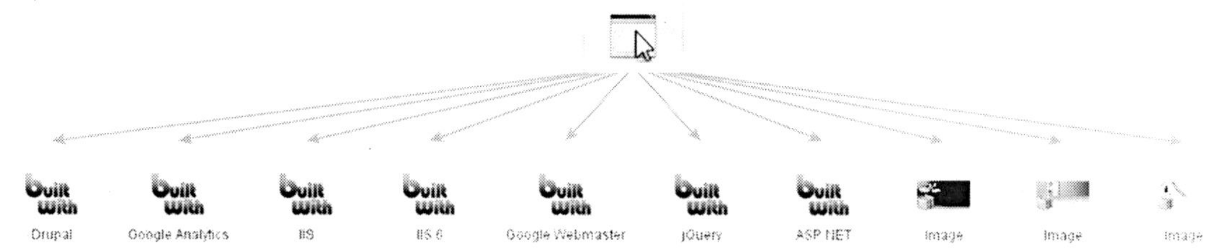

technical and social. Even if the data crawls include plenty of breadth and depth, software users will still need to access Maltego Radium reports to benefit from the full measure of the data extracted. Further, there is still information that is not collected. There will still be ambiguities.

Every research approach involves some limitations to assertions and generalizability. The analysis of electronic networks has multiple ones. The online environment offers numerous potentials for hoaxing. Websites may be spoofed; official Websites may include honeypots; social network accounts may be backed by people, robots, or cyborgs. Various Socio-Technical Systems (STS) may be gamed. People often engage in impression management and spin. Even if information may be extracted, it must be parsed, triangulated, and analyzed for it to have any value. Plenty of information may be accessed publicly, but much

Figure 20. Mapping the domain of Manhattan, Kansas

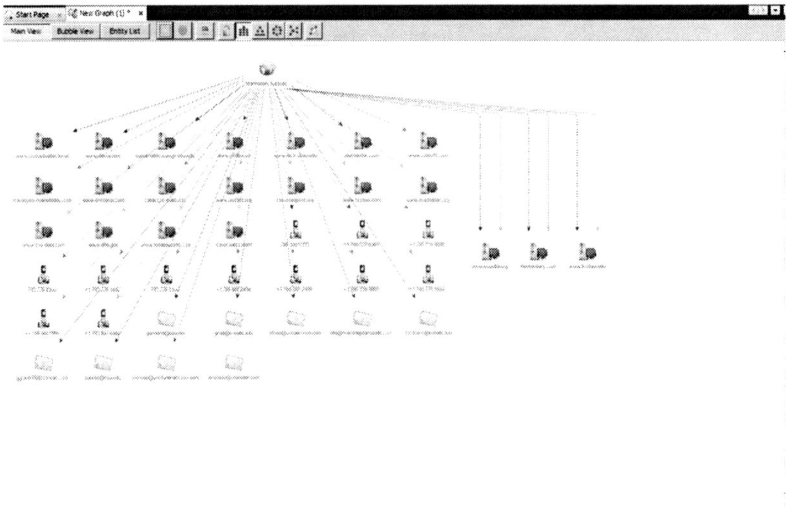

Figure 21. K-State on Facebook

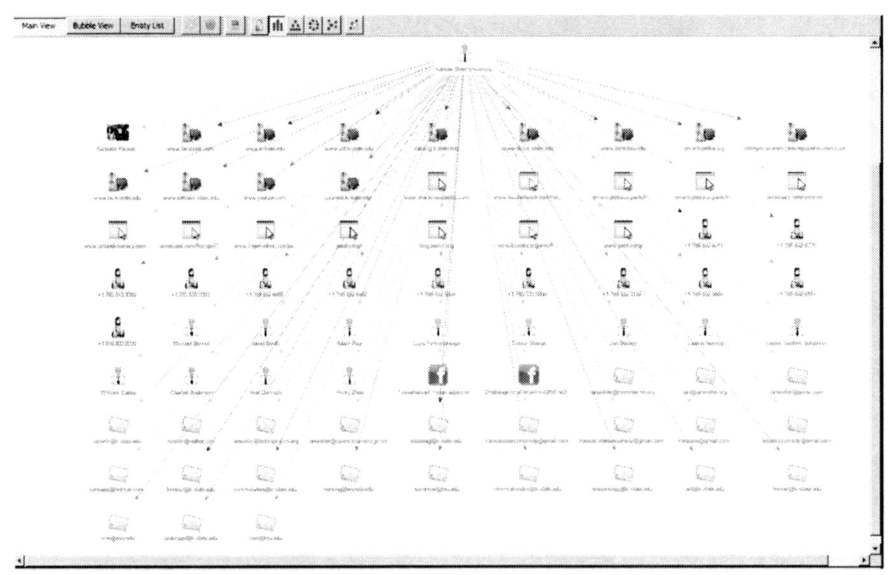

is also occurring in private channels. Much is happening in the "hidden Web."

Also, the online environment is under constant change, so a slice-in-time capture will be limited. Dynamic constant crawls tie up computing resources, though, and result in files that save out in a static way.

Another challenge is that people work in an evolving legal ecosystem. There are differing rules for privacy rights in different regions of the world. University institutional review boards and grant-funding organizations have high standards for any research involving human subjects. These all mean that individuals need to proceed with care when conducting network crawls, especially

Figure 22. The kstate_pres affiliation network on Twitter with ties to an individual

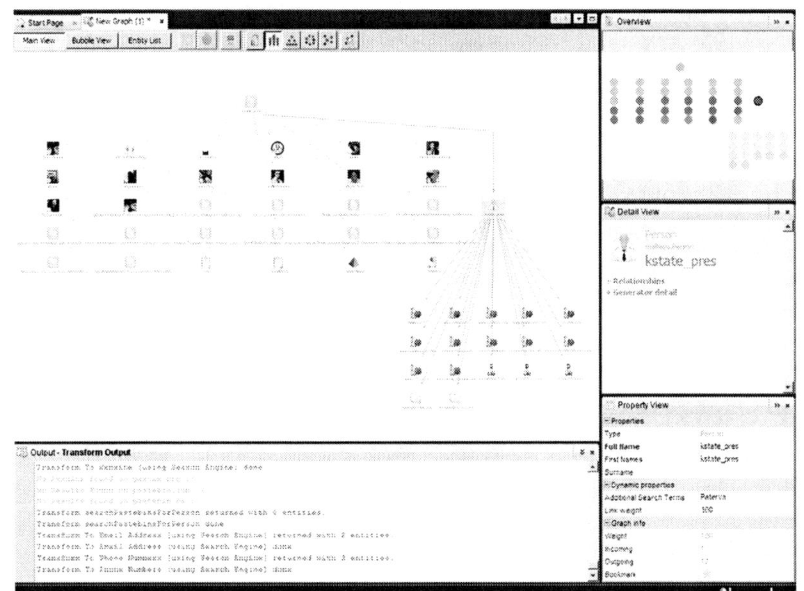

for research in which human identities may be identified.

The software Maltego Radium only captures some information. It cannot capture what is not connected to the Internet and WWW. It cannot crawl what is labeled "private" on various social media platforms. It may be duped into crawling information in honey pots. It does not offer indicators to researchers about which nodes or links to explore in more depth. It also cannot currently trace what information is moving through networks (except limited textual information in microblogging sites). It also cannot perform invisible or stealth crawls without the user revealing some information about himself or herself. There are a number of social media platforms that do not have application programming interfaces (APIs) which allow public access to their data, and that often means much data may not be extracted for analysis.

Another limitation to this approach is that there are high cognitive demands for researchers, who need to be able to wield the tool intelligently and not over-claim or under-claim results. The learning curve is fairly high, even if it's only used for initial discovery, basic pattern recognition, anomaly detection, and hypothesis-making. There has not yet been a consensus agreement of how much of a network needs to be crawled for a generalization to be possible without under-sampling (In the research literature, many researchers crawl all data from large-scale real-world networks for their analyses.).

Finally, this type of computational research—extracting data from social media platforms and analyzing them as sociograms; capturing multimodal details to disambiguate the Internet--approach is fairly new in academia, research, and professional fields. This means that there may be resistance to the findings. This may mean the need for increased work to explain the research approaches and information interpretations.

There may be idiosyncrasies of particular crawls as well. For example, the author strove to use Maltego Radium to find a Twitter account related to a colleague (with his permission) by putting his name in a transform, but the Twitter Digger "machine" in Maltego Radium came up empty in terms of entities. It returned the message: "The account Brent A. Anders does not exist or we have reached the twitter API limits." However, when she used a known Twitter account linked to her colleague, it easily reversed back to her colleague. The "transforms" do not work with equal fluency in both directions. The information that a researcher starts out with may well affect the quality of the information that is discovered (see Figure 23).

FUTURE RESEARCH DIRECTIONS

Mainline organizations in academia stand to benefit from accessing the understructure and interrelationships of various sites, individual accounts, and other types of electronic and public information. This chapter described some of those benefits.

This issue has value in the academic literature because it is important—as part of information literacy and social informatics—to realize what is accessible electronically and how that data may be recalibrated for analytical relevance. It is relevant for applications in academic research. This is relevant also for supporting the many members of the individuals who are part of a university family, with multi-generational learners, professors, researchers, alumni, neighbors, and dedicated fans.

While researchers have been honing their methodologies, based on the various new questions that researchers will ask, there will be new techniques to surfacing, collecting, and analyzing network data. They will be honing their induction, deduction, and inferential analyses of various data sets. They will be better able to assess networks from ever more nuanced pieces of information. They may evolve new ways of visualizing such network information. Further, they may create new methods of strategizing interventions in various networks based on their analysis of structures and other information.

The software tools that enable data extraction and visualization will likely continue evolving. As time progresses, surely there will be more popular mainline tools that enable the crawling of the so-called Hidden Web which is not currently accessible by today's browsers. What is electronically knowable by the general public will increase, with positive and negative externalities. The understandings of various types of networks

Figure 23. An absence of reflexivity in data crawls

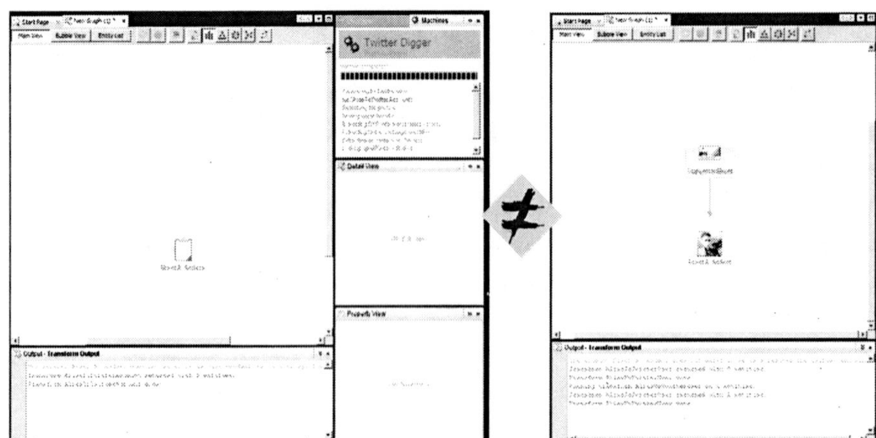

will become more sophisticated. The affordances of newer approaches may lead to some degree of predictivity, which could enhance planning and decision-making.

In the near-term, it looks like social networking platforms may be plateauing. There may be fatigue in terms of the over-sharing phenomenon. Some users of social networking sites have found a point of diminishing returns and a growing lack of interest. Social technologies, and maybe all technologies, tend to be popular for a time and then diminish in popularity. While people's enthusiasm for various technologies and devices will wax and wane, there will be a variety of other types of computing (such as wearable computing) that will enhance human socializing with each other. The analysis of networks will likely be usable in a variety of ways that are as-yet unanticipated today.

CONCLUSION

Electronic network analysis has the potential for a broad range of possible applications in an academic environment beyond penetration testing. The network analysis applications, using Maltego Radium, in this particular chapter are light but may suggest more complex applications. Certainly, practitioners in various respective fields may conceptualize other ways that this tool may be used.

REFERENCES

Aggarwal, C. C., & Yu, P. S. (2012). On the network effect in web 2.0 applications. *Electronic Commerce Research and Applications*, *11*, 142–151. doi:10.1016/j.elerap.2011.11.001.

Arnaboldi, V., Guazzini, A., & Passarella, A. (2013). Egocentric online social networks: Analysis of key features and prediction of tie strength in Facebook. *Computer Communications*. Retrieved April 8, 2013, from http://www.sciencedirect.com/science/article/pii/S0140366413000856

Binder, J., Howes, A., & Sutcliffe, A. (2009). The problem of conflicting social spheres: Effects of network structure on experienced tension in social network sites. In *Proceedings of CHI 2009—Social Networking Sites*, (pp. 965-974). Boston, MA: ACM Press.

Chen, R. (2013). Living a private life in public social networks: An exploration of member self-disclosure. *Decision Support Systems*, 1–8.

Hoser, B., & Nitschke, T. (2010). Questions on ethics for research I the virtually connected world. *Social Networks*, *32*, 180–186. doi:10.1016/j.socnet.2009.11.003.

Lin, J.-W., & Lai, Y.-C. (2013). Online formative assessments with social network awareness. *Computers & Education*, *66*, 40–53. doi:10.1016/j.compedu.2013.02.008.

Rowe, M. (2010). The credibility of digital identity information on the social web: A user study. [Raleigh, NC: WICOW.]. *Proceedings of WICOW*, *10*, 35–42. doi:10.1145/1772938.1772947.

Schaefer, M. (2012). *Return on influence: The revolutionary power of Klout, social scoring, and influence marketing*. New York: McGraw-Hill.

Steinfield, C., Ellison, N. B., & Lampe, C. (2008). Social capital, self-esteem, and use of online social network sites: A longitudinal analysis. *Journal of Applied Developmental Psychology*, *29*, 434–445. doi:10.1016/j.appdev.2008.07.002.

Taleb, N. N. (2010). *The black swan: The impact of the highly improbable*. New York: Random House. (Original work published 2007).

Yu, A. Y., Tian, S. W., Vogel, D., & Kwok, R. C.-W. (2010). Can learning be virtually boosted? An investigation of online social networking impacts. *Computers & Education*, *55*, 1494–1503. doi:10.1016/j.compedu.2010.06.015.

ADDITIONAL READING

Hansen, D. L., Schneiderman, B., & Smith, M. A. (2011). *Analyzing social media networks with NodeXL: Insights form a connected world*. Amsterdam: Elsevier.

KEY TERMS AND DEFINITIONS

Alias: An assumed identity.

Black Box, Gray Box, Crystal Box: Levels of knowledge of a network.

Black Hat: A malicious or villainous (often law-breaking) individual.

Center-Periphery Dynamic: A visual phenomena related to graphs depicting networks in which the most influential node is in the middle and the less connected or active or powerful ones are on the periphery.

Data Crawl: A data extraction.

Data Mining: Sophisticated data processing using statistical algorithms to find patterns in often large data sets.

Diffusion: The spreading of something widely.

Edge: A line or link with arrows showing directionality.

Fat Node: An influential entity.

Focal Node: The main or target entity of interest; a social network hub.

Geodesic Distance: The diameter of a social network, indicated by the distance between the two furthest-apart nodes.

Influence: The ability to effect change on another's values or behaviors.

Link: A tie between entities showing a relationship.

Network Topology: The entities and elements in a network.

Node: An entity; a vertex.

Path: The distance traversed between nodes for the transfer of information or anything else that may be transmitted through a network.

Penetration Testing: The defensive assessment of a network and its potential vulnerabilities by a network defender.

Percolation: The movement of anything transmittable through a network.

Propagation: Dissemination.

Pseudonymity: The maintenance of long-term anonymity.

Social Actors: Individuals or groups that act within a social network.

Social Capital: Benefits derived from cooperation between individuals and groups in a social context.

Social Engineering: In information technology, the manipulation and deception of people to compromise IT systems.

Social Network Analysis: A systems analytic approach to understand the social dynamics of a network, its entities, their interrelationships, and other features of the network.

Topology: Network structure.

White Hat: An ethical individual and law-abider who conducts hacking to benefit the larger community.

Section 4
Cases in Real-World Packaging of Digital Contents for Learning

Chapter 12
Immersion and Interaction via Avatars within Google Street View:
Opening Possibilities beyond Traditional Cultural Learning

Ya-Chun Shih
National Dong Hwa University, Taiwan

Molly Leonard
National Dong Hwa University, Taiwan

ABSTRACT

The optimal approach to learning a target culture is to experience it in its real-life context through interaction. The new 3D virtual world platform under consideration, Blue Mars Lite, enables users to be immersed in existing Google Maps Street View panorama, globally. Google Maps with Street View contains a massive collection of 360-degree street-level images of the most popular places worldwide. The authors explore the possibility of integrating these global panoramas, in which multiple users can explore, discuss, and role-play, into the classroom. The goal of this chapter is to shed new light on merging Google Street View with the 3D virtual world for cultural learning purposes. This approach shows itself to be a promising teaching method that can help EFL learners to develop positive attitudes toward the target culture and cultural learning in this new cultural setting.

INTRODUCTION

Learning through engagement and immersion in cultural context offers promising possibilities for cultural learning. Cultural context plays an important role in contributing to the expansion of English as a Foreign Language (EFL) learners' cultural learning. In the EFL context, the fact that learners are physically situated *outside* the target culture means that teaching cultural content from textbooks in a structured context, e.g., in EFL classrooms, becomes the norm. However, it is well-recognized that culture is best learned when learners are completely immersed in a natural or real-world cultural setting, rather than learning it in the classroom, in an artificial and compartmentalized way. Thanks to innovative new technologies, possibilities exist for target culture learning

DOI: 10.4018/978-1-4666-4462-5.ch012

through immersion in "real-world" settings, even in the EFL context.

Google Maps with Street View allows users to discover the real world via 360-degree street-level imagery (Google Maps Street View, n.d.). Of late, thanks to panorama technology and the debut of Google Street View in 2007, users can explore natural landscapes, cities, rural areas, buildings, and artifacts, worldwide by engaging in virtual sightseeing at street level. Additionally, users can plan, navigate, and enjoy a virtual trip, such as hiking the Grand Canyon, and can visit the interiors of buildings, such as restaurants and stores, using panoramic view virtual tours offered by Google Street Business Photos, on their computers or mobile devices.

Google Street View enables users to explore places in a variety of contexts, worldwide. In the process, it opens up many new and exciting possibilities for language and culture learning, and broadens learners' immersion experiences. The use of Google Street View in daily life is closely linked to language and culture learning, due to the technology's ability to simulate what would otherwise usually only occur through immersion in the real-world context. According to Avatar Languages,

> *...the program [Google Street View] allows us to virtually explore a location and it therefore offers immersive experiences similar to a 3D virtual world. Of course, 3D virtual worlds are also social spaces, where fellow users can meet each other and this is not the case with Street View. ... Google Street View is a useful and everyday tool, so it is easily incorporated into real-life activities that offer language learning opportunities. (Avatar Languages, n.d., para 5)*

Google Street View also provides culture-authentic materials for cultural learning. Learners can be exposed to authentic materials which supply them with authentic inputs. The authentic materials, including visual materials such as street signs, public artworks, ads, artifacts, and realia, stimulate follow-up conversations, communication, and interaction, be it face-to-face or through the use of computer-mediated communication tools. The use of authentic materials plays an important role in fostering cultural learning, and has a beneficial effect on cultural learning. Google Street View brings the real world into the classroom, allows users to employ target language for real-life purposes and to benefit from the cultural immersion, and triggers student-student and student-instructor interactions.

Google Street View is similar to 3D virtual environments, in that both provide "immersive experiences" as mentioned in the previous citation. On the other hand, Google Street View does not provide a social space like Second Life does, in the form of a virtual environment where people can meet, communicate, and interact directly with one another "in-world". As a result, and based on her own experiences, it occurred to the researchers that some users may feel lonely while engaged in Google Street View sightseeing, and might prefer to have company while exploring. For language learners in particular, Street View brings real-world contexts and authentic materials to the language classroom, but is still limited in terms of its beneficial effect due to the inherent lack of social interaction in the street view context. To progress, language learners need to interact with both the context and with other speakers of the target language. Learners' communicative, interactive, and social needs, combined with actual practice, pave the way for cultural learning to take place.

Blue Mars Lite, which incorporates Google Street View into the 3D virtual world, includes a feature called Street View Chat (Blue Mars Lite, n.d.). This feature enables language learners to embody themselves as avatars, move around at will inside Google Street View, visit different Google Street View locations, and share information, interact, and communicate with one another. Street View Chat brings dual benefits to language learners by combining the real-world contexts and authentic materials offered by Google Street View with the social interaction enabled by 3D virtual reality and chat technologies. The synergistic combination of these technologies creates a rich immersive experience for learners.

The objectives of this chapter are to uncover the suitable approaches to teaching culture in this context, to provide an overview of the features of this system, to explore the possibilities of integrating this new system into EFL settings, to describe planned approaches to curriculum development and task-based design, to give concrete examples of tasks which have been designed for cultural learning, and to explore learners' attitudes towards the target culture, and cultural learning in this context.

The study answers the following research questions:

- What attitudes do EFL learners hold with respect to the target culture after taking the virtual tour?
- What are the attitudes of EFL learners toward cultural learning in this new cultural setting?

THE ROLE OF ATTITUDES IN CULTURAL LEARNING

According to Paige, Jorstad, Siaya, Klein, and Colby's (2003) conceptual model of cultural learning, attitude changes can be identified as the development of either favorable or unfavorable attitudes toward (a) target culture, (b) target culture persons, and (c) cultural learning. Further, according to Herek (1986, 2000), attitudes can be broken down into instrumental attitudes, which are concerned with personal *interests*, and symbolic attitudes, which relate to personal *values*. A favorable attitude toward a target culture, persons, and learning about the culture reflects an invisible belief in the value of taking a positive *interest* in cultural differences and in making connections through the cultural learning processes, as well as the *value* of increasing one's understanding and appreciation of the culture. Both instrumental and symbolic attitudes are closely linked to cultural learning. The existence of a positive interest or value plays an important role in exploring cultures and cultural differences (Byram, 1997) and in cultural learning. In this context, an individual's attitude reflects his or her feelings, perceptions, beliefs and values, as they relate to a particular culture. This conceptualization corresponds closely to the definition of attitude as "an explicit indicator of a person's tacit perceptions, beliefs, and values" (Anzai, Dobberfuhl, Matsuzawa, Zimmerman, 2008, p. 14).

Our goal is to describe the learners' attitudes toward the target culture, persons, and toward cultural learning by means of retrospective investigation, in the hope of illuminating any changes and cultural experiences in their interest, their culturally-shaped values, and their thought patterns that come about as a result of a series of virtual tours.

WAYS TO LEARN CULTURE

There are many ways to learn and teach culture, including field trips and travelling, role-playing, simulation, virtual tours, cultural immersion, scavenger hunts, and the integration of podcasts, videos, audio recordings, authentic materials, maps, and other media in the EFL classroom. The context of cultural learning is defined as the setting or situation where cultural learning occurs. Cultural learning can occur in naturalistic contexts or in artificial, structured, classroom settings (Paige et al., 2003). In this study, culture was taught in a context combing both naturalistic and structured settings. The use of Google Street View provided a "real world" context in which learners could virtually immerse themselves and discover culture in the field, naturally. On the other hand, the contextual setting is properly viewed as being slightly artificial because the community formed by an instructor and learners is not a naturally occurring one, and is, in some ways, similar to a classroom setting.

Teaching culture in a language classroom is highly dependent on *what* is to be taught, and *how* the material should be conveyed. To illustrate the processes of teaching and learning about culture, Scarino and Liddicoat (2009) proposed conceptualizing these two processes as two dimensions which give rise to four quadrants when they intersect (see Figure 1). The vertical axis represents two aspects of culture which are situated at its opposite ends: facts and processes. Process is defined "as a dynamic system through which a society constructs, represents, enacts, and understands itself" (Scarino & Liddicoat, 2009, p. 20). Intersecting the vertical axis, the horizontal axis represents two types of cultural content related to cultural learning: 1) artifacts and institutions (i.e., things produced by a society); and 2) practices (i.e., things said and done by members of a society). The diagram shows four ways of teaching culture:

The first quadrant is the most static way of teaching factual knowledge, whereas the fourth quadrant is the most dynamic way of teaching culture, through involving students in the practices of a cultural community.

Figure 1. Methods of teaching culture (adapted from Scarino & Liddicoat, 2009, p. 20)

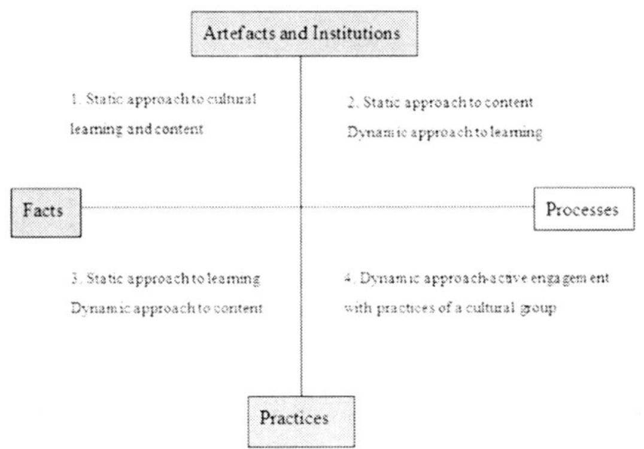

The way in which we view culture influences both the way we teach culture and how we assess cultural learning. Culture is regarded as both a body of factual knowledge and a dynamic system. This study uses a static method of presenting and receiving factual knowledge (e.g., students discovering the arts and artifacts in London through virtual tours), and a dynamic process of ongoing engagement and interaction (e.g., students virtually interacting with native English speakers to experience their lifestyle, hear what they say, and see what they do) in a virtual context.

Students learned about the target culture and specific aspects thereof through cultural immersion, social interaction, negotiation, and involvement within authentic contexts, and observation of culturally relevant features within the virtual context. The dynamic constructivist perspective of cultural learning sees it as a dynamic process of interacting with cultural artifacts and people from the target culture or in it. The outcome of the person-to-person interactions within the socio-cultural context is the students' construction of their own knowledge of the target culture, as well as their development of positive attitudes toward the target culture and cultural learning.

CULTURAL SIMULATIONS AND LEARNING IN VIRTUAL ENVIRONMENTS

Immersive virtual environments are becoming a promising tool for (inter) cultural learning, especially for the acquisition of cultural knowledge and intercultural communication skills (Lane & Ogan, 2009; Ogan & Lane, 2009). The environment situates learners in a simulated cultural context and engages them in the construction of cultural knowledge and experiences through cultural practice and socio-cultural interaction. Lane and Ogan reviewed several virtual environments, such as Croquelandia, Adaptive Thinking and Leadership (ATL), Second China, Tactical

Language and Culture Training System (TLCTS), BiLAT, and VECTOR, built for promoting cultural understanding and/or communication skills. These environments provide "high-fidelity simulation of new cultural settings" (Lane & Ogan, 2009, Abstract section), through visual representation consisting of visible aspects of culture, such as streets, buildings, and artifacts. They also offered narrative-based techniques and virtual characters to trigger learners' motivation, and to increase their cultural practice, interaction, and communication.

The preliminary findings of the above-mentioned empirical studies on previous virtual environments show their potential for increasing usability, i.e., ATL (Raybourn, Deagle, Mendini, & Heneghan, 2005), Spanish pragmatics, i.e., Croquelandia (Sykes, 2008), and cultural knowledge and motivation, i.e., TLCTS (Johnson & Valente, 2008). For example, Second China was developed at the University of Florida within the framework of Second Life. This virtual environment combines an immersive virtual environment and traditional Websites to promote cultural awareness, cultural experiences, and understanding of Chinese culture (Henderson, Fishwick, Fresh, Futterknecht, & Hamilton, 2008). Human characters, called bots, interact with users. This environment presents the tangible aspects of culture and real-world objects, such as a meeting room and desk. Second China provides more direct, authentic, and natural ways to improve learners' understanding of culture-related issues. The results of a peer evaluation of Second China are positive (p. 10).

However, current empirical research related to the effects of virtual environments on cultural learning is still in its infancy. We look forward to seeing the results of follow-up empirical studies on Second China and other virtual environments. More long-term empirical research is needed to fill the current knowledge gap in this field. Previous researchers exerted tremendous effort to create tangible cultural objects such as art work, buildings, and dress, and endeavored to ensure the accuracy of visual representations of a specific culture and to create virtual humans for cultural interaction and communication. However, constructing virtual environments is time-consuming, and the resulting visual representations are artificial. It is impossible to create a virtual environment that provides students with the kind of culturally rich information and high cultural authenticity that they would encounter in a real-world context. The researchers involved in the Second China Project (Henderson et al., 2008) indicated that their project aimed "to blur the lines between a virtual cultural experience and a real-life cultural context" (p. 11). They indicated the following concern: "Although building culturally appropriate artifacts may be an excellent way to reinforce learning, the question as to whether this is a good time investment/learning-outcome payoff remains to be seen" (p. 10). Our study adopts a similar goal and addresses this concern by placing learners in a "hybrid" world (i.e., a "virtual plus real-life") cultural context, while saving time in cultural artifact construction by incorporating real street views and objects in the virtual environment.

CULTURAL LEARNING TASKS AND THE CURRICULUM

The Blue Mars Lite (n.d.) platform provides users with a street view of London (see Figure 2) by combining photos and immersive experiences. Users can virtually walk through and explore London, interacting with avatars controlled by real people. This approach is ideally suited to applications in which target cultural resources are limited to the classroom context, and can be incorporated into task-based activities, including real-world tasks and pedagogical tasks, that offer language and cultural learning opportunities. We combined in-world virtual mixed-reality tasks with preparatory and follow-up tasks involving online resources such as conventional Websites and Web 2.0 tools (including YouTube videos and wikis), as well as asynchronous discussion

Figure 2. Interaction in Google Street View of London

through blogs. Students used these resources to research the historic sites and locations (see Table 1), and used blogs to share, record, and reflect on their language learning and cultural experiences with screenshots. Additionally, virtual scavenger hunts were designed to motivate learners to search for a range of online information, such as maps, audio and video files, and newspapers, in relation to cultural objects or particular themes such as transportation in London or the Tudor dynasty.

For real-life tasks, tourism role-playing allowed students to act as tourists engaged in cultural practices and artifacts. In the later phase, students became tour guides who provided information and cultural interpretation and gave directions to other students. The virtual sightseeing walking tour of London was combined with online resources, such as London audio tours, which were downloaded from related conventional Websites or podcasts. This approach provided easy-to-follow directions and informative commentary when students "walked virtually". For example, students virtually visited the building of a traditional London pub called the Punch Tavern on London's Fleet Street. This is an ideal place to learn more about the culture of Britain through a 3D platform. Students also looked at the interior of the building and learned about British pub food by researching the items on an online menu of the pub provided on the official Website and pretending to order food inside the pub.

Students were guided by a knowledgeable person who empowered them with guidance, introduction, explanation, and cultural insight. According to Lafayette and Schultz (1975, 1997), students gain most cultural insights from directed observation of culture-specific patterns, followed-up by the help of a "knowledge resource person" (Lafayette & Schulz, 1997, p. 580). In this case, a native English speaking instructor served as a perfect language model and a rich source of English cultural information for the learners.

A CASE STUDY

A qualitative case study typically involves a longitudinal study and intensive analysis of complex phenomena, individual units, and their development within their contexts. This study investigates the English learners' attitudes as they reflect their values, beliefs, preferences, and perceptions. We investigated the attitudes of participants by interviewing them and reviewing the written data. We used various data sources to observe multiple facets of intercultural communication in context, and collected videos of intercultural interaction and a corpus of electronic communication transcripts to assess attitudinal development.

Context and Participants

Three EFL (English as a Foreign Language) graduate students (Huan, Chun, and Gran), and one undergraduate student (Emma) participated in this program. Their ages ranged from 21 to 26. Each participant had been at the university for at least two years prior to the program's commencement. The participants were representative of a typical sample of their cohort, and were selected purposefully to ensure that they would represent a rich source of information to provide deep insight into their cultural learning experiences. All

Table 1. Themes and cultural content for learning

Themes /Topics	Cultural Content
Food: Pubs British Food Menus and Ordering	British pub culture, activities, pubs and social life, drinking habits Learning British food vocabulary, developing food likes and dislikes Inside Punch Tavern and navigating the Punch Tavern Website Reading pub menus, ordering from real menus knowledgeably
Tea: Twining's Tea	The origins of British tea culture Intersection of British and local history—the Opium Wars Appreciating tea, British style
Transportation: Modes of Transportation Finding your way around	Learning how to use the London underground and bus systems From Westminster Abbey to the Tower of London--being able to make decisions about how to get from point A to point B Giving and getting directions— Westminster area and British Museum areas Using London transportation Websites for information and to purchase tickets and passes
Geography: Pre-trip orientation, Thames River, London Eye, Hyde Park, Westminster	The Thames as historical and geographic center of London Thames-side walk--using the Thames and its bridges to get oriented Using the London Eye as a jumping off point to get oriented Using Google Street View to get oriented Scavenger Hunt—raising awareness of the surroundings Hyde Park walk—stepping out into the unknown
Institutions: Royal Institutions, Religious Institutions, Government Institutions	British royal institutions and their role in British culture. Palaces, Horse Guards, Royal Parks, the Monarchy Westminster Abbey, St Paul's Cathedral, the Temple Church—Religious history, Henry VIII, and the development of the Church of England. Charles I/Cromwell/ Charles II and the differing strains of Protestantism The history and workings of Parliament, 10 Downing Street, Scotland Yard
Artifacts/ Architecture: Palaces, Churches West End/Regency Tudor Architecture	Development of palace architecture—Norman, English Gothic, Tudor, Georgian, Regency styles Pre-fire London—the City in Tudor times Famous architects and their influences—Inigo Jones, Christopher Wren, (John Nash) Pub architecture and decoration
Historical Events:	The intersection between historical events and the physical and cultural development of London Events: The Romans, Boadicea, The Norman Conquest, Henry VIII and the Church of England, Elizabeth I and Shakespeare, Cromwell, The Great Fire, The Blitz
Historical and Cultural Figures:	An introduction to important figures and their impact on the English identity. Figures: Caesar, Boadicea, Edward the Confessor, William the Conqueror, Henry VIII, Elizabeth I and the Tudor dynasty, Charles I/Cromwell/ Charles II, Inigo Jones, Christopher Wren, Victoria, Elizabeth II, Princess Diana, Darwin, Newton, Dickens, Samuel Johnson, Thomas Twining, Winston Churchill
Lifestyles: London's Neighborhoods Pub Culture Tea Local Shopping Theater Culture	A variety of neighborhood styles: Westminster, Notting Hill, University of London neighborhood, Southwark, etc Pubs and social life Tea as a social custom Contrasts between high-end and university districts, famous outdoor markets, Boots, Tesco The vicissitudes and growth of London theater from Shakespeare to the present day. The New Globe Theater. The vitality of present-day theater in London. Where and how to buy tickets.
Business: Common London Businesses Sticker Shock	Tesco, Boots, Barclay's Bank, Herod's Department Store, Twining's, Pubs, Banks and banking Pounds. Preparing learners for prices and the cost of living in London

participants satisfied the following criteria: he or she had made at least 10 visits to the platform since the beginning of the program; he or she had been an English learner for at least 10 years; he or she had never had been to London physically; and his or her English proficiency level ranged from GEPT Intermediate Level to GEPT Superior Level. The General English Proficiency TEST

(GEPT) (information available at https://www.gept.org.tw/) is a five-level (superior, advanced, high-intermediate, intermediate, elementary) criterion-referenced testing system implemented in Taiwan to evaluate EFL learners' English proficiency.

We incorporated Web 2.0 tools with Google Street View to create a blended learning environment and method that enables situated language learning and collaborative language learning. A native English-speaking teacher initially acted as a tour guide to 4 students who were new to London and its culture. The students started a city walking tour by visiting several historic sites and culturally rich locations in London. The students also completed theme-based tasks (see Table 1) to understand the locations and follow-up tasks to reflect on their cultural immersion experiences through blogs.

Data Collection and Analysis

We conducted a case study to explore EFL graduate students' interaction, writing, and cultural learning processes. Various data collection strategies, including interviews, observations, and collection of written texts (blog entries) and qualitative data analysis, helped reveal the interaction process in collaborative learning groups. Using this data, we investigated the possible development of a virtual community (of practice) and cultural understanding in this innovative setting.

Throughout the data analysis process, we reviewed, coded, and organized the data repeatedly, continually, categorically, and chronologically. We prefabricated a "start list of codes" (as suggested by Miles & Huberman, 1994, p. 58) based on our conceptual framework, which was based on the model of cultural learning developed by previous researchers, as Damen (1987) and Paige et al. (2003) indicated. The starting list of codes was revised and extended in subsequent processes of data analysis, and particularly when new ideas and codes surfaced. We identified and described the categories, patterns, and themes emerging from the data, and compared and contrasted the results (categories and themes) with related literature, particularly the cultural learning model.

Delimitation and Limitation of the Study

Cultural learning generally comprises three domains: cognitive learning, behavioral learning, and affective learning (Paige et al., 2003). Currently, we focused on the aspect of cultural learning: attitudes, and how learner attitudes affect their behavior. It is widely believed that attitudes reflect invisible values, beliefs, feelings, interests, and thinking. There is disagreement, however, between various competing paradigms about how readily such attitudes may actually be measured, and even about whether or not it is possible to measure them empirically at all. It is the opinion of the authors that it would be unrealistic to expect that the virtual tours in this program would result in immediately measureable changes in the learners' attitudes.

In terms of behavioral learning and changes, within the scope of the present study, were primarily focused on learners' retrospectively self-reported changes in behavior (i.e., influence of attitudes on behavior) over the study period. The behavioral aspect of cultural learning can take many years. Moreover, observing and specifically identifying behavioral changes is inherently difficult in this context since participant behavior could only be observed through the avatars, in the sense that only participants' avatars could be observed, and not the actual participants themselves. Hence, we will focus on learner behavior influenced by attitudes in this study.

RESULTS AND DISCUSSION

Attitudes toward the Target Culture, Persons, and Country

Most changes in learner attitudes toward target culture were favorable in this study. The changes identified were observed and reported by the instructor and researchers, self-reported by learners in interviews, and written about by learners in their reflection blog entries after the virtual trips were completed by all the students. Learners' attitudes were identified as positive feelings toward the target culture in this study. Learners' attitudes changed over the course of visiting London virtually, observing objects and interacting with partners and the native English-speaking instructor (all of whom were embodied as avatars) in "virtual London". For example, Huan reported a positive attitudinal change toward the visible aspects of culture and the country after taking the virtual tour:

It's far from what I imagined. I used to think of London as rainy and gray with lots of old houses. Only the palace is a glamorous place I would go. But after touring, it kind of changed my thoughts. I'd like to know more, and visit more places in London. (Huan, blog entry, 20120430)

Positive experiences of Huan's virtual immersion in London generated a desire to visit the target country physically, and to know more about London.

Moreover, positive attitudes, including appreciation, curiosity, interest, and openness were observed. For example, Emma showed her appreciation, interest, openness, and excitement toward typical English food, and Elizabethan buildings, both of which constitute visible aspects of culture:

All of the food looks so good. I've been vegetarian for a while, but I'm willing to go back to eating meat again just to try English food XD !!!. . . the Elizabethan buildings get me really excited. (Emma, blog entry, 20120604)

Learners developed positive attitudes toward the target culture and persons (i.e. native speakers of the target language), and enjoyed interacting with them. Interviews with the students revealed that, on the one hand, the cultural immersion experience gave rise to positive feelings about native English speakers, and consequently, students were motivated to interact with and communicate with native speakers of English. On the other hand, the interaction and communication within the cultural setting built up students' positive attitudes toward native English speakers, and reinforced the students' use of the English language within this context. This result is in agreement with the conclusion of previous studies (e.g., Culhane & Kehoe, 2000), pointing to the favorable effect of learner-native speaker interaction in the target cultural setting on the learners' attitudes toward both the target culture and native speakers. Interactions and attitudes are reciprocal, in the sense that both influence each other, and they are found to have a mutually causal relationship in this study.

Learners also improved their attitudes toward the target culture and toward England in general. The persistence of these positive attitudes was evidenced by learners' heightened interest in all things London- or England-related, whether this meant a desire to further explore London virtually, or an expressed desire to visit London physically, in the real world. All four learners reported that they had never been particularly interested in visiting England before their exposure to London through Google Street View, nor had they ever seriously considered doing so before using the system. After taking the virtual trip, however, they had developed positive attitudes toward London and England, and were motivated to actually visit London in real life. In particular, interviews with Gran and Emma indicated that they paid closer attention to the 2012 Olympics since the games were held in London. Moreover, their excitement was heightened by their ability to recognize and identify locations they had visited virtually while watching TV coverage of the games.

Learner Development of an Ethnorelativistic View of Cultural Differences

The learners began to recognize aspects of the target culture, as well as the differences between the target culture and their own. Students showed themselves to be aware of the cultural differences. For example, "London is very different from Taipei because London has lots of traditional buildings . . . . There are no vendors in the park" (Huan, blog entry, 20120618). Huan went on to say, "I would like to have everything on the menu. They look so tasty to me, except the chicken liver... even in Taiwan I still don't like to eat liver". Similarly, in her blog, Emma also shared her opinions about the differences in the visual aspects of culture, like the appearances of the cities themselves: "I think London is more beautiful and picturesque than some modern cities like Taipei or Hong Kong" (Emma, blog entry, 20120604). Comments made by learners reveal an awareness of cultural differences in terms of the visible aspects of culture, like the food, the buildings, and the overall appearance of a city, as well as an appreciation of the target culture.

In addition to demonstrating their awareness of cultural differences in terms of the visible aspects, they showed an interest in further comparing their own culture and the target culture vis-à-vis the invisible aspects of culture, such as language symbols (e.g., royal titles), social issues (e.g., hierarchical social structures), and behaviors (e.g., being polite and reserved) associated with the cultural community members, as part of the cultural learning process.

The learners tended to view cultural differences in a positive light, and saw the target culture as being rich in resources that aided them in cross-cultural communication. In other words, they developed an ethnorelativist view of the cultural differences between the target culture and their own. It was their immersion in the target culture that fostered learners' ethnorelative attitudes toward it, and this immersion also contributed to their acceptance of cultural differences.

Influence of Attitudes on Behavior

Positive attitudes influenced students' behavior. Specifically, they were motivated to increase their contact with the target culture, both in terms of the people and the country itself. For instance, Huan mentioned in a post-event interview, "I still visited London virtually through the platform after the program [ended]." All of the students also demonstrated a greater desire to visit London physically and even spoke of plans to study English as a result of the increased contact. These results correspond to Garrett, Coupland and William's (2003) proposition that attitudes may be vital inputs and outputs in social action which affect behavior. Thus, attitude serves a double function, as both an outcome of cultural learning and as a cause of a behavioral change.

As mentioned previously, attitudes can be broken down into instrumental attitudes, which relate to personal *interests*, and symbolic attitudes, which refer to personal *values* (Herek, 1986, 2000). The results of this study show that learners developed both subsets of attitudes. In considering the target culture, learners' attitudes reflect their interest, positive feelings, perceptions and beliefs, attribution of value, and overall appreciation. For instance, Emma indicated,

But after touring, I know exactly what it's like. The excitement of seeing a different country without having to spend the money to go abroad also increases students' eagerness to want to learn more. All in all, this has been a great experience, and I've learned so much about London. I also appreciate it more than I ever have! [sic]. Now I want to go there and see it for myself. (Emma, blog entry, 20120618)

As a result of holding positive attitudes, learners were motivated to actively seek out more cultural information and resources, and to change their behavior, for example, in terms of increasing their contact, communication and interaction with (native) English speakers.

Attitudes toward Cultural Learning

Learning culture in this context appears to enhance positive attitudes toward cultural learning. Students reported positive feelings about the cultural learning environment, the topics, the cultural learning content, and the teaching methods. The blended learning environment represented by the integration of Google Street View, the virtual environment, and Web 2.0 tools (including YouTube and blogs), was regarded by the majority of participants in this study as a useful and effective tool for cultural learning. As Emma also indicated,

It's nice being able to tour London in a virtual reality world rather than just reading about it on the Internet, because I can actually see every detail. Today's tour was really good because everyone looked up information and told some stories and history about Westminster, the Thames, and the Bridges of London. (Emma, blog entry, 20120604)

Specifically, learners were impressed with the Google Street View virtual platform, which they described as "rich in cultural learning access and opportunity". They also had good things to say about the virtual tour that was made possible through exploring Google Street View. Emma indicated that the cultural immersive experience made a great impression on her, and infused her with an appreciation:

The very first tour we did left a big impression on me. I didn't know that through using Google Street View one could see cities so clearly, just like I was actually there! What's so much better about doing tours in Google Street View, instead of simply learning English through a book, is that by being able to see things for themselves, students relate better to new ideas, new words, and new cultures. (Emma, blog entry, 20120604)

The excerpt above also shows Emma's appreciation of the cultural immersion program, especially in comparison with the traditional cultural learning process in a classroom setting, "through a book," and "reading about it through the Internet." Her comments express her feeling that when it comes to cultural learning, textbooks cannot compete with learning through exposure to authentic cultural materials. This new way of learning through "naturalistic" settings, or in other words, cultural learning "in the virtual field", fosters student autonomy and motivation, and is more effective than the traditional methods (i.e., learning cultural elements within the textbook contents), as the learners themselves reported. The cultural immersion approach and the use of authentic materials, that is, objects contained in the Street View panorama, for teaching culture within the virtual context are appreciated and endorsed by the learners who underwent the real cultural experiences.

Our incorporation of Web 2.0 tools (including YouTube, wikis, and blogs) into the curriculum meant that learner engagement was prolonged, thus expanding the opportunity for communication and interaction with English speakers, cultural immersion, and cultural learning. For example, learners' explorations and travel experiences in the virtual world inspired them to look for more up-to-date information on British culture through the Internet as a follow-up. In the group interview, learners mentioned having more opportunities for both asynchronous discussion and interaction with target-language-speaking persons, and expressed the view that it was enjoyable to learn culture through communication and interaction with English speakers. Moreover, learners expressed an appreciation of the chance to enhance their cultural learning by communicating asynchronously through blogs. They also saw practical value in learning through cultural engagement and through acquiring additional cultural information using Web 2.0 tools, like wikis.

IMPLICATIONS AND CONCLUSION

The findings of this study have a number of important conclusions and implications for future practice. Firstly, cultural learning in the virtual field via the platform has been found to have a positive influence on attitudes toward the target culture, persons, country, and cultural learning, and the development of an ethnorelativistic view of cultural differences. The platform offers an alternative for teachers who want to incorporate authentic materials into their teaching. Today, classrooms and textbooks are still central to cultural learning and language education, even though textbooks only provide a discrete cultural picture that is "a snapshot, and only one of many through which the culture could be explored and understood" (Kramsch & McConnell-Ginet, 1992, as cited in Paige, Jorstad, Siaya, Klein, & Colby, 2003, p. 40). The platform provides a natural and holistic approach toward cultural learning and teaching.

Secondly, the learners appreciated the cultural elements and learning content within the various contexts of the program, and seemed to enjoy the dynamic and interactive cultural learning methods. Their experiences in the virtual field comprised cultural immersion and cultural learning through interacting with target-language-speaking persons, virtual objects, and authentic materials. The system also enabled learners to interact using the real language and gain experience with the target culture, as mediated by the system and the native English speakers.

Thirdly, the combination of Google Street View and a virtual environment, linked with YouTube and blogs, helped the learners to elaborate, reflect, and extend their ideas and experiences gained in the virtual world, and their group relationships beyond the timeframe of the events held in the virtual world. This combination of technological tools created an ideal situation for learner autonomy as well as for language and cultural learning by doing, participating and interacting. By using blogs, the learners were able to fully express themselves and their autonomy.

Finally, the integration of immersive virtual environment and Web 2.0 tools promoted greater opportunities to form a community of practice, and shaped students' identities as English users and members of a cultural community as they participated in the virtual events and in the virtual community of practice, developed during the ongoing interaction process. A strong sense of cultural community enhanced interactions, commitment, mutual support, and a willingness to share thoughts, ideas and feelings among members. Furthermore, group dynamics were facilitated through prolonged cultural simulation and engagement.

The results echo those of previous studies of the effects of cultural learning in the field or via the experience of studying abroad on cultural learning, for instance, in terms of the development of positive attitudes toward the host or target culture (e.g., Armstrong, 1984; Hansel, 1985; Tsai, 2011). This cultural learning environment integrates a 3D virtual world platform and Google Street View in an attempt to optimize the strengths of both cultural immersion and interaction with culture-authentic materials. This research will serve as a basis for future practice of contextual cultural immersion in virtual environments, and can inform future studies on the application of these technologies to language learning and acquisition. There is still a great deal of opportunity for research into contextual and experiential language learning in this innovative setting.

Familiarizing visitors with any given culture through the experience of virtual travel before they physically encounter it can provide visitors with necessary background formation, and allows them to understand the local people's values, thoughts, feelings, and actions, without being obtrusive. This research demonstrates how the proposed system can be used to situate learners in cultural immersion and virtual travel settings, simulating what learners could expect to encounter in "real view" if they actually visited the locale. The opportunity to practice in the virtual world provides learners with information and simulated experiences, for instance, giving them transportation guidance and travel directions to facilitate real travel in the city. In terms of general practice, user immersion via these technologies opens up possibilities for those considering studying abroad or planning trips to foreign destinations, regardless of their motivations for traveling. Virtual travel can simulate actual travel by allowing users of the proposed system to walk through what is essentially a preview of the target country and culture. Future studies can explore the effects of virtual travel on travelers' experiences, in terms of their understanding the target country and culture, to see whether or not virtual travel facilitates subsequent real travel or makes it easier for travelers to enter the target community.

ACKNOWLEDGMENT

This research has been heavily supported by a grant from the Taiwan National Science Council.

REFERENCES

Anzai, S., Dobberfuhl, P., Matsuzawa, C., & Zimmerman, E. (2008). *Students' cultural knowledge and attitudes before and after studying abroad: Engineering majors in Japan*. Retrieved March 21, 2013, from http://www.unc.edu/clac/documents/presentations/Anzai_Dobberfuhl_Matsuzawa_Zimmerman%20CLAC%202008.pdf

Armstrong, G. K. (1984). Life after study abroad: A survey of undergraduate academic and career choices. *Modern Language Journal*, *68*, 1–6. doi:10.1111/j.1540-4781.1984.tb01535.x.

Avatar Languages. (n.d.). *Google street view for language learning: A guide for teachers*. Retrieved March 21, 2013, from http://www.avatarlanguages.com/teaching/streetview.pdf

Blue Mars Lite. (n.d.). *Blue mars lite: Street view chat*. Retrieved March 21, 2013, from http://create.bluemars.com/wiki/index.php/Blue_Mars_Lite:_Street_View_Chat

Byram, M. (1997). *Teaching and assessing intercultural communicative competence*. Clevedon, UK: Multilingual Matters.

Culhane, S. F., & Kehoe, J. (2000). The effects of an anti-racist role-play program. *Polyglossia*, *3*, 1–8.

Damen, L. (1987). *Culture learning: The fifth dimension in the language classroom*. Reading, MA: Addision-Wesley. Retrieved March 21, 2013, from http://people.ict.usc.edu/~lane/papers/Lane-Ogan-CATS09-VirtualEnvironmentsForCultural-Learning.pdf

Garrett, P. B., Coupland, N., & William, H. (2003). *Investigating language attitudes*. Cardiff, UK: University of Wales.

Google Maps Street View. (n.d.). *Explore the world at street level*. Retrieved March 21, 2013, from http://maps.google.com/intl/en/help/maps/streetview/#utm_campaign=en&utm_medium=van&utm_source=en-van-na-us-gns-svn

Hansel, B. G. (1985). *The impact of a sojourn abroad: A study of secondary school students participating in a foreign exchange program (culture learning, contact travel, educational)*. (Unpublished doctoral dissertation). Syracuse University, New York, NY.

Henderson, J., Fishwick, P., Fresh, E., Futterknecht, F., & Hamilton, B. D. (2008). Immersive learning simulation environment for Chinese culture. In *Proceedings of Interservice/Industry Training, Simulation, and Education Conference*. IITSEC.

Herek, G. M. (1986). The instrumentality of attitudes: Toward a neofunctional theory. *The Journal of Social Issues*, *42*(2), 99–114. doi:10.1111/j.1540-4560.1986.tb00227.x.

Herek, G. M. (2000). The social construction of attitudes: Functional consensus and divergence in the US public's reactions to AIDS. In Maio, G. R., & Olson, J. M. (Eds.), *Why we evaluate: Functions of attitudes* (pp. 325–364). Mahwah, NJ: Lawrence Erlbaum.

Johnson, W. L., & Valente, A. (2008). Tactical language and culture training systems: Using artificial intelligence to teach foreign languages and cultures. In *Proceedings of Innovative Applications of Artificial Intelligence*. IEEE.

Kramsch, C., & McConnell-Ginet, S. (1992). (Con)textual knowledge in language education. In Kramsch, C., & McConnell-Ginet, S. (Eds.), *Text and context: Cross-disciplinary perspectives on language study*. Lexington, MA: Heath & Co..

Lafayette, R. C., & Schultz, R. A. (1975). Evaluating culture learning. In Lafayette, R. C. (Ed.), *The cultural revolution in foreign languages: A guide for building the modern curriculum* (pp. 104–118). Lincolnwood, IL: National Textbook Company.

Lafayette, R. C., & Schultz, R. A. (1997). Evaluating cultural learning. In Heusinkveld, P. R. (Ed.), *Pathways to culture* (pp. 577–594). Yarmouth, ME: Intercultural Press.

Lane, H. C., & Ogan, A. (2009). *Virtual learning environments for culture*. Retrieved March 21, 2013, from http://people.ict.usc.edu/~lane/papers/Lane-Ogan-CATS09-VirtualEnvironmentsFor-CulturalLearning.pdf

Miles, M., & Huberman, A. M. (1994). *Qualitative data analysis*. Thousand Oaks, CA: Sage Publications.

O'Reilly, T. (2005). What is web 2.0. *O'Reilly Network*. Retrieved March 21, 2013, from http://www.oreillynet.com/pub/a/oreilly/tim/news/2005/09/30/what-is-Web-20.html

Ogan, A., & Lane, H. C. (2009). Virtual learning environments for culture and intercultural competence. In Blanchard, E., & Allard, D. (Eds.), *Handbook of Research on Culturally-Aware Information Technology: Perspectives and Models*. Hershey, PA: IGI Global.

Paige, R. M., Jorstad, H. L., Siaya, L., Klein, F., & Colby, J. (2003). Culture learning in language education: A review of the literature. In Lange, D. L., & Paige, R. M. (Eds.), *Culture as the core: Perspectives on culture in second language learning* (pp. 173–236). Raleigh, NC: Information Age Publishing.

Raybourn, E. M., Deagle, E., Mendini, K., & Heneghan, J. (2005), Adaptive thinking & leadership simulation game training for special forces officers. In *Proceedings, Interservice/Industry Training, Simulation and Education Conference*. IITSEC.

Scarino, A., & Liddicoat, A. J. (2009). *Teaching and learning languages: A guide*. Melbourne, Australia: Curriculum Corporation. Retrieved March 21, 2013, from http://www.tllg.unisa.edu.au/lib_guide/gllt_ch2.pdf

Sykes, J. (2008). *A dynamic approach to social interaction: Synthetic immersive environments and Spanish pragmatics*. (Unpublished doctoral dissertation). University of Minnesota, Minneapolis, MN.

Tsai, Y. (2011). Attitudes: A role in the reflection of intercultural learning outcomes. *International Journal of Innovative Interdisciplinary Research*, *1*, 139–149.

ADDITIONAL READING

Baldwin, J. R., Faulkner, S. L., Hecht, M. L., & Lindsley, S. L. (Eds.). (2006). *Redefining culture: Perspectives across the disciplines*. Mahwah, NJ: Lawrence Erlbaum Associates.

Brooks, N. (1968). Teaching culture in the foreign language classroom. *Foreign Language Annals, 1*, 204-217. Retrieved March 21, 2013, from http://www.eric.ed.gov/ERICWebPortal/search/detailmini.jsp?_nfpb=true&_&ERICExtSearch_SearchValue_0=ED022388&ERICExtSearch_SearchType_0=no&accno=ED022388

Brooks, N. (1975). The analysis of foreign and familiar cultures. In Lafayette, R. (Ed.), *The Culture Revolution in Foreign Language Teaching*. Skokie, IL: National Textbook Company.

Byram, M., & Morgan, C. (1994). *Teaching-and-learning language-and-culture*. Clevedon, UK: Multilingual Matters.

Halverson, R. J. (1985). Culture and vocabulary acquisition: A proposal. *Foreign Language Annals, 18*(4), 327–332. doi:10.1111/j.1944-9720.1985.tb01810.x.

Kramsch, C. (1993). *Context and culture in language teaching*. Oxford, UK: Oxford University Press.

Levy, J. (1995). Intercultural design. In Fowler, S. M. (Ed.), *Intercultural sourcebook: Cross-cultural training methods* (pp. 1–15). Yarmouth, ME: Intercultural Press.

Liddicoat, A. J. (2005). Culture for language learning in Australian language-in-education policy. *Australian Review of Applied Linguistics, 28*(2), 1–28.

Lo Bianco, J. (2003). Culture: Visible, invisible and multiple. In Lo Bianco, J., & Crozet, C. (Eds.), *Teaching invisible culture: Classroom practice and theory* (pp. 11–38). Melbourne, Australia: Language Australia Ltd..

Moore, J. (1991). *An analysis of the cultural content of post-secondary textbooks for Spanish: Evidence of information processing strategies and types of learning in reading selections and post-reading adjunct questions*. (Unpublished doctoral dissertation). University of Minnesota, Minneapolis, MN.

Nostrand, H. L. (1974). Empathy for a second culture: Motivations and techniques. In Jarvis, G. A. (Ed.), *Responding to new realities* (pp. 263–327). Skokie, IL: National Textbook.

Omaggio Hadley, A. (1993). *Teaching language in context* (2nd ed.). Boston: Heinle & Heinle.

Robins, R. W. (2005). Psychology: The nature of personality: Genes, culture and national character. *Science, 310*(5745), 62–63. doi:10.1126/science.1119736 PMID:16210523.

Street, B. V. (1993). Culture is a verb. In Graddol, D. et al. (Eds.), *Language and culture* (pp. 23–42). London: BAAL and Multilingual Matters.

KEY TERMS AND DEFINITIONS

Blue Mars Lite: Blue Mars Lite © is a registered trademark of Avatar Reality, Inc. It incorporates Google Street View into the 3D virtual world platform, and includes a feature named "Street View Chat."

Cultural Learning: Cultural learning comprises three domains: cognitive learning, behavioral learning, and affective learning (Paige et al., 2003).

English as a Foreign Language (EFL): Refers to situations where English is taught to people who learn the language for different reasons in non-English-speaking countries.

Google Street View: Google Maps with Street View enable users to discover real locations via 360-degree street-level imagery.

Virtual Environment (VE): The acronym for *virtual environment*. VEs, typically built in Virtual Reality Modeling Language (VRML), are created to support multi-user collaboration and interaction, regardless of distance, and currently enjoy widespread use in educational settings. Participants are embodied as avatars, and can use chat boxes and/or voice chat to communicate with others within VEs.

Panorama: A panorama is a 360-degree view of a physical space in a 3D model. Google Street View provides panoramic 360-degree views of indicated locations.

Web 2.0: The term "Web 2.0" originates from "a brainstorming session between O'Reilly and MediaLive International" (O'Reilly, 2005). Web 2.0, including Web applications, such as blogs, wikis, and video-sharing Web sites, is used to foster collaboration, interaction, communication and information sharing on the World Wide Web.

Chapter 13
How Digital Media like TED Talks Are Revolutionizing Teaching and Student Learning

Gladys Palma de Schrynemakers
Long Island University – Brooklyn, USA

ABSTRACT

Launched in 1984, Technology, Entertainment, and Design (TED) Talks was successfully developed and implemented as a practical way to bring recognized experts together to discuss the latest developments and improve communication and collaboration across these fields. From its embryonic beginning, TED Talks has today expanded exponentially and is now a multi-media vehicle for delivering pioneering work to a global audience. For faculty wishing to bring user-friendly, cutting-edge research and ideas to the classroom, it can be an exciting teaching tool because students can draw from the real life experiences of outstanding professionals who are trailblazers in their fields. This chapter presents assignments that were created using TED Talks and provides a template that can be used to create unique assignments that are compatible with the needs and goals of the course. The template is designed to help faculty craft a learning experience that is embedded in an encouraging environment for innovative approaches and student involvement—where specific student learning objectives exist, along with approaches to assess student learning.

STUDENT LEARNING IN THE 21ST CENTURY

Recently, faculty at my institution, Long Island University/Brooklyn, were engaged in a rather lively discussion about students not doing the assigned class readings and all too often being distracted by their various digital devices. The conversations further escalated to the usual assumption, namely, that many students today are not committed to their education. In such dialogues, two things immediately strike me. First, they seem to occur all the time and not just at my institution, but in many institutions across New York State, where likeminded faculty purport that technology is somehow robbing children in K-12 and college students of their intellectual capacity and somehow responsible for their academic deficiencies. Second, almost all of their *a priori* conjectures concerning the effectiveness and practicality of technology in teaching and learning are the result of unexamined and untested hypotheses and assumptions about how today's students learn. Although there is no direct evidence

DOI: 10.4018/978-1-4666-4462-5.ch013

supporting the notion that technology is antithetical to learning, the discussion nevertheless has advanced into popular literature. For example, in the November 2009 article in Psychology Today, entitled *Is Technology Making Us Dumber?*, the author waxes nostalgic about the good old days of academia, when students knew things because they read "real" books. All these reputed concepts and theories bring home John Dewey's contention in *Democracy and Education* (1966): "If we teach today as we taught yesterday we rob our children of tomorrow." What those who deliver education today throughout the academy need to recognize and adopt is an important practical lesson—our students often communicate best in a familiar digital environment that provides an increasingly richer context for learning. I hasten to emphasize that the inherited teaching methods of the past are not suitable for students now in an age where information exponentially increases at decreasing intervals. If the focus is student learning, as it should be, then it becomes critically important to challenge our students and foster their learning and to do so in ways that promote their personal development. Keeling and Hersh, in *We're Losing Our Minds* (2011), encounter colleges and universities today with the same mode of reasoning, that is, existing just as repositories of knowledge, and their only job is to transmit this knowledge to students. The authors passionately argue that this form of education generates passive non-engagement, and that is why employers are dissatisfied with our graduates, who are often unable to compete effectively in the global market. The premise has been presented in other recent texts like Richard Arum's (2010) controversial *Academically Adrift* and Andrew DelBanco's *College What It Was, Is and Should Be* (2012), all calling for reform in higher education that moves students from simply being "blank slates" to participating in a dialectic that allows them to make associations between material within and across disciplines; as a result, students will be able to think critically about those connections and learn how to problem solve using these various understandings.

Noted columnist Malcolm Freidman and foreign policy professor Michael Mendelbaum, in their recent book, *That Used to be Us* (2011), outline four major issues facing America today, two of which focus on globalization and the instructive power of information technology; however, they recognize that the American educational system is not preparing students to perform in the global arena or to use technology effectively, that is, to elevate all aspects of student learning in an environmental setting familiar to learners. This apparent struggle in the academy, namely, to engage students in a curriculum that appreciates the value of technology in an interconnected world, will be at the heart of how America will fare in the 21st century. Freidman and Mendelbaum are blunt when they opine:

As a country we have not yet adapted to this new reality. We don't think of education as an investment in national growth and national security because throughout our history it has been a localized, decentralized issue, not a national one. Today, however, what matters is not how your local school ranks in its county or state but how America's schools rank in the world (pp. 101-102).

Mark Taylor, like others who agree with this view, points out that:

... new media and communication technologies have triggered explosive growth in the amount of information to which people have ready access. Not only is the quantity of information growing, its substance is also changing. This has important implications for the reorganization of knowledge and, by extension, higher education (p. 112).

The higher education community can no longer assume that long accepted forms of teaching and delivery of information are going to be effective in connecting students to and preparing them for this increasingly changing educational landscape. Coupling inherited pedagogies with traditional modes of learning is no longer successful for the average student in the twenty-first century, where the culture is dominated by the extraordinary growth in information and its accessibility. The academy is uniquely positioned to provide a variety of media, most likely already familiar to students, which can serve as multisensory and multidisciplinary technological resources to be integrated into their formal scholastic experience.

HOW STUDENTS USE TECHNOLOGY TO LEARN

It is understandable that today's students, particularly those who wish to be imaginative and synthetic thinkers, do not conform to the guidelines of the past but instead look to technology as the new way of learning. Increasingly, students today are not learning from print material, as noted by Richard Miller, from Rutger's Writer's House in his You Tube video, *This is How We Think: Learning in Public After the Paradigm Shift*. Therein, he addresses a so-called Network Centric Paradigm for human communication, a recognized shift in the 21st century, where learning goes beyond print to include visuals and other interactive media that individually and collectively will change the dynamic of learning. Once that interaction is changed, the teaching and learning relationship between faculty and student must also change. Faculty like Miller are interested in reconfiguring their teaching in the humanities, English, and writing, specifically to help students be able to construct meaning in an age of information overload. Robert J. Lifton, in his text *The Protean Self* (1999), describes the impact of this age of change on the individual:

We are becoming fluid and many-sided. Without quite realizing it, we have been evolving a send of self-appropriate to the restlessness and flux of our time. This mode of being differs radically from that of the past, and enables us to engage in continuous exploration and personal experiment. (p. 1)

Lifton likens this new condition to Proteus from Greek mythology and refers to this state as the Protean Self and further asserts:

Though variation is the essence of the protean self, that self has certain relatively consistent features. Central to its function is a capacity for bringing together disparate and seemingly incompatible elements of identity and involvement in what I call 'odd combinations,' and for continuous transformation of these elements (p. 5).

This fluidity and constant change may create a sense of fragmentation in students. Moreover, it may also create in them an inability to understand and thread together the many disparate forms of information from print, media, social media, technology, and their educational experiences. Miller asserts that that is the new role of faculty, specifically in the humanities, to provide a framework of understanding that helps students create ways in which these seemingly disparate and ever changing types of information can be understood.

A facilitator of knowledge in a digital learning environment is often a role that many faculty find unfamiliar and even intimidating because their academic environment was one of printed text, disciplinary specificity, and expertise in one area developed over a lifetime of research and collegial interactions at academic conferences. Now they are being asked to be enablers and to expedite learning in a nontraditional setting where information and knowledge are being derived from multiple disciplines and funneled through a myriad of technological platforms at dizzying speeds and volumes. For many in the academy, this is a daunting task that requires a paradigm shift in the way teaching and learning can be accomplished efficiently, successfully, and realistically for students who have become adapted to a world where technology is often their first resource for information. This conclusion is supported by the Educause Center for Applied Research (ECAR) Study of Information Technology, which, in 2012, reported that 75% of students state that technology will help them achieve their academic outcomes. Other relevant data from the same report show that 53% of those participating prefer that their instructors interact face-to-face and through a course management system, while 45% preferred interaction through e-mail or by text messaging (Dahlstrom, 2012).

The new reality is becoming more evident, that the days of faculty simply lecturing and holding office hours are practices of the past that have outlived their efficacy. Even so, the use of technology is not meant to replace the important face-to-face interactions between faculty and their students but to allow for multiple ways of creating opportunities to engage in instruction and learning that go beyond the classroom into a worldwide arena where students become engaged learners. In large measure, this accounts for the success of blended learning models, where technology is a key component of instruction and education and where learning becomes natural through the use, in part, of digital texts and media. ECAR's 2012 study further notes that in the blended environment, "Technology is important to students in terms of how they access course materials and how instructors use technology to engage them in the learning process" (p. 7). In fact, "they expect their instructors to seamlessly integrate technology into their pedagogical practices" (p. 7). This is very different from the recent past, when professors basically used technology as a supplemental tool. Power Point presentations and Clickers are not the only pedagogical supports that elevate student learning and draw learners to participate in discovering their educational opportunities. Today's students are a part of a multi-modular approach to learning, where information arrives digitally from diverse sources and is shared in a variety of ways. The challenge then is to help students create their own practices for organizing and integrating the delivery of information through the new technology so that learning becomes an exercise that is effortless and open.

TED'S MEMETIC TRANSFORMATION

Technology, Entertainment, and Design (TED) started as conferences that were designed to share ideas in a global arena with the hope that the three areas named in its title would become an umbrella for almost any topic. The conferences traditionally feature about 50 speakers, hosting one conference in California and one in Scotland. Speakers come from every field and have included North American presidents, scientists, and artists, who have won every imaginable award. The presenters are given a checklist to prepare their remarks for TED Talks, which must be no longer than 20 minutes and engage the audience through the use of media, technology, or whatever the presenter needs—except Power Points are not allowed.

Today, TED Talks is available on almost any topic and is free online. The topics range from cutting edge technology to the teaching of mathematics to almost any topic of interest we can imagine. A visit to the TED Talks Website http://www.ted.com/ is like stepping into a multidisciplinary and interdisciplinary candy shop for idea junkies. It can be invaluable to any instructor who is interested in infusing curriculum with cutting edge research presented by leaders in the field. The format allows instructors to include these treasures in a multitude of ways into their courses; for example, they can serve as mini-lectures to introduce a topic or as an embedded part of an assignment, where students first view a presentation and then are asked to integrate the piece as a reference in a larger project. (This instructor has also used TED Talks as part of blog assignments.)

HOW TECHNOLOGY IS MOVING FROM AN EDUCATIONAL TOOL TO TRANSFORMATIVE PEDAGOGY

Khanna and Khanna (2012, p. 54) write about a "Hybrid Age," one that replaces the technological age, when technology was simply a tool for learning and functioning. They conclude that "…the "Hybrid Age" is a new sociotechnical era that is unfolding as technologies merge with each other and humans merge with technology—both at the same time." As in any new era marked by significant changes—like the Renaissance, the Industrial Revolution, and the Age of Technology—there occur paradigm shifts that provide a mix of theoretical and practical perspectives for managing a world in transition. For example, the Internet became a household word in the 1990s, but it was not until the first definitive search engine, Google, was available in 1998 that the Internet became an extraordinarily important tool. The term Google is derived from the word Googol, a mathematical designation for the number one followed by 100 zeros—which explains why those responsible for coining the Internet name selected it, namely, to describe a search engine capable of organizing and presenting vast amounts of information. (Google, n.d.) Google not only proved to be a comprehensive and transformative resource for acquiring and retrieving information, but it also resulted in the evolution of a new vocabulary and new perceptions for constructing meaning. Khanna and Khanna (2012) write about this paradigm shift, loosely characterizing it as "coevolution," because the ongoing changes in technology have prompted changes in how humans use technology, for example, through mobile devices, social networks, or learning about complex and immerging theories through TED Talks. Khanna and Khanna (2002) are convinced that what they have identified as an emerging historical trend and called a "Hybrid Era" will eventually inform and advance our view of knowledge into a more multifaceted, connected view of the world. In fact, it is already happening: scanning the offerings on the TED Talks Website will quickly lead to the recognition that cutting-edge and, at times, world-altering ideas are being promulgated by a global community, representing almost every country and not limited by ethnicity, gender, or race.

Moreover, in their paper, *Forms of Literacy Development with Technology in the College Years* (2002), Langer and Kenfelkamp present a notion of a:

Technology Arc [that] serves to address the dilemma of operating within a more dynamic educational system that needs to respond quicker to changes brought on by technology. Providing students with the necessary computer skills are important, but developing a method of measuring an individual's growth and maturity with cultural literacies is critical if institutions of higher education are to meet the ongoing demands of a more dynamic and multicultural society (pp. 5-6).

Langer and Kenefelkamp and Khanna and Khanna write about the synergism that prevails between technology and the learner, a connection that Howard Gardner, in his *Five Minds for the Future* (2008), aptly describes as conceptualizing knowledge in two ways. More specifically, Gardner sees the synthesizing mind involved in "selecting crucial information from the copious amounts available; [and thereafter], arraying that information in ways that make sense to self and others" (p. 155). At the heart of this "mind" is an individual's capacity to integrate new information to one's own knowledge base to expand that base. Similarly, Dewey (1933), like most constructivists, understood that synthesizing requires of learners an ability to understand what they "… see…in its relations to other things: to note how it operates or functions, what consequences follow from it, what cause it" (p. 137). Gardner's "Creating Mind," is compatible with the ideas of Khanna and Khanna vis-à-vis the evolutionary character of this era, when observing that the creating mind:

[goes] beyond existing knowledge and syntheses to pose new questions, offer new solutions, fashion new works that stretch existing genres or configures new ones; creation builds on one or more established disciplines and requires an

informed "field" to make judgments of quality and acceptability (p. 156).

Faculty must recognize that a new framework for informing teaching and learning is finding a place of importance in higher education, that technology is no longer simply a teaching tool but an emerging methodology that engages students in ways that are comprehensive and easy to use. New platforms that incorporate digital media like TED Talks inculcate disciplinary knowledge and, at the same time, offer new ways of applying that knowledge to a larger, more complex arena.

TED Talks, in many ways, is an effective medium platform for creating a synergistic learning environment for students. Ted Wagner, author of *The Global Achievement Gap and Learning to Innovate, Innovating to Learn*, developed an excellent construct for how to improve the educational experience of students. Wagner presents a construct that he calls the three Cs—critical thinking, effective oral and written communication, and collaboration (Wagner, 2010).

Creating assignments using TED Talks can be used as a model to illustrate Wagner's three C's. During any given TED Talks, presenters introduce a topic from a disciplinary lens and within 20 minutes effectively communicate the content of the topic within the discipline; also, they relate the topic to other disciplines and to its relevance in the global community. As part of these presentations, the speakers clearly articulate their thinking, most times bringing new insights into the mix, and how their analyses have assisted them at arriving at new ideas, hypotheses, or theories.

TED Talks engages students by contextualizing real-world issues through an engaging digital visual narrative that often is delivered through a storyline that can be paused and replayed, much like the media they experience in their non-academic lives. Storytelling, e.g., oral history, is a sociable and practical exercise for exchanging ideas and sharing new insights that has served human beings since they started speaking. It is through hearing different narratives and then partaking in a dialogue about said narratives that students begin to engage in a productive and deep understanding that goes beyond mere memorization and recall of information. Alice Walker, writing about the importance of hearing multiple perspectives to achieve a richer and more complex understanding of the world, views everyone as authors, contributing to a shared text. For example, in her book, *In Search of Our Mother's Garden,* she writes:

I believe that the truth about any subject only comes when all sides of the story are put together, and all their different meanings make one new one. Each writer writes the missing parts to the other writer's story. And the whole story is what I am after (Walker, 1983, p. 49).

This shared understanding becomes approachable through digital media like TED Talks—which may well turn out to be the narrative arena for the 21st century—that engage students in learning activities that are at the core of our educational mission. Faculty members creating learning environments that employ as their springboards dynamic and innovative ways for students to make sense of complex and current issues is a clear and practical application worthy of pursuit. Doing so will engage students to reflect on the nature of social change and prepare them to be effective citizens in the ever-shifting landscape of this new century.

CREATING A TEMPLATE FOR LEARNING USING TED TALKS

Higher Education today is immersed in another transformative process that reflects a shift recognizing the value of measuring and assessing student learning to identify what knowledge and skills students require to advance their development as responsible citizens and in their careers. Where traditionally there was an emphasis in the relationship between faculty and content, now the focus is on the content and students—which goes beyond simply receiving a grade. One way to ensure that a clear connection exists between digital and print content and student learning is to construct a template that plans for intentional learning. Experiences that are deliberate and are designed to assist students in constructing knowledge are at the center of the learning template. The ability to make transparent learning points allows students to see the various components or multiple perspectives involved in understanding a topic; this creates an environment for intentional learning. It is no longer Locke's idea that prevails, where students are *tabula rasa*—Latin for clean slate—for teachers to fill with knowledge. Intentional learning involves students in not only learning about the content, but also about critical and contributory underlying elements, thereby making it straightforward for them to connect that knowledge and those skills to effective strategies for a broad array of life experiences.

When instructors are creating a topic, unit, etc., they should begin by laying out the elements to see all the components of the learning. For example, instructors might consider a graphic representation that the author created (see Figure 1.)

The Learning Template (Figure 1) acts as a framework to help instructors design assignments that link student learning objectives to actual learning experiences, e.g., readings, explorations, discussions, etc., and to the tools used to measure the efficacy of the learning. At the core of assessment of student learning are well-articulated learning objectives that focus on what accomplishments are expected of the learner upon completing a learning unit or section of the course. Because learning objectives usually contain words like "the student will be able to synthesize, analyze," instructors will be able to judge whether students have met the requirements of the course through systematic measurements that are rubric driven.

The learning experience may be varied, e.g., viewing a TED Talks, reading materials, writing a digital text, or blogging based on a prompt, and much more. It is, to a large extent, whatever activity the instructor designs to relay the content to the student; however, the experience(s) should result in the construction of some student artifact, e.g., a digital essay, a blog, an exam, an oral presentation, etc. Of course, it is of critical importance that this embedded medium-supplemented format of instruction engage students and help them reach their educational goals. In other words, instructors must assess the efficacy of this teaching design through the use of measures.

The measure is used to evaluate if students have achieved the learning objective set forth in

Figure 1. Learning template (Schrynemakers, 2012)

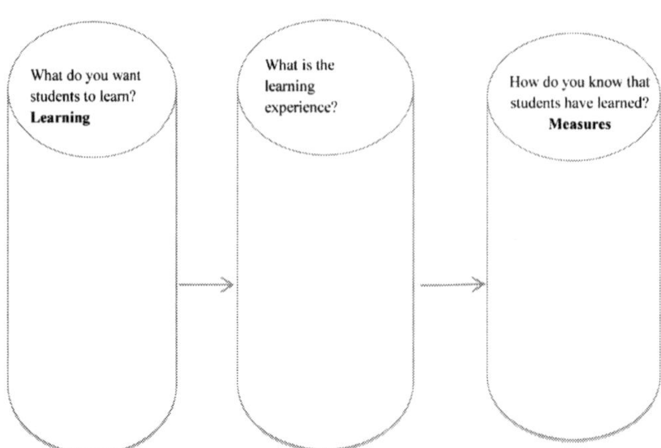

the curriculum or for a specific activity. If well designed, the measure can provide the instructor with invaluable data about what specific learning challenges students are experiencing. Usually, measures include rubrics related to a variety of learning experiences, including essays, papers, performances, etc. More specifically, a rubric, "...is a matrix that explicitly states the criteria and standards for student work. It identifies the traits that are important and describes levels of permanence within each of the traits" (Walvoord,, 2010 p. 81).

Herein is a graphic template (Figure 2) that incorporates digital media, literacy, and assessment. The purposes of this template are to illustrate the connections among the three aforementioned elements—learning objectives, learning experiences, and measures—and how they can be used to help students accomplish their educational goal in learning arena that foster's Wagner's three C's: critical thinking, written communication, and collaboration. The template, which was designed to craft assignments for minority students enrolled in a weekly science seminar, includes academic goals that were very similar to Wagner's three C's. The digital medium, specifically TED Talks, was the interactive vehicle selected for the class. Used first as a form of motivation, it soon became an essential part of the content and the way in which students made connections throughout the weekly unit. The seminars had specific learning goals and objectives.

Overall Learning Goals

- **Critical Thinking:** Students will have the ability to identify, reflect upon, evaluate, integrate, and apply different types of information and knowledge to form independent judgments. Students experience writing and other critical thinking processes as a way to learn.
- **Complexity:** Students will be exposed to an approach to understanding scientific knowledge that distinguishes between ambiguity, nuance, clarity, and precision.
- **Communication:** Students will be required to communicate scientific concepts and experiments effectively through writing protocols and oral presentations; moreover, they will be asked to contextualize their own ideas and those of others using rhetorical analysis, logical reasoning, and information literacy.

Figure 2. Learning template (Schrynemakers, 2012)

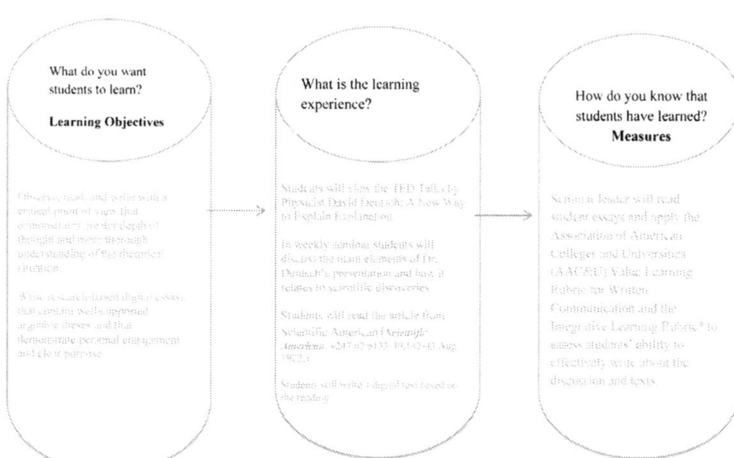

Learning Objectives

- Observe, read, and write with a critical point of view that demonstrates greater depth of thought and more thorough understanding of the rhetorical situation.
- Write research-based digital essays that contain well-supported arguable theses and that demonstrate personal engagement and clear purpose.
- Locate, select, and appropriately use and cite evidence that is ample, creditable, and smoothly integrated into an intellectual position.
- Analyze the rhetorical differences, both constraints and possibilities, of different modes of presentations.
- Reflect more deeply upon the writing process as a mode of thinking and learning that can be specific to the scientific range of writing and thinking tasks.

Herein are samples of students' work that resulted from the Learning Template (see Figure 2).

Scientific Prompt about Reading and TED Talk

Galileo challenged an existing scientific model within a specific political climate. The state used this model to justify its own authority. How did Galileo's theory threaten the established religious, scientific, social and political order? What was the crucial difference between Copernicus' and Galileo's model?

Response #1

Galileo Galilei challenged the Bible's claim that the earth was at the center of the universe. He claimed, like Copernicus, that the universe was heliocentric, or that the sun was the center of the universe and the rest of the planets revolved around it. In turn, Galileo was trialed for heresy since "There was widespread agreement that the truth resided not in astronomy but in the Bible" (Gingerich 134)" during that time. Galileo not only challenged the church's religious teachings, but he also combatted the scientific, social and political structure of his time. By doing so, he paved the way for a new analytical way of thinking in which he based his conclusions on researched topics, instead of using the Bible to support his claims. Galileo's method is known as the "hypothetico-deductive method", where one tests a hypothesis and continues to test it until it becomes more and more convincing (Gingerich 137). His new method of thinking influenced other scientists to not rely solely on beliefs passed down to them, but to question and find answers to their questions themselves.

Galileo challenged Roman Catholic religious beliefs by contradicting the structure of the universe depicted in the Bible. His work was condemned by the church for it undermined the teaching the church had been preaching to its followers for years. It was difficult for the church to accept Galileo's claim because it threatened their power. As a leading power figure, the Roman Catholic Church could not afford to be outwitted by a mere astronomer. Interestingly enough, it became quite obvious that the church's qualm with Galileo was not so much due to his theory, but on his method of arriving at the theory. Gingerich states:

"the Copernican system was not really the issue. The battleground was the method itself, the route to sure knowledge of the world, the question of whether The Book of Nature could in any way rival the inerrant Book of Scripture as an avenue to truth" (Gingerich 137).

Gingerich describes Galileo's method of analytical thinking as "the route of sure knowledge of the world" which emphasizes that for years, the church's followers were led blindly by their religious leaders following the religious teaching in the Bible. The concern of the church was not Galileo's heliocentric claim, but that if proven wrong by one man, its followers would question the validity of the church and all of its teachings.

Due to the social climate of the time, Galileo's teachings were more prone to criticism by the church. The church was suffering from opposition that began in the 1500s. During the time of the Reformation, Copernicus made his heliocentric claim, but it was not deemed heresy by the church since the church had greater concerns, such as Martin Luther's condemning the church for indulgences in 1517. Luther's opposition to the church proved to have a lasting effect on the church's efforts to regain the trust of its people. In 1542, Pope Paul III passed the Holy Roman and Universal Inquisition. In the 1570s, the Index of Prohibited Books was passed, which listed texts deemed inappropriate by the church, and lastly, in 1616, Galileo published *The Starry Messenger*, which restated the heliocentric theory. Galileo's mistake was that he chose to speak out about his theory during a time when the church was seeking to regain its power and image (The Counter-Reformation), so that any claim that opposed the church would spark instant scrutiny by the church.

The major difference between Copernicus' and Galileo's model is that Copernicus' model was never deemed heresy, for he presented it during a time when the church had other matters on its mind. Unfortunately for Galileo, he spoke up during a stressful climate for the church. This, in turn, worked against him and he was censored. The power remained at the hands of the church and the church did everything it could to make sure that it remained that way. Nevertheless, we now know that Galileo's claim was correct. It was his method of hypothetical and analytical thinking which set the path for how scientists and researchers come about concluding their works.

Response # 2

In the article "The Galileo Affair", Galileo's cosmology embraced the theory of Heliocentric Copernican system which was stated that by rearranging the planetary orbs, the sun was at the center of the universe with the other planets and earth revolving around it. The fastest planet Mercury had the orbit closest to the sun, the slowest planet Saturn was the outside and the planets betweens were placed in the order of their periods. Not only did Galileo embrace the Copernican system but also he challenged an existing scientific model of Geocentrism which stated that the earth was being at the center and the other planets including the sun were revolving around the earth. He challenged that the existing scientific was wrong.

His challenge created a big fuss during that time because it was considered as heresy. Galileo's statement was considered the threat to the established religion (Roman Catholic Church) as well because the holy bible clearly stated that the lord set the earth on its foundation and it can never be moved. It was the sun revolving around the earth. There was also a widespread agreement that truth resided not in astronomy but in the Bible since the Book of Scripture had been dictated by God. Therefore, if the statement from the bible was proved wrong, it would make the sacred Scripture false which could then result in people losing their faith in the church and its teaching. Because of that, not only the traditional religion was threatened but also the existing social order was shaken as well.

According to the article, Galileo's theory threatened the established scientific, religion and the social order as well as the political order. During Galileo time, the church was everything to everybody and it held most of the political power as well. Most important officials were the church officials and they wanted to safeguard people's faith so that they could keep their power. By proving that the church teaching was wrong, their existing political order was greatly affected as well.

I think the crucial difference between Copernicus's model and Galileo's model was the fixed and unfixed position of the stars. Copernicus believed that the stars were distant objects that do not revolve around the sun and they were fixed in their own positions. However, when Galileo observed the stars using his telescope, he found that the positions of the stars relative to Jupiter were changing and that it was impossible for them to be fixed in a place. He later found that there were actually four stars that revolving around Jupiter.

Response #3

Some of the greatest scientific discoveries have come from those scientists that many refused to believe. Galileo Galilei was a perfect example of one of these controversial scientists. From Italy, he played a major role in the Scientific Revolution. His famous amount of overwhelming support of the Copernican system challenged not only religion, science, society, but even political order. If it were no for his determination and persistence, the Copernican system would have been long thrown out, along with Galileo's new scientific methodology of hypothesis testing.

The Copernican system is the idea that the Sun is the center of the universe, and all other planets revolve around it. Galileo supported this theory greatly, and for that got punished because it went against the Roman Catholic church idea about how the universe worked. The Catholics believed that the Earth as the middle of the universe, and everything revolved around the Earth, which is known as the heliocentric system. The Catholics believed in this system greatly, and based a lot of their religion off of it. So when Galileo started trying to spread the idea of the Copernican system, people started questioning the Roman Catholic religion as a whole.

Galileo's support of the Copernican system not only challenged religion, but also science, society, and the political order. The main theory about the universe at the time was the heliocentric system, which the Copernican system was a completely different system. This is the theory that at the time almost all of society believed as well, so it again challenged the way that people thought and what they believed in. Even the political order, which was based around the major religion at the time, the Roman Catholic Church, was threatened by this. If people started believing in the Copernican system, then all would be challenged and everything has a whole would have to change.

Galileo did not settle for the induction method as enough evidence for the Copernican system either. He went further and invented the hypothetico-deductive method, in which one tests a hypothetical model, and gains more likelihood of being true as it passes each test successfully. Galileo did this by using a telescope and finding that Venus goes through a complete cycle of phases, meaning that it has to revolve around the Sun and not the Earth. This system is now used widely today, where we come up with a hypothesis and then go through tests to find evidential support to show that our hypothesis is either true or false.

Galileo went through great lengths to try and prove that the Copernican system was true. He challenged everyone and anyone who did not believe him, and put even his very life in danger for what he believed in. Galileo came up with a system for scientific testing, which is now used throughout the field of science everywhere today. Now if only we can take from this and learn today that there can be new ways of truth, even if they challenge what we thought was the truth.

In the Learning Template, the rubrics are used to assess students' written communications and integrative learning skills which were developed by the Association of American Colleges and Universities (AAC&U) through the Value Rubrics Project. These rubrics were developed and normed by faculty from across the country working with members of AAC&U. The rubrics were organized around Essential Learning Outcomes, as a result of the the work of The Liberal Education and America's Promise (LEAP) initiative. The four

Essential Learning Outcomes include Knowledge of Human Cultures and the Physical and Natural World, Intellectual and Practical Skills, Personal and Social Responsibility, and Integrative and Applied Learning. These learning outcomes were developed as a result of previous publications from the Association of American Colleges and Universities: *Greater Expectations: A New Vision for Learning as a Nation Goes to College* (2002), *Taking Responsibility for the Quality of the Baccalaureate Degree* (2004), and *College Learning for the New Global Century* (2007).

The dialectic of the weekly seminar, both written and spoken, is purposefully designed to incorporate the elements Terrel L. Rhodes outlines in Essential Learning Outcomes, including knowledge of human cultures and the physical and natural world, intellectual and practical skills, personal and social responsibility, and integrative and applied learning (p. 2). Outcomes, Rhodes notes, are the skills that should prepare students to meet the challenges of the 21st century. As Carol Geary Schneider noted in Peer Review (2008, Toward Intentionality and Integration), when faculty move toward "engaging students in the implications of knowledge," they are "pulled toward more integrative designs for learning and the equal interest in getting students out in the field to test these skills against real problems" (p. 3).

The analysis of the rubric data assisted the seminar instructors in understanding the learning needs of students and was used to improve student learning. Another equally important aspect for improving student learning was making learning expectations clear to students at the outset; therefore, the Written Communication and Integrated Learning Rubrics are shared with students prior to engaging in seminar readings and assignments. The sharing and the discussions about the rubrics are important steps in assisting students to be intentional learners. Unfortunately, in higher education today, the tenet—how *our students learn is as important as what our students learn*—is not yet fully appreciated, thereby putting the future of our students at risk by not using the new technology to catalyze the transformative ways students learn, create, and adapt. We would do well to pay attention to the inextricable thread connecting learning to technology.

WRITTEN COMMUNICATION VALUE RUBRIC

See Table 1. For more information, please contact value@aacu.org.

Definition

Written communication is the development and expression of ideas in writing. Written communication involves learning to work in many genres and styles. It can involve working with many different writing technologies, and mixing texts, data, and images. Written communication abilities develop through iterative experiences across the curriculum.

Evaluators are encouraged to assign a zero to any work sample or collection of work that does not meet benchmark (cell one) level performance.

INTEGRATIVE LEARNING VALUE RUBRIC

See Table 2. For more information, please contact value@aacu.org.

Definition

Integrative learning is an understanding and a disposition that a student builds across the curriculum and cocurriculum, from making simple connections among ideas and experiences to synthesizing and transferring learning to new, complex situations within and beyond the campus.

Table 1. Written communication value rubric

	Capstone 4	Milestones 3	2	Benchmark 1
Context of and Purpose for Writing *Includes considerations of audience, purpose, and the circumstances surrounding the writing task(s).*	Demonstrates a thorough understanding of context, audience, and purpose that is responsive to the assigned task(s) and focuses all elements of the work.	Demonstrates adequate consideration of context, audience, and purpose and a clear focus on the assigned task(s) (e.g., the task aligns with audience, purpose, and context).	Demonstrates awareness of context, audience, purpose, and to the assigned tasks(s) (e.g., begins to show awareness of audience's perceptions and assumptions).	Demonstrates minimal attention to context, audience, purpose, and to the assigned tasks(s) (e.g., expectation of instructor or self as audience).
Content Development	Uses appropriate, relevant, and compelling content to illustrate mastery of the subject, conveying the writer's understanding, and shaping the whole work.	Uses appropriate, relevant, and compelling content to explore ideas within the context of the discipline and shape the whole work.	Uses appropriate and relevant content to develop and explore ideas through most of the work.	Uses appropriate and relevant content to develop simple ideas in some parts of the work.
Genre and Disciplinary Conventions *Formal and informal rules inherent in the expectations for writing in particular forms and/or academic fields (please see glossary).*	Demonstrates detailed attention to and successful execution of a wide range of conventions particular to a specific discipline and/or writing task (s) including organization, content, presentation, formatting, and stylistic choices	Demonstrates consistent use of important conventions particular to a specific discipline and/or writing task(s), including organization, content, presentation, and stylistic choices	Follows expectations appropriate to a specific discipline and/or writing task(s) for basic organization, content, and presentation	Attempts to use a consistent system for basic organization and presentation.
Sources and Evidence	Demonstrates skillful use of high-quality, credible, relevant sources to develop ideas that are appropriate for the discipline and genre of the writing	Demonstrates consistent use of credible, relevant sources to support ideas that are situated within the discipline and genre of the writing.	Demonstrates an attempt to use credible and/or relevant sources to support ideas that are appropriate for the discipline and genre of the writing.	Demonstrates an attempt to use sources to support ideas in the writing.
Control of Syntax and Mechanics	Uses graceful language that skillfully communicates meaning to readers with clarity and fluency, and is virtually error-free.	Uses straightforward language that generally conveys meaning to readers. The language in the portfolio has few errors.	Uses language that generally conveys meaning to readers with clarity, although writing may include some errors.	Uses language that sometimes impedes meaning because of errors in usage.

Reprinted with permission from Assessing Outcomes and Improving Achievement: Tips and tools for Using Rubrics, edited by Terrel L. Rhodes.

Table 2. Integrative learning value rubric

	Capstone 4	Milestones 3	2	Benchmark 1
Connections to Experience *Connects relevant experience and academic knowledge*	Meaningfully **synthesizes** connections among experiences outside of the formal classroom (including life experiences and academic experiences such as internships and travel abroad) to **deepen understanding** of fields of study and to broaden own points of view.	Effectively **selects and develops** examples of life experiences, drawn from a variety of contexts (e.g., family life, artistic participation, civic involvement, work experience), to **illuminate** concepts/theories/ frameworks of fields of study.	**Compares** life experiences and academic knowledge to infer differences, as well as similarities, and **acknowledge perspectives** other than own.	**Identifies** connections between life experiences and those academic texts and ideas **perceived as similar and related** to own interests.
Connections to Discipline *Sees (makes) connections across disciplines, perspectives*	Independently creates wholes out of multiple parts (synthesizes) or draws conclusions by combining examples, facts, or theories from more than one field of study or perspective.	Independently connects examples, facts, or theories from more than one field of study or perspective.	When prompted, connects examples, facts, or theories from more than one field of study or perspective.	When prompted, presents examples, facts, or theories from more than one field of study or perspective.
Transfer *Adapts and applies skills, abilities, theories, or methodologies gained in one situation to new situations*	Adapts and applies, independently, skills, abilities, theories, or methodologies gained in one situation to new situations **to solve difficult problems or explore complex issues in original ways.**	Adapts and applies skills, abilities, theories, or methodologies gained in one situation to new situations **to solve problems or explore issues.**	Uses skills, abilities, theories, or methodologies gained in one situation in a new situation **to contribute to understanding of problems or issues.**	Uses, in a basic way, skills, abilities, theories, or methodologies gained in one situation **in a new situation.**
Integrated Communication	Fulfills the assignment(s) by choosing a format, language, or graph (or other visual representation) **in ways that enhance meaning,** making clear the interdependence of language and meaning, thought, and expression.	Fulfills the assignment(s) by choosing a format, language, or graph (or other visual representation) **to explicitly connect content and form,** demonstrating awareness of purpose and audience.	Fulfills the assignment(s) by choosing a format, language, or graph (or other visual representation) that **connects in a basic way** what is being communicated (content) with how it is said (form).	Fulfills the assignment(s) (i.e. to produce an essay, a poster, a video, a PowerPoint presentation, etc.) **in an appropriate form.**
Reflection and Self-Assessment *Demonstrates a developing sense of self as a learner, building on prior experiences to respond to new and challenging contexts (may be evident in self-assessment, reflective, or creative work)*	Envisions a future self (and possibly makes plans that build on past experiences that have occurred across multiple and diverse contexts).	Evaluates changes in own learning over time, recognizing complex contextual factors (e.g., works with ambiguity and risk, deals with frustration, considers ethical frameworks).	Articulates strengths and challenges (within specific performances or events) to increase effectiveness in different contexts (through increased self-awareness).	Describes own performances with general descriptors of success and failure.

Reprinted with permission from Assessing Outcomes and Improving Achievement: Tips and tools for Using Rubrics, edited by Terrel L. Rhodes.

Evaluators are encouraged to assign a zero to any work sample or collection of work that does not meet benchmark (cell one) level performance.

CONCLUSION

The 21st century demands of its citizens an array of skills to assist them in understanding the ever-evolving complexity of a global arena. Institutions of higher education can no longer rely on traditional modes of teaching and delivery methods because learning in the 21st century is a generative process that, in large measure, is driven by technology. Therefore, faculty and institutions that fail to appreciate the significance of this paradigm shift will miss the opportunity to serve their students and meet the growing challenges to manage the revitalization of higher education. In the current context of learning through technology, the academy will have to consider seriously the efficacy of remaining tied to the medieval principles of its founding, i.e., with the Kantian notion of autonomy and self-determination. To this point, Charles Taylor (2010) concludes that the:

...new media and communications technologies have triggered explosive growth in the amount of information to which people have ready access. Not only is the quantity of information growing, its substance is changing. This has important implications for the reorganization of knowledge and, by extension higher education (p. 112).

Likewise, McCluskey, and Winter (2012) in *The Idea of the Digital University* note that:

It is a new world, and universities can prepare students not only in new ways but also in better ways. The Web and other digital tools give us the power to educate more citizens in a more economical way. What has been seen as a crisis in higher education can well be looked at as the golden dawn of a new era. We just need the courage and wisdom to see it (p. 201).

Social Media like TED Talks are changing the context of the student experience in higher education, evolving a practical role for technology in the classroom, and creating a familiar and welcoming environment for students. The new and emerging technologies have helped to create bridges between classroom and real world learning, where students contribute to their knowledge base through their individual and collective experiences. We owe it to our students to be well-informed about the tools that can construct a meaningful and effective educational experience for them.

REFERENCES

Arum, R., & Roksa, J. (2011). *Academically adrift: Limited learning on college campuses*. Chicago: University of Chicago Press.

Association of American Colleges and Universities. (2002). *Greater expectations: A new vision for learning as a nation goes to college*. Washington, DC: Association of American Colleges and Universities.

Association of American Colleges and Universities. (2004). *Taking responsibility for the quality of the baccalaureate degree*. Washington, DC: Association of American Colleges and Universities.

Association of American Colleges and Universities. (2007). *College learning for the new global century*. Washington, DC: Association of American Colleges and Universities.

Bolte Taylor, J. (2006). *My stroke of genius*. New York: Viking.

Dahlstrom, E. (n.d.). *ECAR study of undergraduate students and information technology*. Louisville, CO: EDUCAUSE Center for Applied Research. Retrieved from http://www.educause.edu/ecar.

Dewey, J. (1933). *How we think: A restatement of the relation of reflective thinking to the educative process*. Boston: Henry Holt.

Dewey, J. (1966). *Democracy and education*. New York: Free Press.

Educause Learning Initiative. (2008). *Annual meeting, virtual worlds as web 2.0 learning spaces*. Educause.

Friedman, T. L., & Mandelbaum, M. (2011). *That used to be us*. New York: Farrar, Strauss and Giroux.

Gardner, H. (2009). *Five minds for the future*. Boston: Harvard Business School Press.

Google. (n.d.). *Wikipedia*. Retrieved January 12, 2013, from http://en.wikipedia.org/wiki/Google

Keeling, R. P., & Hersh, R. H. (2011). *We're losing our minds: Rethinking American higher education*. New York: Palgrave Macmillan. doi:10.1057/9781137001764.

Khanna, A., & Khanna, P. (2012). *TED hybrid reality: Thriving in the emerging human- technology civilization*. TED.

Langer, A. M., & Knefelkamp, L. L. (2002). *Forms of literacy development with technology in the college years: A scheme for students, faculty and institutions of higher learning*. Paper presented at the Association of American Colleges and Universities Conference on Technology, Learning, and Intellectual Development. Baltimore, MD.

Lifton, R. J. (1999). *The protean self: Human resilience in an age of fragmentation*. Chicago: University of Chicago Press.

McCluskey, F. B., & Winter, M. L. (2012). *The idea of the digital university: Ancient traditions, disruptive technologies and the battle for the soul of higher education*. Washington, DC: Westphalia Press.

Miller, R. E. (2012, November 12). *This is how we think: Learning in public after the paradigm shift*. [Video File]. Retrieved February 6, 2012, from http://www.youtube.com/watch?v=aNDyP2pzE8Q

Perry, W. G. (1999). *Forms of intellectual and ethical development in the college years: A scheme*. San Francisco, CA: Jossey-Bass Publishers.

Rhodes, T. (Ed.). (2010). *Assessing outcomes and improving achievement: Tips and tools for using rubrics*. Washington, DC: Association of American Colleges and Universities.

Rhodes, T. L. (Ed.). (2010). *Assessing outcomes and improving achievement: Tips and tools for using rubrics*. Washington, DC: Association of American Colleges and Universities.

Richardson, W. (2012). *Why school? How education must change when learning and information are everywhere*. Amazon Digital Services, Inc..

Robison, J. E. (2009). Is technology making us dumber? *Psychology Today: Health, Help, Happiness + Find a Therapist*. Retrieved from http://www.psychologytoday.com/blog/my-life-aspergers/200911/is-technology-making-us-dumber

Schneider, C. G. (2008). From the president. *Peer Review, 10*(4), 3.

Suskie, L. A. (2009). *Assessing student learning: A common sense guide*. San Francisco, CA: Jossey-Bass.

Taylor, M. C. (2010). *Crisis on campus: A bold plan for reforming our colleges and universities*. New York: Alfred A. Knopf.

Wagner, T. (2010). *The global achievement gap: Why even the best schools don't teach the new survival skills our children need – And what we can do about it*. New York, NY: Basic Books.

Walker, A. (1983). *In search of our mother's gardens: Womanist prose*. San Diego, CA: Harcourt Brace Jovanovich.

Walvoord, B. E. (2010). *Assessment clear and simple: A practical guide for institutions, departments, and general education*. San Francisco, CA: Jossey-Bass.

Chapter 14
Structuring an Emergent and Transdisciplinary Online Curriculum:
A One Health Case

Shalin Hai-Jew
Kansas State University, USA

ABSTRACT

Subject domains are in constant transition as new research and analysis reveal fresh insights, and occasionally, there may be paradigm shifts or new conceptual models. Transdisciplinary approaches may be understood as such a shift, with new approaches for conceptualization, analysis, and problem solving via recombinations of domain fields. Such transitory paradigm-shifting moments remove the usual touchpoints on which a curriculum is structured. There are often few or none of the accepted sequential developmental phases with identified concepts and learning outcomes in book chapters, thematic structures, and historical or chronological ordering. An emergent curriculum requires a different instructional design approach than those that have assumed curricular pre-structures. Based on a year-and-a-half One Health course build, this chapter offers some insights on the processes of defining and developing an emergent curriculum.

INTRODUCTION

Curriculums in most learning domains are in constant evolution, with the integration of new voices and research informing the current field. Sometimes, the shift in domains occurs at a higher level of abstraction, in a way which integrates or assimilates multiple domains. Occasionally, an instructional design and development team has to work together to create an undefined and emergent curriculum for an online course.

DOI: 10.4018/978-1-4666-4462-5.ch014

This emergent context provides unique design and development challenges. The development cycle may be much longer than typical for the course build, which has to evolve somewhat organically. A range of Subject Matter Expert (SME) talent has to be brought into play to develop the learning contents. The development team (itself cross disciplinary) has to walk a fine line between the objective science-based learning and any perceived advocacy role in promoting the new paradigm. Pedagogical coherence has to be created from potentially disjointed elements, with special considerations for learner needs, given the need for individual sense-making from different learning traditions.

By definition, such learning is not fully defined; rather, it is emerging out of a fluid situation. Emergent learning may well be contested and even rejected by practitioners. Further, emergent curriculums have the potential to affect not only undergraduate and graduate students but also researchers, policy-makers, applied practitioners, and administrative leaders in the world. Historically, an "emergent curriculum" was defined in the context of child learning which integrated elements of the environment into a flexible learning approach. Here, the term is used to denote a curriculum not yet fully defined by those in a domain field. As such, an emergent curriculum is evolving and transitory. It may be accepted or rejected by practitioners.

BACKGROUND

In higher education today, it is very hard to find fields that are not influenced by other domains. Very insular fields are rare, and the norm is interdisciplinary learning. It will be important to define some terms early on. Traditionally, a uni-discipline or mono-discipline consists of a domain level evolving in "isolation" without the cross-fertilization of ideas. This domain involves a specific body of knowledge with its own history, a shared identity of a professional community, common terms, contributing researchers, accepted research methods (modes of inquiry), professional values, research and practitioner methods, and contents.

According to Jantsch (1972), a "multidisciplinarity" approach combines juxtaposed learning between disciplines without clear relational ties between them. In this approach, the disciplines retain their unique identities; a multidisciplinary research project is often "the simple sum of its parts" (Wagner, et al., 2011, p. 16). (By contrast, "pluridisciplinary" or "polydisciplinary" refers to the juxtaposition of disciplines seen to be related or somewhat similar, such as clusters of languages or "math" and "physics".). Multidisciplinarity involves the engagement of several disciplines in sequential or juxtaposed modes.

"Cross-disciplinarity" is typified by "rigid polarization toward specific monodisciplinary concept" with a particular domain emerging in the forefront as contrasted with other domains (Wagner, et al., 2011, p. 16). This approach does not dissolve the boundaries of the respective domains by integrates parts of various domains while allowing one or a few to be dominant.

An "interdisciplinarity" or blended approach is described as having a coordination of disciplines (knowledge and methods) by higher-level concepts that define interrelationships between domains. The interactions between the various disciplines may be at a variety of levels, whether at the level of concepts, methods, terminology, research, or other modes. Such an approach enables the formulation of "a holistic view or common understanding of a complex issue, question, or problem" (Wagner, et al., 2011, p. 16) that lead to more accurate-world understandings for comprehension, analysis, trouble-shooting, research, design, policy-making, and intercommunications and cooperation. Practically, interdisciplinarity is "the combination of different perspectives to tackle a common problem" (Sillitoe, 2004, p. 8).

Finally, there is a supra-domain approach: "transdisciplinarity" describes "multilevel coordination of (an) entire education / innovation system" that is integrated and formally structured (Jantsch, 1972, p. 15). Transdisciplinary connections are built from axiomatic understandings of the world that help bring together various domains of study for value-added research. An integrative "transdisciplinary" framework emerges from a worldview that moves beyond the human-created boundaries of a learning domain. This approach enables the creation of new knowledge. It enables reaching across professional and academic groups to practitioners in the field and those in the broader public (who may be involved in policy decisions, for example). Transdisciplinary practice involves three main approaches: transformative praxis, constructive problem-solving and real-world engagement ("Transdisciplinary studies," Feb. 24, 2012). In the research literature, these categories are described as elements on a continuum and include some overlap.

Taken individually, these concepts and practices have been in application from ancient times particularly since learning domains are constantly being defined and re-defined. In many modern areas of study and practice (e.g., bioengineering, biochemistry, astrophysics, eco-toxicology, informatics, agro-ecology, ecosystem health, engineering, and biomedicine, among others), there are inherent assumptions of cooperation across domain fields. Formally, these disciplinarity terms have been evolving for decades in application to curriculum development. For example, in 1970, Jean Piaget introduced the term and practice of "transdisciplinary" inquiry.

Engaging the world: A core rationale for mixing disciplines is that single stand-alone disciplines do not sufficiently explain the world in its complexity. Transdisciplinary research (TR) reflects a systems approach to the world which offers a broader conceptualization of problem framing that is inclusive of various individuals with differentiated specialties and skill sets: "TR strives to grasp the relevant complexity of a problem, taking into account the diversity of both everyday world and academic perceptions of problems, linking abstract and case-specific knowledge, and developing descriptive, normative and practical knowledge for the common interest" (Hadorn, Pohl, & Bammer, 2010). Accompanying these different skill sets are techniques, information, models, and approaches, which may shed new light.

Practical deliverables: The main rationale for combining domain approaches is to provide new mental models / conceptual models, techniques, data structures, policy design and implementation, problem-solving methods, and research—ultimately for the betterment of people.

Inter- and trans-disciplinary approaches employ abstract knowledge structures or "high-level ontologies to support information integration" (Lampe, Riede, & Doerr, 2008, p. 4:2). One way to understand interdisciplinary science research involves the analysis of co-citations as "a form of discourse" to identify points of overlap (Small, 2010, p. 839) as well as the authors that are collaborating or advancing the work across disciplines. Mapping knowledge structures from different domains may identify areas of intractable differences as well. However, even if some issues may be irreconcilable between domains, there may still be some smaller areas of coordination, cooperation, and co-research.

Mixed-discipline work (used here to suggest a combination of domain approaches) suggests a need for clear data and information structures. Further, it may be understood that there are natural interdependencies between knowledge domains. Discrepancies in terminology need to be explored and explicated. A shared understanding of language is needed for the bridge-building between learning domains. In such blending, there will be points of consensus as well as disagreement. Three cognitive activities in the "juncture of disciplines" are "overcoming internal monologism or mono-disciplinarity, attaining provisional integration, and questioning the integration as necessarily partial" (Nikitina, 2005, p. 389).

The need for social network structures to solve problems: The integration of various domains is achieved through SMEs and professionals in the various fields who have the transdisciplinary soft skills to collaborate widely and effectively. Stokols (2006) conceptualizes these collaborations on three main axes: "(1) collaboration among scholars representing different disciplines; (2) collaboration among researchers from multiple fields and community practitioners representing diverse professional and lay perspectives; and (3) collaboration among community organizations across local, state, national, and international levels" (p. 63). Individuals need good relationships for coordination and interdisciplinary work (Cummings & Kiesler, 2008, p. 438).

One transdisciplinary problem-solving approach involves using "breadth-first" to define problems from a variety of perspectives and then "Long Tail" strategies that involve "unlimited knowledge" and large pools of unique learning through formal and non-formal routes (Domik & Fischer, 2010, p. 95).

BARRIERS AND BRIDGES TO TRANSDISCIPLINARY WORK

The research literature identifies a range of challenges to inter-disciplinary and transdisciplinary work. A group of researchers writes about how interdisciplinary science research has carried the "burdens of expense, intrusion, and lack of reproducibility year-upon-year" (Wagner, et al., 2011, p. 14).

Barriers to cross-discipline integration: Transdisciplinary collaborations, also known informally as "(discipline) boundary work," have been described as "*highly labor intensive* and often evoke *tensions and conflicts* among participants [e.g., stemming from their different disciplinary world views, interpersonal styles, (and) department affiliations]" (Stokols, 2006, p. 68).

The culture and organization of academia are seen as barriers, with faculty members actively seeking out opportunities "to learn about research of colleagues that might complement their own" (Lélé & Norgaard, 2005, p. 968). The protectionism of various administrators and faculty researchers may make collaborating across departmental lines more difficult. Individuals trained into a discipline often spend much of their academic careers immersing in their respective fields. If they remain in academia, they work in very hierarchical environments which may not encourage lateral collaborations:

Not only do professors and students need to work laterally across an organization that is typically very hierarchical in nature, often finding that deans and department heads are unwilling to commit their own resources to benefit other divisions, but this disciplinary department structure is a schema that extends well beyond any individual institution to discourse communities reinforced by professional societies, journals, and the like (Boden, Borrego, & Newswander, 2011, p. 742).

Some have argued that interdisciplinary research may make some sciences more appealing to female students and increase their retention (Rhoten & Pfirman, 2007). Others have worked to introduce transdisciplinarity early on in a graduate curriculum in order to change the culture of academia to be more receptive to this approach (to socialize them into this approach) (Felt, Igelsböck, Schikowitz, & Völker, 2012). Some researchers suggest that transdisciplinary research is a critical skill for graduate students to expand career options (Golde & Gallagher, 1999); it is seen as a progressive approach (Rhoten & Parker, 2004) and a "hallmark of contemporary knowledge production and professional life" (Mansilla & Duraising, 2007, p. 215). However, there is a widespread sense of career risk in engaging in transdisciplinary (often comparative) research when novice researchers have to work to establish themselves in their selected domain.

Collaborators working on different campuses face additional challenges from the geographical distance. Cummings and Kiesler (2008) cite two studies that showed that "over 500 interdisciplinary research projects have documented comparatively poor outcomes of more distributed projects and the failed coordination mechanisms that partly account for these problems," which suggest that a lack of co-location of a team doing transdisciplinary work may cause further strains on the team, in terms of both "coordination and relationships" (p. 439). As a balancing point, though, many grant funders are more supportive of projects that involve several campuses and Principal Investigators (PIs). A further barrier may be expressed as researchers go to publish or disseminate their work, "whether those objects are individual scientists, papers, tools or materials" (Small, 2010, p. 835).

Finally, transdisciplinary collaborators require a full skill set—not only specialist knowledge but the ability to collaborate with others from a variety of domains. This transdisciplinarity may be conceptualized also as individuals who cross-train in multiple domains for competitive advantage. Such types of multi-domain learning are not uncommon through undergraduate studies (majors and minors; double or triple majors) as well as graduate programs (with many professional studies bringing law or business or other elements to complement the field studies). Some universities offer customized degree programs that offer more free-form learning with very high-level requirements instead of closely-defined sequences. Transdisciplinary collaborations require "*extensive preparation, practice, and continual refinement*" (Stokol's italics) (Stokol, 2006, p. 69). Such individuals require self-awareness and meta-cognition (factors of emotional intelligence) in order to work through the challenges of understanding other mind sets and differences. They require the skills to monitor group processes.

Researchers have pointed out how individuals from dissimilar epistemological traditions may experience tensions from the incongruence from different conceptual models. In order to handle such stresses, teams engaged in transdisciplinary work must be attentive to the process of collaboration. Each member must be able to suspend their own epistemic beliefs and handle interpersonal conflict (Vanasupa, McCormick, Stefanco, Herter, & McDonald, 2012). They must be able to finesse and negotiate meanings across disciplines in an intercultural context (Woods, 2007) while preserving constructive work relationships. Team members also need to articulate their own domain field and evolving learning. While team members must maintain a sense of openness and curiosity, they must also demonstrate "interdisciplinary communicative competence," which includes "conceptual competence; competence in negotiating meaning; competence in interdisciplinary text production; knowledge; skills of interpreting and relating; skills of discovery and interaction; attitudes; critical disciplinary awareness" (Woods, 2007, p. 860). Prior interdisciplinary collaborations inform and develop this skill set.

One piece of advice comes from a team that has worked on building cross-disciplinary science-based simulations. They advise:

Approach the project with humility. Even though the scientists on the team may be world-class experts in their respective component fields, they are all likely to be amateurs when it comes to the system as a whole. It is worth remembering that a distinguished group of component experts does not guarantee a distinguished system team. In fact, since laypeople often have a deep and holistic understanding of their local environments, we scientists may be no more 'expert' than they are, even though their knowledge is not necessarily scientific. All team members must take time to probe and query each other's approaches, assumptions, and methods. More important, they must be willing to have their own assumptions and statements probed by others. This requires humility, a willingness to be challenged by team members outside one's own area, and an openness to learning from such transactions (Nicolson, Starfield, Kofinas, & Kruse, 2002, p. 383).

Research on teaming has highlighted the benefits of physical proximity that enables spontaneous and routine communication, to support collaboration. People's familiarity with their colleagues reduces uncertainty about how others may behave. Such relationships may enable people to come to agreement and to collaborate with a deeper sense of earned trust. Such relationships may lower the reluctance into exploring other domains.

Finally, transdisciplinary practitioners may not be fully cognizant of where their teaching, research, and learning may lead. This suggests that practitioners need to be comfortable with a chaotic and unpredictable work space and an openness to challenging deeply held foundational ideas.

Bridges to transdisciplinarity: There are multiple points of entry to transdisciplinary work. The challenges of drawing learning, theory, and practices from multiple domains may be partially mitigated by some "bridges" to ease the work of transdisciplinary teams. Simply, depending on the domains involved, people may lay the cognitive groundwork for a transdisciplinary framework. They may work towards changing the culture of academia to incentivize mixed disciplinary pursuits; they may work on restructuring the organization to enable such work. Information and Communication Technology (ICT) may enable stronger teaming. Finally, formal and informal training may enhance transdisciplinary collaboration skill sets.

Cognitive groundwork: One important bridge to support transdisciplinary work involves the creation of the cognitive groundwork, which explains the cross-domain potentials. One example involves topic mapping between domains to identify areas of similarity and overlap. Using this conceptualization, there may be particular fields and practitioners that are more likely to be able to successfully achieved transdisciplinary collaborations. The degrees of differences between domains may cause a larger rift that may be more difficult to bridge whereas similar domains may more easily cohere (Rafols & Meyer, 2010, as cited in Wagner, et al., 2011, p. 16) in a kind of content-level homophily.

This mapping may involve the shared language or terminology understandings; it may involve the building of shared knowledge structures or ontologies; it may involve the uses of analogies. Such expressions may extend to data visualizations. Some of the work may be conceptual, such as thought experiments, position papers, scenarios, or theoretical models. More sophisticated mapping may include simulations that embody integrated disciplinary perspectives with clear multidisciplinary linkages expressed. Such models may codify knowledge and analysis from inter-related disciplines to create transparent understandings (Nicolson, Starfield, Kofinas, & Kruse, 2002). Creating such models illuminate what is known and also what is unknown, which contributes to transdisciplinary understandings. These authors suggest that it's preferable to design a "suite of models" in lieu of an all-purpose synthesis model (Nicolson, Starfield, Kofinas, & Kruse, 2002, p. 380), which may result in extensive encapsulated complexity (and diminished human understandings). Nicolson, et al. (2002) emphasize the importance of sensitivity analysis at every stage of the modeling, to test for the effectiveness of the model: "Sensitivity analysis is the only available means of determining what goes into the model and what level of detail is necessary. It is an essential tool for estimating the likely effects of alternative hypotheses for system processes" (Nicolson, Starfield, Kofinas, & Kruse, 2002, p. 382).

Perhaps multiple domain fields share ethical guidelines or professional practices. Perhaps there is equipment used in multiple fields. Perhaps there are shared research questions or a common problem that is being solved.

Transdisciplinary research in a range of mixed fields may offer insights not only about a larger issue in the world but may provide direction for those who want to engage in that type of research. Separate lines of research already exist in terms of transdisciplinary research and curriculums.

Cultural and organizational changes in academia: The culture of academia focuses on in-depth domain specializations for experts, who define their respective niches and often work in those general areas for much of their careers. The value systems in academia view comparative or domain-boundary-crossing as somewhat lesser endeavors than discoveries in particular domain fields. One way to strive for cultural change may be to spark conversations about possibilities for transdisciplinary work. An encouragement of professional cooperation instead of domain (turf)-based competition may encourage more cross-field collaboration.

Structurally, universities and colleges are deeply hierarchical. To encourage lateral collaborations across departments and colleges, the institutions of higher education may benefit from a flatter hierarchy. While some funding agencies encourage cross-institutional collaborations, some will not because of the increased sense of risk to the project. Institutions may work out ways to better share the "spoils" of various grants and funding sources. The existence of respected transdisciplinary publications may further change incentive structures for engaging in such cross-boundary research. One researcher suggested the importance of "credible platforms" for interdisciplinary communication so that such scientific endeavors may persist and have an impact (Wear, 1999, p. 299). Professional societies may host cross-disciplinary conferences that are inclusive but also thematically coherent. Institutions of higher learning may consider cross-disciplinary work as a critical part of a tenure package. Some research has found that a high degree of specialization may result in a decrease in promotion prospects (Leahey, Keith, & Crockett, 2010).

Information and Communication Technologies (ICT): The World Wide Web (WWW) and Internet involve a range of enablements that intuitively may support mixed disciplinarity. For one, academics have formal and informal publication profiles that are widely available. The work of many is deeply searchable and high-profile (except for those whose works may be embargoed). Information and communication technologies mitigate geographical distances and enable rich mediated communications and collaborations. Knowledge structures may be expressed in a variety of ways using text and image structures (like wikis), which may be highly interactive. Social networking sites enable people to connect with each other from across many physical and psychological distances. With the plurality of knowledge, maintaining artificial domain boundaries may be harder now than before.

Formal and informal training: The weight of the research literature suggests that collaborating on transdisciplinary teams involves plenty of challenges. These are difficult skill sets to attain and maintain. In order to socialize researchers into these approaches, it helps to create various points of entry. For example, various mainline and comparative journals may feature writing about such research. Universities and colleges may offer graduate-level courses that introduce such techniques while offering a survey level of the related domain knowledge and methods. (Graduate-level students are thought to have both sufficient domain knowledge and research abilities to be able to start putting such transdisciplinary ideas to use.) Funding organizations may continue to encourage cross-disciplinary work. Institutions of higher education may offer refresher courses to maintain mixed disciplinary collaboration skills as well as content-specific insights in a variety of fields for mixed disciplinary researchers.

Figure 1 highlights the basic research literature about various types of mixed disciplinary in a vertical continuum at the left. Particular bridges aid practitioners in surmounting barriers to mixed disciplinary work. At the far right are some of the deliverables that have been mentioned in the research literature in relation with multi-disciplinary and transdisciplinary work.

The previous section highlights the research literature on mixed disciplinary work. Interdisciplinary courses have been popular over the past three decades, since the mid 1970s (Nowacek, 2005). What follows describes a recent project to build a graduate-level course on One Health that integrates transdisciplinary approaches for the emergent curriculum.

Figure 1. Barriers and bridges to mixed disciplinary collaborations and deliverables

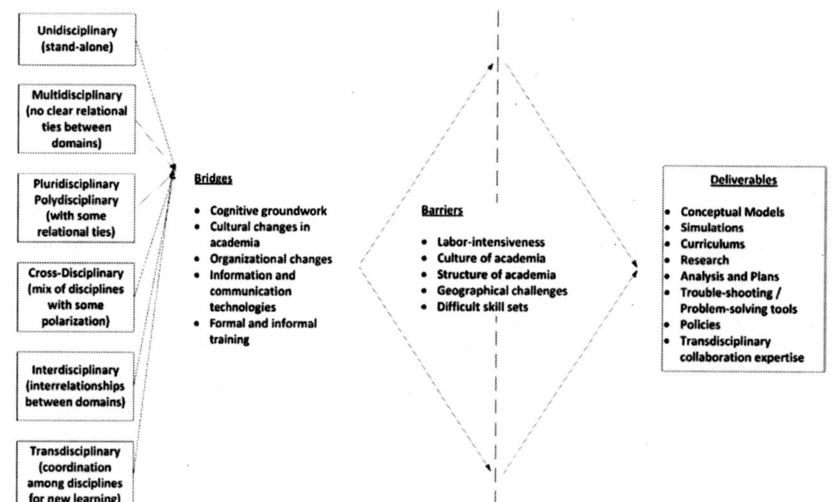

BUILDING A ONE HEALTH COURSE

At Kansas State University, in early 2011, a small development team gathered to start work on a One Health course. The concept of One Health is that human, animal, and environmental health is deeply intertwined. This concept is anchored in the fact zoonotic diseases may be transmitted between species from animals to humans (sometimes through vectors—living agents that transmit disease) and from humans to animals (through "reverse zoonosis"). The Centers for Disease Control and Prevention note that "approximately 75% of recently emerging infectious diseases affecting humans are diseases of animal origin; approximately 60% of all human pathogens are zoonotic" ("National Center for Emerging and Zoonotic Infectious Diseases," Sept. 7, 2012). The costs of zoonotic diseases on society is high (Narrod, Zinsstag, & Tiongco, 2012). The way a problem is framed already implicitly sets some boundaries around the problem. The boundaries specify what will be attended to, what will be ignored and what will be marginalized (Midgley 2000). In that sense, the understanding of zoonotic diseases cannot be understood from the closed framework of human health in isolation but needs to consider a range of factors. After all, ecological systems contain interdependent elements, with nuanced mutual effects.

Further, combating emerging infectious diseases must be strategized "in terms of an open, dynamic system operating at multiple levels" (Parkes, et al., 2005, p. 261). To fully understand pathogen origins and transmission into people, it is critical to understand shared diseases in humans and animals as well as the impacts of the environment. Further, since maintaining health across species and the environment involves informing and cooperation with the broader public, it is important that correct understandings are established. There is plenty of documentation of people misunderstanding science and misdirecting public expenditures (Mnookin, 2011).

One Health then is a potentially mobilizing term that emphasizes the need for professional collaborations from a range of SMEs from many fields: veterinary medicine, human medicine, the biological sciences, food safety and security, and others. Here, the health of animals and the environment are valuable and important in their own right and also in the implications for all in terms of One Health.

The course description was finalized shortly before the course launched. It was evolved over the development lifespan of the project. It reads:

"One Health" encompasses the complex interrelationships among humans and animals, humans and the environment, and animals and the environment. This course provides a broad-based introduction to One Health, incorporating original videos of leading subject matter experts and researchers, case studies, and scientific readings. It addresses zoonotic diseases (those that may be transferred between humans and animals) and environmental issues that impact human, animal, and ecosystem health. Topics include disease surveillance, the human-animal bond, the built environment, disaster response, sanitation, rural/suburban/urban interface, and food safety and security ("Introduction to One Health Syllabus," 2012).

Further, the course learning objectives show the breadth of information coverage. In a sense, this course provides a "survey" view of where One Health may branch in the future:

1. Become familiar with the One Health concept and the respective interrelationships among human health, animal health, and \ environmental health.
2. Identify diseases with zoonotic potential and their routes of transmission.
3. Define the role of One Health in food safety and defense.
4. Demonstrate how a variety of natural and human-made environmental issues influence human health, and how communities impact the environment.
5. Demonstrate how a variety of natural and human-made environmental issues affect animal health, and how animal populations affect the environment.
6. Identify issues of society and nature that exemplify One Health and describe methods by which these may be addressed ("Introduction to One Health Syllabus," 2012).

The course had to be designed with scaffolding for the MDs (medical doctors) and DVMs (Doctors of Veterinary Medicine) enrolled in the course as well as non-majors, who could well prefer a practical and applied curriculum that may benefit their own world-awareness and health decisions and behaviors.

In Fall Semester 2012, this course was offered in a multi-disciplinary way in three areas: Biology (BIOL), Clinical Sciences (CS), and Diagnostic Medicine/Pathobiology (DMP).

THREE AREAS FOR AN EMERGENT COURSE CURRICULUM

To illuminate the instructional design strategies used, this emergent course build section focuses on three main areas:

1. The cross-disciplinary development team and subject matter experts (SMEs).
2. The organic content structure and broad sourcing.
3. The strategic design for learners.

1. Cross-Disciplinary Development Team and Subject Matter Experts (SMEs)

The development team, itself cross-disciplinary, involved members from different bureaucratic units on campus. This course development was led by a Principal Investigator (PI) who was a high administrator on campus and a geneticist by academic field. A professor of clinical sciences, a veterinarian with a One Health background, and an instructional designer formed the core team. Additional support work was achieved by two videographers linked to the College of Veterinary Medicine. The core design team was co-located on the campus; however, a variety of SMEs from a variety of geographic locations provided contents.

The team started meeting once or twice a month early on; as the project progressed to its final stages, team members met several times a week. The team members read the main text, which was published just the year prior in 2010 (Peter M. Rabinowitz and Lisa A. Conti's *Human-Animal Medicine: Clinical Approaches to Zoonoses, Toxicants and Other Shared Health Risks* [Saunders, Elsevier]). This helped set the foundational understandings for the team; however, even though the book was fairly recent, the research had already progressed well beyond the confines of the text. Editorial decisions also meant that the text focused on some elements more than others.

Instead of beginning with a project stylebook to establish standards early on in the project, the group evolved consensus-based standards. These standards resulted in science-based standards for research; citation methods (based on the American Association for Microbiology's citation method); slideshow and video templating; documentation standards for copyright releases; and a range of other standards.

The team purposively set itself up to be a learning organization. As the team worked through various parts of the curriculum, they would email article links and files to each other. There were healthy discussions about the content during the face-to-face meetings during which content was vetted and edited, with one member or another commenting, "I didn't know that" or "That's interesting…" or "I wonder…." The group members strove to be objective in their responses and non-partisan. This process mean more time was expended in the development cycle; instead of a fast prototype, the course build evolved much more slowly. The long cycle would only be possible for well-funded online course developments.

The project lead and PI emphasized the need to set high information standards for all academic works referenced in the learning materials. She personally delved into dozens of articles in order to pursue full accuracy. She also worked according to a clear information hierarchy (more below). She set the clear standard that the course curriculum would follow the research literature. The focus was on content validity much more than on dazzling IT technological innovations.

As an instructional design project, this involved a very hands-on PI whose stature and contacts across campus were critical to the project's success. A majority of the video contents were created through interviews of various SMEs linked to the campus and also those off campus (but with ties to K-State faculty and administrators). All had national and international standing in their respective fields. Like a jigsaw assignment, they all added insights to One Health. The roles of these area experts were to introduce key concepts in their respective areas and introduce their own research interests. The questions used for the interviews were brainstormed by the team and then co-evolved with the interview subject. The finalized videos omitted the questioner's questions, and only the answers ran (the team edited the video using verbatim transcriptions). Other SMEs were featured in videos when several members of the team attended a One Health conference out-of-state and lined up a video team from the campus to attend also.

Figure 2 shows the critical role of various members of the team with public-facing sides. The principal investigator had critical ties with the funding organizations, internal and external subject matter experts, and the assessment agency assessing the project. The two isolate nodes of the videographers show that they did not engage with external entities directly. The one pendant node belongs to third-party sources of copyright contents, with copyright pursuit achieved by the instructional designer. The two members who are the fulcrum of the project are the PI and the veterinarian / One Health administrator, who have more ties than the others.

Figure 2. The one health development team and its relationship with external entities

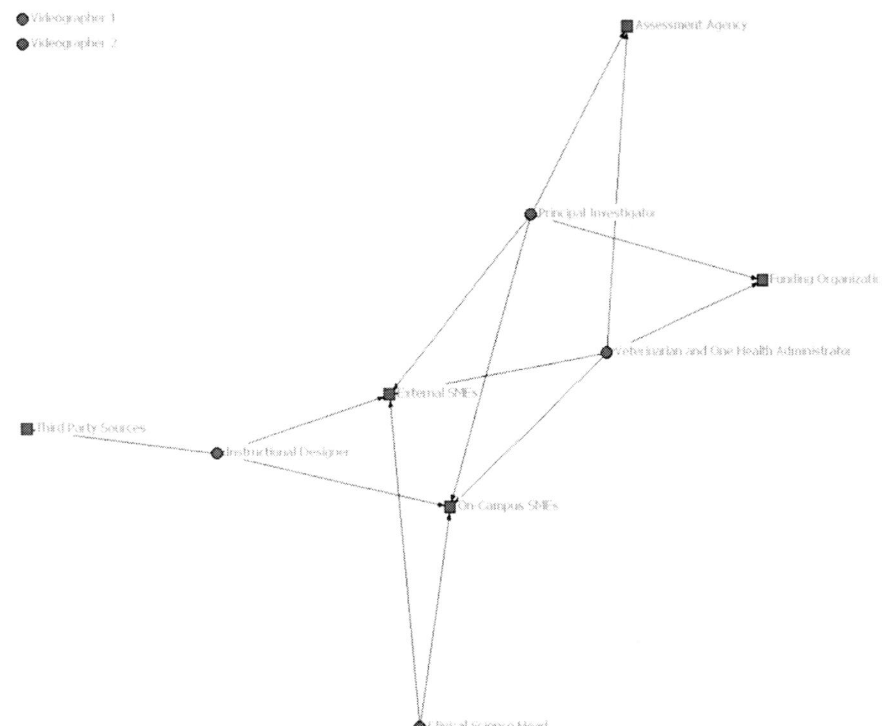

2. Organic Content Structure and Broad Sourcing

The development team started developing the online course while creating the authorizing documents for the course (which would have to go through Faculty Senate approval). The team proceeded with a simple ontology—the three spokes of the implied relationships in One Health: relationships among humans and animals; relationships among humans and the environment, and relationships among animals and the environment.

Organic content structure: The contents of each of those relationships would evolve based on the available SMEs and the available research. The idea was that the videotaped interviews of the SMEs and the slideshows would augment and complement the textbook.

The introductory week included optional slideshows to enable learners to refresh knowledge for the course. This included a slideshow on microbiology and one on disease models. The team worked to align the textbook readings, the filmed interviews, the slideshows, and even the "One Health in the News" articles with links. Some of the readings were medical case studies from the Centers for Disease Control "Morbidity and Mortality Weekly Report" (MMWR), which highlighted the practical aspects of One Health approaches based on real-world diseases. The team pursued videos, photos, and scientific articles that were relevant to the course contents for copyright releases; other sources were access through perma-linking or deep linking.

A highly simplified course outline follows with the three general topic areas:

1. Relationships among Humans and Animals
   a. The role of globalization in emerging diseases

  b. The human-animal bond
  c. Introduction to global public health
  d. Sustaining global surveillance and responsiveness to emerging diseases
  e. Comparative medicine
  f. Zoonotic diseases (organized around routes of transmission and with many resources focused on particular zoonotic diseases)
  g. Animals as sentinels
  h. Foodborne illnesses
  i. Foodborne safety, defense and security
  j. Safe food processing
2. Relationships among Humans and the Environment
  a. The built environment and human disease concerns
  b. Indoor air quality
  c. Natural environment disease concerns
  d. Heavy metals and trace minerals in the environment
  e. Mycotoxins
  f. The built environment: physical activity, health, and safety
  g. The design of homes for the human life span
  h. Walkability
  i. Multiple and reciprocal levels of human-environment interaction
3. Relationships among Animals and the Environment
  a. The built environment and animal disease concerns
  b. Wetland ecology
  c. Wildlife habitat encroachment
  d. Introduction of non-native species
  e. Invasive species
  f. Climate change and effects on animals
  g. Animal disaster management
  h. Bio and agro-terrorism (and risk communication)

As such, the weekly modules were structured topically. This meant that each week's work combined the various learning objects (slideshows, video presentations, and assigned readings) with the appropriate linked assignments, to create a fairly coherent subject-based unit of learning.

A more systematic content analysis enables more in-depth description of the course curriculum. This provides the development team with a perspective of their work that they likely had not fully achieved given the immersion in the specific details. These approaches may offer meaningful insights about both the concept of One Health and the nature of a multi-disciplinary curriculum.

Visualizing the curriculum: This same high-level view of the curriculum may be expressed as a two-mode node-link diagram. This is a two-mode affiliation network in the sense that the main areas (most connected nodes) are the three central organizing relationships of the course: (1) humans and animals, (2) animals and the environment, and (3) humans and the environment. The other nodes represent specific contents that relate to these three main areas. As such, they are more specific.

Figure 3 expresses the three main sections of the course as three main centralized nodes in this content analysis informational "network". While the main nodes—Humans and Animals, Animals and the Environment, and Humans and the Environment—are specially linked to the contents of their sections, there are still interconnections between the various aspects of the curriculum. These interconnections bolster the concept of One Health or the interlinking between humans, animals, and the environment. The "Optional" link is an added section which is a "pendant" node at the periphery of the network, which represents the opt-in aspect of the related learning. (The figure was created using UCINET 6® of Analytic Technologies.)

To achieve a broad view of the topic, the development team had two members who developed the contents, and the two lead PIs vet and critique the learning contents. As indicated by the node-link diagram above, some of the learning contents included some overlapping details. While the development team tried to keep excessive repetition out of the curriculum, sometimes, it was

Figure 3. One health curricular content analysis

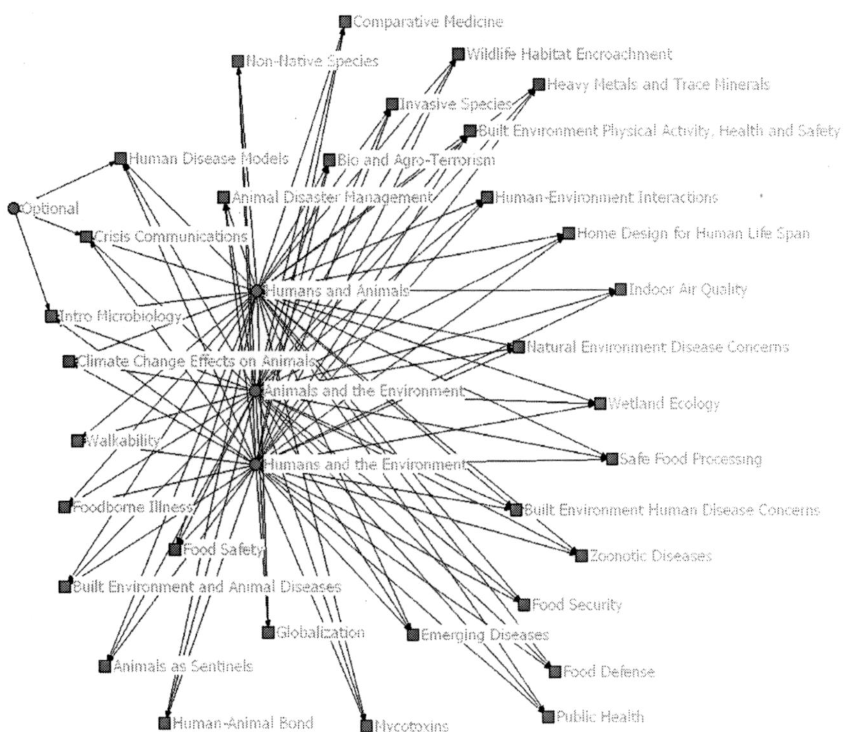

necessary to address health issues in multiple places. For example, the care of food animals was covered in sections dealing with bio- and agro-terrorism as well as food security, emerging diseases, and animal disaster management (A few of the nodes above were manually adjusted for text label clarity.).

Broad information sourcing: The nature of the various topics meant that the development team had to pursue open-source resources online (namely, government agencies) for images and articles. For example, the Centers for Disease Control and Prevention's Public Health Library (PHIL) offered some helpful images. The World Health Organization (WHO) offered a fine starting point for various disease research and more globalist imagery. The Federal Emergency Management Agency (FEMA) provided helpful images in their Photo Library. General Creative Commons releases enabled wide usage of publicly sources imagery. The National Academy of Sciences had well-researched articles that benefitted the development of the slideshows. The CDC's MMWR offered a range of case studies. Case studies provide a way of promoting cross-disciplinary collaboration (Stauffacher, 2010).

Team self-sourcing: The development team also invested hundreds of hours to conduct secondary research for self-developed slideshows with alt-texted images, precise metadata, documented copyright releases, and clear citations. Because of the breadth of expertise needed, the assumption taken was that it was critical to avoid the cognitive illusion of WYSIATI ("What You See is All There Is"), to use Dr. Daniel Kahneman's term. That meant that the instructional designer had to find and review often over a hundred or more articles in a field in order to select the 20 – 30 used as main sources in a slideshow; the others would serve as background information (or were not directly relevant to the slideshow angle or were too specific to the topic).

Team members went out to take photos at county fairs, public streets (for images of "bulb-outs and pedestrian islands"), an auction barn, and a farm. Local and state government provided images of what a stop-order movement might look like in the case of a contagious animal disease outbreak. Many resources were pulled from credible government human and animal health sites, such as the Centers for Disease Control and Prevention (CDC), World Health Organization (WHO), Office of International des Epizooties (OiE, the World Organisation for Animal Health), United States Department of Agriculture (USDA), and Defra (Department for Environment, Food and Rural Affairs for the UK). Case studies were drawn from the CDC's Morbidity and Mortality Weekly Report (MMWR) collection.

The work was done in the order that certain resources became available. For example, video interviews were scheduled based on the availability of the principals. Or, slideshows on certain topics were developed based on related themes and topics, to fit the team's learning in that area (Certain team members already had extensive scientific knowledge, but other members of the team had to acquire the learning as they proceeded.).

The draft course content was placed in a work site in the university's Learning / Course Management System (L/CMS). That course site was the location also of the finalized course. To meet legal requirements, the team strove to follow all laws regarding intellectual property (attaining proper rights releases and maintaining documentation of these), accessibility (alt-texting all images; transcribing all videos), privacy rights (attaining signed releases from those involved in the course videos), libel (vetting contents), and others.

Another way to visually depict the contents of this course involves using a content analysis tool expressed as a Wordle™. Figure 4 shows a data visualization that collates various textual contents.

Figure 4. A content analysis of the textual contents (using Wordle™)

Here, the textual contents of the course—the slideshows, syllabus, video transcripts, course directions, assignment rubrics, and transition texts—were dropped into the free Wordle™ (text analysis and data visualization) program, which analyzes the "quantitative structure" of textual contents. Multimedia was represented by the text of the machine-readable transcriptions. What were not included were open-book quizzes (which are randomized), alt-texting (of info-rich images), assigned readings, assigned cases, and an advertising flyer for the course. Words eliminated from the Wordle™ word cloud included "Dr.," which was used frequently in the transcripts. "Time stamp" was also eliminated. The word "cont." was also deleted because it had a high listing because of the continuation of topics between slides in a slide who. Finally, filler words like "like" and "just" were also eliminated. What resulted were 144,796 words over 484 pages of textual contents extracted from the finalized contents of the course build. The resulting data visualization from word frequency appearances (resulting in larger-size words) is the following.

This "word cloud" data visualization (a light quantitative approach as the "coding scheme") evokes some of the complexity and breadth of the topic. Ideally, this content analysis would include the textbook contents, which would involve hundreds of pages of additional contents (but also the editorial hand of the two respective authors). (The image is used here thanks to the liberal copyright policy of Wordle.net.)

The visualization highlights some of the essentials of the threshold concept of One Health (the core unifying idea that is a pre-requisite to understanding this) as well as the threshold knowledge (set of core concepts to understand the mixed disciplinary field) underpinning its approach. If this word cloud shows anything, it does capture the intertwined nature of One Health, with human and animal diseases closely related (or in many cases, caused by the same pathogen). There are many implied environmental dependencies on each other. While diseases and pathogens were covered in the course, the framing of it was much more accessible based on lived experiences, cases, research, and observations.

To be more specific, and to show the focus on various disease concerns, the following mind maps (spatial layout diagrams) show the three segments of the course and some of the disease concerns raised in each segment.

Above, the reverse zoonoses section was alluded to but not fully developed in the finalized curriculum.

The related mind maps (or "word trees") in Figures 5 – 7 provide a cursory and macro-level (instructional designer) overview. The actual learning materials were micro-level in-depth slideshows with accurate imagery and research citations throughout. These were bolstered by subject-specific filmed interviews. Additional resources were included at the end. (These were created using the open-source software tool FreeMind 0.9.0.)

Figure 5. A mind map of some of the diseases of concern in the "humans and animals" segment

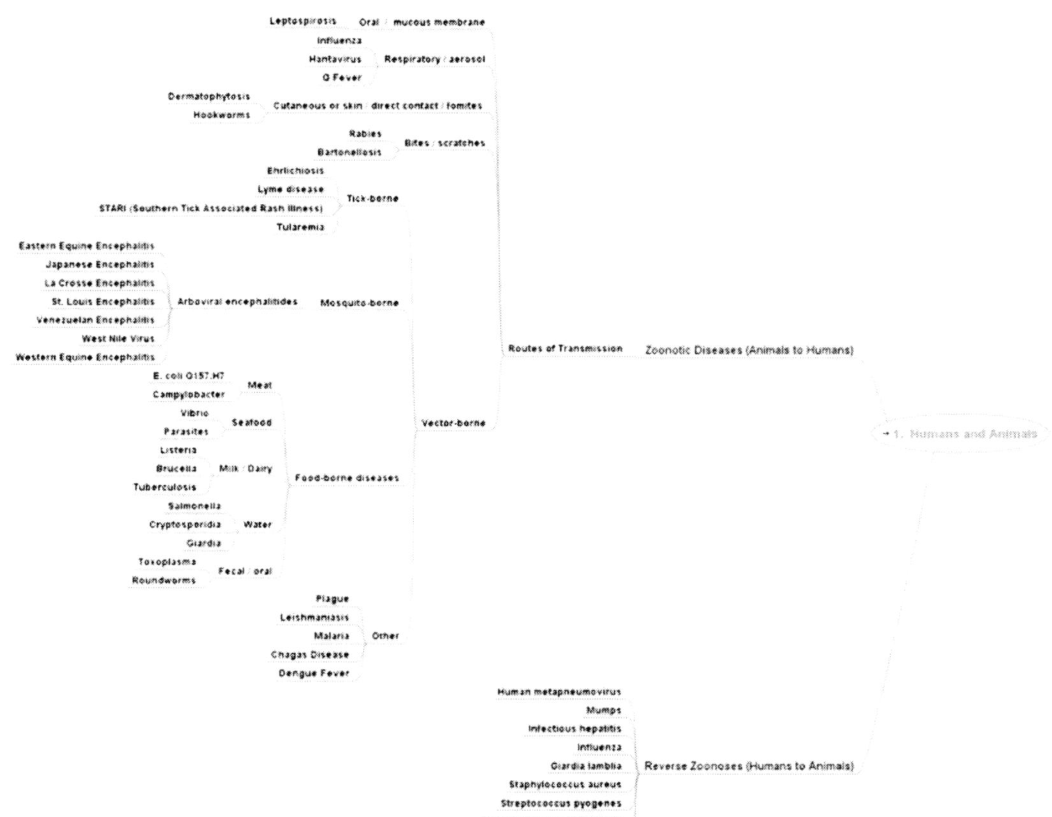

Figure 6. A mind map of some of the diseases of concern in the "animals and environment" segment

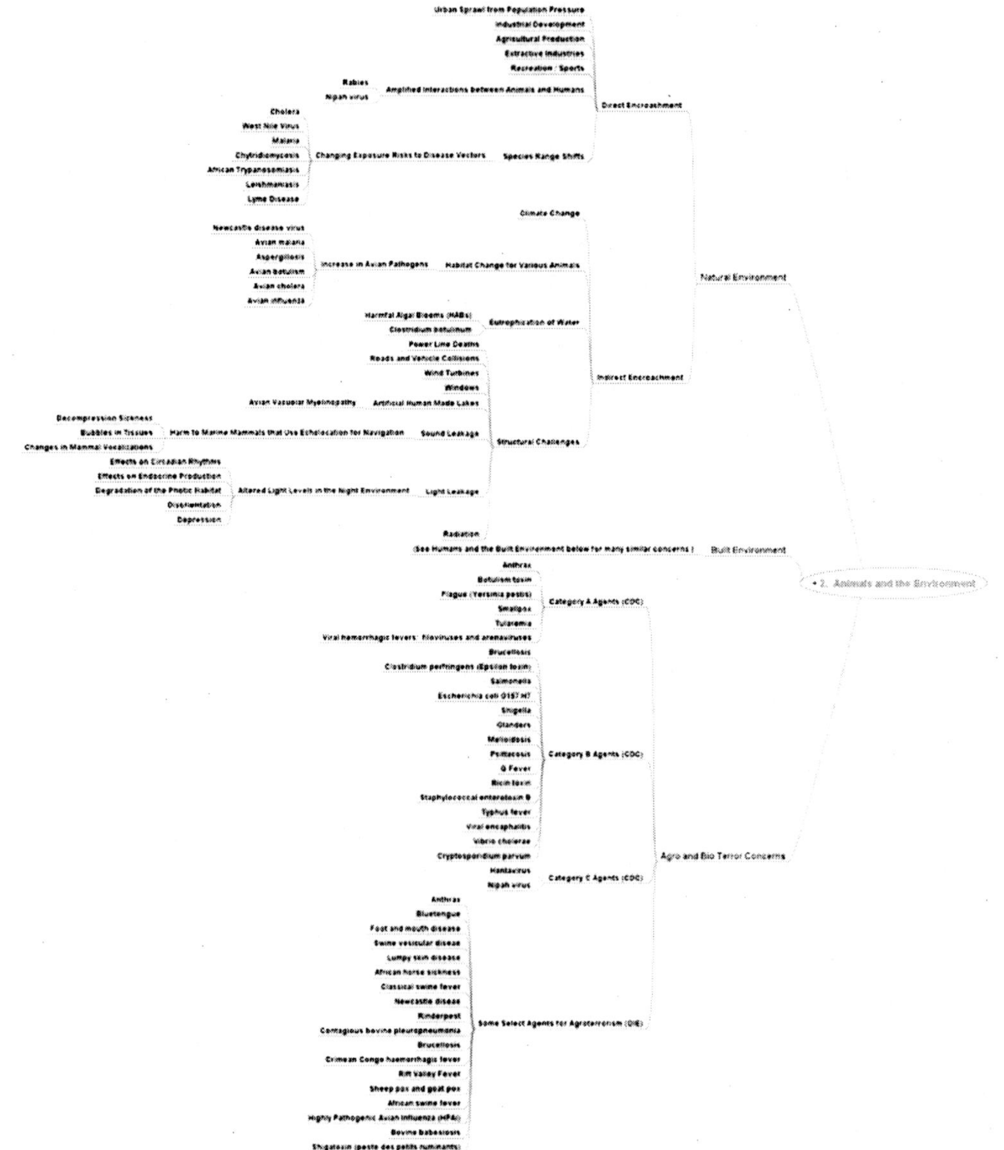

Some latent content analyses: These visualizations provide an overview of the explicit and manifest contents. In terms of latent contents, based on the author's work on the project and reevaluation of the contents based on these visualizations, there are some embedded concepts. A One Health approach adheres to scientific methods for knowability. Each of the different areas have shared and unique tools and equipment for research. The solid focus on respected method is part and parcel of the need to balance against human subjectivity-based error. In the biological sciences, there are humans and then "non-human animals," which acknowledge the biological nature of people and their relationship to animals; it also acknowledges the importance of people ("speciesism"), in general. In this same vein, while One Health may seem "political" (in terms of its sug-

Figure 7. A mind map of some of the diseases of concern in the "humans and environment" segment

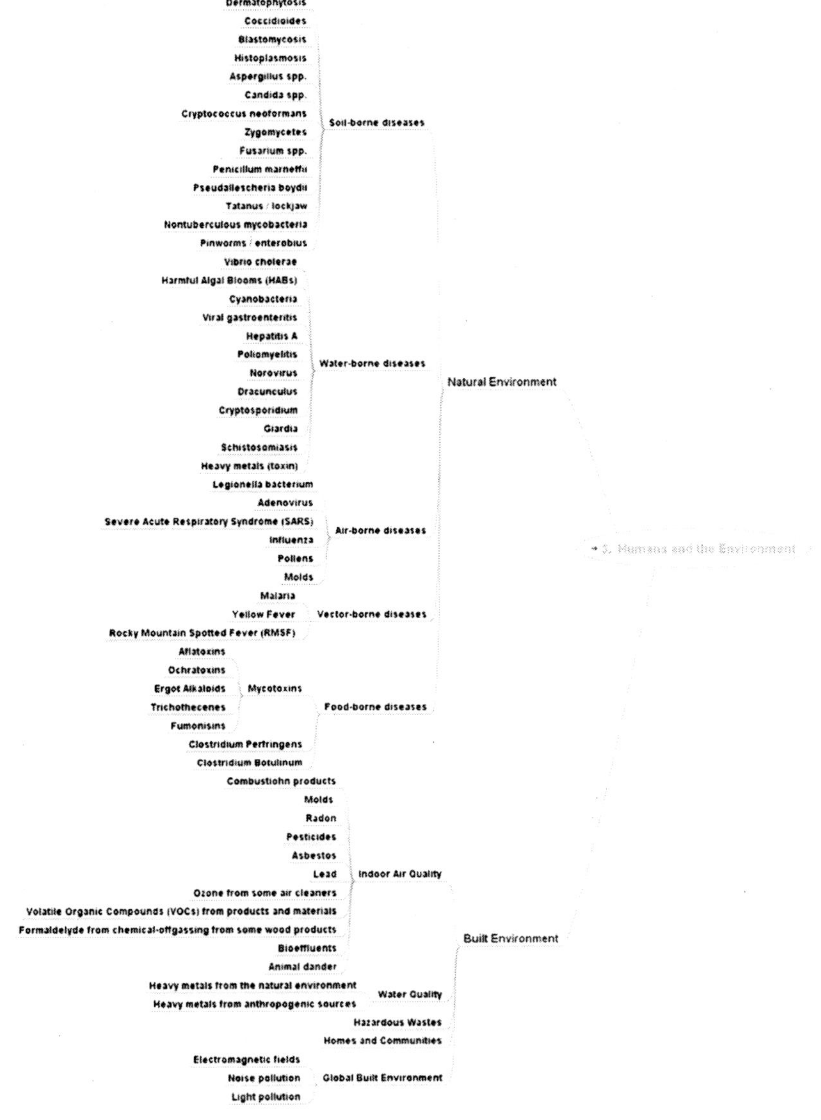

gested priorities and approaches), the development team took great pains to avoid politicized or activist stances. The concept is that the facts will speak, and what people interpret from those and how they proceed, will be in their professional and personal purviews. A One Health approach requires the build-up of knowledge and capabilities among researchers. There will have to be clear cost-benefit calculations for educational administrators. There seems to be a built-in gradualism to this transdisciplinary concept and approach. Another latent concept involves the power of complexity and system effects, the idea that various phenomena affect other phenomena to varying degrees. Another latent concept involves the critical need for respectful intercommunications and collaborations among professionals to push the field forward. Finally, the approach of One Health is practical. The idea is to strive for applied approaches that may enhance decision-making and processes. These four main values infuse the curriculum.

Templating to contain and present the multidisciplinary contents: To present the contents, two simple and familiar structures were used. The main one was the slideshow construct, which was evolved by the team. This contained the proper branding to align with university policies (in terms of the logos used and the correct shades of the school purple). The basic order was as follows: a title slide, learning objectives, contents, transition slides, alt-texting of all images, proper citation methods of all research (cited by both links and the American Society for Microbiology citation method), and additional resources (links) (see Figure 8).

The videos were captured based on customized questions (developed by the team) and asked of the subject matter experts. These interviews had a simple back-end structure, involving the presenter's self-introduction, descriptions of their respective fields, an explanation of their research work, and anticipated critical research questions within their domain fields. Given the open semi-structured questions of interviews, the actual interviews (between Dr. Jodi Freifeld and the interview subject) developed in a variety of directions. Then, the development team went through transcripts and selected out contents that were not absolutely necessary, and sometimes, they reordered the remaining contents for logical (if not chronological sequential) coherence.

3. Strategic Design for Learners

For an emergent science-based curriculum, there is a strong need for foundational convergent learning (of facts) and then the innovations of divergent learning (for the innovative transdisciplinary aspects). For the convergent fact-based learning, the development team integrated science-based articles; research-based slideshows; SME videos; and other readings. They brought in CDC MMWR case analyses as well as other cases to acclimate learners to the case format used in the medical

Figure 8. A Templated Slideshow Structure (with a SlideSorter view of "Comparative Medicine")

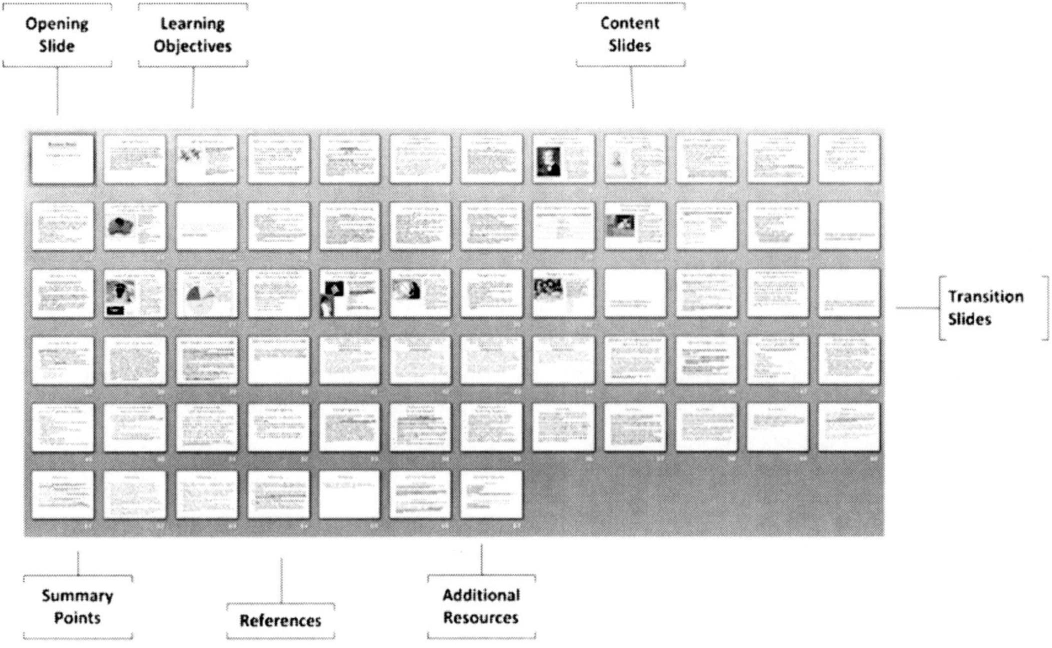

and public health professions and to introduce them to case-based reasoning.

To introduce innovation, learners were assigned a term research project with a fairly open-ended approach to topic selection (any disease or issue related to One Health) in order to benefit learners based on their particular backgrounds and unique interests. (The course is designed for individuals who already work in public health, students pursuing veterinary medicine, students pursuing graduate public health degrees, and practicing physicians and veterinarians. In the first semester of the course being offered, multiple individuals with MDs enrolled along with others from the prior demographic groups.) The results of this assignment will be posted broadly to the class, so the learners will be able to learn from their peers. The design and development team set clear standards for valid information sources, so the students will acquire some secondary research skills and familiarize themselves with some of the respected sources in the field. To socialize learners into One Health, learners were encouraged to explore professional organizations and government agencies related to the various topics. (This was done through an "Additional Resources" section at the ends of the various topical slideshows.)

The Message Board was employed to first "break the ice" among the distance learners. Then, there were discussion questions to encourage learners to synthesize and integrate various aspects of the learning. The students were asked to interact with each other around the learning contents. The instructor would interact in depth with her students as well.

The following timeline expresses the basic sequentiality of the designed learning. Table 1 shows the developmental sequencing of the course curriculum.

A shared information hierarchy: Mixed-disciplinary curriculums may be enhanced with points of commonality. In this particular course, a core underlying assumption involves the values of scientific inquiry and research. While researchers may use different equipment and methodologies, they still share underlying values about how information may be arrived at in a credible way. These values emerged as the team worked together to co-create the slideshows. The gold standard for research involves laboratory experiments with proper procedures. Meta-analyses and analyses offer interpretive value. Local cases, because they tend to have limited generalizability, come next in this hierarchy; these are valuable because they are based on experiences and observations. Theoretical papers, models, and simulations offer hypotheticals and projections; these encapsulate a range of research. Many of these are not yet tested. Papers that show the testing of models would be considered research papers. Position papers offer formal and advocacy stances on an issue. Delphi studies and expert interviews (and panel "discussions") are considered fairly limited because of the format and limitations of sources. Crowd-sourced information (in open wikis and blogs) without citations is at the lowest level of the information hierarchy.

The information used in course materials builds the credibility of the transdisciplinary concept. In that light, it is critical that only the best supported factual information should be used. (Especially with emergent learning, the course should be designed to control for possible negative learning or misunderstandings. It is critical not to push a science beyond where it will go, but it's also important to "amplify" research where possible.) The development team worked to ensure that issues were thoroughly addressed and that the proper terminologies were used. Because of the emergent nature of the contents, the team worked to identify gaps in information for thoroughness. The team members also "spotted" each other in terms of the accuracy of representation, to ensure that incorrect inferences would be less likely for the learners.

The difficulty of applying critical thinking into a complex domain field further emphasizes the need for proper training, especially given

Table 1. "introduction to one health" timeline

Section	Slideshows	Videos	Readings	Assignments
Week 1: Course Intro	Intro to Microbiology Intro to Disease Models	"One Health" "The Role of a Public Health Officer" "A Look at One Health History"	Course Outline Syllabus Instructor Self-Intro "One Health in the News" (current readings) Assigned Readings from the Text	Student Self-Introductions in the Message Board
Section 1: HUMANS AND ANIMALS				
Week 2: Globalization and the Human-Animal Bond	The Role of Globalization in Emerging Diseases Comparative Medicine	The Human-Animal Bond Global Public Health Sustaining Global Surveillance	Assigned Readings from the Text "One Health in the News" (current readings)	
Week 3: Zoonotic Diseases—Routes of Transmission	Zoonotic Diseases: Routes of Transmission	Be Aware of Diseases You and Your Pets Can Share Leptospirosis Rabies: Johnny the Puppy Toxoplasmosis	Assigned Readings from the Text "One Health in the News" (current readings)	
Week 4: Zoonotic Diseases: Vector-borne Diseases and Sentinel Animals	Zoonotic Diseases 2: Vector-borne Diseases Animals as Sentinels	Ehrlichiosis and Anaplasmosis West Nile Virus	Assigned Readings from the Text "One Health in the News" (current readings)	Interactive Discussion Questions
Week 5: Zoonotic Diseases: Foodborne Illness	Zoonotic Diseases 3: Foodborne Diseases	Shiga Toxin Producing E. Coli	Assigned Readings from the Text "One Health in the News" (current readings) Case Study Readings	Case Study Analysis 1
Week 6: Food Safety, Defense, and Security	Food Safety, Defense, and Security	Food Safety Antibiotic Residues Milk Safety Safe Meat Processing	Assigned Readings from the Text "One Health in the News" (current readings)	Quiz 1
Section 2: HUMANS AND THE ENVIRONMENT				
Week 7: The Built Environment Disease Concerns	Built Environment Disease Concerns	Indoor Air Quality Lead Poisoning	Assigned Readings from the Text "One Health in the News" (current readings)	
Week 8: The Natural Environment Disease Concerns	Natural Environment Disease Concerns	Blue-Green Algae Heavy Metals and Trace Minerals Mycotoxins	Assigned Readings from the Text "One Health in the News" (current readings)	
Week 9: The Built Environment, Physical Activity, Health, and Safety	Built Environment Effects on Physical Activity	Design of the Built Environment Design of Homes for the Human Life Span Walkability	Assigned Readings from the Text "One Health in the News" (current readings)	Interactive Discussion Questions
Week 10: Multiple and Reciprocal Levels of Human-Environment Interaction	Multiple and Reciprocal Levels of Human-Environment Interaction	Maintaining Human Health in Short-term Concentrations of People Rocky Mountain Spotted Fever	Assigned Readings from the Text "One Health in the News" (current readings)	Quiz 2

continued on following page

Table 1. Continued

Section	Slideshows	Videos	Readings	Assignments
Section 3: ANIMALS AND THE ENVIRONMENT				
Week 11: Animals in the Built Environment	Animals in the Built Environment	Wetland Ecology Exercising with Pets Lead Toxicity in Livestock	Assigned Readings from the Text Case Study Readings "One Health in the News" (current readings)	Case Analysis 2
Week 12: Wildlife Habitat Encroach-ment (and) Intro of Non-Native Species	Wildlife Habitat Encroachment The Introduction of Non-Native Species	Wildlife Encroachment Invasive Species	Assigned Readings from the Text "One Health in the News" (current readings)	Interactive Discussion Question 3
Week 13: Climate Change and Effects on Animals (and) Animal Disaster Management	Climate Change Effects on Animals	Pets in Disasters Livestock in Disasters Sampling Crab Larvae in the Gulf of Mexico	Assigned Readings from the Text "One Health in the News" (current readings)	
Week 14: Bio- and Agro-Terrorism	Bio- and Agro- Terrorism	Bio- and Agro- Terrorism and Emerging Diseases Food Protection and Defense	Assigned Readings from the Text "One Health in the News" (current readings)	Quiz 3
Week 15: Term Paper and Wrap-up	Term Paper Rubric	N/A	Case Study Readings "One Health in the News" (current readings) Original Student Research (secondary research)	Term Paper (An Original Case Analysis)

that the human mind has "intrinsic tendencies toward illusion, distortion, and error" (van Gelder, 2005, p. 45). Initiation into the various domain fields occurs through the acquisition of language, common practices, professional ethics, and methodologies.

Course soft launches and soft-pedaling the One Health message: In creating a course around an emergent and potentially controversial topic, the leader of the project decided on a soft launch, which included a presentation to an out-of-state funding organization, flyers posted around the campus (and the two branch campuses) and posted on Websites, and emails from deans to their respective staff and college graduate students. Further, the group worked with a public relations professional from the Division of Continuing Education to place an article about the course in the university news online publication, *K-State Today,* and a note was placed on the One Health Kansas Website. The PI took due caution not to over-reach in terms of going for a splashy national-level publication, at least not in the first offering in Fall Semester 2012. With a topic that is emergent, there is a potential for missteps that may alienate potential adopters of the transdisciplinary One Health approach. In that sense, narrowcasting the outreach made much more sense than widespread broadcasting.

In that light, it makes sense to modulate the launch. After all, it's the in-field(s) practitioners that will set the pace for any advancement in mixed disciplinary work; they will have to work out what is considered normative practices within their domain standards. Ideologies (with policy implications, such as a pro-human / animal / environment health stance) may be extrapolated from the One Health course curriculum, but these were not points emphasized during the course build.

The data array was used to inform a social network diagram showing the marketing efforts that were done and then which ones were the most successful (in terms of bringing in actual students). While there is a value in publicizing the work, the bottom line has to be the value of the online course for students.

Table 2 maps the actual tools that were effective in resulting in actual student enrollments for the two-credit graduate-level course. This type of analysis informs marketing outreach strategies.

As can be seen by the fragmented social network, Figure 9 the actual students who enrolled in the course were reached through direct contacts from emails to their deans, who distributed the message to their respective faculty and academic advisors. Two students were recruited by contacts made with an out-of-state health clinic (organization) which provided some limited funding to the course development. The flyers around campus elicited a few phone calls of interest, but none of those resulted in a direct enrollment. A range of endeavors, indicated at the top left of the diagram, stand as isolate nodes. They did not contribute to the enrollment of the first-semester of enrolled learners.

Faculty selection: Optimally, in selecting faculty members for the course, as in the selection of subject matter experts during the development phase, it's critical to bring in individuals who are solidly achieved in their respective fields. In academia, generalists are seen to go into administration; specialists achieve in their respective fields and earn credibility that way. Further, they must have a broader sense of the transdisciplinary realm (in this case, One Health, public health, and environmentalism). A mix of both specialist and generalist knowledge is required for effective subject matter focus.

Defining what One Health means in applied work: In terms of what One Health means in terms of research methodologies and collaborations, there was very little in the research literature that addressed this issue. This may be that the approach is a nascent one. How this concept manifests in education, research, and applied practice will be defined by subject matter experts who pursue this collaboration.

To illustrate this concept, the following is a filled radar chart that expresses how different domain fields may come into play for a particular (theoretical) problem-solving challenge. Figure 10 posits three theoretical scenarios: (1) an emerging zoonotic human disease scenario, (2) a mass animal disease outbreak scenario, and

Table 2. The data array for course outreach and marketing

	Student 1	Student 2	Student 3	Student 4	Student 5	Student 6	Student 7
One Health Kansas Website	0	0	0	0	0	0	0
Article in K-State Today	0	0	0	0	0	0	0
Article in Local Manhattan Mercury Newspaper	0	0	0	0	0	0	0
Flyers around K-State Main Campus	0	0	0	0	0	0	0
Flyers around K-State Olathe Branch Campus	0	0	0	0	0	0	0
Flyers around K-State Salina Branch Campus	0	0	0	0	0	0	0
Emails to the College Deans	1	1	1	1	1	1	1
Connections with Out-of-State Funder / Health Clinic	0	0	0	0	0	0	0

Figure 9. A social network diagram of the outreach, publicity, and recruitment (a two-mode network)

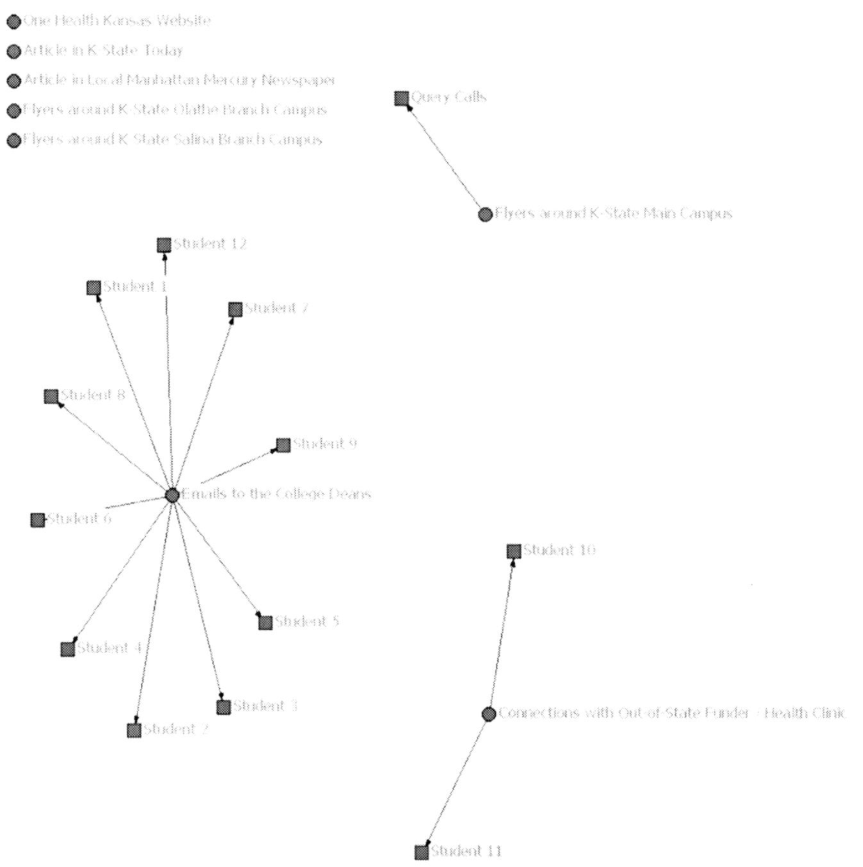

(3) an industrial pollution scenario. This chart then shows a variety of domain fields which may have particular insights for analysis and problem-solving. The numbers in this chart are fictitious, and the scenarios themselves are fictitious, but this image is to show how mixed disciplinarity through professional intercommunications and collaboration may enhance how people engage shared challenges.

Figure 10 shows how different domain areas may provide more in-depth insights than other fields. For those working on real-world health challenges, they will have to work strategically to include those who may include insights that are most critical. Further, almost all the various fields are conceptualized as having some impact. This illustration is conceptual, but real-world scenarios may be mapped to a similar conceptualization with varying levels of expertise brought to bear.

PROLIFERATION OF ONE HEALTH IDEAS

Finally, to understand the proliferation of One Health ideas, there are several ways to conduct explorations via the Internet. One tool, NodeXL enables the extraction of microblogging data from Twitter and the presentation of the details in a social network diagram. Figure 11 shows two main clusters of microblogging (Tweeting, in this case) about One Health. There is high centralization and density in the center, but the social network

Figure 10. One Health scenarios and mixed disciplinary contributions to analysis and problem-solving (a filled radar chart)

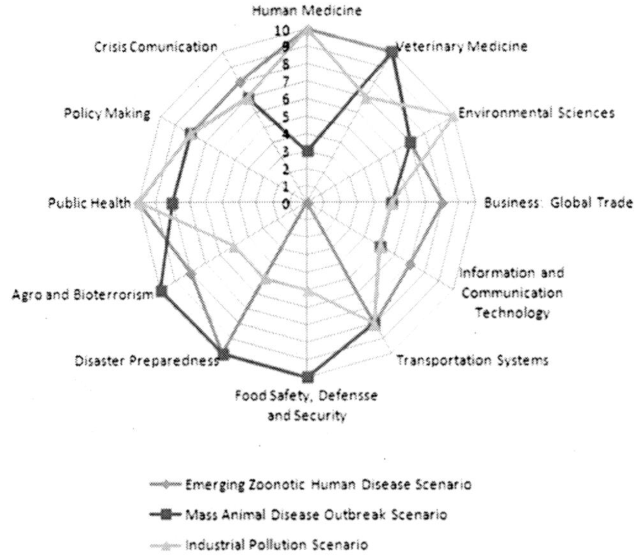

Figure 11. Microblogging about One Health in the Twitterverse (per NodeXL and the Harel-Koren fast multiscale visualization)

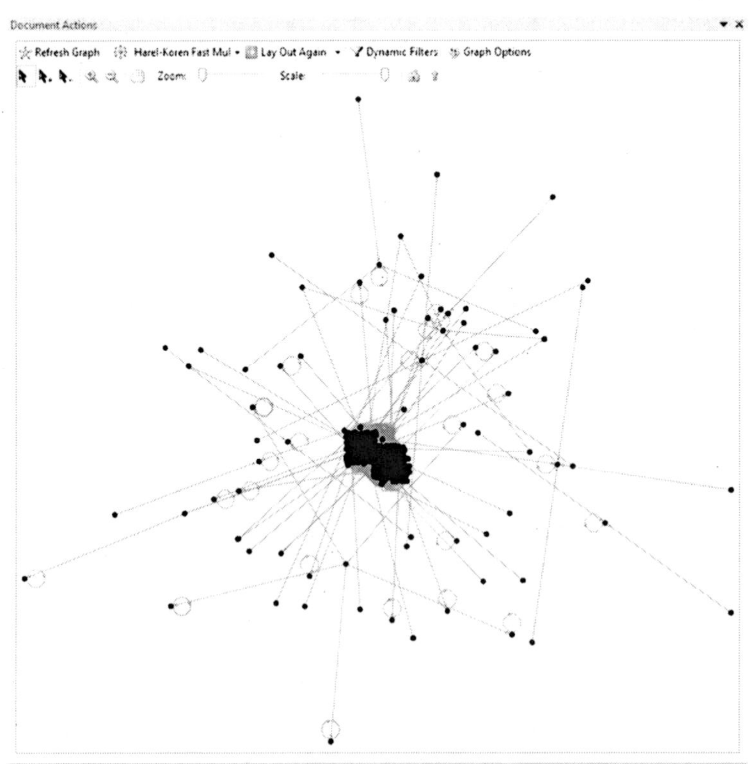

quickly thins out, in this Harel-Koren Fast Multiscale visualization.

Table 3 shows the data behind this directed graph. The network is a fairly close one, with the geodesic distance (the shortest distance between the most extreme nodes) at only 3 skips or degrees of separation. The average geodesic distance is only .4 degrees of separation, which suggests overall reachability of the others in this social network surrounding "One Health". This is a small online community of likely initiates to the issue. For "one health" to proliferate further as an issue of awareness, much less practice, there will have to be much wider proliferation. In terms of reciprocated vertexes (nodes), only 1% mutually follow each others Tweets, which means that there are likely a few leaders whom many follow, without the leaders necessarily following their followers (in a reciprocal way). Just a small percentage of nodes follow each other. The average density of connections is 7 nodes in this network.

Another way of presenting Table 3 data is through the Fruchterman-Reingold force-based algorithm. This visualization in Figure 12 shows a few central nodes that are connected to others, but most are followers in the periphery who subscribe to the messages of a few.

Another approach is to use the Maltego tool to analyze the Internet presence of the One Health Initiative Website. Figure 13 shows an organizational site with some connections to a few organizations and food safety Websites. For it to achieve global reach, it will need to have more global partners and more buy-in. The sophistication of the site itself is minimal, with only 4 nodes of variant content types.

The uses of various tools to surface new information from Internet and Web presences will be critical to getting a sense of the proliferation of ideas and practices. Deeper analyses of the various nodes and Websites of the partner organizations would contribute more specific data. To enhance such searches, of course, it would help

Table 3. Microblogging about One Health: the graph metrics (per NodeXL)

Graph Metric	Value
Graph Type	Directed
Vertices	1000
Unique Edges	983
Edges With Duplicates	66
Total Edges	1049
Self-Loops	977
Reciprocated Vertex Pair Ratio	0.014285714
Reciprocated Edge Ratio	0.028169014
Connected Components	934
Single-Vertex Connected Components	899
Maximum Vertices in a Connected Component	12
Maximum Edges in a Connected Component	19
Maximum Geodesic Distance (Diameter)	3
Average Geodesic Distance	0.404511
Graph Density	7.10711E-05
Modularity	Not Applicable
NodeXL Version	1.0.1.229

Figure 12. Microblogging about One Health in the Twitterverse (per NodeXL and the Fruchterman-Reingold force-based visualization)

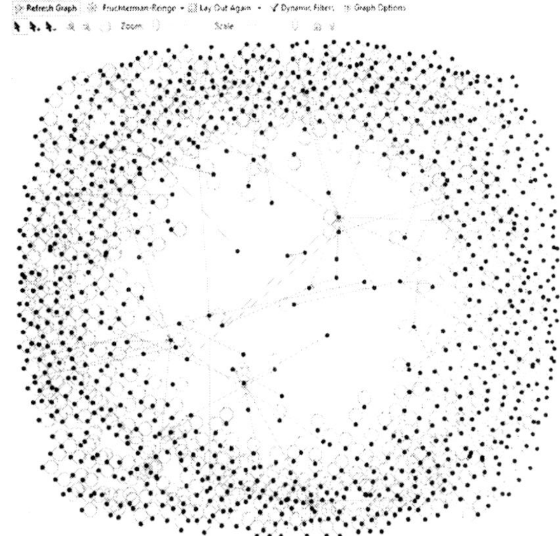

Figure 13. The One Health initiative website (through a Maltego "all transforms" analysis)

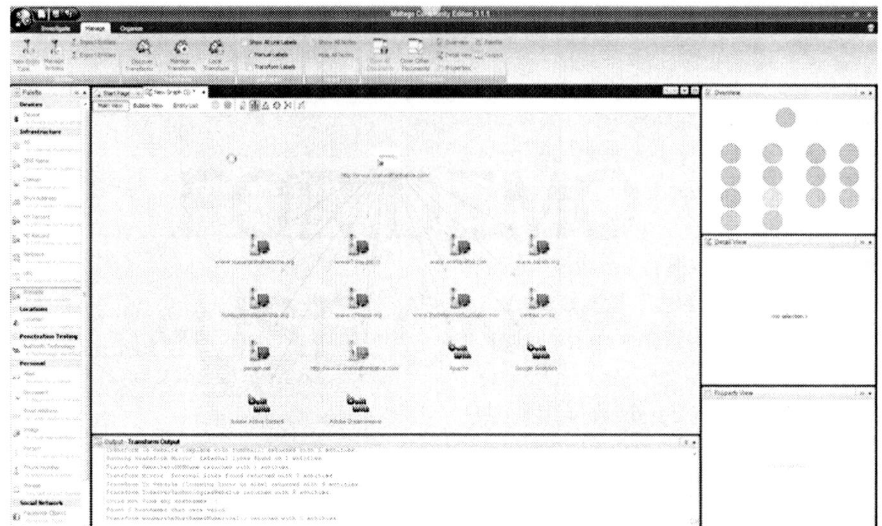

to query insiders who may serve as informants about their respective fields and perspectives.

LEVELS OF ABSTRACTION FOR MIXED DISCIPLINARY WORK

Beyond the specific "use case" of One Health, the learning from this curricular build offers some insights regarding mixed disciplinary work. One way to conceptualized mixed disciplinary work may be in three levels of abstraction: concrete / specific (observable), connective undefined middle (methodological), and high abstraction (conceptual). See Figure 14.

At the base level are concrete / specific elements, grounded in observable details. These specific elements come from empirical observations in the world and in experimental contexts. Some aspects may be quantifiable. All should be describable. These specific elements include tangible data, case studies, research findings, examples, and mixed terminology; often, the findings are expressed in tangibles like publications in the various fields.

The connective undefined middle consists of methodological approaches to mixed disciplinary work. These include collaborative teaming and intercommunications methodologies; academic and organizational workplace cultures and structures (including funding and rewards—like recognition, scholarships, publications); information and communication technology (ICT), model design and development, research methodologies, and equipment. This is the connective layer that explores high abstractions as well as the concrete phenomena of the world.

In terms of high abstraction, these would include theories that highlight similarities between domains. Testable hypotheses may also be fairly abstract. Models, both conceptual (expert) and mental (novice or amateur) ones, tend towards abstraction. Simulations, which are actualized models, too, may be fairly abstract in presentation and predictiveness. Ontologies or knowledge structures tend to be high-level in order to be inclusive of a variety of information. (The metadata describing the terms and information artifacts must be inclusive of multiple domain fields.) Decision trees may vary in terms of abstraction levels, but these often are designed with sufficient abstract flexibility for greater transferability and application to a variety of circumstances. High abstraction elements organize information and identify relationships.

Endeavors for mixed disciplinary approaches often seem to originate at the grounded observable level, which is then abstracted into concepts. The follow-on work involves the methodological level—or the work that connects the conceptual and the observable, with revisions made to the conceptual as more concrete research is completed. One may move from the grounded level to the abstract using inductive logic (moving from the specific to the general); one may move from the high abstraction level to the grounded using deductive logic (reasoning from the general to the specific). As with most science research, there is no final "proof"; rather, transdisciplinary fields move towards pseudo-conclusions based on the weight of the available evidence.

This visualization helps in the analysis of what progress has been made in a particular mixed disciplinary approach. One caveat: transdisciplinary evolution of various fields will likely be case-specific to the particular transdisciplinary "overlay." How this work evolves and the benefits it offers will depend in larger part on the work of the various professionals in the fields.

In terms of "unit of analysis," future researchers may conduct content analysis in various ways. One way may be from a particular discipline or even a team member or learner (ego perspective) as a unit of analysis. Perhaps transdisciplinary curriculums may be explored. Analysts may identify a taxonomy of necessary knowledge among various domain fields to describe what is needed to advance a field: theirs will necessarily require an intimate knowledge of the states of the domain fields to build this high-level transdisciplinary view in order to identify gaps. Another may involve the published cross-disciplinary research done in a transdisciplinary area. That research involves specific-level data (Level 1: Concrete / Specific). Researchers may analyze a range of strategies that serve as connectivity between the concrete and the high-abstract (Level 2: Connective Undefined Middle). These involve bridging strategies between the various domains. Finally, researchers may engage various abstract models, ontologies, and decision-trees (Level 3: High Abstraction).

Figure 14. Mixed disciplinarity elements in three levels of abstraction

3. High Abstraction	Conceptual • Theories • Testable hypotheses • Models (conceptual and mental) • Simulations • Ontologies / knowledge structures • Decision trees and structures
2. Connective Undefined Middle	Methodological • Mixed disciplinarity collaborative methodologies (teaming and intercommunications) • Academic and organizational workplace cultures and structures (including funding and rewards) • Information and Communication Technology (ICT) • Model design and development • Research methodologies • Equipment
1. Concrete / Specific	Observable • Data (tangible) • Case studies • Research findings • Examples • Mixed terminology

FUTURE RESEARCH DIRECTIONS

As for this One Health course, it is a gateway course that may lead to a number of professions. To understand this better, it would be critical to map lead-up courses and lead-away courses from "Introduction to One Health." Further, understanding the various skill clusters linked to successful application of One Health would add another dimension to people's understandings.

In a sense, this course is a conversation starter in academia, to encourage a multi-disciplinary approach to complex health phenomena. The approach is non-deterministic and strategically ambiguous, which allows those in various research and applied capacities to define what One Health means in their respective areas.

To "map" where the state of One Health is currently, it may be helpful to conduct a Delphi study of the experts in the field working on One Health issues. (Appendix A offers a draft set of questions that could be the core of a Delphi study.) Further, there may be a qualitative content analysis (expressed as a node-link diagram) of the broadly available One Health publications (books and articles). Or, there may be an analysis of publications based on abstracts (summaries) alone, of the corpus / corpora data, which is currently not very extensive as the approach is a nascent one.

Transdisciplinary collaborations will likely continue to play a critical role in academic work. Currently, such work is designed as an overlay on multiple fields that transform the domains in unique ways. Future research may delve into different methods for transdisciplinarity, such as faculty and staff interdisciplinary clusters used to advance pure and applied research tracks.

Currently, this transdisciplinary approach generally affects graduate students, faculty, and researchers. Undergraduate students, who do not usually begin studying in their majors until their junior and senior years, may not be the best candidates for multi-disciplinary research until they are firmly grounded in a domain and its technicalities; however, the converse could also be argued: that undergraduates would benefit from exposure to multiple-domain research and practices as a tool to help them discern differences between domains.

In a sense, it may be argued that each case of transdisciplinary work is *sui generis* or unique onto itself, with irreducible insights. Any transdisciplinary collaboration may be a one-off, a short-run phenomenon, or part of a long-term trend. On the other hand, there may be transferable takeaways based on research that may benefit other projects. Practitioners may observe other bridges that enhance the transdisciplinary work. Such team members may migrate their transdisciplinary skill sets to other collaborative projects.

CONCLUSION

This chapter described the instructional design strategies behind the building of a complex emergent curriculum that drew from a number of domain fields. This described how a cross-disciplinary team used a variety of strategies to actualize the transdisciplinary curriculum. Some of those strategies may be transferable to other transdisciplinary curricular endeavors. Further, this chapter offered some ideas about how to conceptualize the approach to an emergent, transdisciplinary curriculum.

ACKNOWLEDGMENT

Thanks to Drs. Beth A. Montelone (lead PI), Robert L. Larson (co-PI), and Jodi Freifeld (instructor), the heart of the design and development team. Thanks also to videographers Kent Nelson and Joseph Chapes. This "Intro to One Health" project was one of the toughest curricular builds that I have been a part of because of the unique challenges of the biological sciences, the research, the stratospheric standards, and the long development cycle. In retrospect, the "emergent" and "transdisciplinarity" features added to the complexity of the instructional design. All said, I am also deeply proud of the resulting One Health course. I learned a lot about the subject areas and know the importance of continuing learning.

REFERENCES

Boden, D., Borrego, M., & Newswander, L. K. (2011). Student socialization in interdisciplinary doctoral education. *Higher Education*, *62*, 741–755. doi:10.1007/s10734-011-9415-1.

Cummings, J. N., & Kiesler, S. (2008). Who collaborates successfully? Prior experience reduces collaboration barriers in distributed interdisciplinary research. In *Proceedings of the Computer-Supported Collaborative Work* (CSCW '08), (pp. 437-446). San Diego, CA: ACM.

Domik, G., & Fischer, G. (2010). Coping with complex real-world problems: Strategies for developing the competency of transdisciplinary collaboration. In *Proceedings of KCKS 2010*. IFIP AICT.

Felt, U., Igelsböck, J., Schikowitz, A., & Völker, T. (2012). Growing into what? The (un-)disciplined socialisation (sic) of early stage researchers into transdisciplinary research. *Higher Education*. doi: doi:10.1007/s10734-012-9560-1.

Golde, C. M., & Gallagher, H. A. (1999). The challenges of conducting interdisciplinary research in traditional doctoral programs. *Ecosystems (New York, N.Y.)*, *2*(4), 281–285. doi:10.1007/s100219900076.

Hadorn, G. H., Pohl, C., & Bammer, G. (2010). Solving problems through transdisciplinary research. In R. Frodeman, J. T. Klein, & C. Mitcham (Eds.), *The Oxford Handbook of Interdisciplinarity*. Retrieved from csid.unt.edu/files/HOI%20 Chapters/Chapter_30_HOI.doc

Jantsch, E. (1972). Inter- and transdisciplinary university: A systems approach to education and innovation. *Higher Education*, *1*(1), 7–37. Retrieved from http://www.jstor.org/stable/3445957 doi:10.1007/BF01956879.

Lampe, K.-H., Riede, K., & Doerr, M. (2008). Research between natural and cultural history information: Benefits and IT-requirements for transdisciplinarity. *ACM Journal on Computing and Cultural Heritage,* 1(1), 4:1 – 4:22.

Leahey, E., Keith, B., & Crockett, J. (2010). Specialization and promotion in an academic discipline. *Research in Social Stratification and Mobility*, *28*, 135–155. doi:10.1016/j.rssm.2009.12.001.

Lélé, S., & Norgaard, R. (2005). Practicing Interdisciplinarity. *Bioscience*, *55*(11), 967–975. doi:10.1641/0006-3568(2005)055[0967:PI]2.0.CO;2.

Mansillka, V. B., & Duraising, E. D. (2007). Targeted assessment of students' interdisciplinary work: An empirically grounded framework proposed. *The Journal of Higher Education*, *78*(2), 215–237. Retrieved from http://www.jstor.org/stable/4501203 doi:10.1353/jhe.2007.0008.

Mnookin, S. (2011). *The panic virus: A true story of medicine, science, and fear*. New York: Simon & Schuster.

Narrod, C., Zinsstag, J., & Tiongco, M. (2012). A One Health framework for estimating the economic costs of zoonotic diseases on society. *EcoHealth*. Retrieved from http://www.ncbi.nlm.nih.gov/pmc/articles/PMC3415616/

National Center for Emerging and Zoonotic Infectious Diseases. (2012). Retrieved from http://www.cdc.gov/ncezid/

Nicolson, C. R., Starfield, A. M., Kofinas, G. P., & Kruse, J. A. (2002). Ten heuristics for interdisciplinary modeling projects. *Ecosystems (New York, N.Y.)*, *5*, 376–384. doi:10.1007/s10021-001-0081-5.

Nikitina, S. (2005). Pathways of interdisciplinary cognition. *Cognition and Instruction*, *23*(3), 389–425. doi:10.1207/s1532690xci2303_3.

Nowacek, R. S. (2005). A discourse-based theory of interdisciplinary connections. *The Journal of General Education*, *54*(3), 171–195. Retrieved from http://www.jstor.org/stable/27798019 doi:10.1353/jge.2006.0006.

Parkes, M. W., Bienen, L., Breilh, J., Hsu, L.-N., McDonald, M., & Patz, J. A. et al. (2005). All hands on deck: Transdisciplinary approaches to emerging infectious disease. *EcoHealth, 2*, 258–272. doi:10.1007/s10393-005-8387-y.

Rhoten, D., & Parker, A. (2004). Risks and rewards of an interdisciplinary research path. *Science, 306*(5704), 2046. doi:10.1126/science.1103628 PMID:15604393.

Rhoten, D., & Pfirman, S. (2007). Women in interdisciplinary science: Exploring preferences and consequences. *Research Policy, 36*, 56–75. doi:10.1016/j.respol.2006.08.001.

Sillitoe, P. (2004). Interdisciplinary experiences: Working with indigenous knowledge in development. *Interdisciplinary Science Reviews, 29*(1), 6–23. doi:10.1179/030801804225012428.

Small, H. (2010). Maps of science as interdisciplinary discourse: Co-citation contexts and the role of analogy. *Scientometrics, 83*, 835–849. doi:10.1007/s11192-009-0121-z.

Stauffacher, M. (2010). Beyond neocorporatism? Transdisciplinary case studies as a means for collaborative learning in sustainable development. *Environmental Sociology,* 201 – 216. Retrieved from http://link.springer.com/chapter/10.1007/978-90-481-8730-0_12?null

Stokols, D. (2006). Toward a science of transdisciplinary action research. *American Journal of Community Psychology, 38*, 63–77. doi:10.1007/s10464-006-9060-5 PMID:16791514.

Transdisciplinary Studies. (2012, Feb. 24). *Wikipedia*. Retrieved from http://en.wikipedia.org/wiki/Transdisciplinary_studies

Van Gelder, T. (2005). Teaching critical thinking: Some lessons from cognitive science. *College Teaching, 53*(1), 41–46. doi:10.3200/CTCH.53.1.41-48.

Vanasupa, L., McCormick, K. E., Stefanco, C. J., Herter, R. J., & McDonald, M. (2012). Challenges in transdisciplinary, integrated projects: Reflections on the case of faculty members' failure to collaborate. *Innovations in Higher Education, 37*, 171–181. doi:10.1007/s10755-011-9199-3.

Wagner, C. S., Roessner, J. D., Bobb, K., Klein, J. T., Boyack, K. W., & Keyton, J. et al. (2011). Approaches to understanding and measuring interdisciplinary scientific research (IDR): A review of the literature. *Journal of Informetrics, 165*, 14–26. doi:10.1016/j.joi.2010.06.004.

Wear, D. N. (1999). Challenges to interdisciplinary discourse. *Ecosystems (New York, N.Y.), 2*(4), 299–301. doi:10.1007/s100219900080.

Woods, C. (2007). Researching and developing interdisciplinary teaching: Towards a conceptual framework for classroom communication. *Higher Education, 54*(6), 853–866. doi:10.1007/s10734-006-9027-3.

ADDITIONAL READING

Rabinowitz, P. M., & Conti, L. A. (2010). *Human-animal medicine: Clinical approaches to zoonoses, toxicants and other shared health risks*. Maryland Heights, MO: Saunders, Elsevier.

KEY TERMS AND DEFINITIONS

Agroterrorism: The use or threatened use of biological agents (such as pathogens) to cause disruption to agriculture (or food production) to achieve political aims.

Animal Disease Models: Biology-based uses of animals to study human diseases and other health issues.

Bioterrorism: The intentional release of biological, chemical or radiological agents against a sector of agriculture to promote a political agenda.

Built Environment: Human-created living spaces.

Climate Change: A long-term change in the earth's weather conditions.

Comparative Medicine: The formal study of similarities between veterinary (animal) and human medicine, such as the application of animal models for the study of disease progression or drug effects.

Content Analysis: The study of a body of information.

Cross-Disciplinary: The integration of respective domains without dissolving their individual boundaries; may tend towards one of the discipline over the others.

Delphi Method: Consultation with experts in a field to better forecast the near-future.

Domain: An academic discipline or subject matter.

Emergent: Coming into being, forthcoming; evolving.

Encroachment (Direct): Human incursions into animal environments (such as through the building of housing developments; mining; livestock raising on pristine lands).

Encroachment (Indirect): Human actions that have indirect effects on animal habitat, such as through air / light / sound pollution; the introduction of invasive species; the misuse of antibiotics leading to drug-resistant bacteria).

Food Defense: The guarding and maintenance of a nation's food supply and food production processes from intentional adulteration or tampering.

Food Safety: The guarding of a food supply from unintentional adulteration or tampering through quality control and healthy food practices.

Food Security: Access to sufficient nutritious food for healthy living.

Global Warming: The gradual increase in the earth's atmospheric temperature.

Globalization: Global integration through mass travel, trade, and inter-communications.

Habitat: A niche in which animals are adapted.

Interdisciplinary: Between learning domains.

Interdisciplinary Cluster: A group of faculty and staff who co-conduct pure and applied research to advance a field.

Microbiology: The study of microorganisms.

Multidisciplinary: Involving a number of domains or disciplines.

Natural Environment: Living (biotic) and non-living (abiotic) things on earth; spaces which have not been affected by direct human actions.

One Health: The approach of considering the interrelationships between humans and animals, animals and the environment, and humans and the environment for a holistic approach to research, public health, and other endeavors.

One Medicine: The study of health and disease across human and animal species; a concept created by Dr. Calvin Schwabe.

Organic: Evolving naturally or inherently from a source.

Pluri-Disciplinary (Poli-Disciplinary): The juxtaposition of somewhat-related disciplines.

Public Health: The prevention of disease and the maintenance of health among a human population through the promotion of proper nutrition, healthcare, exercise, and other factors.

Reverse Zoonoses: A contagious disease that can transfer from humans to animals.

Routes of Transmission: The ways that diseases may be transmitted.

Subject Matter Experts (SMEs): Content or area expert.

Threshold Concept: An idea that is critical to the mastery of a subject or approach.

Threshold Knowledge: A set of threshold concepts.

Transdisciplinary: A framework of study, research, and practice that incorporates and synthesizes a range of disciplines.

Zoonotic Disease: A contagious disease that can transfer from animals to humans.

APPENDIX A

A (Proposed) Delphi Study Regarding One Health

Demographics

- What is your professional role and professional field?
- How long have you been working in this professional field in a professional capacity?
- Does your background have a natural fit or tie with One Health?
- What city, state (province) or country do you reside in?

One Health

What is your relationship to the concept of One Health?

- Have you ever applied One Health concepts and practices in your work life? Would you please elaborate?
- Have you heard of One Health? If you have, when did you first hear of One Health? What was the context?
    - Website
    - Article
    - Media coverage
    - Conference presentation
    - Conversation
    - Other
- From your perspective, what is One Health?
- Please list at least 10 words which come to mind when you think of One Health. Please write them in the order of most salient to least salient.
- What do you see as some of the implications of One Health in your profession / discipline?
- What are some examples of One Health that you see in your professional field / discipline?
- Do you see One Health as a salient approach in your domain field? Why or why not?
- How do you see One Health changing various professions?
- How do you see One Health affecting curriculums for today's learners?
- What domain fields would you benefit from if you were to take a multidisciplinary / interdisciplinary or transdisciplinary One Health approach?
- What are the implications of One Health in your professional life? Does One Health change how you analyze or problem-solve? Does it affect your learning and understandings? Does it affect your everyday work practices? Please elaborate.
- What are some of the implications of One Health In your (current and future) professional life?
- What are some contemporary research questions in One Health in your professional field? Why?
- Is One Health an idea (or framework) that has the power to mobilize people? Why or why not?

Name Release Permission:

Finally, would you be willing to have your name linked to your responses in a publication of the results of this Delphi study? (Your decision will not affect whether your comments will be recorded. They will be. However, without your permission, your responses will not be linked to your name.)

- Yes
- No

Section 5
Digital Packaging for Young Learners

Chapter 15
Identification and Analysis of Primary School Children's Knowledge Acquisition:
Using Knowledge Visualization Scenarios and Information Visualization Methodology

Søren Eskildsen
Aalborg University, Denmark

Kasper Rodil
Aalborg University, Denmark

Matthias Rehm
Aalborg University, Denmark

ABSTRACT

Measuring a learning effect can be a difficult task and is not made any easier with all the parameters that can be taken into account. This chapter provides an insight into what to consider as interesting parameters when evaluating an interactive learning tool. The authors introduce a visual approach to enlighten children and teachers. This is done by visualizing logging data that has been collected during learning sessions with the Virtual Savannah software. They do not leave out traditional means like observation and usability testing, since they believe a holistic view is important, and a single method of data collection is not enough to base conclusions on. To understand the authors' approach, a short introduction on various perspectives on visualization is essential. The authors also discuss how multimedia can be used on a cognitive level to satisfy more pupils with different learning styles. Lastly, the authors present their approach and results from an in situ evaluation on primary school children.

DOI: 10.4018/978-1-4666-4462-5.ch015

INTRODUCTION

A zoo presents its visitors with living animals such as roaring lions, majestic giraffes and playful elephants. This constitutes a rich multimodal experience for the visitor enhancing his knowledge about the animals by observing them walk or feed. Still, he gets only a somewhat distorted perspective on what it means to be a lion because of the following features of the zoo experience:

- **Confined space:** The space restrictions on the animals' habitats in the zoo inhibit the visitor to experience relevant spatial behavior of the animals, e.g. migration patterns across the Savannah due to climatic conditions.
- **Small number of animals:** Most animals live in larger social environments, e.g. zebras are rarely found individually but wander the Savannah in large herds. In a zoo this social environment is often much smaller inhibiting the visitor from experiences social behavior between the animals.
- **Different routines:** A large part of an animal's life in the wild is dedicated to finding food. This essential routine that has relevant percussions on the animal's behavior is alleviated in the zoo environment, where food is served according to the dietary requirements of the inhabitants. Again, this inhibits the visitor from experiencing essential behavior of the animals.
- **Different environment:** Animals in the zoo live in designed environments that may easily lack features that are found in the animal's original habitat, e.g. selection of plants does not mirror the wild conditions. Thus, the visitor experience lacks the relation between the animal and its environment and has e.g. to acquire the knowledge that elephants prefer Acacia trees through additional information channels.

The Zoo embraces this challenge by providing the casual visitor with factual information, often in the form of text plates adjacent to the animal habitats. Additionally, they run educational programs often tailored to school children, where they are presented with factual knowledge in lessons before they visit the animals.

In the first part of this chapter, we examine how this factual knowledge can be conveyed in a more exploratory manner. As a means to this end we developed an interactive system for knowledge visualization allowing for instance expressing the speed of a cheetah's kill, explaining the hunting patterns of lions and transferring knowledge on animal migration. Our research project collaborates with a zoo with more than 400,000 average visitors per year and approximately 10,000 school children partake in learning programs partly situated in respective public schools and partly in the zoo's educational facilities.

The second part of the chapter focuses on a different type of visualization, i.e. information visualization. To gain insight into how the children use and navigate the virtual environment developed for them; their interactions with the system have been logged. This information is extremely valuable in deciding if the children discovered the knowledge implemented in the system and which kind of media they prefer to acquire this knowledge. Information visualization needs different methods and tools, and in the second part of the chapter we are going to explore the value of some of them.

Listed below are key points investigated in this chapter:

- An investigation of methods on how to gain insights into children's usage of an interactive learning system.
- How the integration of knowledge and information visualization on the one hand strengthens the applicability and evaluation of the system and on the other hand impact the approaches incorporated in the proposed learning environment.

Learning with Visualization Systems

One of the primary goals of Zoological gardens is knowledge transfer by sharing valuable insight into animal habitats, poaching and the consequences relating to man-nature interference. There are two aspects with knowledge transfer, one is presenting the given subject in the most understandable way and secondly presenting it in an appealing way to attract as many visitors to secure the economic future of the zoo.

Various projects on enhancing the knowledge transfer have been attempted through visualization. The visualization principles were introduced within the business domain; due to the high return on investment if the transfer of knowledge succeeds, and being a fairly new method, many do not yet use the full potential that visualization offers. Several research projects are combining the focus on enhancing visitors' experience and learning in environments like zoo's and museums.

- **Reason:** New technologies, which then in return generate new possibilities of educational systems.
- **Goal:** Capture the attention of people and educate them, by utilizing these new possibilities.

Pumpa and Wyeld (2006) reason for developing a virtual system for allowing users to step into the Aboriginal dream world. The mapping and representation of indigenous knowledge is created through 3D graphics. Their reasoning behind having it structured within a virtual world is that the Aboriginals use their environment as an active part of the knowledge transfer. The learner can with the system take part alongside with the Aboriginals and experience how they use the landscape and an array of objects found within the system to their advantage. This knowledge would otherwise not be available to tap into by reading books, but since the 3D visualization supplies narrative information about how objects became a part of their culture, which were necessary to ensure the continued existence. This attempt of knowledge transfer is an example on how a learning environment in a 3D engine could be executed. This approach has been a great inspiration for our work. Staying within the 3D visualization approach the E-junior project by Wrzesien and Raya (2010) introduces a virtual reality environment for teaching children about the Mediterranean and its sea-life. Their qualitative assessment shows an increase in engagement, willingness and joy in participating in this new method of experiencing their learning curriculum. The project still needs to show any significant increase in the actual learning compared with traditional learning methods. In their documentation users are asked to solve questionnaires in a prior, during and post setup. E-junior is an approach to solve the same case as the Virtual Savannah, but with very extensive use of technology. The E-junior project is a Virtual Reality installation, which requires huge facilities along with personnel to maintain the expensive equipment. Accessible technology like touch screens have made information systems more feasible, and their robustness is very suitable for public environments and direct interaction removes the need for peripherals. Lehn, Hindmarsh, Luff and Heath (2007) present a usage of the touch screen interaction technology within Tate Britain museum of art. Their field observations of visitors' actions and interactions have shown that visitors found the installation very popular. The installation featured a drawing activity, where a single user would reveal the work of John Constable, by touching different parts on the screen, whereby a large projection reveals part by part the painting on the wall as the user progresses.

A different art form, other than what the Tate Modern museum is displaying, is cave paintings that are an ancient method of knowledge visualization. At the "Center for the Interpretation of Cave Art" in Ulldecona, Spain, Kourakis and Parés (2010) presented a multi-user virtual heritage application that allowed children to explore and experience the hunting strategies assimilated from cave paintings. They have transformed ancient paintings of hunting patterns by using modern visualization methods, with the purpose of transferring ancient knowledge to elementary school children. They used a 2.4m x 1.8m touch screen setup for display and an interaction device, were the interaction part was done through a defined set of finger gestures. As a result of their observations they found that the children were able to interact successfully. It can be discussed whether the solution of keeping the graphics as cave paintings actually do depict how the actual hunting strategies was conducted. But due to their other focus of explaining the cave paintings accordingly this might not suit a 3D visualization study directly.

The potential of tabletops as interaction and collaboration device in classrooms was explored by AlAgha, Hatch, Ma, and Burd (2010) with a teacher-centric approach. The outcome of their research showed a method that enables multiple users to participate in a lecture conducted by the teachers, while students use touch tables separately from the main table used by the teacher. Furthermore the system lets the teacher monitor the individual screen of students onto the main screen. During feedback from the evaluation session, a teacher noted a useful feature of logging every action and then reviewing it afterwards, in that this would help to reflect on the teachers own practice. This would require the system to present the results of the logging in a less time consuming manner. A solution could be to visualize the data.

An approach to provide visitors of zoos an array of multimedia information is the use of WEB-MOZIS presented by Michel, Plass, Tschritter, and Ehlers (2008). Their solution is to create a system for Pocket PCs and Smart Phones that allows the user to retrieve information about animals situated in the case study zoo of Osnabrück. A database system on a server processes all information, such as position of the visitor within the zoo in order to provide content information about the animals. Information is presented as an interactive 3D world and as 2D Web-Mapping to the visitor. The 3D information changes from Google Maps photos with an overlay of 3D animals and buildings within the zoo to small 3D scenes of animal habitats.

VISUALIZATION

Knowledge transfer is currently taking place between Aalborg Zoo's educational staff and the school children, without any visualizations of the greater context like the African savannah's ecology. As a result of this, an investigation of how a visualization system could solve or present the lack of greater context would be legitimate. This type of visualization is referred to as knowledge visualization and this topic will be covered in a further extent later on in this section. Everyday we experience how visualization can help to communicate across barriers, such as language and cultural differences. But visualization can have limitations when it is given a certain value not familiar to "outsiders." To explore the terms used throughout the chapter the next sections will discuss them separately and compare them afterwards.

Knowledge Visualization

Knowledge visualization as a term was introduced by Tergan, Keller, and Burkhard (2006) as a field of research, due to the lack of research on transferring knowledge within the business knowledge management domain. The term is defined as "*...a field of study that investigates the power of visual formats to represent knowledge. It aims at supporting cognitive processes in generating, representing, structuring, retrieving, sharing, and using knowledge*" (Tergan, Keller, & Burkhard, 2006, p. 168). In other words: The use of visual formats such as sketches, diagram, images, interactive visualizations etc. to improve the transfer of knowledge or simplify it. As a result of investigating information and understanding the meaning of datasets, a person becomes knowledgeable about the findings. This finding demands a structure to be presented as knowledge to another person; in a context like business this would normally be through diagrams. Meyer (2009) states that the goal of knowledge visualization is to use visual representations to improve the transfer and creation of knowledge.

Knowledge visualization can be segmented into 6 different groups. Eppler and Burkhard (2004) and Da and Jianping (2009) identified these segments as:

- Heuristic Sketches
- Conceptual Diagrams
- Visual Metaphors
- Knowledge Animations
- Knowledge Maps
- Domain Structures

The most fitting description to the Virtual Savannah is Knowledge Animations, which is described as being a computer based visualization that enables users to interact with different types of information or media. Da and Jianping (2009) have investigated how visualization technics, if applied correctly, affect the ability to transfer knowledge. Their investigation leads to one conclusion. By using visualization, when trying to provide information or knowledge, it will greatly increase the knowledge transfer. It is interesting to pursue this statement by examining interactive visualization or knowledge animation to see whether these can provide better learning experience, since the learner is able to decide what knowledge and information they would like to be presented with. An example is described by Eppler and Burkhard (2004), on an interactive visualization as a tool which emulates the New York Stock Exchange in order to let the user supervise and control the exchange dynamically by visual cues. Animating information or data sets will allow users to observe behavior of individual entities or the global context. This can translate into the Virtual Savannah since it provides knowledge at both levels. In the Virtual Savannah's global context animals are migrating for food or fresh water and each individual animal or relevant object can be inspected (see Figure 1). Aalborg Zoo does not have the necessary means to cover every animal on the savannah nor to provide enough details as is possible in a virtual solution. Knowledge visualization would solve and even enhance already known material, but in greater detail or with another perspective.

Figure 1. A migrating herd crossing the Masai Mara River in the virtual savannah

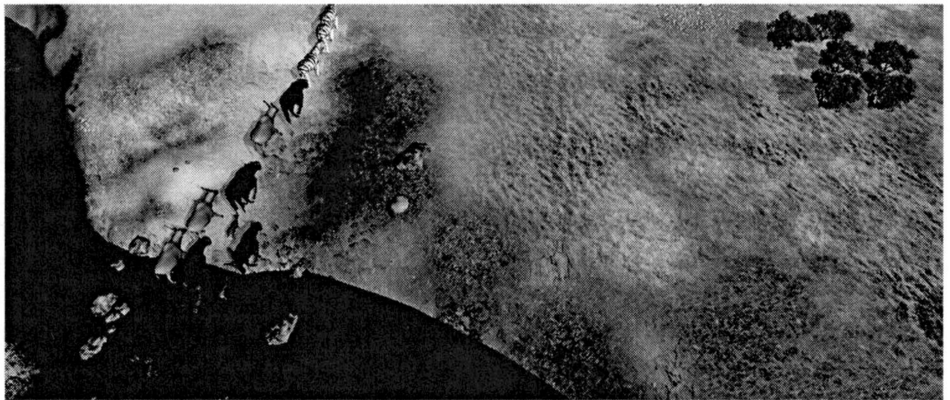

Information Visualization

Information Visualization visualizes vast amounts of data or very abstract data that may become more transparent or easier to recognize clusters, trends or outliers according to Tergan, Keller, and Burkhard (2006). Crime mapping is a great example of information visualization. The National Institute of Justice of the United States defines crime mapping as: plotting crimes in specific segments to a map in order to visualize and analyze any crime incident patterns. This could help identify problems in neighborhoods or to extract patterns of certain crimes. Mapping of crimes has been used as a method to visualize patterns or trends in many decades, but done by hand with pins on large paper maps, which are not easily reorganized if specific relations are wanted to be depicted together. This has changed with Google Maps applications like CrimeReports and the official CompStat used by the police in New York and other major cities in the US. The information like street names alone would perhaps not provide any indications on patterns unless seen in another context, like an overview of a city as the mapping tools provide.

Information visualization can be generated by the data from an evaluation, which has neither predetermined patterns nor results to deliver. Research done by Rick, Harris, Marshall, Fleck, Yuill, and Rogers (2009) describes how children design together on a multi-touch table by using activity logs to plot images showing interaction with the system. Their system allowed the participants to design their own classroom by adding chairs, tables and themselves as avatar placeholders. From logging of touch position and different actions available, they were able to see that most of the work conducted was within the classroom environment and not in the staging areas of the system. The study further showed that, as expected, the reach of each student played a vital role on what and where they touched the tabletop. The important features of information visualization are correlating data or facts; with the purpose of recognizing patterns or trends worth investigating. This can be useful if set into an educational context like the Virtual Savannah, since it will provide information about how solid the system is built and in its final state may provide the teacher with information about each child.

Differences between Knowledge and Information

Meyer (2009) describes data and facts as information if analyzed in order to provide a meaning. Examples on data or facts: "It is raining" and "the grass is green". This is two different facts and if combined they represent information for example about a specific period of the year at African savannah. Information is then the understanding of the effects or causes of the data or facts. To possess knowledge of a subject is defined as having acquired facts, information, and skills through an experience or education. This knowledge can be both the theoretical or practical understanding of a subject. Tergan, Keller, and Burkhard (2006) formulated the most important difference between knowledge and information as: *"...information is outside the brain and knowledge is inside"* (Tergan, Keller, & Burkhard, 2006, pp. 168). It is a cognitive process to shape information into knowledge, which can be externalized by means of structured visualizations as seen on tube maps. This is similar in the Virtual Savannah, with 3D representations of animals migrating and eating from trees as externalized knowledge visualization and further the system can be used to produce logs of each user's navigation and interaction, which can be presented as information visualization. The important classifications on Knowledge Visualization and Information Visualization are listed here:

- **Knowledge Visualization**: What the user sees and experiences within the system (requires a cognitive process)
- **Information Visualization:** Visualizing the user's activities while interacting with the system (data which have been processed)

LEARNING WITH MULTIMEDIA

The methods for teaching children about the world they are about to actively partake in and understand have for many decades been instructed from a dominant role; the teacher. The means to acquire information and structure knowledge have been focused on oral lecturing, written notes and/or memorization of formulas and grammatical rules. The verbal part of European teaching has been a strong focus since J. Gutenberg introduced movable type printing in the year 1493. In these current digital years new media and methods to organize and structure information have seen the light of day. This modern toolbox offers animations, advanced graphical systems, the possibility to present an audience with information unhinged from space and time limitations, and it has all been made publicly accessible with the rapid growth of the Internet. Smartphones enable children and adults to tap into that digital reservoir while riding on a bus, browse e-books from a tablet or conduct remote studies via Webcam. The modern printing press was for many years restricted to the wealthy families and the church, now for a relatively little amount of money, it is possible to have fun and to learn from the world. The amount of information currently being presented from a diversified range of tools and media do not make the problem to be focused around "Where to find information?", but "Where to find the *right* information?" It is not only obvious that to attract children to teaching material it has to be innovative and motivating, but also suit individual needs. As described by McCue (2005), the amount of time children use watching television could at least be complimented with something meaningful. Indeed a daunting task, but maybe the modern toolbox holds parts of the solution.

The Multimedia Toolbox

The term multimedia deals with combining various types of media, which in the simplest form could be a piece of text accompanied with an illustration. Through the focus on computers, multimedia is very much considered to be digital and the work described here will also deal with it in that sense, and the definition we choose for it is the digitally combined product of multiple media. Multimedia can be everything from a person watching online lectures to games and infotainment, which makes it a very broad definition. We therefore argue for not only focusing on the multimedia as a whole, but by investigating the components that make up a specific digital multimedia product.

The popular phrase "a picture is better than 1000 words" is in our opinion only part of the truth, if so is a video with 30 frames per second then better than 30,000 words? Hardly not, and as we will explain later on, the placing of the picture or a narrated supplement is equally important. The work described in Mayer's book on multimedia learning (2005) stand as seminal research on the topics regarding aforementioned areas and delivers interesting insights in the cognitive process behind how the brain segregates stimuli and different modalities into semantic meaning using complimentary processing loops. We also draw parallels to Baddeley's (1992) working memory theory and theory on cognitive load to understand our product's possible impact or the danger in just producing redundant information, which end users can't assimilate into knowledge.

How Do We Process Multimedia Input?

Mayer (2005) provides insights into how the processes of visual and auditory stimuli can serve as instructional message tools for learning and presenting information.

Figure 2 shows how Mayer's theory on cognitive processing relates to a multimedia presentation. In this example the focus is only on the two modalities as it relates not only to our case study, but are the two most common types of presented media. The user of a given system is usually first

Figure 2. Cognitive theory of multimedia learning (re-visualized by authors)

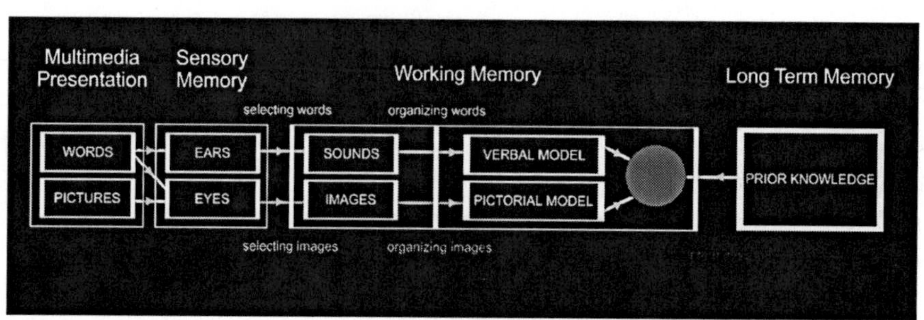

presented with either a verbal or visual information output. In the case of narrated content the ears are the perceptual system sensing this kind of stimuli. Verbal information can also be presented as written text, which is sensed by the eyes. Finally visualized information is sensed by the eyes. The sensory memory organizes and processes it into working memory. Baddeley's theory (1992), on working memory describes the system for shortly storing information as the 'Working Memory' (WM). It functions a bit like memory blocks (RAM) in a computer and is a main storage for input to be processed. In parallel to RAM the WM is a limited storage device, which can only keep little amount of information at a time before sending it further in the system. Or when new information is added which exceeds capacity some of this information will be discarded. The WM is the center for intentional behavior and is structured by two slave systems. These two systems termed *the visuo-spatial sketchpad* and the *phonological loop* deal with separate domains. The visuo-spatial sketchpad deals with visual perception and actions, and the phonological loop is basis for speech processing and active memory.

When WM is full of pictorial stimuli it creates a pictorial model of what has been seen. Imagine to be asked to draw a horse. You take your sketchbook and sit close to the horse starting to draw. It is impossible to draw the horse from only looking at it once, which is directly related to the limited capacity of your mental pictorial storage. The same goes for verbal information such as narrated or written text. After the models have been created and organized new stimuli can be sensed and so on. The important part of this model is the dual channel approach it is crucial to understand how to optimize a multimedia product with respect to the end user. Miller empirically tested his theory on finite memory, which he termed cognitive load. Mayer has conducted research on this topic; Mayer and Moreno (1998), and his results show that students can improve their learning if two modalities can complement each other, but indeed also obstruct each other if not used wisely. Especially redundancy can occur, but redundant information can also improve the performance of the student. The works presented by Mayer and Moreno (1998), show how the auditory stimuli mediated as narrative content can improve students' learning when played in parallel to visual illustrations. It also indicates that by playing narrated audio combined with pictorial stimuli the learning outcome is improved in comparison with written and pictorial stimuli combined. An example of this combination could be online video tutorials, where skilled professionals give insights into their working process for instance in graphic design. By narrating good ideas and tips, and concurrently showing how to create the ideas, the watcher gets an insight into the reflections behind the choices and learns the practice in one step. Alternatively, the watcher could watch a row of pictures combined with a body of text. This could function well for the watcher, but as the abstraction of information rises it gets increasingly more complicated to perform even simple tasks.

The integration from media into knowledge is a process where previously acquired knowledge structures, called schemata (Kohls & Scheiter2008), is compared with new information. Tuning is when the schema is inadequate in guiding your interaction, and therefore you must adjust it to function in the new mental environment. Restructuring is when you need to construct a new schema due to the fact that you have no prior structure/experiences to aid you in this new context/environment. These three processes are in a constant and continuous time loop, and could be understood as the old saying: "You are never too old to learn." The schemata are located in the Long Term Memory, which capacity is considered to be infinite. In contradiction to Long Term Memory the information process in our WM is only stored as inputs for 20-30 seconds.

How Does Theory on Cognition Relate to the Virtual Savannah?

How do the theory on cognition converge into the restructuring of the Virtual Savannah, and what design implications does it bring? We design from the perspective: "A user is an individual, with individual strengths and weaknesses." In the specific case of the Virtual Savannah, information is placed as singular entities to interact with. In the recent version of the system, we explore how we can segregate different types of media meaningfully and without clustering information as Mayer's research argue against. This not only suits the purpose of moving our design away from the already implemented text plates currently placed in Aalborg Zoo, but also allows users of the system to more actively choose their specific media of interest. The system should also facilitate the possibility to gain different levels of knowledge. The system should provide users with a better understanding through the use of multimedia than through text and pictures alone, by constructing semantic knowledge from key areas of our system. We witnessed during our 'fly on the wall' session in the zoo, that the children memorized factual information from their pre-training in the schools (this argument has later been backed up by educational staff at the zoo). We therefore wish to explore how the system can give children an understanding of the bigger picture and how this can be verified. Although previous tests did not show crucial usability errors, we wish to color our interface design with a more explicit use and presentation of media. The clustering of information, which in fact was decreasing the working memory of the user, thus we will attempt to segregate the types of information more lucidly. The method for structuring visual information is known as the contiguity principle, and is a design approach to minimize cognitive load. An example could be a slideshow presentation with figures, colors, graphs and text scattered all around the screen. The mere sight of this type of 'sharing knowledge' can draw the breath from most students, whereas a well-designed slideshow where images and text relate, and are used wisely with respect to the media's intrinsic strengths and weaknesses can be much easier to follow and understand. In essence we are reluctant in using all available media in a 'media blitz,' where we obstruct our initial product goals with too much information. Another important aspect in this development cycle is to tentatively measure and investigate whether the system is applicable in a learning environment.

THE CASE STUDY: AALBORG ZOO

Zoologists at Aalborg Zoo possess a large portion of domain knowledge about the animal kingdom, environmental issues and consequences of human – nature interference. They are intrinsically and politically motivated to teach the public and school children about these important topics and transfer this knowledge through a diverse range of methods. Before personnel optimization and budget cut-downs, the staff had time to elaborate these topics for visitors of the park by simply being present to enlighten by sharing knowledge near the animal cages. To supplement the direct customer contact a large selection of wooden boards are placed all around the park to inform and elaborate visitors on the animals. During a meeting with the zoo, they stated openly their concern of the fact that people do not read their signs and that they do not have time to talk to visitors due to the demand for an optimized workplace. They don't feel that the visitors have an improved user experience by reading wooden boards and the park naturally needs to make its value proposition competitive with other theme parks and tourist sites in the area.

The zoo in Aalborg teaches public school classes via humor and pedagogical means about aforementioned areas in the zoo (see Figure 3).

The children are, prior to this teaching taught by their own teachers about the animals partly with material sent as preparation literature from the zoo and by material the teachers decide by themselves. During these sessions of 45 min. with normally around 25 children per session, the transfer of knowledge is conducted with not much more than basic theory and the limits the time sets makes it hard to ensure an optimal transfer. The pupils are only included in the dialogue when directly asked, and the quantity of children makes one-to-one difficult.

Figure 3. A teaching session from Aalborg zoo's educational department

We attended two of these sessions to experience for ourselves how the transfer is conducted and to see how the children responded to this snippet of animal curriculum. It was obvious that the children were well prepared and responded with basic informational answers to questions regarding the types of species living in Africa, special features about some of the animals etc. The teacher from the zoo tried to illuminate political areas regarding poaching, breeding and consequences of human interference. During this short window of knowledge transfer, the focus was on anecdotes and the overall situation regarding species on the savannah. After the session the teacher told us, that he usually varies in presenting various parts of the curriculum to the different classes to allow him variance in teaching, but he stated that every part of the curriculum is important and his window is too short to deliver a deeper rooted understanding of the animals and their habitat. Although being a contextual learning process, where the children are presented with living snakes, lion furs, the possibility to see close confined animals in cages, they can't see the big picture with running herds and open terrains, and construct it into semantic knowledge.

The Setting of the Virtual Savannah

The investigation in this study centers around the virtual savannah's impact on teaching school children with the aforementioned multimedia toolbox and how this can be used by the teachers to understand individual children's preferences of media. In our formulation of hypotheses, we wanted to examine children's prior knowledge on the subject of the African savannah and compare this over time to get an insight into retention and acquired knowledge while using the Virtual Savannah as a learning device. Having developed a logging tool we wanted to investigate; from an inductive point of view, how the children used and navigated our system. Being influenced by information visualization, we actively sought to uncover methods to gain insights into data, which are impossible to collect through traditional qualitative methods of measuring. This can, maybe, give some insights into further development or help us gain a deeper understanding regarding design of placement of information in the system, user patterns in navigating the virtual world or as triangulation for test results. The following pages explore from qualitative and quantitative methods, how our system is perceived from children, subject experts (zoologists) and teachers (primary school teachers) in the system's domain. Firstly, we elaborate on core design decisions behind the prototype and logging system. Secondly, we describe and discuss reflections, results, observations, analysis and methods behind an in situ test conducted with a class of 10-11 year olds at a Danish public school.

Hypothesis

- **H^A:** Children with low prior knowledge on African animals have increased knowledge about African animals after using the Virtual Savannah.
- **H0:** Children with low prior knowledge on African animals do not have increased knowledge about African animals after using the Virtual Savannah.

HOW WE MEASURE THE USER

The intention of this study is not to focus solely on one type of measurement (qualitatively or quantitatively), but try to combine these two approaches into a more holistic picture of the children's use of the system (see Figure 4). We strongly believe that deeper insights into user behavior and active use of the system is an important, even necessary component to be able to optimize design, increase usability and aid in understanding the human-machine relationship, especially regarding learning scenarios.

Figure 4. Illustrates how quantitative and qualitative evaluation can tell about your product from different angles and thereby provide information you would not have found by using one method

Observation

Observation can be conducted in mainly two different ways, in a controlled environment or take place in the field. There are pros and cons for either method according to Sharp, Rogers, and Preece (2007). Our test on school children invites an approach, which will be least intrusive to them, given the scenario. It would therefore be ideal to have each child conduct the test on a touch-screen setup at home or in a lesson, but since our objective is to measure them individually with no classmate support and the restriction of having only two touch-screens this would not be a feasible solution. We choose a combination of situating it in the school lesson context and a small controlled environment for testing purposes, which they can relate to in order to reconciling them with our test setup and presence. The purpose of having more data gathering beyond the already existing data logging and assignments is to analyze, whether our developed prototype supports its tasks and goals well enough in terms of usability.

This approach is therefore a direct observation in a semi controlled environment and consists of a video camera setup together with facilitator taking notes. Figure 5 depicts the two similar test setups. The framework used to structure each session is as follows:

1. Present the user with the assignment sheet and ensure they have done one prior.
2. Have them fill out the sheet until first assignment.
3. Present the system to them and write in their name.
4. Let them start the system when they have read/seen the intro screen.
    a. This is done separately for each of the three assignments.
5. Help on system error or questions regarding the system (not assignment questions) else observe/note their interaction.

The observation setup allowed the video camera to be positioned in a way that made it possible to record their body language and the actual actions performed within the system.

To avoid the many downsides of conducting the observation as a qualitative study only, we take the approach of doing it as a performance measure. Performance measuring described by Dumas and Redish (1999) is quantitative data gathering i.e. how many errors they produce during a certain task. The logging system counts how many times something is touched, but not whether it was intentional or an error. Our analysis was therefore based upon finding the answers to the following list of usability issues:

1. Number of unintended selections.
2. Number of calls for help.
3. Time spent with the system.
4. Time spent in text, picture, video and sound menu.
5. Observation of frustration.
6. Observation of confusion.
7. Observation of satisfaction.

By observing almost 4 hours of video material and numerous pages of logging details from the system, we can paint a picture of how each child used the virtual savannah.

Figure 5. A rendered overview of the in situ setup, which shows how the camera position could capture body language and interaction

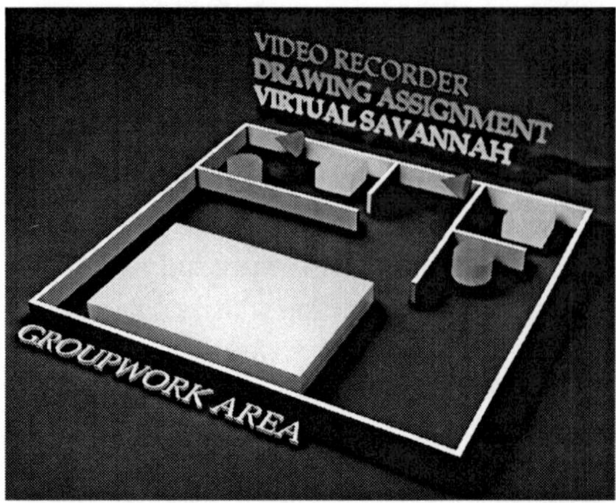

The Logging System

In field research or lab studies users are often subjected to being video recorded, interviewed, and asked to answer questions for shedding some light on the actual system's strong and weak points. By observing users, the developers can record and note gestures and facial expressions, or by placing cameras strategically, it is possible to almost reconstruct the entire span of user actions with moving pictures to get a deeper understanding into the chronology and logics behind user behaviors and actions. All these evaluation methods are beside their qualitative nature, hard to conduct without 'noise' or heavily colored subjective conclusions, and can prove to be tedious to analyze and time consuming to setup. Although many methodologies help in understanding the use of a system, it often tends to be imprecise with respect to qualitatively logging user information. Another implication of traditional logging of user behavior is that test participants can act much differently (Hawthorne effect) when filmed and watched by system designers, than when being alone in the original intended settings for the system. There are still plenty of important upsides by qualitatively observing interactions and/or video.

To gain an insight into the answering of specific questions for the children, and their use of the system, we have designed and developed a system to quantitatively record elements of user behavior and actions. Data logging not only brings transparency into the test but also how it can help in understanding the data and indeed also how inspections of our data can prevent us from drawing incorrect conclusions for our hypotheses. Our idea behind developing an internal observational component is not only to be able to inspect users, but also inspect why they score as they do in their written assignments intended for evaluating the system. The latter is mainly developed with the educator in mind. With the inclusion of an internal logging component it also aids in understanding users joining a course as an online remote study scenario or to extract valuable information from a publicly used system after a period of time. This can have multiple purposes such as benchmarking how many users the system has (true popularity based on active usage and not on e.g. registered users), how learning differentiates with various media and various teaching methods over time or it can reveal parts of a system, which users never use, which could indicate irrelevant content, hard to reach content (usability) or unpopular information such as text about animals versus videos about animals.

WRITTEN ASSIGNMENTS

To measure if learning occurs by using the system and provide any feedback to the educators, it is important to establish the children's prior knowledge on the subject about the African savannah and animal migration. The various media in a multimedia product are perceived and processed differently. It has been a focus on not filling working memory due to our presentation of various kinds of information. We only present users with one media at a time. The visualized information has been added in our system as an element we wish to use for teaching purposes instead of traditional solutions with plain text and pictures. As an example, migrating animals show by their actions that they migrate, and the animations of elephants eating from acacia trees add to this corpus of visualized knowledge. It has therefore been logical for us to measure children's knowledge by segregating the assignments accordingly. To measure prior knowledge the children complete the assignments without guidance one week before the test, then once more concurrently while using the system and finally they must complete the same set of assignments one week after the test. Having them complete the same set three times brings possibilities to investigate if any difference in the individual scoring occur, and we can compare retention from using the system and a week later. The great advantage with the logging system is that it is now possible to inspect every completed assignment, and directly see if their answers are based on guessing or if the information was seen, but not understood correctly. If they understood the assignment and the presented information, and we can see if they got their knowledge from video, text, pictures, or watching the savannah. It is also possible to see how long their interactions for the different assignments were, which could shed some light into the scoring as well.

The questions have been conferred with the educational staff in Aalborg Zoo. This has the purpose of tailoring the curriculum to the zoo's needs, as well as ensuring that the material has the quality needed to deliver the expected knowledge about the African ecology and migrating herds.

Assignment 1

"Which 4 African animal species migrate together for long distances?" The correct information behind this assignment is tailored exclusively to the visual channel. The children must inspect the virtual world to find those exact four animals migrating together. Figure 6 depicts the implementation. The significant difference between the test group's prior knowledge and retained knowledge one week after the test indicate that the children assimilated knowledge about the subject, although only being subjected to the system for a short duration of time.

Assignment 2

"Why don't these four animals stay in the same place all year round?" This assignment is made visual in two places in the system. To further enhance the visuals a weather system is producing rain and thunder. There is constant rainfall in the northern part to symbolize growth of grass; this feature can be toggled on and off. Firstly, we wish to see if the rain has any impact on the pupil's answering, which will be facilitated through a follow up question at the test after the pupil has completed the task. Secondly, we wish to see if the test group understands the diversity in the terrain as why animals migrate. Figure 7 depicts the northern part of the savannah, where it rains and the environment is lush. The results indicate that the test group's scores show no significant change. Through navigation data collected by our logging system, we can see that only 3 children actually moved downwards where the difference between lush and dry is visualized. It is impossible to conclude that the test group did or did not acquire their knowledge from visualized information; hence, the majority did not explore the savannah for this particular assignment.

Figure 6. The great migration consists of 4 different animals. This figure shows all four, which the children have to name in order to answer assignment 1

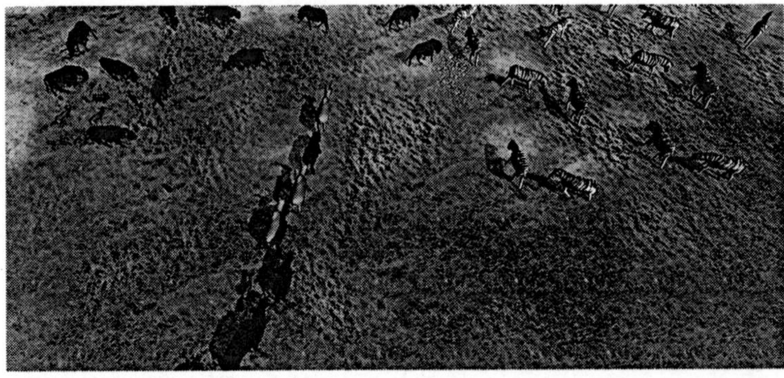

Figure 7. A weather system is built into the program to provide real clues to assignment 2

Assignment 3: Part One

"What do elephants eat?" The purpose of the assignment is two-tailed, where the first part examines how the users find these spatially located sources (animals) of information; and heavily based on the logging system tracking of usage with the Virtual Savannah. The answer is available both visually and textually in the system. This allows the user for actively using our GUI, hence also testing it for any usability errors. Figure 8 depicts the implementation of the first part. 15 out of 19 children navigated in areas where elephants were placed. 8 of them have been categorized into using knowledge visualization for answering. 7 of them answered, according to analysis criteria, correctly. The 7 remaining children used the GUI for providing an answer, and 6 children provided a correct answer.

Assignment 3: Part Two

"How tall can a male giraffe become?" The answer is only placed as episodic information, which can be found in the GUI by interacting with a giraffe. The giraffes located in the system are placed amongst a group of trees in the upper right corner. This assignment, besides being a test of the children's ability to find factual knowledge, was designed explicitly to force the users to find giraffes in the system. We thereby hoped to collect some interesting data from our logging component to give us answers on how children navigate an unexplored virtual world. Figure 9 depicts the implementation of part two. 13 out of 19 children navigated where the giraffes were placed. Despite the nature of the question, 4 still answered by using visual means. 3 were incorrect, and the one correct is by us classified as a guess. She did not answer it correct in step 1, which indicates that the answer was not coming from prior knowledge. 9 children used the GUI as foundation for answering. All of them answered correctly. 6 of the 9 did not show any prior knowledge regarding the question. 6 of the 9 retained the correct answer one week after the test (two did not complete assignments at step 3).

Assignment 4

Covering most of the assignments with known and very adapted methods to measure and evaluate, we explored another way to measure the children on their understanding of the great migration scenario; before, during and after the use of the Virtual Savannah. Our approach is inspired by the works of Wagoner and Jensen (2010), who conducted an evaluation in London Zoo during the Formal Learning program situated at the zoo, which is their equivalent to the schooling program in Aalborg Zoo. Their work was focused at obtaining primary school pupils' understanding of animal

Figure 8. Elephants gathered around acacia trees to feed on them

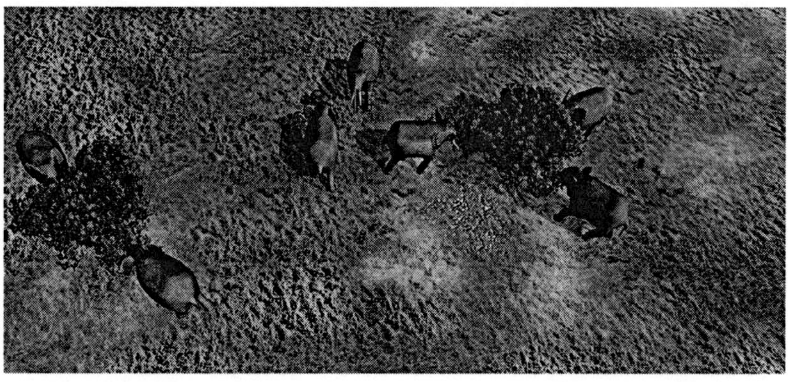

Figure 9. As the elephants giraffes need to feed and this is also from the acacia tree, but the giraffes are placed in the opposite side of the map to entice the children to navigate over a greater distance

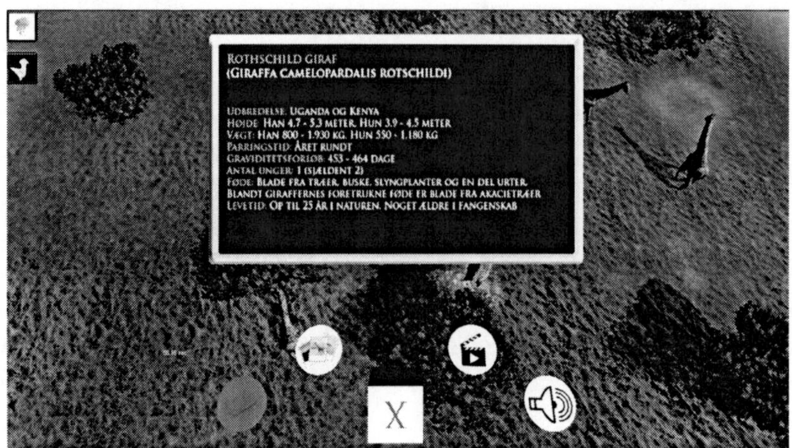

habitats. To get insights into this understanding, children were asked to draw the animals' habitats. They are arguing that this may help to visualize a change in the children's knowledge. We had an open mind and inductive approach on what the children will draw and what we would be able to interpret from them. Wagoner and Jensen had about a third of their children doing a noticeable change in the drawings. We judged that 4 of 19 answers had an important change in their drawings. On Figure 10, a user's progress is depicted, these submissions are very detailed savannah drawings compared with other submitted drawings. What is noticeable beyond the details is the addition of a river and the perspective change.

VISUALIZATION OF THE USER

Until now we have presented how Knowledge Animations can be used to visualize greater contexts of the ecology of the African savannah, but the Virtual Savannah should also provide an additional layer for the teacher. This layer can help identify guesses and point towards preferred learning styles. Here we discuss and provide a solution by answering this question: What do we visualize and how should we interpret these visualizations?

What Do We Visualize and How Should We Read Them?

On Figure 11 (left) a depiction of all the children's navigation data has been plotted from the first part

Figure 10. Prior, VS, and post drawings, which depict the addition of elements like the river along with herds crossing of it

Figure 11. Left: sum of 19 children's navigation while solving assignment 3; right: sum of 16 children's navigation while actively solving assignment 3

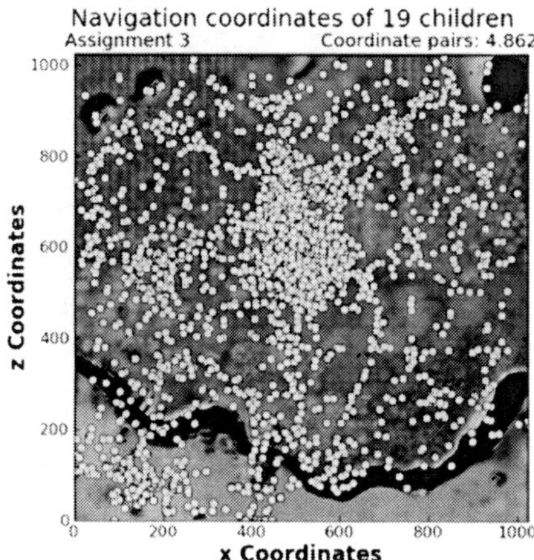

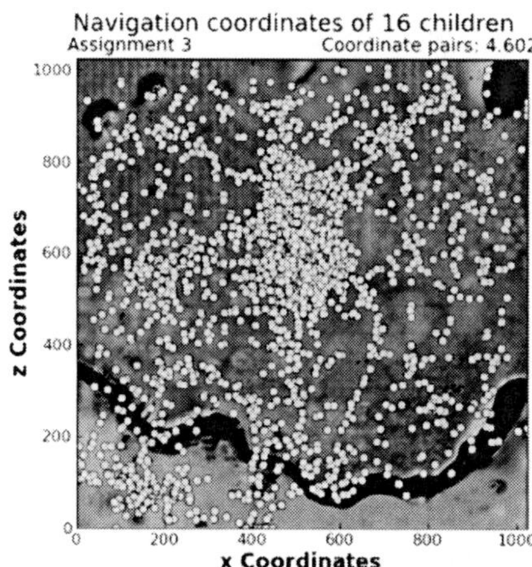

of assignment 3 overlaying an x, z perpendicular screen grab of the virtual world presented in the Virtual Savannah. The coordinates are collected every 500ms, and the spatial data now presented as information visualization, can reveal in greater detail how the users navigated during the test. The units in the virtual world correspond to the axes. By inspecting the plot, it is now visualized where the children did or did not move to. This information can be utilized for the placement and impact of information presented in the system. From a teacher's point of view it can help investigating why the pupils answer as they do. If they never saw the information, how could they have learned from it? In our specific case it can provide insights into how the children scored in their assignments. The strength of an accumulated sum of coordinates being visualized is that qualitative inspections based upon quantitative data is possible. Being only interested in users navigating the virtual world, Figure 11 (right) is a plot of all the individuals (16 of 19 children) moving away from the center area of virtual savannah in an attempt to seek answers for the specific assignment. The three children sorted out, did not actively try to find the animals, therefore we exclude them from the inspection of navigation.

It is obvious from Figure 11, that although having plotted the exact coordinates and removed ca. 200 logs from 3 users not navigating outside the center, the interpretation is quite difficult to make. It does show a precise mapping from where the users have been in the virtual world, as points are slowly adding up, but it is almost impossible to visually segregate between the two figures. For assignment 3 it can be concluded that none was in the lower right corner, and density seems much higher around the center of the screen. This states that many logs were collected at these places of clustering, but we cannot interpret based on this type of visualization, how many logs per unit there are, and it does not say how the users moved around in terms of finding the animals. From the design of the assignments, we can correlate with the placement of animals, which the children need to find to solve the assignment. Qualitatively we can say that Figure 11 indicates that there is a clustering around these animals, which implies that some of the children found the animals. What the visualization depict, is where users are represented spatially and does not bring any insights into answering temporally where they have been the most, or the longest. Why is it important? It is important to investigate if the plots above are generated by random navigation or if it is possible to deduct patterns about virtual places, which the user have certain interest for. This could help establishing if some users actually found the animals, which could be used for triangulation of scores they achieved. From the visualization depicted on Figure 11, it cannot be concluded if a user has spent enough time for one log, or the user stayed dormant for 10 minutes.

All the coordinates are sorted into a 1024, 1024 matrix, and 'red' coloring is indicating 100%, which is the unit with most logs. The intensity plot shown as Figure 12 depicts an unbiased weighting of logs, and the data used for this plot is consistent with Figure 11. By filtering the data we lose the precision depicted in the first figures, hence only inspecting qualitatively, but by weighting it is possible to slightly see trends appearing. The 'red' coloring now visualizes where the maximum of areas are, and 'deep blue' indicate areas least visited. The strength is that we can visually see intensity, but it also leaves areas with few logs as a diminishing little weight, making it almost impossible to see. We reason, that users must have spent less time navigating than being in a certain area reading text, watching video, etc. If that is valid, then it would be interesting to see what impact the 'deep blue' areas have.

To dissect the data we approached the problem of finding trends (if they are there), by searching through all the lower represented coordinates. Currently there is a pool of data, which is a sum of movement and stationary interactions. To discard the highest values; the places where there is a large representation of logs, and only focus on areas with few points, it is possible to see other parts of the data qualitatively. Figure 13 depicts the data, where all units with 50% of the max (unit with the most logs) are set to be 100%, which allows the sparsely represented units to have a larger weight in the

Figure 12. Intensity plot of 16 children actively navigating as they try to solve assignment 3

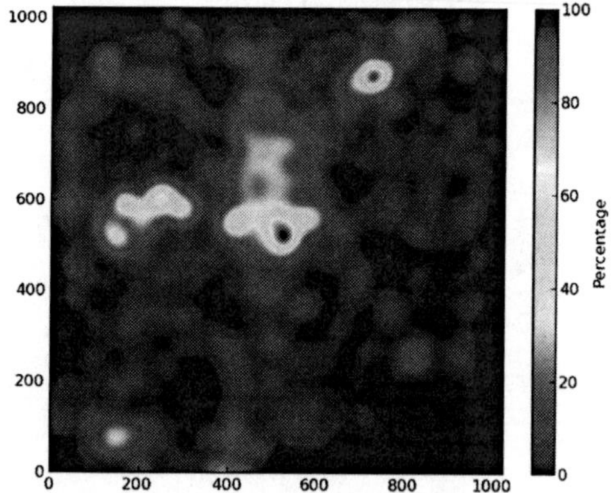

equation. Subsequently, Figure 13 depicts a 25% weighting as well.

If Figure 13 is correlated with our actual placement of the animals on the savannah shown on Figure 14, and then compares the intensity plots, it is visible, that the users to a certain extent have been in these areas of interest. It also indicates, qua the relative large amount of logs in the center, that the children search in the close vicinity of where they start in the system. It is clear that a larger amount of coordinates are logged in the vertical left side of the middle, than on the right. This could indicate that the majority of the children are right-handed; hence, they naturally drag to their right. For further studies it is an important observation, hence placing of information should reflect this in the design phase.

The Virtual Savannah is bridging knowledge visualization with traditional media, and by approaching it with methods to create information visualization, hidden layers and trends can appear. If constructing, e.g. a virtual museum, the methods described above could support developers with valuable visualizations on what the visitors prefer in sense of exhibitions. The findings in this document support understanding the

Figure 13. Illustrating how a 50% and 25% weighting would change the regions of interest

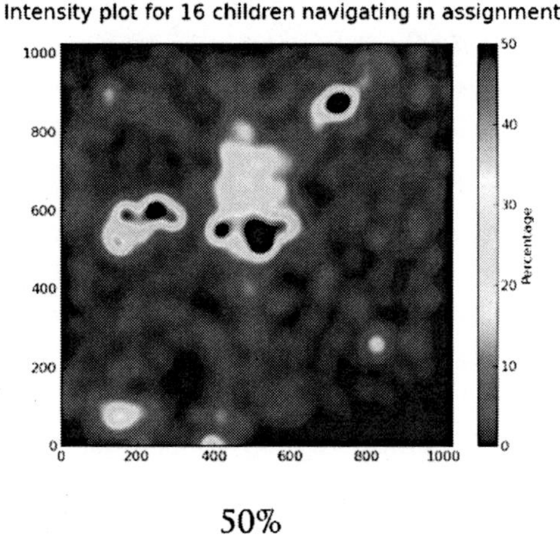

50%

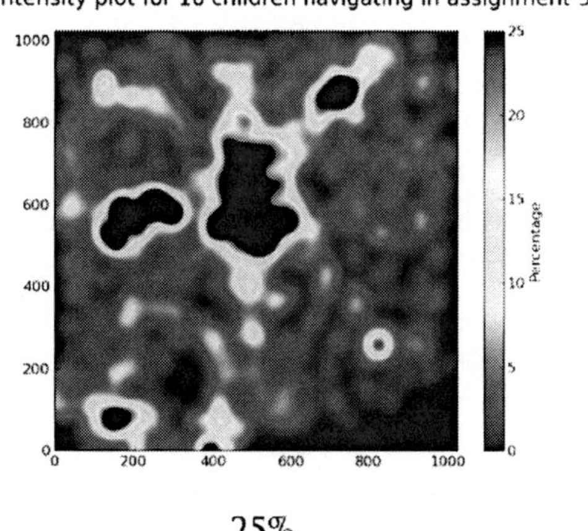

25%

importance of how users behave. We strongly believe that this triangulation can be fused into the design and test of 3D virtual learning systems. It could also prove useful for teachers evaluating students on a subject similar to the Virtual Savannah, where visualizations could spare the teacher from manually inspecting how and why students answered as they do.

Figure 14. Screen grab of the actual placement of animals represented as white dots

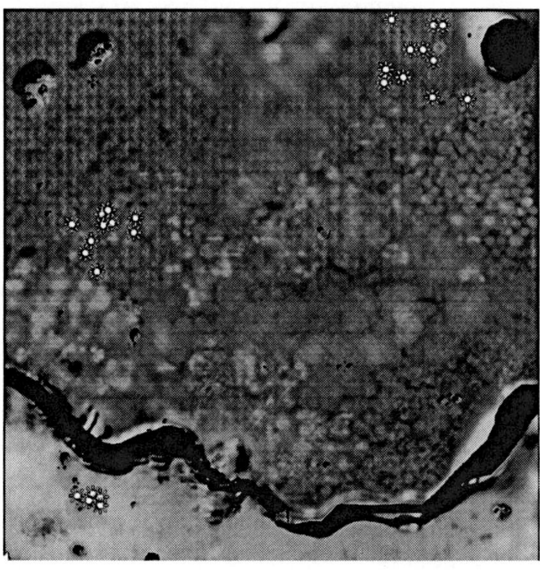

DISCUSSION

The main objective of this case study was to investigate, if the implemented prototype could serve as a multimedia learning tool in public schools and thereby provide a platform to investigate how the learning could be measured by visualizing it for teachers. Having gained access to the target group, which normally can be difficult, we chose to use the children's prior knowledge as control for the findings during the in situ test. Subsequently, we used the prior knowledge as control for how much the children knew one week after the test. In studies with a larger timescale, it would be interesting to measure a higher number of classes on different schools. Prior to unrolling such a large setup, it would still rely on a thorough investigation of usability, methodology of the test and first results, which are presented here. An approach could be to compare the Virtual Savannah with traditional teaching with books, but first off, we do not see the system as something replacing books, but more as a supplement to traditional methods, hence results based on comparison would provide little meaning. As said by a teacher in a follow up interview, regarding the question (translated by authors) "Is the Virtual Savannah useful as a part of the teaching material subjecting learning about the African savannah?"

(Reply - translated by the authors) "Yes – absolutely. It is a fantastic supplement to the teaching." The teacher supports the idea on using it as a supplement, for pre-training children prior to being enrolled in the educational program at the zoo. The educational staff at the zoo was highly interested in the investigation, and having investigated this in situ, we believe that similar systems has promising future potential. Given the premises for the analysis and test, our results show that the test group has significantly better results compared to their prior knowledge. This supports the Virtual Savannah's potential to be a system and an approach, where it is possible; through efficient design and implementation, to assimilate knowledge. The significant results comparing prior knowledge and retention support our belief that the children actually learned from using the system. Although further studies could investigate if this has been stored in the long-term memory for a long period, or if it is quickly forgotten again.

If the system functions as intended, why conduct a usability evaluation? During our usability evaluation and reflection notes from the test, we experienced that some children still unintentionally activated trees in their navigation around the virtual world (termed the Midas touch). The results from the test did not reflect this, but it is for a future investigation an important finding. If our results were obstructed by graver usability errors, the end results based on the assignments could have ended useless. The only possibility to find and correct these errors was through the usability evaluation. For the next iteration, it has proven useful, and has aided in detailing a full picture of the entire user experience.

The logging system is in the authors' opinion more important than we first predicted while developing it. We now see it as a potential framework to include in other iterations of the system, but indeed also in other applications. Specifically, the possibility to create a tool for the teacher to easily inspect how his pupils perform and use a given system could prove valuable. Through information visualization these details could, in a less time consuming way, provide the teacher with a more holistic picture of the individual pupil compared with e.g. undetailed SATs or assignments similar to those we used for testing. Having used it as a supplement for understanding how the children used, and specifically navigated the system, we believe that tests designed to focus on the logging system's abilities could provide interesting findings into behavior and navigation. For example, the logging system could serve as a profiler for users of an information system. If it was possible to find certain trends among users, the system itself could re-order on data provided from the logging. Imagine a virtual museum or interactive game, where information is dynamically placed and tailored to the individual user. The navigation maps could easily provide information on how players of a game moved through levels; it could show clusters indicating player difficulties/bottlenecks. It could be a valuable tool in the post investigation of a system used, if placed i.e. in a new environment, then after a period of time the developers could extract data and fuse these findings into the design or re-implementation phases.

The collaboration with Aalborg Zoo has provided a much inspiring platform to conduct work on. For example, the assignments created for the test are directly representing curriculum the zoo wishes to convey and it was interesting to fuse zoo curriculum into our scientific approach of evaluating users. The representatives were ensuring that the curriculum we designed was valid, but it generated many thoughts on how to test it. We strongly believe that without the multifaceted test, we would have been left with only a fragment of the overall picture. For example, we do not believe that the findings in the drawing exercise are strong on their own, but could in future studies be compared with how African children visualize animals, which to a certain point would be more familiar to them. Such a cross-cultural study could provide pointers on how children of same age perceive differently, and to inspect which facts Western children have learned through other media sources.

REFERENCES

AlAgha, I., Hatch, A., Ma, L., & Burd, L. (2010). Towards a teacher-centric approach for multi-touch surfaces in classrooms. In *Proceedings of the ACM International Conference on Interactive Tabletops and Surfaces*, (pp. 187-196). New York, NY: ACM.

Baddeley, A. (1992). Working memory. *Science, 255*(5044), 556–559. doi:10.1126/science.1736359 PMID:1736359.

Da, Z., & Jianping, Z. (2009). Knowledge visualization - An approach of knowledge transfer and restructuring in education. In *Proceedings of the 2009 International Forum on Information Technology and Applications* (vol. 3, pp. 716-719). Washington, DC: IEEE Computer Society.

Dumas, J. S., & Redish, J. C. (1999). *A practical guide to usability testing*. Exeter, UK: Intellect Ltd..

Eppler, M. J., & Burkhard, R. A. (2004). *Knowledge visualization: Towards a new discipline and its fields of application. Università della Svizzera italiana*. Faculty of Communication Sciences, Institute for Corporate Communication.

Kohls, C., & Scheiter, K. (2008). The relation between design patterns and schema theory. In *Proceedings of the 15th Conference on Pattern Languages of Programs* (PLoP '08). New York, NY: ACM.

Kourakis, S., & Parés, N. (2010). Us hunters: Interactive communication for young cavemen. In *Proceedings of the 9th International Conference on Interaction Design and Children*, (pp. 89-97). New York, NY: ACM.

Lehn, D. V., Hindmarsh, J., Luff, P., & Heath, C. (2007). Engaging constable: revealing art with new technology. In *Proceedings of the SIGCHI Conference on Human Factors in Computing Systems*, (pp. 1485-1494). New York, NY: ACM.

Mayer, R. E. (2005). *The Cambridge handbook of multimedia learning*. Cambridge, UK: Cambridge University Press. doi:10.1017/CBO9780511816819.

Mayer, R. E., & Moreno, R. (1998). A split-attention effect in multimedia learning: Evidence for dual processing systems in working memory. *Journal of Educational Psychology, 90*(2), 312–320. doi:10.1037/0022-0663.90.2.312.

McCue, P. (2005). The crucial role of animated children's educational games. In *Proceedings of ACM SIGGRAPH 2005*. New York, NY: ACM.

Meyer, R. (2009). Knowledge visualization. In *Proceedings of the Media Informatics Advanced Seminar on Information Visualization*. Media Informatics.

Michel, U., Plass, C., Tschritter, C., & Ehlers, M. (2008). WebMozis - Web-based and mobile zoo information system - A case study for the city of osnabrueck. *The International Archives of the Photogrammetry: Remote Sensing and Spatial Information Sciences, 37*(Part B4), 839–843.

Pumpa, M., & Wyeld, T. G. (2006). Database and narratological representation of Australian aboriginal knowledge as information visualisation using a game engine. In *Proceedings of the International Conference on Information Visualisation (IV'06)*, (pp. 237-244). IEEE Computer Society Press.

Rick, J., Harris, A., Marshall, P., Fleck, R., Yuill, N., & Rogers, Y. (2009). Children designing together on a multi-touch tabletop: An analysis of spatial orientation and user interactions. In *Proceedings of the 8th International Conference on Interaction Design and Children*, (pp. 106-114). New York, NY: ACM.

Sharp, H., Rogers, Y., & Preece, J. (2007). *Interaction design: Beyond human-computer interaction*. New York: John Wiley & Sons Ltd..

Tergan, S.-O., Keller, T., & Burkhard, R. A. (2006). Integrating knowledge and information: Digital concept maps as a bridging technology. *Information Visualization*, *5*, 167–174. doi:10.1057/palgrave.ivs.9500132.

Wagoner, B., & Jensen, E. (2010). Science learning at the zoo: Evaluating children's developing understanding of animals and their habitats. *Psychology & Society*, *3*(1), 65–76.

Wrzesien, M., & Raya, M. A. (2010). Learning in serious virtual worlds: Evaluation of learning effectiveness and appeal to students in the e-junior project. *Computers & Education*, *55*(1), 178–187. doi:10.1016/j.compedu.2010.01.003.

Chapter 16
Evaluating a Technique for Improving Letter Memory in At-Risk Kindergarten Students

Carol Stockdale
ARK Institute of Learning, USA

ABSTRACT

This chapter focuses on a process for improving letter naming. Numerous studies have established the correlation between fluent letter naming and reading in young children (Badian, 2000; Catts, 2001; Faust, Dimitrovsky, & Shacht, 2003; Terepocki, Kruk, & Willows, 2002; Mann & Foy, 2003). Two schools using the same reading program were selected for the study. The 125 kindergarten children attending these schools were screened for letter naming fluency. The low scoring individuals in each school were randomly assigned either to a treatment or control group for the study. Pretesting addressed rapid letter recall, color naming, object naming, and receptive vocabulary. The children in the treatment groups received twelve twenty-minute instructional sessions teaching the children to attend to the distinctive features (unique parts) of each letter. The students in the treatment groups made significant gains in letter naming speed and accuracy compared to the control groups. Receptive language scores improved. Other measures had no significant correlation with letter naming proficiency in posttests.

INTRODUCTION

The goal of this study is to evaluate a method for helping students form a stable orthographic image for letters. Rapid letter naming is a complex skill that requires linking a verbal label to a recognized visual image. Maryanne Wolf describes this skill as "one of the best predictors of reading performance" (Wolf, 2000, p. 179). This skill is important for kindergarten children. Rebecca Treiman studied the role of naming letters for young children extensively. She concludes that prereaders and beginning readers use the names of letters as a means of connecting printed words with spoken words (Treiman & Rodriguez, 1999). In a study addressing the foundation of literacy, Treiman found that preschool and kindergarten children benefited from both letter-name and letter-sound relationships, but she concluded that letter naming was more helpful to them than the letter-sounds. In fact, she stated that the non-reader could only use the letter-name link as a tool (Treiman, 2000).

A number of studies further suggest that difficulty in naming letters correlates with reading problems (Ehri, 1982, 1983; Roberts, 2003; Trei-

DOI: 10.4018/978-1-4666-4462-5.ch016

man, Weatherston, & Berch, 1994). Studies linked to naming difficulty indicate:

- Naming difficulty, as related to alphabetic knowledge, is a primary obstacle to reading.
- Letter knowledge predicts reading abilities.
- Dyslexic students make more naming errors than nondyslexic students.

Given the value of letter naming, techniques that address this skill can have consequence for improving instruction.

LETTER NAMING

In 1998, The National Research Council produced *Preventing Reading Difficulties in Young Children* (Snow et al. 1998) which outlined three "stumbling blocks" children may encounter impeding their route to becoming successful readers. The Council itemized these difficulties as understanding the alphabetic principle, transferring spoken language skills to reading, and remaining motivated to read when the process is so challenging. The first block children encounter is difficulty understanding the alphabetic principle—the concept that written spellings systematically represent spoken words. This concept includes letter naming (Badian, 2000; Terepocki, Kruk, & Willows, 2002; Mann & Foy, 2003; Lyon 1999).

A variety of other studies underscore the importance of alphabetics to develop reading skills (Badian, 2000; Catts, 2001; Faust, Dimitrovsky, & Shacht, 2003; Terepocki, Kruk, & Willows, 2002; Mann & Foy, 2003; Lyon 1999; Ehri, 1982, 1983; Roberts, 2003; Treiman, Weatherston, & Berch, 1994). These researchers examined the fundamental role of alphabetic through various lens. They focused on the foundational process of letter recall as it related to rapid naming (Catts, 2001) or to the reading process in terms of developmental stages (Ehri, 1982, 1983). Others looked at naming difficulty as a factor for dyslexic students (Faust, Dimitrovsky, & Shacht, 2003). Letter recall was the central point of many studies (Badian, 2000; Terrepocki, Kruk & Willows, 2002; Mann & Foy, 2003; Lyon, 1999) while letter naming as related to word recognition was studied by others (Roberts, 2003; Treiman, Weatherston, & Berch, 1994). Alphabetics importance to the development of reading skills has been broadly considered.

Other literature affirms the value of letter knowledge in predicting reading abilities. Badian found that letter naming and sentence memory were two preschool measures that added most to the prediction of reading at each grade level (Badian, 2000). Badian added that while not as strong as letter naming and sentence memory, preschool orthographic ability contributed to prediction of reading and spelling. A study on the relationship between letter naming and phonological awareness identified phoneme manipulation as closely associated with letter knowledge and letter sound knowledge, thus underscoring the importance of letter naming (Mann & Foy, 2003). From studying the reading process, Ehri indicated that letter knowledge became automatic before word recognition. She further concluded that kindergarten students' knowledge of letter names was the best single predictor of reading achievement at the end of first grade, better even than IQ (Ehri, 1982).

A study of the relationship between naming difficulties, phonological awareness and reading disabilities used a "Tip Of the Tongue" (TOT) model (Faust, Dimitrovsky & Schacht, 2003). A child in this model viewing letters or words might say, "It is on the tip of my tongue, but I cannot think of it." In this study, children with dyslexia made more naming errors and either did not know or could not name the items due to TOT compared to typical readers.

These studies intrigue educators in many settings. Do children who have difficulty naming letters also have problems with other naming tasks? Do the children who struggle to name letters later demonstrate dyslexia or other learning disorders? In addition to the auditory and attentional processes involved in letter naming, is there a visual process that contributes to the ability to rapidly name letter forms? Do children who have trouble naming letters have difficulty forming stable letter images? Whatever the causes of letter naming difficulty, can children who have limited ability to recall letter names improve this skill through the use of a prescribed procedure?

In *Overcoming Dyslexia,* Shaywitz wrote, ". . .the reading circuitry includes brain regions dedicated to processing the visual features, that is, the lines and curves that make up letters, and to transforming the letters into the sounds of language and to getting to the meaning of words" (Shaywitz, 2003, p. 78). Beginning readers must select and differentiate these lines and curves to identify letters.

LETTER IMAGING

Nanci Bell has written extensively regarding the essential partnership of the auditory and visual components of the decoding process. She defines symbol imagery as the ability to visualize letters in words noting, "Symbol imagery is visual memory for letters, seeing letters in your mind's eye; however, unless directly stimulated, it may not occur for children and adults, and what's more, it will be interrupted with instruction in only the phonetic aspect of word" (Bell, 2001, p. 51). From Bell's perspective, phonemic awareness and symbol imagery are "mates in the sensory system for language processing, specifically, literacy development" (Bell, 2001, p. 31).

The procedure used in this study was designed to improve memory for letter images. The conceptual base for this procedure was based on initial work at Cornell University by Eleanor Jack Gibson. She conducted studies directed at learning how children acquired knowledge of letterforms (Garner, 1979; Gibson & Walker, 1984; Pick, 1979; Pick, 1992). She concluded that specific attributes, but not the entire letterform, contributed to the identification process. Gibson named these attributes "distinctive features." In addition to Gibson's premise regarding the role of specific distinguishing attributes, feature detection studies describing how animals, notably frogs, perceived form and movement (Hubel & Wiesel, 1979) also contributed to the idea of shaping the input students used when learning to identify letters.

DISTINCTIVE FEATURES

During two decades, educators in a medical center developed and refined distinctive feature techniques. These techniques were based on the systematic identification of features unique for each letter that at-risk students used to build stable memories for letters (Stockdale & Possin, 2001, p. 129). Early probes indicated that students with learning problems often selected features that were not distinctive. They might select the same features for the letter "d" and the letter "b" or "h" or even "y." On the other hand, if taught features that were indeed distinctive, the students could then more successfully identify the intended letter.

The procedure also incorporated another aspect of perception described by Robert McKim in his courses on problem solving at Stanford University. He said, "Most of us experience seeing as a passive, 'taking in' process. In fact perception is an active, pattern-seeking process that is closely allied to the act of thinking" (McKim, 1972, p. 12). These words indicated that if simply looking at the letters was insufficient to identify distinctive features, the student's letter input needed to be shaped. The pattern seeking nature of perception must be recognized and formed into an active student centered process.

At the medical center, the educators discovered that simply looking at the letters or the features did not routinely produce effective recall in their at-risk students. But displaying the features for a short time and then covering the display with a white card was effective. When the duration of the exposure of the features was approximately .5 second, the student then had to actively use an internal scan to recall the display and name the letter. This was the approximate time it took for a teacher to flip a card up and down to expose and then hide the stimulus (features). These procedures became a part of clinic instruction and were shared with the interested classroom teachers of clinic children. They were also taught to educators in graduate courses on reading and spelling problems. No one remembers who first called the process used at the clinic "symbol stabilization."

Could this method of instruction help kindergarten students with restricted naming skills *before* encountering obstacles with reading and spelling? Could educators without specialized training in learning disorders carry out this procedure in a limited time period? Could this treatment occur without disrupting the regular classroom day? These questions prompted the study reported here to evaluate symbol stabilization with entering kindergarten students.

METHOD

Participants

The population for the study was kindergarten students from one public and one private school in the Puget Sound region of Washington State. The selected children spoke English as their first language. The administrators and teachers had 5 or more years of experience. The school and district populations reflected diversity in race, culture, and economic levels. Both schools used the *Read Well K* curricula (Sophris West, 2004). The three kindergartens in each school were included in the study. Students from these classes were given a screening test for letter naming fluency. The students with the lowest scores on the letter-naming test were the population addressed in the study. Each student in the low scoring group was assigned a number. A blind draw from this group by an uninvolved adult made the random selections. Half of the students in the low scoring group in each school were thus randomly assigned to the intervention group, and half were assigned to the control group.

Measures

Letter Naming Fluency (LNF) of the Dynamic Indicators of Basic Early Literacy Skills (Good & Kaminski, 2002)

The University of Oregon developed the Dynamic Indicators of Basic Early Literacy Skills (DIBELS) measures based upon the essential early literacy domains discussed in both the National Reading Panel (NRP, 2000) and National Research Council (Snow, et al., 1998) reports to assess student development of phonological awareness, alphabetic understanding, and automaticity and fluency with the code. The measures are described by the developers as reliable and valid indicators of early literacy development and predictive of later reading proficiency (Good & Kaminski, 2002). The screening measure selected from the DIBELS targets letter naming. It is a short (one minute) fluency measure that examines a student's automaticity, or fluency, in recognizing a series of random letters. The examiner gives the student a page of letters and one minute to identify as many letters as possible.

Comprehensive Test of Phonological Processing (CTOPP) (Wagner, Torgesen, & Rashotte, 1999)

The CTOPP version for five- and six-year-olds includes composites for phonological awareness, rapid naming, and phonological memory. The phonological awareness composite is measured by three subtests: Elision, blending words, and sound matching. The Elision Subtest asks the student to omit part of a word. "Say toothbrush.

Now say toothbrush without saying tooth" (p. 2). The Blending Words Subtest uses tape-recorded words presented in parts. The student hears "num" and "ber" and is asked to say the assembled word (number) (p. 4). The Sound Matching Subtest is also oral. The teacher points to a picture and says the name of the item (sock). Then the student is asked to point to a picture from an array with the same sound and/or to say the name of the picture (p. 5). The rapid naming composite includes two tests: Rapid Color Naming (p. 3) and Rapid Object Naming (p. 7). The student is timed for speed with a stopwatch during the naming tests. One function of these measures is to examine naming in a broader context. A second function is to examine whether phonological awareness correlates with letter naming.

Peabody Picture Vocabulary Test (PPVT) (Dunn, & Dunn, 1997)

The examiner says the test word (running), and the student selects the best match for the word from four pictures. The test is well established for validity and reliability and has been further evaluated for cultural bias. The function of the measure is to determine whether these kindergarten children have limited receptive vocabulary. Is there evidence of general language problems that could contribute to difficulty with language subskills such as letter naming?

Testing Personnel

Four persons conducted the testing and treatment. All had previous professional experience with standard testing and controlled measurement procedures and were trained in the specific processes and theory used in this study. These administrators rehearsed stages of treatment, applied written markers for movement from one stage to another and reported student performance in writing for each session. If questions arose, the test administrators also had ready access to help.

Site

Each kindergarten had an established site in an alcove near the entry door with a table and chairs for work with teaching assistants or volunteers. These sites were familiar to the children and in use at intervals throughout the day. These sites were used for the one-on-one testing and treatment in this study.

Testing Procedure

1. Three kindergarten classes from each school participated. The English-speaking students in the classes at each school were given *Letter Naming Fluency of the Dynamic Indicators of Basic Early Literacy Skills* (Good & Kaminski, 2002). The acronym, LNF/DIBELS, is used to refer to this measure. The scores of students from each school were recorded and examined for natural clusters.
2. 30 children from across the three classrooms at each school with the lowest scores on the LNF/DIBELS screening measure were identified as the school-wide sample.
3. 15 of the 30 children in each school-wide sample were randomly assigned to the control group and 15 of the children were assigned to the treatment group.
4. The 15 children in each treatment group and the 15 children in each control group were pretested using:
    a. Peabody Picture Vocabulary Test (PPVT-form A) (Dunn & Dunn, 1997).
    b. Comprehensive Test of Phonological Processing (CTOPP)(Wagner, Torgesen, & Rashotte, 1999).
5. **Intervention:** Each student in the treatment groups received symbol stabilization training during 12 sessions of 20 minutes duration over the course of approximately one month.
6. The children in each treatment group were post tested using:

   a. Peabody Picture Vocabulary Test (PPVT-form B) (Dunn & Dunn, 1997).
   b. Comprehensive Test of Phonological Processing (CTOPP) (Wagner, Torgesen, & Rashotte, 1999).
7. The children in each control group were post tested using:
   a. Peabody Picture Vocabulary Test (PPVT-form B) (Dunn & Dunn, 1997).
   b. Comprehensive Test of Phonological Processing (CTOPP) (Wagner, Torgesen, & Rashotte, 1999).
8. The scores of the treatment and control groups were analyzed and compared.

One student from the treatment group completed the study a week after the other children due to absences. One student in the treatment group and one student in the control group dropped out of kindergarten during the period of the study. The completed study included 29 students in the treatment group and 29 students in the control group.

Treatment Procedure

Children in the treatment group typically met with their treatment administrator for 20-minute sessions three times a week. The treatment was completed in a month unless student absences extended the duration into another week.

Equipment

1. Raised plastic upper and lower case letters.
2. Cards with printed upper and lower case letters.
3. Notebooks of letters in distinctive feature form.
4. Cards with words representing related families.
5. A box with hand holes for holding and examining plastic letters without seeing the letters.
6. 3 x 5 cards for visual notes.

Treatment Stages

The treatment administrator was trained to monitor progress of each child through the 4 possible stages of instruction. The stages have been identified during clinic work with children (Stockdale & Possin, 2001, p. 129). Mastery of a stage meant that the child could complete the behavior asked for by the questions. Upon mastery, the child was immediately moved on to the next level of treatment even if part way through a session.

Stage 1: Recognition or matching activities (administrator supplies the label for the letters):

1. Can the student identify visual similarities and differences in both 3-dimensional plastic letters and 2-dimensional printed letters?
2. Can the student recognize and match the same letter in both upper and lower case form?
3. Can the student differentiate letters by touching them?

Stage 2: Recall or descriptive language activities. The administrator models descriptive language. Student describes the distinctive features of the letters:

1. Can the student describe features of the letter he is touching?
2. With the administrator's modeling, can the student draw picture clues that help him recall a letter name?
3. Can the student visually identify the distinctive features of individual letters?

Stage 3: Recreate or naming activities to refine letter memory and to build fluency:

1. Can the student sustain letter naming for 2 minutes?
2. Can the student name letters clusters from seeing their distinctive features?

Stage 4: Expand letter naming to pattern discernment by finding and naming Word Families:

1. Can the student discover similar 3-letter patterns in words? These patterns are called families.
2. Can the student name the family and draw a cue that helps him remember the family?
3. Can the student read the words in the family after naming the cue (pattern of 3 letters)?

Matching Letters

The initial letter matching activity uses plastic 3-dimensional letters and cards with the pictures of the letters. The student is handed a letter and matches it to the appropriate card or to another letter as the administrator says the name of the letter and the student repeats the name. The array of letters and the pace for identification is gradually increased (see Figure 1).

Tactile Letter Identification

The administrator introduces the activity by asking the student to close her eyes. The administrator places the lower case letter "o" in the student's hand and asks the student to describe the object. (This letter has been mastered in the matching activity.) They discuss the characteristics of the letter—round or curvy, hole-in-the-middle. The administrator explains that these are features that tell your fingers what they are feeling. This is explained as similar to recognizing faces by how the eyes and nose and other features are shaped. The student's task is to select the important features of each letter that will tell her fingers what they are feeling. This is practiced on two or three highly distinctive letters. Usually this includes such letters as "l", "c", and "t." The box with hand holes is introduced (see Figure 2).

The box allows the administrator to monitor how the student handles the letters. The student is given the letters that were discussed and is asked to identify them by touch alone. This is the time to shape "how" the student handles the letters. The preferred hand is used to stroke or feel the letter held in the other hand. The student describes the features that informs her of which letter is in her hand. The administrator uses the term "features" and explains that fingers are good at finding features. More letters are given to the student and their features are identified. If the student cannot name the letter, but can select features, the administrator supplies the name. Both upper and lower case letters are used during this activity to help kindergarten children differentiate and name both cases.

Figure 1. Matching letters

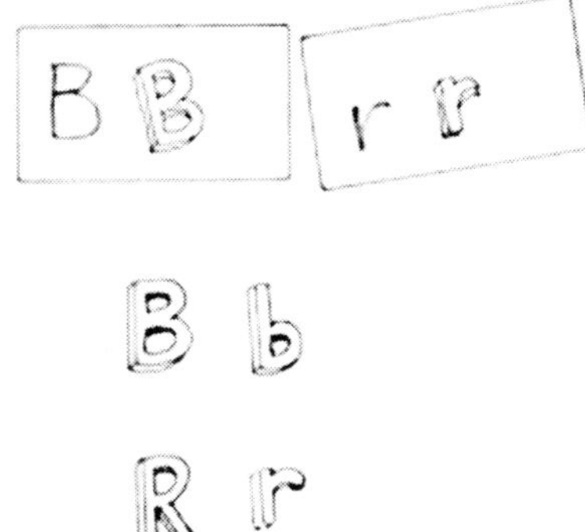

Figure 2. Hand holes box

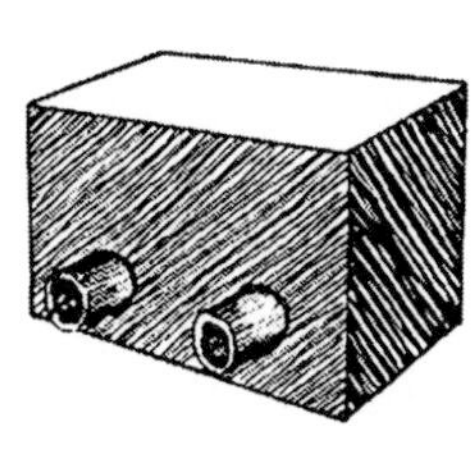

Descriptive Language Links Image to Letter Names and to Distinctive Features

Using their new knowledge of distinctive features, the students in each treatment group begin identifying the letters by touch (tactile input). They put their hands into the box with "hand holes" so they can feel the letters, one at a time. The students' task is to identify and name the letters by touch. At the back of the box, the administrator observes and monitors the student's handling of the letters and shapes the task to keep the focus on selecting letter differences. For instance, the administrator can arrange confusing letters in the correct orientation or even place the letter in the child's hand. Similar letters such as "p" and "d" or "g" and "q" can thus be selected out for comparison. If the student does not know a letter, the administrator prompts by asking, "What do you feel?" The emphasis is on differentiating features by touch. At this stage naming is important but secondary to selecting differentiating features.

Drawing Picture Cues to Link Meaning and Letter Names

Students draw images for letters that are difficult to name. Images help students recall letter names (labels) they find hard to remember. The image must trigger the name. The administrators encourage the students to think of an image to help them recall the label. If the student has difficulty thinking of one, the administrator suggests several and the student chooses one to use as a cue. Some students need to draw a picture of their image on a 3 x 5 card and write the letter on the back. The images need to be within the everyday vocabulary of the student. For instance, an administrator suggested a blue jay to cue the name of the letter "j." The student rejected this choice and selected "jail." After drawing a circle with a few vertical lines across it, she said that was her cue for "j."

Figure 3. Picture cue

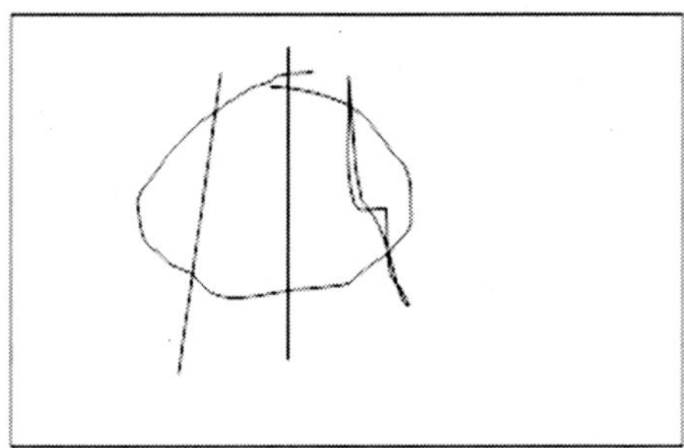

She was correct in that she could then name the letter correctly each time (see Figure 3).

Administrator and student develop language for the different features, such as "bumps" for "m" and "n" and "tall lines." for "l" and "d." The kindergarteners use their own words. Several children in the study needed to learn descriptive words for slanted lines such as "k," "y," etc. Some called them "slanty lines," or "hill lines." The child learns to describe distinctive features in his or her own words. The child's descriptive words must link both the features and the image of the letter to be useful as naming cues. (Children have images for their own words.) Once the words are established, the administrator, who also cues the child if other words are used during the lessons, consistently applies each student's descriptive language. The student is now ready to move on to seeing letters by their distinctive features alone.

Distinctive Features in Visual Form

Eyes, the students are told, can tell letters by seeing only the important parts just as fingers can tell a letter by finding important parts. The students see cards with the black distinctive features marked on the shaded letters. The student points to the important parts (features) for several letters (see Figure 4).

Figure 4. Distinctive feature card (Stockdale & Possin, 2001, p. 129)

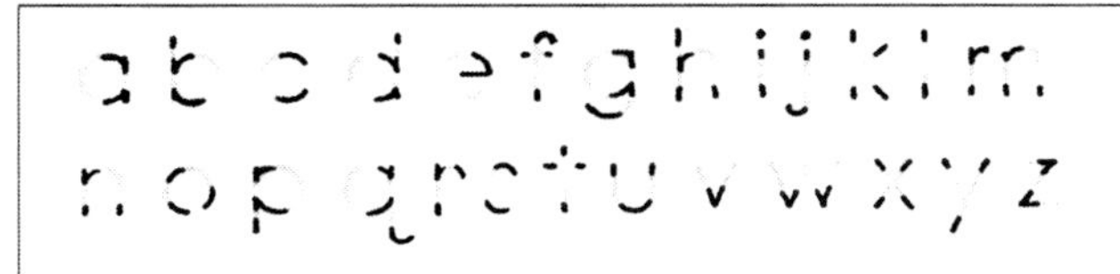

Distinctive Feature Notebook

The student is introduced to a notebook that initially presents just the distinctive features of one letter on each page. The student then names each letter after a brief glance (.5 second). After one letter is readily identified, the features of two letters are displayed for identification. The letters in the notebook are in pattern groups found in words. This distinctive feature notebook emphasizes lower case letters.

There are three distinctive feature notebooks. The first contains individual letters only; the second contains 24 pages of the most commonly occurring 2-letter patterns such as blends, vowel teams, or digraphs that emerging readers will encounter. The third notebook contains 3 and 4-letter patterns, primarily prefixes and suffixes. The student progresses sequentially through each notebook. Mastery is defined as the ability to name each letter or letter pattern after the .5 second display. Most students mastered the first notebook in two sessions. Two and three letter patterns required more exposure and practice (see Figure 5).

Figure 5. Distinctive feature notebook displaying 2 letters (http://www.arkinst.org/resources.asp)

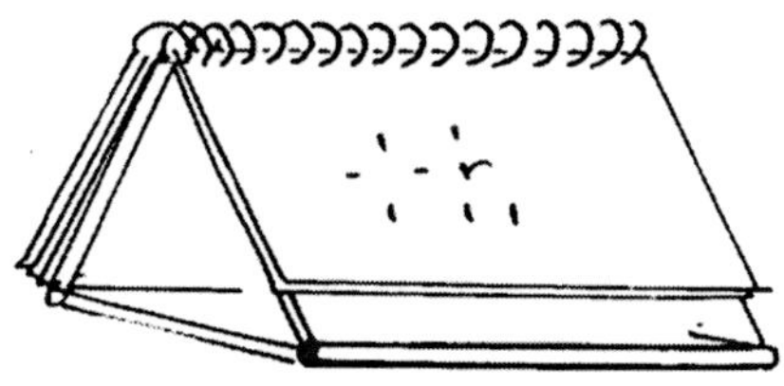

Word Families

Once the three notebooks have been mastered, the student moves into the final stage which involves recognizing and naming word families (See Figure 6). Students learn to identify three-letter word patterns, or "word families," by sorting a group of words into "families" that have the same letter patterns, such as "ack," "ill," or "ump." This step asks the child who can now differentiate letters to apply the sorting step to groups of letters.

The procedure involves the following steps. Initially, the student is given only 2 cards and asked to find the parts of the words that are alike. For example, the student is given cards with the word "hill" on one card and "pillow" on the other and asked to find the letters that are the same. The administrator then reads the family name and it becomes the "ill" family. The student reads the cards and may want or need to make a picture note for the family name.

The student progresses from identifying the same letter pattern or "family" in two words to finding the pattern in various locations in five words. Soon the student can sort similarities within 5-word families. The student names the letters in the family, learns the family name, draws a picture note as a cue for the letter pattern and read words containing the pattern. The "ill" family might include what is shown in Figure 6.

This process requires careful and selective visual scan from the student. Therefore, the "ill" family includes the pattern placed in different locations within the word in the symbol stabilization process. The "ill" pattern is intended to cue *visual* recall of the word rather than the phonetic

Figure 6. A word family

hill	village	gorilla	spill	pillow

decoding process. Two and three syllable words are important to be sure that the child is scanning the entire word to find the "ill" pattern.

When moving on to more word families, the task is initially limited to 4 cards representing 2 patterns. After the child sorts the two patterns, the administrator reads the words with the child. By the second or third exposure, many of the children read the entire family cueing from the basic 3-letter "family" pattern.

In summary, the treatment administrators moved each child in the treatment group through the 4 stages of instruction at that child's individual pace. At the first stage that meant seeing and feeling similarities and differences and matching identical letters and upper case with lower case letters. The second stage required the student to describe the distinctive features of letters and to name letters from these features. Stage three asked the students to sustain letter naming and to identify clusters of letters from their distinctive features. Finally, in stage 4, students identified 3-letter patterns in words as word families, developed cues for the family, and read words using the cue pattern.

At the conclusion of the 12 sessions of treatment, posttest measurement began with both the control group and the treatment group. This meant readministrating the *Letter Naming Fluency of the Dynamic Indicators of Basic Early Literacy Skills (LNF/DIBELS)* (Good & Kaminski, 2002), *Peabody Picture Vocabulary Test (PPVT-form B)* (Dunn & Dunn, 1997), and the subtests of the *Comprehensive Test of Phonological Processing (CTOPP)* (Wagner, Torgesen, & Rashotte, 1999). PPVT- Form B was used to minimize the effect of initial testing. All of the classrooms used the Read Well-K (SophrisWest 2004) curricula. Times for treatment were chosen to minimize interference with reading instruction.

RESULTS

Treatment students made significant gains in their letter naming scores. They also advanced in receptive vocabulary. Fifteen of the 29 students in the treatment group completed 3 stages and were in the fourth stage by the conclusion of the sessions. They were reading words in word families.

Children progressed in the treatment at different rates. The study reports both the pace and achievement levels of students in the treatment plan.

Measurements

The scores on the DIBELS letter-naming test of the treatment and control groups at the beginning of the school year were very similar (Table 1).

The 7.7 mean of the Control Group was very similar to the 8.0 mean of the Treatment Group on the letter-naming test. The probability that this difference is significant ($t = -2.1, p = .87$) indicates that it is unlikely that these two groups differ ap-

Table 1. Means for treatment and control groups at pretest

Level	Participants (*N*)	Std Dev	Mean
Control groups	29	6.8	7.7
Treatment groups	29	6.4	8.0

Table 2. Mean for treatment and control groups at posttest

Level	Participants (*N*)	Std Dev	Mean
Control groups	29	10.4	15.5
Treatment groups	29	12.4	24.0

preciably. Large standard deviations reflect substantial individual differences in the participants' scores.

The posttest scores of the Treatment and the Control Groups on the DIBELS letter-naming test differ significantly at the conclusion of the treatment period as shown in Table 2. The means differed statistically significantly, t = 6.6, p = .01. The mean of the Treatment Group was 54.8% higher than the mean of the Control Group. Groups that started out with similar mean scores posted significantly different mean scores at the conclusion of the treatment.

Symbol stabilization procedures resulted in improved letter naming by the kindergarten students who participated as members of the treatment group. The large standard deviation score reflects the wide range of scores in both groups.

Pace of Treatment

Initial DIBELS/LNF mean scores for children in the treatment and control groups was 8 or a bit less. The sample was diverse in ability with the ability to speak English being the only qualification. Figure 7 illustrates the progression and pace of the treatment students during the 12 sessions. Mastery of a stage meant that the child could complete the behavior asked for by the questions. The child was immediately moved on to the next level of treatment even if part way through a session.

Figure 7. Pace of treatment

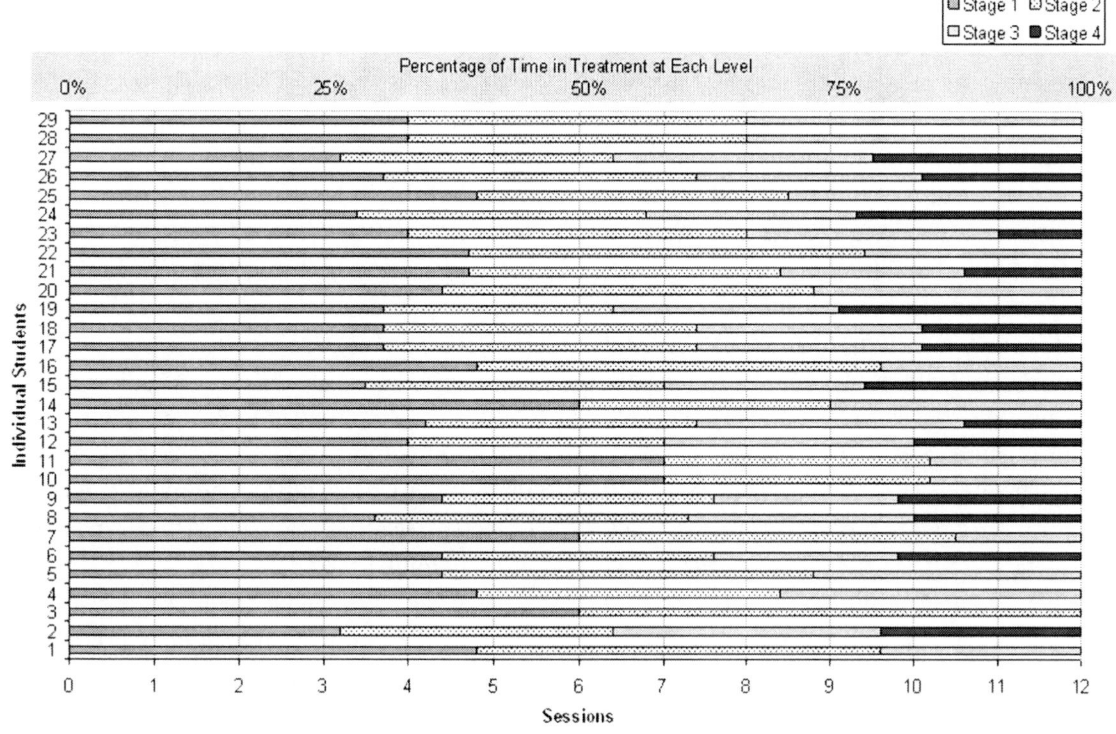

All the students began at stage 1 with matching activities during which the administrator supplied the label for the letters. All of the 29 children were still in this stage at the end of the first week and their 3rd session.

- Can the student identify visual similarities and differences in both 3-dimensional plastic letters and 2-dimensional printed letters?
- Can the student recognize and match the same letter in both upper and lower case form?
- Can the student differentiate letters by touching them?

By the end of the second week and 6th session, 27 of the children were judged able to identify visual similarities and differences in both plastic and printed letters, match upper and lower case letters, and differentiate letters by touch. Now they were working on the following skills:

- Can the student describe features of the letter he is touching?
- With the administrator's modeling, can the student draw picture clues that help him recall a letter name?
- Can the student visually identify the distinctive features of individual letters?

By the end of the third week and 9th session, 22 of the children were deemed able to recognize specific distinctive features by touch and by sight and describe the features in their own words after discussion with the administrator. They could also label letters and made personal cues for challenging letters. They were in the 3rd stage and working on activities to refine letter memory and build fluency. A wide array of letters was spread before them either in plastic or print form and they named letters for 2-minutes or until all of letters in the array had been successfully named. They also were learning to recognize pairs and groups of letters in distinctive feature form. Six of the other 7 children were far along into the second stage or nearly ready to move into the third stage. One child was only midway into the second stage. To determine moving the student to the final stage, the administrator asked:

- Can the student sustain letter naming for 2 minutes?
- Can the student name letters clusters from seeing their distinctive features?

During their last week, one child remained in stage 2 of the treatment, 13 children were in stage 3 and 15 children were in the 4th stage. These students could discern patterns in words and name them as families, create personal drawings for cues to recall challenging families, and read some or all of the words in a family. The administrators evaluated progress with these questions:

- Can the student discover similar 3-letter patterns in words? These patterns are called families.
- Can the student name the family and draw a cue that helps him remember the family?
- Can the student read the words in the family after naming the cue (pattern of 3 letters)?

All of the children could name the upper and lower case letters although some of them cound not do so instantly (see Figure 7).

Naming Relationships

What is the relationship between letter naming and other naming tasks? Does naming ability or inability cross tasks from letters to colors or to objects? Did the treatment in this study affect other naming scores?

In order to exam the effect of intervention on each of the language measures, we conducted a one-way MANOVA with intervention as the between subjects variable (treatment vs. control) and five dependent variables (percentage change in the PPVT, RCN, and ROM, and change in overall score of the DIBELS and ELISON). As expected, a significant difference between the intervention and control groups was not found (F (6,32) = 2.145, p =.075).

Although, the MANOVA revealed no significant differences at the .05 level, because the observed p-value approached significance, we conducted follow up one-way ANOVA tests as a conservative approach to see if individual tests may have been producing contradictory change or otherwise obscuring actual test score/percentage change differences. As can be seen from Figure 1, we found a significant difference between intervention groups for both percentage change on the PPVT (F (1,38) = 4.532, p =.04, η^2 =.11) and change on the DIBELS (F(1,38) = 6.978, p =.012, η^2 =.16). Specifically, the treatment group scored significantly higher on both tests. However, no other significant differences on the other three language tests were revealed (see Figure 8).

Relationship between Color Naming and Letter Naming

The scores of the kindergarten students in the study at the beginning of the school year did not indicate a correlation between color naming and letter naming. In fact the analysis indicated r = –.05 correlation, which, although slightly negative, is not significant. Two months into the school year, posttest scores showed a moderate positive correlation at the r = .29 level. For two months these children were exposed to color names and letter names each day. The labels have become more familiar. In addition, the children have been asked to respond to direction during this time. “Take out your red crayon.” “Find the letter ‘A’ on the worksheet; color it red.” Given the intense daily focus on letter naming in all of the kindergartens, and the use of color names for tasks, the children had extensive opportunity to learn the labels for both colors and letters. The fact that the correlation remained only moderate suggests that each task is determined by a variety of factors.

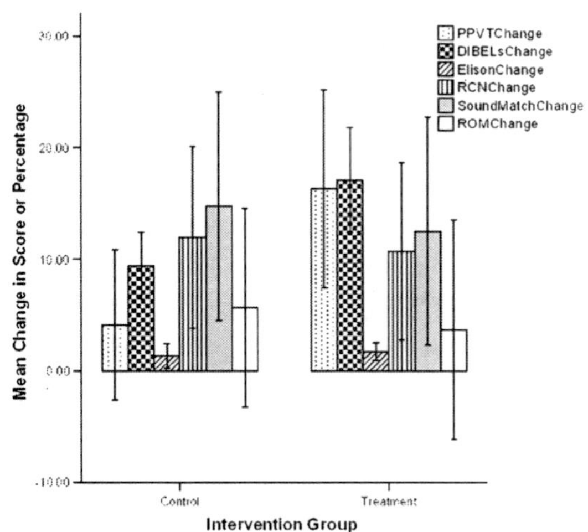

Figure 8. Mean change in score or percentage on the five different language tests for both the treatment and control groups. Standard error bars are included.

Relationship between Object Naming and Letter Naming

The scores correlating object naming with letter naming produced relationships similar to those between letter naming and color naming. The correlation at the beginning of the school year was r = –.03. The percentage of variance accounted for (r^2) is thus less than .1 percent. Two months into the school year, posttest scores showed a moderate correlation of r = .33 level. Some of the same factors that affect color naming also affect object naming. The students had experience in following directions and responding to questions. However, unlike direct color instructions, they did not rehearse naming “pencil,” “star,” “boat,” or the other names. Responding to a timed task was apparently somewhat easier after two months of kindergarten. However, the fact that the correlation remained only moderate suggests that each task is determined by a variety of factors.

Relationship between Object Naming and Color Naming

The CTOPP object naming test uses pictures of common objects such as "boat," "star," and "pencil." The names are rehearsed prior to testing. All of the children were able to name the objects. The same process was used for the color testing. However, several children did not recall the names of all the colors. Despite this difference, the parallels between object naming and color naming were notable. Using both scores at the beginning of the year and two months into the school year, the correlation between Rapid Color Naming and Rapid Object Naming of r = .64 level describes a moderate to strong relationship. This would suggest that naming colors and objects is a more similar task than naming letters and colors or letters and objects for the children in this sample.

Relationship between Receptive Vocabulary and Letter Naming

The Peabody Picture Vocabulary Test (PPVT) (Dunn 1997), during which the student selects pictures to illustrate words spoken by the examiner, is designed to measure receptive vocabulary. Is there a relationship between letter naming scores and receptive vocabulary? At the beginning of the year the pretest scores of letter naming and vocabulary correlated only at r = .20 (NS) significance suggesting very slight predictive correlation. The posttest scores two months into the school year were r = .34, in the weak to moderate correlation range. This relationship was further explored in the one-way ANOVA. The PPVT increased along with the improved letter naming (DIBELS).

Relationship between Sound Matching, a Phonological Skill, and Letter Naming

The National Reading Council report (NRP, 2000b) strongly endorses direct instruction focused on phonological awareness and phonics instruction. The question of whether this instruction will also support letter naming is informed by the relationship of the CTOPP Sound Matching subtest and the letter naming of the DIBELS test. The pretest data was collected during the early days of the school term. The correlation was then very slight between these kindergarten students' skill in naming letters (DIBELS) and their ability to match sounds prior to instruction (r = .10). However, there was substantial variation in the Sound Matching skills of these students. The standard deviation of 17.9 illustrates the unevenness of performance.

The posttest data was collected after 2 months of kindergarten. The relationship of the students' ability to name letters and their skill in matching sounds to pictures remained limited, although there was change from the pretest period. All of the children were receiving instruction in the sounds that go with letters. However, progress with this skill was uneven. In fact, 11 children had higher scores on Sound Matching at pretest than at posttest, suggesting that they did not progress in keeping with the higher expectations that go with their increase in age. This influences correlation in that all of the children improved their letter naming scores (DIBELS). The Standard Deviation is high at 22.1. The correlation between the skills expresses at the weak positive level (r = .21). This suggests that the two skills do not operate on the same factors.

Does Sound Matching develop separately and largely unaffected by letter naming treatment? Table 3 suggests that there is significant relationship (p =.005) to time, suggesting that the children in the study progressed from the early days of school to the second sampling approximately 2 months later. Both the Treatment and the Control Groups came along together in this growth in that the relationship of group assignment to change is not significant (p = .7) as shown in the effect tests. This result, too, would suggest that Sound Matching to pictures operates from different factors than letter naming.

Table 3. Analysis of variance: time and treatment vs. control on letter naming (DIBELS)

Factor	Participants (N)	DF	p Value
Time	58	1	0.01
Treatment or Control	58	1	0.15
Treatment or Control*Time	58	1	0.73

At the conclusion of the study, DIBELS/ LNF measures indicated that the children in the treatment group could name letters with greater speed and fluency than could the children in the control group. The difference was significant. The post testing also indicated that the PPVT test of receptive vocabulary was higher to a significant degree in keeping with the DIBELS score. No other language test indicated a significant difference.

DISCUSSION

The symbol stabilization technique requires the student to:

- Build meaning for the visual form of letters and to link that form to a label.
- Construct a personal image base for letters.
- Link his own descriptive language to the visual form and the letter label.
- Practice an intentional scan centered on feature detection.
- Make a broad memory base for letters that includes visual, tactile, and verbal attributes.

Letter naming is important for the beginning reader. Researchers identify letter naming difficulty as highly predictive of future reading problems (Badian, 2000; Catts, 2001; Faust, Dimitrovsky, & Shacht, 2003; Terepocki, Kruk, & Willows, 2002; Mann & Foy, 2003; Lyon, 1999; Ehri, 1982, 1983; Roberts, 2003; Treiman, Weatherston, & Berch, 1994). Apparently, other skills can develop independent of letter naming. This finding suggests that letter naming has unique attributes that merit instructional focus.

The test data indicated that letter naming involves features that set it apart from other naming tasks and from sound matching activities. Marilyn Adams suggests several reasons for letter naming importance including that letter naming is incorporated into instructional programs. She concludes, "There is a significant mnemonic disadvantage to trying to develop the visual identities of letters without giving each a unique and perceptually distinct label" (Adams, 1990). This uniqueness is in keeping with the focus of researchers who look to letter naming problems as a possible predictor of reading difficulty (Badian, 1998: Badian, et al., 1991; Berninger, et al., 1999; Catts, 2001; Catts, et al., 2003; Meyer, et al., 1998; Neuhaus, 2002). Neuhaus (2002) underscores the importance of letter naming in the summary statement, "Automatic letter recognition is the key to automatic word recognition" (p. 31).

Innovative practices, such as symbol stabilization, are needed for children with atypical learning needs. Acknowledging that letter-naming skills vary substantially among kindergarten students is a first step. These naming differences were true for children in the study without previous classroom experience and also for children who had attended preschool. Educators need to be aware that letter naming is difficult for some of their students so that they can provide the necessary differentiated instruction. Educators may move step by step through a reading curriculum without adapting the process for those who need special attention. In clinical practice, 4th and 5th grade children still often display highly unstable letter memory.

The data from this study suggest that shaping the visual features to which students attend can improve recall of letter names. Naming is a memory activity. Reinforcing attention to the specific features by using the student's own descriptive language is an important component in the recall process. The study also underscores the premise that learning is an active rather than a passive process. The treatment processes in this study demanded individual actions and allowed for students to create their own responses. Instruction must incorporate and value action.

Symbol stabilization helped children recall letters. Letter memory was shaped for students who initially did not readily recall letter names. Bell states, in regard to what she refers to as the "Visual and Auditory Circles" and their roles in decoding, "It is not and either/or issue . . . it is an integration of processes and integration can occur only if the underlying sensor-cognitive functions are intact . . ." (Bell, 2001, p. 48). Symbol imagery, she notes, is imperative for skilled word processing. Students in this study developed efficient perception of letters. Half of the children in the treatment group moved from letter perception to beginning reading in twelve twenty-minute sessions.

In summary, with only 4 hours of instruction most children in the control groups moved from little or no letter naming ability to naming all 52 letters. The results were consistent for each of the instructional groups despite the fact that 2 of the 4 test administrators had never taught kindergarten or reading. The children made major advances in a short period of time, and with a minimum of expense. This significant gain by the children in the treatment group demonstrates that letter memory can be shaped efficiently by using an instructional process that focuses on identifying distinctive features. Fifteen of the children in the study were able to complete the process, moving from letters to letter patterns and were reading words after four hours of instruction. This achievement exceeded expectations for a heterogeneous school population of children selected as least able to name letters prior to the study.

FUTURE DIRECTIONS

This study was conducted outside the classroom with one student at a time. However, classroom teachers can set aside a small study center where an aide or volunteer conducts the same steps with individuals or with small groups of children. The protocol is applicable so long as the essential features of the instruction are met.

There are implications for further research. This study indicates that letter naming is a specific skill that does respond to direct instruction and that strengthening the capacity to visualize letters and to develop a unique verbal label for letter images is beneficial to the letter naming process. Other studies need to repeat this study at the kindergarten level and at other age levels. Long-range follow-up studies need to determine whether the students who have difficulty learning to read are the same students who had difficulty naming letters in kindergarten. It would also be useful to know whether the students who received treatment in symbol stabilization develop reading problems down the line. Israeli researchers, Faust et al. (2003), suggested that children with dyslexia demonstrated naming problems. A further long-range study could examine the subset of students who develop the markers of dyslexia and possible links with children who had naming problems in kindergarten. Directed and specific early intervention is both wise and frugal.

REFERENCES

Adams, M. (1990). *Beginning to read: Thinking and learning about print*. Cambridge, MA: MIT Press.

Badian, N. A. (1998). A validation of the role of preschool phonological and orthographic skills in the prediction of reading. *Journal of Learning Disabilities*, *31*(5), 472–481. doi:10.1177/002221949803100505 PMID:9763776.

Badian, N. A. (2000). Do preschool orthographic skills contribute to prediction of reading. In Badian, N. A. (Ed.), *Prediction and Prevention of Reading Failure* (pp. 31–56). Baltimore, MD: York Press, Inc..

Badian, N. A., Duffy, F. H., Als, H., & McAnulty, G. B. (1991). Linguistic profiles of dyslexic and good readers. *Annals of Dyslexia*, *41*, 221–245. doi:10.1007/BF02648088.

Bell, N. (1997). *Seeing stars: Symbol imagery for phonemic awareness, sight words and spelling*. San Luis Obispo, CA: Gander Publishing Company.

Berninger, V. W., Abbott, R. D., Zook, D., Ogier, S., Lemos-Britton, Z., & Brooksher, R. (1999). Early intervention for reading disabilities: Teaching the alphabet principle in a connectionist framework. *Journal of Learning Disabilities*, *32*(6), 491–503. doi:10.1177/002221949903200604 PMID:15510439.

Catts, H. W. (2001). Estimating the risk of future reading difficulties in kindergarten children. *Language, Speech, and Hearing Services in Schools*, *32*(1), 4–8. doi:10.1044/0161-1461(2001/004).

Catts, H. W., Hogan, T. P., & Fey, M. E. (2003). Subgrouping poor readers on the basis of individual differences in reading-related abilities. *Journal of Learning Disabilities*, *36*(2), 151–164. doi:10.1177/002221940303600208 PMID:15493430.

Distinctive Feature Flip Notebooks and Display Stand. (n.d.). Retrieved from http://www.arkinst.org/resources.asp

Dunn, L. M., & Dunn, L. M. (1997). *PPVT-III Peabody picture vocabulary test* (3rd ed.). Washington, DC: American Guidance Service.

Ehri, L. C. (1982). *State of the art address: Learning to read and spell*. Paper presented at the American Psychological Association Annual Meeting. Washington, DC.

Ehri, L. C. (1983). *A critique of five studies on letter-name knowledge and learning to read*. Columbus, OH: Merrill.

Faust, M., Dimitrovsky, L., & Shacht, T. (2003). Naming difficulties in children with dyslexia: Application of the tip-of-the-tongue paradigm. *Journal of Learning Disabilities*, *36*(3), 203–215. doi:10.1177/002221940303600301 PMID:15515642.

Garner, W. R. (1979). Letter discrimination and identification. In Pick, A. D. (Ed.), *Perception and Its Development* (pp. 111–144). Hillsdale, NJ: Lawrence Erlbaum Associates, Publishers.

Gibson, E. J., & Walker, A. S. (1984). Development of knowledge of visual-tactual affordance of substance. *Child Development*, *55*, 453–460. doi:10.2307/1129956 PMID:6723444.

Good, R. H., & Kaminski, R. A. (Eds.). (2002). *Dynamic indicators of basic early literacy skills* (6th ed.). Eugene, OR: Institute for the Development of Educational Achievement. Retrieved from http://dibels.uoregon.edu/

Hubel, D., & Wiesel, T. (1979, September). Brain mechanisms of vision. *Scientific American*, 150–162. doi:10.1038/scientificamerican0979-150 PMID:91195.

Lyon, G. R. (1999). *The NICHD research program in reading development, reading disorders and reading instruction*. Retrieved from http://www.ncld.org/research/keys99_nichd.cfm

Mann, V. A., & Foy, J. G. (2003). Phonological awareness, speech development, and letter knowledge in preschool children. *Annals of Dyslexia*, *53*, 149–173. doi:10.1007/s11881-003-0008-2.

McKim, R. H. (1972). *Experiences in visual thinking*. Monterey, CA: Brooks/Cole Publishing Company.

Meyer, M. S., Wood, F. B., Hart, L. A., & Felton, R. H. (1998). Selective predictive value of rapid automatized naming in poor readers. *Journal of Learning Disabilities*, *31*(2), 106–117. doi:10.1177/002221949803100201 PMID:9529781.

Neuhaus, G. F. (2002, Winter). What does it take to read a letter? *Perspectives*, 6–8.

Neuhaus, G. F., & Swank, P. R. (2002). Understanding the relations between RAN letters subtest components and word reading in first grade students. *Journal of Learning Disabilities*, *35*(2). doi:10.1177/002221940203500206 PMID:15490743.

NRP. (2000b). Report of the national reading panel teaching children to read: Report of the subgroups. Washington, DC: NICHD, NIFL, Department of Education.

Pick, A. D. (Ed.). (1979). *Perception and its development: A tribute to Eleanor J. Gibson*. Hillsdale, NJ: Lawrence Erlbaum Associates.

Pick, H. L. Jr. (1992). Eleanor J. Gibson: Learning to perceive and perceiving to learn. *Developmental Psychology*, *28*(5), 787–794. doi:10.1037/0012-1649.28.5.787.

Roberts, T. A. (2003). Effects of alphabet-letter instruction on young children's word recognition. *Journal of Educational Psychology*, *95*(1), 41–51. doi:10.1037/0022-0663.95.1.41.

Shaywitz, S. M. D. (2003). *Overcoming dyslexia*. New York: Alfred A. Knopf.

Snow, C. E., Burns, M. S., & Griffin, P. (1998). *Preventing reading difficulties in young children*. Washington, DC: Committee on the Prevention of Reading Difficulties in Young Children, National Research Council.

Sophris West. (2004). *Read well k*.

Stockdale, C., & Possin, C. (2001). *The source for solving reading problems*. East Moline, IL: LinguiSystems, Inc..

Terepocki, M., Kruk, R. S., & Willows, D. M. (2002). The incidence and nature of letter orientation errors in reading disability. *Journal of Learning Disabilities*, *35*(3), 214–233. doi:10.1177/002221940203500304 PMID:15493319.

Treiman, R. (2000). The foundations of literacy. *Current Directions in Psychological Science*, *9*, 89–92. doi:10.1111/1467-8721.00067.

Treiman, R., & Rodriguez, K. (1999). Young children use letter names in learning to read words. *Psychological Science*, *10*, 334–338. doi:10.1111/1467-9280.00164.

Treiman, R., Weatherston, S., & Berch, D. (1994). The role of letter names in children's learning of phoneme-grapheme relationships. *Applied Psycholinguistics*, *15*, 97–122. doi:10.1017/S0142716400006998.

Wagner, R. K., Torgesen, J. K., & Rashotte, C. A. (1999). *The comprehensive test of phonological processing (CTOPP)*. Austin, TX: Pro-Ed, Inc..

Wolf, M. (2007). *Proust and the squid: The story and science of the reading brain*. New York: HarperCollins.

Compilation of References

Acquisti, A., & Gross, R. (2006). *Imagined communities: Awareness, information sharing, and privacy on the Facebook*. Retrieved from http://link.springer.com/chapter/10.1007%2F11957454_3?LI=true

Adamic, L., & Adar, E. (2005). How to search a social network. *Social Networks*, *27*, 187–203. doi:10.1016/j.socnet.2005.01.007.

Adams, M. (1990). *Beginning to read: Thinking and learning about print*. Cambridge, MA: MIT Press.

Aggarwal, C. C., & Yu, P. S. (2012). On the network effect in web 2.0 applications. *Electronic Commerce Research and Applications*, *11*, 142–151. doi:10.1016/j.elerap.2011.11.001.

Agrawal, R., & Srikant, R. (1994). Fast algorithms for mining association rules in large databases. In J. B. Bocca, M. Jarke, & C. Zaniolo (Eds.), *Proceedings of the International Conference on Very Large Data Bases* (pp. 487-499). San Francisco, CA: Morgan Kaufmann.

Agrawal, R., & Srikant, R. (1995). Mining generalized association rules. In *Proceedings of the International Conference on Very Large Data Bases* (pp. 407-419). San Francisco, CA: Morgan Kaufmann.

Agrawal, R., Imieliski, T., & Swami, R. (1993). Mining association rules between sets of items in large databases. *SIGMOD Record*, *22*(2), 207–216. doi:10.1145/170036.170072.

AlAgha, I., Hatch, A., Ma, L., & Burd, L. (2010). Towards a teacher-centric approach for multi-touch surfaces in classrooms. In *Proceedings of the ACM International Conference on Interactive Tabletops and Surfaces*, (pp. 187-196). New York, NY: ACM.

Alm, A. (2009). Blogging for self-determination with L2 learner journals. In Thomas, M. (Ed.), *Handbook of research on web 2.0 and second language learning* (pp. 202–221). Hershey, PA: IGI Global. doi:10.4018/978-1-60566-190-2.ch011.

American Association of Poison Control Centers. (n.d.). *Annual reports*. Retrieved December 18, 2012, from http://www.aapcc.org/annual-reports/

Anonymous, . (1984). Needlestick transmission of HTLV-III from a patient infected in Africa. *Lancet*, *2*(8146), 1376–1377. PMID:6150372.

Antenos-Conforti, E. (2009). Microblogging on Twitter: Social networking in intermediate Italian classes. In Lomicka, L., & Lord, G. (Eds.), *The next generation: Social networking and online collaboration in foreign language learning* (pp. 59–90). San Marcos, TX: CALICO.

Anzai, S., Dobberfuhl, P., Matsuzawa, C., & Zimmerman, E. (2008). *Students' cultural knowledge and attitudes before and after studying abroad: Engineering majors in Japan*. Retrieved March 21, 2013, from http://www.unc.edu/clac/documents/presentations/Anzai_Dobberfuhl_Matsuzawa_Zimmerman%20CLAC%202008.pdf

Armstrong, G. K. (1984). Life after study abroad: A survey of undergraduate academic and career choices. *Modern Language Journal*, *68*, 1–6. doi:10.1111/j.1540-4781.1984.tb01535.x.

Armstrong, K., & Retterer, O. (2008). Blogging as L2 writing: A case study. *AACE Journal*, *16*(3), 233–251.

Arnaboldi, V., Guazzini, A., & Passarella, A. (2013). Egocentric online social networks: Analysis of key features and prediction of tie strength in Facebook. *Computer Communications*. Retrieved April 8, 2013, from http://www.sciencedirect.com/science/article/pii/S0140366413000856

Arnold, N., Ducate, L., & Kost, C. (2009). Collaborative writing in wikis: Insights from culture projects in intermediate German classes. In Lomicka, L., & Lord, G. (Eds.), *The next generation: Social networking and online collaboration in foreign language learning* (pp. 115–144). San Marcos, TX: CALICO.

Arum, R., & Roksa, J. (2011). *Academically adrift: Limited learning on college campuses*. Chicago: University of Chicago Press.

Ashton, C. M., Houston, T. K., Williams, J. H., Larkin, D., Trobaugh, J., Crenshaw, K., & Wray, N. P. (2010). A stories-based interactive DVD intended to help people with hypertension achieve blood pressure control through improved communication with their doctors. *Patient Education and Counseling*, *79*(2), 245–250. doi:10.1016/j.pec.2009.09.021 PMID:19833472.

Association of American Colleges and Universities. (2002). *Greater expectations: A new vision for learning as a nation goes to college*. Washington, DC: Association of American Colleges and Universities.

Association of American Colleges and Universities. (2004). *Taking responsibility for the quality of the baccalaureate degree*. Washington, DC: Association of American Colleges and Universities.

Association of American Colleges and Universities. (2007). *College learning for the new global century*. Washington, DC: Association of American Colleges and Universities.

Auer, M. R. (2011). The policy sciences of social media. *Policy Studies Journal: the Journal of the Policy Studies Organization*, *39*(4), 709–736. doi:10.1111/j.1541-0072.2011.00428.x.

Austin, P. E., Dunn, K. A., Kesler, C., & Brown, C. K. (1995). Discharge instructions: Do illustrations help our patients understand them? *Annals of Emergency Medicine*, *25*(3), 317–320. doi:10.1016/S0196-0644(95)70286-5 PMID:7532382.

Avatar Languages Blog. (n.d.). *SurReal language quests*. Retrieved January 31, 2013, from http://www.avatarlanguages.com/blog/surreal-language-quests/

Avatar Languages. (n.d.). *Google street view for language learning: A guide for teachers*. Retrieved March 21, 2013, from http://www.avatarlanguages.com/teaching/streetview.pdf

Back, M. D., Stopfer, J. M., Vazire, S., Gaddis, S., Schmukle, S. C., Egloff, B., & Gosling, S. D. (2010). *Facebook profiles reflect actual personality, not self-idealization*. Psychological Science Online First. doi:10.1177/0956797609360756.

Baddeley, A. (1992). Working memory. *Science*, *255*(5044), 556–559. doi:10.1126/science.1736359 PMID:1736359.

Badian, N. A. (1998). A validation of the role of preschool phonological and orthographic skills in the prediction of reading. *Journal of Learning Disabilities*, *31*(5), 472–481. doi:10.1177/002221949803100505 PMID:9763776.

Badian, N. A. (2000). Do preschool orthographic skills contribute to prediction of reading. In Badian, N. A. (Ed.), *Prediction and Prevention of Reading Failure* (pp. 31–56). Baltimore, MD: York Press, Inc..

Badian, N. A., Duffy, F. H., Als, H., & McAnulty, G. B. (1991). Linguistic profiles of dyslexic and good readers. *Annals of Dyslexia*, *41*, 221–245. doi:10.1007/BF02648088.

Baird, A. D., Scheffer, I. E., & Wilson, S. J. (2011). Mirror neuron system involvement in empathy: A critical look at the evidence. *Social Neuroscience*, *6*(4), 327–335. doi:10.1080/17470919.2010.547085 PMID:21229470.

Baldi, M., Baralis, E., & Risso, F. (2005). Data mining techniques for effective and scalable traffic analysis. In *Proceedings of the International Symposium on Integrated Network Management* (pp. 105-118). IEEE Press.

Ballanteyne, R., Bain, J. D., & Packer, J. (1999). Researching university teaching in Australia: Themes and issues in academics' reflections. *Studies in Higher Education*, *24*(2), 237–257. Retrieved from http://search.ebscohost.com.er.lib.k-state.edu/login.aspx?direct=true&db=tfh&AN=1973925&site=ehost-live doi:10.1080/03075079912331379918.

Bandura, A., Ross, D., & Ross, S. A. (1961). Transmission of aggression through imitation of aggressive models. *Journal of Abnormal and Social Psychology, 63*(3), 575–582. doi:10.1037/h0045925 PMID:13864605.

Baralis, E., Cagliero, L., Cerquitelli, T., D'Elia, V., & Garza, P. (2010). Support driven opportunistic aggregation for generalized itemset extraction. In *Proceedings of the 2010 IEEE Conference on Intelligent Systems* (pp. 102-107). IEEE Press.

Baralis, E., Cagliero, L., Cerquitelli, T., Garza, P., & Marchetti, M. (2009). Context-aware user and service profiling by means of generalized association rules. In *Proceedings of the Conference on Knowledge and Engineering Systems* (pp. 50-57). Springer.

Baralis, E., Cagliero, L., Cerquitelli, T., & Garza, P. (2012). Generalized association rule mining with constraints. *Information Sciences, 194*, 68–84. doi:10.1016/j.ins.2011.05.016.

Bastiaansen, J. A. C. J., Thioux, M., & Keysers, C. (2009). Evidence for mirror systems in emotions. *Philosophical Transactions of the Royal Society B. Biological Sciences, 364*(1528), 2391–2404. doi:10.1098/rstb.2009.0058 PMID:19620110.

Bates, M. J. (2005). Berrypicking. In Fisher, K. E., Erdelez, S., & McKechnie, L. (Eds.), *Theories of Information Behavior*. Medford, NJ: Information Today.

Bechara, A., Damasio, A. R., Damasio, H., & Anderson, S. W. (1994). Insensitivity to future consequences following damage to human prefrontal cortex. *Cognition, 50*(1), 7–15. doi:10.1016/0010-0277(94)90018-3 PMID:8039375.

Belkin, N. J. (1980). Anomalous states of knowledge as a basis for information retrieval. *The Canadian Journal of Information Science, 5*, 133–143.

Bell, N. (1997). *Seeing stars: Symbol imagery for phonemic awareness, sight words and spelling*. San Luis Obispo, CA: Gander Publishing Company.

Benevenuto, F., Rodrigues, T., Cha, M., & Almeida, V. (2011). Characterizing user navigation and interactions in online social networks. *Information Sciences*.

Berardi, M., Lapi, M., Leo, P., & Loglisci, C. (2005). Mining generalized association rules on biomedical literature. In *Proceedings of the 18th International Conference on Innovations in Applied Artificial Intelligence* (IEA/AIE'2005). London: Springer-Verlag.

Berninger, V. W., Abbott, R. D., Zook, D., Ogier, S., Lemos-Britton, Z., & Brooksher, R. (1999). Early intervention for reading disabilities: Teaching the alphabet principle in a connectionist framework. *Journal of Learning Disabilities, 32*(6), 491–503. doi:10.1177/002221949903200604 PMID:15510439.

Binder, J., Howes, A., & Sutcliffe, A. (2009). The problem of conflicting social spheres: Effects of network structure on experienced tension in social network sites. In *Proceedings of CHI 2009—Social Networking Sites*, (pp. 965-974). Boston, MA: ACM Press.

Bishop, T. (2004). *Microsoft notebook: Wiki pioneer planted the seed and watched it grow*. Retrieved from http://www.seattlepi.com/business/158020_msftnotebook26.html

Blanchard, J., Guillet, F., & Briand, H. (2003). Exploratory visualization for association rule rummaging. In *Proceedings of the 4th International Workshop on Multimedia Data Mining MDM/KDD2003*, (pp. 107-114). Washington, DC: MDM/KDD.

Blattner, G., & Friori, M. (2009). Facebook in the language classroom: Promises and possibilities. *International Journal of Instructional Technology & Distance Learning, 6*(1). Retrieved January 31, 2013, from http://www.itdl.org/journal/jan_09/article02.htm

Blue Mars Lite. (n.d.). *Blue mars lite: Street view chat*. Retrieved March 21, 2013, from http://create.bluemars.com/wiki/index.php/Blue_Mars_Lite:_Street_View_Chat

Boden, D., Borrego, M., & Newswander, L. K. (2011). Student socialization in interdisciplinary doctoral education. *Higher Education, 62*, 741–755. doi:10.1007/s10734-011-9415-1.

Bolte Taylor, J. (2006). *My stroke of genius*. New York: Viking.

Borau, K., Ullrich, C., Feng, J., & Shen, R. M. (2009). Microblogging for language learning: Using Twitter to train communicative and cultural competence. In M. Spaniol et al. (Eds.), *8th International Conference on Web Based Learning - ICWL 2009* (pp. 78–87). Berlin: Spinger-Verlag. Retrieved January 31, 2013, from http://www.carstenullrich.net/pubs/Borau09Microblogging.pdf

Borgatti, S. P. (2005). Centrality and network flow. *Social Networks*, *27*, 55–71. doi:10.1016/j.socnet.2004.11.008.

Borgatti, S. P. (2006). A graph-theoretic perspective on centrality. *Social Networks*, *38*, 466–484. doi:10.1016/j.socnet.2005.11.005.

Borgatti, S. P., Everett, M. G., & Freeman, L. C. (2002). *UCInet for windows: Software for social network analysis*. Boston, MA: Harvard.

Borg, S. (1994). Language awareness as a methodology: Implications for teachers and teacher training. *Language Awareness*, *3*(2), 61–71. doi:10.1080/09658416.1994.9959844.

Bower, B. L. (2001). Distance education: Facing the faculty challenge. *Online Journal of Distance Learning Administration*, *4*(2).

Bower, G. H., Black, J. B., & Turner, T. J. (1979). Scripts in memory for text. *Cognitive Psychology*, *11*(2), 177–220. doi:10.1016/0010-0285(79)90009-4.

Braverman, J. (2008). Testimonials versus informational persuasive messages: The moderating effect of delivery mode and personal involvement. *Communication Research*, *35*(5), 666–694. doi:10.1177/0093650208321785.

Brewer, D. D. (2000). Forgetting in the recall-based elicitation of personal and social networks. *Social Networks*, *22*, 29–43. doi:10.1016/S0378-8733(99)00017-9.

Brickman, P. (1978). Is it real? In Harvey, J. H., Ickes, W., & Kidd, R. F. (Eds.), *New directions in attributional research* (*Vol. 2*, pp. 5–34). Hillsdale, NJ: Lawrence Erlbaum Associates.

Buccino, G., Baumgaertner, A., Colle, L., Buechel, C., Rizzolatti, G., & Binkofski, F. (2007). The neural basis for understanding non-intended actions. *NeuroImage*, *36*, T119–T127. doi:10.1016/j.neuroimage.2007.03.036 PMID:17499159.

Buelow, M. T., & Suhr, J. A. (2009). Construct validity of the Iowa gambling task. *Neuropsychology Review*, *19*(1), 102–114. doi:10.1007/s11065-009-9083-4 PMID:19194801.

Byram, M. (1997). *Teaching and assessing intercultural communicative competence*. Clevedon, UK: Multilingual Matters.

Cadez, I., Heckerman, D., Meek, C., Smyth, P., & White, S. (2000). Visualization of navigation patterns on a web site using model-based clustering. In R. Ramakrishnan, S. J. Stolfo, R. J. Bayardo, & I. Parsa (Ed.), *Proceedings of the 6th ACM SIGKDD International Conference on Knowledge Discovery and Data Mining (KDD 2000)* (pp. 280-284). Boston, MA: ACM Press.

Cagliero, L. (2011). Discovering temporal change patterns in the presence of taxonomies. *IEEE Transactions on Knowledge and Data Engineering*, 99.

Cagliero, L., & Fiori, A. (2013). Generalized association rule mining from Twitter. In *Intelligent Data Analysis*. Amsterdam: IOS Press.

Campbell, A. (2003). Weblogs for use with ESL classes. *The Internet TESL Journal, 9*(2).

Campbell, A. (2007). Motivating language learners with Flickr. *The Internet TESL Journal, 11*(2).

Capocchi Ribeiro, M. A. (2002). *An interactionist perspective to second/foreign language learning and teaching*. (ERIC Document Reproduction Service No. ED 469392. Cashmore, P. (2006). *Second life +web 2.0= virtual world mashups!* Retrieved January 31, 2013, from http://mashable.com/2006/05/30/second-life-Web-20-virtual-world-mashups/

Catanese, S. A., De Meo, P., Ferrara, E., Fiumara, G., & Provetti, A. (2011). Crawling Facebook for social network analysis purposes. In *Proceedings of WIMS '11*. Sogndal, Norway: WIMS.

Catts, H. W. (2001). Estimating the risk of future reading difficulties in kindergarten children. *Language, Speech, and Hearing Services in Schools*, *32*(1), 4–8. doi:10.1044/0161-1461(2001/004).

Catts, H. W., Hogan, T. P., & Fey, M. E. (2003). Subgrouping poor readers on the basis of individual differences in reading-related abilities. *Journal of Learning Disabilities*, *36*(2), 151–164. doi:10.1177/002221940303600208 PMID:15493430.

Ceynowa, K. (2011). *Mobile applications, augmented reality, gesture-based computing and more – Innovative information services for the internet of the future: The case of the Bavarian state library*. Retrieved from http://conference.ifla.org/past/ifla77/122-ceynowa-en.pdf

Chakravarthy, S., & Zhang, H. (2003). Visualization of association rules over relational DBMSs. In *Proceedings of the 2003 ACM symposium on Applied Computing* (pp. 922–926). ACM.

Chaminade, T., Zecca, M., Blakemore, S. J., Takanishi, A., Frith, C. D., & Micera, S. et al. (2010). Brain response to a humanoid robot in areas implicated in the perception of human emotional gestures. *PLoS ONE*, *5*(7), e11577. doi:10.1371/journal.pone.0011577 PMID:20657777.

Chang, H.-C. (2010). A new perspective on Twitter hashtag use: Diffusion of innovation theory. In *Proceedings of ASIST 2010*. Pittsburgh, PA: ASIST.

Chang, C. (2008). Increasing mental health literacy via narrative advertising. *Journal of Health Communication*, *13*(1), 37–55. doi:10.1080/10810730701807027 PMID:18307135.

Chapman, B. F., & Henderson, R. G. (2010). E-learning quality assurance: A perspective of business teacher educators and distance learning coordinators. *Delta Pi Epsilon Journal*, *52*(1), 16–31.

Chen, Y. C. (2009). *The effect of applying wikis in an English as a foreign language (EFL) class in Taiwan*. (Doctoral Dissertation). University of Central Florida, Orlando, FL. Retrieved January 31, 2013, from http://etd.fcla.edu/CF/CFE0002227/Chen_Yu-ching_200808_PhD.pdf

Chen, R. (2013). Living a private life in public social networks: An exploration of member self-disclosure. *Decision Support Systems*, 1–8.

Cheong, M., & Lee, V. (2009). Integrating web-based intelligence retrieval and decision-making from the twitter trends knowledge base. In *Proceedings of the Second ACM Workshop on Social Web Search and Mining* (pp. 1-8). ACM Press.

Chernoff, H. (1973). The use of faces to represent points in k-dimensional space graphically. *Journal of the American Statistical Association*, *68*(342), 361–367. doi:10.1080/01621459.1973.10482434.

Cho, H., Gay, G., Davidson, B., & Ingraffea, A. (2007). Social networks, communication styles, and learning performance in a CSCL community. *Computers & Education*, *49*, 309–329. doi:10.1016/j.compedu.2005.07.003.

Choi, J. (2009). Asian English language learners' identity construction in an after school literacy site. *Journal of Asian Pacific Communication*, *19*(1), 130–161. doi:10.1075/japc.19.1.07cho.

Christakis, N. A., & Fowler, J. H. (2009). *Connected: The surprising power of our social networks and how they shape our lives*. New York: Little, Brown and Company.

Chu, Z., Gianvecchio, S., Wang, H., & Jajodia, S. (2010). Who is tweeting on Twitter: Human, bot, or cyborg. In *Proceedings of ACSAC '10*. Austin, TX: ACSAC.

Chur-Hansen, A., & McLean, S. (2006). On being a supervisor: the importance of feedback and how to give it. *Australasian Psychiatry*, *14*(1), 67–71. PMID:16630202.

Clay, M. (1999). Development of training and support programs for distance education instructors. *Online Journal of Distance Learning Administration*, *2*(3).

Connolly, T., & Reb, J. (2005). Regret in cancer-related decisions. *Health Psychology*, *24*(4S), S29–S34. doi:10.1037/0278-6133.24.4.S29 PMID:16045415.

Cook, T. (2008). Saskatchewan child nearly killed by riding mower. *The Canadian Press*. Retrieved November 28, 2012, from: http://www.thestar.com/News/Canada/article/427950

Cotton, B. (2009). Innovation networks: A report on creating a specialist professional social network, offline and online, to foster innovation in the new media sector. [LNCS]. *Proceedings of Online Communities*, *5621*, 312–321. doi:10.1007/978-3-642-02774-1_34.

Couturier, O., Mephu Nguifo, E., & Noiret, B. (2005). A formal approach to occlusion and optimization in association rules visualization. In *Proceedings of VDM of IEEE 9th International Conference on Information Visualization*. IEEE Press.

Cox, K. (2001). Stories as case knowledge: Case knowledge as stories. *Medical Education, 35*(9), 862–866. doi:10.1046/j.1365-2923.2001.01016.x PMID:11555224.

Culhane, S. F., & Kehoe, J. (2000). The effects of an anti-racist role-play program. *Polyglossia, 3*, 1–8.

Cumming, G. S., Barnes, G., Perz, S., Schmink, M., Sieving, K. E., & Southworth, J. … Van Holt, T. (2005). An exploratory framework for the empirical measurement of resilience. Ecosystems, 8, 975- 987. DOI: doi:10.1007/s10021-005-0129-z.

Cummings, J. N., & Kiesler, S. (2008). Who collaborates successfully? Prior experience reduces collaboration barriers in distributed interdisciplinary research. In *Proceedings of the Computer-Supported Collaborative Work* (CSCW '08), (pp. 437-446). San Diego, CA: ACM.

Cummings, J. N., & Cross, R. (2003). Structural properties of work groups and their consequences for performance. *Social Networks, 25*, 197–210. doi:10.1016/S0378-8733(02)00049-7.

Cummings, R. E. (2008). What was a wiki and why do i care? A short and usable history of wikis. In Cummings, R. E., & Barton, M. (Eds.), *Wiki Writing: Collaborative Learning in the College Classroom*. Ann Arbor, MI: University of Michigan Press. doi:10.3998/dcbooks.5871848.0001.001.

Cuzzocrea, A., Song, I.-Y., & Davis, K. C. (2011). Analytics over large-scale multidimensional data: The big data revolution! In A. Cuzzocrea, I.-Y. Song, & K. C. Davis (Eds.), *Proceedings of the ACM 14th International Workshop on Data Warehousing and On-Line Analytical Processing (DOLAP 2011)* (pp. 101-104). Glasgow, UK: ACM Press.

Da, Z., & Jianping, Z. (2009). Knowledge visualization - An approach of knowledge transfer and restructuring in education. In *Proceedings of the 2009 International Forum on Information Technology and Applications* (vol. 3, pp. 716-719). Washington, DC: IEEE Computer Society.

Dahlstrom, E. (n.d.). *ECAR study of undergraduate students and information technology*. Louisville, CO: EDUCAUSE Center for Applied Research. Retrieved from http://www.educause.edu/ecar.

Dal Cin, S., Zanna, M. P., & Fong, G. T. (2004). Narrative persuasion and overcoming resistance. In Knowles, E. S., & Linn, J. A. (Eds.), *Resistance and persuasion* (pp. 175–191). Mahwah, NJ: Lawrence Erlbaum Associates.

Damasio, A. R., Tranel, D., & Damasio, H. (1991). Somatic markers and the guidance of behavior: Theory and preliminary testing. In Levine, H. S., Eisenberg, H. M., & Benton, A. L. (Eds.), *Frontal lobe function and dysfunction* (pp. 217–229). New York: University Press.

Damen, L. (1987). *Culture learning: The fifth dimension in the language classroom*. Reading, MA: Addision-Wesley. Retrieved March 21, 2013, from http://people.ict.usc.edu/~lane/papers/Lane-Ogan-CATS09-VirtualEnvironmentsForCulturalLearning.pdf

De Nooy, W., Mrvar, A., & Batagelj, V. (2011). *Exploratory social network analysis with Pajek: Structural analysis in the social sciences*. Cambridge, UK: Cambridge University Press. doi:10.1017/CBO9780511996368.

de Wit, J. B. F., Das, E., & Vet, R. (2008). What works best: Objective statistics or a personal testimonial? An assessment of the persuasive effects of different types of message evidence on risk perception. *Health Psychology, 27*(1), 110–115. doi:10.1037/0278-6133.27.1.110 PMID:18230021.

De Young, R., & Monroe, M. C. (1996). Some fundamentals of engaging stories. *Environmental Education Research, 2*(2), 171–187. doi:10.1080/1350462960020204.

Deci, E., & Ryan, R. (1985). *Intrinsic motivation and self-determination in human behavior*. New York: Plenum. doi:10.1007/978-1-4899-2271-7.

Decrem, B. (2006). Introducing flock beta 1. *Flock official blog.*

Deen, B., & McCarthy, G. (2010). Reading about the actions of others: Biological motion imagery and action congruency influence brain activity. *Neuropsychologia, 48*(6), 1607–1615. doi:10.1016/j.neuropsychologia.2010.01.028 PMID:20138900.

Delp, C., & Jones, J. (2008). Communicating information to patients: The use of cartoon illustrations to improve comprehension of instructions. *Academic Emergency Medicine, 3*(3), 264–270. doi:10.1111/j.1553-2712.1996.tb03431.x PMID:8673784.

Dennis, M. R., & Babrow, A. S. (2005). Effects of narrative and paradigmatic judgmental orientations on the use of qualitative and quantitative evidence in health-related inference. *Journal of Applied Communication Research*, *33*(4), 328–347. doi:10.1080/00909880500278137.

Denscombe, M. (2001). Critical incidents and the perception of health risks: The experiences of young people in relation to their use of alcohol and tobacco. *Health Risk & Society*, *3*(3), 293–306. doi:10.1080/13698570120079895.

Dervin, B. (1976). *Information for sense-making*. Paper presented to the Symposium of the Committee on Public Information in the Prevention of Occupational Cancer, National Research Council, National Academy of Sciences. Washington, DC.

Deursen, A. V., & Visser, E. (2002). The reengineering wiki. In *Proceedings 6th European Conference on Software Maintenance and Reengineering* (CSMR), (pp. 217-220). IEEE Computer Society.

Deutschmann, M., Panichi, L., & Molka-Danielsen, J. (2009). Designing oral participation in Second Life: A comparative study of two language proficiency courses. *ReCALL*, *21*(2), 206–226. doi:10.1017/S0958344009000196.

Dewey, J. (1933). *How we think: A restatement of the relation of reflective thinking to the educative process*. Boston: Henry Holt.

Dewey, J. (1966). *Democracy and education*. New York: Free Press.

di Pellegrino, G., Fadiga, L., Fogassi, L., Gallese, V., & Rizzolatti, G. (1992). Understanding motor events: A neurophysiological study. *Experimental Brain Research*, *91*(1), 176–180. doi:10.1007/BF00230027 PMID:1301372.

Dignum, F., & Kuiper, R. (1999). Specifying deadlines with continuous time using deontic and temporal logic. *International Journal of Electronic Commerce*, *3*(2), 67–85. Retrieved from http://www.jstor.org/stable/27750885.

Dillard, A. J., Fagerlin, A., Cin, S. D., Zikmund-Fisher, B. J., & Ubel, P. A. (2010). Narratives that address affective forecasting errors reduce perceived barriers to colorectal cancer screening. *Social Science & Medicine*, *71*(1), 45–52. doi:10.1016/j.socscimed.2010.02.038 PMID:20417005.

Dippold, D. (2009). Peer feedback through blogs: Student and teacher perceptions in an advanced German class. *ReCALL*, *21*(1), 18–36. doi:10.1017/S095834400900010X.

Distinctive Feature Flip Notebooks and Display Stand. (n.d.). Retrieved from http://www.arkinst.org/resources.asp

Domik, G., & Fischer, G. (2010). Coping with complex real-world problems: Strategies for developing the competency of transdisciplinary collaboration. In *Proceedings of KCKS 2010*. IFIP AICT.

Doyle, T. (2011). *Learner-centered teaching: Putting the research on learning into practice*. Sterling, VA: Sylus Publishing.

Drossaert, C., Boer, H., & Seydel, E. (1996). Perceived risk, anxiety, mammogram uptake, and breast self-examination of women with a family history of breast cancer: The role of knowing to be at increased risk. *Cancer Detection and Prevention*, *20*(1), 76–85. PMID:8907207.

Ducate, C. L., & Lomicka, L. L. (2005). Exploring the blogosphere: Use of web logs in the foreign language classroom. *Foreign Language Annals*, *38*(3), 410–421. doi:10.1111/j.1944-9720.2005.tb02227.x.

Ducate, C. L., & Lomicka, L. L. (2008). Adventures in the blogosphere: From blog readers to blog writers. *Computer Assisted Language Learning*, *21*(1), 9–28. doi:10.1080/09588220701865474.

Dumas, J. S., & Redish, J. C. (1999). *A practical guide to usability testing*. Exeter, UK: Intellect Ltd..

Dunn, L. M., & Dunn, L. M. (1997). *PPVT-III Peabody picture vocabulary test* (3rd ed.). Washington, DC: American Guidance Service.

Durugbo, C. (2012). Modeling user participation in organisations as networks. *Expert Systems with Applications*, *39*, 9230–9245. doi:10.1016/j.eswa.2012.02.082.

Ebner, M., Mühlburger, H., Schaffert, S., Schiefner, M., Reinhardt, W., & Wheeler, S. (2010). Getting granular on Twitter: Tweets from a conference and their limited usefulness for non-participants. In Reynolds, N., & Turcsányi-Szabó, M. (Eds.), *KCKS 2010, IFIP AICT 324* (pp. 102–113). IFIP International Federation for Information Processing. doi:10.1007/978-3-642-15378-5_10.

Educause Learning Initiative. (2008). *Annual meeting, virtual worlds as web 2.0 learning spaces*. Educause.

Efron, M., & Winget, M. (2010). Questions are content: A taxonomy of questions in a microblogging environment. In *Proceedings of ASIST 2010*. Pittsburgh, PA: ASIST.

Ehri, L. C. (1982). *State of the art address: Learning to read and spell*. Paper presented at the American Psychological Association Annual Meeting. Washington, DC.

Ehri, L. C. (1983). *A critique of five studies on letter-name knowledge and learning to read*. Columbus, OH: Merrill.

ELATEwiki. (n.d.). Retrieved from http://www.ELATEwiki.org

ElearningFacultyModules.org. (n.d.). Retrieved from http://elearningfacultymodules.org

Elger, C. E., & Lehnertz, K. (1998). Seizure prediction by non-linear time series analysis of brain electrical activity. *The European Journal of Neuroscience*, *10*(2), 786–789. doi:10.1046/j.1460-9568.1998.00090.x PMID:9749744.

Ellison, N. B., Steinfield, C., & Lampe, C. (2007). The benefits of Facebook 'friends': Social capital and college students' use of online social network sites. *Journal of Computer-Mediated Communication*, *12*, 1143–1168. doi:10.1111/j.1083-6101.2007.00367.x.

Elola, I., & Oskoz, A. (2010). Collaborative writing: Fostering foreign language and writing conventions development. *Language Learning & Technology*, *14*(3), 51–71. Retrieved January 31, 2013, from http://llt.msu.edu/issues/october2010/elolaoskoz.pdf

Engelfriet, J., & Treur, J. (2002). Linear, branching time and joint closure semantics for temporal logic. *Journal of Logic Language and Information*, *11*, 389–425. doi:10.1023/A:1019999621456.

Eppler, M. J., & Burkhard, R. A. (2004). *Knowledge visualization: Towards a new discipline and its fields of application. Università della Svizzera italiana*. Faculty of Communication Sciences, Institute for Corporate Communication.

Ertmer, P., Richardson, J., Lehman, J., Newby, T., Cheng, X., Mong, C., & Sadaf, A. (2010). Peer feedback in a large undergraduate blended course: perceptions of value and learning. *Educational Computing Research*, *43*(1), 67–88. doi:10.2190/EC.43.1.e.

Erwin, D. O., Ivory, J., Stayton, C., Willis, M., Jandorf, I., & Thompson, H. et al. (2003). Replication and dissemination of a cancer education model for African American women. *Cancer Control*, *10*(5), 13–21. PMID:14581900.

Ezingeard, J., & Bowen-Schrire, M. (2007). Triggers of change in information security management practices. *Journal of General Management*, *32*(4), 53–72.

Farkas, M. (2010). *Your reality, augmented*. Retrieved from http://americanlibrariesmagazine.org/columns/practice/your-reality-augmented March, 2013.

Faust, M., Dimitrovsky, L., & Shacht, T. (2003). Naming difficulties in children with dyslexia: Application of the tip-of-the-tongue paradigm. *Journal of Learning Disabilities*, *36*(3), 203–215. doi:10.1177/00222194030360030l PMID:15515642.

Fayyad, U., Grinstein, G. G., & Wierse, A. (2001). *Information visualization in data mining and knowledge discovery*. San Francisco, CA: Morgan Kaufmann Publishers Inc..

Felt, U., Igelsböck, J., Schikowitz, A., & Völker, T. (2012). Growing into what? The (un-)disciplined socialisation (sic) of early stage researchers into transdisciplinary research. *Higher Education*. doi: doi:10.1007/s10734-012-9560-1.

Field, K., & O'Brien, J. (2010). Cartoblography: Experiments in using and organizing the spatial context of micro-blogging. *Transactions in GIS*, *14*(s1), 5–23. doi:10.1111/j.1467-9671.2010.01210.x.

Fine, P., Eames, K., & Heymann, D. L. (2011). Herd immunity: A rough guide. *Clinical Infectious Diseases*, *52*(7), 911–916. doi:10.1093/cid/cir007 PMID:21427399.

Fisher, S. L., & Ford, J. K. (2006). Differential effects of learner effort and goal orientation on two learning outcomes. *Personnel Psychology*, *51*(2), 397–420. doi:10.1111/j.1744-6570.1998.tb00731.x.

Fontaine, R., & Rogers, W. (2011). Internet freedom: A foreign policy imperative in the digital age. Washington, DC: Center for a New American Security.

Ford, E. S., Zhao, G., Tsai, J., & Li, C. (2011). Low-risk lifestyle behaviors and all-cause mortality: Findings from the national health and nutrition examination survey III mortality study. *American Journal of Public Health*, *101*(10), 1922–1929. doi:10.2105/AJPH.2011.300167 PMID:21852630.

Franco, C. (2008). Using wiki-based peer-correction to develop writing skills of Brazilian EFL learners. *Novitas-ROYAL*, *2*(1), 49–59.

Friedman, T. L., & Mandelbaum, M. (2011). *That used to be us*. New York: Farrar, Strauss and Giroux.

Fry, B. (2007). *Visualizing data*. Sebastopol, CA: O'Reilly Media.

Gardner, H. (2009). *Five minds for the future*. Boston: Harvard Business School Press.

Garner, W. R. (1979). Letter discrimination and identification. In Pick, A. D. (Ed.), *Perception and Its Development* (pp. 111–144). Hillsdale, NJ: Lawrence Erlbaum Associates, Publishers.

Garrett, P. B., Coupland, N., & William, H. (2003). *Investigating language attitudes*. Cardiff, UK: University of Wales.

Gendolla, G. H. E., & Koller, M. (2001). Surprise and motivation of causal search: How are they affected by outcome valence and importance? *Motivation and Emotion*, *25*(4), 327–349. doi:10.1023/A:1014867700547.

Gibson, E. J., & Walker, A. S. (1984). Development of knowledge of visual-tactual affordance of substance. *Child Development*, *55*, 453–460. doi:10.2307/1129956 PMID:6723444.

Gibson, R., & Zillmann, D. (1994). Exaggerated versus representative exemplification in news reports. *Communication Research*, *21*(5), 603–624. doi:10.1177/009365094021005003.

Gilbert, D., Chen, H. L., & Sabol, J. (2008). Building learning communities with wikis. In Cummings, R. E., & Barton, M. (Eds.), *Wiki Writing: Collaborative Learning in the College Classroom*. Ann Arbor, MI: University of Michigan Press.

Glanz, K., Resch, N., Lerman, C., Blake, A., Gorchov, P., & Rimer, B. (1992). Factors associated with adherence to breast-cancer screening among working women. *Journal of Occupational and Environmental Medicine*, *34*(11), 1071–1078. doi:10.1097/00043764-199211000-00008 PMID:1432296.

Glanz, K., Rimer, B. K., & Viswanath, K. (Eds.). (2008). *Health behavior and health education: Theory, research, and practice*. San Francisco, CA: Jossey-Bass.

Gleicher, F., Boninger, D. S., Strathman, A., Armor, D. A., Hetts, J. J., & Ahn, M. (1995). With an eye toward the future: The impact of counterfactual thinking on affect, attitudes and behavior. In Roese, N. J., & Olson, J. M. (Eds.), *What might have been: The social psychology of counterfactual thinking* (pp. 283–304). Mahwah, NJ: Lawrence Erlbaum Associates.

Godwin-Jones, R. (2003). Blogs and wikis: Environments for on-line collaboration. *Language Learning & Technology*, *7*(2), 12–16.

Godwin-Jones, R. (2008). Web-writing 2.0: Enabling, documenting, and assessing writing online. *Language Learning & Technology*, *12*(2), 7–13.

Golde, C. M., & Gallagher, H. A. (1999). The challenges of conducting interdisciplinary research in traditional doctoral programs. *Ecosystems (New York, N.Y.)*, *2*(4), 281–285. doi:10.1007/s100219900076.

Goldstein, J., & Roth, S. F. (1994). Using aggregation and dynamic queries for exploring large data sets. In E. Dykstra-Erickson & M. Tscheligi (Eds.), *Proceedings of the SIGCHI Conference on Human Factors in Computing Systems (CHI 2004)* (pp. 23-29). Boston, MA: ACM Press.

Good, R. H., & Kaminski, R. A. (Eds.). (2002). *Dynamic indicators of basic early literacy skills* (6th ed.). Eugene, OR: Institute for the Development of Educational Achievement. Retrieved from http://dibels.uoregon.edu/

Google Maps Street View. (n.d.). *Explore the world at street level*. Retrieved March 21, 2013, from http://maps.google.com/intl/en/help/maps/streetview/#utm_campaign=en&utm_medium=van&utm_source=en-van-na-us-gns-svn

Google. (n.d.). *Wikipedia*. Retrieved January 12, 2013, from http://en.wikipedia.org/wiki/Google

Graesser, A. C., Hauft-Smith, K., Cohen, A. D., & Pyles, L. D. (1980). Advanced outlines, familiarity, and text genre on retention of prose. *Journal of Experimental Education*, *48*(4), 281–290.

Greene, K., & Brinn, L. (2003). Messages influencing college women's tanning bed use: Statistical versus narrative evidence format and a self-assessment to increase perceived susceptibility. *Journal of Health Communication*, *8*(5), 443–461. doi:10.1080/713852118 PMID:14530147.

Green, M. C., & Brock, T. C. (2000). The role of transportation in the persuasiveness of public narratives. *Journal of Personality and Social Psychology, 79*(5), 701–721. doi:10.1037/0022-3514.79.5.701 PMID:11079236.

Green, M. C., & Brock, T. C. (2002). In the mind's eye: Transportation-imagery model of narrative persuasion. In Green, M. C., Strange, J. J., & Brock, T. C. (Eds.), *Narrative impact: Social and cognitive foundations* (pp. 315–341). Mahwah, NJ: Lawrence Erlbaum Associates.

Green, M. C., & Brock, T. C. (2005). Persuasiveness of narratives. In Brock, T. C., & Green, M. C. (Eds.), *Persuasion: Psychological insights and perspectives* (2nd ed., pp. 117–142). Thousand Oaks, CA: Sage Publications.

Grinstein, G., Pickett, R. M., & Williams, M. G. (1989). EXVIS: An exploratory visualization environment. In *Proceedings of Graphics Interface '89*. London: IEEE.

Grothmann, T., & Reusswig, F. (2006). People at risk of flooding: Why some residents take precautionary action while others do not. *Natural Hazards, 38*(1), 101–120. doi:10.1007/s11069-005-8604-6.

Guo, L., Tan, E., Chen, S., Zhang, X., & Zhao, Y. E. (2009). Analyzing patterns of user content generation in online social networks. In *Proceedings of the 15th ACM SIGKDD International Conference on Knowledge Discovery and Data Mining*, (pp. 369-378). ACM.

Hadorn, G. H., Pohl, C., & Bammer, G. (2010). Solving problems through transdisciplinary research. In R. Frodeman, J. T. Klein, & C. Mitcham (Eds.), *The Oxford Handbook of Interdisciplinarity*. Retrieved from csid.unt.edu/files/HOI%20Chapters/Chapter_30_HOI.doc

Hai-Jew, S., & McHaney, R. W. (2010). ELATEwiki: Evolving an e-learning faculty wiki. In Luppicini, R., & Haghi, A. K. (Eds.), *Cases on Digital Technologies in Higher Education: Issues and Challenges*. Hershey, PA: IGI Global. doi:10.4018/978-1-61520-869-2.ch001.

Hall, M., Frank, E., Holmes, G., & Pfahringer, B. (2009). The WEKA data mining software: An update. *ACM SIGKDD Explorations Newsletter, 11*(1), 10–18. doi:10.1145/1656274.1656278.

Halvorsen, A. (2009). Social networking sites and critical language learning. In Thomas, M. (Ed.), *Handbook of research on web 2.0 and second language learning* (pp. 237–255). Hershey, PA: IGI Global. doi:10.4018/978-1-60566-190-2.ch013.

Hamasaki, M., Matsuo, Y., Nishimura, T., & Takeda, H. (2009). Ontology extraction by collaborative tagging. In *Proceedings of World Wide Web* (pp. 427–437). IEEE.

Hammig, B., Childers, E., & Jones, C. (2009). Injuries associated with the use of riding mowers in the United States, 2002-2007. *Journal of Safety Research, 40*(5), 371–375. doi:10.1016/j.jsr.2009.07.005 PMID:19932318.

Han, J., Pei, J., & Yin, Y. (2000). Mining frequent patterns without candidate generation. In *Proceedings ACM-SIGMOD International Conference Management of Data* (pp. 1-12). ACM Press.

Han, J., & Fu, Y. (1999). Mining multiple-level association rules in large databases. *IEEE Transactions on Knowledge and Data Engineering, 11*(5), 798–805. doi:10.1109/69.806937.

Hanneman, R. A., & Riddle, M. (2005). *Introduction to social network methods*. Riverside, CA: University of California.

Hansel, B. G. (1985). *The impact of a sojourn abroad: A study of secondary school students participating in a foreign exchange program (culture learning, contact travel, educational)*. (Unpublished doctoral dissertation). Syracuse University, New York, NY.

Hansen, D., Smith, M. A., & Schneiderman, B. (2011). EventGraphs: Charting collections of conference connections. In *Proceedings of the 44th Hawaii International Conference on System Sciences*. IEEE.

Hansen, D. L., Schneiderman, B., & Smith, M. A. (2011). *Analyzing social media networks with NodeXL: Insights from a connected world*. Amsterdam: Elsevier.

Harp, S. F., & Mayer, R. E. (1998). How seductive details do their damage: A theory of cognitive interest in science learning. *Journal of Educational Psychology, 90*(3), 414–433. doi:10.1037/0022-0663.90.3.414.

Harrison, R., & Thomas, M. (2009). Identity in online communities: Social networking sites and language learning. *International Journal of Emerging Technologies & Society, 7*(2), 109–124.

Hastall, M. R., & Knobloch-Westerwick, S. (2012). Severity, efficacy, and evidence type as determinants of health message exposure. *Health Communication*. doi: doi:10.1080/10410236.2012.690175 PMID:22809248.

Hattie, J., & Timperley, H. (2007). The power of feedback. *Review of Educational Research, 77*(1), 81–112. doi:10.3102/003465430298487.

Havre, S., Hetzler, E., Whitney, P., & Nowell, L. (2002). Themeriver: Visualizing thematic changes in large document collections. *IEEE Transactions on Visualization and Computer Graphics, 8*, 9–20. doi:10.1109/2945.981848.

Heer, J., Kong, N., & Agrawala, M. (2009). Sizing the horizon: the effects of chart size and layering on the graphical perception of time series visualizations. In *Proceedings of the 27th International Conference on Human Factors in Computing Systems (CHI 2009)* (pp. 1303-1312). Boston, MA: ACM Press.

Heider, F. (1958). *The psychology of interpersonal relations*. New York, NY: John Wiley & Sons. doi:10.1037/10628-000.

Heisler, G. (1974). Ways to deter law violators: Effects of levels of threat and vicarious punishment on cheating. *Journal of Consulting and Clinical Psychology, 42*(4), 577–582. doi:10.1037/h0036709.

Henderson, J., Fishwick, P., Fresh, E., Futterknecht, F., & Hamilton, B. D. (2008). Immersive learning simulation environment for Chinese culture. In *Proceedings of Interservice/Industry Training, Simulation, and Education Conference*. IITSEC.

Henttonen, K. (2010). Exploring social networks on the team level—A review of the empirical literature. *Journal of Engineering and Technology Management, 27*, 74–109. doi:10.1016/j.jengtecman.2010.03.005.

Hepp, M., Siorpaes, K., & Bachlechner, D. (2007, September). Harvesting wiki consensus: Using wikipedia entries for knowledge management. *IEEE Internet Computing*, 54–65. doi:10.1109/MIC.2007.110.

Heptonstall, J., Gill, O. N., Porter, K., Black, M. B., & Gilbart, V. L. (1993). Health care workers and HIV: Surveillance of occupationally acquired infection in the United Kingdom. *CDR Review, 3*(11), R147–R158. PMID:7694732.

Herbert, M. J., & Harsh, C. M. (1944). Observational learning by cats. *Journal of Comparative Psychology, 37*(2), 81–95. doi:10.1037/h0062414.

Herek, G. M. (1986). The instrumentality of attitudes: Toward a neofunctional theory. *The Journal of Social Issues, 42*(2), 99–114. doi:10.1111/j.1540-4560.1986.tb00227.x.

Herek, G. M. (2000). The social construction of attitudes: Functional consensus and divergence in the US public's reactions to AIDS. In Maio, G. R., & Olson, J. M. (Eds.), *Why we evaluate: Functions of attitudes* (pp. 325–364). Mahwah, NJ: Lawrence Erlbaum.

Heymann, P., Ramage, D., & Garcia-Molina, H. (2008). Social tag prediction. In *Proceedings of the 31st Annual International ACM SIGIR Conference on Research and Development in Information Retrieval* (pp. 531-538). ACM Press.

Hilage, T. A., & Kulkarni, V. (2012). Review of literature on data mining. *International Journal in Research and Reviews in Applied Sciences, 10*(1), 1–14.

Hipp, J., Myka, A., Wirth, R., & Guntzer, U. (1998). A new algorithm for faster mining of generalized rules. In *Proceedings of the 2nd European Symposium on Principles of Data Mining and Knowledge Discovery* (pp. 72–82). IEEE.

Hirvela, A. (1999). Collaborative writing: Instruction and communities of readers and writers. *TESOL Journal, 8*(2), 7–12.

Hofschroer, M. (2012). Friends helps global television audience learn English. *Marketwire*. Retrieved from http://www.marketwire.com/press-release/friends-helps-global-television-audience-learn-english-1732657.htm

Hong, Y. (2011). *Narrative and frame in health communication: The influence of narrative transportation to promote detection behavior.* (Unpublished masters thesis). University of Alabama, Tuscaloosa, AL.

Horizon Report. (2011). Retrieved from http://wp.nmc.org/horizon2011/sections/augmented-reality/#0

Hoser, B., & Nitschke, T. (2010). Questions on ethics for research I the virtually connected world. *Social Networks*, *32*, 180–186. doi:10.1016/j.socnet.2009.11.003.

Houston, T. K., Cherrington, A., Coley, H. L., Robinson, K. M., Trobaugh, J. A., & Williams, J. H. et al. (2011). The art and science of patient storytelling—Harnessing narrative communication for behavioral interventions: The ACCE project. *Journal of Health Communication*, *16*(7), 686–697. doi:10.1080/10810730.2011.551997 PMID:21541875.

Houts, P. S., Doak, C. C., Doak, L. G., & Loscalzo, M. J. (2006). The role of pictures in improving health communication: A review of research on attention, comprehension, recall, and adherence. *Patient Education and Counseling*, *61*(2), 173–190. doi:10.1016/j.pec.2005.05.004 PMID:16122896.

Hsu, H. Y., & Wang, S. K. (2009). The effect of using blogs on college students' reading performance and motivation. In T. Bastiaens et al. (Eds.), *Proceedings of World Conference on E-Learning in Corporate, Government, Healthcare, and Higher Education 2009* (pp. 1308–1313). Chesapeake, VA: AACE.

Hubel, D., & Wiesel, T. (1979, September). Brain mechanisms of vision. *Scientific American*, 150–162. doi:10.1038/scientificamerican0979-150 PMID:91195.

Huberman, B. A., Romero, D. M., & Wu, F. (2008). Social networks that matter: Twitter under the microscope. *Social Computing Laboratory, HP Labs*. Retrieved on Feb. 9, 2013, from http://www.hpl.hp.com/research/scl/papers/twitter/

Iacoboni, M. (2009). Imitation, empathy, and mirror neurons. *Annual Review of Psychology*, *60*, 653–670. doi:10.1146/annurev.psych.60.110707.163604 PMID:18793090.

Jabbi, M., Bastiaansen, J., & Keysers, C. (2008). A common anterior insula representation of disgust observation, experience and imagination shows divergent functional connectivity pathways. *PLoS ONE*, *3*(8), e2939. doi:10.1371/journal.pone.0002939 PMID:18698355.

Jamner, M. S., Wolitski, R. J., & Corby, N. H. (1997). Impact of a longitudinal community HIV intervention targeting injecting drug users' stage of change for condom and bleach use. *American Journal of Health Promotion*, *12*(1), 15–24. doi:10.4278/0890-1171-12.1.15 PMID:10170430.

Janhonen, M., & Johanson, J.-E. (2011). Role of knowledge conversion and social networks in team performance. *International Journal of Information Management*, *31*, 217–225. doi:10.1016/j.ijinfomgt.2010.06.007.

Jantsch, E. (1972). Inter- and transdisciplinary university: A systems approach to education and innovation. *Higher Education*, *1*(1), 7–37. Retrieved from http://www.jstor.org/stable/3445957 doi:10.1007/BF01956879.

Johnson, W. L., & Valente, A. (2008). Tactical language and culture training systems: Using artificial intelligence to teach foreign languages and cultures. In *Proceedings of Innovative Applications of Artificial Intelligence*. IEEE.

Jose, P. E., & Brewer, W. F. (1984). Development of story liking: Character identification, suspense and outcome resolution. *Developmental Psychology*, *20*(5), 911–924. doi:10.1037/0012-1649.20.5.911.

Jung, G., & Lee, B. (2010). Analysis on social network adoption according to the change of network topology: The impact of 'Open API' to adoption of Facebook. In *Proceedings of the 12th International Conference on Electronic Commerce (ICEC), Roadmap for the Future of Electronic Business* (pp. 23 – 32). ICEC.

Jung, J. Y. (2009). Attention, awareness, and noticing: The role of consciousness and the selective fossilization hypothesis. *Teachers College, Columbia University Working Papers in TESOL &. Applied Linguistics*, *9*(2), 58–59.

Kaplan, R. D. (2012). *The revenge of geography: What the map tells us about coming conflicts and the battle against fate*. New York: Random House.

Kaplan, S. A., Bradley, J. C., & Ruscher, J. B. (2004). The inhibitory role of cynical disposition in the provision and receipt of social support: The case of the September 11th terrorist attacks. *Personality and Individual Differences*, *37*, 1221–1232. doi:10.1016/j.paid.2003.12.006.

Keegan, D. (1996). *Foundations of distance education*. New York: Routledge.

Keeling, R. P., & Hersh, R. H. (2011). *We're losing our minds: Rethinking American higher education*. New York: Palgrave Macmillan. doi:10.1057/9781137001764.

Keim, D. A. (2006). Challenges in visual data analysis. In E. Banissi, K. Börner, C. Chen, G. Clapworthy, C. Maple, A. Lobben, J. Zhang (Eds.), *10th International Conference on Information Visualisation (IV 2006)* (pp. 9-16). London, UK: IEEE Press.

Keim, D. A. (2000). Designing pixel-oriented visualization techniques: Theory and applications. *IEEE Transactions on Visualization and Computer Graphics*, *6*, 59–78. doi:10.1109/2945.841121.

Keim, D. A. (2002). Information visualization and visual data mining. *IEEE Transactions on Visualization and Computer Graphics*, *8*, 1–8. doi:10.1109/2945.981847.

Keller, J. M. (1987). Development and use of the ARCS model of instructional design. *Journal of Instructional Development*, *10*(3), 2–10. Retrieved from http://www.jstor.org/stable/pdfplus/30221294.pdf doi:10.1007/BF02905780.

Keller, J., & Suzuki, K. (2004). Learner motivation and e-learning design: A multinationally validated process. *Journal of Educational Media*, *29*(3). doi:10.1080/1358165042000283084.

Kember, D., Ho, A., & Hong, C. (2008). The importance of establishing relevance in motivating student learning. *Active Learning in Higher Education*, *9*(3), 249–263. Retrieved from http://alh.sagepub.com.er.lib.k-state.edu/content/9/3/249.full.pdf doi:10.1177/1469787408095849.

Kessler, G. (2009). Student-initiated attention to form in wiki-based collaborative writing. *Language Learning & Technology*, *13*(1), 79–95. Retrieved January 31, 2013, from http://llt.msu.edu/vol13num1/kessler.pdf

Kessler, G., & Bikowski, D. (2010). Developing collaborative autonomous language learning abilities in computer mediated language learning: Attention to meaning among students in wiki space. *Computer Assisted Language Learning*, *23*(1), 41–58. doi:10.1080/09588220903467335.

Keysers, C., & Gazzola, V. (2009). Expanding the mirror: Vicarious activity for actions, emotions, and sensations. *Current Opinion in Neurobiology*, *19*(6), 666–671. doi:10.1016/j.conb.2009.10.006 PMID:19880311.

Keysers, C., Kaas, J. H., & Gazzola, V. (2010). Somatosensation in social perception. *Nature Reviews. Neuroscience*, *11*(6), 417–428. doi:10.1038/nrn2833 PMID:20445542.

Khanna, A., & Khanna, P. (2012). *TED hybrid reality: Thriving in the emerging human- technology civilization*. TED.

King, E. S., Balshem, A., Ross, E., Rimer, B., & Seay, J. (1995). Mammography interventions for 65- to 74-year-old HMO women: Program effectiveness and predictors of use. *Journal of Aging and Health*, *7*(4), 529–551. doi:10.1177/089826439500700404 PMID:10165968.

Koenraad, A. L. M. (2007). *3D and language education*. Retrieved January 31, 2013, from http://www.koenraad.info/vrall-2/3d-and-language-education-1/view

Koenraad, A. L. M. (2008). How can 3D virtual worlds contribute to language education? Focus on the language village format. In *Proceedings of the 3rd International WorldCALL Conference (WorldCALL 2008)*. Retrieved January 31, 2013, from http://www.koenraad.info/vrall-2/how-can-3d-virtual-worlds-contribute-to-language-education/view

Kohls, C., & Scheiter, K. (2008). The relation between design patterns and schema theory. In *Proceedings of the 15th Conference on Pattern Languages of Programs* (PLoP '08). New York, NY: ACM.

Kolb, D. A. (1984). *Experiential learning: Experience as the source of learning and development*. Upper Saddle River, NJ: Prentice-Hall.

Kolcz, A. (2012). Large scale learning at Twitter. In Simperl, E. et al. (Eds.), *ECWC 2012 (LNCS) (Vol. 7295)*. Berlin: Springer.

Koller, D. (2012). What we're learning from online education. *TEDGlobal*. Retrieved from http://www.youtube.com/watch?v=U6FvJ6jMGHU

Kourakis, S., & Parés, N. (2010). Us hunters: Interactive communication for young cavemen. In *Proceedings of the 9th International Conference on Interaction Design and Children*, (pp. 89-97). New York, NY: ACM.

Kozma, R. (1991). Learning with media. *Review of Educational Research*, *61*(2), 179–211. doi:10.3102/00346543061002179.

Krackhardt, D. (1987). Cognitive social structures. *Social Networks*, *9*, 109–134. doi:10.1016/0378-8733(87)90009-8.

Kramsch, C., & McConnell-Ginet, S. (1992). (Con)textual knowledge in language education. In Kramsch, C., & McConnell-Ginet, S. (Eds.), *Text and context: Cross-disciplinary perspectives on language study*. Lexington, MA: Heath & Co..

Krashen, S. (1981). *Second language acquisition and second language learning*. Oxford, UK: Pergamon Press.

Krashen, S. (1982). *Principles and practice in second language acquisition*. Oxford, UK: Pergamon.

Kratzer, J., Leenders, R. T. A. J., & Van Engelen, J. M. L. (2010). The social network among engineering design teams and their creativity: A case study among teams in two product development programs. *International Journal of Project Management*, *29*, 428–436. doi:10.1016/j.ijproman.2009.09.007.

Kraut, R., Egido, C., & Galegher, J. (1988). *Patterns of contact and communication in scientific research collaboration*. ACM Press. doi:10.1145/62266.62267.

Kreuter, M. W., Holmes, K., Alcaraz, K., Kalesan, B., Rath, S., & Richert, M. et al. (2010). Comparing narrative and informational videos to increase mammography in low-income African American women. *Patient Education and Counseling*, *81*(Suppl), S6–S14. doi:10.1016/j.pec.2010.09.008 PMID:21071167.

Kuang, C. (n.d.). Five to-die-for augmented reality shopping apps. *FastCompany*. Retrieved from http://www.fastcodesign.com/1313133/five-to-die-for-augmented-reality-shopping-apps

Kuhlthau, C. C. (2001). The use of theory in information science research. *Journal of the American Society for Information Science and Technology*, *52*, 62–73. doi:10.1002/1532-2890(2000)52:1<62::AID-ASI1061>3.0.CO;2-J.

Kumar, N., Keogh, E., Lonardi, S., & Ratanamahatana, C. A. (2005). Time-series bitmaps: A practical visualization tool for working with large time series databases. In *Proceedings of the 5th SIAM International Conference on Data Mining (SDM 2005)* (pp. 531-535). Newport Beach, CA: SIAM.

Kuriscak, L. M., & Luke, C. L. (2009). Language learner attitudes toward virtual worlds: An investigation of Second Life. In Lomicka, L., & Lord, G. (Eds.), *The next generation: Social networking and online collaboration in foreign language learning* (pp. 115–144). San Marcos, TX: CALICO.

Kyes, K. B., Brown, I. S., & Pollack, R. H. (1991). The effect of exposure to a condom script on attitudes toward condoms. *Journal of Psychology & Human Sexuality*, *4*(1), 21–36. doi:10.1300/J056v04n01_04 PMID:12317687.

Lafayette, R. C., & Schultz, R. A. (1975). Evaluating culture learning. In Lafayette, R. C. (Ed.), *The cultural revolution in foreign languages: A guide for building the modern curriculum* (pp. 104–118). Lincolnwood, IL: National Textbook Company.

Lafayette, R. C., & Schultz, R. A. (1997). Evaluating cultural learning. In Heusinkveld, P. R. (Ed.), *Pathways to culture* (pp. 577–594). Yarmouth, ME: Intercultural Press.

Lampe, K.-H., Riede, K., & Doerr, M. (2008). Research between natural and cultural history information: Benefits and IT-requirements for transdisciplinarity. *ACM Journal on Computing and Cultural Heritage,* 1(1), 4:1 – 4:22.

Lane, H. C., & Ogan, A. (2009). *Virtual learning environments for culture*. Retrieved March 21, 2013, from http://people.ict.usc.edu/~lane/papers/Lane-Ogan-CATS09-VirtualEnvironmentsForCulturalLearning.pdf

Langer, A. M., & Knefelkamp, L. L. (2002). *Forms of literacy development with technology in the college years: A scheme for students, faculty and institutions of higher learning*. Paper presented at the Association of American Colleges and Universities Conference on Technology, Learning, and Intellectual Development. Baltimore, MD.

Lanier, J. (2010). *You are not a gadget*. New York: First Vintage Books.

Larkey, L. K., & Gonzalez, J. (2007). Storytelling for promoting colorectal cancer prevention and early detection among Latinos. *Patient Education and Counseling*, *67*(3), 272–278. doi:10.1016/j.pec.2007.04.003 PMID:17524595.

Larkey, L. K., Lopez, A. M., Minnal, A., & Gonzalez, J. (2009). Storytelling for promoting colorectal cancer screening among underserved Latina women: A randomized pilot study. *Cancer. Culture and Literacy*, *16*(1), 79–87. PMID:19078934.

Lau, A. (2006). *Family warns of lawn mower dangers after girl loses foot.* Retrieved November 28, 2012, from http://www.newsnet5.com/dpp/news/Family-Warns-Of-Lawn-Mower-Dangers-After-Girl-Loses-Foot

Lau, R. Y. K., Song, D., Li, Y., Cheung, T. C. H., & Hao, J. (2009). Toward a fuzzy domain ontology extraction method for adaptive e-learning. *IEEE Transactions on Knowledge and Data Engineering*, *21*(6), 800–813. doi:10.1109/TKDE.2008.137.

Lave, J., & Wenger, E. (1991). *Situated learning: Legitimate peripheral participation.* Cambridge, UK: Cambridge University Press. doi:10.1017/CBO9780511815355.

Leahey, E., Keith, B., & Crockett, J. (2010). Specialization and promotion in an academic discipline. *Research in Social Stratification and Mobility*, *28*, 135–155. doi:10.1016/j.rssm.2009.12.001.

Lee, L. (2008). Focus-on-form through collaborative scaffolding in expert-to-novice online interaction. *Language Learning & Technology, 12*(3), 53–72. Retrieved January 31, 2013, from http://llt.msu.edu/vol12num3/lee.pdf

Lee, L. (2010). Exploring wiki-mediated collaborative writing: A case study in an elementary Spanish course. *CALICO Journal*, *27*(2), 260–276.

Lehn, D. V., Hindmarsh, J., Luff, P., & Heath, C. (2007). Engaging constable: revealing art with new technology. In *Proceedings of the SIGCHI Conference on Human Factors in Computing Systems*, (pp. 1485-1494). New York, NY: ACM.

Lélé, S., & Norgaard, R. (2005). Practicing Interdisciplinarity. *Bioscience*, *55*(11), 967–975. doi:10.1641/0006-3568(2005)055[0967:PI]2.0.CO;2.

Leonard, C., Burke, C. M., O'Keane, C., & Doyle, J. S. (1997). Golf ball liver: Agent orange hepatitis. *Gut*, *40*(5), 687–688. PMID:9203952.

Leuf, B., & Cunningham, W. (2001). *The wiki way: Quick collaboration on the web.* Boston: Addison-Wesley.

Leung, C.-S., Irani, P., & Carmicheal, C. (2008). Wifisviz: Effective visualization of frequent itemsets. In *Proceedings of the VIII IEEE International Conference on Data Mining (ICDM '08)*, (pp. 875–880). IEEE Press.

Li, X., Guo, L., & Zhao, Y. (2008). Tag-based social interest discovery. In *Proceedings of the 17th International Conference on World Wide Web* (pp. 675-684). ACM Press.

Li, Z., Han, J., Ji, M., Tang, L.-A., Yu, Y., Ding, B., … Kays, R. (2011). Movemine: Mining moving object data for discovery of animal movement patterns. *ACM Transactions on Intelligent Systems Technologies, 2*, 37:1–37:32.

Lifton, R. J. (1999). *The protean self: Human resilience in an age of fragmentation.* Chicago: University of Chicago Press.

Lim, L. (2013). Friends will be there for you at Beijing's central perk. *National Public Radio*. Retrieved from http://www.npr.org/2013/01/23/170074762/friends-will-be-there-for-you-at-beijings-central-perk

Lin, J.-W., & Lai, Y.-C. (2013). Online formative assessments with social network awareness. *Computers & Education*, *66*, 40–53. doi:10.1016/j.compedu.2013.02.008.

Liu, B., Hsu, W., Wang, K., & Chen, S. (1999). Visually aided exploration of interesting association rules. In *Proceedings of the 3rd Pacific-Asia Conference on Knowledge Discovery and Data Mining* (pp. 380-389). IEEE.

Liu, B., Ma, Y., & Lee, R. (2001). Analyzing the interestingness of association rules from the temporal dimension. In *Proceeding of the International Conference on Data Mining*, (pp. 377-384). IEEE Press.

Liu, Y., & Salvendy, G. (2005). Visualization to facilitate association rules modeling: A review. *Ergonomia IJE&HF*, *27*(1), 11–23.

Long, M. (1985). Input and second language acquisition theory. In Gass, S., & Madden, C. (Eds.), *Input in second language acquisition* (pp. 177–393). Rowley, MA: Newbury House Publishers, Inc..

Long, M. (1996). The role of the linguistic environment in second language acquisition. In Ritchie, W., & Bhatia, T. (Eds.), *Handbook of second language acquisition* (pp. 413–468). San Diego, CA: Academic. doi:10.1016/B978-012589042-7/50015-3.

Lord, G. (2008). Podcasting communities and second language pronunciation. *Foreign Language Annals*, *41*(2), 364–379. doi:10.1111/j.1944-9720.2008.tb03297.x.

Lund, A. (2008). Wikis: A collective approach to language production. *ReCALL*, *20*(1), 35–54. doi:10.1017/S0958344008000414.

Lyon, G. R. (1999). *The NICHD research program in reading development, reading disorders and reading instruction*. Retrieved from http://www.ncld.org/research/keys99_nichd.cfm

Majchrzak, A., Wagner, C., & Yates, D. (2006). *Corporate wiki users: Results of a survey*. Paper presented at the Symposium on Wikis. New York, NY.

Malfait, N., Valyear, K. F., Culham, J. C., Anton, J. L., Brown, L. E., & Gribble, P. L. (2010). fMRI activation during observation of others' reach errors. *Journal of Cognitive Neuroscience*, *22*(7), 1493–1503. doi:10.1162/jocn.2009.21281 PMID:19580392.

Malouff, J., Thorsteinsson, E., Schutte, N., & Rooke, S. E. (2009). Effects of vicarious punishment: A meta-analysis. *The Journal of General Psychology*, *136*(3), 271–286. doi:10.3200/GENP.136.3.271-286 PMID:19650522.

Mann, V. A., & Foy, J. G. (2003). Phonological awareness, speech development, and letter knowledge in preschool children. *Annals of Dyslexia*, *53*, 149–173. doi:10.1007/s11881-003-0008-2.

Mansillka, V. B., & Duraising, E. D. (2007). Targeted assessment of students' interdisciplinary work: An empirically grounded framework proposed. *The Journal of Higher Education*, *78*(2), 215–237. Retrieved from http://www.jstor.org/stable/4501203 doi:10.1353/jhe.2007.0008.

Mario, C., & Talia, D. (2003). The knowledge grid. *Communications of the ACM*, *46*(1), 89–93. doi:10.1145/602421.602425.

Mark, B., & Coniam, D. (2008). Using wikis to enhance and develop writing skills among secondary school students in Hong Kong. *System*, *36*, 437–455. doi:10.1016/j.system.2008.02.004.

Mar, R. A., & Oatley, K. (2008). The function of fiction is the abstraction and simulation of social experience. *Perspectives on Psychological Science*, *3*(3), 173–192. doi:10.1111/j.1745-6924.2008.00073.x.

Marsh, J. (1992). Menace or motivator? International Central Institute for Youth and Educational Television, 12(2).

Mathioudakis, M., & Koudas, N. (2010). TwitterMonitor: Trend detection over the twitter stream. In *Proceedings of the 2010 International Conference on Management of Data* (pp. 1155-1158). ACM Press.

Mayer, R. (1998). Systematic thinking fostered by illustration in scientific text. *Journal of Educational Psychology*, *81*, 240–246. doi:10.1037/0022-0663.81.2.240.

Mayer, R. E. (2005). *The Cambridge handbook of multimedia learning*. Cambridge, UK: Cambridge University Press. doi:10.1017/CBO9780511816819.

Mayer, R. E. (2009). *Multimedia learning* (2nd ed.). New York: Cambridge University Press. doi:10.1017/CBO9780511811678.

Mayer, R. E., & Moreno, R. (1998). A split-attention effect in multimedia learning: Evidence for dual processing systems in working memory. *Journal of Educational Psychology*, *90*(2), 312–320. doi:10.1037/0022-0663.90.2.312.

Mayer, R., & Anderson, R. (1991). Animations need narrations: An experimental test of dual-coding hypothesis. *Journal of Educational Psychology*, *83*, 484–490. doi:10.1037/0022-0663.83.4.484.

Mayer, R., & Anderson, R. (1992). The instructive animation: Helping students build connections between words and pictures in multimedia learning. *Journal of Educational Psychology*, *84*(4), 444–452. doi:10.1037/0022-0663.84.4.444.

Mayer, R., & Gallini, J. (1990). When is an illustration worth ten thousand words? *Journal of Educational Psychology*, *82*, 715–726. doi:10.1037/0022-0663.82.4.715.

McBride, C. M., Emmons, K. M., & Lipkus, I. M. (2003). Understanding the potential of teachable moments: The case of smoking cessation. *Health Education Research*, *18*(2), 156–170. doi:10.1093/her/18.2.156 PMID:12729175.

McCarty, S. (2009). Social networking behind student lines in Japan. In Thomas, M. (Ed.), *Handbook of research on web 2.0 and second language learning* (pp. 181–201). Hershey, PA: IGI Global. doi:10.4018/978-1-60566-190-2.ch010.

McCluskey, F. B., & Winter, M. L. (2012). *The idea of the digital university: Ancient traditions, disruptive technologies and the battle for the soul of higher education*. Washington, DC: Westphalia Press.

McCue, P. (2005). The crucial role of animated children's educational games. In *Proceedings of ACM SIGGRAPH 2005*. New York, NY: ACM.

McHaney, R. W. (2009). Implementation of ELATEwiki. *EDUCAUSE Quarterly*, *32*(4). Retrieved from http://www.educause.edu/EDUCAUSE+Quarterly/EDUCAUSEQuarterlyMagazineVolum/Implementation-ofELATEwiki/192968.

McHaney, R. W. (2011). *The new digital shoreline: How web 2.0 and millennials are revolutionizing higher education*. Stylus Publishing.

McHaney, R. W. (2012a). The web 2.0 mandate for a transition from webmaster to wiki master. In *Open-Source Technologies for Maximizing the Creation, Deployment, and Use of Digital Resources and Information* (pp. 193–218). Hershey, PA: IGI Global. doi:10.4018/978-1-4666-2205-0.ch012.

McHaney, R. W. (2012b). *Web 2.0 and social media for business*. Ventus.

McKim, R. H. (1972). *Experiences in visual thinking*. Monterey, CA: Brooks/Cole Publishing Company.

McPherson, M., Smith-Lovin, L., & Cook, J. M. (2001). Birds of a feather: Homophily in social networks. *Annual Review of Sociology*, *27*, 415–444. Retrieved from http://www.jstor.org/stable/2678628?origin=JSTOR-pdf doi:10.1146/annurev.soc.27.1.415.

McQueen, A., Kreuter, M. W., Kalesan, B., & Alcaraz, K. I. (2011). Understanding narrative effects: The impact of breast cancer survivor stories on message processing, attitudes, and beliefs among African American women. *Health Psychology*, *30*(6), 674–682. doi:10.1037/a0025395 PMID:21895370.

Mediawiki. (2012). Category: MediaWiki configuration settings. *MediaWiki*. Retrieved from http://www.mediawiki.org/wiki/Category:MediaWiki_configuration_settings

MediaWiki.org. (2012). Retrieved from http://www.mediawiki.org/wiki/MediaWiki

Mendoza, M., Poblete, B., & Castillo, C. (2010). Twitter under crisis: Can we trust what we RT? In *Proceedings of the Workshop on Social Media Analytics (SOMA '10)*, (pp. 71-79). Washington, DC: SOMA.

Meng, H. S., & Fong, S. (2010). Visualizing e-government portal and its performance in WEBVS. In *Proceedings of the Fifth International Conference on Digital Information Management (ICDIM)* (pp. 315-320). IEEE Press.

Metaferia, T. F. (2012). Using blogs to promote reflective language learning. *Journal of Language and Culture*, *3*(3), 52–55.

Meyer, R. (2009). Knowledge visualization. In *Proceedings of the Media Informatics Advanced Seminar on Information Visualization*. Media Informatics.

Meyer, E. T., & Schroeder, R. (2009). Untangling the web of e-research: Towards a sociology of online knowledge. *Journal of Informetrics*, *3*, 246–260. doi:10.1016/j.joi.2009.03.006.

Meyer, M. S., Wood, F. B., Hart, L. A., & Felton, R. H. (1998). Selective predictive value of rapid automatized naming in poor readers. *Journal of Learning Disabilities*, *31*(2), 106–117. doi:10.1177/002221949803100201 PMID:9529781.

Michel, U., Plass, C., Tschritter, C., & Ehlers, M. (2008). WebMozis - Web-based and mobile zoo information system - A case study for the city of osnabrueck. *The International Archives of the Photogrammetry: Remote Sensing and Spatial Information Sciences*, *37*(Part B4), 839–843.

Miles, M., & Huberman, A. M. (1994). *Qualitative data analysis*. Thousand Oaks, CA: Sage Publications.

Miller, R. E. (2012, November 12). *This is how we think: Learning in public after the paradigm shift.* [Video File]. Retrieved February 6, 2012, from http://www.youtube.com/watch?v=aNDyP2pzE8Q

MineSet. (2012). Retrieved from www.sgi.com/software/mineset

Mioduser, D., & Dagan, O. (2007). The effect of alternative approaches to design instruction (structural or functional) on students' mental models of technological design processes. *International Journal of Technology and Design Education*, *17*, 135–148. doi:10.1007/s10798-006-0004-z.

Mislove, A., Koppula, H. S., Gummadi, K. P., Druschel, P., & Bhattacharjee, B. (2008). Growth of the Flickr social network. In *Proceedings of WOSN '08*. Seattle, WA: ACM.

Mnookin, S. (2011). *The panic virus: A true story of medicine, science, andfear*. New York: Simon & Schuster.

Mokdad, A. H., Marks, J. S., Stroup, D. F., & Gerberding, J. L. (2004). Actual causes of death in the United States, 2000. *Journal of the American Medical Association*, *291*(10), 1238–1245. doi:10.1001/jama.291.10.1238 PMID:15010446.

Molenberghs, P., Cunnington, R., & Mattingley, J. B. (2012). Brain regions with mirror properties: A meta-analysis of 125 human fMRI studies. *Neuroscience and Biobehavioral Reviews*, *36*(1), 341–349. doi:10.1016/j.neubiorev.2011.07.004 PMID:21782846.

Monmonier, M. (1990). Strategies for the visualization of geographic time-series data. *Cartographica: The International Journal for Geographic Information and Geovisualization*, *27*(1), 30–45. doi:10.3138/U558-H737-6577-8U31.

Morrison, I., Lloyd, D., Di Pellegrino, G., & Roberts, N. (2004). Vicarious responses to pain in anterior cingulate cortex: Is empathy a multisensory issue? *Cognitive, Affective & Behavioral Neuroscience*, *4*(2), 270–278. doi:10.3758/CABN.4.2.270 PMID:15460933.

Morrison, I., Tipper, S. P., Fenton-Adams, W. L., & Bach, P. (2012). Feeling others' painful actions: The sensorimotor integration of pain and action information. *Human Brain Mapping*. doi:10.1002/hbm.22040 PMID:22451259.

Mukamel, R., Ekstrom, A. D., Kaplan, J., Iacoboni, M., & Fried, I. (2010). Single-neuron responses in humans during execution and observation of actions. *Current Biology*, *20*(8), 750–756. doi:10.1016/j.cub.2010.02.045 PMID:20381353.

Myers, M. L., Iscoe, C., Jennings, C., Lenox, W., Minsky, E., & Sacks, A. (1981). *Public version: Federal trade commission staff report on the cigarette advertising investigation.* Washington, DC: Federal Trade Commission. Retrieved October 12, 2012, from http://legacy.library.ucsf.edu/tid/jdr92d00/pdf

Mynard, J. (2007). A blog as a tool for reflection for English language learners. *ASIAN EFL Journal*, *24*, 1–6.

Naaman, M., Becker, H., & Gravano, L. (2011). Hip and trendy: Characterizing emerging trends on Twitter. *Journal of the American Society for Information Science and Technology*, *62*(5), 902–918. doi:10.1002/asi.21489.

Narrod, C., Zinsstag, J., & Tiongco, M. (2012). A One Health framework for estimating the economic costs of zoonotic diseases on society. *EcoHealth*. Retrieved from http://www.ncbi.nlm.nih.gov/pmc/articles/PMC3415616/

National Center for Emerging and Zoonotic Infectious Diseases. (2012). Retrieved from http://www.cdc.gov/ncezid/

National Institute for Occupational Safety and Health. (n.d.). *Fatality assessment and control evaluation (FACE) program.* Retrieved December 12, 2012, from http://www.cdc.gov/niosh/face/default.html

Neuhaus, G. F. (2002, Winter). What does it take to read a letter? *Perspectives*, 6–8.

Neuhaus, G. F., & Swank, P. R. (2002). Understanding the relations between RAN letters subtest components and word reading in first grade students. *Journal of Learning Disabilities*, *35*(2). doi:10.1177/002221940203500206 PMID:15490743.

Nicolson, C. R., Starfield, A. M., Kofinas, G. P., & Kruse, J. A. (2002). Ten heuristics for interdisciplinary modeling projects. *Ecosystems (New York, N.Y.)*, *5*, 376–384. doi:10.1007/s10021-001-0081-5.

Nikitina, S. (2005). Pathways of interdisciplinary cognition. *Cognition and Instruction*, *23*(3), 389–425. doi:10.1207/s1532690xci2303_3.

Norman, G. R., & Brooks, L. R. (1997). The non-analytical basis of clinical reasoning. *Advances in Health Sciences Education : Theory and Practice*, *2*(2), 173–184. doi:10.1023/A:1009784330364 PMID:12386407.

Notari, M. (2006). How to use a wiki in education: Wiki-based effective constructive learning. In *Proceedings of the 2006 International Symposium on Wikis* (pp. 131-132). New York: Association for Computing Machinery.

Novak, J. D. (2009). *Learning, creating, and using knowledge: Concept maps as facilitative tools in schools and corporations*. Mahwah, NJ: Taylor and Francis.

Nowacek, R. S. (2005). A discourse-based theory of interdisciplinary connections. *The Journal of General Education*, *54*(3), 171–195. Retrieved from http://www.jstor.org/stable/27798019 doi:10.1353/jge.2006.0006.

NRP. (2000b). Report of the national reading panel teaching children to read: Report of the subgroups. Washington, DC: NICHD, NIFL, Department of Education.

O'Donnell, C. R., O'Donnell, L., San Doval, A., Duran, R., & Labes, K. (1998). Reductions in STD infections subsequent to an STD clinic visit: Using video-based patient education to supplement provider interactions. *Sexually Transmitted Diseases*, *25*(3), 161–168. doi:10.1097/00007435-199803000-00010 PMID:9524995.

O'Reilly, T. (2005). What is web 2.0. *O'Reilly Network*. Retrieved March 21, 2013, from http://www.oreillynet.com/pub/a/oreilly/tim/news/2005/09/30/what-is-Web-20.html

Oatley, K., & Gholamain, M. (1997). Emotions and identification: Connections between readers and fiction. In Hjort, M., & Laver, S. (Eds.), *Emotion and the arts* (pp. 263–298). New York: Oxford University Press.

Obstfeld, D. (2005). Social networks, the Tertius iungens orientation, and involvement in innovation. *Administrative Science Quarterly*. Retrieved from http://asq.sagepub.com/content/50/1/100.abstract. doi: 10.2189/asqu.2005.50.1.100

Occupational Safety and Health Administration. (n.d.a). *Accident inspection number 311958839*. Retrieved May 15, 2012, from http://www.osha.gov/pls/imis/establishment.inspection_detail?id=311958839

Occupational Safety and Health Administration. (n.d.b). *Fatality and catastrophe investigation summaries*. Retrieved December 12, 2012, from http://www.osha.gov/pls/imis/accidentsearch.html

OCLC. (2012). *Libraries as read/write services*. Retrieved from http://www.oclc.org/research/events/dss/marchionini.html

Ogan, A., & Lane, H. C. (2009). Virtual learning environments for culture and intercultural competence. In Blanchard, E., & Allard, D. (Eds.), *Handbook of Research on Culturally-Aware Information Technology: Perspectives and Models*. Hershey, PA: IGI Global.

Oliver, K. (2010). Integrating web 2.0 across the curriculum. *TechTrends*, *54*(2), 50–60. doi:10.1007/s11528-010-0382-7.

O'Malley, J. M., & Chamot, A. J. (1990). *Learning strategies in second language acquisition*. Cambridge, UK: Cambridge University Press. doi:10.1017/CBO9781139524490.

Overview of Smartphone Augmented Reality Applications for Tourism. (n.d.). Retrieved from http://www.ifitt.org/admin/public/uploads/eRTR_SI_V10i2_Yovcheva_Buhalis_Gatzidis_63-66.pdf

Paige, R. M., Jorstad, H. L., Siaya, L., Klein, F., & Colby, J. (2003). Culture learning in language education: A review of the literature. In Lange, D. L., & Paige, R. M. (Eds.), *Culture as the core: Perspectives on culture in second language learning* (pp. 173–236). Raleigh, NC: Information Age Publishing.

Parker, K. R., & Chao, J. T. (2007). Wiki as a teaching tool. *Interdisciplinary Journal of Knowledge and Learning Objects,* (3), 57-72.

Parkes, M. W., Bienen, L., Breilh, J., Hsu, L.-N., McDonald, M., & Patz, J. A. et al. (2005). All hands on deck: Transdisciplinary approaches to emerging infectious disease. *EcoHealth*, *2*, 258–272. doi:10.1007/s10393-005-8387-y.

Pennington, N., & Hastie, R. (1991). A cognitive theory of juror decision making: The story model. *Cardozo Law Review*, *13*, 519–557.

Penuel, W. R., Means, B., & Simkins, M. (2000). The multimedia challenge. *Educational Leadership*, *58*(2), 34–38.

Perry, R. W., & Lindell, M. K. (2008). Volcanic risk perception and adjustment in a multi-hazard environment. *Journal of Volcanology and Geothermal Research*, *172*(3), 170–178. doi:10.1016/j.jvolgeores.2007.12.006.

Perry, W. G. (1999). *Forms of intellectual and ethical development in the college years: A scheme*. San Francisco, CA: Jossey-Bass Publishers.

Peterson, M. (2006). Learner interaction management in an avatar and chat-based virtual world. *Computer Assisted Language Learning*, *19*(1), 79–103. doi:10.1080/09588220600804087.

Pick, A. D. (Ed.). (1979). *Perception and its development: A tribute to Eleanor J. Gibson*. Hillsdale, NJ: Lawrence Erlbaum Associates.

Pick, H. L. Jr. (1992). Eleanor J. Gibson: Learning to perceive and perceiving to learn. *Developmental Psychology*, *28*(5), 787–794. doi:10.1037/0012-1649.28.5.787.

Pillemer, D. (2003). Directive functions of autobiographical memory: The guiding power of the specific episode. *Memory (Hove, England)*, *11*(2), 193–202. doi:10.1080/741938208 PMID:12820831.

Pillemer, D. B. (2001). Momentous events and the life story. *Review of General Psychology*, *5*(2), 123–134. doi:10.1037/1089-2680.5.2.123.

Pinkman, K. (2005). Using blogs in the foreign language classroom: Encouraging learner independence. *The JALT CALL Journal*, *1*(1), 12–24.

Pliske, R., & Klein, G. (2003). The naturalistic decision-making perspective. In Schneider, S. L., & Shanteau, J. (Eds.), *Emerging perspectives on judgment and decision research* (pp. 559–585). New York: Cambridge University Press. doi:10.1017/CBO9780511609978.019.

Polichak, J. W., & Gerrig, R. J. (2002). Get up and win! Participatory responses to narrative. In Green, M. C., Strange, J. J., & Brock, T. C. (Eds.), *Narrative impact: Social and cognitive foundations* (pp. 71–95). Mahwah, NJ: Lawrence Erlbaum and Associates.

Pramudiono, I., & Kitsuregawa, M. (2004). FP-tax: Tree structure based generalized association rule mining. In *Proceedings ACM SIGMOD Workshop on Research Issues in Data Mining and Knowledge Discovery* (pp. 60-63). ACM Press.

Priem, J., & Costello, K. L. (2010). How and why scholars cite on Twitter. In *Proceedings of ASIST 2010*. Pittsburgh, PA: ASIST.

Pumpa, M., & Wyeld, T. G. (2006). Database and narratological representation of Australian aboriginal knowledge as information visualisation using a game engine. In *Proceedings of the International Conference on Information Visualisation (IV'06)*, (pp. 237-244). IEEE Computer Society Press.

Radhakrishnan, A. (2009). *9 semantic search engines that will change the world of search*. Retrieved from http://www.searchenginejournal.com/semantic-search-engines/9832/

Raith, T. (2009). The use of weblogs in language education. In Thomas, M. (Ed.), *Handbook of research on web 2.0 and second language learning* (pp. 274–291). Hershey, PA: IGI Global. doi:10.4018/978-1-60566-190-2.ch015.

Ramachandran, S., Jensen, R., & Sincoff, E. (2010). Simulation development and authoring: Why abstraction matters. In *Proceedings of the Interservice/Industry Training, Simulation, and Education Conference*. ITSEC.

Raybourn, E. M., Deagle, E., Mendini, K., & Heneghan, J. (2005), Adaptive thinking & leadership simulation game training for special forces officers. In *Proceedings, Interservice/Industry Training, Simulation and Education Conference*. IITSEC.

Rey, G. D. (2012). A review of research and a meta-analysis of the seductive detail effect. *Educational Research Review*, *7*, 216–237. doi:10.1016/j.edurev.2012.05.003.

Rhodes, T. L. (Ed.). (2010). *Assessing outcomes and improving achievement: Tips and tools for using rubrics*. Washington, DC: Association of American Colleges and Universities.

Rhoten, D., & Parker, A. (2004). Risks and rewards of an interdisciplinary research path. *Science*, *306*(5704), 2046. doi:10.1126/science.1103628 PMID:15604393.

Rhoten, D., & Pfirman, S. (2007). Women in interdisciplinary science: Exploring preferences and consequences. *Research Policy*, *36*, 56–75. doi:10.1016/j.respol.2006.08.001.

Richardson, W. (2009). *Blogs, wikis, podcasts, and other powerful web tools for classrooms* (2nd ed.). Thousand Oaks, CA: Corwin Press.

Richardson, W. (2012). *Why school? How education must change when learning and information are everywhere*. Amazon Digital Services, Inc..

Rick, J., Harris, A., Marshall, P., Fleck, R., Yuill, N., & Rogers, Y. (2009). Children designing together on a multi-touch tabletop: An analysis of spatial orientation and user interactions. In *Proceedings of the 8th International Conference on Interaction Design and Children*, (pp. 106-114). New York, NY: ACM.

Ricketts, M. (2007). *The use of narratives in safety and health communication*. (Unpublished doctoral dissertation). Kansas State University, Manhattan, KS.

Ricketts, M., Shanteau, J., McSpadden, B., & Fernandez-Medina, K. M. (2010). Using stories to battle unintentional injuries: Narratives in safety and health communication. *Social Science & Medicine*, *70*(9), 1441–1449. doi:10.1016/j.socscimed.2009.12.036 PMID:20176428.

Rizzolatti, G., & Fabbri-Destro, M. (2009). The mirror neuron system. In Bernston, G. G., & Cacioppo, J. T. (Eds.), *Handbook of neuroscience for the behavioral sciences* (*Vol. 1*, pp. 337–357). Hoboken, NJ: John Wiley and Sons, Inc. doi:10.1002/9780470478509.neubb001017.

Rizzolatti, G., & Sinigaglia, C. (2010). The functional role of the parieto-frontal mirror circuit: Interpretations and misinterpretations. *Nature Reviews. Neuroscience*, *11*(4), 264–274. doi:10.1038/nrn2805 PMID:20216547.

Roberts, T. A. (2003). Effects of alphabet-letter instruction on young children's word recognition. *Journal of Educational Psychology*, *95*(1), 41–51. doi:10.1037/0022-0663.95.1.41.

Robison, J. E. (2009). Is technology making us dumber? *Psychology Today: Health, Help, Happiness + Find a Therapist*. Retrieved from http://www.psychologytoday.com/blog/my-life-aspergers/200911/is-technology-making-us-dumber

Rook, K. S. (1986). Encouraging preventive behavior for distant and proximal health threats: Effects of vivid versus abstract information. *Journal of Gerontology*, *41*(4), 526–534. doi:10.1093/geronj/41.4.526 PMID:3722739.

Rook, K. S. (1987). Effects of case history versus abstract information on health attitudes and behaviors. *Journal of Applied Social Psychology*, *17*(6), 533–553. doi:10.1111/j.1559-1816.1987.tb00329.x.

Ropinski, T., Oeltze, S., & Preim, B. (2011). Visual computing in biology and medicine: Survey of glyph-based visualization techniques for spatial multivariate medical data. *Computer Graphics*, *35*(2), 392–401. doi:10.1016/j.cag.2011.01.011.

Rosen, L., & Kato, K. (2006). *Building community, improving oral proficiency: A wiki case study*. Retrieved January 31, 2013, from http://www.actfl.org/files/ACTFL06handouts/Session371.pdf

Rowe, M. (2010). The credibility of digital identity information on the social web: A user study.[Raleigh, NC: WICOW.]. *Proceedings of WICOW*, *10*, 35–42. doi:10.1145/1772938.1772947.

Sadoski, M. (2001). Resolving the effects of concreteness on interest, comprehension, and learning important ideas from text. *Educational Psychology Review*, *13*(3), 263–281. doi:10.1023/A:1016675822931.

Santiesteban, A. J., & Koran, J. J. (1977). Acquisition of science teaching skills through psychological modeling and concomitant student learning. *Journal of Research in Science Teaching*, *14*(3), 199–207. doi:10.1002/tea.3660140304.

Saxenian, A. (1994). *Regional advantage: Culture and competition in silicon valley and route 128*. Boston: Harvard University.

Scarino, A., & Liddicoat, A. J. (2009). *Teaching and learning languages: A guide*. Melbourne, Australia: Curriculum Corporation. Retrieved March 21, 2013, from http://www.tllg.unisa.edu.au/lib_guide/gllt_ch2.pdf

Schaefer, M. (2012). *Return on influence: The revolutionary power of Klout, social scoring, and influence marketing*. New York: McGraw-Hill.

Schank, R. C., & Abelson, R. P. (1977). *Scripts, plans, goals, and understanding*. Hillsdale, NJ: Lawrence Erlbaum Associates.

Scharle, A., & Szabo, A. (2000). *Autonomy in language learning: A guide to developing learner responsibility*. Cambridge, UK: Cambridge University Press.

Schmidt, R. W. (1990). The role of consciousness in second language learning. *Applied Linguistics*, *11*(2), 129–158. doi:10.1093/applin/11.2.129.

Schmidt, R. W. (1993). Consciousness, learning and interlanguage pragmatics. In Kasper, G., & Blum-Kulka, S. (Eds.), *Interlanguage pragmatics* (pp. 21–42). Oxford, UK: Oxford University Press.

Schneider, C. G. (2008). From the president. *Peer Review*, *10*(4), 3.

Schon, D. (1983). *The reflective practitioner: How professionals think in action*. London: Temple Smith.

Seitzinger, J. (2006). *Be constructive: Blogs, podcasts, and wikis as constructivist learning tools*. Learning Solutions e-Magazine.

Selwyn, N. (2009). Faceworking: Exploring students' education-related use of Facebook. *Learning, Media and Technology*, *34*(2), 157–174. doi:10.1080/17439880902923622.

Sharp, H., Rogers, Y., & Preece, J. (2007). *Interaction design: Beyond human-computer interaction*. New York: John Wiley & Sons Ltd..

Shaywitz, S. M. D. (2003). *Overcoming dyslexia*. New York: Alfred A. Knopf.

Sherer, M., & Rogers, R. W. (1984). The role of vivid information in fear appeals and attitude change. *Journal of Research in Personality*, *18*(3), 321–334. doi:10.1016/0092-6566(84)90016-3.

Sillitoe, P. (2004). Interdisciplinary experiences: Working with indigenous knowledge in development. *Interdisciplinary Science Reviews*, *29*(1), 6–23. doi:10.1179/030801804225012428.

Simoff, S. J., Behlen, M. H., & Mazeika, A. (2008). Visual data mining: An introduction and overview. In Simoff, S. J., Behlen, M. H., & Mazeika, A. (Eds.), *Visual Data Mining (LNCS)*. Springer-Verlag. doi:10.1007/978-3-540-71080-6_1.

Simpson, O. (2013). *Supporting students in online, open & distance learning*. New York: Routledge.

Singhal, A., Cody, M. J., Rogers, E. M., & Sabido, M. (Eds.). (2004). *Entertainment education and social change: History, research, and practice*. Mahwah, NJ: Lawrence Erlbaum.

Size Limits on Twitter Import. (2012). Retrieved from http://nodexl.codeplex.com/discussions/348565

Slater, M. D., & Rouner, D. (2002). Entertainment-education and elaboration likelihood: Understanding the processing of narrative persuasion. *Communication Theory*, *12*(2), 173–191.

Small, H. (2010). Maps of science as interdisciplinary discourse: Co-citation contexts and the role of analogy. *Scientometrics*, *83*, 835–849. doi:10.1007/s11192-009-0121-z.

Smith, M. (2013). *A cloud large-data processing function? NodeXL discussion board*. Retrieved Feb. 12, 2013, from http://nodexl.codeplex.com/discussions/428064

Smith, M. A., Schneiderman, B., Milic-Frayling, N., Rodrigues, E. M., Barash, V., & Dunne, C. … Gleave, E. (2009). Analyzing (social media) networks with NodeXL. In *Proceedings of C&T '09*, (pp. 255-263). University Park, PA: C&T.

Smith, G. A., & Committee on Injury and Poison Prevention. (2001). Technical report: Lawn mower-related injuries to children. *Pediatrics*, *107*(6), e106. doi:10.1542/peds.107.6.e106 PMID:11389304.

Smith, H., & Higgins, S. (2006). Opening classroom interaction: the importance of feedback. *Cambridge Journal of Education*, *36*(4), 485–502. doi:10.1080/03057640601048357.

Snow, C. E., Burns, M. S., & Griffin, P. (1998). *Preventing reading difficulties in young children*. Washington, DC: Committee on the Prevention of Reading Difficulties in Young Children, National Research Council.

Soares, D. A. (2008). Understanding class blogs as a tool for language development. *Language Teaching Research*, *12*(4), 517–533. doi:10.1177/1362168808097165.

Solomon, M. Z., & DeJong, W. (1988). The impact of a clinic-based educational videotape on knowledge and treatment behavior of men with gonorrhea. *Sexually Transmitted Diseases*, *15*(3), 127–132. doi:10.1097/00007435-198807000-00001 PMID:2465581.

Solomon, M. Z., DeJong, W., & Jodrie, T. (1988). Improving drug-regimen adherence among patients with sexually transmitted disease. *The Journal of Compliance in Health Care*, *3*(1), 41–56.

Sophris West. (2004). *Read well k.*

Speer, N. K., Reynolds, J. R., Swallow, K. M., & Zacks, J. M. (2009). Reading stories activates neural representations of visual and motor experiences. *Psychological Science*, *20*(8), 989–999. doi:10.1111/j.1467-9280.2009.02397.x PMID:19572969.

Sriphaew, K., & Theeramunkong, T. (2002). A new method for finding generalized frequent itemsets in association rule mining. In *Proceedings of the VII International Symposium on Computers and Communications* (pp. 20-26). ACM Press.

Stangor, C., & McMillan, D. (1992). Memory for expectancy-congruent and expectancy-incongruent information: A review of the social and social developmental literatures. *Psychological Bulletin*, *111*(1), 42–61. doi:10.1037/0033-2909.111.1.42.

Stanley, G. (2006). Podcasting: Audio on the internet comes of age. *Teaching English as a Second or Foreign Language, 9*(4). Retrieved January 31, 2013, from http://www-writing.berkeley.edu/TESL-EJ/ej36/int.html

Stapel, D. A., Reicher, S. D., & Spears, R. (1994). Social identity, availability and the perception of risk. *Social Cognition*, *12*(1), 1–17. doi:10.1521/soco.1994.12.1.1.

Stapel, D. A., & Velthuijsen, A. S. (1996). Just as if it happened to me: The impact of vivid and self-relevant information on risk judgments. *Journal of Social and Clinical Psychology*, *15*(1), 102–111. doi:10.1521/jscp.1996.15.1.102.

Stauffacher, M. (2010). Beyond neocorporatism? Transdisciplinary case studies as a means for collaborative learning in sustainable development. *Environmental Sociology,* 201 – 216. Retrieved from http://link.springer.com/chapter/10.1007/978-90-481-8730-0_12?null

Steele, J., & Iliinsky, N. (Eds.). (2010). *Beautiful visualization: Looking at data through the eyes of experts.* Cambridge, MA: O'Reilly Media.

Steinfield, C., Ellison, N. B., & Lampe, C. (2008). Social capital, self-esteem, and use of online social network sites: A longitudinal analysis. *Journal of Applied Developmental Psychology*, *29*, 434–445. doi:10.1016/j.appdev.2008.07.002.

Sterling G. (2009). Retrieved from http://searchengineland.com/augmented-reality-is-also-a-form-of-search-23859

Sterling, B. (2013). *Augmented reality: New patent allows for Google Glass to control appliances.* Retrieved from http://www.wired.com/beyond_the_beyond/2013/03/augmented-reality-new-patent-allows-google-glass-to-control-appliances/

Stockdale, C., & Possin, C. (2001). *The source for solving reading problems.* East Moline, IL: LinguiSystems, Inc..

Stokes, J. P. (1983). Predicting satisfaction with social support from social network structure. *American Journal of Community Psychology*, *11*(2), 141–182. doi:10.1007/BF00894363.

Stokols, D. (2006). Toward a science of transdisciplinary action research. *American Journal of Community Psychology*, *38*, 63–77. doi:10.1007/s10464-006-9060-5 PMID:16791514.

Sun, Y. (2009). Voice blog: An exploratory study of language learning. *Language Learning & Technology*, *13*(2), 88–103.

Suskie, L. A. (2009). *Assessing student learning: A common sense guide.* San Francisco, CA: Jossey-Bass.

Sykes, J. (2008). *A dynamic approach to social interaction: Synthetic immersive environments and Spanish pragmatics.* (Unpublished doctoral dissertation). University of Minnesota, Minneapolis, MN.

Sykes, J. M. (2009). Learner requests in Spanish: Examining the potential of multiuser virtual environments for L2 pragmatic acquisition. In Lomicka, L., & Lord, G. (Eds.), *The next generation: Social networking and online collaboration in foreign language learning* (pp. 115–144). San Marcos, TX: CALICO.

Taleb, N. N. (2010). *The black swan: The impact of the highly improbable*. New York: Random House. (Original work published 2007).

Tal-Or, N., Boninger, D. S., Poran, A., & Gleicher, F. (2004). Counterfactual thinking as a mechanism in narrative persuasion. *Human Communication Research*, *30*(3), 301–328. doi:10.1111/j.1468-2958.2004.tb00734.x.

Tan, P., Kumar, V., & Srivastava, J. (2002). Selecting the right interestingness measure for association patterns. In *Proceedings ACM SIGMOD International Conference on Knowledge Discovery and Data Mining* (pp. 32-41). ACM Press.

Tan, P.-N., Steinbach, M., & Kumar, V. (2005). *Introduction to data mining*. Reading, MA: Addison-Wesley.

Taylor, M. C. (2010). *Crisis on campus: A bold plan for reforming our colleges and universities*. New York: Alfred A. Knopf.

Terepocki, M., Kruk, R. S., & Willows, D. M. (2002). The incidence and nature of letter orientation errors in reading disability. *Journal of Learning Disabilities*, *35*(3), 214–233. doi:10.1177/002221940203500304 PMID:15493319.

Tergan, S.-O., Keller, T., & Burkhard, R. A. (2006). Integrating knowledge and information: Digital concept maps as a bridging technology. *Information Visualization*, *5*, 167–174. doi:10.1057/palgrave.ivs.9500132.

Thorndike, E. L. (1898). Animal intelligence: An experimental study of the associative processes in animals. *Psychological Monographs*, *2*(4), 1–109. doi:10.1037/h0092987.

Thrasher, J. F., Arillo-Santillán, E., Villalobos, V., Pérez-Hernández, R., Hammond, D., & Carter, J. et al. (2012). Can pictorial warning labels on cigarette packages address smoking-related health disparities? Field experiments in Mexico to assess pictorial warning label content. *Cancer Causes & Control*, *23*(S1), 69–80. doi:10.1007/s10552-012-9899-8 PMID:22350859.

Tinsworth, D. K., & McDonald, J. E. (2001). *Special study: Injuries and deaths associated with children's playground equipment*. Washington, DC: U.S. Consumer Product Safety Commission.

Tong, S. T., Van Der Heide, B., Langwell, L., & Walther, J. B. (2008). Too much of a good thing? The relationship between number of friends and interpersonal impressions on Facebook. *Journal of Computer-Mediated Communication*, *13*, 531–549. doi:10.1111/j.1083-6101.2008.00409.x.

Toyoda, E., & Harrison, R. (2002). Categorization of text chat communication between learners and native speakers of Japanese. *Language Learning and Technology*, *6*(1), 82-99. Retrieved January 31, 2013, from http://llt.msu.edu/vol6num1/pdf/toyoda.pdf

Transdisciplinary Studies. (2012, Feb. 24). *Wikipedia*. Retrieved from http://en.wikipedia.org/wiki/Transdisciplinary_studies

Treiman, R. (2000). The foundations of literacy. *Current Directions in Psychological Science*, *9*, 89–92. doi:10.1111/1467-8721.00067.

Treiman, R., & Rodriguez, K. (1999). Young children use letter names in learning to read words. *Psychological Science*, *10*, 334–338. doi:10.1111/1467-9280.00164.

Treiman, R., Weatherston, S., & Berch, D. (1994). The role of letter names in children's learning of phoneme-grapheme relationships. *Applied Psycholinguistics*, *15*, 97–122. doi:10.1017/S0142716400006998.

Tsai, Y. (2011). Attitudes: A role in the reflection of intercultural learning outcomes. *International Journal of Innovative Interdisciplinary Research*, *1*, 139–149.

U. S. Consumer Product Safety Commission. (2010). *Public playground safety handbook (CPSC Publication No. 325)*. Washington, DC: Author.

U. S. Consumer Product Safety Commission. (n.d.a). *National electronic injury surveillance system (NEISS) on-line*. Retrieved November 15, 2012, from http://www.cpsc.gov/library/neiss.html

U. S. Consumer Product Safety Commission. (n.d.b). *Riding lawn mowers: Document no. 588*. Retrieved November 15, 2012, from http://www.cpsc.gov/cpscpub/pubs/588.pdf

Ubel, P. A., Jepson, & Baron, J. (2001). The inclusion of patient testimonials in decision aids: Effects of treatment choices. *Medical Decision Making*, *21*(1), 60–68. doi:10.1177/0272989X0102100108 PMID:11206948.

University of Utrecht. (2009). *NIFLAR project home page*. Retrieved January 31, 2013, from http://cms.let.uu.nl/niflar

Van Gelder, T. (2005). Teaching critical thinking: Some lessons from cognitive science. *College Teaching*, *53*(1), 41–46. doi:10.3200/CTCH.53.1.41-48.

Vanasupa, L., McCormick, K. E., Stefanco, C. J., Herter, R. J., & McDonald, M. (2012). Challenges in transdisciplinary, integrated projects: Reflections on the case of faculty members' failure to collaborate. *Innovations in Higher Education*, *37*, 171–181. doi:10.1007/s10755-011-9199-3.

Veletsianos, G. (2012). Higher education scholars' participation and practices on Twitter. *Journal of Computer Assisted Learning*, *28*, 336–349. doi:10.1111/j.1365-2729.2011.00449.x.

Vickers, H. (2007a). *SurReal language quests*. Retrieved January 31, 2013, from http://avatarlanguages.com/blog/?p=14

Vickers, H. (2007b). SurReal quests: Enriched, purposeful language learning in second life. *The Knowledge Tree*. Retrieved January 31, 2013, from http://kt.flexiblelearning.net.au/tkt2007/Ed.-15/surreal-quests-enriched-purposeful-language-learning-in-second-life

Vogel, V. G., Graves, D. S., Vernon, S. W., Lord, J. A., Winn, R. J., & Peters, G. N. et al. (1990). Mammographic screening of women with increased risk of breast cancer. *Cancer*, *66*(7), 1613–1620. doi:10.1002/1097-0142(19901001)66:7<1613::AID-CNCR2820660728>3.0.CO;2-E PMID:2208012.

Vollman, D., Khosla, K., Shields, B. J., Beeghly, B. C., Bonsu, B., & Smith, G. A. (2005). Lawn mower-related injuries to children. *The Journal of Trauma*, *59*(3), 724–728. PMID:16361919.

Vollman, D., & Smith, G. A. (2006). Epidemiology of lawn mower-related injuries to children in the Unted States, 1990-2004. *Pediatrics*, *118*(2), 273–278. doi:10.1542/peds.2006-0056.

Voss, J. F., Wiley, J., & Sandak, R. (1999). On the use of narrative as argument. In Goldman, S. R., Graesser, A. C., & Vandenbroek, P. (Eds.), *Narrative comprehension, causality, and coherence: Essays in honor of Tom Trabasso* (pp. 235–252). Mahwah, NJ: Lawrence Erlbaum and Associates.

Vroom, V. (1964). *Work and motivation*. New York: Jon Wiley & Sons.

Vygotsky, L. S. (1987). Thinking and speech. In R. W. Rieber & A. S. Carton (Eds.), The collected works of L. S. Vygotsky: Vol. 1: Problems of general psychology (pp. 39-285). New York: Plenum.

Vygotsky, L. S. (1978). *Mind and society: The development of higher psychological processes*. Cambridge, MA: Harvard University Press.

Wagner, C. S., Roessner, J. D., Bobb, K., Klein, J. T., Boyack, K. W., & Keyton, J. et al. (2011). Approaches to understanding and measuring interdisciplinary scientific research (IDR): A review of the literature. *Journal of Informetrics*, *165*, 14–26. doi:10.1016/j.joi.2010.06.004.

Wagner, R. K., Torgesen, J. K., & Rashotte, C. A. (1999). *The comprehensive test of phonological processing (CTOPP)*. Austin, TX: Pro-Ed, Inc..

Wagner, T. (2010). *The global achievement gap: Why even the best schools don't teach the new survival skills our children need – And what we can do about it*. New York, NY: Basic Books.

Wagoner, B., & Jensen, E. (2010). Science learning at the zoo: Evaluating children's developing understanding of animals and their habitats. *Psychology & Society*, *3*(1), 65–76.

Walker, A. (1983). *In search of our mother's gardens: Womanist prose*. San Diego, CA: Harcourt Brace Jovanovich.

Walvoord, B. E. (2010). *Assessment clear and simple: A practical guide for institutions, departments, and general education*. San Francisco, CA: Jossey-Bass.

Wang, S., & Vasquez, C. (2012). Web 2.0 and second language learning: What does the research tell us? *CALICO Journal, 29*(3), 412–430.

Warren, S. J., Barab, S. A., & Dondlinger, M. J. (2008). A MUVE towards PBL writing: Effects of a digital learning environment designed to improve elementary student writing. *Journal of Research on Technology in Education, 41*(1), 121–147.

Warren, S. J., Stein, R. A., Dondlinger, M. J., & Barab, S. A. (2009). A look inside a muve design process: Blending instructional design and game principles to target writing skills. *Journal of Educational Computing Research, 40*(3), 295–321. doi:10.2190/EC.40.3.c.

Watson, H. J., & Wixom, B. H. (2007). The current state of business intelligence. *IEEE Computer, 40*(9), 96–99. doi:10.1109/MC.2007.331.

Watts, D. J. (2003). *Six degrees: The science of a connected age*. New York: W.W. Norton & Company.

Wear, D. N. (1999). Challenges to interdisciplinary discourse. *Ecosystems (New York, N.Y.), 2*(4), 299–301. doi:10.1007/s100219900080.

Weare, K. (1992). The contribution of education to health promotion. In Bunton, R., & Macdonald, G. (Eds.), *Health promotion: Disciplines, diversity and developments* (pp. 102–125). New York: Routledge.

Web 2.0. (n.d.). *Wikipedia*. Retrieved January 31, 2013, from http://en.wikipedia.org/wiki/Web_2.0

Weiner, B. (1974). *Achievement motivation and attribution theory*. Morristown, NJ: General Learning Press.

Weinstein, N. D. (1989). Effects of personal experience on self-protective behavior. *Psychological Bulletin, 105*(1), 31–51. doi:10.1037/0033-2909.105.1.31 PMID:2648439.

Wicker, B., Keysers, C., Plailly, J., Royet, J. P., Gallese, V., & Rizzolatti, G. (2003). Both of us disgusted in my insula: The common neural basis of seeing and feeling disgust. *Neuron, 40*(3), 655–664. doi:10.1016/S0896-6273(03)00679-2 PMID:14642287.

Wiki. (n.d.). *Wikipedia*. Retrieved January 31, 2013, from HTTP://EN.WIKIPEDIA.ORG/WIKI/WIKI

Wikipedia. (2012, November 30). *Wikipedia*. Retrieved from http://en.wikipedia.org

Willems, R. M., & Casasanto, D. (2011). Flexibility in embodied language understanding. *Frontiers in Psychology, 2*(116), 1–11. PMID:21713130.

Wittel, A. (2001). Toward a network sociality. *Theory, Culture & Society, 18*(6), 51–76. doi: doi:10.1177/0263 27601018006003.

Wölfl, S. (2005). Events in branching time. *Studia Logics: An International Journal for Symbolic Logic, 79*(2), 255–282.

Wolf, M. (2007). *Proust and the squid: The story and science of the reading brain*. New York: HarperCollins.

Wong, P. C., Whitney, P., & Thomas, J. (1999). Visualizing association rules for text mining. In *Proceedings of the 1999 IEEE Symposium on Information Visualization* (INFOVIS '99), (pp. 120-128). Washington, DC: IEEE Computer Society.

Woods, C. (2007). Researching and developing interdisciplinary teaching: Towards a conceptual framework for classroom communication. *Higher Education, 54*(6), 853–866. doi:10.1007/s10734-006-9027-3.

Woolf, S. H., & Aron, L. (Eds.). (2013). *U.S. health in international perspective: Shorter lives, poorer health*. Washington, DC: National Academies Press.

WordNet Lexical Database. (2012). Retrieved from http://wordnet.princeton.edu

World Health Organization. (2011). *Global status report on noncommunicable diseases 2010*. Geneva, Switzerland: WHO.

Wright, S. S., & Kyes, K. B. (1996). The effects of safer-sex stories on college students' attitudes toward condoms. *Journal of Psychology & Human Sexuality, 8*(4), 1–18. doi:10.1300/J056v08n04_01 PMID:12347910.

Wrzesien, M., & Raya, M. A. (2010). Learning in serious virtual worlds: Evaluation of learning effectiveness and appeal to students in the e-junior project. *Computers & Education, 55*(1), 178–187. doi:10.1016/j.compedu.2010.01.003.

Wu, S., Hofman, J. M., Mason, W. A., & Watts, D. J. (2011). Who says what to whom on Twitter. In *Proceedings of the World Wide Web 2011*. Hyderabad, India: IEEE.

Xue, Y., Zhang, C., Zhou, C., Lin, X., & Lin, Q. (2009). An effective news recommendation in social media based on users' preference. In *Proceedings of the International Workshop on Education Technology and Training* (pp. 627-631). IEEE Computer Society.

Yahia, B., Mephu, S., & Nguifo, E. (2004). Emulating a cooperative behavior in a generic association rule visualization tool. In *Proceedings of the16th IEEE International Conference on Tools with Artificial Intelligence (ICTAI'04)*. Boca Raton, FL: IEEE Press.

Yang, M. T., Cheng, Y. R., & Shih, Y. C. (2011). Facial expression recognition for learning status analysis. In *Proceedings of the International Conference on Human-Computer Interaction (HCI 2011)* (LNCS), (vol. 6764, pp. 131-138). Orlando, FL: Springer.

Yang, S. H. (2009). Using blogs to enhance critical reflection and community of practice. *Journal of Educational Technology & Society*, *12*(2), 11–21.

Yin, Z., Li, R., Mei, Q., & Han, J. (2009). Exploring social tagging graph for web object classification. In *Proceedings of the 15th ACM SIGKDD International Conference on Knowledge Discovery and Data Mining* (pp. 957-966). ACM Press.

Yu, A. Y., Tian, S. W., Vogel, D., & Kwok, R. C.-W. (2010). Can learning be virtually boosted? An investigation of online social networking impacts. *Computers & Education*, *55*, 1494–1503. doi:10.1016/j.compedu.2010.06.015.

Zabrucky, K. M., & Moore, D. (1999). Influence of text genre on adults' monitoring of understanding and recall. *Educational Gerontology*, *25*(8), 691–710. doi:10.1080/036012799267440.

Zabrucky, K., & Ratner, H. H. (1992). Effects of passage type on comprehension monitoring and recall in good and poor readers. *Journal of Literacy Research*, *24*(3), 373–391. doi:10.1080/10862969209547782.

Zeitlin, L. R. (1994). Failure to follow safety instructions: Faulty communications or risky decisions? *Human Factors*, *36*(1), 172–181. PMID:8026839.

Zentall, T. R. (2011). Social learning mechanisms: Implications for a cognitive theory of imitation. *Interaction Studies: Social Behaviour and Communication in Biological and Artificial Systems*, *12*(2), 233–261. doi:10.1075/is.12.2.03zen.

Zentall, T. R. (2012). Perspectives on observational learning in animals. *Journal of Comparative Psychology*, *126*(2), 114–128. doi:10.1037/a0025381 PMID:21895354.

Zorko, V. (2009). Factors affecting the way students collaborate in a wiki for English language learning. *Australasian Journal of Educational Technology*, *25*(5), 645–665.

About the Contributors

Shalin Hai-Jew works as an instructional designer at Kansas State University. She teaches for Washington Online and Walla Walla Community College. She has B.A.s in English and Psychology and an M.A. in English from the University of Washington, in Seattle. She has an Ed.D. (2005) from Seattle University, where she was a Morford Scholar. She was a tenured professor at Shoreline Community College. She has taught in Jiangxi Normal University in Nanchang, Jiangxi Province, from 1988 – 1990, and at Northeast Agriculture University, in Harbin, Heilongjiang Province, from 1992 – 1994, the latter two years with the United Nations Volunteers of the United Nations Development Programme (UNDP). She has edited several academic books. She has published widely. She is a non-degree seeking graduate student at K-State.

* * *

Brent A. Anders: Brent Anders, M.Ed., is a Senior Electronic Media Coordinator for the Office of Mediated Education at Kansas State University. His work includes: educational media consulting (working directly with instructors and departments), as well as videography/filmmaking (directing, capturing, editing, and final production). Additionally Anders works directly with live-Webcasting and Web accessibility/usability. Anders has a Bachelor's degree in Psychology (human computer interaction focus), and a Master's degree in Education with an instructional technology focus. Currently, Anders is pursuing a PhD in Adult Education. Anders also serves in the Army National Guard as a Master Sergeant. His primary military duty is that of Chief Instructor, managing the military education at the Kansas Regional Training Institute. His additional duty is that of Senior Instructor for the 80-hour Army Basic Instructors Course (ABIC). This course teaches sergeants and officers how to properly instruct soldiers within a class setting using proven effective means of education. Anders has contributed to multiple published works dealing specifically with higher education. The focus of these publications has ranged from video and graphics to motivation and the use of emotion to enhance educational success. Anders has been in the education field for over 15 years dealing with military training, distance education, educational media, and higher education in general.

Rosemary Boggs is a Program Coordinator with the Division of Continuing Education at Kansas State University. She facilitates the delivery and coordination of the College of Education courses and programs offered via distance, including courses offered face-to-face in locations other than the Kansas State University campus. Rosemary serves as liaison with the College of Education faculty and staff for all distance education concerns/needs, which includes coordinating the development of new classes and programs for online learning. She coordinates the marketing of the College of Education distance graduate programs for K-12 personnel, for educators working with adult learners, and for academic advisors in higher education. Rosemary also assists students in these programs with application and enrollment issues, as well as providing any assistance to them that a distance student may need. She has been active in helping develop asynchronous training for faculty who teach through distance delivery systems. She is the co-chair of the E-Learning Faculty Modules committee and has been instrumental in working with faculty to develop the Stand Alone Modules in the E-Learning Faculty Module Wiki. Rosemary has a bachelor's degree from the University of Illinois and a master's of education from South Dakota State University. Boggs has been recognized for her commitment to continuing education through the Division of Continuing Education Employee Recognition Award in 2008 and the Regional UPCEA Continuing Educator Award in 2012. Rosemary was a member of the Chamber of Commerce Manhattan Leadership Class of 2010. Previously, Boggs was a seasonal educator at Sunset Zoo in Manhattan, Kansas, was employed by South Dakota State University, and worked for the Brookings, South Dakota, K-5 school program. She was also a 4-H and Youth Development Advisor in Illinois. Her lifelong goal has been to help others achieve additional skills and knowledge through educational activities. Boggs is a firm believer in volunteerism and volunteers her time with organizations that strive to better the lives of less fortunate people. She and her husband have two daughters who they enjoy visiting in Minneapolis and Chicago. She enjoys traveling, gardening, reading, and all Kansas State University sporting events.

Luca Cagliero has been a research assistant at the Dipartimento di Automatica e Informatica of the Politecnico di Torino since March 2012. He holds a Master degree in Computer and Communication Networks and a PhD in Computer Engineering from Politecnico di Torino. His current research interests are in the fields of Data Mining and Database Systems. In particular, he has worked on structured and unstructured data mining by means of classification and association rule mining algorithms. His current research interests are mainly focused on Bayesian and associative classification of structured data, generalized itemset mining, textual document summarization, social network mining and analysis, recommendation systems, and genetic data mining.

Søren Eskildsen is a research assistant at Department of Architecture, Design, and Media Technology at Aalborg University, Denmark. His main topics of research are within visualization methods, HCI, mobile interaction, and serious games. He obtained his B. Sc (2009) and M.Sc. (2011) in Medialogy at Aalborg University, which lead to his current position as research assistant at Aalborg University. He is currently working on mobile context tracking in perspective to different use cases like, language learning and collaborative creation.

Rob Gibson is currently the Director of Learning Technologies at Emporia State University, a moderately-sized university located in Emporia, KS. In this role, he and his team provide a variety of learning technology support for faculty, staff, and students, including the learning management system; video production; Web conferencing and streaming media support; instructional design services; training and development; classroom support services; research support; and other related services. He has served in this capacity since 2008. Gibson has worked in higher education since 1988. He began his career at the University of Wyoming working with early distance education systems that utilized phone lines to serve graphics and voice to students located in remote state locations. After completing his first master's degree, he moved to Wichita State University where he served as the instructional designer for a television-based distance education system in the early 1990s. In 1995—the dawn of Web browsers—Gibson and a faculty member from Nursing Informatics designed and developed what is thought to be the first online course in Kansas – well before course management systems. He later worked for a small Liberal Arts College before accepting a position at CU Online located at the University of Colorado – Denver and Health Sciences Center. He has published numerous peer-reviewed articles and book chapters, and actively promotes educational technology through a variety of social media outlets. Gibson holds undergraduate degrees in business administration and commercial art, a Master of Science degree in Instructional Technology and Design, a Doctor of Education in Instructional Technology and Distance Education, and is currently completing an MBA with particular emphasis in information technology and project management. An early champion of online course delivery, Rob elected to pursue his doctoral degree in the late 1990s when online programs were still the exception rather than the norm. His dissertation research investigated the effectiveness of various faculty development programs regarding online learning. Gibson has been an early and consistent champion of emerging technologies that have the potential to shape education. His research interests include gesture-based computing, augmented reality, usability analysis, online learning, instructional systems design, learning theory, and competency-based learning. He serves on several product advisory boards and has been the recipient of outstanding course development awards. He also holds multiple certifications from Quality Matters.

William H. Hsu is an associate professor of Computing and Information Sciences at Kansas State University. He received a B.S. in Mathematical Sciences and Computer Science and an M.S.Eng. in Computer Science from Johns Hopkins University in 1993, and a Ph.D. in Computer Science from the University of Illinois at Urbana-Champaign in 1998. At the National Center for Supercomputing Applications (NCSA) he was a co-recipient of an Industrial Grand Challenge Award for visual analytics of text corpora. His research interests include information visualization, predictive analytics, data mining, machine learning, and probabilistic reasoning, with applications to information extraction, time series prediction, biomedical informatics, geoinformatics, and digital humanities. Published applications of his research include spatiotemporal event detection for veterinary epidemiology, crime mapping, and opinion mining; analysis of heterogeneous information networks; document analysis; and sentiment analysis. Current work in his lab deals with: topic detection and tracking from news articles and social media; learning, visualizing, and reasoning with domain-adaptive models of large natural language corpora; structured information extraction; and graphical models of probability and utility for information security. Dr. Hsu has published over 45 refereed conference and journal papers and book chapters, and has over 30 additional publications.

Molly Leonard is an Echols Scholar graduate of the University of Virginia and has been an ESL teacher in Hualien, Taiwan, for more than 25 years. Over that period of time she has honed her teaching skills in classes large and small, with students ranging in age from 4 to 84 and in level from those who didn't know the word "Hello," to bilingual speakers. While she teaches every language skills area, her primary focus is on training students in listening and speaking, and in Taiwan learner-specific materials development. In recent years, she has found herself employing the computer in her teaching at exponentially increasing levels, most particularly since the advent of Web 2.0. She has recently returned to school and is presently a master's degree student in applied English at National Dong Hwa University in Hualien, Taiwan, working under the guidance of Professor Ya-Chun Shih to enhance her understanding and knowledge of Web 2.0 and computer-assisted language learning.

Naeem A. Mahoto received Master degree in Computer Engineering from Mehran University of Engineering and Technology Jamshoro, Pakistan, and Ph.D in Control and Computer Engineering from Politecnico di Torino, Italy. He works in the field of data mining and bioinformatics. His research interests are focused on pattern extraction, classification of electronic records in the medical domain. His research activities are also devoted to summarization of Web documents and social network analysis.

Roger McHaney, professor of management information systems, is an expert on use of technology and the ways Web 2.0 and tech-savvy millennials are impacting higher education and learning. He also develops distance education teaching and learning techniques. His work has been published in top business and education journals. He is a frequent keynote speaker and has lectured internationally in locations including in India, New Zealand, China, United Kingdom, Italy, Greece, Belgium, and The Netherlands. McHaney currently holds the Daniel D. Burke Chair for Exceptional Faculty at Kansas State University where teaches courses in digital business, management of information systems, information resources management, software development, and enterprise computing. His areas of research include Web 2.0 in education and business, technologies used by millennials, discrete event simulation, education simulation systems, computer-mediated communication systems, and organizational computing. His ongoing research includes studies on how social media is impacting business and education, distance learning techniques, business applications in virtual worlds such as Second Life, message board language complexity, and development of online training simulations. McHaney was recognized for his excellence in teaching by being named K-State's 2006-2007 Coffman Chair for University Distinguished Teaching Scholars. As Coffman Chair, he collected various distance learning techniques being used across campus and compiled an online educational resource that makes the transition to distance learning easier for faculty and staff. He is co-founder and wiki master of ELATEWiki.org and has recently authored the book *The New Digital Shoreline: How Web 2.0 and Millennials are Revolutionizing Higher Education*. He earned both bachelor's and master's degrees from Lake Superior State University in northern Michigan, and a doctorate in computer information system and quantitative analysis from the Sam M. Walton College of Business at the University of Arkansas. He is currently working on projects that investigate how technology and Web 2.0 impact higher education. It is his dream to eventually be able to teach all his classes from his retreat on the shore of Lake Huron in Michigan's Upper Peninsula. Roger is married and has three children, all of whom are currently attending universities.

Matthias Rehm is associated professor for media technology at Aalborg University where he works on cultural aspects of HCI, Social Robotics, and Mobile Interaction. Prior to that, he has worked at Augsburg University at the lab for multimedia concepts and applications where he has been leading several international projects in the area of multimodal interactive systems. His research interests include embodied conversational agents, cultural aspects of human computer interaction, modeling of social behavior as well as multimodal user interfaces. Rehm has published over 50 papers in the area of human-centered computing.

Mitch Ricketts is the Health, Safety, and Environmental Quality Coordinator for Research and Extension at Kansas State University. In this capacity, he conducts public health interventions and manages workplace safety in research, academic, and manufacturing settings throughout Kansas. In addition, he is a member of the Graduate Faculty—teaching courses on the Web and in traditional classroom environments. He has worked in the fields of education and public health for over 30 years. Early in his career, he served as a public school teacher and counselor in grades 7-12 (with a B.S.Ed. in social science and a M.S. in counseling from Pittsburg State University). He was later employed by a governmental agency in Kansas to promote environmental stewardship and the prevention of injuries to students and employees in public schools (using his M.S. in occupational safety management from the University of Central Missouri). In 2007, he earned a Ph.D. in cognitive and human factors psychology from Kansas State University. His dissertation examined the role of narratives in health communication. As a Board Certified Safety Professional, he has served in official advisory roles for the American Society of Safety Engineers, Kansas Childhood Lead Advisory Council, Central States Center for Agricultural Safety and Health, Kansas Department of Emergency Management, and many other agencies. He has authored a number of Cooperative Extension Service publications and peer-reviewed journal articles.

Kasper Rodil is a Ph.D student at Department of Architecture, Design, and Media Technology at Aalborg University, Denmark. His main research topics are Indigenous Knowledge Management Systems, HCI, cross-cultural interface design, Participatory Design, 3D visualization for Communication, and Localization of Design. After obtaining his B.Sc and M.Sc. in Medialogy at Aalborg University, he took a position as Post Graduate Research Fellow at the Polytechnic of Namibia. He is currently one of the anchors of a project to preserve indigenous knowledge in Namibia and creator of www.IndiKnowTech.org.

Gladys Palma de Schrynemakers, Associate Provost at LIU/Brooklyn, directs the Collegiate Science Technology Program (CSTEP) and was Principal Investigator (P.I.) for Predominantly Black Institutions (PBI) Undergraduate STEM Grant, both prepare undergraduate minority and economically disadvantaged students to enter the STEM fields. As the Executive Vice President of APACS, Association of Administrators of CSTEP and STEP, she works closely with over 200 CSTEP/STEP directors and program staff to create a statewide professional development network for diverse students in high school, college/university to enter into STEM and licensed professions. She is the P.I. for the New York State's Smart Scholars Early College High School. This program specifically engages groups of students who historically have not had access to college. She Co-Chairs the annual Teaching Narrative Conference at the Brooklyn Campus, an event that focuses on teaching narratives as a form of inquiry about student learning. Dr. Schrynemakers serves as a member of the Leadership Team for Integrative Assessment of the Imagine America Initiative. During her 23-year career with the university, she has secured over 9 million dollars in grants, taught social science research, and published frequently in peer-reviewed venues on theory and practice of constructing knowledge and assessment.

Ya-Chun Shih was born in Taiwan. She received her M.A. and Ph.D. degrees in Curriculum and Instruction (Bilingual Education emphasis) from Pennsylvania State University in 1997 and 2000, respectively. In 2001, Dr. Shih joined the faculty of National Hualien University of Education, located near the world-famous Taroko Gorge, as Assistant Professor of English Language Teaching. In 2009, the University was renamed as National Dong Hwa University. She is currently Assistant Professor in the Department of English at National Dong Hwa University, Hualien, Taiwan, and one of the Computer-Assisted Language Learning (CALL) practitioners. She has pursued a wide range of technology-supported language learning issues, including serving as an instructor, instructional designer, researcher, journal reviewer, guest speaker, advisor, and committee member on related issues. Under Dr. Shih's leadership, the VEC3D (3D Virtual English Classroom), an interdisciplinary research team of instructional designers and computer science experts, designed and developed a variety of innovative language learning platforms. The VEC3D innovation started with an inspired idea for contextual language learning. Dr. Shih and her research team are expanding beyond the traditional language learning environments and methods by incorporating technology into daily lessons and communicative activities. Her current research focuses on integrating virtual reality technologies and language learning in education. She has investigated the effect of Virtual Reality Assisted Language Learning (VRALL) on students' achievement of English as a foreign language. She has also explored issues related to the use of 3D Collaborative Virtual Environments (CVEs) within a social and cultural context. The central research issues for the VEC3D project include research on (non)verbal communication, developing communicative competence, and cultural awareness. Her research has been heavily supported by a grant from the Taiwan National Science Council.

Lynda Spire is an assistant dean in the Kansas State University Division of Continuing Education. Her responsibilities include the supervision of the credit coordination staff that facilitates the development and delivery of the online courses offered to distance students. A significant part of her responsibilities include development of services offered by the division to the K-State distance students and faculty. She has headed several project teams to create or improve services to the faculty and students. One of the team projects include the creation of the ELATE Wiki that was created in 2009 and has been used by teachers across the nation as they share teaching tips, ideas, and methods. Spire was instrumental in the creation and production of the K-State E-Learning Faculty Modules wiki that was developed by team members drawn from across Kansas State University. In addition, Spire works with a team to produce the *Leading Edge*, an electronic newsletter designed to open the traditional campus to distance students, the Virtual Graduation, the Student Service Satisfaction Survey, and the DCE honors and Awards program. She has led multiple efforts to promote quality in online courses and programs on the campus including presentations, production of a K-State Quality Checklist, and faculty communication tools. Spire is involved in many K-State campus activities including the President's Commission for Multicultural Affairs, the Committee for Academic Policies and Procedures, the University Assessment Facilitators, the Coordinating Committee for People with Disabilities, and the Steering Committee for the Women of K-State. In addition, she is a member of the Manhattan Convention and Visitor's Bureau Steering Committee and the University Professional Continuing Education Association. Spire earned a bachelor's degree from West Texas A&M University and a master's from Kansas State University.

Carol Stockdale is the founder and director of the ARK Institute of Learning in Tacoma, Washington. The ARK provides clinic services to children and adults and trains educators. The ARK mission is to translate practical tools and methods from the clinic setting to classrooms and homes where students struggle to learn. Stockdale has taught at university and secondary levels. Her research focuses on the role of visual perception in the acquisition of academic skills and combines her interest in visual perception and art with her interest in how individuals learn. Stockdale received a Bachelor of Science degree from Iowa State University, and a Masters of Arts from the University of Puget Sound. She has an Ed.D. from Seattle University. She has coauthored books on reading problems and on visual-spatial disorders. She speaks and presents papers about learning problems at national conferences. Stockdale is the mother of three adult sons and the grandmother of six.

Index

A

Adaptive Curriculum 47, 67
Adaptive Thinking and Leadership (ATL) 269
Add-In 127, 161
Aggregate Manipulator (AM) 187
Agroterrorism 328
Alphabetic Principle 355-356
Anecdote 1, 4-5, 10, 22, 35
Application Programming Interface (API) 58, 161
Archives 93-95, 97-98, 101-102, 186, 353
Association Rule Mining 164-167, 169-170, 172, 178-180, 182
Augmented Reality 57-58, 93, 95-98, 100-102, 121
Aurasma 97-99
automapped tree hierarchies 246

B

Big Data 154, 184-186, 189-190, 196-197
BiLAT 270
Black Hat 264
Blog Assisted Language Learning (BALL) 71, 91
Blue Mars Lite 266-267, 270, 278, 280
Branching Logic 47-49, 66, 68-69, 218

C

Centrality 123, 161, 192, 198-199, 216, 220, 222, 224, 226, 244-245
Cluster 134, 141, 161, 220, 227-228, 231, 243, 329
Collaborative Virtual Environment (CVE) 91
Computer Assisted Language Learning (CALL) 91
Conjunction 48, 69, 73, 79, 85, 125, 174
Content Analysis 64, 120, 145, 310-312, 325-326, 329
Convergence 49, 51, 69, 100-101, 192
Coreference resolution 191
Counterfactual Thinking 21-22, 27, 32, 35
Cultural Learning 71-72, 75, 78, 82, 84, 266-271, 273, 275-277, 279-280

D

Data Analytics 51, 184, 187, 196
Data Crawl 127, 134-135, 139-140, 142-145, 147, 150, 157, 161, 248, 264
Data Extraction 125, 132, 134, 140, 143, 161, 222, 245, 247-248, 250-251, 253, 255, 258, 262, 264
Data Harvesting 161
Data Mining and Knowledge Discovery 164, 179-180, 182
Data Visualization 166, 182, 184, 188, 201, 231, 248, 250, 312
Decision Juncture 61, 69
Delphi Method 329
Digital Learning Objects (DLOs) 47, 49, 56, 61
Distinctive Feature 355, 357, 360, 363, 366, 371
Divergence 48-49, 51, 55-56, 68-69, 279
Domain Name System 247
Dynamic Query (DQ) 187

E

Eigenvector Centrality 161
E-Learning Faculty Modules 103-105, 107, 109, 112-113, 115-116, 203, 218-221, 238-240
E-LearningFacultyModules.org 103, 108
Electronic Network Analysis 241, 245-246, 248-250, 263
embedded links 115
Emergent Curriculum 216, 299-300, 305, 326
Encroachment 310, 329
Engagement 12, 24, 37, 44, 72, 78, 120-121, 129, 266, 269, 276-277, 290, 300-301, 335
English as a Foreign Language (EFL) 71, 86, 92, 266, 281
Equivalence 161, 200, 226, 228-229
Exclusive Disjunction 66, 69

F

Facebook 71-74, 78, 80-82, 86, 91, 120-121, 126, 129, 133, 145, 151, 159-160, 242, 247, 258, 260, 263
Facial Expression Recognition 71, 79-80, 84, 90, 92

Feedback 37-38, 40-41, 43-46, 63, 66, 87, 104, 205, 223, 336, 345
Flickr 42, 71-72, 74-75, 78, 80-82, 86, 120, 126, 147-148, 152-154, 160
Foot and Mouth Disease (FMD) 193
Frequent Itemset 182

G

Gated Assignment 69
Generalized Rule Graph 165, 173-175
Geocentrism 291
geocomputation 196
Geodesic Distance 143-144, 161, 244, 264, 323
Geographic Information System (GIS) 189
geolocation 157, 241, 246-247
Globalization 283, 309, 329
Google Street View 266-268, 271, 273-274, 276-278, 280-281
Graph nodes 165, 169

H

Health Communication 1-2, 6, 15, 22, 25, 27-28, 31, 35, 46
Health Education 27, 29, 34-35
Heterogeneous Information Networks (HIN) 192
Heterophily 122, 161
Hidden Ties 241
homophily 161, 199, 225, 243, 304
Human-Computer Information Retrieval (HCIR) 94

I

Identification 16, 28, 30, 35, 141, 147, 155, 185, 191, 246-247, 249-250, 333, 357, 361, 363, 371
Information Search Process (ISP) 93
Information visualization 166, 179-180, 182, 184-185, 187-188, 195, 333-334, 338, 342, 349-350, 352-354
innovative policies 96
Instructional Design 38, 46-49, 68, 90, 106, 198-199, 202-203, 205, 216, 218, 222-223, 299, 307-308, 326
Instructional Design Projects 198, 202, 218
Isomorphic Equivalence 229
Itemset Generalization Process 172, 182

K

Keyhole Markup Language (KML) 189

L

launch strategy 115
Logical Connectives 48, 69
Logical Disjunction 48, 69

M

malicious damage 115
Maltego Radium 241, 246-248, 250, 256, 258-259, 261, 263
Massively Online Open Course (MOOC) 196
Mass-Personal 161
Mediated Contents for Learning 282
MediaWiki 103, 106, 109, 118
microblogging sites 121, 123, 128-129, 241, 246, 261
Microsite 47, 49, 56, 60-61, 67, 69
mining algorithm 167, 172
Mirror Neuron 1, 8-9, 20, 25, 31, 35
Mobile Applications 93, 96, 101-102
monodisciplinary 300
Multidisciplinarity 300
Multimedia Learning 1, 14, 29, 35, 46, 339-340, 351, 353
Multiplex Relations 229

N

Named Entity Recognition (NER) 190, 195
Narrative 1, 6, 12, 15, 23-29, 31-36, 201, 220, 244, 287, 335, 340
Network science 198-199, 212
Node-Link Diagram 65, 161, 199-200, 227, 231, 310, 326
NodeXL 120, 125-128, 133-135, 143, 153, 158-161, 225, 248, 264, 321-323
Nonbiological Affinity 229
Nonymous 150, 162, 247
N-Step Neighborhood 229
Null Dyads 229

O

Online Connectivity 241
Online Learning 47, 50, 54, 57, 67, 106, 199, 206, 299
Online Learning Design 299
Organic Design 299
Orthography 355

P

Panorama 266-267, 276, 281
Parable 1, 35
Paradigm Shift 196, 284, 286, 296-297, 299

Percolation Theory 230
Perfect Hierarchy 230
periphery 122, 199, 205, 207-208, 229-230, 243, 250, 264, 310, 323
Personalization 2, 187
phonological loop 340
pluridisciplinary 300
polydisciplinary 300
positive Word-of-Mouth (pWOM) 245
Predictive Analytics 162, 189, 230
Profile (Learner) 69
Pseudonymity 241, 264

R

Random walk 162
Reachability 230, 323

S

Satisfaction 37-38, 40-42, 44-45, 129, 160, 242, 344
Scale-Free Networks 230
Second Life (SL) 92
semantic heterogeneity 189
Short Message Service (SMS) 123, 130
Small World Phenomena 231
Smartphones 96, 98, 339
Social Network Analysis 120-129, 155-165, 181, 183, 198-199, 213, 222-225, 245, 248, 264
Social Network Analysis (SNA) 155, 162, 245
Social Presence 129
sociogram 198, 200-202, 226, 229, 231
sousveillance 244
spam 108, 115, 121, 181
spatial database management system (SDBMS) 188
Spatiotemporal 184, 188-189, 191-192, 196
Special Collections 58, 93, 95, 97-98, 100-101
Stochastic 59, 69, 221
Story 1, 10, 12-16, 20-24, 28, 30-36, 59, 287, 327, 372
Structural Hole 200, 231
Structural Prestige 217, 231
Subnetwork 228, 231
Symbol Stabilization 355-359, 363, 365, 369-370
Systems View 198, 223

T

taxonomy 23, 159, 165, 167-175, 182-183, 325
Technology, Entertainment, and Design (TED) 282, 285
Topology 155, 159, 162, 222, 264
Transportation 27-28, 36, 95, 271, 278
Transposition 231
Trellis Graphic 231
Triad Census 231
Triadic Closure 231
tuples 195
Twitpics 246, 256-257
Twitter 71-86, 120-128, 130-150, 159-182, 246-262, 321
Twitter Generalized Rule Visualizer (TGRV) 164-165, 174

U

Undirected Lines 231
Universal Classes 231
User-Generated Content (UGC) 164, 168

V

Valued Graph 231
Vector 121, 226, 232, 270
Vertex 127, 228-232, 264
Vicarious Learning 1, 36
Virtual Environment 72, 75-77, 80-82, 85, 90-92, 266-267, 270, 276-277, 281, 334
Virtual Reality 91, 93, 97, 268, 276, 281, 335
Visual Data Mining 166, 179-180, 183
Visualization 64, 120, 123, 132-145, 152, 155, 164-169, 173-190, 192, 194-197, 201-203, 214, 218-221, 229, 231, 246, 248-251, 262, 312-313, 322-325, 333-354
visuo-spatial sketchpad 340

W

Wayfinding 54, 69, 96-97
Weak Link 232
Web 2.0 71-76, 78, 80, 82-92, 104-105, 118, 121, 145, 245, 263, 270-277, 279, 281, 297
White Hat 246, 264
WordNet 164-165, 169-170, 175, 181

X

Xor 66, 69

Y

YouTube 40, 69, 73, 120, 126, 146, 151, 270, 276-277, 297

Z

Zoonotic Disease 329